D0337553

Early Childhood Curriculum

Developmental Bases for Learning and Teaching

Sue C. Wortham
University of Texas
at San Antonio

Merrill
Prentice Hall

Upper Saddle River, New Jersey
Columbus, Ohio

Library of Congress Cataloging-in-Publication Data

Wortham, Sue Clark,
    Early childhood curriculum : developmental bases for learning and teaching / Sue C.
Wortham.—3rd ed.
        p. cm.
    Includes bibliographical references and index.
    ISBN 0-13-091424-X
    1. Early childhood education—Curricula. 2. Curriculum planning. 3. Child
development. I. Title.

LB1139.4.W67 2002
372.19—dc21   2001034542

Vice President and Publisher: Jeffery W. Johnston
Executive Editor: Ann Castel Davis
Associate Editor: Christina Kalisch
Editorial Assistant: Keli Gemrich
Production Editor: Sheryl Glicker Langner
Production Coordination: Clarinda Publication Services
Design Coordinator: Diane C. Lorenzo
Photo Coordinator: Sandy Lenahan
Cover Designer: Melissa Cullen
Cover photo: Super Stock
Production Manager: Laura Messerly
Director of Marketing: Kevin Flanagan
Marketing Manager: Amy June
Marketing Coordinator: Barbara Koontz

This book was set by in Helvetica and Zapf Humanist by The Clarinda Company. It was printed and bound by
R. R. Donnelley & Sons Company. The cover was printed by The Lehigh Press, Inc.

Photo Credits:
1, 5, 15, 25, 49, 180, 188, 303, 310, 341, 346, 361, 397, 405, 415: Scott Cunningham/Merrill; 11, 32, 241,
271: Barbara Schwartz/Merrill; 23, Library of Congress; 53, 285: Dan Floss/Merrill; 73, 79, 82, 119, 123, 135, 147,
155, 190, 217, 257, 349, 384: Anne Vega/Merrill; 94, 136, 194, 203, 220, 236, 289, 294, 297: Sue and Marsal
Wortham; 115, 265, 391, 412: Anthony Magnacca/Merrill; 163, 325: Todd Yarrington/Merrill; 183, Shirley Zeiberg/PH
College; 333, Tom Watson/Merrill.

Pearson Education Ltd., *London*
Pearson Education Australia Pty. Limited, *Sydney*
Pearson Education Singapore Pte. Ltd.
Pearson Education North Asia Ltd., *Hong Kong*
Pearson Education Canada, Ltd., *Toronto*
Pearson Educación de Mexico, S.A. de C.V.
Pearson Education—Japan, *Tokyo*
Pearson Education Malaysia Pte. Ltd.
Pearson Education, *Upper Saddle River, New Jersey*

Copyright © 2002, 1998, 1994 by Pearson Education, Inc., Upper Saddle River, New Jersey 07458. All rights
reserved. Printed in the United States of America. This publication is protected by Copyright and permission should be
obtained from the publisher prior to any prohibited reproduction, storage in a retrieval system, or transmission in any
form or by any means, electronic, mechanical, photocopying, recording, or likewise. For information regarding
permission(s), write to: Rights and Permissions Department.

Merrill
Prentice Hall

10 9 8 7 6 5 4 3 2 1
ISBN: 0-13-091424-X

This third edition of *Early Childhood Curriculum: Developmental Bases for Learning and Teaching* was written for teachers of children from infancy to 8 years of age. It was prepared in response to the need of present and future teachers to understand the role of the child's development in the curriculum. The curriculum discussed is planned for the very youngest children, whether in a child-care, private preschool, or public school setting. The children from birth to age 8 who attend early childhood programs are diverse in their development. Teachers in the primary grades in elementary schools are particularly aware of the difficulty in providing successful learning experiences for children who come to them from diverse backgrounds and with a range of abilities, especially at a time when children may be expected to cover learning objectives more rapidly than in the past. In this edition, more attention is given to how diversity affects development and how life changes can affect young children.

Regardless of the child's age, the teacher needs to understand that the nature of the child's development has implications for the kinds of experiences that are appropriate. Likewise, teachers can benefit from understanding the role of developmental theories in the practice of teaching in an early childhood program. The developmental curriculum presented is strongly based on the work of Jean Piaget; however, in this third edition, more emphasis is given to the work of Lev Vygotsky that includes the social dimensions of learning and the role of the teacher to scaffold and support the child's progress. Urie Bronfenbrenner's conceptualization of the role of the family and community in the child's development complements the constructivist theories of Piaget and Vygotsky.

This text is also about the issues of bridging and making transitions; it offers information and suggestions for bridging theory and practice, and it includes suggestions for guiding children through transitions in developmental stages, especially as they move from preschool into the primary grades. The important transition from preliteracy into literacy and the appropriate strategies that teachers can use are examples of curriculum content presented.

Chapters 1 through 3 establish the background setting and context for the early childhood curriculum that will be described. Chapter 1, "The Changing Role of the Teacher in Developing Curriculum for Diverse Populations," discusses the diversity of children entering early childhood programs; likewise, it describes the teacher's changing role in developing curriculum for very young children. Chapter 2, "Historical and Theoretical Bases for Appropriate Programs in Early Childhood Settings," reviews the historical heritage of early childhood education to include the theoretical bases that inform early childhood curriculum. Chapter 3, "The Need for Quality Programs in Early Childhood Education," discusses national goals for quality early childhood programs in the United States. A discussion of how classical and contemporary theories inform quality programs is followed by examples of model programs that have international importance.

The developmental foundation of curriculum is introduced in Chapter 4, "Developmental Characteristics of Young Children from Birth to 8 Years: Implications for Learning." Continuity of development is traced in young children from birth to 8 years with implications for learning experiences to foster cognitive, physical, language, and social-emotional development. Characteristics of development are explained with regard to the sensorimotor, preoperational, and concrete operational periods.

Chapters 5 and 6 address programs for infants and toddlers. Chapter 5, "Organizing Infant–Toddler Programs," traces the history of programs for infants and toddlers and describes the characteristics of a model program for infants and toddlers today. Chapter 6, "Infant–Toddler Curriculum: Birth to Age 2," discusses how development is nurtured in physical, cognitive, language, and social development and suggests activities that can be used with very young children.

The next three chapters address the developmental needs and programming for preschool children ages three through five. Chapter 7, "A Developmental Model for Preschool Programs," addresses the elements needed in a quality developmental program for preschool children. It describes the characteristics of such a model and the way in which it is implemented. Chapter 8, "Preschool Curriculum: Ages 3 to 5: Language and Cognitive Development," describes curriculum for those developmental domains, while Chapter 9, "Preschool Curriculum: Ages 3 to 5: Social and Physical Development," presents curriculum for the social and physical domains. Each of these chapters discusses the role of play, the environment, and the teacher for development and provides examples of activities and thematic unit topics.

Chapters 10 through 12 move to programs for children from age 5 to 8. Chapter 10, "A Model for Programs for Children Ages 5 to 8," describes how developmental changes during those three years have implications for the way quality curriculum and instruction are designed and implemented as children make the transition into the concrete operational period and toward literacy. The characteristics and implementation of an ungraded primary model are presented. Chapter 11, "The Transitional Curriculum: Ages 5 to 8: Language Arts, Mathematics, and Science," and Chapter 12, "The Transitional Curriculum: Ages 5 to 8: Social Studies and Physical Education," discuss the goals and topics that are the foundations for each of the curriculum content areas.

Finally, Chapter 13, "Teaching in the Real World," takes a final look at the world of early childhood teachers as they encounter and address problems and possibilities present in early childhood programs today. Readers are introduced to the realities of practice experienced by contemporary teachers. These teachers often struggle with making decisions within the context of many kinds of programs from different philosophical perspectives and within their own developmental stages. New teachers entering the field will find both opportunities and frustrations as they join teachers who are working to provide quality programs for the very youngest of children in our society.

The four appendices provide examples of thematic, integrated curriculum. Appendix A is an example of a preschool unit on seeds. Appendix B describes a unit on farm animals for kindergarten. The unit in Appendix C is designed for a multiage class that includes kindergarten and the primary grades. This unit is based on the storybook *If You Give a Mouse a Cookie* (Numeroff, 1985). The last unit in Appendix D is planned for the primary grades and is based on *Alexander and the Terrible, Horrible, No Good, Very Bad Day* (Viorst, 1972). Each of the units is organized using the processes described in Chapters 7 and 10.

Acknowledgments

I am especially indebted in this section to my colleague Blanche Desjean-Perrotta who provided many suggestions for changes and improvements. She has been using the text for several years and has reflected upon how the text can best be of assistance to her students. In addition, she teaches her class at an elementary school where she and the students are in constant contact with the opportunities and challenges faced by the early childhood teachers on that campus.

I also wish to thank the reviewers of the third edition who also made suggestions that reflected their own careful considerations of how to refine content and ensure currency of the ideas presented. The reviewers were Douglas C. Godwin, Texas A&M University; Beth Ridge, Concordia University (IL); and Asha Saini, University of Nebraska at Kearny.

As always I am indebted to Ann Davis, my editor, who offers support and expresses confidence that I can see the project to completion with my own vision of what I want to communicate to readers. I appreciate the freedom she provides for me to work as freely as possible. I also would like to thank Christina Kalisch, Associate Editor, and production staff who patiently helped me to iron out inconsistencies and my convoluted writing style: Sheryl Langner, Production Editor; Sandy Lenahan, Photo Coordinator; and Emily Autumn, Production Coordinator at Clarinda Publication Services.

In the first two editions, I discussed my daughter-in-law who questioned my total preoccupation in writing this text. She had difficulty imagining that the result was worth the time spent and suggested that I take up knitting instead. In the second edition, I mentioned that she had returned to school to become a Spanish teacher and was preoccupied with studying herself. Now I must report that Mary Blanche is an instructor of Spanish at the college level and is totally obsessed with teaching and college life. I still am not interested in knitting, but I did watch my sister latch hook a wall hanging last fall. That is close enough for the moment.

The Prentice Hall Companion Website: A Virtual Learning Environment

Technology is a constantly growing and changing aspect of our field that is creating a need for content and resources. To address this emerging need, Prentice Hall has developed an online learning environment for students and professors alike—Companion Websites—to support our textbooks.

In creating a Companion Website, our goal is to build on and enhance what the textbook already offers. For this reason, the content for each user-friendly website is organized by topic and provides the professor and student with a variety of meaningful resources. Common features of a Companion Website include:

For the Professor—

Every Companion Website integrates **Syllabus Manager™**, an online syllabus creation and management utility.

- **Syllabus Manager™** provides you, the instructor, with an easy, step-by-step process to create and revise syllabi, with direct links into Companion Website and other online content without having to learn HTML.
- Students may log on to your syllabus during any study session. All they need to know is the web address for the Companion Website and the password you've assigned to your syllabus.
- After you have created a syllabus using **Syllabus Manager™**, students may enter the syllabus for their course section from any point in the Companion Website.
- Clicking on a date, the student is shown the list of activities for the assignment. The activities for each assignment are linked directly to actual content, saving time for students.
- Adding assignments consists of clicking on the desired due date, then filling in the details of the assignment—name of the assignment, instructions, and whether or not it is a one-time or repeating assignment.
- In addition, links to other activities can be created easily. If the activity is online, a URL can be entered in the space provided, and it will be linked automatically in the final syllabus.
- Your completed syllabus is hosted on our servers, allowing convenient updates from any computer on the Internet. Changes you make to your syllabus are immediately available to your students at their next logon.

For the Student—

Topic Overviews—outline key concepts in topic areas

Web Links—general websites related to topic areas as well as associations and professional organizations

Read About It—timely articles that enable you to become more aware of important issues in early childhood education

Learn by Doing—put concepts into action, participate in activities, complete lesson plans, examine strategies, and more

For Teachers—access information that you will need to know as an in-service teacher, including information on materials, activities, lessons, curriculum, and state standards

Visit a School—visit a school's website to see concepts, theories, and strategies in action

Electronic Bluebook—send homework or essays directly to your instructor's email with this paperless form

Message Board—serves as a virtual bulletin board to post—or respond to—questions or comments to/from a national audience

Chat—real-time chat with anyone who is using the text anywhere in the country—ideal for discussion and study groups, class projects, etc.

To take advantage of these and other resources, please visit the *Early Childhood Curriculum: Developmental Bases for Learning and Teaching*, Third Edition, Companion Website at

www.prenhall.com/wortham

CONTENTS

CHAPTER ONE

The Changing Role of the Teacher in Developing Curriculum for Diverse Populations   1

Introduction   2

Who are the Children Served in Early Childhood Programs?   2

Children in Early Childhood Programs Are Diverse   2

Early Childhood Programs and At-Risk Learners   7

The Complex Nature of Settings for Early Childhood Programs   13

Public School Programs   14

Nonpublic School Programs   15

Continuing Complexity in Preschool Programs   16

The Changing Role of the Teacher in Developing Curriculum for Early Childhood Programs   18

The Role of the Teacher in Developing Curriculum for Diverse Populations   18

Multicultural Curriculum   18

Curriculum for Children from Diverse Family Environments   19

Curriculum for Children with Special Needs   19

The Role of the Teacher in Involving Parents in Curriculum Development   19

The Role of the Teacher in Addressing Conflicts Between Theory and Practice in Curriculum Development   20

Summary   20

Study Questions   21

CHAPTER TWO

Historical and Theoretical Bases for Appropriate Programs in Early Childhood Settings   23

Historical Roots of Early Childhood Education   24

Rural Schools   24

The Evolution of Early Childhood Education   25

The Progressive Era   27

Nursery School and Child Care Movements   28

The Influence of Maria Montessori   29

Urbanization of Public Schools   29

A Period of Innovation: The 1950s and 1960s   30

The Evolution of Early Childhood Programs for Populations at Risk   31

African American Education   32

Latino Education   32

Native American Education   33

Minority Education During Depression and War Years   33

Early Childhood Programs for Children with Disabilities   33

Intervention and Compensatory Programs in the 1960s and 1970s   34

Theoretical Bases of Development   35
Maturational Theory   35
Psychoanalytic Theory   36
Behaviorist Theory   37
Social Learning Theory   39
Cognitive-Developmental Theory/Constructivism
   39

**Early Childhood Curriculum Practices Today:
   Historical Influences Revisited   42**
The Expanding Role of Early Childhood
   Education   43
Parental Interest in Learning in the Early
   Childhood Years   43
Expansion of Child Care   44
Expansion of Preschool Programs in Public
   Schools   45

Summary   46

Study Questions   48

CHAPTER THREE

The Need for Quality Programs in Early Childhood Education   49

Introduction   50
Challenges to Quality in Early Childhood
   Programs   50

**Goals for Quality Early Childhood
   Programs   51**
Staff Training, Licensing, and Funding   51
Characteristics of Quality Programs   52

**How Classical and Contemporary Theories
   Inform Quality Early Childhood Programs
   54**
Applying Classical Theories   54
Theory and Cultural Relevance: Ecological
   Theory   56
Gardner's Theory of Intelligence   56

**Models of Quality Early Childhood
   Programs   58**
Developmentally Appropriate Practices
   (DAP)   58

High/Scope Curriculum   64
Reggio Emilia   67
The Project Approach   72

Summary   75

Study Questions   77

CHAPTER FOUR

Developmental Characteristics of Young Children from Birth to 8 Years: Implications for Learning   79

Birth to 2 Years: The Sensorimotor Stage   80
Cognitive Development   80
Physical Development   81
Language Development   81
Social-Emotional Development   81

**Characteristics and Competencies: Birth to
   6 Months   83**

**Characteristics and Competencies: 6 to
   12 Months   84**

**Characteristics and Competencies: 12 to
   18 Months   87**

**Characteristics and Competencies: 18 to
   24 Months   87**

**Infant and Toddler Development:
   Implications for Learning   89**

Ages 2 to 5: The Preoperational Stage   92
Cognitive Development   92
Physical Development   93
Language Development   93
Social-Emotional Development   94

**Characteristics and Competencies:
   2 to 5 Years   96**

**Development in the Preschool Years:
   Implications for Learning   98**

**Age 5 to 8 Years: The Transition from
   Preoperations to Concrete Operations   107**
Cognitive Development   108
Physical Development   109

Language Development   109
Social-Emotional Development   110

Characteristics and Competencies in Children Ages 5 to 8 Years: Implications for Learning and Instruction   111
Cognitive Development   111
Physical Development   111
Social-Emotional Development   112

Summary   112

Study Questions   113

CHAPTER FIVE

Organizing Infant–Toddler Programs   115

The Evolution of Infant–Toddler Programs   116
Infants and Toddlers Prior to the Twentieth Century   116
Infants and Toddlers in the Twentieth Century   117
Infants– and Toddlers Today   121

Considerations for Developing Models for Infant–Toddler Programs   125
Theoretical Bases for Infant–Toddler Programs   125

Characteristics of a Quality Infant–Toddler Model   127
The Role of Quality Caregivers   127
The Role of the Environment   127
The Role of Play   129
The Role of Routines   132
The Role of Parents   134
Planning and Managing the Infant–Toddler Developmental Experiences   136
The Role of Thematic Curriculum for Infants and Toddlers   138
The Role of Assessment in Infant–Toddler Programs   139

Summary   144

Study Questions   145

CHAPTER SIX

Infant–Toddler Curriculum: Birth to Age 2   147

Curriculum for Physical Development   148
Nurturing Physical Development in Infants and Toddlers   148

Curriculum for Cognitive Development   155
Nurturing Cognitive Development in Infants and Toddlers   155

Curriculum for Language Development   163
Nurturing Language Development in Infants and Toddlers   163

Curriculum for Social Development   171
Nurturing Social Development in Infants and Toddlers   171

Curriculum for the Expressive Arts   176
Nurturing Expressive Arts Development in Infants and Toddlers   176

Summary: A Word of Caution   180

CHAPTER SEVEN

A Developmental Model for Preschool Programs   183

Introduction   183
The Difference Between Theory and Practice   183

Considerations for Developing a Model for Preschool Education   185
Principles of Child Development   185
Balanced Curriculum   186
Parent, Teacher, and Child Relationships   186
Assessment and Accountability   187
Diversity in Children and Families   187

Characteristics of a Quality Developmental Model   187
Developmentally Appropriate Practices (DAP): Using Principles of Development   189
The Inclusive Classroom   190

The Culturally Responsive Classroom   191
The Integrated Classroom   191
The Teacher's Role   191
The Role of the Environment   192
The Role of Play   193
The Role of the Daily Schedule   194

Planning and Managing Instruction   195
Understanding Developmental-Thematic
   Curriculum   196
Roles of Developmental-Thematic
   Curriculum   197
Designing Developmental-Thematic Curriculum
   Units   198
Implementing Developmental-Thematic
   Curriculum   211
Arranging the Environment   211

**The Role of Assessment in Preschool
   Programs   212**
Assessment of Child Development and
   Learning   212
Assessment of Children in Preschool
   Programs   213
Assessment of Program Components   214

Summary   215

Study Questions   215

CHAPTER EIGHT

**Preschool Curriculum: Ages 3 to 5:
Language and Cognitive Development   217**

Introduction   218

Curriculum for Language Development   218
How Young Children Develop Language   218
Forms of Language   219
Language Differences in the Preschool
   Years   220

Planning for Language Development   222
The Role of Play in Language
   Development   222
The Role of Teacher in Language Development
   and Literacy   223

The Role of Parents in Language
   Development   223
The Role of Environment in Language
   Development and Literacy   224

**Designing Curriculum for Language
   Development   225**
Experiences That Promote Expressive
   Language   225
Experiences That Promote Receptive
   Language   227

Developing Foundations for Literacy   227
Resolving the Issues in Beginning Literacy
   Instruction   228
What Does the Young Child Need to Know to
   Develop Literacy?   228

Goals for Literacy   230
Emergent Writing   230
Emergent Reading   235

**Designing Language Curriculum for Children
   with Disabilities and Language
   Differences   237**

Curriculum for Cognitive Development   241
How Young Children Develop Concepts   242
Planning for Cognitive Development   242
Goals for Cognitive Development: Mathematics
   and Science   244
The Role of the Teacher in Cognitive
   Development   245
The Role of the the Environment and Play in
   Cognitive Development   246

**Designing Curriculum for Cognitive
   Development   247**

**The Integrated Curriculum for Language and
   Cognitive Development   257**
Using Children's Literature as a Focus for
   Integrated Curriculum   258
Using Thematic Units as a Focus for Integrated
   Curriculum   258
Activities for a Unit on Seeds   258

**Designing Cognitive Curriculum for Children
   with Disabilities   262**

Summary   263

Study Questions   264

CHAPTER NINE

Preschool Curriculum: Ages 3 to 5: Social and Physical Development 265

Curriculum for Social Development 266
Understanding Social Development 266
Life Changes That Affect Social
   Development 266
Planning for Social Development 268
Goals for Social Science 270
The Role of Play in Social Development 272
The Role of the Environment in Social
   Development 273
The Role of the Teacher in Social
   Development 274
Designing Curriculum for Social
   Development 275
Designing Curriculum for Social Science 276
Designing Integrated Curriculum in Social
   Science 277
Designing Integrated Curriculum for Children's
   Life Changes 282

Curriculum for Physical Development 283
Understanding Physical Development 285
Planning for Physical Development 287
The Role of Play in Physical
   Development 287
The Role of Environment in Physical
   Development 288
The Role of the Teacher in Physical
   Development 289

**Designing Curriculum for Physical
   Development 291**
The Integrated Curriculum for Physical
   Development 294
Designing Physical Development Activities for
   Children with Disabilities 297
Summary 298
Study Questions 299

CHAPTER TEN

A Model for Programs for Children Ages 5 to 8 301

**The Significance of Developmental Changes
   in the Primary Grades 302**
Physical Development 302
Cognitive Development 303
Social and Emotional Development 303

The Role of Play in the Primary Grades 304

**Describing Appropriate Curriculum for
   Children Ages 5 to 8 305**

**Describing a Curriculum for Continuing
   Developmental Needs 305**

**The Upgraded Primary: A Model for Children
   Ages 5 to 8 307**
The British Infant School Model 309
Team Teaching 309
Multiage Grouping 310

**Characteristics of the Ungraded Primary
   Model 311**
Ungraded Classrooms 311
Developmental Curriculum 311
Integrated Curriculum 311
Systematic Instruction 311
Cooperative Learning Groups 312
Peer Teaching 312

Planning and Managing Instruction 312
The Role of the Environment 313
Designing Thematic Curriculum 314
Implementing Thematic Curriculum 326
Incorporating Systematic Instruction 329

**The Role of Assessment in Kindergarten and
   Primary Grades 331**
The Purposes of Assessment in Kindergarten and
   Primary Grades 331
Summary 335
Study Questions 336

CHAPTER ELEVEN

The Transitional Curriculum: Ages 5 to 8: Language Arts, Mathematics, and Science   339

Curriculum for Language Arts   340
The Continuing Process of Language
   Development   341
Addressing the Language Needs of Diverse
   Speakers   341
Designing Curriculum for Language
   Development   343
Cooperative Learning Groups   344
The Continuing Process of Literacy
   Development   346
The Language Arts Program for Children
   Ages 5 to 8   346
Organizing the Language Arts Program   352
Content-Area Grouping   353
Accommodating the Learning Differences of
   Students with Special Needs   358

Curriculum for Mathematics   359
Trends and Issues in Mathematics   360
Organizing the Mathematics Program   364
Designing Curriculum for the Mathematics
   Program   368
Accommodating Learning Differences Among
   Students   371

Curriculum for Science   372
How Young Children Learn About
   Science   372
Trends and Issues in Science   373
Planning the Science Program   374
Incorporating the Science Process   375
The Role of the Environment   375
The Role of the Teacher   376
Organizing the Science Program   377
Designing Curriculum for the Science
   Program   378
Integrated Experiences That Promote
   Science   380

**Integrating Curriculum in Language Arts,
   Mathematics, and Science   381**

Summary of Activities   382
Summary   383
Study Questions   387

CHAPTER 12

The Transitional Curriculum: Ages 5 to 8: Social Studies and Physical Education   389

Curriculum for Social Studies   390
Social Development for Ages 5 to 8   390
Activities for Nurturing Continued Social
   Development   392
Social Studies Curriculum in Kindergarten and
   the Primary Grades   393
Goals for Social Studies   393
Designing Curriculum for Social Studies   397
Designing Integrated, Thematic Units in Social
   Studies   402

Curriculum for Physical Education   402
Physical Development of Children
   Ages 5 to 8   402
Planning for Physical Development   404
Designing Curriculum for Physical Development
   and Education   405
The Integrated Curriculum for Physical
   Development   406

Summary   410
Study Questions   411

CHAPTER 13

Teaching in the Real World   413

Beth   414
Renee   415
Yolanda   415
Susan   415
Rollo and Nancy   416

Gladys   416

Hector   417

Loretta   417

Loisa   418

A P P E N D I X   A

Preschool Unit: Seeds   419

A P P E N D I X   B

Preschool Unit: Farm Animals   429

A P P E N D I X   C

Kindergarten-Primary Unit: *If You Give a Mouse a Cookie*   439

A P P E N D I X   D

Primary Unit: *Alexander and the Terrible, Horrible, No Good, Very Bad Day*   449

References   457

Name Index   479

Subject Index   485

The Changing Role of the Teacher in Developing Curriculum for Diverse Populations

C H A P T E R   O B J E C T I V E S

As a result of reading this chapter you will be able to:

1. Understand how the early childhood years and early childhood education have acquired new importance in a new century.
2. Describe ways in which young children in early childhood programs represent diversity.
3. Explain the role of the teacher in developing curriculum for children in today's early childhood programs.

Introduction

These are significant years in a new century for programs in early childhood education. The importance of the early childhood years for the development of young children and for later success in school has been documented extensively. Likewise, ample evidence documents the effect that quality early childhood programs have for providing the types of experiences that promote successful learning in elementary school (Bowman, Donovan, & Burns, 2000; Carnegie Corporation of New York, 1994, 1996).

Policymakers are becoming aware of the significance of early childhood education and how it enhances development and learning in America's children. As a result, funding for preschool programs is increasing each year. Some experts believe that by 2010 free preschool education will be available for all children (Adler, 1998).

This book was written for teachers and future teachers of children from birth to age eight. It will help teachers of young children become informed about quality educational programs. One purpose of this book is to describe how teachers can develop curriculum and learning experiences that are appropriate for the young children they teach.

The purpose of this chapter is to serve as an introduction to early childhood curriculum. To address this purpose, we need to understand the young children who attend early childhood programs. They will be described in terms of diversity. Thus, we will look at how the role of teachers is changing in terms of the differences in children who attend early childhood programs. We will also look at how such programs are diverse and how they are changing to meet the needs of children and their families in today's world. In addition, we will discuss how the role of teachers is changing as early childhood settings become more complex.

Finally, we will look at how the role of the teacher is evolving to respond to the changing needs of children, families, and society in a new century. When developing curriculum for young children, teachers in all types of settings face new challenges to develop quality programs for all young children (Kagan & Neuman, 1997). Change in education is now the rule in contemporary schools, just as it is in other facets of society. Early childhood curriculum and instruction in today's and tomorrow's programs are responses to the issues that confront the community, educators, and families in a period of continuing transition.

In the following section, we will explore the types of children who attend early childhood programs. We will look at differences in these children and the types of diversity they represent. Next, we will discuss children who are "at risk" for not succeeding in school and some of the factors that cause them to be at risk.

Who Are the Children Served in Early Childhood Programs?

Is it possible to describe a "typical class" of children in an early childhood classroom today? Probably not. Prior to the 1960s a kindergarten class was likely to enroll mostly white, middle-class children with fairly similar backgrounds whose parents could pay for their children to attend. Now, early childhood programs serve all types of children from all types of families and many different types of neighborhoods. Children come from different ethnic groups, might speak different languages, and live within a variety of cultures. In other words, the children who attend today's early childhood programs are diverse.

Children in Early Childhood Programs Are Diverse

What does diversity mean? *Webster's Ninth Dictionary* defines diversity as the condition of being different. Diversity has always been a characteristic of young children in preschool programs. In the past, some children have been considered as "different," and different meant "less" compared with the perception of the characteristics of most of the children in the class. Thus, diversity could have negative connotations.

Today, diversity in children adds to the richness of experiences that are possible in early childhood classrooms. Difference can be a positive trait in children. David Elkind declares that we are now in a postmodern era of education when we are interested in particular children, rather than typical children. He explains differences as follows:

> What has come to the fore in postmodern times is the awareness of the importance of difference. In the modern era, difference was often seen from the standpoint of superiority. Non-Western societies, as an illustration were regarded as inferior to Western 'civilizations' because they had not progressed as far. This notion of superiority was implicit in the concept of the United States of America as a "melting pot" in which people (inferior) cultures would be melted down and then poured into a mold from which each would be dropped out as a purified, standard American. Today, however, we recognize that people do not melt and that other cultures, ethnic groups, and races are to be appreciated and valued rather than dissolved into some common amalgam. The postmodern conception of America as a cultural "rainbow" celebrates the valuation of difference, in contrast to the feeling of superiority inherent in the modern conceptions of social progress and of the melting pot. (Elkind, 1997, 242)

What are some of the differences that children have which represent diversity in the classroom? In the paragraphs that follow we want to discuss cultural, ethnic, and language differences. Then we will address differences in ability, differences in family environments, and factors that can cause children to be at risk for difficulties with learning and adjustment to preschool and school experiences.

Cultural Differences

Every child is a member of a cultural group. The group can be as small as a family unit or as large as a nation. Subcultures exist within a culture. In the United States, there are multitudes of cultures and subcultures. For example, many citizens of the United States belong to a Hispanic culture. Because Hispanic Americans might have come from Mexico, Central America, South America, or Puerto Rico, they represent cultures unique to those areas of the world.

A person's social group, religion, and race can contribute to his culture. When the United States was first being settled, the original immigrants to America came from Europe; as a result, the United States is strongly influenced by European cultures. However, Native American cultures were present before the first settlers arrived.

Today children in early childhood classrooms represent cultures from all parts of the world. If children come from a family that has lived in the United States for many generations, they are probably more familiar with the mainstream American culture. Yet many families who have lived in this country for generations represent American culture while retaining the culture of the country of their forebears.

Ethnic Differences

Children can be diverse in that they represent different ethnic groups or different races. Children can have an African American, Asian, Hispanic, or European background, to name a few. Many children represent more than one ethnic or racial group, and thus they have a mixed ethnic heritage.

✦ Lucy Wu

Lucy Wu is six years old. Her parents came to the United States from Vietnam when they were teenagers. Lucy's mother went with her family to Houston, where they were sponsored by a Lutheran church; her father's family also went to Houston to stay with relatives until they could get settled. Lucy's mother and father met in a local community college. They worked in a small grocery store that her father's family opened in a leased building in an older neighborhood in eastern Houston. Recently, the store burned as a result of faulty wiring. The contents of the store were not insured; thus, Lucy's mother is working as a housekeeper in a local motel and her father is working at a drive-in grocery until the debts are paid and they can try to get another start in a family business. Lucy and her parents are living temporarily with her maternal grandparents in a small apartment until they can afford their own place again. ✦

Language Differences

Although English is the dominant language spoken in the United States, many children come from homes where another language is spoken. Children in early childhood programs may be speakers of Chinese, Japanese, and Vietnamese if they are from an Asian family. Likewise children may speak Spanish, Russian, Polish, or many other languages when they enter an early childhood classroom. While it is true that the majority of children in the United States speak English, many children either speak another language as their first language or can speak more than one language.

Children in early childhood classrooms currently represent both individual and global diversity. Teachers of these young children must understand the complexity of cultural, racial, ethnic, and language diversity when preparing curriculum and instruction for their students. Awareness of such differences has broadened in the last several decades. Eugene Garcia (1995,

p. 157) described the experience of one teacher's 21 years at the same elementary school in California:*

> When she took that initial fifth-grade assignment, she was teaching at one of many Los Angeles suburbs, and her students and her community was almost all middle class, white, English-speaking, third- to fourth-generation European immigrants. They were all much like herself.
>
> In that short first decade of her professional career, the Los Angeles metropolitan area extended itself beyond her suburb to create new suburbs, and her community became a haven for recently arrived Mexican immigrants and other Spanish-speaking immigrants from the southwestern United States. In that decade, the majority of students in her class changed. African-American students speaking a distinct English dialect, most of them immigrants from the southern United States, joined students who spoke Spanish in their working-class homes and commuted regularly between the United States and Mexico. Their immigrant parents, like the parents of her students earlier, had come to this locale to find employment and achieve a higher standard of living. Although they were not like her, she felt just as committed to these new students as she had felt toward her first students.

In addition, the influx of new immigrants and refugees to the United States has widened the diversity of groups entering the schools. Families have come from Cuba, Central America, Indochina, Eastern Europe, the former Soviet Union, and many other regions as political crises, wars, and changes in government leadership have forced families to seek safety and economic opportunity in other countries. Children

---

*E. Garcia, "The Impact of Linguistic and Cultural Diversity on America's Schools" in *Making a Difference for Students at Risk*, edited by M. C. Wang and M. C. Reynolds (p. 157). Copyright © 1995 by Corwin Press. Reprinted by permission of Sage Publications, Inc.

from these families entering early childhood programs bring unique cultural experiences to their new nation. Their parents range from professionals with affluent circumstances to uneducated people from underdeveloped nations. Some of these children are either under foster parent care, have been adopted by American parents, or are otherwise of a race that is different from that of the parents. Morever, mixed-race adoptions are becoming more common in this country. Teachers of the future will need a broad understanding of the differences in nationality, culture, and life events that affect every child entering their classrooms (DiMartino, 1989; Wardle, 1990).

Differences in Family Environments

As mentioned earlier, early childhood education prior to the 1960s, particularly in public schools, was oriented to the middle-class child (Weber, 1984). The child was assumed to come from an intact family with both parents present in the home. The typical mother did not work outside the home and devoted her time and energy to the family. In recent decades many factors have affected the makeup of the family structure. In addition to families in which a father and mother are present, there are single-parent families, stepfamilies, and blended families (which result from multiple marriages or cohabitation, where children from two or more family combinations live as a single family), and teenage parents.

Billy and Bobby

Billy and Bobby are two-year-old twins. Their mother, Susan, is seventeen and not married. They live in the family room in the basement of Susan's parents' home in Evansville, Indiana. Susan works at a Kmart department store during the day and attends night school three evenings a week. She receives a check each month through Aid to Families with Dependent Children. Billy and Bobby stay in a family day home during the day; their grandmother takes care of them on the evenings when Susan attends school.

Susan and her mother have recently been fighting over the amount of time Susan has been out on dates each week with her new boyfriend. Susan believes she is going to have to move out.

Her boyfriend is not working and does not want to get married and have the responsibility of the twins. In addition, Susan needs to get a job before her monthly checks are ended. At the moment, Billy and Bobby face an uncertain future. ✦

Children live with a single parent for various reasons, divorce being the most common. Although dual custody is a frequent possibility when parents divorce, most children spend the majority of their lives with one parent. Fathers who are single parents are increasing in number, as are split-custody decisions where siblings are divided between the parents. Single adults are now able to adopt children as well as act as foster parents to children needing temporary homes. In addition, children may live with a grandparent when the parents are unable or unwilling to care for their children. The number of children living in single-parent homes has increased dramatically in recent decades. Edelman (1989) reported that 8.9 million children under the age of ten lived in single-parent households, a 48 percent increase from the six million reported in the early 1980s.

Although the pre-1970 perception that the father was the breadwinner and the mother maintained the home and cared for the children was never true for many families, the percentage of mothers employed outside the home has risen dramatically since the 1970s. In 1993, 59.6 percent of married women with children under age six were working outside the home (Children's Defense Fund, 1994). By 1999, 61.8 percent of married women with children under six were working outside the home. A major concern is that 60 percent of these mothers had infants under age one (Children's Defense Fund, 2000).

Whether the working mother is a single parent or married, the changes in family lifestyle can cause problems for family members. The majority of working women in the United States provide half or more of the family's financial resources. Working parents are faced with time management problems, concerns for quality child care, and the matter of balancing priorities between work and home. Children from families in which both parents or the single parent are employed face adjustments that may range from attending a combination of child-care and educational settings each day, to self-caring before and after school, to accepting family responsibilities (Children's Defense Fund, 2000; O'Neil, 1991).

Working parents often find it difficult to meet with teachers for conferences or attend school meetings. They must frequently hurry their children and themselves as they seek to reconcile family and work schedules. Families are learning how to manage work and other responsibilities. Carpooling children to and from school, sharing afterschool care, and developing flexible work schedules are helping families to attend to the needs of their children. Many schools now offer before- and after-school care as well as training and support groups for parenting skills and other issues that are unique to working parents. Many employers are learning that it is in their best interest to support employees when they need to attend a school conference or meet with child care staff during the day. Early childhood centers in turn have provided extended hours and evening care for children of parents who work in the evening, rather than during the day.

✦ Raul

Raul is in the second grade and lives in a suburb outside of Orlando, Florida. Both of his parents work and commute into Orlando early each morning. When Raul started having problems in school and resisted having to go to a child care center for after-school care, his parents began to work to solve the difficulties. Fortunately, Raul's father can have flexible hours at his workplace. Now Raul's father leaves at 5:30 each morning and returns by 3:30 in the afternoon to be at home when Raul returns from school on the bus. After Raul has had time for a snack, he and his father work on his homework together. Raul's father would like not to have to leave for work so early in the morning, but Raul has benefitted from the change. He is doing better in school and usually has time to play outside with some neighborhood friends before his mother arrives home and prepares dinner for the family. ✦

Differences in Learning Needs

Children enter school as unique individuals. They bring with them their experiences from their homes and communities. They also bring their own combination of interests, styles of learning, rate of development, and personalities. They may be children who are visual learners who need to see new information in addition to hearing about it. Some children may need to have instructions given one step at a time, whereas others may benefit from receiving all of the instructions at one time. Some children will be very shy or assertive. As a group they represent a range of aptitudes for learning, as well as strengths and weaknesses that may be so minor that they are hidden or so extreme that they are serious impediments. Despite their differences, children are all similar in that they have hopes of being successful students. The first years in early childhood classrooms are important because it is during this time that children form perceptions of themselves and their competence as individual students and as members of groups of students.

Many children have exceptionally high aptitudes and abilities. They have a high potential for learning that allows them to learn quickly and often independently. They are self-starters and voracious in their desire to acquire information. They can accomplish by themselves much of what is to be learned. The teacher's responsibility with children having high learning potential is to keep them challenged and help them discipline themselves to work to achieve their best without being pushed unreasonably to excel.

Other children are also competent, but they are steady rather than fast-paced learners. They do consistently well in school and are a stable influence on the other children in the class. These students may have occasional difficulties but are easily redirected toward a positive outcome in their class experiences.

Some children enter school with disabilities. The disabilities can range from developmental delay and mental retardation to various types of physical disabilities. These children present many types of individual learning needs that are unique to their own conditions.

As we have seen from the information presented on differences in young children, many kinds of diversity can be present in early childhood classrooms. Although diversity is a positive characteristic in children, the teacher is challenged to address the unique needs of each child. In addition, some children are at risk for learning difficulties because of some of the conditions in their lives and development. In the next section, we will explore some of the factors that cause some children to be at risk for development and learning problems.

Early Childhood Programs and At-Risk Learners

Young children tend to be resilient. They are able to cope with positive and negative influences in their lives with a minimum of difficulty. However, other children experience more difficulty when faced with challenges and traumatic events. These children are at risk for problems in development and learning; that is, they might have negative outcomes in personal development and school achievement because of stressors in their lives.

Children of Divorced Families

Some children of divorced families may be at risk for learning difficulties. Such children are more likely to become juvenile delinquents, have trouble in school, need psychiatric help, and experience depression, loneliness, low self-esteem, and low achievement. During the first two years after a divorce, children are often neglected because the parent who is to care for them is overworked, absorbed with problems of surviving, and trying to cope with meeting the increased responsibilities of single parenting (Clark-Stewart, 1989). Some of the children will also have to adjust to a new step-parent and siblings in a stepfamily. An additional factor may be reduced family income because of the altered economic circumstances caused by the divorce.

Although the effects of experiencing a divorce may or may not be long-lasting (Wallerstein, Lewis, & Blakeslee, 2000), the classroom teacher must be sensitive to the trauma these children are experiencing. Teacher support is needed to reassure the affected students that they are valued at school and that school life will provide some consistency in their young lives. The school community can also provide support to the large numbers of young children and their parents who are affected by separation and divorce each year.

✦ The Hemphill Family

Robert and Cathy Hemphill have a blended family. Four years ago, they divorced their spouses and planned to remarry. Robert's children, Kenneth and Katy, soon adjusted to the idea. Their mother remarried within a year after the divorce and was planning to have another baby. Kenneth was six and Katy was four when their parents divorced.

Cathy's three children resented their mother's divorce. Cathy's children, Matthew, Emily, and Eric were 13, 11, and 10, respectively, when their parents divorced. They had to move from a large home with a swimming pool and guesthouse to a small house with only one bathroom.

Cathy and Robert decided to wait until Cathy's children had accepted the divorce and the idea of a stepfather. Unfortunately, after three years, Cathy's oldest son was still very angry and Cathy decided that additional time would not make a difference.

Robert and Cathy have been married for almost two years. They have moved to a three-bedroom home with a large family/game room. Eric and Kenneth have become great pals. Matthew is in high school and playing football. He seems comfortable living in a blended family and enjoys his stepfather. Emily is in high school as well and is an excellent student. All five of the children participate in sports. Robert is working to build another bedroom for Kenneth and Eric to share. The boys are helping him on the weekends. Cathy's children live with her and spend some weekends with their father. Kenneth and Katy live with their mother and spend weekends with their father. Because they just live a few miles down the road, they are with Robert and Cathy frequently on weekdays as well. ✦

Children of Teenage Parents

Children of teenage parents can also be at risk. Many of these parents are barely more than children themselves, with little in the way of parenting skills or financial resources. The teen birth rate actually dropped in the 1970s and remained stable in the 1980s. In 1991 the teen birth rate rose for the fifth year in a row to 62.1 births per 1000 (Children's Defense Fund, 1994). Fortunately by 1997, the rate had fallen to 52.3 births per 1000 (Children's Defense Fund, 2000).

Children born to teenage mothers are more likely to live in a one-parent home at or below the poverty level than those born to older women. Their mothers are likely to be unemployed or working at low-paying jobs. Because of the stressful circumstances for the mothers, children are likely to be at risk from poor nutrition, inadequate housing, and inappropriate parenting. Children entering school from a home headed by a teenage parent frequently need security, nutritious meals, and positive experiences, which the parent is often unable to provide. The parent in turn may need support and assistance from the school in finding social services and in learning how to help the child.

Homeless Children

When attention first focused on the growing numbers of homeless people in the United States, those affected were described as mentally ill individuals who had been released from mental institutions with no local services to provide the assistance they needed. Others without homes were drug- or alcohol-addicted individuals or vagrants who did occasional work. Within the last few decades, the homeless population has come to include families who have lost their homes for a variety of reasons (Eddowes & Hranitz, 1989). By 1997, there were a total of about 850,000 homeless children and youths nationally, 625,330 of them school-age and 216,391 of preschool age (Office of Elementary and Secondary Education, U.S. Department of Education, undated). In 1999 it was estimated that 12 percent of homeless children were placed in foster care, and 22 percent of homeless children lived apart from their immediate family in foster care or with a relative (Better Homes Fund, 1999).

✦ Cassandra

Cassandra is four years old. She and her parents had been living in an old farm house ten miles from Natchez, Mississippi. Her father worked on a nearby farm, but it was recently sold by the owner. Cassandra, her two older brothers, and her parents then moved into Natchez, where they are now staying with Cassandra's aunt. The home is large, but Cassandra's four cousins make

a total of ten people living in the home. Many of Cassandra's toys and clothes are in a storage building behind the house.

Cassandra's mother found work at a dry cleaner's, but her father is still looking for work. Her aunt heard of a vacancy in the Head Start program located near her home and is going to take Cassandra to the center to enroll her in the program. Cassandra's brothers have been enrolled in an elementary school, but they feel like strangers and make excuses not to attend classes. ✦

The reality of life for many of the working poor is that financial security is impossible, even if both parents work. These families live marginal lives that are governed by the availability of work. If one parent loses employment, then the rent cannot be paid and the family must move. Any combination of financial problems, such as the serious illness of a family member or an unexpected expense, can wipe out the family's resources. Another difficulty for the working poor is the unavailability of affordable housing. The decreased availability and deterioration of low-cost housing has made it impossible for many families to afford rent for even the most modest apartment or home (Eddowes & Hranitz, 1989). Providing quality education to homeless children is a challenge because of the transient nature of homeless families (Quint, 1994).

As families join the ranks of the homeless, children become victims of their living conditions. Many homeless families are forced to seek housing in shelters that are not designed for children. Shelters are frequently located in old buildings or houses; consequently, they may not be equipped to provide minimum safety standards for infants and young children.

Homeless children usually have to give up their toys and other items that provide security. It is difficult for them to attend school because of the transient nature of their existence. As a result, regular school attendance is impossible

Teaching Stressed Children

The difficult part of teaching is not the academics. The difficult part is dealing with the great numbers of kids who come from emotionally, physically, socially, and financially stressed homes. Nearly all of my kindergarten kids come from single-parent families. Most of the moms really care for their kids but are very young, undereducated, and financially strained. Children who have had no breakfast or who are fearful of what their mom's boyfriends will do the them—or to their moms—are not very good listeners or cooperative partners with teachers or their peers. We are raising a generation of emotionally stunted and troubled youth who will in turn raise a generation of the same. What is the future of this country when we have so many needy kids? (A kindergarten teacher in Minnesota, quoted by Boyer, 1989, p. 73.)

for many. They are frequently teased by schoolmates who do not understand their plight. If they are able to attend school, their teachers need to be aware of and sensitive to their stress. Like many other populations of at-risk children, they need nutritious meals at school, particularly because shelter meals are not usually prepared for the needs of growing children. For some, the mere availability of food may be uncertain outside of the school (Eddowes & Hranitz, 1989). Special planning is required in every community if homeless children are not to become invisible and forgotten (McCormick & Holden, 1992).

Fortunately, communities and schools are responding to the needs of homeless children. In some cities, special schools have been established to serve children while they are in a shelter. Some cities have acquired apartments for homeless families and help the parents obtain job training and child care. The families are able to stay in the apartments until they can pay for more permanent housing. Organizations such as Habitat for Humanity build modest homes using volunteer labor and donated funds to provide affordable housing for low-income families. Healthcare has been improved through expansion of insurance coverage for low-income families through the Children's Health Insurance Program (CHIP). However, although 2 million children were enrolled in CHIP by September 1999, millions of eligible children still had not been reached (Children's Defense Fund, 2000).

Children Living in Other Stressful Situations

Many children live in stressful home environments which place them at risk for difficulties in development and learning. Some of these stress factors include parents with substance abuse problems, and homes where violence, neglect, and abuse occur that affect young children.

Children who live in a home where the adults are addicted to alcohol or chemicals live in a stressful environment. Parents who are under the influence of drugs or alcohol are more likely to neglect or abuse their children than those who are not addicted.

Domestic violence occurs in every socioeconomic, racial, and ethnic group. Shelters for battered women and children are necessary in most midsize and larger communities to provide a haven for victims of domestic violence. Violence in schools also affects young children. Between 1989 and 1995, the percentage of children who felt unsafe in school or when they were traveling between home and school increased. This is still true even though schools are experiencing a decline in school violence (Children's Defense Fund, 2000).

Violence also results from children having access to guns. Homicide is now a leading cause of death for children between ages 5 and 14. Moreover, more than 300 children died in accidental shootings in 1997 (Children's Defense Fund, 2000).

Schools and teachers have a particularly important responsibility when teaching children who are at risk for neglect or abuse. Children who are dressed inappropriately or who frequently attend school in dirty clothing may exhibit other symptoms of neglect. Similarly, children who have been physically, sexually, or mentally abused may show signs of their condition that may alert the teacher that the child's situation may need to be reported to the proper authorities. Children who are frequently bruised, exhibit burn marks, or have other unusual physical characteristics may have been physically abused. Schools need to help children who are experiencing abuse or neglect; such children may be unable to attend to learning. Schools must take responsibility for these children, because teachers may be the adults outside the family who have the most frequent and consistent contact with the children and are most likely to have an opportunity to initiate intervention. There are indications that the number of neglected and abused children will continue to rise in the immediate future. It is estimated that as many as 500,000 children are abused each year. Many more cases may go unreported. For these children, schools are a haven and possibly their only source of security (Austin, 2000; Santrock, 1997).

Children Who Have Disabilities

Children who have physical and emotional conditions that can affect their learning are frequently described as having special needs. Physical impairments include hearing and visual disabilities as well as other physical disabilities. Hearing impairments range from slight to severe and affect speech and language development (Mayer, 1996; Moran, 1996; Patterson & Wright, 1990). Visual impairments such as near-sightedness (myopia) and farsightedness (hyperopia) can be corrected with eyeglasses. More severe visual impairments include conditions such as congenital cataracts or glaucoma and atrophy of the optic nerve, all of which can have more serious implications for hindrances to learning (Silberman, 1996).

Some students can be seriously disabled by mental retardation or emotional disturbance. Emotionally disturbed children are characterized by an inability (not related to a physical disability) to benefit from instruction. They have difficulty relating to their peers and exhibit wide variations in mood (Edwards & Simpson, 1996). Children with mental retardation have a condition that affects academic learning differently, depending on the amount of retardation. Children with mild retardation are described as educable mentally retarded, and those with moderate retardation are characterized as trainable mentally retarded. Children with severe or profound mental retardation also may have serious physical conditions that require extensive medical attention and services from time of birth (Brown & Yoshida, 1996).

Some children exhibit learning difficulties that are not associated with mental retardation. They have difficulty academically and sometimes socially and do not respond to the usual instructional methods. Children with this condition are described as learning disabled but may also be characterized as hyperactive, perceptually disabled, brain injured, dyslexic, or neurologically impaired (Graham, Harris, Reid, & Kandel, 1996). A more recent and currently popular label for hyperactivity is attention deficit disorder (ADD) (Buchoff, 1990) or attention deficit hyperactivity disorder (ADHD) (Barkeley, 1989).

Children with special needs exhibit many different types of possible interference with learning, as well as variations in the seriousness of the interference. Many of the children can be served by or at least included in the regular classroom within the instructional program used with other students. Other conditions are severe enough to require the services of a special teacher or a combination of specialists to provide therapy or instruction (or both) that is planned for the students' individual needs. Children with special needs also need to interact and learn in the regular classroom as much as possible with their nondisabled peers. Different processes have been used to accomplish this goal. *Mainstreaming* was the first process used to introduce children to a regular classroom for a part of the school day. In *reverse mainstreaming*, children without disabilities were introduced to a classroom serving children with disabilities for part of the day. The current practice is to use *inclusion*, also known as *integration*, where all children are enrolled in the regular preschool or

school program (Odem & Diamond, 1998; Udell, Peters, & Templeman, 1998). An individual program is planned for each student with special needs to determine the balance needed between special services and experiences in the regular classroom (Meyen, 1996a; Wang, Reynolds, & Walberg, 1994–1995).

Marilee

Marilee is five years old and entering kindergarten. She was born with deformities in both her legs. She has been in special programs since she was a baby and has had physical therapy all of her life. Today she walks with the aid of a walker and has a brace on one leg. Marilee is looking forward to kindergarten. She will be attending school a few blocks from her home with many of her friends who live nearby. Marilee's teacher is familiar with her special needs and has made a home visit to talk to Marilee and her parents. Marilee hardly seems to be aware that she has a disability. She can play outdoors with her friends, and finds her brace and walker to be a bit of a bother. She is not self-conscious about her condition and has a smile for everyone. +

At-Risk Children May Need Intervention Programs

Children who are at risk academically need early intervention to remediate the negative factors that can affect their ability to learn. Because early intervention is most effective in eliminating or minimizing risk factors, early childhood programs—many beginning in infancy—enhance the possibilities that children can overcome the conditions in their lives that can negatively affect their learning (Children's Defense Fund, 2000; Taylor, Willits, & Lieberman, 1990).

Early childhood education is very important for children who are at risk academically or have a disability. Early intervention with any kind of risk factor or impairment is important to maximize the child's opportunity to overcome, minimize, or adapt to the disability. Whether the young child is at risk because of economic, physical, or social factors, early attention to the problem is essential. If the child is experiencing more than one risk factor, the possibility of long-term damaging consequences multiplies (Schorr, 1989). Early modification or elimination of risk factors is essential to prevent permanent damage to the child's outcomes.

The Child Mental Health Foundations and Agencies Network has published a list of factors that can put a child at risk for negative school outcomes. They are as follows (Peth-Pierce, 2000, p. 5):

- Low birth weight and neurodevelopmental delays
- Other medical problems
- Difficult temperament and personality (e.g., hyperactivity or aggressive behavior)
- Family composition (e.g., divorce, remarriage)
- Low level of maternal education
- Parental substance abuse
- Immigrant status
- Minority status
- Low socioeconomic status
- Maltreatment
- Problematic maternal relationship history
- Psychophysiological markers (e.g., indicators of changes in the brain or other organs that limit child's cognitive and regularity capacities)
- Insecure attachments in early years
- Child care by someone other than the mother (e.g., child care facility)
- Characteristics of kindergarten and first grade classes (e.g., large class sizes, fewer parent-teacher meetings)

There are also factors that mediate against poor outcomes by children who are at risk (Peth-Pierce, 2000, p. 8):

- Residence with both parents or remarriage after divorce
- Higher cognitive functioning of the child

- Easier temperament of the child
- Child's self confidence
- Emotional support from alternative caregiver
- Higher level of maternal education
- Cooperative parental coping (maintaining positive relationships with child)
- Stable, organized, and predictable home environment
- High-quality daycare at an early age (for children who have insecure attachments to a primary caregiver)
- A secure attachment in infancy and early history of positive functioning
- Larger number of classroom friends
- Social support and internal perceptions of control (for girls only)
- Warm and open relationships with kindergarten teachers

The children who attend preschool programs are diverse, as we have seen from the description of factors that cause children to be diverse and factors within diversity that can cause children to be at risk for difficulties in learning. The settings that serve preschool children are also diverse; however, they are becoming more integrated as we will see in the next section.

The Complex Nature of Settings for Early Childhood Programs

Early childhood education encompasses the years from birth through age eight. The teacher who is preparing to teach children of these ages can be overwhelmed by the various types of settings that serve such children. The majority of primary-age children attend school in some type of institutional setting, be it public, private, or parochial. (Home schooling, where parents conduct instruction with their own children, is a growing method of education but still accounts for only a small percentage of children.) Preschool children, on the other hand, can attend a variety of programs, including those offered by schools, parochial institutions, agencies, corporations, and hospitals.

The role of teachers varies in the programs, as does their salary. Teacher preparation requirements and licensing also can be very different. Financing for the programs ranges from publicly funded schools and projects to settings that are entirely supported by fees paid by parents. For purposes of this discussion, the programs have been categorized as public school programs, nonpublic school programs, Head Start, and child care programs.

Public School Programs

Kindergarten Programs

Public schools have served children under the age of six for more than a century through kindergarten classrooms. The purpose for kindergarten has evolved through the decades during which it as been associated with the public schools. Designed as a program for five-year-olds, it was originally developed following the philosophy and methods of Friedrich Froebel in the nineteenth century. Not all states have kindergartens in their public schools, but as the trend toward expanding early childhood programs in public schools continues, more states are establishing kindergarten classrooms.

In the 1940s and 1950s, kindergartens were perceived as programs for middle-class children. Since the 1960s, however, they have served all populations of children. They have been joined by preschool programs that serve children who are at risk for academic failure (Coleman, 1990). These newer programs can include pre-kindergarten or other programs for four-year-olds, bilingual programs, classes for children with special needs, and extended-care programs.

Pre-kindergarten Programs

Pre-kindergarten programs have been established in some states for four-year-old children who have language or cognitive delays. Pre-

kindergarten children are usually from low-income homes and sometimes from homes where the primary language is not English, and they attend programs that emphasize learning experiences to develop the language and concepts needed for later success in school.

Bilingual Programs

Bilingual programs serve children who speak a language other than English. Although bilingual programs may begin in the preschool years, they usually extend into the elementary grades. In school districts where non–English-speaking children enter school for the first time beyond the intermediate grades, bilingual education may be offered at the secondary level.

Programs for Children with Special Needs

Children who are falling behind in achievement in the elementary grades can receive supplementary instruction through a federally funded program title Chapter I (formerly Title I) and other federal programs. Children who are not demonstrating adequate achievement in mathematics and reading receive additional instruction beyond that provided by the regular classroom teacher.

Children with special needs are also served in preschool classes. At-risk preschool children can be served in programs funded by Chapter I funds. Children are also screened and identified for early childhood special education programs for early intervention that can begin at age three for children with disabilities. Following the development of an Individualized Education Plan (IEP) for each child, the special education teacher and classroom teacher conduct the program with other specialists to optimize the child's potential to learn and develop skills to compensate for the disability (Wolery, 1994).

Extended-Care Programs

Many schools are now implementing extended care before and after classes for students needing child care during out-of-school hours

(Kagan, 1989). These programs can be developed and conducted by school-based personnel or by a community agency that works in a cooperative manner with the school district. Parents can enroll their child in the program; the fees they pay support the payment of program expenses.

Nonpublic School Programs

Parochial and private schools frequently have preschool programs. The starting age may be about three years old, and the program may have a class for three-, four-, and five-year-olds for a few hours each day. Other programs are called nursery schools or mother's-day-out programs and are not offered every day. Preschool programs can also be offered by a local college or university and be labeled as a laboratory school or child development center.

Head Start

Head Start is a publicly funded program. Developed in the 1960s for intervention with at-risk minority and low-income children, it is a comprehensive program that addresses the educational, nutritional, and social needs of such children. It can be associated with public school districts or conducted as a separate program through a community agency. The large number of children served by Head Start has increased in recent years. In 1993, 36 percent of at-risk children had been served. An increase of $550 million for Head Start in fiscal year 1994 enabled tens of thousands of children to be

added to the Head Start program (Children's Defense Fund, 1994). In 1999, over 800,000 children were being served by Head Start programs, representing about 50 percent of the children who were eligible (Children's Defense Fund, 2000).

Child Care

Child care has grown to become a major industry in the United States as a result of the rising numbers of working mothers. In 1987, 52 percent of mothers of children under age five were employed, compared with only 14 percent in 1950. By 1999, as mentioned earlier, 64 percent of mothers with children under age six were in the labor force (Children's Defense Fund, 2000). With many children needing care while their mothers work, there are various types of settings that provide child care.

Family child care is characterized by child care provided in an individual home. The provider cares for a small number of children and has adapted the home to accommodate the children who come to the home each day. In contrast, center-based child care involves a setting that serves larger numbers of children, usually divided by age groups. The children are assigned to classrooms for their age level, and the room is equipped for the programmatic and developmental needs that are characteristic for that age.

Child care centers are established in various community contexts. Centers that are conducted as businesses may range from a single center to a chain of more than one hundred centers. Child care is also provided at church settings. The church sponsors the child care program or leases the facilities to an individual or group during the week. Employer-sponsored child care is also a growing service (Magid, 1989). Large companies or corporations may build a center or negotiate with an existing center to serve the children of their employees. Another option is for a cluster of companies, such as a group located in an industrial park, to

collectively sponsor a center that provides care to children of workers in the sponsoring companies (O'Neil & Foster, 2000). Hospitals frequently offer child care facilities for employees' children but may also provide service for chronically ill children in the community.

Employer-sponsored care may or may not be provided at a reduced rate for employees. Convenience of location may be the primary consideration for the parent. Federally supported child care, in contrast, funds child care for low-income parents and assists them in obtaining job training or employment that will allow them to become wage earners, rather than continue as welfare recipients. In 1993, the Child Care and Development Block Grant was passed, which had a positive effect on the availability of quality child care for low-income parents (Children's Defense Fund, 1994). Although care for infants and preschool children while parents work is the primary service provided by child care centers, educational programs are also conducted.

Continuing Complexity in Preschool Programs

It must be obvious to the reader by now that it is a difficult task to describe early childhood programs in neat categories. In reality, over time, programs have had to modify and provide additional services to adapt to the changing needs of families. Public schools are accepting pre-kindergarten children and are offering child care, and child care centers are strengthening their instructional programs. Private preschools are also extending their programs to include child care. The field is becoming comprehensive, and the various components are no longer able to function as separate entities (Bowman, Donovan, & Burns, 2000). Both education and care must be adequate in all programs.

Growing numbers of children are in programs that are part of public education. An estimated 1 million pre-kindergarten children were enrolled in public schools in 1999 (Clifford,

Early, & Hills, 1999). Forty-two states served approximately 725,000 pre-kindergarten children in 1998–99 (Schulman, Blank, & Ewen, 1999). The pre-kindergarten programs included voluntary pre-kindergarten, special education pre-kindergarten, Head Start, Even Start, and pre-kindergarten programs for 260,000 at-risk children funded by Title I funds (Hinkle, 2000).

A major concern about early childhood programs is the variation in quality among program options. Many programs do not have sufficient quality because of underfinancing, inadequate teacher pay, which leads to a high turnover rate, inadequate regulation, and uncoordinated training mechanisms (Kagan & Neuman, 1997). Major efforts are being made to improve the disparities in quality. The Quality 2000 Initiative resulted in the publication of *Years of Promise: A Comprehensive Learning Strategy for America's Children*

(Carnegie Corporation of New York, 1996). A similar project conducted by the U.S. Department of Education resulted in the report, *Eager to Learn: Educating Our Preschoolers* (Bowman, Donovan, & Burns, 2000). Both publications provide recommendations for program improvement that include program quality, child outcomes, curriculum, parent involvement, assessment, professional development, credentialing of teachers, program licensing, and development of program standards by individual states.

Because there are various types of early childhood settings and because early childhood programs vary within a community, between communities, and among different areas of the nation, early childhood teachers work under diverse circumstances. How teachers in early childhood programs design and implement curriculum and instruction in their own program

Bright Beginnings

The Bright Beginnings Initiative is a literacy rich program that serves 2000 students in 25 locations in the Charlotte-Mecklenburg School District in North Carolina. The goal of the initiative is to ensure that 85 percent of students in the district from all racial and economic backgrounds read at or above grade level by third grade.

The Bright Beginnings Program and Double Oaks Pre-Kindergarten and Family Resource Center serves 400 children and is also an example of how different types of early childhood programs and agencies can work together to provide a high quality pre-kindergarten program for at risk children. In addition to the Bright Beginnings program, the Even Start/Family Independence Initiative and a family resource center are housed at Double Oaks. Other community groups that participate or support the Bright Beginnings Initiative include the Charlotte Speech and Hearing and United Way, Head Start, Mecklenburg County Health Department, and Smart Start. Two churches, Myers Park Methodist Church, and St. Gabriel's Catholic Church, donate funds for the Learning Gallery at the center.

Although it is not possible to describe all of the programs and services that take place at Double Oaks, the Bright Beginnings Initiative has shown some initial positive results. The 1997–98 class performed consistently better on the kindergarten assessment conducted at the end of the school year than a similar group of children who did not participate in Bright Beginnings.

Source: *U.S. Department of Education Community Update, 80,* 6–7 (2000).

setting depends on their unique backgrounds and experiences and the way in which their individual teaching styles fit into the particular environment where they work with young children. The early childhood teacher seeking employment will want to be aware of the different possibilities that are available in the community. In addition, the teacher entering the profession will want to be aware of the philosophy and approach being used in the early childhood setting where employment is sought to determine what type of a program is in place or being developed. Many teachers feel that they have no choice, that they must take whatever teaching opportunity is available. If this is the case, and the program is not appropriate, the teacher might work toward improving the situation or seek a better position in another setting. On the other hand, the teacher might have the opportunity to join a group of teachers who are in the process of restructuring their program and curriculum to be developmentally appropriate. Moreover, there are early childhood settings in many states that have been offering developmentally appropriate quality programs for many years. The teachers hired to join this type of setting have the advantage of being able to learn from fellow teachers.

The Changing Role of the Teacher in Developing Curriculum for Early Childhood Programs

It is clear that many challenges face tomorrow's teachers of young children in the early childhood years. Gone are the days when young children could be perceived as coming from similar homes and family backgrounds. Gone are the days when curriculum and instruction for young children could be designed from a commercial program prepared by a specialist in some distant city. No longer can the teacher be concerned only with the instructional program when work-

ing with a classroom of young children. The teachers of tomorrow will develop educational programs for diverse populations of students. They will acknowledge and appreciate student differences and involve their families in the program. A major challenge will be to learn how to design a curriculum that is appropriate for all young children and compatible with their development and interests, as well as their unique needs. Development of high-quality programs for young children will include design of a curriculum that is dynamic, child-centered, and responsive to the diverse populations that are represented in each classroom.

The Role of the Teacher in Developing Curriculum for Diverse Populations

Every classroom of small children is diverse. No matter what the background of the children, even if their circumstances seem to be similar, their individual families are different, with varied family routines, rituals, and observances. If the children come from more varied ethnic groups, and cultures, the diversity will be more pronounced. These and other consideration are kept in mind when preparing learning experiences in the early childhood classroom.

Multicultural Curriculum

There is now an emphasis on a multicultural curriculum in early childhood programs in recognition of the diversity of young children. One focus of a multicultural curriculum has been to study different cultures around the world: a social studies curriculum might include the study of, for instance an African culture, the Eskimos, or the culture in a South American country. The definition of *multicultural curriculum* intended here is more specific to the developmental needs of young children in the early childhood years.

The multicultural curriculum reflects the cultural representation within the group of children in a particular classroom (Diaz-Soto, 1999). Topics studied incorporate the unique reflections of those topics in the child's family. If foods are being studied, family recipes can represent the multicultural makeup of the classroom. The multicultural curriculum celebrates the contributions of the cultures of children who are learning together at a particular time in their lives (Au & Kawakami, 1991).

Curriculum for Children from Diverse Family Environments

Earlier in the chapter, the complex diversity of family environments in which children live was discussed. Children come to early childhood programs from all types of housing arrangements and family structures. Their parents represent many kinds of employment or lack thereof. Some of the children come from very secure family lifestyles, whereas others are experiencing stress that can originate from many causes. Although children from every socioeconomic group can come from stressful home environments, children living at the poverty level are more likely to be affected by multiple sources of stress. Teachers of young children need to be sensitive to how the program designed for these children demonstrates awareness of their needs and provides continuity and support when needed. The curriculum for social development is particularly relevant when accommodating differences in family environments.

Curriculum for Children with Special Needs

Although public school programs are most likely to serve children with special needs within a preschool or primary-grade program, other early childhood settings also serve children with disabilities or other types of expectionalities. The teacher of young children not only needs to be aware of the adaptations that must be made to accommodate a child with special needs in the classroom environment but also must consider how learning experiences can be prepared to

include the child's special learning needs. Children with ADHD may work better in small rather than large group activities. Children with limited vision will need to have visual activities modified to take advantage of their best avenue for exploring the environment. Each child with special needs will have individual strengths and requirements that will be factors in how the teacher and other students can assist him.

The Role of the Teacher in Involving Parents in Curriculum Development

As discussed earlier in the chapter, various factors are causing changes in family lifestyles and structures. Many of the changes have put families under stress. Teachers in early childhood programs must be more perceptive and sensitive to the needs young children may bring to school that reflect possibly stressful family circumstances. Therefore, teachers will want to know and involve parents and families in their programs (Carnegie Corporation of New York, 1996). Changes in family lifestyles require that different types of programs be available to fit individual family requirements. Cooperation between program and family will be necessary if the unique needs of individual family circumstances are to be fulfilled. (Bowman, Donovan & Burns, 2000; Hinkle, 2000).

There are more important reasons for involving parents in the early childhood program. The extensive research conducted on intervention programs for young children in recent decades has revealed that parent involvement is an essential factor in successful programs. The majority of parents of young children are employed, and they need information on how they can help their children. They also may need help in understanding how important their role is for the child's success in development and learning (Boyer, 1989). Parents may need training in parenting skills or help in seeking assistance for themselves or their children. Supportive partnership relationships among the teachers, other early childhood program staff members and the family are important ingredients in the development of a successful program to better serve the child (Carnegie Corporation of New York, 1996; Kagan & Neuman, 1997).

Parents can also make a very important contribution to the school. In addition to assisting the teacher or staff within possible time limitations, parents can give valuable input to the development of the school curriculum. Parents can serve as resources for learning experiences and share their interests and skills with teachers and children. They can provide needed assistance to the teacher in organizing materials and other resources for the instructional program. Parents can help teachers understand their interests and goals for their child's development and learning while serving as a source of support for the teacher in developing the best possible program for the child (McCormick, 1990).

The Role of the Teacher in Addressing Conflicts Between Theory and Practice in Curriculum Development

Early childhood settings have evolved different traditions. As discussed, early childhood programs today are moving toward a comprehensive, overlapping system as educators seek to develop quality programs that are responsive to changing family needs. The task of developing quality programs for young children is complex. The teacher not only must plan the program for all types of children but also must understand the contributions of various types of early childhood settings, the contributions of research to the development of quality program models, and the relationships between theory and practice in program planning.

Over the course of the history of early childhood education, various theories and influences have affected how programs are designed for young children. These historical and theoretical factors will be discussed in Chapter 2. In the twenty-first century, teachers are experiencing a complex task in determining how best to use current theories and influences to teach young children. Research on how children develop and learn has come into conflict with educational programs to accelerate children's learning in early childhood classrooms. Teachers of young children are groping to understand the implications of these conflicting approaches and will be working to resolve the resulting issues in the years to come. The purpose of this textbook is to help practicing and future teachers understand variables that influence the development of appropriate programs for young children. It also is intended to assist teachers and future teachers of young children in sorting out the issues and developing the knowledge and ability to develop quality instructional programs.

Summary

We are just beginning to understand the challenges and opportunities that young children bring to early childhood programs. Because we are a nation of people whose origins are from many nations, we represent many cultures, ethnic groups, races, and languages. Children enter early childhood settings from families that also represent the full range of economic levels, from poverty to affluence. Their potential for learning is affected by their intellectual aptitude as well as other negative and positive conditions in the family. Their ability to fully participate in the program may be affected by physical handicaps. Children who have an individual or family situation that can be a deterring factor in their participation and learning in a program are said to be at risk. Some children have several risk factors in their lives that compound the possibility that they will later experience difficulty in school.

Because the early childhood years between birth and age eight are very important in the formation of the child's potential for development and learning, early childhood programs can make a major difference in preventing or remediating a risk factor. Various early childhood programs located in public schools, private institutions, and community agencies provide services that aim to reduce risk factors for preschool and primary school children.

Growing numbers of preschool children, including infants, require weekday care while their parents are at work. Because of this growing need, various settings—ranging from family child-care homes, for-profit child care centers, churches, and schools—are providing care to accommodate these young children in the preschool years. School-age children may need extended care before and after school until their parents are able to return home with them. The separation between caregiving and educational programs is diminishing as early childhood settings expand and adapt their programs to fit family requirements.

Teachers in these varied settings work with children in the same age ranges. Although the purpose for establishing their program originally may have been distinctly different from that for other programs, services and educational programs offered by early childhood settings now tend to be more similar because of the characteristics they share in meeting contemporary family needs. Teachers and caregivers in all settings will want to be perceptive to the positive and negative factors that affect each young child and to what their roles should be in helping the child continue to develop and learn to his or her full potential.

This chapter discussed many variables that contribute to the diversity in young children. Indeed, the reader may come away with the impression that there is "something wrong" with almost every child who is in the early childhood years. That is not the case. A large percentage of children come from stable, happy homes and are in good health. Even if they have experienced divorce, economic downturn, or a health condition, they may exhibit no characteristics that indicate that they are having problems. Similarly, not all children from low-income homes

exhibit limited potential as a result of the home environment. It would be equally unbalanced to give the impression that most young children in early childhood programs are similar to the precocious, well-adjusted children in family sitcoms on television. Nevertheless, it is important for those preparing for or engaged in the teaching and care of young children to be knowledgeable about and sensitive to the conditions in the young child's life to which they will respond in planning their instructional program. Teachers in early childhood programs have many challenges and opportunities when they work with the complexity of factors that affect each student.

Teachers in the future will have complex roles; moreover, they will be in partnership with the parents and other persons who may be serving and influencing the child's development and learning. They will be developing a curriculum for young children that will facilitate physical, social-emotional, and cognitive development and learning. They will be teaching the "whole child" in whichever early childhood setting they have chosen.

Study Questions

1. Why do teachers of young children need to get to know their students before they enter the early childhood program?
2. What kind of information can teachers obtain from the parents and their children that will help them in designing their instruction program?
3. What factors will teachers in early childhood programs need to consider when determining the type of setting in which they would like to teach?
4. Why do teachers of young children need to understand risk factors that can affect young children's success in elementary school?

5. Why do students from low-income homes sometimes need nearly intervention programs prior to the elementary years?

6. What are the implications of cultural and ethnic differences in young students for planning the instructional program?

7. Family environments are changing because of social and economics factors. What are some of these changes, and how can young children be affected by them?

8. Why are young children who are born to teenage mothers likely to have more than one condition that puts them at risk during the preschool years?

9. How can it be that contemporary lifestyles are stressful in all types of families and at all income levels?

10. Why is the population of homeless children increasing? What are the effects of homelessness on young children?

11. How can inappropriate adult lifestyles negatively affect young children?

12. How are children most affected by the increasing violence in U.S. society?

13. Why will teachers and settings serving children in the early childhood years have expanding responsibilities for children and families in instructional or caregiving programs throughout the 2000s and beyond?

14. How can children vary mentally and physically in their ability to learn?

15. What is meant by the term *exceptional children?*

16. How are early childhood programs especially helpful for children who are at risk academically or have some type or exceptionality?

17. How are the varied early childhood settings that serve preschool children different yet also increasingly more similar?

18. Why are public schools expanding their programs for the preschool years?

19. Why will teachers of young children under age eight need to continually learn about curriculum development for early childhood programs?

20. Why is ongoing communication with parents essential for teachers in early childhood programs?

21. Teachers frequently report that parents are too busy to become involved with school programs. How and why should teachers find ways to convince parents of how vital their interaction and participation is for their child's progress in school?

22. How is the field of early childhood education both challenging and potentially exciting as we begin a new century?

Historical and Theoretical Bases for Appropriate Programs in Early Childhood Settings

CHAPTER OBJECTIVES

As a result of reading this chapter, you will be able to

1. Describe the historical bases of different types of early childhood programs.
2. Explain six theories of development—and be able to compare them.
3. Discuss how today's early childhood programs reflect their history and roots.

Chapter 1 discussed the diversity among the children who attend early childhood programs. Included was a discussion of the variety of early childhood programs available to serve the needs of the diverse population of young children. These programs of various types have a rich heritage and reflect the contributions of leaders in the field. They also represent the work of theorists who studied the course of child development and the nature of children's learning.

In this chapter, we will review history and explore the people, trends, and movements that have shaped the field of early childhood education as it is today. In the sections that follow, we will first survey the historical roots of early childhood education. Then we will look at the history of early childhood programs for particular populations of young children. This task is difficult because public schools, child care settings, private preschools, programs for at-risk children, and programs for children with disabilities have histories that overlap and have similar influences. The history of early childhood education can be described as a fabric with many threads that form the whole. Each of the different components has a piece in the fabric formed by some threads. The sections that follow provide the historical roots of early childhood education in an overview of the field. Then, we will trace individual components that include the evolution of programs for children whose development and learning are at risk and of programs for children with disabilities within their historical contexts.

Historical Roots of Early Childhood Education

For many years after this country was first settled, there were no schools for older elementary-age children, much less for those who were of primary age and younger. The priority for education in the colonies in the seventeenth century before the American Revolution was to establish colleges and then academies that would prepare young men for university work. Harvard University was established in 1636, followed by William and Mary, Princeton, and others. Later, secondary schools were established. All early educational institutions were for white male students (Snyder, 1972).

Younger children were taught in the home. Children of the poor were trained through apprenticeships for a vocation or labored in factories, in mines, or on farms. It was not until the nineteenth century, after the Civil War, that public school systems were developed with access to education for all populations.

Dame schools were the first educational settings available for children in the early childhood years during the colonial period. A group of parents paid an unmarried or widowed woman to teach their children in her home. The children received instruction in reading and writing. The Bible was the common source for instruction. Girls were also taught household skills, whereas boys learned skills needed for farming (Bonn, 1976).

Rural Schools

Rural schools were established to provide education as the new nation expanded across the West and in the South during the nineteenth century. Based on the agricultural calendar, schools frequently were in session only during the winter months when weather prevented outdoor farm work. The Northwest Ordinances of 1784, 1785, and 1787 allowed public lands to be leased to benefit public schools. Students as young as three years and as old as those in late adolescence were served in one-room schoolhouses. Uneducated adults and older farm workers frequently attended school when their work and the weather permitted. The closing of one-room schools occurred at the end of the nineteenth century as the country became urbanized and school districts were consolidated. Children younger than age six were gradually excluded from attendance in the rural schools (Gulliford, 1984).

✦ Early Childhood Education in the One-Room School

In the mid-nineteenth century, the school year was divided into two terms. The typical summer term extended over five months, from May to August or September. The winter term varied from state to state, depending on local planting and harvesting times; it generally began after harvest in November and continued until just before spring plowing, usually around early April. After 1900 the school year was standardized into one nine-month term, beginning in September and ending in May.

The ages of the students varied considerably. Before the Civil War, children in rural areas were sent to school at the age of three or four, partly to get them out of the house and partly because parents believed that the school was an exten-

sion of the family and, therefore, the proper place for children. In Ohio between 1845 and 1864, children of three or four began learning how to spell. Older girls and boys would watch over their younger brothers and sisters. By observing the other students in the classroom, the four-year-olds learned basic skills (Gulliford, 1984, p. 47). ✦

The Evolution of Early Childhood Education

The history of early childhood education in this country reflects influences dating to the eighteenth century in Europe. In the Middle Ages, children did not have a childhood as we perceive it today. Children worked alongside their parents at a very early age to provide food and clothing needed for survival. It was not until Jean-Jacques Rousseau (1762–1911) wrote the novel *Emile* (1762) that the development of the child was considered a separate stage in life. Rousseau's belief in nature and in the child's right to the period called *childhood* had a great impact on education. Rousseau believed in a natural approach to educating children that would permit growth without interference and restrictions.

Johann Pestalozzi, a Swiss educator, is considered the first early childhood teacher. Influenced by Rousseau's perceptions of children and childhood, Pestalozzi established several schools for poor and orphaned children (Braun & Edwards, 1972).

The German educator Friedrich Froebel was in turn influenced by Pestalozzi. He visited Pestalozzi's school in Yverdun occasionally. Although he was unable to understand clearly what Pestalozzi was trying to achieve, he was able to develop his own philosophy of how children should learn, and he used his ideas to establish the first school with an organized curriculum for preschool children. Froebel created the *Kindergarten,* or "child garden," because he believed that his classes were gardens for children rather than school rooms. He believed that part of each day should be spent in play; the rest of the day was spent on a teacher-directed curriculum based on what Froebel called *gifts and occupations.* Gifts were to be handled by the child to achieve a sense of reality, whereas occupations were used to train the eye, hand, and mind. Examples of gifts were yarn balls of bright colors. One occupation was weaving using strips of paper (Braun & Edwards, 1972).

In the United States, the kindergarten movement marked the introduction of the first program designed specifically for children younger than age six. It was brought to this country by one of Froebel's students, Mrs. Carl Schurz, who began a kindergarten in her own home in Watertown, Wisconsin, in 1855 (Snyder, 1972). The first kindergartens were private and organized for children whose parents could afford to pay tuition, but as the kindergarten movement became more popular, kindergartens for poor children were established in settlement houses, churches, and wherever an advocate could find a space where a kindergarten could be opened (Weber, 1969).

Kindergartens soon became affiliated with public schools. In 1873, the first public school kindergarten was established in the St. Louis

public schools by Superintendent William T. Harris and Susan Blow, a leader in the kindergarten movement. Gradually, as more kindergartens were absorbed into the public school system, private and philanthropic kindergartens were discontinued. The kindergarten program itself changed as students of the child-study movement clashed with traditionalists who felt that Froebel's methods must be maintained without any change. Leaders of the new field of psychology and of the child-study movement that evolved after 1890 taught new information about child development and the purposes of education; this information influenced teachers to reconsider how young children should be taught (Braun & Edwards, 1972; Weber, 1969).

Although the history of early childhood education in the twentieth century reflected the contributions of American psychologists and educators, European influences continued. Rousseau viewed the child as a competent, self-initiated learner and the teacher as a facilitator. His awareness of developmental stages and stage-related learning and views of the child informed later approaches to early childhood education.

Pestalozzi promoted the importance of the parents in the child's learning. He saw the child's moral, physical, and intellectual development as the purpose of his work. He trained older children to tutor young children and taught them how to use variations in teaching strategies with their younger peers. Pestalozzi himself used direct instructions, modeling, and advance organizers in his teaching strategies—strategies that have reappeared in more current theories and approaches to teaching (Williams, 1999).

In fact, many of the approaches and innovations of the twentieth century were influenced by Europeans such as Pestalozzi, Froebel, Rousseau and others from the eighteenth and nineteenth centuries as well as Piaget and Vygotsky in the twentieth century. Moreover, many of the values and beliefs in how young children should be treated had a permanent influence on the view of children in the United States that still affects our advocacy for children in American society.

Susan Blow and Changes in the Kindergarten Movement

The kindergarten movement was very popular in the United States and Canada. As the numbers of kindergarten teachers grew, they began meeting as a part of National Education Association conferences each year. In 1892 the International Kindergarten Union (IKU) was organized as a separate organization in Sarasota Springs, New York. The IKU was later to become The Association for Childhood Education International (ACEI). In the early years of the new organization, Froebelian methods were generally accepted by the membership. Nevertheless, advocates of the child-study movement soon began to question the traditionalists at IKU meetings. Susan Blow was one of the Frobelians who argued to retain Froebel's methods in American kindergartens. In 1898, heated arguments were presented by conference participants for both sides. According to accounts of the meeting, Susan Blow was the most popular speaker, as reported by the press:

> *The breeziest greeting of the day was that given to Miss Susan E. Blow. . . . She was armed to mow down some new-fangled notions labelled "Progressive," and she slashed them right and left with bristling weapons to the delight of the convention. . . . She believed in the old introspection. She ridiculed the absurdities of mathematical measurements of psychological faces and declared that under this physiological psychology experiments with children became the teacher's sport. . . . She didn't object to looking to individual characteristics, but it was on the basis of what was universal, along the basis of the common humanities alone, that it was possible to educate the child,*

> *and it was not on the narrow basis of his own individual idiosyncrasies. The criticisms made by Miss Blow delivered with her particular emphasis carried the Convention off its feet, and the applause was long.* (The Philadelphia Inquirer, January 13, 1898, quoted in Snyder, 1972, pp. 70–71) ✦

The Progressive Era

During the 1920s and 1930s, which were considered to be a part of the Progressive Era in education, educational leaders and psychologists used their work in child study to propose teaching methods for preschools and elementary schools. Whereas early public schools in the nineteenth century had stressed reading, writing, and mathematics skills with an emphasis on rote learning, new leaders such as John Dewey, Alice Temple, Patty Smith Hill, Francis Parker, and William Heard Kilpatrick proposed that schooling for young children should be more child-centered and meaningful. John Dewey proposed that the classroom should be a miniature community where children could engage in purposeful learning related to the society in which they lived. The child-centered curriculum proposed by progressive educators included study through projects and preparation for life as adults. Children took responsibility for their learning, and teachers involved them in instructional planning.

Patty Smith Hill's Legacy for the Kindergarten

If Susan Blow was a staunch defender of the traditional kindergarten following Froebelian methods, Patty Smith Hill had a major role in the development of the kindergarten model that persisted from the Progressive Era until the Civil Rights era in the 1960s. She taught for many years at Columbia Teacher's College, where Blow was also a professor. Hill, however, was influenced by John Dewey's philosophy of education and Edward Thorndike's interest and research in measurement and learning.

Throughout her tenure at Teacher's College, Hill pursued her interest in improving the kindergarten by experimenting and by studying young children in the classroom. At the same time that Teacher's College led the way in teacher training in the United States, Hill was recognized as a major leader in kindergarten education. She published extensively on kindergarten curriculum and programs, and her influence in kindergarten classrooms had a lengthy history. If Froebel was the father of kindergarten, Hill was the mother of the Progressive kindergarten in the United States. (Snyder, 1972) ✦

One of the influential leaders in the child-study movement was Arnold Gesell, a student of G. Stanley Hall, who had originated child-study research at university-based centers. Gesell did extensive study of children at Yale University and contributed the first descriptions of children at different chronological ages based on normative data. His theory of child development, called the *maturational theory*, was based on the belief that the child unfolded like a flower and developed readiness for learning as she matured (Gesell & Ilg, 1946). Gesell's influence was strong during the 1930s through the 1950s. The maturational theory had a major influence on the evolution of public school organization and curriculum during those decades.

✦ The Nature of Arnold Gesell's Norms of Development

Gesell's major scientific effort related to the establishment of norms of behavior. He wrote of the Yale Clinic, "The major research is directed toward a normative charting of behavior devel-

opment," with the direct purpose of developing "norms of growth."

No one asked the important question of the nature of the population utilized for the derivation of norms. The population of children studied at the Yale Clinic was of "high average or superior intelligence" and came from homes of "good or high socio-economic status." Essentially, Gesell used children of adults in the academic community. (Weber, 1970, pp. 14–15) ✦

Nursery School and Child Care Movements

Other sources also influenced early childhood education in the early decades of the nineteenth century. The nursery school movement that originated in England with the work of the McMillan sisters was adopted in the United States; nursery schools were established in this country as part of the child-study movement. Such schools had been developed to improve health and nutrition for preschool children from families living in poverty in England; thus, they were similar to the day nurseries developed in this country for custodial care that were later to become child care programs.

The child care movement dates back to the middle of the nineteenth century. The early years of child care in a group setting cannot be separated from other early childhood programs, because of the overlap in programs. Philanthropic, religious, and organizational groups who were concerned about immigrant, orphaned, or neglected children became known as "child savers" because they established programs to save poor children through parent training, playground development, nursery schools, and day nurseries. Often these programs resided in the same buildings as kindergartens. Frequently, children attended more than one program each day (Cremin, 1988).

By the 1930s, philanthropic schools were declining in number. Conversely, the child care movement continued to expand as poor families needed somewhere to place children during the depression years. The advent of World War II saw a continuation of the need for child care as women worked in the war effort (Wortham, 1992).

✦ A Broader View of Child Care

The myth of the full-time American mother as the eternal model does not fit the complex realities of the past any more than it does the practices of the present, and many of the options that exist today have had previous incarnations in only slightly different form. For example, colonial apprenticeship was to a large extent male child care, part of a little-known tradition of men as nurturers. It was also an early form of foster care, particularly for poor young children whose families could not provide for them.

On the plantation, slave children too young to work in the fields were dropped off in the morning to be looked after in groups, a situation oddly suggestive of today's day care for the children of working mothers. Wealthy white children, with their legendary mammies, evoke a long legacy of shared mothering with more than one woman at the center of the picture. (Youcha, 1995, p. 13) ✦

The Influence of Maria Montessori

Dr. Maria Montessori, a leader in early childhood education in Italy, also influenced educators in the United States. Dr. Montessori was the first woman to earn a degree in medicine in Italy. In 1907, she was invited to start a school in a slum in Rome. Montessori believed in training of the senses. The curriculum she designed for preschool children from low-income households included activities that were developed for the sense of touch, as well as for thermal, visual, and auditory senses. Her materials were didactic (and interesting as well as educational when used over and over) and self-correcting. Although Montessori's approach to early education was not received well in the 1920s, when it was first introduced in the United States, her method became popular in private and parochial schools after 1950. Her sensorial materials were later adapted by special education teachers to facilitate the learning of children with disabilities (Braun & Edwards, 1972).

Urbanization of Public Schools

Urbanization of public schools after 1900 brought other changes as well. As small school districts consolidated and urban schools became larger, the graded school came into being. Although rural schools had teachers who taught whatever levels were needed by the students, consolidated schools and graded schools focused on one age or grade. With the advent of standardized, commercially produced curriculum designed for graded elementary schools, teachers were trained for grade-level teaching, with expectations of what the children should be able to accomplish in a particular grade.

Beginning with the early years when kindergartens became part of primary schools, there were differences between the philosophies and teaching approaches held by kindergarten teachers and elementary school teachers. The source of their training was different, as was their approach to the needs of their students. Although kindergarten teachers had a tradition of Froebelian training that was later influenced and modified by training in child development, primary-grade teachers were the product of teachers' colleges and normal schools, where the emphasis in teacher preparation was in teaching methodology. The differences continued until recent decades, as universities and colleges maintained separate programs for child development and public elementary school training. Kindergarten teachers have had, and continue to have, a mixed identity, as they are part of both levels of education (Granucci, 1990).

A Period of Innovation: The 1950s and 1960s

The 1950s and 1960s brought a new group of psychologists and educators whose work focused on the importance of the early years of childhood for later development and learning. Benjamin Bloom, Jean Piaget, J. McVicker Hunt, and Jerome Bruner were some of the leaders of the period who emphasized the significance of the early years in child development. Bloom (1964) found that the first five years were the most rapid period of development and the most significant in determining the course of further development. He believed that deprivation during the preschool years could have serious consequences for both cognitive and affective development. Jean Piaget also believed that the nature of the experiences provided a child during the early years could make a difference in the child's intellectual development. Piaget proposed that the child constructed knowledge through active interaction with the environment. The child proceeds through stages of cognitive development as an active initiator of learning, and responses to information depend on the level of understanding at that stage of development (McCarthy & Houston, 1980; Schickedanz, Schickedanz, Hansen, & Forsyth, 1993). Hunt (1961) further supported Piaget's proposal of the role of experience during the early years. He questioned the notion of fixed intelligence and suggested that early experiences were important for the development of intelligence. Quality encounters with the environment during the early years make a higher adult level of intellectual capacity possible.

Bruner was also concerned with the development of cognition. Like Piaget, he believed that there were transitions in a child's intellectual development. For Bruner, the child first represented knowledge using visual imagery, or "iconic representation," to more abstract "symbolic representation." He was also influenced by Lev Vygotsky in that he believed that culture plays a central role in cognition and that school is a cultural setting for learning. He emphasized the importance of language in mediating learning, again similar to Vygotsky's view of the importance of language in cognitive development (Anglin, 1973).

In the 1960s, federal intervention programs, intended to enhance learning for children from deprived environments, brought a new emphasis to the importance of the early childhood years. Projects such as Head Start, Follow Through, and Home Start; programs funded for migrant and bilingual children; and programs for children with special needs all had research components. Projects involved experimentation into theories of learning and development of innovative approaches to curriculum and instruction. Although early evaluation reports of the Head Start program were disappointing when measuring long-term intellectual gain, longitudinal studies found positive outcomes for students who had been in Head Start, compared with their peers who had not been enrolled in the program (Berrueta-Clement, Schweinhart, Barrett, Epstein, & Weikart, 1984). The instructional materials and teaching methods developed in these projects in the 1960s were used in early childhood programs, particularly public school programs, in the 1970s. Younger children were also served in public school settings when federal programs funded school districts to establish classrooms for migrant children as young as age four. Preschool children who were at risk for inadequate achievement in the primary grades—including children with disabilities and other special needs—were served in early intervention and compensatory programs.

Developers of policy and curriculum in elementary education also reacted to the national revolution in education, sparked by the Cold

War and the launching of *Sputnik* by the Soviets. In an effort to improve public education, there was an emphasis on mathematics and science in the curriculum. At the same time, federal funding for children who were considered to be "disadvantaged" brought new expectations for teachers to teach according to students' individual needs. In the 1970s, innovations in instruction, many of which were federally funded, were available to schools to explore new models and teaching strategies. The Open Classroom, Individually Guided Education, and Competency-Based Instruction were a few of the instructional innovations used in elementary schools. The Open Classroom was based on the concept of open education borrowed from the British educational system. Instruction was child-centered, with the teacher serving in the role of instructional facilitator. Learning centers were used in elementary classrooms. In addition, new schools were designed without interior walls to provide large, open learning areas where teachers and students from multiple classrooms learned together.

Individually Guided Education was a process of individualized instruction that used a team of teachers to plan and implement instruction based on individually paced instruction. Teams of teachers often worked in an open environment, although it was not a requirement of the process. Competency-Based Instruction also was a form of individually paced education. It was based on specific learning objectives, and progress through the curriculum was based on mastery of the sequenced objectives.

In spite of the influx of information and curriculum methods and materials brought into the public schools from federally funded programs, differences in philosophy and methodology continued to exist between programs for children under age six and programs for children in the primary grades. Such differences had an impact on how problems in implementing school reform were addressed in the 1980s and 1990s (Morgan, 1989).

The Evolution of Early Childhood Programs for Populations at Risk

In the preceding section that addressed the historical routes of early childhood education, information was given on how intervention programs were initiated in the 1960s and 1970s to address the special learning needs of children who were at risk for failure in public school. At-risk populations included children from poverty homes, children from homes where a language other than English was spoken, and children who had disabling conditions. Federally funded programs were implemented to provide compensatory and intervention programs for at-risk children. Compensatory programs were supplementary to the regular instruction provided in the public schools. They were intended to give children from disadvantaged environments extra help in their educational program. Intervention programs, to the contrary, were designed to serve children with disabilities or who were at risk for developing a disability. Intervention programs were and are intended to make a difference in the child's developmental outcome. A series of legislative acts in the 1960s first funded these programs to address the needs of infants and young children who were at risk for learning as a result of a variety of conditions and circumstances. Some of the infant programs that resulted from this legislation are described in Chapter 5. Before the 1960s, efforts to address the needs of young children in at-risk populations were minimal and extremely limited.

Concerns for the successful education of children from at-risk populations emerged slowly. From the early years of educational efforts in this country, it was recognized that children of the poor deserved the support of those with more advantages in life. Thus, programs were established by philanthropists for urban children living in poverty who were too young to go to school. Conversely, children of the poor also labored for long hours in dangerous occupations until compulsory education laws finally were enacted and

enforced and the Fair Labor Standards Act passed in 1938 ended child labor. In addition, before the 1950s and 1960s, little attention was paid to differences in school achievement between poor and minority children and their middle-class peers (Wortham, 1992).

African American Education

Children from minority populations were likely to be at risk for learning because of poverty, but they had the additional misfortune to attend separate and lower-quality schools than their white peers. Until segregation was abolished during the Civil Rights era, African American and many Hispanic children attended segregated schools.

Before the Civil War, there were schools in both the North and South for African American children, particularly before the Revolutionary War. After that war, and until after the Civil War, teaching of African American children was forbidden by law (Farmer, 1976). After the Civil War, southern whites opposed the establishment of schools for African American children. In the early 1900s, segregated schools were legalized, and it was not until after World War II that these conditions of inferior schooling changed.

Latino Education

Children of Latino families suffered a similar fate in attending separate and inferior schools before the 1960s. Although their education was not segregated by law, they attended neighborhood schools where all of the children were Mexican American. Fewer financial resources were directed toward these schools.

Native American Education

Native American children also attended separate schools. Their schooling was under the jurisdiction of the U.S. government. During the nineteenth century, one-room schoolhouses on the reservations were run by missionaries. A system of boarding schools away from the reservations was also established by the end of the nineteenth century. These children were forced to leave their homes and culture and adopt different names and wear different clothing in an effort to acculturate them to mainstream American life (Snapper, 1976).

Minority Education During Depression and War Years

The decades of the 1930s and 1940s were particularly difficult for minority children. During the depression years, Native American children lived in poverty as a result of broken treaties that left Native American families with severe economic problems. More positively, the federal government changed its policy of trying to integrate Native American children into American society and focused on preserving their languages, arts, and heritage. However, Native American children still attended separate schools, and little attention was given to improving their education until the Civil Rights movement in the 1960s and 1970s.

During World War II, Japanese-American children living on the west coast were relocated into internment camps because of the fear that Japanese-Americans would assist the Japanese effort in the war. Of the approximately 112,000 Japanese Americans relocated, more than 30,000 were children under age 15. There were no plans for schooling the children, and

although schools were established by 1942, they were makeshift arrangements with no school furniture, materials, supplies, or books, and few qualified teachers (Wishon & Spangler, 1990).

Hispanic families became migrant workers during the depression and war years, traveling from one region of the United States to another to engage in the planting and harvesting of agricultural crops. Poorly educated and hampered by language difficulties, the migrant labor way of life minimized young children's opportunities for education. Living conditions were primitive, and children worked alongside their parents in the fields. Although efforts were made after World War II to improve living conditions and education for migrant worker families, their problems continued. Mechanization of crop harvesting increasingly minimized working opportunities after the 1940s (Wortham, 1992).

Early Childhood Programs for Children with Disabilities

The first efforts to provide programs for children with disabilities came much earlier than those for other at-risk populations. In 1898, at the convention of the National Education Association, Alexander Graham Bell proposed that programs for students with disabilities be established in the public schools. In fact, the earliest programs were in separate institutions. Thomas Gallaudet, a teacher, established the American Asylum for the Deaf in West Hartford, Connecticut, in 1817 after visiting a school for the deaf in Paris. In 1826, The New England Asylum for the Blind in Boston was established after Dr. John D. Fisher persuaded the Massachusetts State Legislature to appropriate funds for the institution. Later, in 1871, a day school for students with severe hearing impairments was also established in Boston, followed by a class for mentally retarded children in Providence, Rhode Island, in 1896. Four years later, a school for children with physical disabilities was established in Chicago.

A public school teacher, Elizabeth Farrell, initiated the first public school program for children with disabilities in New York City. She demonstrated how these children should be taught as individuals and according to their disabilities. She organized an ungraded class and later initiated classes for younger children. In 1922, she organized the Council for Exceptional Children (Gross & Gross, 1976).

The early efforts to serve children with disabilities were predominantly through residential schools. As more was learned about the potential of these children, institutional programs were found to be inadequate. A combination of raised expectations for children with disabilities and concerns about abuse and neglect in residential schools led to the conviction that children with disabilities would benefit from higher quality education. Thus, when in the 1960s and 1970s, the segregation of minority children was seen as illegal and unequal, children with disabilities were also included in the efforts to provide equal education for all children (Cremin, 1988). The programs funded during those two decades included intervention and compensatory categories of programs.

Intervention and Compensatory Programs in the 1960s and 1970s

With the advent of the Civil Rights movement, many efforts were made to improve education for children at risk for difficulties in school. At the preschool level, Project Head Start began as a summer program in 1965, and it was soon expanded into a year-long program. It included appropriate learning experiences for children, health care, meals, and parent education. It was joined by a Migrant Program to serve children whose parents migrated each year following the harvesting of crops across the United States; a Home Start program that extended early education and parental participation into the home; and a variety of other programs with similar purposes (McCarthy & Houston, 1980).

Kindergarten and primary-grade programs were also affected by compensatory programs such as the migrant programs. The Bilingual Education Act (1974) was funded to comply with a court-mandated ruling that school districts must establish special language programs for non–English-speaking children. The Elementary and Secondary Education Act of 1965 also provided funding to assist schools in the education of poor children.

At the same time that programs to serve children's individual needs were being funded and implemented, concerns arose about labeling children and putting them into special programs. With compensatory programs, the concern was that the supplementary instruction was replacing regular instruction, rather than being used as a resource for special assistance. There was also a major concern about putting children into special education programs. Large numbers of children were being channeled into special education programs because of difficulties they were experiencing in the regular classroom, rather than because of an identified disability. Biases in categorizing children as needing special education services resulted in large numbers of African American and Hispanic children being relegated to special education programs. Jane Mercer (1973) and Christine Sleeter (1986) researched and reported about poor and minority children who were trapped in special education programs, a practice that continues today (King, Chipman, & Cruz-Janzen, 1994).

The growing conviction that the separation and isolation of children with disabilities was inappropriate and that they would do better if they were educated alongside their peers led to the passage of the Education of All Handicapped Children Act of 1975 (PL 94-142). The act mandated that handicapped students be mainstreamed as much as possible with their nondisabled peers. Schools were required to screen, diagnose, and plan for the individual needs of each student (Deiner, 1993). More recently, inclusion has been initiated whereby students—

with support from special education personnel—are assigned to the classroom where they would have been placed if they had not had a disability.

From these beginnings in the 1960s and 1970s, early childhood programs were established, expanded, and modified over the years to provide compensatory and intervention services to children beginning in the early childhood years. Studies of the programs documented their effectiveness in leading to more positive developmental outcomes for young children. Guralnick (1989) reported that intervention programs within the first three years of life may be significantly effective, while Hanson and Lynch (1989) proposed from their research that early intervention may remediate a primary handicap or prevent the development of a secondary handicap.

Studies of Head Start and early childhood special education programs demonstrated their effectiveness. One research finding was that children who attended Head Start might have improved developmental status (Lazar & Darlington, 1982), and children who attended preschool programs were less likely to need special education services later and were less likely to become delinquent (Barnett & Escobar, 1990; Schweinhart & Weikart, 1985). Today, preschool and elementary school children may attend Head Start, pre-kindergarten, kindergarten, early childhood special education, bilingual, and migrant programs. Continual evaluation of these programs leads to revisions in policies and practices to further improve the outcomes for young children at risk.

Theoretical Bases of Development

As the field of child study has advanced, psychologists and philosophers have developed different theories on the nature of development and on the influence of such theories regarding how children develop and learn. Although some of these views have been important since the 1950s, other ideas were the result of the child-study movement or coincided with the establishment of child-study efforts around 1900.

Each of the theories involves a different way of approaching child development, and the conflict among theories has led to difficulties in developing the most appropriate model of instruction for children in early childhood programs. Maturational theory focuses on physical and intellectual development, whereas psychoanalytic and psychosocial theories are concerned with social and emotional, or personality, development. Behaviorist and social learning theories focus on intellectual and personality development. Cognitive-developmental theory is concerned with intellectual development and how it affects cognitive and social growth. Each of the theories has relevance for child development and learning; nevertheless, none offers a complete explanation for all aspects of development. More important, the various theories significantly affect how parents, caregivers, and teachers understand development and learning.

Maturational Theory

The early observations of children that were made in an effort to understand their development were led by G. Stanley Hall, who wrote an article titled "The Contents of Children's Minds" (1883). Observation of children and subsequent descriptions of babies and young children were expanded by many researchers; however, Arnold Gesell, a student of G. Stanley Hall, is credited with establishing norms for the ages at which behaviors emerged in young children, as described earlier in this chapter (Gesell & Ilg, 1946). Gesell, a physician, conducted his work at the Yale Clinic of Child Development. He collected data on the effects of maturation in children and subsequently explained development and learning based on his theory of maturation.

Gesell believed that skills such as walking, talking, and learning to read occurred as a result of the individual child's biological timetable. Biological readiness, rather than any influence of experience, was the predominant factor in the child's ability to learn (Weber, 1984). Gesell's norms or average ages of attainment made him very influential in the 1920s through the 1940s.

Gesell's work on developmental norms by chronological age coincided with the urbanization of elementary schools in the first decades of the twentieth century. As one-room schools with multi-age classes gave way to consolidated schools with several classrooms for each grade level, curriculum became more centralized. Gesell's descriptions of children's maturity levels and readiness for learning at chronological ages informed curriculum developers on how to design curriculum for different grade levels. In addition, some of the general principles of growth developed by Gesell remain important today. For example, Gesell described that growth proceeds from the head to the tail (cephalocaudal) and from the body to the extremities such as the hands and feet (proximodistal).

While Gesell made important contributions to the field of early childhood education, his data on developmental norms may not be appropriate for application to the diversity of children today. Moreover, Piaget's cognitive developmental theory in later decades better described individual cognitive development rather than by chronological age. The role of the environment on cognitive development also was not addressed in Gesell's maturational theory.

Nevertheless, there is a continuing influence of maturational theory reflected in the unfortunate practice of evaluating a child's "readiness" for placement in kindergarten or first grade in elementary schools. This practice follows the belief that some children are ready for school while others lack the needed maturity (National Association of Early Childhood Specialists in State Departments of Education, 2000).

Jolene

Jolene is six years old. She is the fifth child in her family. Her mother and father both work at a vegetable canning factory. Work is not steady throughout the year, and there are times when the family must go on welfare until they are rehired. Jolene has been cared for by a neighbor who has other neighborhood children in her care. She is not licensed, and the number of children in her care changes frequently. She provides toys for the children and has a swing set outside that was purchased for her own children. The children are entertained most of the day with television.

When Jolene was enrolled in school, she was evaluated using a readiness test. In addition, a teacher talked with Jolene and engaged her in some activities. She found that Jolene does not know her alphabet and has limited ability in language. The two first-grade teachers are concerned about Jolene's placement, but they do not agree on whether she should be placed in kindergarten or first grade. One of the teachers believes that since Jolene has not attended kindergarten, that is the correct placement. She believes that Jolene is not ready for first grade. The other teacher disagrees. She pointed out that Jolene's limitations are due to a lack of experiences and not because Jolene is incapable of learning with her peers. She notes that placing Jolene in kindergarten places her a year behind her peers. Is the situation an issue of readiness or lack of opportunity? Is the solution to place Jolene in kindergarten or to provide a learning environment that will facilitate her development and learning at the first-grade level? ✦

Psychoanalytic Theory

The Austrian physician Sigmund Freud was investigating social and personality development in the early part of the twentieth century. Freud believed that sexual energy is the force that influences children's behavior and that children progress through a series of psychosexual stages. In his psychoanalytic theory, Freud (1925) proposed that personality development is composed of the instincts of id, ego, and superego and that these three components control the child's innate drives to release sexual energy through oral gratification, warmth, love, pleasurable body sensations, and elimination of body wastes. If the child's instincts are not under- or overgratified by parents, the child will progress naturally through oral, anal, phallic, latent, and genital stages (Morrison, 1988; Schickedanz et al., 1993).

Psychosocial Theory

Erik Erikson, a student of Freud, developed his theory of psychosocial development based on Freud's work. Erikson (1963) proposed that the child's personality development is strongly determined by social contexts such as the family and school, and that the individual's interactions with environmental influences within eight life stages create her personality.

Erikson believed that the individual's adaptation at each developmental stage determines personality growth. The resolution of the conflict at each stage determines the course of personality development. In each stage it is necessary to positively resolve the life crisis at that stage if the next stage is to be resolved successfully. In the early childhood years, the child progresses through the stages of trust versus mistrust, autonomy versus shame and doubt, initiative versus guilt, and industry versus inferiority. Psychosocial theory helps parents and teachers to understand young children's emotional and social needs and how adults can support positive outcomes in the child's development. Figure 2.1 lists Erikson's stages of psychosocial development in the early childhood years and describes important adult behaviors that affect the child's resolution of each stage.

✦ Hyperactivity: ADHD or a Factor of Emotional Development?

A group of kindergarten and primary-grade teachers are discussing the children in their classrooms. It is the first month of school, and the teachers are comparing notes on the numbers of children they have who are hyperactive or who have adapted poorly to school routines. One teacher comments that the school has more children each year who are ADHD and require Ritalin so that they can function in the classroom. She wonders aloud what is going on that more children each year enter school who are unable to attend in class.

Some of the other teachers point out that there are other factors that are affecting these children. Some of the children come from homes where child abuse has been documented frequently. Others have single parents or might be living with grandparents because the parents are not able to care for them. Drug use is common in the neighborhood, as is alcoholism. The emotional status of these children is in question.

The principal asks the teachers to review what they understand to be the emotional needs of young children in the preschool years. Is it possible that many of these children are exhibiting emotional needs in their inability to participate appropriately in the classroom? Is medication the answer to the restlessness and inappropriate behavior of all of these children? ✦

Behaviorist Theory

Behaviorist theory stemmed from the work of Ivan Pavlov, the Russian physiologist who determined that animals could learn new physiological responses to the environment through stimuli. Pavlov used the process of conditioning to teach a dog to salivate at the sound of a bell by

STAGE	AGE	CHARACTERISTICS
1. Trust versus mistrust	Birth to 18 months	If the infant's needs are met by loving, dependable adults, trust is developed. If adults fail to meet the infant's needs, mistrust develops.
2. Autonomy versus shame and doubt	18 months to 3 and a half years	If the child is allowed to explore and develop a sense of self as an individual, autonomy develops. If parents are rigid, severe in toilet training, and impatient, the child will develop a sense of shame and doubt.
3. Initiative versus guilt	3 and a half to 6 years	Physical and mental abilities expand. If the child is encouraged to explore and parents encourage sociodramatic play and imaginative thought, the child will develop initiative. If parents are restrictive and punitive, the child will develop a sense of guilt.
4. Industry versus inferiority	6 to 12 years	Achievement becomes important. If adults help the child find learning and achievement rewarding, the child develops a sense of industry. If the child does not experience success in achievement, a sense of inferiority develops.

FIGURE 2.1   Erikson's psychological stages of development in the early childhood years.

ringing the bell each time food was offered. Because the dog salivated each time the food was offered, it became conditioned to salivate each time the bell rang, even when food was no longer offered (Schickedanz et al., 1993).

Later behaviorists applied the so-called S–R (stimulus-response) theory to children and their development. For current behaviorists, the critical factors in growth and development are the environment and the opportunity to learn. Learning is continuous, results from the reward

system in the environment, and is unrelated to ages and stages. The direction of behavior is shaped through control of the learning environment and the individual's experiences (Morrison, 1988).

Through B. F. Skinner's work (1953), behaviorist theory was applied to parenting and schooling. Skinner proposed that if the environment is arranged to facilitate the desired behavior, and expectations are set for that behavior, then the child will be influenced to use the appropriate behavior. Adult rewards for appropriate behavior will strengthen or condition the behavior. According to Skinner, because all behavior is learned, it can be shaped or modified. Strategies for behavior modification are based on reinforcement. When appropriate behaviors are rewarded, the behavior is reinforced and chances that the behavior will be repeated are increased. Punishment is used to discourage the reoccurrence of an undesirable behavior. However, punishment affects unwanted behaviors only temporarily and should be used infrequently. Parents and teachers of young children have found the concept of positive reinforcement especially helpful in managing behavior. Praising the young child for an appropriate behavior is more effective than inadvertently reinforcing a behavior that the adult wants the child to stop using. For example, if a parent buys a toy in the grocery store to stop his two preschoolers from fighting, he may find himself faced with inappropriate behavior the next time the children are shopping with him. The children have learned that the parent will reward them for misbehaving. Likewise, the teacher who picks up and holds the toddler who is disturbing story time has reinforced the unwanted behavior by singling out the child for attention. Parents and teachers find that unwanted behavior is best ignored whenever possible and that appropriate behavior should be strengthened through positive reinforcement.

Social Learning Theory

More recently, behavioral theorists have expanded the nature of learning to include imitation and observation. Social learning theorists such as Albert Bandura (Bandura & Walters, 1963) believe that many behaviors are not learned through shaping but develop through the individual's reactions to and interpretations of situations. The same stimulus or situation will elicit different responses depending on the individual's interpretation of the event. Verbal instruction, plus the individual's observations within a social context, affect that individual's expectations, abilities, and other inner qualities used to determine his response. Thus, a child who observes another child being punished for an inappropriate behavior can learn the appropriate response. Likewise, the child can learn a new behavior by imitating another child who is using the behavior correctly.

 Terry and Julio

Terry and Julio are playing in the manipulative center in the class for three-year-olds. Julio cannot manage to string large colored beads on a shoelace. A teacher notices Julio's difficulty and comes over to show him how to hold the string and push a bead over the end of the shoelace. Terry, who has been working on a puzzle, watches the teacher showing Julio how to string beads. He puts the puzzle away and gets another shoestring. Watching Julio intently, he attempts to put beads on the string. After losing several beads, he finally gets one on and pushes it to the end of the shoelace. He now attempts to duplicate the pattern of colored beads that Julio has placed on his shoestring. ✦

Cognitive-Developmental Theory/Constructivism

Jean Piaget

The cognitive-developmental view of development has had a major influence on the understanding of how children acquire and use knowledge. Jean Piaget's work has extended our understanding of how cognition develops. Piaget's (1963) studies of cognition led him to propose that children have different levels of understanding at different ages. Further, and more important, according to cognitive-developmental theory, the child has an active role in development. Unlike maturational theory, which proposes that biological readiness controls the ability to learn, or behaviorist theory, which suggests that the environment shapes behavior and learning, cognitive-developmental theory holds that the child's interaction with the environment and cognitive organization of experiences result in intelligence. The emphasis of this theory is on the child's thought processes when learning is occurring. The child's knowledge is constructed gradually as continued experiences permit an expanded understanding of the information encountered.

Piaget proposed that children pass through a fixed sequence of stages in cognitive development. Within each stage, both the quantity of information and quality of knowledge increase.

Piaget believed that knowledge is acquired and changes over time when the child takes in new information through assimilation and by incorporating or accommodating the new information into the existing knowledge structure called a *scheme*. The schemes are organized mental patterns that represent behaviors and actions. For infants, schemes are very concrete, whereas for older children, the schemes become more sophisticated and abstract. Through the process of assimilation and accommodation, the child not only acquires new knowledge, but reorganizes existing knowledge. The child is constructing knowledge; therefore, Piaget's theory is also called a *constructivist* approach to development. As the child progresses through stages of development, cognitive styles of organizing and structuring knowledge change. The child's mode or quality of thinking is different in each stage.

In the early childhood years, the child moves through the sensorimotor and preoperational stages of development. The sensorimotor stage begins at birth and continues until about 18 months. The infant acquires information by acting upon the environment using physical actions and the senses. In the preoperational stage of development, a major milestone is the ability to use symbolic thinking. The child is able to use symbolism to have one object represent another. Later, the child is able to symbolize at a more abstract level. In this stage, the child is controlled by perception. For example, a young child might believe that a cloud is alive because it can move through the sky.

According to cognitive-developmental theorists, the early childhood years end when the child moves from the preoperational to the concrete operational stage of development. In the concrete operational stage, the child is able to use logical thinking and can learn using symbols, such as in learning to read (Weber, 1984). Figure 2.2 describes the sensorimotor, preoperational, and concrete operational stages of development.

While Piaget's work was perhaps the most significant in helping us understand intellectual growth, there are questions about the specifics of his theory. Some cognitive skills emerge earlier than Piaget described; in addition, evidence has shown that the emergence of some skills is on a different timetable in some-Nonwestern cultures. Other concerns focus on information that some individuals never achieve the stage of formal operations (Rogoff & Chavajay, 1995).

Lev Vygotsky

The work of Lev Vygotsky, a Russian psychologist, is called the Vygotskian approach. It is also classified as constructivist because Vygotsky, like Piaget, also believed that children construct knowledge. He died at the young age of 38 from tuberculosis but published extensively before his death. American psychologists became aware of his work when his book *Thought and Language* (1932/1962) was translated into English in 1962.

Whereas Piaget proposed that children construct knowledge from interaction with the environment, Vygotsky believed that social interaction plays a significant role in learning. For Vygotsky, both physical and social interaction are necessary for development. The adult plays an important role as social mediator; moreover,

STAGE	AGE	DESCRIPTION
Sensorimotor	Birth to 18 months	The infant acquires knowledge through physical actions. Understanding is constructed by coordinating sensory experiences and physical actions.
Preoperational	2 to 7 years	The young child acquires and represents knowledge through symbolic actions such as speaking words. The child is able to use symbolic thinking that is also intuitive. Understanding is controlled by perception.
Concrete operational	7 to 11 years	The child is able to acquire knowledge symbolically and logically. The child reasons logically about concrete events. Logical thinking replaces intuitive thought as long as the concrete objects or events are present.

FIGURE 2.2   Piaget's stages of cognitive development in the early childhood years.

the teacher must identify what the child actually understands. The social environment includes the child's family, school, community, culture—all of the social contexts that are reached by the child. Cultural differences affect the way the child thinks, as do the structures of the individual family. Vygotsky took the importance of the child's context a step further to include the child's cultural and individual history. The child shares mental processes within the social context and learns by sharing experiences through interacting with others. The child learns by sharing activities with others first, followed by individual experiences (Vygotsky, 1978).

Also in contrast with Piaget, Vygotsky believed that learning leads development. While Piaget proposed that the child's level of thought and stage of development control mental abilities, Vygotsky argued that learning must occur for development to advance. The child's developmental level must be considered, but accumulation of learning facilitates development.

Vygotsky conceptualized the relationship between learning and development through his Zone of Proximal Development (ZPD). He believed that development is a continuum of behaviors. The development of behavior has two levels; what the child can perform independently (independent performance) and the level that the child can achieve with help (assisted performance). The zone of proximal development describes the continuum between assisted performance and independent performance. Assisted performance includes the help of the adult or peer. The teacher assists the child's acquisition of independent behavior by helping the child directly or indirectly. As the child makes progress in achieving at the independent level, the zone of proximal development also moves higher (Bodrova & Leong, 1996). The behaviors that the teacher uses to assist the child to support learning and development are termed *scaffolding*. The teacher provides instruction, materials in the environment, and other experiences to support the child and enable the child to acquire competencies and continue to move to new competencies (Berk & Winsler, 1995).

Early Childhood Curriculum Practices Today: Historical Influences Revisited

The field of early childhood education reflects its history. Beginning with Rouseau and Pestalozzi through periods of later influence, early childhood education as a field has maintained and yet modified all of the advances that have fashioned what it is today (Lanser & McDonnell, 1991). Although the curriculum practices at a private preschool or Montessori school may be very different from those at a public school or child care center, early childhood education encompasses all of these contributions of programmatic approaches to the field. The history of early childhood education curriculum practices can be thought of as cumulative. Teachers in early childhood programs are more likely to take an eclectic approach to instruction whereby the methods and materials used reflect the many positive influences in this history of such education.

The history of public school curriculum practices can be represented as more of a pendulum. During different periods, teaching practices have reflected trends of the time, and some of those trends have been extremely different. Early public schools stressed reading, writing, and mathematics skills with an emphasis on rote learning. Later, John Dewey's influence resulted

in a more child-centered approach (Dewey, 1899). Children were to take responsibility for their learning, and teachers were to involve them in instructional planning. This trend came to be called *progressive education*, and it increased in popularity in the 1930s and 1940s at all levels of public education.

The 1960s and 1970s were a period of innovation and experimentation in schooling as educators attempted to improve educational achievement for diverse populations of children. The federal government funded intervention and compensatory education projects targeted at improved achievement for children who were at risk for learning.

By the 1980s, the pendulum was again moving to more traditional teaching methods. With the loss of federal funding and a down-turn in national economics and Scholastic Apptitude Test (SAT) scores, a new reform movement sometimes called Back to Basics was embraced on a national level. Some states and school districts implemented any of a variety of measures—including tighter academic standards, elimination of social promotion, increased retention in grades, and an emphasis on the instruction of basic skills to be measured by standardized tests—to solve some of the problems that were thought to be caused by lax instructional methods and a lack of rigor in the curriculum. Whole-class instruction (rather than instruction geared to the individual student) based on state-mandated curriculum objectives was the trend in some states.

In the 1980s and 1990s an interest emerged in moving to all-day kindergartens; however, part of the movement was based on teaching basic skills to better prepare children for elementary school and required standardized tests. The purpose for expanding kindergartens and using a more formal curriculum was to accelerate academic achievement.

The reaction against this movement by early childhood education specialists was strong. Declaring that those who advocated that academic achievement could be accelerated failed to understand how cognitive development affects learning, a counter movement supporting "developmentally appropriate" curriculum emerged. The widely discussed and widely used term "Developmentally Appropriate Practices" (DAP) was proposed in a position paper and subsequent publications by the National Association for the Education of Young Children (NAEYC) (Bredekamp, 1987).

Even as DAP gained recognition and popularity in the 1990s, it too was challenged as being too focused on white, middle-class children. As awareness of cultural and ethnic differences became more prevalent in early childhood programs, DAP was challenged as not being responsive to all children. Moreover, the issues of inclusion arising from the enrollment of children with disabilities into regular classrooms brought new conflicts concerning the use of DAP (Williams, 1999).

At the end of the twentieth century, these issues evolved into new approaches to early childhood curriculum. The leaders of this movement, known as "early childhood reconceptualists," are concerned with the role of play in the curriculum, inequities in curriculum in meeting the needs of children from diverse backgrounds and with diverse abilities, and lack of access for all children to some early childhood settings (Mallory & New, 1994; Williams, 1999).

In the latter half of the 1990s, the NAEYC revised its position statement and guidelines for DAP (Bredekamp & Copple, 1997). Although the revisions did address some of the original concerns, much work remains to be done to ensure that all children receive an early childhood education that is both developmentally and individually appropriate.

The Expanding Role of Early Childhood Education

Early childhood education is in a period when attention is again being focused on the impor-

tance of the early years, a focus that is coming from different sources; nevertheless, the renewed emphasis on early childhood programs is enhancing possibilities for better funding and program improvement. This interest comes from parents concerned about the growth and development of their own children and public schools that are eligible for federal and state funding for new early childhood programs. It also comes from the child care industry and privately funded preschool programs that are expanding to meet the needs for care and programming for infants, toddlers, and preschool children. Mitchell (1989, p. 666) proposed that the high level of interest in early childhood programs stems from the following:

1. The increased demand for child care from the growing numbers of working mothers in all income groups
2. Concern about present and future productivity, international competitiveness, and the changing nature of the workforce, which will include more women and be characterized by greater ethnic and racial diversity as the minority becomes a majority
3. The centrality of child care among efforts to move mothers off AFDC support and into the labor force
4. A desire to provide a better start for poor children in school and in life
5. An accumulating body of evidence that high-quality, early childhood programs have long-term positive effects for disadvantaged children and high cost-benefit ratios (on the order of five to one)

Parental Interest in Learning in the Early Childhood Years

Parents are becoming increasingly interested in their children's opportunity for learning in the preschool years. Parents are aware that the early childhood years are important for their children's academic achievement. More parents are buying books on parenting and child development to acquire information on what kinds of experiences they should provide for their children. There is a high level of interest in parenting classes among some parent populations. Affluent parents frequently enroll their babies in physical development classes, swimming classes, and other programs advertised to enhance the growth and learning of infants and toddlers. Whether these programs are a wise choice is a separate issue (Elkind, 1987), but their success does indicate that parents are interested in providing good experiences in the early years.

As more parents are placing their children in child care during the day by necessity or by choice, parental concern extends to the educational program offered by caregiving centers (Gullo, 1990; Kagan, 1989). Although child care was once thought of as a service for the poor so that mothers could seek employment, today all types of parents seek quality caregiving programs for their babies and preschool children. According to Mitchell (1989), parents want choices. Parents have different needs for caregiving programs. They want child care centers to be affordable, convenient, and easy to choose, and they want them to reflect their own values and child-rearing practices.

Father Love

The widely held cultural construction of fatherhood in America—especially prior to the 1970s—has two strands. Historically, the first strand asserted that fathers are ineffective, often incompetent, and maybe even biologically unsuited to the job of child-rearing . . . . The second strand asserted that fathers' influence on child development is unimportant, or at the very most peripheral or indirect. . . . . Because researchers internalized these cultural beliefs as their own personal beliefs, fathers were essentially ignored by mainstream behavioral science until late in the 20th century. The 1970s through the 1990s, however, have seen a revolution in recognizing fathers and the influence of their love on child development. . . . The net effect of these influences has been to draw attention to the fact that father love sometimes explains a unique, independent portion of the variation in specific child outcomes, over and above the portion explained by mother love. In fact, a few recent studies suggest that father love is the sole significant predictor of specific outcomes, after removing the influence of mother love. (Rohner, 1998, p. 158)

Expansion of Child Care

Providers in the child care industry are becoming aware of the importance of quality programming as a part of caregiving. The title "day care" is rapidly being abandoned by centers as they seek to be identified as facilities with a good educational program for young children. Terms such as *enrichment*, *school*, and *discovery* or *creative* are increasingly used as part of the name of child care centers. People involved in child care are now aware that when parents look for a center, convenience is not their sole priority. They look for cleanliness, characteristics of the staff, the quality of materials available to the children, and the type of learning activities that are used with the children.

The child care industry is expanding because of the increasing numbers of children needing care. In fact, the number of children needing care is overwhelming the care that is available. By

1999, it was estimated that 13 million children under age six spend some time each day in the care of someone other than their parents (Children's Defense Fund, 2000; McMullen, 1999).

In addition to availability of child care, a major concern is the quality of child care programs. Abundant research has demonstrated that quality care is very important, particularly for children from low-income homes. Studies have demonstrated that children who attend quality child care programs prior to entry in elementary school receive long-lasting benefits in school achievement. Moreover, children also benefit from participating in quality after-school programs (Frank Porter Graham Child Development Center, 1999; Children's Defense Fund, 2000).

Unfortunately, the reality is that the quality of a majority of settings is poor or inadequate. The quality of some settings jeopardizes children's healthy development (Carnegie Corporation of New York, 1994; Galinsky, Howes, Kantor, & Shinn, 1994). In addition, the cost of quality child care is beyond the means of many families. Because they cannot afford to send their children to a quality program, parents of modest or moderate means have to send their children to less expensive and often lower quality child care centers.

The federal government became more aware of the need for expanded and improved care in the early 1990s. In 1991, the Child Care and Development Block Grant was approved and funded by Congress to provide states with new money to subsidize child care for low-income families (Children's Defense Fund, 1991). The 2000 federal budget provided for continued funding of the Child Care and Development Block Grant at $1.82 billion, while the Social Services Block Grant (Title XX), which states use to support child care, was cut from $1.9 billion to $1.775 billion (Children's Defense Fund, 2000).

Public schools are a growing resource for children needing care before and after school.

Hymes (1990) reported that in 1989, 17 percent of the public school districts in this country offered some form of child care or allowed child care groups to use school buildings for that purpose. In 1999, 1.7 million children were attending some type of after-school program that included public school programs, community center programs, church programs, and child care center programs.

Child care is part of the early childhood program system in this country. As caregiving institutions increase their perception that they are a part of the field of early childhood education, many will continue to improve their programming to maintain a respected position in the field. Evidence of this trend can be found in the growing numbers of child care centers seeking national accreditation through the NAEYC. The Department of Education has more global goals for improvement of programs for preschool children to include children in child care programs as reflected in the National Research Council's report, *Eager To Learn: Educating Our Preschoolers* (Bowman, Donovan, & Burns, 2000). The goal for all preschool programs, including child care programs, is to improve the quality of education for young children.

Expansion of Preschool Programs in Public Schools

In recent years, public schools have expanded many of their preschool early childhood intervention programs. One major expansion has been in pre-kindergarten programs for four-year-old children at risk for low achievement in the elementary grades. Mitchell (1989) reported that in 1979 only 7 states had appropriated funds for preschool programs, but by 1989 31 states had appropriated funds for state-initiated programs. In 1999, only 9 states had no state-initiated prekindergarten initiatives, while the remaining 41 states had a total of 58 preschool programs (Children's Defense Fund, 2000).

Federal funding has broadened support for early childhood and early intervention programs. The Elementary and Secondary School Improvement Act of 1988 reauthorizing Chapter I funds created Even Start, a joint parent-child education program. The purposes of Even Start were to improve adult literacy and offer early childhood education to children between one and seven years of age. In addition, Chapter I funding expanded the migrant program to include three- and four-year-olds.

The services to children with disabilities and special needs that were initiated with PL 94-142 in the 1970s were joined in the 1980s by extended services mandated by PL 99-457 to infants and toddlers and their families (Kagan, 1989). PL 94-142, the Individuals with Disabilities Act, guaranteed all children with disabilities the right to an appropriate education in a free public school and placement in the least restrictive learning environment. Because this law required that preschool programs be provided for children under the age of six, both public schools and Head Start programs initiated revised preschool programs to include children with disabilities.

Preschool programs for children with disabilities were further expanded under PL 99-457 that authorized two new programs: the Federal Preschool Program and the Early Intervention Program. Under this new law states had to prove that they are meeting the needs of all children with disabilities if they wish to receive federal funds. The Federal Preschool Program also extends the right of children with disabilities to children between the ages of three and five. Although children could be served in various types of settings under these laws, school districts provide many of the services in preschool classrooms.

The Americans with Disabilities Act (ADA) passed in 1990 (Stein, 1993), and the amendments to PL 94-142 have had an additional impact on the education of young children with disabilities. Under the ADA, all early childhood programs must be prepared to serve children with special needs. Facilities and accommodations for young children, including outdoor play environments, must be designed, constructed, and altered appropriately to meet the needs of young children with disabilities. The cumulative effect of these laws has advanced the civil rights of children with disabilities and resulted in the inclusion of young children in preschool and school-age programs. As a result, early childhood programs must use *inclusion*, whereby all children learn together with the goal that the individual needs of all children will be met (Wolery & Wilbers, 1994).

As the field of early childhood education continues to extend and expand, programs for young children are beginning to overlap and merge. It is becoming obvious that the tradition of labeling of types of early childhood programs is outdated. A new conceptualization of a comprehensive field of early childhood education that encompasses all types of programs is emerging. One possible term is an "early childhood ecosystem" that requires new ways of relating and interacting among various system components (Kagan & Rivers, 1991; Mitchell, 1989). Before public school early childhood programs can address membership in an early childhood ecosystem, they must resolve problems within their own school systems, particularly the programs serving children between the ages of four and eight. These age groups in the public schools are the subject of much concern and debate because of current practices in instruction and policies of promotion and retention that are adversely affecting students. In the next chapter, we will study these issues and how they affect students, teachers, and parents.

Summary

Early childhood education has a rich and varied history. Today's early childhood programs are equally varied and have historical ties with one another. Early childhood classrooms in each historical period have been affected by the social, economic, and political trends of the time. In addition, educational trends at the elementary and secondary levels have had an effect on early childhood programs as well.

Each historical period has had thinkers and leaders that have led the way. The roots of early childhood education can be traced back to Europe to Rousseau, Pestalozzi, and Froebel. Their influence traveled to this country, which had yet to establish its own leadership in the colonial period and early years of the new nation. As this country was settled and populations moved west, all levels of education had influences that were distinctly American. As public schools were established and improved, kindergartens, and later preschool classes, became part of public education. At the same time, child care became a field in early childhood education. Education for young children with disabilities was initiated before the turn of the twentieth century. Programs for children who are at risk for difficulties in learning did not begin until the Civil Rights movement after World War II.

Early childhood education has not always been of the same quality for all young children. Children of African American and Latino parents attended schools that were separate from their Anglo peers until the 1960s. Children of Native Americans were educated within a separate system run by missionaries and the U.S. government until after World War II.

Early childhood education has evolved through cycles and trends. These periods have responded to the work of psychologists, results of child study research, and governmental legislation. Federal funding had an influence on nursery schools during the Great Depression in the 1930s, child care for mothers working in the war effort in the 1940s, and federal compensatory and intervention programs established to help children at risk because of disabilities or environmental factors in the 1960s and 1970s.

Most recently, a back-to-basics movement resulted in a return to an academic approach to instruction that has been countered in early childhood education with a concern about programs that are more appropriate for the development of young children.

Today's early childhood programs reflect current trends and influences. Child care is an ever growing field as more mothers enter the workplace. Public schools offer a variety of programs for children under age six to meet the needs of young children with different cultural and language backgrounds, different abilities, and different conceptual and language development levels. Attempts are being made to provide classrooms that will enhance the development and learning of young children to better prepare them for success in elementary and secondary education.

As was true in earlier periods, today's early childhood settings are influenced by an eclectic combination of theories and educational leaders. The wave of psychological theories that blossomed in the 1950s produced trends that inform today's settings. The names of Piaget, Bloom, Skinner, Erikson, Hunt, and Vygotsky—along with many others—are familiar to the early childhood educator. The theories that have been put into practice in each early childhood setting depend on the purpose of the program, the needs of the young children being served, and the instructional approach that is desired.

An overriding concern for all of the programs is to provide quality experiences. A current concern is whether programs are appropriate for the child's developmental levels. Indicators of quality programs that are developmentally appropriate have been widely embraced in the field of early childhood education. The history of this source of influence and issues surrounding implementation of programs that are appropriate for young children are discussed in Chapter 3.

Study Questions

1. Children younger than 3 years of age were included in settings that served young children prior to 1900. Trace these settings, and describe how the very young were included and served.
2. What type of education was provided in one-room schools? What instructional approaches predominated?
3. Why did one-room schoolhouses close? What types of curricula and instruction were developed as the country urbanized and schooling became more centralized?
4. Who were the educational leaders who influenced early childhood education prior to 1900? What were their contributions?
5. Why did kindergartens become part of the public schools? What issues affected kindergarten programs as kindergarten teachers interacted with primary-grade teachers?
6. The child-study movement and progressive education movement gave direction to educational reform between 1900 and 1950. How did these two movements influence early childhood education?
7. When and how did group care of preschool children begin? Why has it continued to expand in recent decades?
8. Explain the difference between intervention and compensatory programs. What is the purpose of each, and who is served in each type of program?
9. How did the Head Start movement use the work of theorists? How have early childhood programs benefitted from Head Start models?
10. Why were the decades of the 1960s and 1970s considered to be a period of innovation in education? What were the contributions of this period?
11. Who are the children considered to be at risk for delayed development and learning? Describe programs that serve at-risk children in the early childhood years.
12. How does the history of the education of minority children help us to understand why the civil rights movement included reform in elementary education? How do programs implemented during the civil rights movement affect early childhood programs today?
13. Are early childhood special education programs that provide early intervention successful? What evidence do we have that children who attend these programs have benefitted?
14. What are some contributions that we gained from Arnold Gesell? What are some limitations of his maturational theory?
15. Why do teachers need to give as much importance to the emotional development of young children as to their cognitive development? What theorists inform our understanding of these domains of development?
16. How do Piaget and Vygotsky contribute to the constructivist approach to learning? How are they alike and different in their perception of how young children develop and learn?
17. Describe some factors that have contributed to the growth and expansion of early childhood programs in the 1980s and 1990s.
18. What challenges face early childhood educators today? What factors make it difficult to have the same level of quality in all early childhood programs?

CHAPTER THREE

The Need for Quality Programs in Early Childhood Education

CHAPTER OBJECTIVES

As a result of reading this chapter you will be able to

1. Discuss why it is difficult for all types of programs to achieve the same level of quality.
2. Describe why teacher preparation is an important factor in conducting quality programs.
3. Explain 5 principal characteristics of quality programs.
4. Understand how theories of learning and development inform quality programs.
5. Discuss and compare at least 3 examples of quality programs.

Introduction

In Chapter 2 a major topic was the many types of early childhood programs that are available for children. Also discussed was the growing trend for these many types of programs to overlap. For example, many Head Start programs are now housed in public schools and it is becoming more common for public schools to offer before-school and after-school care to help working parents. The purpose of this chapter is to further explore the concept of early childhood education as one comprehensive program, where all types of settings that serve young children are interrelated and share commonalities in quality of program. However, there are currently some challenges to establishing quality in all programs. Until these challenges are resolved, the issue of program quality cannot be satisfactorily addressed. We will also explore characteristics of quality programs and some current models that exhibit these characteristics.

Challenges to Quality in Early Childhood Programs

Differences in Training and Preparation

There are significant variations in requirements for teacher preparation among types of early childhood programs. Public school early childhood programs require teachers to have a college degree and some type of licensure as a minimum requirement for teaching. At the other extreme, some privately funded preschools and child care programs require nothing beyond a high school diploma to become a teacher. Now, with the emphasis on education as well as care, all teachers of preschool children need to have more preparation and training if quality is to be available in all types of early childhood settings. This is especially important now that all types of programs enroll children from diverse backgrounds and those who have disabilities or other special needs.

Differences in Sources and Levels of Funding

The types of funding available to early childhood settings is as varied as the settings themselves. Child care centers are primarily funded by parents. However, child care settings sponsored by religious institutions or corporations frequently subsidize fees paid by parents. In addition, there is now federal funding disseminated by the states to provide support for centers that serve low-income families.

Public schools receive funding from the local, state, and federal level, depending on the types of programs offered in the early childhood programs. Schools that have early childhood intervention programs, such as bilingual programs, pre-kindergarten programs for children with limited language and concept development or children with special needs, receive funding beyond the state level.

Head Start programs are entirely funded by the federal government. If they are associated with a public school, then the funding comes from the federal government, but the district might match federal funds by providing classrooms and other in-kind resources for the program.

These differences in funding sources directly affect what resources are available to the programs. Child care centers that serve affluent parents can charge higher fees and are likely to have the highest quality programs. Middle- and low-income families are less able to pay for care for their children. The resources available to centers who serve these children will be at a lower level. These centers are less likely to have the materials and equipment that are available at centers with more resources.

Differences in Teacher Salaries

The level of income the teacher earns in an early childhood program has a direct effect on the quality of the program. Programs that hire people with lower levels of education and pay minimum wages experience high rates of turnover in staff. The training provided to teachers who are poorly paid is not likely to be enough for them to remain at the center and gain the experience needed to become a knowledgeable teacher.

Settings such as public schools require the highest educational level to become a teacher. Moreover, they are likely to pay the highest level of salary for early childhood teachers. The result is that the programs with the highest expectation for teacher preparation are likely to provide the most adequate level of income. This in turn means that the teachers are more likely to continue in their position and improve their teaching competencies.

Is the assumption to be made, then, that all public school programs are of a high quality and other types of settings are of a lower quality? Not at all. There are programs of high and low quality in all types of early childhood settings; nevertheless, these challenges in resources, training, and pay can have a major effect on whether the programs can provide the best kinds of experiences for young children. In the next part of this chapter we will look at what it means to have a program of high quality. We will explore some of the characteristics of a quality program that all early childhood settings should reflect in the twenty-first century and how theories of development contribute to quality in curriculum and instruction for young children. Finally, we will learn about some models of quality programs that we can draw from in developing a quality curriculum for young children.

Goals for Quality Early Childhood Programs

As we begin a new century, we have many sources of information about quality programs for young children. The goals that we set for early childhood education are ambitious and will take time to achieve. Experts in the field

have described many of the characteristics of a quality program. They have collaborated in several efforts to establish how quality programs can be characterized. The descriptions include components such as curriculum, teacher preparation and training, assessment and accountability, relationships with students and parents, knowledge of child development, access to adequate funding, and provisions for licensing of teachers and governance. In the following sections we will first discuss goals for funding, licensing, and governance. The different components of a quality programs will follow.

Staff Training, Licensing, and Funding

Licensing and Training

An approach to bridging the differences in teacher training among early childhood programs, is to establish different levels of training and licensing. Kagan and Neuman (1997) reported on the proposed types of training and licensing as developed in the Quality 2000 Initiative. In discussing early childhood caregiving settings, it was proposed that there be an associate educator license, educator license, and administrator license. The associate level would require at least a Child Development Associate (CDA) credential with a practicum with children and certification in pediatric first aid. The Educator's license would require an associate's or bachelor's degree in early childhood education or child development plus the practicum, certification in pediatric first aid, and demonstration of competency in working with children and families. The administrator's license would require at least a bachelor's or master's degree to include at least 15 hours in early childhood administration as well as the competencies required for the lower levels of credentialing.

The goal for improving program licensing would include national licensing guidelines that do not currently exist. In addition, licensing at the state level could be improved by eliminating the exemptions from regulations and enforcing the requirements for licensing. Another recommendation is to streamline the licensing of facilities (Kagan & Neuman, 1997).

If staff training and preparation are to be improved, it will necessary for state licensing boards, colleges and community organizations, and other institutions that share in training to collaborate in redesigning curricula to address early childhood content and pedagogy needed by all early childhood professionals.

Program Funding

If adequate funding is to be provided for all early childhood settings, new ideas for acquiring funding will have to be generated. Kagan and Neuman (1997) suggest that funding requirements to conduct quality programs will have to be established. Then options to increase funding at the federal and state level should be explored to include individual and corporate income taxes, new sales and excise taxes, using school aid formulas such as those currently used for elementary education, and other strategies to raise funds. Public assistance for low-income families would be part of the mix.

Characteristics of Quality Programs

The features of a quality program stem from several components that include principles of child development, a balanced curriculum, relationships between parents, teachers, and children, assessment and accountability, and consideration for diversity in children and families. These characteristics of quality programs will be discussed in this part of the chapter.

Principles of Child Development

One piece of a framework for a quality program is the understanding and application of how young children develop and learn. Curriculum and learning experiences should be based on principles of child development. Not only do teachers use knowledge of maturation and cog-

nitive changes in young children, but continuing research, such as new findings from brain research, should inform program planning (Bowman, 1999).

An understanding of child development also includes individual, cultural, and environmental differences in development. Children vary in the rate of development; moreover, personality differences and cultural expectations affect a child's developmental style. Quality programs attend to variations in development and make sure that learning opportunities are available for individual needs.

Eduardo

Eduardo is in a second-grade classroom. He cannot read and has a very limited speaking vocabulary. When Eduardo entered kindergarten, he was administered a language test that suggested that his dominant language was Spanish. He was placed in a bilingual classroom where Spanish was the language of instruction. Eduardo made very little progress in kindergarten and first grade. When Eduardo engages in social conversation with his peers and talks with his teacher, he uses English.

Mr. Sanchez, Eduardo's teacher, is perplexed as how to help Eduardo. Is he having difficulty because he was mislabeled as a Spanish speaker in kindergarten? Did the preschool program fail to meet his needs? Another alternative is that Eduardo has delayed development in language and cognition and should be receiving special services. What should be the nature of curriculum designed for Eduardo? +

Balanced Curriculum

A quality program includes experiences in all developmental domains. Curriculum addresses the whole child. To achieve balance, learning experiences include content in reading, mathematics, and science, as well as physical activities, music, art, and drama. The balance in curricu-

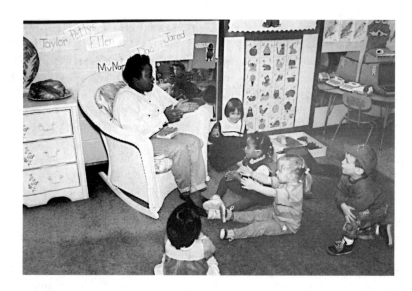

lum extends to the inclusion of skills in addition to expanding the child's understanding of the world. The child needs the opportunity to construct knowledge and apply knowledge in meaningful ways. The Committee on Early Childhood Pedagogy in preparing *Eager to Learn* (Bowman, Donovan, & Burns, 2000, p. 8) suggest the following elements for curriculum development:

- Teaching and learning will be most effective if they engage and build on children's existing understandings.
- Key concepts involved in each domain of preschool learning (e.g., representational systems in early literacy, difference between count numbers and fractions, causation in the physical world) must go hand in hand with information and skill acquisition.
- Metacognitive skill development allows children to learn more deliberatively. Curricula that encourage children to reflect, predict, question, and hypothesize (Examples: How many there will be after two more are added? What happens next in the story? Will it sink or float?) set them on course for effective, engaged learning.

All types of teaching strategies are used within a balanced curriculum. There are opportunities for children to initiate activities as well as teacher-initiated and directed activities. Children are also given opportunities to learn from each other and the environment (Bowman, Donovan, & Burns, 2000).

Parent, Teacher, and Child Relationships

Quality programs initiate and support relationships with parents and their children. Parents can be effective partners in the child's education if there is regular communication and interaction between the school or center and the home. Programs can support parents and help them to do a good job with their children; conversely, parents can provide valuable information and assistance to the early childhood program. The center can be welcoming place for parents with resources and learning opportunities. The parents should be considered as equal participants in the program and engage in program governance (Bowman, 1999; Kagan & Neuman, 1997).

Assessment and Accountability

Quality programs use assessments carefully with young children. It is important for programs to be able to measure successful outcomes for both children and the program as a whole. How to achieve such assessment can be problematic. Program planners need to establish clear goals and desired results for both evaluation and accountability purposes, as well as for program planning for groups and individual children. However, successful strategies that are appropriate for young children are difficult to develop.

Because children under age six are in a rapid, sporadic, and uneven course of development, assessment results, particularly those used with standardized tests, can misrepresent a child's learning. Moreover, the general dissatisfaction with standardized tests and the unclear quality of emerging performance assessments pose a challenge for early childhood programs. Quality programs use a variety of assessment approaches with preschool children to include teacher-designed assessments, observation, and judicious selection of standardized tests for specific purposes that will benefit the children and improve program planning (Bowman, Donovan, & Burns, 2000; Kagan & Neuman, 1997; Wortham, 2001d).

Diversity in Children and Families

A quality program provides opportunities for children and families to express their own cultural values and practices, but to also learn about other cultures. The program helps children to understand cultural similarities and differences. Children will need to use what they bring from their own cultures to become active learners in acquiring information in new cultures. This is particularly important when children and families need to become a part of a more mainstream culture at the center or school and the community at large. They need to use what they already know to acquire new knowledge and skills (Bowman, 1999; Kagan & Neuman, 1997).

How Classical and Contemporary Theories Inform Quality Early Childhood Programs

We have just described some characteristics of a quality early childhood program. Now we will turn to the role of theories of development in organizing quality programs. To accomplish this, we need to design a comprehensive theory of development that includes both classical and contemporary theories. What, then, should be our theoretical bases for designing quality programs for young children? How shall we establish a theoretical foundation that includes variations in development that young children bring to early childhood programs? First, we will review the role of the classical theories of development discussed in Chapter 2. Then we will consider how other models of development can add to our quest for a more inclusive or comprehensive approach to understanding young children's development and learning. We want to understand development in an expanded form that incorporates differences in development beyond the typical American perceptions.

Applying Classical Theories

Maturational Theory

This text is based on the development of young children; therefore, consideration of Arnold Gesell's maturational theory and norms for development is important. Chapter 2 discussed the significance of the emergence of developmental behaviors on a chronological timetable and how Gesell described average ages for the child's attainment of these behaviors. Educators need to understand the nature of chronological development (Gesell & Ilg, 1946). Nevertheless, Gesell's norms are based on a very select population of children. Further, cultural and socioeconomic factors affect the developmental process or developmental expectations of young children. For example, study of preschool children enrolled in Reggio Emilia schools in Italy demonstrated that young children can engage in long-term projects with intense intellectual attention, contrary to the American notion that preschool children have short attention spans and must have frequent changes in activities. Likewise, in Japanese preschool classrooms, purposefully limited supplies and materials are used as strategies for cooperative behavior. This is in contrast to the Western view that young children's egocentrism limits their ability to consider the interest of others and to work and play cooperatively (New, 1993, 1994).

Cognitive-Developmental Theory

Piaget's notions of development and learning can be used to modify Gesell's biological theory of development, which does not account for the effects of early experiences on the child's development. For Piaget, cognition is not merely based on chronological ages but is focused on the child's active attempts to make meaning of his or her world. From Piaget we also understand that the style of the child's thinking changes as the child matures and develops individually through cognitive stages. The child's active engagement in interaction with the world is responsible for his or her ability to construct knowledge. The perception of development gained from Piaget's theory is centered in the child and the nature of the experiences that are available to the child. Hence, in descriptions of the learning process using Piaget's cognitive-developmental theory, this process is frequently referred to as child-centered.

Piaget's cognitive-developmental theory did not address the cultural contexts of development or the influence of the child's social environment. Vygotsky believed that the child's construction of knowledge is influenced by past and present social interactions; it is socially mediated. He further proposed that some knowledge is spontaneously learned by the child, while other

knowledge must be taught within the context of the school experience. Further, knowledge acquired at school depends on the teaching roles used by the teacher. The teacher uses a range of strategies to facilitate the child's construction of knowledge (Bodrova & Leong, 1996).

Psychosocial Theory

An inclusive model of development includes the child's emotional development. Through Erikson's psychosocial theory of development, the child's stages of socioemotional development can be understood. And, through Erikson's position that the child resolves those stages positively or negatively, we can comprehend how some children vary in social and emotional development. Children's extreme variations in emotional development that are present in early childhood classrooms can partially be explained through Erikson's work.

Behaviorist Theory

How does our inclusive model of development recognize the developmental diversity of children with disabilities? How do we apply existing theories to children who have extremes of development outside the norms established by Gesell or the stages of development described by Piaget? For example, children with mental delay do not naturally acquire concepts and skills. They learn through teacher instruction and repeated practice and reinforcement. Likewise, children who have mobility impairments may not be able to explore their physical environment. They may not have the opportunity to experience how their body fits into space or to develop the physical skills described as norms for their chronological age. They may require environmental adaptations or planned activities to experience knowledge that other children can discover for themselves. For example, a toddler with mobility impairment does not explore a room from different perspectives like more mobile peers. Experiences of being under a table or climbing onto a sofa are not possible. Therefore, if the child is to learn perceptions of space, then caregivers must plan for those experiences.

Children with developmental limitations cannot always initiate their own learning. However, they too need a child-centered curriculum that the teacher or caregiver must plan to provide. The adult must have a directive role in planning and carrying out the activities that will enable the child to acquire skills and concepts.

It can be seen from the preceding examples that there is a role for the behaviorist approach within a more inclusive approach to development. Furthermore, aspects of the child-centered classroom for children without disabilities may be addressed by behaviorist strategies. Although teachers of young children desire that appropriate behavior should be an intrinsic motivation, in reality, behaviorist strategies for behavior management are a useful starting point for establishing appropriate classroom behaviors.

Theory and Cultural Relevance: Ecological Theory

An inclusive theory of development must include cultural influences on the development of young children. Our concept of the influence of the child's environment on development and learning must be broadened to understand how the environments that young children live in can be very different. The environment experienced by each child depends on many factors. Our outmoded perceptions of children's development and reconstruction of knowledge must expand to include diversity of environment. What is more important, our definition of quality programs for young children must focus on diversity of cultural environment when planning for a child-centered curriculum.

Advocates of developmentally appropriate practices promote the concept of curriculum that is age and individually appropriate. More important is the cultural relevance of learning. Vygotsky's premise that the social context in which the child learns is a significant factor moves beyond the common assumptions about what is appropriate for young children. The child's social context can include the following (Bodrova & Leong, 1996, p. 9):

1. The immediate interactive level, that is, the individual(s) the child is interacting with at the moment
2. The structural level, which includes the social structures that influence the child, such as the family and school
3. The general cultural or social level, which includes features of society at large, such as language, numerical systems, and the use of technology

Bronfenbrenner's (1979, 1986) ecological theory of development has a more complex explanation of the role of culture and environment. His sociocultural view of development includes five environmental systems: the microsystem, the mesosystem, the exosystem, the macrosystem, and the chronosystem. The child resides at the center of the systems (Figure 3.1). Interaction with the systems expands as the child develops and moves increasingly into the environment beyond the family. The microsystem includes the family, school, church, and neighborhood. The mesosystem reflects the interactions between the elements of the microsystem. The exosystem includes friends of the family, mass media, neighbors, and community services. An example of the influence of the exosystem would be local government that might include policies that affect family life. The macrosystem is the culture of the larger community in which the child lives.

Gardner's Theory of Intelligence

Yet another dimension can be added to a more inclusive theory of development. Howard Gardner (1983) has described intelligence in terms of seven types: verbal skills, mathematical skills, ability to spatially analyze the world, movement skills, insightful skills for analyzing others, and

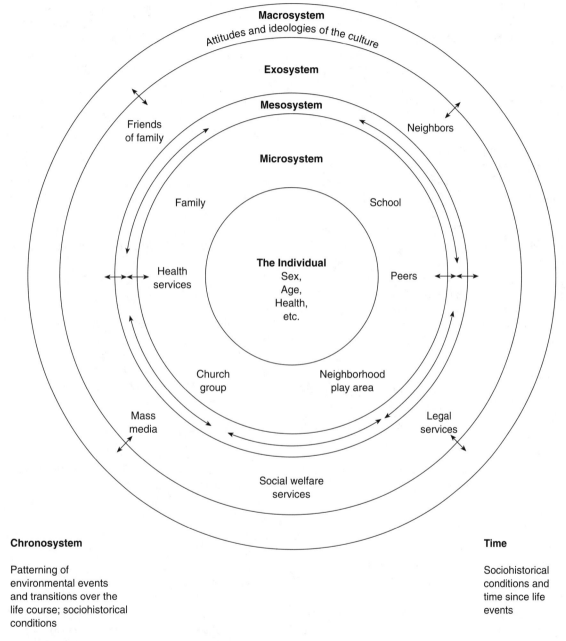

Macrosystem
Attitudes and ideologies of the culture

Exosystem

Mesosystem

Microsystem

Friends
of family

Neighbors

Family

School

The Individual
Sex,
Age,
Health,
etc.

Health
services

Peers

Church
group

Neighborhood
play area

Mass
media

Legal
services

Social welfare
services

Chronosystem

Patterning of
environmental events
and transitions over the
life course; sociohistorical
conditions

Time

Sociohistorical
conditions and
time since life
events

FIGURE 3.1 Bronfenbrenner's ecological theory of development.
Source: Adapted from *Children* (p. 47), by J. W. Santrock, 1997. Reproduced with permission of the
McGraw-Hill Companies.

musical skills. More recently, he has added an eighth intelligence, naturalistic intelligence (Checkley, 1997). Gardner believes that children may have different strengths in intelligence. He also believes that environmental factors can affect the development of the intelligences. Each of the eight types of intelligence can be destroyed by brain damage, and musical intelligence, especially, can be developed at an early age in a musically inclined child. He also believes that parents play an important role in the early years in whether a child will develop the potential for a form of intelligence.

Gardner proposes that it is very important for teachers to take the individual differences in children very seriously. Teachers can guide children in using their minds well. Understanding of the intelligences should be linked with a curriculum focused on understanding where the child is able to apply what they have learned in new situations. Gardner's description of the eight intelligences is shown in Figure 3.2.

Gardner's theory also reminds us that we are educating the whole child. Young children in early childhood programs should have experiences in the fine arts as well as in cognitive, motor, and social development if all of their capabilities are to be developed. In the next part of this chapter, we will learn about some approaches and models to early childhood programs that incorporate the components of quality in addition to applying classical and contemporary theories.

Models of Quality Early Childhood Programs

How have classical and contemporary theories of development and learning informed some examples of quality programs today? How have the developers of these models conceptualized programs of high quality for young children? In this section, four high-quality early childhood programs will be described. Some of the programs originated in the United States:

High/Scope, the Project Approach, and the NAEYC model for Developmentally Appropriate Practices (DAP). The Reggio Emilia Approach originated in Reggio Emilia, Italy, and is being adapted in the United States and other countries. High/Scope was first developed for intervention with impoverished children in the 1960s and has a longitudinal research record that supports its success with at-risk children. Reggio Emilia, the Project Approach, and DAP were developed for all populations of young children. Reggio Emilia settings serve preschool children, and High/Scope, the Project Approach, and DAP models serve preschool and primary-grade children. We will begin with the DAP model, which is the most widely used in the United States.

Developmentally Appropriate Practices (DAP)

The DAP model is a framework for appropriate practices that should be used with young children in early childhood programs, rather than a specific curriculum. The DAP approach evolved as a response to the negative effect of the school reform movement in the 1970s and 1980s.

The History of DAP

In the late 1970s and during the 1980s, a period of educational reform swept the United States. The major concern was that American students did not achieve as well as their counterparts in Japan and European countries.

Efforts to reform the public school systems began with the secondary schools. Increased credits for graduation, tightened standards for grading, and competency testing were some policies carried out by individual states to increase achievement and raise the level of learning. As the reform movement continued to expand, similar policies were passed for elementary schools. State departments of education established curriculum standards to be followed by all schools; such standards included the instructional objectives that were to be used

The Intelligences, in Gardner's Words

• Linguistic intelligence is the capacity to use language, your native language, and perhaps other languages, to express what's on your mind and to understand other people. Poets really specialize in linguistic intelligence, but any kind of writer, orator, speaker, lawyer, or a person for whom language is an important stock in trade highlights linguistic intelligence.

• People with a highly developed logical-mathematical intelligence understand the underlying principles of some kind of a causal system, the way a scientist or a logician does; or can manipulate numbers, quantities, and operations, the way a mathematician does.

• Spatial intelligence refers to the ability to represent the spatial world internally in your mind—the way a sailor or airplane pilot navigates the large spatial world, or the way a chess player or sculptor represents a more circumscribed spatial world. Spatial intelligence can be used in the arts or in the sciences. If you are spatially intelligent and oriented toward the arts, you are more likely to become a painter or a sculptor or an architect than, say, a musician or a writer. Similarly, certain sciences like anatomy or topology emphasize spatial intelligence.

• Bodily kinesthetic intelligence is the capacity to use your whole body or parts of your body—your hand, your fingers, your arms—to solve a problem, make something, or put on some kind of a production. The most evident examples are people in athletics or the performing arts, particularly dance or acting.

• Musical intelligence is the capacity to think in music, to be able to hear patterns, recognize them, remember them, and perhaps manipulate them. People who have a strong musical

intelligence don't just remember music easily—they can't get it out of their minds, it's so omnipresent. Now, some people will say, "Yes, music is important, but it's a talent, not an intelligence." And I say, "Fine, let's call it a talent." But, then we have to leave the word *intelligent* out of *all* discussions of human abilities. You know, Mozart was damned smart!

• Interpersonal intelligence is understanding other people. It's an ability we all need, but is at a premium if you are a teacher, clinician, salesperson, or politician. Anybody who deals with other people has to be skilled in the interpersonal sphere.

• Intrapersonal intelligence refers to having an understanding of yourself, of knowing who you are, what you can do, what you want to do, how you react to things, which things to avoid, and which things to gravitate toward. We are drawn to people who have a good understanding of themselves because those people tend not to screw up. They tend to know what they can do. They tend to know what they can't do. And they tend to know where to go if they need help.

• Naturalist intelligence designates the human ability to discriminate among living things (plants, animals) as well as sensitivity to other features of the natural world (clouds, rock configurations). This ability was clearly of value in our evolutionary past as hunters, gatherers, and farmers; it continues to be central in such roles as botanist or chef. I also speculate that much of our consumer society exploits the naturalist intelligences, which can be mobilized in the discrimination among cars, sneakers, kinds of makeup, and the like. The kind of pattern recognition valued in certain of the sciences may also draw upon naturalist intelligence.

FIGURE 3.2 Howard Gardner's multiple intelligences.
Source: From "The first seven . . . And the eighth. A conversation with Howard Gardner," by K. Checkley, 1997, *Educational Leadership, 55*, p. 12. Reprinted with permission from ASCD. All rights reserved.

at every grade level. Accountability for student learning was measured by standardized tests, and school districts within a state were compared for levels of student achievement. Standards for achievement were raised, and teachers were required to teach more curriculum content that was more difficult than in the past in an effort to increase achievement results.

When academic reform policies reached early childhood classrooms, the developmental nature of young children's learning conflicted with practices that were being initiated as part of educational reform. There was a consistent escalation of academic demand on both kindergartners and first graders (Shepard & Smith, 1988). This practice was referred to as a "push-down" curriculum (Day, 1988). As states set a high priority on test scores, curriculum and instruction were further modified to ensure that students would do well on test scores (Bredekamp & Shepard, 1989).

The increased amount of curriculum content and testing had a negative effect on young children. As the percentage of children who did not do well in first grade increased, measures were taken to solve the problem. Children were placed in transitional classrooms, denied school entry, or retained in kindergarten. Instead of teaching children using strategies that were appropriate for their level of development, schools were holding children responsible for failing (Bredekamp & Shepard, 1989). These practices became labeled as "inappropriate practices" (Bredekamp & Rosegrant, 1992; Nason, 1991; Shepard & Smith, 1990).

The Initial Development of DAP

The effects of the back-to-basics movement on early childhood programs did not continue unchallenged. The NAEYC began to address the issue of developmentally appropriate teaching and testing practices in the mid-1980s. A series of position papers describing developmentally appropriate teaching and testing practices was issued by the organization. Relevant articles were published frequently in the organizational journal *Young Children*. In 1987, *Developmentally Appropriate Practice in Early Childhood Programs Serving Children from Birth Through Age 8* (Bredekamp, 1987) was published. It provided indicators of appropriate practice for all ages from birth through age eight and was supported by the National Council of Teachers of Mathematics, the National Association of Elementary School Principals, and the National Association of State Boards of Education. Subsequently, a position statement regarding guidelines for appropriate curriculum content and assessment (NAEYC & National Association of Early Childhood Specialists in State Departments of Education [NAECSSDE], 1991) was endorsed or supported by 10 national or regional organizations. The Association for Childhood Education International published *Developmental Continuity across Preschool and Primary Grades* (Barbour & Seefeldt, 1993), which provides teachers in both preschool and primary grades with additional information on appropriate instruction for children in early childhood years.

Guidelines for DAP. The *Guidelines for Appropriate Curriculum Content and Assessment in Programs Serving Children Ages 3 Through 8* (NAEYC & NAECSSDE, 1991) were developed in response to the widespread school reform movement in the 1980s. Although major national organizations issued position papers and calls for a change in curriculum, the two organizations issuing the guidelines proposed that these efforts were not achieving real change in curriculum and assessment practices in primary grades in the elementary school. The earlier publication, *Developmentally Appropriate Practice in Early Childhood Programs Serving Children from Birth Through Age 8* (Bredekamp, 1987), was intended to provide clear guidance on how to teach children in the early childhood years, whereas the guidelines were intended to provide assistance on what to teach and how to assess young children's development and learning.

The theoretical underpinnings for the guidelines were based primarily on the theories of Piaget (1963), Erikson (1963), and Vygotsky (1978). Piaget described knowledge as physical, logical-mathematical, and social-conventional. Logical-mathematical knowledge is mentally constructed within the child, while physical knowledge is observable reality. Social-conventional knowledge is related to conventions of society.

Vygotsky differentiated between spontaneous concepts and school-learned concepts. Spontaneous concepts are those learned by the child through direct experience, similar to how Piaget described acquisition of knowledge. Conversely, school-learned concepts require instruction and assistance from the teacher. Moreover, the social context of learning with peers plays a role in the child's learning (Bodrova & Leong, 1996). The guidelines propose, then, that children construct their learning from the environment as well from adults. Learning is interactive between children and adults. Both teacher and children inform the other. The theoretical underpinnings of the guidelines for DAP resulted in the following assumptions about interactive learning and teaching:

1. Children learn best when their physical needs are met and they feel psychologically safe.
2. Children construct knowledge.
3. Children learn through social interaction with adults and other children.
4. Children's learning reflects a recurring cycle that begins in awareness and moves to exploration, to inquiry and, finally, to utilization.
5. Children learn through play.
6. Children's interests and "need to know" motivate learning.
7. Human development and learning are characterized by individual variation (NAEYC & NAECSSDE, 1991, pp. 25–27).

In 1992, the NAEYC published *Reaching Potentials: Appropriate Curriculum and Assessment for Young Children*, Volume 1 (Bredekamp & Rosegrant, 1992), followed by *Reaching Potentials: Transforming Early Childhood Curriculum and Assessment*, Volume 2 (Bredekamp & Rosegrant, 1995). Volume 1 further describes appropriate curriculum and assessment, with descriptions of a transformational curriculum. Included in the volume are chapters on the needs of children who are diverse in ability, culture, and language. Volume 2 further describes the transformational curriculum in terms of content areas. Through these publications, NAEYC further explained DAP and clarified questions about DAP. The two additional publications notwithstanding, concerns and questions about DAP continued to mount.

Although there appeared to be widespread acceptance of DAP in the field of early childhood education, there were questions as to how well DAP was being carried out, even among those who said they believed in the model and were using it. Others questioned the applicability of DAP with all young children, especially those with disabilities and those from different cultures. There were criticisms of some of the statements made by the developers of DAP, as reported in the publications related to understanding and using DAP. NAEYC authors responded to the concerns and criticisms and have revised their discussions of DAP in more recent publications.

✦ Arlene Penneybaker

Arlene Penneybaker is a kindergarten teacher in a large suburban school serving middle-class families. She has been teaching for 15 years and prides herself on keeping up with trends in early childhood education. She attends local workshops and conferences and looks for teaching ideas in magazines that come to her school.

Arlene talks about DAP. She is concerned that first- and second-grade teachers are too academic and do not understand the developmental needs of their students. When Arlene was asked to have a university student complete an internship in her classroom, she readily agreed. The principal had recommended Arlene because she uses DAP. Therefore, the university supervisor was perplexed when her student complained about Arlene's academic expectations for her students. When observing in Arlene's class, the supervisor noted that children spent most of the morning working on writing worksheets where they copied letters or filling in mathematics workbook pages. The teacher proudly pointed out that her learning centers were nicely equipped and well-organized. However, they were used principally as a reward for children who completed their work in a timely manner. The supervisor made plans to have discussions with Arlene to determine her understanding of DAP. +

Revisions in DAP. There are strong indications that the developers of DAP are sensitive to the concerns and issues that have been raised about its limitations. In *Reaching Potentials: Appropriate Curriculum and Assessment for Young Children* (Bredekamp & Rosegrant, 1992), various authors began to address issues related to the applicability of DAP guidelines for all young children. Bowman (1992) discussed the characteristics of minority children and how programs for them needed to be both developmentally and culturally appropriate. Derman-Sparks (1992) built on Bowman's understandings about the needs of minority children and described how an antibias, multicultural curriculum could be designed to meet the needs of minority children. Hills (1992) discussed assessment strategies that are viable for young children and how authentic and performance assessments can be useful for children who are diverse in language, culture, and abilities. Wolfe (1992) addressed how bilingual education could help young children with language differences achieve their potential.

Early childhood teachers and early childhood special education teachers are working collabo-ratively in many settings to include children with disabilities with their nondisabled peers. Through inclusion, teachers of both populations of children are merging their approaches to serving children within the classroom. The adjustments that must be made to adapt to changing roles and responsibilities indicate that advocates for DAP must continue to refine and expand how the model is carried out in classrooms that serve children from diverse backgrounds. A recent effort to meet the challenge is through the *Guidelines for Preparation of Early Childhood Professionals* developed by the NAEYC, the Division for Early Childhood of the Council for Exceptional Children (DEC/CEC), and the National Board for Professional Teaching Standards (NBPTS)(National Association for the Education of Young Children, 1996). A chapter of the *Guidelines* is devoted to the preparation of early childhood special education teachers; however, the qualifications needed to teach children who are culturally and linguistically diverse are not addressed.

Finally, the NAEYC has published a revision of the original 1987 volume on DAP, now titled *Developmentally Appropriate Practice in Early Childhood Programs* (Bredekamp & Copple, 1997). In this new edition, many of the concerns and issues discussed earlier have been addressed. The current context of programs that serve children who present diversity that is complex and extensive is incorporated into the content of the book. A multiple approach to appropriate practices is based on broader perspectives of how young children can be served appropriately. More emphasis is placed on individual rather than chronological needs. Similarly, more attention is given to professional decision-making by teachers, rather than advocating what is appropriate or inappropriate in every classroom.

Understanding the DAP Approach

Many factors influence the quality of an early childhood program, including (but not limited to) the extent to which knowledge about how children develop and learn is applied in program practices. DAP result from the process of professionals making decisions about the well-being and education of children based on at least three important kinds of information or knowledge:

1. What is known about child development and learning—knowledge of age-related human characteristics that permits general predictions within an age range about what activities, materials, interactions, or experiences will be safe, healthy, interesting, achievable, and also challenging to children;
2. What is known about the strengths, interests, and needs of each individual child in the group to be able to adapt for and be responsive to inevitable individual variation; and
3. Knowledge of the social and cultural contexts in which children live to ensure that learning experiences are meaningful, relevant, and respectful for the participating children and their families (Bredekamp & Copple, 1997, pp. 8–9).

This excerpt from the 1997 revised position statement in *Developmentally Appropriate Practices in Early Childhood Programs* reflects the broadened approach taken by the NAEYC in redefining how appropriate practice includes serving the developmental needs of all young children. This approach includes a leadership role for teachers who make the decisions about planning a curriculum for young children that is appropriate to their individual development. The process is a synergetic interaction between teacher roles and the child's encounter with meaningful curriculum.

As defined in this approach (Bredekamp & Rosegrant, 1992, p. 32), meaningful curriculum

- is based on how children learn and addresses the entire learning cycle;
- reclaims the whole child and redefines *child-centered*;
- provides depth of understanding and promotes conceptual development through integrating experiences;

- is individually appropriate, based on children's needs and interests;
- derives from the knowledge base of the disciplines and has intellectual integrity; and
- results from interactive teaching.

The curriculum is based on a learning cycle whereby children become aware, explore and inquire, and then utilize new information. It is a process of learning that begins at a simple discovery level and continues in more depth and complexity until the child is able to use and apply information. Figure 3.3 illustrates the continuing process in the learning cycle.

Meaningful learning occurs within an integrated curriculum based on the integrated nature of development described by the developers as transformational curriculum. Integrated curriculum includes skills development as well as opportunities for child-initiated interests and activities. The role of the teacher is to plan for children's individual needs and interests using a range or continuum of roles. The continuum ranges from nondirective teacher behaviors through supporting or mediating behaviors, to directive activities whereby the teacher engages in teacher-directed roles, such as demonstrating and direct instruction. In keeping with the intent of the DAP approach, teaching is interactive whereby the teacher coordinates, orchestrates, and facilitates learning with active participation on the part of the children (Bredekamp & Copple, 1997). Figure 3.4 illustrates the continuum of teacher roles.

The new 1997 guidelines stress that the NAEYC is not attempting to describe a particular curriculum, but is providing a framework for appropriate curriculum development within the guidelines. The new guidelines were informed with input from many leaders in early childhood curriculum models to include the developers of High/Scope, Reggio Emilia, and The Project Approach. We will now turn to a description of each of these models.

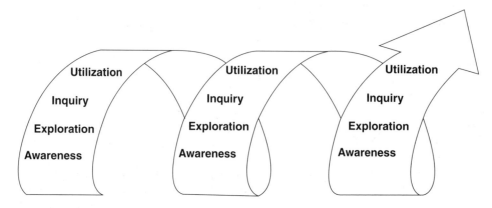

FIGURE 3.3 The learning cycle.
Source: From "Conceptual Frameworks for Applying the Guidelines" by S. Bredekamp and T. Rosegrant in *Reaching Potentials: Appropriate Curriculum and Assessment for Young Children* (Vol. 1, p. 32), edited by S. Bredekamp and T. Rosegrant, 1992, Washington, DC: National Association for the Education of Young Children. Copyright 1992 by the National Association for the Education of Young Children. Reprinted with permission.

High/Scope Curriculum

History of High/Scope

The High/Scope model began as The Cognitively Oriented Curriculum (Weikart, Rogers, Adcock, & McClelland, 1971). The original purpose of the model was to serve at-risk children from poor neighborhoods in Ypsilanti, Michigan, in 1962. David Weikart, the developer of the model, became concerned with the failure rate of high school students from poor neighborhoods in the Ypsilanti Public Schools. One of Weikart's conclusions as to the causes of low achievement was attendance at elementary schools in poor neighborhoods.

Although the Ypsilanti Public Schools did not pursue establishing a program to address the problem, Weikart and colleagues decided to establish an intervention program to prepare three- and four-year-olds for elementary schools. This initial project was called the Perry Preschool Project. From the beginning of the intervention model, Weikart developed a research project to compare the progress of chil-

dren in the project with that of children from the same neighborhoods who did not attend the project.

In 1967, a second research effort, the Preschool Curriculum Demonstration Project, was initiated. This research project compared three different curriculum models that were part of the evolving Head Start movement: the Cognitively Oriented Curriculum (the High/Scope Model), the Language Training Curriculum (the Direct Instruction Model), and the Unit-Based Curriculum (the Nursery School Model) (Schweinhart, Weikart, & Larner, 1986; Weikart, Epstein, Schweinhart, & Bond, 1978). In 1970, this study found that children in all three models performed well on both IQ tests and later school achievement tests.

In 1970, Weikart left the Ypsilanti Public Schools and established the High/Scope Educational Research Foundation. Through this foundation, the model has continued to develop from the 1970s to the present. Over the years, three major publications described the evolving High/Scope Preschool Educational Approach:

NONDIRECTIVE	MEDIATING	DIRECTIVE
Acknowledge / Model / Facilitate / Support / Scaffold / Co-construct / Demonstrate / Direct		

FIGURE 3.4 Teaching continuum.
Source: From "Conceptual Frameworks for Applying the Guidelines" by S. Bredekamp and T. Rosegrant in *Reaching Potentials: Appropriate Curriculum and Assessment for Young Children* (Vol. 1, p. 39) edited by S. Bredekamp and T. Rosegrant, 1992, Washington, DC: National Association for the Education of Young Children. Copyright 1992 by the National Association for the Education of Young Children. Reprinted with permission.

The Cognitively Oriented Curriculum: A Framework for Preschool Educators (1971), by David Weikart, Linda Rogers, Carolyn Adcock, and Donna McClelland; *Young Children in Action* (1979), by Mary Hohmann, Bernard Banet, and David Weikart; *and Active Learning Practices for Preschool and Childcare Programs* (1995), by Mary Hohmann and David Weikart. The High/Scope Research Foundation has also produced films, videotapes, booklets, and other supportive materials. In addition, the work of the Foundation has addressed how the model can be applied in elementary schools and how families are an integral part of the model.

The purpose for the High/Scope project has expanded over the years. As the title of the 1995 publication states, the model is now intended for children from diverse backgrounds and cultures. High/Scope programs serve children with special needs and children from all socioeconomic levels. In addition, the model has been adapted for use in Latin America, Australia, and Europe (Hohmann, Banet, & Weikart, 1979).

Results of longitudinal research of the model spanning the 1960s through the 1990s have documented the benefits for children and their families (Schweinhart, Barnes, & Weikart, 1993). The latest study of 27-year-olds who participated in the preschool program found that fewer participants had been arrested, and more had higher earnings and owned their own homes. More participants owned second cars, and more graduated from high school or received General Education Development Certificates, compared with peers who did not participate in the preschool program (Hohmann & Weikart, 1995).

Christopher

It was the day before Halloween in Christopher's multiage classroom. The classroom serves children who are five, six, and seven years old. Christopher is six and has Down syndrome. Christopher is included into a classroom that uses the High/Scope approach with the support of a paraprofessional educator who is assigned to him.

On this day before Halloween, the teacher read a story about a witch who hated Halloween that was part of a class project on holidays. Christopher sat on the floor in front of the teacher and listened attentively as he gazed at the pictures when the teacher displayed them during the story. After the story was over, the teacher explained the activity to follow that would give the children the opportunity to describe the beginning, middle, and end of the story using writing or art materials. Children were paired to complete the assignment. Christopher and a classmate were given pictures photocopied from the book to put into order. They were to dictate the parts of the story to the paraprofessional educator who would record their statements. It soon became apparent that Christopher and his partner were the only students using pictures; nevertheless, none of the children seemed to be aware of any difference in their activity. Christopher's partner ably gave assistance and demonstrated complete acceptance of her role in working with him. +

Development of the High/Scope Curriculum

When the developers of the High/Scope Model began their plans for curriculum development, they established three criteria (Hohmann & Weikart, 1995, p. 4):

1. A coherent theory about teaching and learning must guide the curriculum development process.
2. Curriculum theory and practice must support each child's capacity to develop individual talents and abilities through ongoing opportunities for active learning.
3. The teachers, researchers, and administrators must work as partners in all aspects of curriculum development to ensure that theory and practice receive equal consideration.

The primary theory used was that of Piaget and also the many theorists who interpreted and translated Piaget's work. J. McVicker Hunt's research (*Intelligence and Experience*, 1961) was a primary focus in the original stages of development. As the original framework of the curriculum model evolved, principles of the curriculum were defined with the following components (Hohmann & Weikart, 1995, pp. 4–5):

- *Active learning*—Through active learning—having direct and immediate experiences and deriving meaning from them through reflection—young children construct knowledge that helps them make sense of their world.
- *Key experiences*—creative, ongoing interactions with people, materials, and ideas that promote children's mental, emotional, social, and physical growth.
- *Plan-do-review* process— . . . Teachers in the Perry Preschool Project provided time for the children to plan their play activities, carry

them out, and reflect on what they had done. . . .
- *Parent component*—Through home visits, teachers offered ideas about learning and child development to parents without directly "teaching" either the children or the parents.

Using these basic elements, the curriculum has evolved over four decades to the model that is used today. In the following section we will examine the High/Scope model in more detail.

Understanding the High/Scope Model

Active learning and key experiences form the core of the High/Scope Model. In addition, there are four elements that support active learning: adult-child interaction, learning environment, daily routines, and assessment.

Adult-Child Interaction. Adults play a supportive role in the High/Scope preschool program. Adults use positive interaction strategies such as sharing control with children, supporting children's play, focusing on children's strengths, and forming authentic relationships with children. In addition, they use encouragement and a problem-solving approach to deal with everyday situations in the classroom.

Learning Environment. The environment also plays a major role in the model. The environment is arranged into interest areas to support the interests of the students. Activities that are provided in the environment include pretending and role play, sand and water play, language arts experiences, math activities such as counting and sorting, and physical activities that include building, climbing, and dancing. Teachers have the responsibility to select appropriate materials, make those materials accessible to the children in an organized manner, and provide storage for the materials. Materials that are provided include found, natural, commercial, and homemade materials.

Daily Routines. The daily routine also supports active learning. Model planners believe that a consistent routine is important. The plan-do-review process described earlier forms the structure for the routine whereby children plan what they want to do before they select and engage in activities. At the conclusion of their work period, they review what they have accomplished. Adults engage in group experiences with children through small-group and large-group activities based on children's experiences and key experiences that structure the curriculum. Large-group time is used for music and movement, projects, story reenactments, and group discussions.

Assessment. Over the years of implementation, the High/Scope Research Foundation has developed an assessment model that focuses on observation as the major tool for understanding children's development and learning. Assessment includes keeping daily anecdotal notes and daily planning sessions using a team approach to interacting with and observing children. The High/Scope Child Observation Record (COR)(1992) is used to document and report children's progress.

The High/Scope model has been described within a wheel of learning. Active learning is at the center of the wheel with the four components of the model supporting the center. Figure 3.5 shows the visual representation of the High/Scope model.

Reggio Emilia

Whereas the High/Scope model is based on "active learning," Reggio Emilia schools reflect "active education." Both of these approaches support Piaget's perception of cognitive development "as a process of ongoing adaptation to one's environment (Staley, 1998, p. 21). And, although the Reggio Emilia schools evolved in Italy, their constructivist approach is consistent with theories that also influence contemporary American models.

History of Reggio Emilia

> The Reggio system can be described succinctly as follows: It is a collection of schools for young children in which each child's intellectual, emotional, social, and moral potentials are carefully cultivated and guided. The principal educational vehicle involves youngsters in long-term engrossing projects, which are carried out in a beautiful, healthy, love-filled setting (Gardner, 1996, p. x).

Early childhood care and education in Italy has a long history that began as charitable and religious centers for infants and preschool children in the nineteenth century. After 1867, Froebel's kindergartens began to have an influence followed by progressive educators at the beginning of the twentieth century. During the first half of the twentieth century, preschool education was controlled by the Catholic Church. It was not until the end of the second world war that parent-run schools within municipal systems were established (Edwards, Gandini, & Forman, 1996).

During the 1950s, Italian educators were influenced by progressive educators John Dewey and Celestin Freinet from France. In Bologna, Bruno Ciari was invited to direct their city school system. The progressive education system Ciari established in Bologna provided leadership for the budding early childhood programs in Italy. Ciari believed "that education should liberate childhood energy and capacities and promote the harmonious development of the whole child in all areas—communicative, social, affective, and with respect to critical and scientific thinking" (Edwards, Gandini, & Foreman, 1996, p. 16).

The evolution of the Reggio Emilia preschool model was initiated in the days immediately after the end of the World War II in 1945. In the following months, Loris Malaguzzi and local parents established the first school in a war-torn country without resources. Bricks were salvaged from bombed houses and the first buildings were constructed by the parents. From these

FIGURE 3.5 High/Scope wheel of learning.
Source: From *Educating Young Children* (p. 6), by M. Hohmann and D. Weikart, 1995, Ypsilanti, MI: High/Scope Press. Copyright 1995 by High/Scope Press. Reprinted with permission.

first tentative efforts, the system of Reggio Emilia schools was established. In the first years, educators and parents worked to develop the program based on projects designed by the teachers. After Malaguzzi visited the Rousseau Institute in Geneva, Switzerland, the schools began to reflect Piaget's theory and perceptions of children's cognitive development.

Despite ongoing struggles for many years with the Catholic Church over how schools would be administered, in 1967 all the parent-run schools came under the administration of the municipality of Reggio Emilia, and in 1972 the rules and regulations developed to govern the parent-run

schools of Reggio Emilia were passed by the City Council. This milestone marked acknowledgement of the Reggio Emilia approach after 10 years of development. Nevertheless, the Catholic establishment continued to challenge the city-run schools. After five months of public debate and interchanges within the schools, the issue of direction and control of the preschools in Reggio Emilia was resolved (Malaguzzi, 1996).

In the last 30 years, the schools of Reggio Emilia have continued to evolve and develop. The model has been influenced by the work of contemporary theorists and writers that include Urie Bronfenbrenner, Lev Vygotsky, Erik Erikson,

Howard Gardner, and Jerome Bruner. The model has gained international recognition and visitors have traveled from all over the world to experience and understand this model for early childhood education.

Development of the Reggio Emilia Model

The Reggio Emilia Model was first conceptualized using Piaget's theory of cognitive development. The child's development in quality of thinking helped in designing the school in which children are active learners. However, as Reggio Emilia educators continued to study Piaget's perception of constructivism, they had some concerns about his approach. They felt that Piaget's theory isolates the child and undervalues the adult's role in promoting cognitive development. They were also concerned about social interaction and that cognitive, affective, and moral judgement were described as parallel tracks. Therefore, in addition to understanding and incorporating Piaget's theory, model developers incorporated Vygotsky's work. They were particularly interested in Vygotsky's theory in how thought and language work together when the child is forming ideas and making a plan of action. Further, they were interested in Vygotsky's Zone of Proximal Development, the distance between the child's current capacities and the child level of potential development. The contributions of these two thinkers and others mentioned earlier guided the evolution of the Reggio Emilia Model (Malaguzzi, 1996).

The theoretical bases of the Reggio Emilia Model are focused on how the young child learns. Reggio Emilia schools used the term "active education" using Piaget's description of cognitive development as a process of ongoing adaptation to the environment. The schools are considered by Malaguzzi as "amiable" because they encourage movement, interindependence, and interaction. Emphasis is placed on the relationships between teachers, parents, and children in the active process of learning (Staley, 1998).

Understanding the Reggio Emilia Approach

The Reggio Emilia Model can be described in terms of eight principles (Cadwell, 1997, pp. 5–6):

- *The child as protagonist.* Children are strong and capable. All children have preparedness, potential, curiosity, and interest in constructing their learning, negotiating with everything their environment brings to them. Children, teachers, and parents are considered the three central protagonists in the educational process (Gandini, 1996).
- *The child as collaborator.* Education must focus on each child in relation to other children, the family, the teachers, and the community, rather than on each child in isolation (Gandini, 1993). There is an emphasis on work in small groups. This practice is based on the social constructivist model that supports the idea that we form ourselves through our interaction with peers, adults, things in the world, and symbols (Lewin, 1995).
- *The child as communicator.* This approach fosters children's intellectual development through a systematic focus on symbolic representation, including words, movement, drawing, painting, building, sculpture, shadow play, collage, dramatic play, and music, which leads children to surprising levels of communication, symbolic skills, and creativity (Edwards et al., 1996). Children have the right to use many materials in order to discover and communicate what they know, understand, wonder about, question, feel, and imagine. In this way, they make their thinking visible through their many natural "languages." A studio teacher, trained in the visual arts, works closely with children and teachers in each school to enable children to explore many materials and to use a great number of languages to make their learning visible.
- *The environment as third teacher.* The design and use of space encourage encounters,

communication, and relationships (Gandini, 1993). There is an underlying order and beauty in the design and organization of all the space in a school and the equipment and materials within it (Lewin, 1995). Every corner of every space has an identity and a purpose, is rich in potential to engage and to communicate, and is valued and cared for by children and adults.

- *The teacher as partner, nurturer, and guide.* Teachers facilitate children's exploration of themes, work on short- and long-term projects, and guide experiences of joint, open-ended discovery and problem-solving (Edwards et al., 1996). To know how to plan and proceed with their work, teachers listen and observe children closely. Teachers ask questions; discover children's ideas, hypotheses, and theories; and provide occasions for discovery and learning (Gandini, 1993).

- *The teacher as researcher.* Teachers work in pairs and maintain strong, collegial relationships with all other teachers and staff; they engage in continuous discussion and interpretation of their work and the work of children. These exchanges provide ongoing training and theoretical enrichment. Teachers see themselves as researchers preparing documentation of their work with children, whom they also consider researchers. The team is further supported by a *pedagogista* (pedagogical coordinator) who serves a group of schools (Gandini, 1993).

- *The documentation as communication.* Careful consideration and attention are given to the presentation of the thinking of the children and the adults who work with them. Teachers' commentary on the purposes of the study and the children's learning process, transcriptions of children's verbal language (i.e., words and dialogue), photographs of their activity, and representations of their thinking in many media are composed in carefully designed panels or books to present

the process of learning in the schools. The documentation serves many purposes. It makes parents aware of their children's experience. It allows teacher to better understand children, to evaluate their own work, and to exchange ideas with other educators. Documentation also traces the history of the school and the pleasure in the process of learning experiences by many children and their teachers (Gandini, 1993).

- *The parent as partner.* Parent participation is considered essential and takes many forms. Parents play an active part in their children's learning experience and help ensure the welfare of all the children in the school. The ideas and skills that the families bring to the school and, even more important, the exchange of ideas between parents and teachers, favor the development of a new way of educating, which helps teachers to view the participation of families not as a threat but as an intrinsic element of collegiality and as the integration of different wisdoms (Spaggiari, 1996).

In keeping with these principles, the Reggio Emilia model will be discussed in terms of the environment, the role of teachers, the role of parents, the role of the child, the curriculum, and assessment.

The Environment. Reggio Emilia schools are designed to encourage social and cognitive development. The physical environment is planned to facilitate interactions between children as well as between teachers and parents.

Gandini (1996) uses the Diana School as an example of the design of Reggio Emilia schools. A main common space, a *piazza*, is surrounded by areas used for different purposes that open to the *piazza*. An important space is the *atelier*, described as a workshop or studio, which is used to work on projects and to explore new and familiar materials and tools. In addition, each age group has a large classroom with a mini-*atelier* attached.

Glass is used extensively to connect interior spaces as well as create a continuity between the indoor and outdoor environments. There are also spaces where children can spend time alone. The arrangement is designed to facilitate constructive exploration of materials and for work on projects and themes. A major purpose of the space is to display and document the children's work.

The Role of the Teaching Staff.   There are three adult roles in Reggio Emilia: the *atelierista*, the *pedagogista*, and teachers. Adults in each of these roles interact with the children, parents and community, and each other.

The *atelierista* uses a background in art to work with children in the *atelier* as they engage in painting, drawing, working with clay, and using other techniques and materials. The *atelierista* helps children communicate and represent what they are learning in their project work. The *atelierista* also talks daily with teachers, *pedagogisti*, and teachers to help them understand the children's artwork and how they learn (Vecchi, 1996).

The *pedagogisti* have multiple responsibilities. They are important in coordinating communications with parents and visitors, as well as engaging teachers in new advances in theory and practice. The *pedagogisti* serve as facilitators for the exchange of ideas between teachers, both within a school and among different schools. Work with teachers includes identifying new themes and activities for professional development. Most importantly, the *pedagogisti* work to develop relationships with parents and to set up meetings so that parents can be involved in planning and creating curriculum projects (Filippini, 1996).

The teacher's role is to work with the children. Teachers focus on children's work, rather than as instructors to the children. Teachers and children are equally involved in the progress of work, materials and techniques being used, and the ideas being explored. Classroom teachers

work with the *atelierista* as partners in facilitating children's work. They work as partners in the exchange of ideas of how to further children's work with materials and discussions (Cadwell, 1997).

The Role of the Child.   A major portion of children's time is spent on project work. They use art materials to represent what they understand and how they are using creativity to reconstruct knowledge. These representations and communications have been described as the languages of children. Katz (1996) believes that preschool children in Reggio Emilia schools are able to use visual representation to communicate ideas, understandings, feelings, and observations much earlier than American children.

In addition to project work, children engage in all types of spontaneous play, blocks, acting out plays, and outdoor play. Some children also engage in art activities during free play periods. Children spend much of the day interacting and socializing with classmates and adults (Katz, 1996).

The Curriculum.   The curriculum of Reggio Emilia is described as emergent. That is, the teachers do not plan objectives and learning activities in advance. Rather, they first study the characteristics of the children as well as their aptitudes, needs, and interests. In addition, the staff meets weekly to continue sharing knowledge of the children in their planning (Katz, 1996).

In planning the curriculum teachers lay out general educational objectives. They formulate hypotheses of what could happen based on their knowledge of the children. The relationships between children, parents, the community, and culture are also considered. Based on children's backgrounds and interests, curriculum themes or projects are initiated. Thereafter, the processes of interactions with children and adults, observation, and documentation of children's work, and discussions among all of the participants to include staff members, parents, and children, are used for ongoing planning and implementation of the curriculum. Children are equal participants in planning the curriculum and evaluating the progress of the work. Each project can start from a suggestion, a child's idea, or a significant event (Rinaldi, 1996).

Assessment. Much has already been said about documentation, the record of children's work. Products of projects or themes are reflected in the children's artwork. In addition, ongoing discussions between staff members and with the children provide continuous assessment of the curriculum and children's progress. Teachers and *atelieristas* keep daily anecdotal records of what the children are doing and the steps that will be taken in guiding the children through further efforts. The display of children's work on the walls of the school plus discussions and written information form the assessment of children's progress as well as self-evaluation by children and teachers.

The Reggio Emilia model has been of interest to educators from many countries. The approach has been implemented in the United States for over a decade. Lacking the longitudinal experience of Italian educators in the evolution of the approach, American projects have had to implement the process slowly and carefully with attention to differences in a new setting (Cadwell, 1997; Forman, Lee, Wrisley, & Langley, 1996; Gillespie, 2000; LeeKeenan & Nimmo, 1996; New, 1996; Staley, 1998).

The Project Approach

The Project Approach has many similarities to the Reggio Emilia Model in that both use projects as a focus for children's learning and use children's participation of curriculum themes. However, the Project Approach was developed separately from Reggio Emilia. The developers of the Project Approach acknowledge the influence of Reggio Emilia in recent years and have

included Reggio Emilia ideas on documentation of children's work.

History of the Project Approach

The developers of the Project Approach base their approach in their work with young children in England and the United States plus their interactions with colleagues in other countries. Their model has its roots in the original project work advocated by Dewey and Kilpatrick during the Progressive Era of education in the United States (Stewart, 1986). They also refer to Isaac's descriptions of children's work in England (Isaacs, 1966).

Another influence on the model is open education which was popular in the 1970s and 1980s as well as the work in British Infant Schools (Helm & Katz, 2001; Katz & Chard, 1989).

The developers, Lillian Katz and Silvia Chard, state that a motivation for designing their model stemmed from the dominance of mindless activities in the early years of schooling. They perceived the Project Approach to be a context that would encourage the child's mind to be "engaged, challenged, and enriched" (Katz & Chard, 1989, p. xi). They believed that the use of projects could be incorporated as part of a total curriculum based on the preferences of individual schools.

The first publication to explain the approach was *Engaging Children's Minds: The Project Approach* (Katz & Chard, 1989). As the original authors engaged in work with teachers in classrooms, their ideas about the uses of the Project Approach continued to evolve. In 1992, Sylvia Chard developed a guide to help teachers learning how to implement the approach. This guide, *The Project Approach: A Practical Guide for Teachers* (Chard, 1992), was followed by a teacher's course, *The Project Approach: A Practical Course for Teachers* (Chard, 1994a), and more recently, *The Project Approach: A Second Practical Guide for Teachers* (Chard, 1994b).

In response to concerns by teachers and administrators that at-risk children with less readiness for school need formal academic exercises rather than project work, additional publications were produced to address the issue. *Young Investigators: The Project Approach in the Early Years* (Helm & Katz, 2001) and *Engaging Children's Minds: The Project Approach* (2nd ed.) (Katz & Chard, 2000) addressed more recent issues and incorporated ideas gained from Reggio Emilia.

Development of the Project Approach

Katz and Chard took a similar approach to that of the NAEYC when explaining DAP. Like the NAEYC, Katz and Chard countered many of the practices used with young children that they considered to be detrimental. They examined practices that asked children to engage in activities that are not in the best interests of young children such as rituals using the calendar and workbooks with paper-and-pencil tasks. They contrasted acquisition of knowledge or contents of mind with dispositions or habits of mind.

One concern is with formal instruction as opposed to learning through exploration and direct experience. A preference of this approach is that learning experiences help children to develop social and communicative competence. Most important, desirable dispositions, or enduring habits of mind such as humor, generosity, and helpfulness are desired rather than negative dispositions such as quarrelsomeness, callousness, and avarice (Katz & Chard, 1989). Katz and Chard cite research (Dweck, 1986) that disposition to learn can be put at risk by "too much emphasis on skilled performance in academically oriented curricula" (Katz & Chard, 1989, p. 38). Likewise, they propose that academically oriented curricula do not permit all children to be successful.

Rather than directly basing their approach on theorists, the authors have looked to curriculum research. Using this research, they base their model on several aspects of children's develop-

ment and learning: the role of interaction in learning; the value of informality; and a variety of teaching methods.

The Role of Interaction. Social interaction facilitates learning and promotes the development of social competence, which implies that young children should be engaged in active, expressive learning processes with other children. Mind-engaging activities should occur whereby young children interact with new concepts and ideas. Such interactions should be based on their own experiences and the real environment.

The Value of Informality. The belief is that the more informal the learning environment, the more children can express their understandings and teachers can access these understandings. The informality should be balanced so that children can make appropriate progress in learning. This would include the ability of children to evaluate their own work and better understand their own progress. The informal approach to curriculum would include spontaneous play and project work (Katz & Chard, 1989).

Variety of Teaching Methods. The authors propose that if children are to develop a disposition for learning, then a variety of teaching methods should be used. Their thinking is that different teaching strategies will promote successful learning with diverse children. Further, they propose that the younger the children, the greater the variety of strategies that should be used by the teacher.

Katz and Chard believe the Project Approach promotes the positive qualities of development and learning that they described. They summarized the advantages of the Project Approach as follows (Katz & Chard, 1989, p. 49):

> Project work takes into account the acquisition of knowledge, skills, dispositions, and feelings. It can provide learning situations in which context and content-enriched interactions and conversations can occur about matters familiar to the children. Project work can provide activities in which children of many different ability levels can contribute to the ongoing life and work of the group. Working together on projects also provides situations and events in which social skills are functional and can be strengthened. Because project topics are drawn from children's interest and familiar environments, the knowledge acquired can have real cultural relevance for them. Last but not least, we advocate the project approach because it provides continuous challenges for teachers and thus can contribute to making the teachers' work interesting and professionally satisfying.

Understanding the Project Approach

A project is an in-depth investigation of a topic worth learning more about. The investigation is usually undertaken by a small group of children within a class, sometimes by a whole class, and occasionally by an individual child. The key feature of a project is that a research effort deliberatively focuses on finding answers to questions about a topic posed either by the children, the teacher, or the teacher working with the children (Katz, 1994, p. 1).

On the surface, the projects just described sound very much like the projects engaged in by teachers and children in Reggio Emilia schools. A major difference is that the classroom teacher generally has the major responsibility in the Project Approach versus a staff collaboration strategy used in Reggio Emilia schools. A second difference is the more obvious organization of projects in the Project Approach. This organizational structure can be discussed in terms of three phases of projects (Chard, 1994b; Helm & Katz, 2001).

The Curriculum: Three Phases of Projects. The first phase of a project has as its purpose to select a project. Once a topic has been identified by a teacher, child, or teacher and children together, planning for the project commences. Teachers conduct preliminary planning by developing a teacher planning web to think about ways the project might develop. Sometimes this process includes a topic web or curriculum web. This process permits the teacher to evaluate whether the topic of the study has merit and identify resources that might be used in developing a topic. If it is determined that the topic is viable, the teacher works with the children to find out what they currently understand about the topic and what new information they would like to learn about the topic. This process can also include a webbing process.

The second phase is initiated after the room has been prepared to investigate the topic. As part of the beginning of the second phase the webs are reviewed, a field-site is selected for the investigation of the topic, and planning with site personnel and other adults who will help with the investigation is conducted. If particular skills are needed for the investigation, they are introduced and practiced before the investigation begins.

The investigation begins with a field-site visit. Children are encouraged to observe and ask questions as they interact with site personnel. They engage in sketching and drawing on site as part of their investigation. Children can also use counting and writing to document data they have found at the site. After the field-site visit, the children discuss the trip or are debriefed about the site visit. Materials and sources of data, such as photographs or videos, can be viewed as part of the discussion. The investigation continues with children engaging in various types of activities as part of their project work. The children represent what they have learned through writing, drawing, construction, dancing, and dramatic play. At this point, the children and teachers might review the webs or develop a re-web to evaluate their progress on the project and identify new questions or directions for the project.

The third phase has as its purpose to end the project. A culminating event is planned to share the results of the project. Student work is displayed, and parents, students from other classrooms, and teachers might participate in the culminating event. Documentation of the achievements of the projects that include student portfolios, project products, teacher observations, student self-reflections, and written narratives are used to document the project topic (Helm & Katz, 2001). Chard (1994) describes five features of the three phases to include group discussions, field work, representation, investigation, and display, which are similar to the three phases used to trace the progress of development of a project.

Assessment. Beyond culminating events to finalize work on a project, documentation is recommended as the approach to assessment of children, teachers, and the curriculum. The documentation used is more specific and varied than the documentation used with Reggio Emilia. Five strategies are used to document children's progress: portfolios, individual or group products, observations, children's self-reflections, and narratives of learning experiences. Each of these types of assessment contribute to understanding children's progress and interests, ongoing assessment of the progress of the project and changes that might be made, and evidence of children's work that can be shared with parents and others.

Helm and Katz (2001) suggest reasons that documentation is appropriate for the project approach. First, they believe that documentation is most valuable as a guide for teachers in the progress of the project. Documentation can also provide evidence of all domains of development as well as provide a framework for teachers to organize observations and recording children's developmental progress. Documentation demonstrates how children learn from active engagement in activities and materials that are relevant; moreover, they show how learning is an interactive process between adults and children. Finally, documentation can show how integrated learning experiences within project work provide insights into children's learning.

Summary

This chapter began with the idea that the need for quality programs is extremely important if children are to be successful learners. In this current decade of a new century, efforts are being made to describe how these quality programs can be actualized. In trying to achieve this quality, one requirement proposed is that there be improved standards for training and licensing of teachers. This goal can be difficult to achieve because requirements for education and training vary widely among types of early childhood programs and among states.

Several characteristics have been proposed to describe quality programs. Inclusion of principles of child development is basic to quality as is a balanced curriculum that addresses all domains of development. Parent relationships with the school are significant as well as a healthy interaction between parents, teachers, and children. A quality program has a clear plan for assessment and accountability. This evaluation would include children's progress, assessment of teacher planning and interaction with children, and ongoing evaluation of the program. Understanding and addressing the diversity of children and families are also significant if a program is to demonstrate quality. Programs should be developed based on the needs, interests, and backgrounds of the children present in the class. These diversity factors can include ethnicity, culture, language, and family values.

Classical and contemporary theories inform quality programs today. The views of how children develop and learn as posited by Arnold Gesell's maturation theory, Piaget's cognitive-developmental theory, Erikson's psychosocial theory, and Skinner's behaviorist theory have informed early childhood programs for many decades. A more comprehensive view of development and learning has been due to the influence of Lev Vygotsky's approach to constructivism and the role of culture in learning as well as Urie Bronfenbrenner's work on the influence of the child's family, community, and other factors in the larger environment. Most recently, Howard Gardner's position that there are different types of intelligences has resulted in a closer look at individual differences in children, their interests, aptitudes, and abilities.

We have more than a few models of early childhood programs that represent the characteristics of quality discussed in the chapter. All of these models have commonalities in how they have incorporated theory into practice with constructivism as a key feature. The models have different origins, but have also influenced each other.

DAP provides guidelines for good practice with young children, but does not advocate a particular curriculum. This program originated in the United States as a response to the increasing emphasis on academics in early childhood classrooms. The Project Approach had a similar purpose for its development, but reflects equal influence from England and the United States.

The High/Scope curriculum has a longer history in that it was first conceptualized in the 1960s. Over the decades it has continued to be refined and expanded. The curriculum model developed within this approach reflects the work of Piaget and constructivism. It has expanded to both infancy and toddler levels as well as into the elementary school. The model is used in many countries and has continued to provide guidance to educators seeking to incorporate child-initiated learning into their program.

The Reggio Emilia model had its origins in Italy in the community of Reggio Emilia. The program dates back to the end of World War II when parent-run schools were established in the post-war years of the 1940s. Heavily influenced by Piaget, Vygotsky, Bronfenbrenner, and others, Reggio Emilia schools use projects, extensive work using art media, and development of curriculum following children's interests. Reggio Emilia is limited to the preschool years, with strong involvement and support by parents. It has captured the interest of educators from all over the world who travel to Italy each year to visit the schools and take ideas home to their own programs.

In Chapter 4 we will look at the course of development in young children from birth through the primary-grade years. After reviewing how children develop within the cognitive, social-emotional, and physical domains, curriculum models for the levels of development in the early childhood years will be presented in subsequent chapters in the text. These examples of how teachers can implement quality programs will reflect the influence of both the theories and the models that have been presented in this chapter.

Study Questions

1. Why is there a difference in quality among different types of early childhood programs? Describe causes of these differences.
2. How important are differences in money resources to developing quality in programs? Explain.
3. How can quality in early childhood programs be determined? Describe some characteristics of quality.
4. How important are parents in today's early childhood programs? How do you believe parents should participate in early childhood programs?
5. What is meant by diversity in children? Explain some types of diversity that children can bring to the classroom.
6. How do theories influence program development in early childhood classrooms? Can theories with a different view of development and learning all have some influence on a classroom? Explain how this can happen.
7. Discuss two theories that address cultural differences in development and learning. Why should they be included when developing curriculum and instruction?
8. Explain what is meant by Developmentally Appropriate Practices (DAP). Why was DAP developed in the United States?
9. Why has DAP been revised in the last 10 years? Discuss at least three issues that led to revision.
10. Explain why DAP is not a curriculum.
11. Why was the High/Scope curriculum developed?
12. Describe four principles of the High/Scope curriculum.
13. How are "active learning" in the High/Scope curriculum and "active education" in the Reggio Emilia model similar?
14. When and why were Reggio Emilia schools developed?
15. Explain the importance of the child's role in Reggio Emilia as described in the eight principles of the model.
16. What is documentation in Reggio Emilia? How is documentation used?
17. How are the roles of *atelieristi* and *pedagogisti* in Reggio Emilia different than teacher roles in the other models?
18. Compare and contrast the nature of curriculum in Reggio Emilia and the Project Approach.
19. How do DAP and the Project Approach have similar purposes for model development?
20. Why is understanding the nature of projects key to implementation of the Project Approach?
21. How do the three phases of project development explain the process used in curriculum development in the classroom? Explain these phases.
22. How are all of the models presented similar in theoretical bases? Explain how all of the theories are complementary.

Developmental Characteristics of Young Children from Birth to 8 Years: Implications for Learning

CHAPTER OBJECTIVES

As a result of reading this chapter, you will be able to:

1. Describe the characteristics and competencies of infants and toddlers.
2. Describe the characteristics and competencies of children from ages 2 to 5 years.
3. Describe the transitional nature of development in children from ages 5 to 8 years.
4. Discuss how the characteristics of competencies of each age level have implications for learning and instruction.

The twentieth century was a period of research concerned with how infants and young children develop and learn. The child study movement established at the turn of the century involved researchers interested in developing information about the physical, social, emotional, cognitive, and language development of children. Investigators at various institutions of higher education in the United States accumulated extensive information on child development. This type of information continues to be gathered in the twenty-first century, with brain research a notable example. The interest in child development and the factors that affect such development and growth has not waned. Instead, research efforts build on earlier data collection. Changing conditions create a demand for investigative studies on how sociological and economic factors affect young children in the early childhood years.

This chapter contains a description of the child's development from birth to age 8; it also describes how the developmental stages affect the way in which the child learns. The work of developmental theorists, as described in earlier chapters, applies to explanations of development in this chapter. Developmental characteristics of children who are developing normally are different from those of young children with diverse abilities and disabilities. Remember also that development can vary because of socioeconomic status.

Birth to 2 Years: The Sensorimotor Stage

This section provides information on development during the first 2 years. Development is discussed under the categories of cognitive, physical, language, and social-emotional development.

Cognitive Development

Piaget (1963) described the first stage of cognitive development as the sensorimotor stage because infants come to know and understand their world by using their senses and physical actions. That is, infants construct understanding by using sensorimotor schemes, by using innate reflexive actions such as sucking. Sensorimotor schemes in turn help infants acquire new ways of interaction. As the infant continually engages in reflexive action, behavior becomes more complex and predictable.

During the sensorimotor stage, the infant moves through six substages of development, beginning with the *reflexive* stage. Reflexive actions in the first stage are gradually replaced by voluntary actions in the second stage, named the *primary circular reactions* stage. In the third stage, *secondary circular reactions,* the infant increases responses to people and objects, initiates activities, and develops object permanency. In the fourth stage, which involves *coordination of secondary circular reactions,* the infant actively searches for hidden objects and comprehends the meaning of simple words.

At the beginning of the second year, the fifth stage, *tertiary circular reactions,* commences. The toddler spends time experimenting with objects and begins to understand space, time, and causality. During the last stage, *symbolic representation* occurs. The toddler now can mentally represent objects within symbolic imitative behavior (Morrison, 1988). The sensorimotor substages might be described as follows:

- Reflexive (birth to 1 month): The neonate primarily uses reflexes for learning.
- Primary circular reactions (1 to 4 months): The infant repeats pleasurable behaviors and coordinates reflexes.
- Secondary circular reactions (4 to 10 months): The infant discovers new capabilities by chance and repeats them (e.g., accidentally hits crib mobile; repeats the action intentionally). Cause and effect are learned.
- Coordination of secondary circular reactions (10 to 12 months): The child is able to apply schemes or learned behavior to new situations; attains object permanence

(i.e., knows that objects exist even when they cannot be seen).

- Tertiary circular reactions (12 to 18 months): The child experiments with cause and effect; repeats behaviors to achieve variety (e.g., repeatedly drops toy from high chair).
- Symbolic representation (18 to 24 months): The child begins to think before acting; can use imagery to represent objects and action (e.g., pretends to drink from cup).

The infant at first uses reflex actions such as sucking and grasping. When the reflexes can be coordinated, the infant can intentionally grasp and pick up objects. After object permanence is achieved, the infant can remember actions and locate objects. The infant learns that he can cause events to happen and can retain a mental image of events and objects that have been experienced (Lawton, 1988; Morrison, 1988; Schwartz & Robison, 1982; Seefeldt & Barbour, 1998).

Physical Development

In their first 2 years, infants and toddlers achieve more physical growth and development than in any other period of their childhood. By their first birthday, they triple their birth weight and acquire mobility skills that include crawling, standing, and walking. During the second year, they practice and refine mobility skills. Motor development proceeds in proximodistal development (from the center of the body out to the fingers). Cephalocaudal development emerges (from the top of the body down to the legs). By the age of 5 months, they can reach and grasp a toy. Fine and gross motor development are controlled through biological maturation and stimulation and opportunities for physical activities.

Teething begins at about 7 months and is completed at 3 years, when the full set of "baby" teeth has erupted. Bladder and bowel control are not achieved until age 2½ or 3 years. Boys are more likely to achieve control at a later age than girls (Santrock, 1997).

Language Development

In the first 2 years, infants and toddlers move from prelinguistic utterances to the use of primitive sentences. Crying and cooing during the first few months evolve to babbling at about 5 or 6 months. Babbling includes the intonation patterns of the language by about 10 months, with the first real word occurring soon thereafter. Use of single words or holophrastic speech for many types of meaningful communication is gradually extended at about 18 months to combinations of two- and three-word utterances. With what is called telegraphic speech, toddlers express more complex thoughts through intonation and various combinations of the words they are rapidly adding to their vocabulary (Menyuk, 1969).

Social-Emotional Development

In infancy, the emotional tie between infant and parent or caregiver is called *attachment*. A positive attachment is crucial in the social and emotional development of the infant and toddler. Parental behavior, as well as the child's temperament, can affect development. Inappropriate parental behavior can cause anxious/avoidant or anxious/ambivalent patterns of attachment (Connell & Goldsmith, 1982). Anxious/ambivalent children are wary of strangers and new situations and have difficulty separating from the mother. Anxious/avoidant children, to the contrary, have no difficulty in separating from the mother; moreover, they show little preference for the parent over a stranger and may ignore the mother. For example, a toddler who was abused as an infant or whose needs were neglected shows anxious attachment in a child-care setting by fussing frequently. He or she might become fearful if routines or caregivers are changed. Neglected infants experience unresponsiveness on the part of parents, whereas abused babies experience harsh and negative care by parents (George & Main, 1979; Wallach & Caulfield, 1998). Children with anxious attachment histories are at a higher risk for developing

later emotional difficulties, including emotional dependency, aggression, inattention, or hyperactivity. During the preschool years, children who were anxiously attached as infants are at increased risk for becoming bullies or victims of bullies (Troy & Sroufe, 1987).

Temperament refers to differences in emotional development that lead to personality over a period of time. At birth, infants have temperament that is only a pattern of moods and responsiveness. Three basic types of temperament can be described. *Easy* children have predominantly positive moods and are calm and predictable. *Difficult* children, to the contrary, show a lot of negative emotion, are easily distracted, and are unpredictable. *Slow-to-warm-up* children respond negatively to new events initially, but adapt over time. They do not exhibit the negative intensity of difficult children, but take longer to adapt than do easy children (Chess & Thomas, 1977).

Social development during the first 2 years includes the development of social signals among peers. Social style in toddlers is related to attachment history; toddlers with secure attachment histories relate more positively toward peers. Prosocial behavior, or empathy, the understanding of another person's feelings, begins to emerge at about 12 months, when babies respond to the distress of others. At twelve months they show distress themselves, and by 18 months, they can try to comfort a distressed peer. Children of parents who have been nurturing and responsive are more likely to respond to the distress of another person (Schickedanz et al., 1993).

The sensorimotor period is one of rapid development in physical, language, and social development. The pages that follow discuss infant and toddler development, followed by checklists that list some major milestones and behavioral characteristics for each age period. The sections on characteristics and competencies describe the attributes that children in each age group have in common; in addition, the lists also describe individual differences in children. These sections are included to help readers who may not have had extended experience with young children acquire a realistic picture of what children are like at each age. In addition, readers can become familiar with what can be expected in behaviors and abilities. It is also important to remember that the description for any age group is general. Each child is unique and develops on an individual timetable.

Characteristics of age levels from birth through 5 years are discussed in the sections that follow; also included are the Wortham Developmental Checklist for Infants and Toddlers and the Frost-Wortham Developmental Checklists for the Preschool Years. The lists are for caregivers, parents, and teachers to use to further understand the normal characteristics in physical, social-emotional, and cognitive development for various age groups. The checklists may be consulted to determine if the child is achieving the listed behaviors during the normal age ranges. Similarly, parents, teachers, and caregivers can refer to the lists for suggestions about appropriate activities that can be conducted with the child. The checklists can be used in early childhood settings or by parents to record achievement of developmental milestones or mastery of listed competencies in the preschool years. Checklists have boxes in which the child's developmental progress can be tracked. The information to be recorded may vary depending on the context in which the checklists are used; therefore, the labels for recording progress may be changed to reflect the characteristics the user wishes to document. For example, the infant and toddler checklists might have boxes for dates of mastery, rather than dates of observation.

Preschool checklists might have boxes to indicate when relevant activities or lessons were conducted.

The checklists may also be adapted for use with children with special needs. PL 99-457 extends the guarantee of a free appropriate education for young children, beginning in infancy. Intervention for infants and toddlers with disabilities is funded through the Infants and Toddlers Program. Intervention plans for children with special needs can include checklists of characteristics adapted for the Individualized Education Program (IEP) for that child. Children with mental delay will progress through the categories of cognitive development much later than will children with normal intelligence; nevertheless, teachers of children with mental delay can also use the checklists to determine the developmental needs of children whose chronological age is different from their mental age. Children with physical disabilities may also be working on motor skills that are typical of younger children with normal development; teachers can adapt the checklist to include the physical characteristics that the child has the potential to develop. They can then use it for record keeping and reporting progress to parents. Because each child with special needs is different, teachers and specialists will need to determine potential abilities and use developmental checklists to fit the profile of the individual student.

Characteristics and Competencies: Birth to 6 Months

The newborn baby is often described as being helpless. In many ways he or she is. For the first few weeks of life, the baby seemingly sleeps, eats, and cries only. The mother or other adult must take care of the infant's needs. However, in spite of physical helplessness, newborn babies can develop a relationship with the family members and others in their life. They can see faces and hear voices. The baby responds to voices by turning his head or quieting to listen.

The new infant communicates his needs by crying and using facial expressions and body movements. Later, smiling, cooing, and gurgling are used to attract and hold the attention of significant people. The baby signals the need to withdraw from an interaction by turning his head away, yawning, crying, or fussing.

Babies come with all kinds of temperaments. From the beginning weeks of life, babies have unique personalities. Some enjoy being held or cuddled, whereas others do not respond to these activities. Each has his own style of being. Infant temperament has been classified into three types: the easy child, the slow-to-warm-up child, and the difficult child (Thomas, Chess, & Birch, 1970). Each type of infant has different personality and temperament characteristics that affect his moods, responsiveness, and activity levels. An infant's personality can affect adult interaction. Adults react positively and negatively to infant personalities, which in turn can cause difficulties for the infant. Parents and caregivers can have a positive effect on the infant's and toddler's emerging personalities by recognizing personality differences and modifying their responses positively and appropriately. This is especially true with the child who is classified as difficult (Soderman, 1985).

Figure 4.1 provides a checklist for the developmental characteristics in the newborn child until about 6 months of age. Because no two infants develop at the same rate, the time line will differ for individual babies.

✦ Hunter

Hunter is 9 months old. He can be characterized as having a slow-to-warm-up temperament. When he was a very young infant, Hunter was very serious. He did not smile easily, and he studied other people in his environment. Both of Hunter's parents are professionals. Hunter's father manages real estate, and his mother is an accountant. Hunter stays with a nanny during the day. Now that he is approaching his first birthday, Hunter is physically very active, eager to explore, and obviously larger than average. ✦*

Characteristics and Competencies: 6 to 12 Months

During the second 6 months of life, the baby experiences one of the most significant periods of growth and development in the entire life cycle. In physical development, the infant learns to sit, crawl, stand, and perhaps walk. Fine motor development allows the child to explore and manipulate toys and other objects by putting them in the mouth and performing other actions that permit learning the physical properties. The baby is very interested in his or her body while practicing motor skills such as rocking on hands and knees or clapping. The child may begin to feed him- or herself and imitates the physical actions of other family members.

The baby enjoys increasing social interactions with others. Babbling, smiling, and making gestures such as waving are used to initiate and respond to social encounters. The baby also uses gestures and tone of voice to communicate wants and needs. Also, the baby is gaining an understanding of the language and intonation used by others and can respond to simple commands, particularly, "No." As the first birthday approaches, he or she may be able to use a few simple words.

A significant stage in social-emotional development is based on the attainment of memory. The baby begins to recognize and react negatively to the presence of strangers. The baby also develops a new awareness of separation from the mother and other family members and fusses and cries when separation occurs. For a period of time, the infant may be more selective about social interactions and be wary of entering new situations.

Figure 4.2 is a checklist for babies 6 to 12 months old; it lists the new competencies the baby acquires in physical, cognitive, and social-emotional development during the second half-year of life.

AGE: BIRTH TO 6 MONTHS

PHYSICAL-COGNITIVE DEVELOPMENT	Date	Date	Date
1. Lifts head when held at shoulder			
2. When on stomach lifts or turns head			
3. Follows a moving person or object with eyes			
4. Looks at suspended object			
5. Grasps and holds a person or object for several seconds			
6. Moves arms and legs actively			
7. Sits in lap with support			
8. Closes hand on dangling toy			
9. Learns to roll over			
10. Looks at objects and realistic pictures			
11. Uses eye-hand coordination in reaching			
12. Turns head to sound of bell or rattle			
13. Plays with hands and feet			
14. Brings object to mouth			
SOCIAL-EMOTIONAL DEVELOPMENT			
1. Looks attentively at an adult			
2. Adjusts body to the way the adult holds him/her			
3. Responds to talking, smiling, touching			
4. Quiets when picked up			
5. Stops crying when someone plays with him/her			
6. Vocalizes in association with pleasure, displeasure, eagerness, and satisfaction			
7. Cries to get a bottle, attention, or to be held			
8. Knows familiar people or things by sight or voice			
9. Chuckles and laughs			

FIGURE 4.1 Wortham development checklist: Infants and toddlers, birth to 6 months

AGE: 6 TO 12 MONTHS			
PHYSICAL-COGNITIVE DEVELOPMENT	Date	Date	Date
1. Sits alone			
2. Transfers object from one hand to another			
3. Drinks from a cup			
4. Picks up small things with thumb and forefinger			
5. Uncovers hidden toy			
6. Looks at picture book			
7. Holds two toys			
8. Imitates speech sounds			
9. Creeps or gets from one place to another			
10. Attains sitting position independently			
11. Stands holding on			
12. Walks holding on			
13. Drops or places objects into a container			
14. Manipulates objects			
15. Says single words such as "mama" and "dada"			
16. Imitates actions			
17. Attempts self-feeding with a cup and spoon or fingers			
SOCIAL-EMOTIONAL DEVELOPMENT			
1. Shows likes or dislikes of people, objects, places			
2. Plays with image in mirror			
3. Understands "No"			
4. Responds to presence of a new person			
5. Squeals with joy or pleasure			
6. Demonstrates anxiety over departure of parents			
7. Enjoys and plays games with others (e.g., "Pat-a-Cake")			
8. Uses motions or gestures to communicate (holds out arms to be picked up)			

FIGURE 4.2 Wortham developmental checklist: Infants and toddlers, 6 to 12 months

Characteristics and Competencies: 12 to 18 Months

The months after the first birthday are an exciting period of development for the toddler. New abilities enable the child not only to get around without assistance but also to communicate using language. Freed from the dependence of infancy, the toddler literally blooms as he practices and masters emerging competencies.

Learning to walk affords the toddler true mobility. By 18 months, he not only will leave tentative steps behind and walk well but will also learn to climb stairs and throw a ball. Fine motor development enables the toddler to become more proficient at feeding himself and to learn a few skills in putting on and removing clothing.

Although gestures are still used to communicate wants, emerging language permits the child to use words to interact verbally with others. The baby understands more language than he can speak; nevertheless, the baby can name things in the environment and use words to initiate and respond to adult language.

Motor skills help the child to carry out new abilities in cognitive development. The toddler uses mobility and dexterity to expand exploration and manipulation of things in the environment. Through active play with toys and independent movement, the toddler enlarges his understanding of the world and the things that are available for play activities. Language and motor skills enhance the child's social and emotional development. The toddler exchanges words for crying when he needs or wants something. The toddler initiates social interactions with others more freely and can control the length of the interactions with others by advancing or withdrawing physically.

The characteristics listed in Figure 4.3 describe the toddler's development during the first 6 months of the second year. As the characteristics of development become more complex, the descriptions of development can be put into categories. Thus, physical-cognitive development now

is divided into motor development, language development, and cognitive development.

 ## Katilynn

Sixteen-month-old Katilynn looks like a little angel but behaves just the opposite. Even before she could move around, she wiggled and squirmed. She was not interested in infant toys and only briefly interested in anything else. Now that Katilynn can walk and climb, nothing is safe. She is into everything she can reach. She is a happy toddler but a source of exasperation for her parents. Katilynn is definitely on the go, but her parents are reluctant to take her to restaurants and other public places that will restrict her activities. She defies confinement. She will not sit in a high chair and stubbornly ignores all attempts to curb her behavior. Her attention span is still very brief, and constant activity fills her busy day. ✦

Characteristics and Competencies: 18 to 24 Months

During the second half of the second year, the toddler seems to have an inexhaustible source of energy. Development of new abilities seems to be constant and rapid. A few weeks brings many changes in motor development, language, cognitive learning, and social development. The child develops simultaneously in more than one area as he tries out new competencies.

The older toddler is physical, or "on the go." He can now run, climb, and accomplish some self-help skills in dressing and washing. The child is proficient in feeding himself and engages in all physical activities with enthusiasm.

Language development is accelerating. The child can make himself understood by using words and is expanding the number of words he or she can string together when talking. Role playing or

AGE: 12 TO 18 MONTHS

PHYSICAL-COGNITIVE DEVELOPMENT	Date	Date	Date
Motor Development			
1. Throws ball			
2. Builds two-block tower			
3. Walks well			
4. Walks backward			
5. Walks up stairs (with difficulty)			
6. Removes clothing (with difficulty)			
7. Takes off shoes and socks			
8. Uses spoon with little help			
9. Turns pages in a book			
10. Drinks from cup or glass unassisted with some spilling			
11. Scribbles			
Language Development			
1. Says single words (may add two and three words)			
2. Points to a body part on request			
3. Imitates words			

FIGURE 4.3 Wortham developmental checklist: Infants and toddlers, 12 to 18 months

pretending now includes talking as the toddler begins to verbalize what he is doing while playing. More words are used correctly, although the toddler uses the same vocabulary to express many different thoughts.

Toys and problem-solving activities are appealing to the competent toddler as he is able to apply past experiences to new learning situations. The toddler is learning to work simple puzzles and is developing an awareness of concepts such as color, shape, and number.

Social awareness allows the toddler to enjoy group activities. Although the toddler is just be-

ginning to interact in play activities with other children, he or she is aware of others and is expanding interactions with peers and adults.

The toddler is eager, interested, challenging, quick, busy, full of energy, and, for adults, exhausting. Toddlers require constant supervision as they explore and experiment with their new abilities. This is the age with the highest potential for toddler accidents, as they move through one of the peak periods of growth and learning. Figure 4.4 lists characteristics of the child during the second half of the second year and describes the toddler's continuing development.

Language Development	Date	Date	Date
4. Responds to a single request			
5. Says the names of at least five things			
Cognitive Development			
1. Pursues and retrieves a toy that is out of sight			
2. Puts objects in and out of container			
3. Role plays with familiar objects			
4. Recognizes and responds to self in mirror			
5. Solves simple puzzles or constructions			
SOCIAL-EMOTIONAL DEVELOPMENT			
1. Cooperates in games with caregivers			
2. Offers objects to another person			
3. Plays independently or in parallel play			
4. Helps with simple tasks			
5. Maintains interest in activities for longer periods			
6. Looks at speaker who is talking			
7. Carries, hugs toys			

FIGURE 4.3 *(continued)*

Infant and Toddler Development: Implications for Learning

Adults who are responsible for children during the first 2 years of life have the opportunity to facilitate growth and development within an exciting time of beginnings. Whereas infants used to be considered as helpless human beings, they are now described as capable and competent. Weiser (1987) stated: "This new baby is capable of selecting stimuli to which to respond or ignore, to physically withdraw from an external cause of pain, or to react with total body movement to internal distress" (p. 22). White and Watts (1973) wrote: "The 10- to 18-month period of life is in effect a critical period for the development of the foundations of competence" (p. 245).

Parents, teachers, and caregivers can best serve as facilitators of competence and learning if they understand how the child grows and develops during the first years. Although young infants cry and need to be fed, changed, and burped, they can also coo, attract the adult's attention, use their body to express themselves, and enjoy social

AGE: EIGHTEEN TO TWENTY-FOUR MONTHS	Date	Date	Date
PHYSICAL-COGNITIVE DEVELOPMENT			
Motor Development			
1. Washes and dries hands			
2. Builds tower of three to four cubes			
3. Kicks ball forward			
4. Throws ball overhand			
5. Walks up steps			
6. Runs			
7. Pounds and rolls clay			
8. Jumps			
9. Removes clothing			
10. Drinks from cup or glass			
11. Uses spoon			
12. Climbs furniture, play equipment			
Language Development			
1. Combines two to three different words			
2. Follows two or three directions			
3. Names pictures			
4. Imitates adult speech without prompting			

FIGURE 4.4   Wortham development checklist: infants and toddlers, 18 to 24 months

interactions with others. Toddlers are busy and active. They are noisy and interested in everything.

During physical development, motor and perceptual skills need to be encouraged. Motor skills include running, jumping, using alternate feet on stairs, and manipulating construction toys. Adults need to provide opportunities and activities to encourage the use of both large and fine motor skills. The baby uses the five senses of hearing, tasting, seeing, smelling, and touching to learn about the world. Activities and opportunities to explore using the senses should be included in daily experiences.

The child learns concepts through exploration and exposure to new experiences in cognitive and language growth. Through the development of language, the child becomes able to commu-

	Date	Date	Date
Language Development			
5. Engages in make-believe telephone conversation			
6. Uses at least fifteen different words correctly			
Cognitive Development			
1. Demonstrates perception of correct function of toy			
2. Solves a two- or three-piece puzzle			
3. Places correct shape in shape box			
4. Uses housekeeping toys			
5. Recognizes self in photograph			
6. Matches familiar objects by color			
7. Matches familiar objects by shape			
8. Understands "one more"			
9. Returns toy to correct place			
SOCIAL-EMOTIONAL DEVELOPMENT			
1. Uses words to make wants known or express feelings			
2. Puts away toys on request			
3. Engages in affectionate interchanges with adults and children			
4. Sings with adults or other children			
5. Shows interest in exploring new places			

FIGURE 4.4 *(continued)*

nicate and express him- or herself. Adults need to plan for opportunities to explore toys, nature, and home and school environment, books, and other items that can enrich children's understanding of their world and expand their receptive and expressive vocabulary.

Social growth includes the development of emotions, the management of fears, and the development of a sense of self. Because babies are in a stage of trust versus mistrust, adults can enhance a positive outlook and confidence by providing a dependable, consistent environment in which they can flourish. Babies need to experience continuity and security in their daily lives that will allow them to become explorers and discoverers. Additional information on how adults can facilitate development and learning with infants and toddlers will be discussed in Chapters 5 and 6.

✦ Koby

Koby, Katilynn's brother, is 4 years old. He fits in the category of the easy child. He has always been agreeable and able to adjust to changes in routines, caregivers, and playmates. He has his own ideas about his choices of activities and clothes. He has preferred to dress like his dad since he was a toddler and usually sports a hat.

Koby recently had his first experience on a soccer team. He finally learned not to lie down on the field during the second half of the game at the end of the season. As the first grandchild on both sides of the family, he usually had extended family representation at the soccer games. Koby now attends a preschool program at a local elementary school. ✦

Ages 2 to 5: The Preoperational Stage

Between the ages of 18 months and 2 years, the toddler enters the preoperational stage. The older toddler, between the ages of 2 and 3, is making a transition from babyhood into the preschool years. By age 2½, the toddler is developmentally closer to the preschool 3-year-old than to the younger 2-year-old toddler. Because 2-year-olds are typically preoperational in their thinking, their development is included with that of preschoolers 3 to 5 years of age. Similarly, children between the ages of 6 and 7 are making a transition into the concrete operational stage. Although they are progressing through the latter stages of preoperational thinking, their development is discussed with primary school–aged children (Santrock, 1997).

Cognitive Development

Children who have reached the preoperational stage have entered a new period of thought; that is, they can use symbolism, or pretending. They are able to represent objects and events mentally.

However, they are controlled by their perceptions. They focus on appearances. They are also limited in that they center on one characteristic at a time and see things from their own egocentric point of view.

Within the preoperational stage is the symbolic function substage. This substage occurs between the ages of 2 and 4. Symbolic thought allows the child to mentally picture things that are not present. Young children who have achieved symbolic function can use art experiences, especially scribbling, to represent things in their environment such as houses, trees, flowers, and people. Symbolism also allows them to engage in pretend play.

Egocentrism in this substage results in the child's inability to distinguish between his own perspective and the perspective of another child or adult. In play, the child assumes that other children share his feelings and thoughts. The child may have difficulty relating to another child's ideas or emotions that are different from his own.

Children in the symbolic function substage also believe that inanimate objects are alive and capable of action. Thus, they are likely to think, for example, that clouds are propelling themselves in the sky. They might also believe, for instance, that a rock or tree can take action or cause something to happen.

Between the ages of 4 and 7, the preoperational child enters the intuitive thought substage, when primitive reasoning begins. The child's thought process is changing from one of symbolic thinking to intuitive, or inner, thinking. The child can organize objects into primitive collections but is unable to use categories of classification in a consistent manner. As a result, the child might start organizing an array of objects by a color, then change to another color or move to arranging by shape or size. This primitive system of organization is caused by centration. The child tends to center, or focus, on one characteristic or attribute. Two attributes cannot be considered at one time. As a result, the child may change from one attribute to another when trying to organize a group of objects. Once the child is able to move beyond centering, levels of thought characteristic of the concrete operational stage—such as classification and seriation—can emerge (Santrock, 1997; Schickedanz et al., 1993).

Children between the ages of 2 and 5 need opportunities to explore. Parents and caregivers can provide experiences for cognitive development through excursions in the nearby environment as well as trips of longer distances. Children also benefit from experiences with books, pictures, and concrete materials related to concepts in their world. Activities with materials combined with conversations facilitate their process of sorting out and internalizing information and ideas.

Physical Development

As children move from toddlerhood to the preschool years, they begin to lose their chubby appearance. Their bodies become more proportional as they get taller and thinner. In a slower rate of growing, they gain about 3 pounds a year and grow approximately 2½ inches.

Children at this stage become agile at climbing, running, and jumping. Later, they can master hopping, skipping, and galloping as they achieve more coordination and control. They acquire some mastery of throwing and catching a ball and move from marked-time climbing of stairs to using alternate feet when both ascending and descending.

Preschoolers gain more fine motor control over hands and fingers and use this control to develop skills in drawing, cutting, coloring, and pasting. They can put on and remove some clothing items, and they enjoy using their developing fine motor skills to become independent.

Indoor and outdoor play environments can provide opportunities for practice of motor skills. Three-year-olds can build block towers and work simple puzzles. They are constantly on the move outdoors as they ride tricycles, move up and down play structures, learn to pump a swing, and run in the playground while pretend playing. Rough-and-tumble play occurs, particularly in boys

(DiPietro, 1981), whereas girls are more likely to enjoy using fine motor skills in, for example, scribbling or playing with puzzles. When playing outdoors, boys are more active than girls and use more space in their play. Girls are more likely to prefer indoor play using fine motor skills in manipulative or art activities (Frost, 1992, Johnson, Christie, & Yawkey, 1999; Wortham, 2001b).

Adults facilitate physical development by providing daily opportunities for gross motor play both indoors and outdoors. In addition to providing space and equipment for gross motor exercise, adults can engage in games and activities that will extend preschoolers' interests and attempts to try new skills. Many manipulative toys attract preschoolers to engage in fine motor activities. Adults need to provide a selection of puzzles, small construction toys, and art media that will entice young children to work with fine motor skills. Because first attempts with scissors and crayons may prove difficult, adults provide support and encouragement through activities that permit the child to enjoy the process.

Language Development

After the age of 2, young children move beyond telegraphic speech in that they are able to use longer and more complete sentences. They are learning morphological rules. This is evidenced by their use of plural and possessive forms of nouns and verb endings. They make errors in the use of rules, such as overgeneralizations (e.g., they might apply inappropriate verb endings when using the past tense).

In syntax or sentence construction, children learn the proper word order for asking questions. Their sentences become more complex as they expand their vocabulary and expressive speech. They are gradually able to use negative sentences (Brown, 1973).

At about 3 years of age, young children begin to understand and use rules of conversation. They are able to talk about things that are not present; consequently, they can use language as they

words per day. After age 5, the rate of acquisition of new word meanings accelerates.

Development in writing and reading, or literacy, is also an important area between the ages of 2 and 5. Literacy is important in the infant and toddler years and is encouraged when parents and other caregivers share books, stories, and pictures with babies. When parents point out labels on a food product, indicate why they are making a grocery list, or explain how they can find a telephone number in the directory, they are helping develop the child's understanding of the functions of reading and writing (Dailey, 1991).

Building on oral language development with books and environmental print, preschool children develop strategies for becoming literate. When parents and teachers talk with children about things the children are interested in and take them on outings that will expose them to new experiences and information, they are helping the child build conceptual foundations and language that is later used in reading and writing (Mavrogenes, 1990). As a result of their experiences, children gradually come to understand that print, not just pictures, gives meaning to books. They come to recognize print, as well as knowledge of the spacing between words, and that individual letters are used to form words (Fields & Spangler, 2000).

Young children also develop literacy through writing efforts. They use scribbles, mock letters, letter reversals, and other print efforts as part of their natural growth toward literacy. Preschool children use trial and error and hypothesis testing in their journey to understand reading and writing, just as they do in acquiring oral language. Their literacy emerges gradually as they engage in reading and writing experiences each day (Lindfors, 1987; Morrow, 1997).

Social-Emotional Development

Between the ages of 2 and 5, young children gradually learn how to become part of a social group. A major task during these years is socialization. This process of socialization is affected by

engage in pretend play or talk about imaginary people and things. As prosocial awareness develops, 4-year-olds are able to understand others' feelings or needs expressed in conversations. Four-year-olds can also vary their speech style when talking to different audiences such as younger children, peers, or adults (Gleason, 1988).

Word meanings develop continuously. Young preschoolers use environmental contexts to understand the meaning of new words. Locative expressions such as "on" and "under" emerge between ages 2 and 3, but others such as "beside" and "between" take longer to understand and use. Santrock (1997) reported that between the ages of 1 and 5 the child learns an average of five parenting styles, relationships with siblings and peers, and family and environmental conditions. To become successful members of social groups, young children must learn appropriate behaviors. They must learn what behaviors their parents desire them to use, how to interact with their siblings, and how to successfully play with friends. One major accomplishment is the acquisition of prosocial behaviors when the young child uses cooperating, sharing, and helping behaviors (Doescher & Sugawara, 1989). Another desired behavior is the development of respect for others. Despite the contrary influences of society and television, adults in young children's environment help them acquire appropriate social behaviors that demonstrate respect by modeling and reinforcing concern for others (O'Brien, 1991).

Parenting styles will affect how the child learns self-control and meets parental expectations. Parents may be authoritarian, authoritative, or permissive (Baumrind, 1971). Authoritarian parents place firm limits on children and expect them to follow their directions, whereas authoritative parents, in addition to using limits and controls, encourage their children to be independent. Permissive parents can be indulgent or indifferent (Maccoby & Martin, 1983). Permissive-indulgent parents place few controls on their children but are involved with them, whereas permissive-indifferent parents are not involved in their children's lives. Whichever style is used, consistency or inconsistency in parenting behaviors will affect the child's social and emotional development. The child needs dependable guidelines in the long process of acquiring self-discipline. If the parent and teacher approach the discipline process indifferently or vacillate in how they guide the child's behavior, then the child's confusion may result in inappropriate behavior.

The parent or other adult can teach the child social skills in a variety of ways. Styles of guiding or correcting behaviors may include instruction, inductive reasoning, reinforcement, or punishment. These parenting strategies can have either positive or negative consequences in the child's long-term social development. If positive guidelines are to be communicated to the child, parents and teachers will want to focus on teaching the child appropriate behavior rather than on punishment of inappropriate behavior (Clewett, 1988).

At the age of 2, the older toddler is learning how to interact with peers through play. He is moving from engaging in mostly solitary play or parallel play near another child to gradually increasing the frequency and level of interaction with children in play activities. Peers are important sources of socialization in that they help the child learn how to fit into group situations outside the family. Young children learn how to engage successfully in social play largely through trial and error. They discover it is less successful to hit than to offer a toy when trying to gain acceptance in a play group. Cooperation and sharing become recognized as successful social behaviors. Parents and teachers can help young children acquire successful social behaviors by discussing such behaviors and modeling appropriate peer relationships.

During the preschool years, the young child is exposed to both negative and positive social influences. Children can learn aggression as well as prosocial behavior. Various influences in their lives help mold the socialization characteristics they acquire. Changing social influences affect which socialization patterns the child will ultimately adopt. Because the child is in the stage that Erikson describes as initiative versus guilt, the child is in the process of discovering what kind of person he will become. The child is beginning to develop a conscience. The child's initiative and enthusiasm will result in both rewards and punishments from parents. Whether the child will resolve this stage with initiative or guilt is influenced by how the parents respond to the child's attempts at independence and self-control. If parents can set effective limits yet encourage children's curiosity, children will develop a positive outlook about their ability to manage self-control. If parents and teachers are punitive and controlling,

	Introduced	Progress	Mastery
CONCEPT DEVELOPMENT			
Identification, Discrimination, and Classification Skills			
1. Discriminates between two smells			
2. Verbalizes that smells are "different"			
3. Discriminates between sounds and verbalizes that they are "difforent"			
4. Identifies sounds verbally			
5. Points to different food objects on request			
6. Discriminates differences in the shape of objects (round, square, triangular)			
7. Discriminates differences in the size of objects (big/little, long/short)			
8. Classifies objects by weight (heavy/light)			
9. Classifies objects by height (tall/short)			
Math: Quantitative and Problem Solving			
1. Manipulates and experiments with simple machines			
2. Counts by rote from 1 to 5			
3. Forms creative designs with materials			
4. Uses construction materials for multiple purposes			
5. Perceives objects from different visual perspectives			
LANGUAGE DEVELOPMENT			
Oral Language			
1. Produces language that is mostly intelligible			
2. Recognizes and verbally labels common objects			
3. Responds correctly to simple instructions involving locations in the classroom			
4. Uses sentences of four to five words			
5. Asks questions to gain problem-solving information			

FIGURE 4.5   Frost-Wortham development checklist: Level III (pp. 96–98)

children will possibly doubt their ability to achieve independence (Clewett, 1988; Sodermann, 1985). Television, changing family patterns, working mothers, quality of child care, and school settings all contribute to the environmental influences that socialize the child positively and negatively.

Characteristics and Competencies: 2 to 5 years

As children move through the preschool years, development is more individually paced. In the preoperational period, development may be more

	Introduced	Progress	Mastery
DRAMATIC PLAY			
1. Imitates grownups (plays house, store, and so forth)			
2. Expresses frustrations in play			
3. Creates imaginary playmates			
4. Engages in housekeeping			
5. Paints and draws symbolic figures on large paper			
6. Builds simple structures with blocks			
7. Uses transportation toys, people toys, and animal toys to enrich block play			
8. Imagines any objects as the object he wants (symbolic function)			
SOCIAL PLAY AND SOCIALIZING			
1. Engages in independent play			
2. Engages in parallel play			
3. Plays briefly with peers			
4. Recognizes the needs of others			
5. Shows sympathy for others			
6. Attends to an activity for 10 to 15 minutes			
7. Sings simple songs			
MOTOR DEVELOPMENT			
Gross Movement			
1. Catches a ball with both hands against the chest			
2. Rides a tricycle			
3. Hops on both feet several times without assistance			
4. Throws a ball 5 feet with accuracy			
5. Climbs up a slide and comes down			
6. Climbs by alternating feet and holding on to a handrail			
7. Stands on one foot and balances briefly			

FIGURE 4.5 *(continued)*

rapid in one area than in another. Developmental change is more dependent on the individual child's maturation and experiences than on chronological age. In discussing developmentally appropriate practice in programs for 3-year-olds, Bredekamp (1987) described the developmental continuum in the preschool years: "At 2½, many children begin to display skills and behaviors most typical of 3-year-olds. Thus, children between 2½ and 3½ years of age are often similar developmentally; and some 3½-year-olds share traits of 4s" (p. 47).

To accommodate a developmental continuum, the checklists in Figures 4.5 (pp. 96–98),

	Introduced	Progress	Mastery
8. Pushes a loaded wheelbarrow			
9. Runs freely with little stumbling or falling			
10. Builds a tower with 9 or 10 blocks			
Fine Movement			
1. Places small pegs in pegboards			
2. Holds a paintbrush or pencil with the whole hand			
3. Eats with a spoon			
4. Buttons large button on his or her own clothes			
5. Puts on coat unassisted			
6. Strings bead with ease			
7. Hammers a pound toy with accuracy			
8. Works a three- or four-piece puzzle			

FIGURE 4.5 *(continued)*

4.6 (pp. 99–102), and 4.7 (pp. 104–107) describe children within three levels of development, rather than by chronological age. The checklists are an adaptation of the Frost-Wortham developmental checklists (Wortham, 1984) that were originally organized by developmental category. In this context, they have been arranged by level of development, with categories of development grouped together within each level. The language and reading development skills in Level V have been updated to reflect the whole-language, or emergent literacy, approach to reading and writing.

The checklist items include characteristic accomplishments or behaviors for each level. They are not intended to be all-inclusive. For example, in the area of concept development, typical concepts the child can learn at a given level are described, yet many more concepts could be added.

The categories of development are further delineated when compared with those on the infant and toddler checklists. Cognitive development is now more specifically described as concept development and math (quantitative and problem-solving). Concept development is further divided into identification, discrimination, and classification skills.

Language development has been categorized as oral language at Levels III and IV. At Level V, it is further divided into language and vocabulary, oral comprehension, and emergent reading and writing.

Social and emotional development is described under social play and socializing and is also reflected in the continued complexity of social interactions in dramatic play.

Physical development is now categorized as motor development. Gross and fine motor skills are described as gross movement and fine movement.

Development in the Preschool Years: Implications for Learning

The older toddler and preschool child in the preoperational period undergo dramatic growth in development between the ages of 2 and 5. They are active learners in every aspect of their devel-

	Introduced	Progress	Mastery
CONCEPT DEVELOPMENT			
Identification, Discrimination, and Classification Skills			
1. Points to basic shapes (circle, square, rectangle, triangle) on request			
2. Names basic shapes:			
a) circle			
b) square			
c) triangle			
d) rectangle			
3. Labels tastes verbally			
4. Identifies primary colors (red, yellow, blue)			
5. Identifies likenesses and differences in two or more objects (shape, size, color)			
6. Discriminates differences (opposites) in:			
a) sound (loud/soft)			
b) amount (full/empty)			
7. Identifies spatial relationships:			
a) far/near			
b) in/out			
c) front/back			
d) high/low			
8. Identifies and discriminates time relationships:			
a) before/after			
b) earlier/later			
9. Identifies and discriminates actions:			
a) run			
b) walk			
c) jump			
10. Classifies objects by more than one property			
11. Reverses simple operations:			
a) stacks/unstacks/restacks			
b) arranges/disarranges/rearranges			
12. Classifies by condition:			
a) hot/cold			
b) wet/dry			

FIGURE 4.6 Frost-Wortham developmental checklist: Level IV (pp. 99–102)

	Introduced	Progress	Mastery
13. Identifies and discriminates value relationships:			
a) right/wrong			
b) good/bad			
c) pretty/ugly			
d) sad/happy			
Math: Quantitative and Problem-Solving			
1. Counts by rote from one to ten			
2. Demonstrates the concept of numbers through 5			
3. Orders the numbers 1 to 5			
4. Understands the concepts of first and last			
5. Identifies:			
a) penny			
b) nickel			
c) dime			
6. Compares differences in dimension (taller/shorter, longer/shorter, thinner/wider)			
7. Demonstrates one-to-one correspondence			
LANGUAGE DEVELOPMENT			
Oral Language			
1. Uses simple position words such as "over" and "under"			
2. Uses simple action words such as "run" and "walk"			
3. Uses complete sentences			
4. Uses language for specific purposes (directions, information)			
5. Verbalizes routine events ("We're going out to play.")			
6. Averages five-word sentences			
7. Follows simple sentences			
8. Repeats nursery rhymes			
DRAMATIC PLAY			
1. Role plays in the housekeeping center			
2. Role plays some adult occupations			
3. Participates in dramatization of familiar stories			
4. Uses puppets in self-initiated dialogues			

FIGURE 4.6 *(continued)*

	Introduced	Progress	Mastery
5. Differentiates between real and make-believe			
6. Pretends dolls are real people			
7. Constructs (paints, molds, and so forth) recognizable figures			
8. Participates in finger plays			

SOCIAL PLAY AND SOCIALIZING

1. Leaves the mother readily			
2. Converses with other children			
3. Converses with adults			
4. Plays with peers			
5. Cooperates in classroom routines			
6. Takes turns and shares			
7. Replaces materials after use			
8. Takes care of personal belongings			
9. Respects the property of others			
10. Attends to an activity for 15 to 20 minutes			
11. Engages in group activities			
12. Sings with a group			
13. Is sensitive to praise and criticism			

MOTOR DEVELOPMENT

Gross Movement

1. Balances on one foot			
2. Walks a straight line forward and backward			
3. Walks a balance beam			
4. Climbs steps with alternate feet without support			
5. Climbs on jungle gym			
6. Skips haltingly			
7. Throws, catches, and bounces a large ball			
8. Stacks blocks vertically and horizontally			
9. Creates recognizable block structures			
10. Rides a tricycle with speed and skill			

	Introduced	Progress	Mastery
Fine Movement			
1. Pounds and rolls clay			
2. Puts together a five-piece puzzle			
3. Forms a pegboard design			
4. Cuts with scissors haltingly; pastes			
5. Eats with a fork correctly			
6. Holds a cup with one hand			
7. Puts a coat on a hanger or hook			
8. Manipulates large crayons and brushes			
9. Buttons buttons and zips zippers haltingly			

FIGURE 4.6   *(continued)*

opment. They need constant experiences to help them refine emerging social, cognitive, physical, and language competencies. Improved large and fine motor control allows them to become more independent. They need indoor and outdoor play activities that will encourage practice and enjoyment of their motor skills.

The curiosity of the preschool child is nurtured through the provision of field trips, exploration of the natural environment, experiences and discovery with real materials, and opportunities for creativity and expression through music, drama, and various art media. The reading of books, storytelling, and other literary experiences will spark their interest in writing and reading their own stories and the stories and books written by others.

Preschool children learn social skills through opportunities to interact with members of the family and to play with peers. As a result of social interaction, they learn self-control as well as sharing, helping, playing together, and successfully resolving problems with family and friends. The child learns these social skills both within the home and at caregiving or school environments that foster the development of positive social relationships. The young child needs time to work and play with family members and other children with modeling, discussion, and encouragement, which will help the child learn to use positive rather than negative social behaviors. Adults provide the personal and environmental support that facilitates learning and growth in social and all other areas of development. More detailed information on how teachers facilitate development and learning in the preschool years will be discussed in Chapters 7 to 9.

 Miles and Elizabeth

Miles and Elizabeth are siblings. Miles is almost 5 years old, and Elizabeth is 8. Their mother is of Hispanic ancestry and their father is Anglo. Neither the children nor their parents speak any language other than English, although they hear grandparents and other extended family members speaking Spanish. Their father works as a graphic artist and their mother is a dental assistant. Both children have been in child care since they were young infants. Elizabeth is now in the second grade, and Miles will enter kindergarten next fall.

Elizabeth can be described as somewhat shy and eager to please. She participates in dancing lessons and Brownie Scouts. Her teachers find her a cooperative and diligent student. She enjoys Bar-

bie dolls, books, and art activities. She is enjoying trying out her new skills in writing and spelling by describing the pictures she creates.

Miles engages in rough-and-tumble outdoor play with his friends. He lives in a neighborhood full of boys his age who spend many hours playing together in the evenings and on weekends. Wheel toys and other props facilitate "superhero" and other fantasy play themes that move across the yards of homes on their block. Miles enjoys playing with miniature vehicles and is able to keep himself occupied for long periods of time in self-initiated play when he is indoors. He is easy to manage if firm limits are set for his behavior. ✦

Understanding the Implications of Brain Research

Early childhood educators have understood the importance of the early years for development and learning for many decades. This significance was made apparent by the work of researchers such as Jean Piaget, Jerome Bruner, and others who studied the course of development in young children. Differences in development between children from homes where parents were educated and economically successful and children from low-income homes were significant. The growing data on at-risk children during the 1960s were a major impetus for funding for federal intervention programs.

Extensive evidence exists on the importance of appropriate nutrition, health, and learning experiences during the early childhood years for later success in school. More recently, brain research has supported this premise. Researchers have studied how the brain continues to grow and develop after birth. More significantly, researchers have explained how synapses in the brain are formed during the early childhood years, whereas unused connections are pruned away between the years of early childhood and age 10 (Zero to Three & The Ounce of Prevention Fund, 2000). Some educators who have studied brain research have proposed that the early years of brain plasticity provide temporary "windows of opportunity" for child development that will later be lost when the pruning process begins.

There are fundamental problems with this assumption. Bruer (1999) warns that incorrect assumptions are being made about the sensitive periods for learning. He reports there is no scientific evidence that more learning takes place while dendrite connections are being expanded than after pruning takes place. To the contrary, he proposes that more learning occurs after age 10 than before and perhaps learning is more efficient after brain activity is stabilized.

What, then, are the merits of brain research? Information on brain development has expanded our understanding of how an optimal family environment in the very early years enhances a child's development. Likewise, quality early childhood programs facilitate ongoing development in the preschool and primary grade years. The importance of rich opportunities to explore and interact with the environment support brain development. All of the information on early childhood and development developed during the second half of the twentieth century are supported by brain research. Nevertheless, we must be cautious in following educational claims for toys and activities that will expand a child's brain development during sensitive periods. Rather, we should continue to support sound experiences that will enhance development and learning in the early childhood years and beyond (Bruer, 1999; O'Donnell, 1999).

	Introduced	Progress	Mastery
CONCEPT DEVELOPMENT			
Identification, Discrimination, and Classification Skills			
1. Identifies spatial relationships:			
a) top/bottom			
b) over/under			
2. Identifies and discriminates value relationships (like/dislike)			
3. Identifies and discriminates time relationships:			
a) morning/noon/night			
b) today/tomorrow			
c) yesterday/today			
4. Labels smells verbally			
5. Identifies colors (green, orange, purple, brown, black, white)			
6. Identifies the simple properties of an object (color, shape, size)			
7. Classifies colors by intensity (dark/light, darker than/lighter than)			
8. Classifies foods (fruits, vegetables, meat)			
9. Classifies tastes (sweet, sour, salty)			
10. Classifies surfaces by textures (smooth, rough, soft, hard)			
11. Identifies and classifies common objects by shape (circle, rectangle, triangle, oval, square)			
12. Seriates (arranges) objects by size			
13. Classifies by function:			
a) food/eat			
b) vehicle/ride			
Math: Quantitative and Problem-Solving			
1. Counts to fifty			
2. Demonstrates the concept of numbers through 10			
3. Orders the numbers 1 to 10			
4. Writes numbers for sets 1 to 10			
5. Identifies pairs of familiar objects (shoes, socks, gloves, earrings)			
6. Groups objects into sets of equal number			
7. Compares elements of unequal sets (more than/fewer than)			

FIGURE 4.7   Frost-Wortham developmental checklist: Level V (pp. 104–107)

	Introduced	Progress	Mastery
8. Combines (adds) the total number in two small groups			
9. Uses ordinal concepts up through concept of third			
10. Identifies:			
a) penny			
b) nickel			
c) dime			
d) quarter			
11. Compares distance (height, width) to an independent object			
12. Compares volumes in separate containers			
13. Tells time to the hour			

LANGUAGE DEVELOPMENT

Oral Language

	Introduced	Progress	Mastery
1. Communicates ideas, feelings, and emotions in well-formed sentences			
2. Uses the correct form of more verbs in informal conversation			
3. Uses the correct prepositions to denote place and position			
4. Uses most personal pronouns correctly			
5. Explains the operation of simple machines			
6. Uses language to get what she or he wants			
7. Can follow instructions containing three parts			

Reading Readiness

Language and Vocabulary

	Introduced	Progress	Mastery
1. Listens to and follows verbal directions			
2. Identifies the concept of word			
3. Identifies the concept of letters			
4. Invents a story for a picture book			

Oral Comprehension

	Introduced	Progress	Mastery
5. Locates elements in a picture (tallest, largest, and so forth)			
6. Retells in the correct sequence a story read to him			
7. Reorganizes pictures to show the correct story sequence			
8. Answers recall questions about a story			
9. Draws analogies from a story to his own experience			
10. Makes value judgements about story events			

	Introduced	Progress	Mastery
Emergent Reading and Writing			
11. Tells experiences for an experience story			
12. Follows left-to-right progression as an adult reads			
13. Identifies recurring words on an experience chart			
14. Suggests titles for experience stories			
15. Uses invented spelling to write stories			
16. "Reads" familiar storybooks			
DRAMATIC PLAY			
1. Role plays a wide variety of roles in the housekeeping center and in other centers			
2. Role plays on the playground			
3. Role plays a variety of adult occupations			
4. Recognizes that pictures represent real objects			
5. Participates in a wide variety of creative activities: finger plays, rhythm band, working with clay, painting, outdoor play, housekeeping, singing, and so forth			
6. Produces objects at the carpentry table and tells about them			
7. Produces art objects and tells about them			
8. Searches for better ways to construct			
9. Builds complex block structures			
SOCIAL PLAY			
1. Completes most self-initiated projects			
2. Works and plays with limited supervision			
3. Engages in cooperative play			
4. Listens while peers speak			
5. Follows multiple and delayed directions			
6. Carries out special responsibilities (e.g., feeding animals)			
7. Listens and follows the suggestions of adults			
8. Enjoys talking with adults			
9. Can sustain an attention span for a variety of duties			
10. Evaluates his work and suggests improvements			

FIGURE 4.7 *(continued)*

	Introduced	Progress	Mastery
MOTOR DEVELOPMENT			
Gross Movement			
1. Catches and throws a small ball			
2. Bounces and catches a small ball			
3. Skips on either foot			
4. Skips rope			
5. Hops on one foot			
6. Creates Tinkertoy and block structures			
7. Hammers and saws with some skill			
8. Walks a balance beam forward and backward			
9. Descends stairs by alternating feet			
Fine Movement			
1. Cuts and pastes creative designs			
2. Forms a variety of pegboard designs			
3. Buttons buttons, zips zippers, and ties shoes			
4. Creates recognizable objects with clay			
5. Uses the toilet independently			
6. Eats independently using a knife and fork			
7. Dresses and undresses independently			
8. Holds and manipulates pencils, crayons, and brushes of various sizes			
9. Combs and brushes hair			
10. Works a 12-piece puzzle			

Age 5 to 8 Years: The Transition from Preoperations to Concrete Operations

The ages from 5 to 8 are described here as transitional because the young child is experiencing several kinds of transitions. In terms of schooling, the child is making a transition from home, child care, or preschool into a public or private elementary setting. If the school has preschool classes for 4- and 5-year-old students, the transition is being made from preschool into primary classrooms.

The child is also making developmental transitions. Although the child is in the last years of early childhood, he is gradually moving from preoperations into concrete operations. Development is uneven during this period, both within the individual child and when comparing children of the same chronological age.

It is during this transitional period between preschool and primary grades that the historical heritage of American schooling comes into conflict with developmental theories of how young children learn during the early childhood years. American primary grades have traditionally been organized by chronological age. Following Gesell's description of norms for different ages, educators and curriculum developers in the years from 1930 to the 1950s organized instruction in the primary grades to complement the child's abilities at ages 6, 7, and 8. The organizational pattern by chronological age persists today, with the expectation that children should be prepared to learn using similar curriculum and tasks as their chronological peers. The problems encountered by young children in successfully achieving in spite of individual developmental characteristics are further complicated by the continuing escalation of curriculum difficulty as a response to school reform, discussed in Chapter 1. The lack of flexibility in adapting curriculum to individual developmental characteristics has resulted in difficulties for both teachers and students in the primary grades, especially in first grade. The need to understand the nature of development and the implications for learning are particularly significant in the years between ages 5 and 8.

Cognitive Development

Between the ages of 5 and 8, children move from the preoperational stage into the concrete operational stage. Some current researchers disagree with Piaget's position that concrete operations occur at about age 7 and have demonstrated that some children can achieve conservation at much earlier ages than was previously thought. Similarly, young children acquire concrete operational concepts gradually, rather than as a synchrony in development, as Piaget believed (Beilin, 1989). There is much individual variation in when and how children move from preoperations to concrete operations. It can begin in some children as young as age 4, but it is a gradual process, with characteristics of concrete operations emerging differently in young children (Santrock, 1997).

As young children make the transition to concrete operations, the quality of their thinking changes. They cease evaluating situations based on perception and begin to use logic and mental operations to understand their experiences. This advance in thinking leads to improvement in memory and length of time at each task.

The ability to conserve is the central characteristic that signals the child's achievement of the concrete operational stage. Whether the conservation activity involves number, mass, length, volume, or other type of quantity, the child who can conserve understands that the physical appearance of something does not change its quantity. The classic conservation task involving the quantity of liquid usually comes to mind as an example. The child understands that changing the width and height of the container holding the liquid does not change the original amount of the liquid. Also, rearranging an array of objects does not change the number of objects.

The ability of the child to think logically using specific thinking skills leads to his ability to think about and solve problems mentally; nevertheless, children are limited to things they are familiar with or can see. They are not yet able to think or solve problems as adults do (Bredekamp, 1987; Bredekamp & Copple, 1997).

Children in the concrete operational stage are able to use mental strategies to learn new information. They can use rehearsal of information to store the information in memory. They can also play with their thoughts to think about thinking. Called metacognition, this thinking strategy permits the child to make up jokes or play games that require planning strategies (Santrock, 1997; Schickedanz et al., 1993). Regardless of the child's new sophistication in thinking skills, the process of learning new information remains the same. The child reconstructs knowledge through active involvement with information. New information is not acquired through rote memory but through engaging in experiences and modifying what is already understood using individual processes and learning paces.

Physical Development

As children move from kindergarten into the primary years, they grow more slowly than during the preschool years. Weight gain occurs in the muscles; the average weight gain is 5 to 7 pounds a year. The trunk and legs grow more rapidly than the head; the legs grow longer and the trunk becomes slimmer. Muscle tone improves, and boys are usually stronger than girls.

Children begin to lose their first teeth at age 6 and have their permanent teeth by age 11 or 12. Their facial appearance becomes longer and slimmer as the face and jaw become more balanced with the upper part of the head.

During the primary years, children refine their gross and fine motor skills. They gain better control of their bodies and have longer attention spans. Handwriting skills are acquired through expressive art activities and opportunities for emergent writing experiences. Gross motor skills are developed through sports, games, and other physical activities. Children need to be active because they become fatigued if long periods of sitting are required. The change and progress in motor development are steady and predictable if children have plenty of opportunity for fine and gross motor experiences. They need opportunities for running, jumping, bicycling, and learning sports such as baseball and gymnastic activities such as using a balance beam. For fine motor skills, they need abundant experiences with art, including drawing, painting, working with clay, cutting, and playing with manipulative materials (Santrock, 1997; Schickedanz et al., 1993).

Language Development

The process of language development in the years from 5 to 8 is similar to that of motor development. Children are refining and extending the language learned in the preschool years. They have mastered the basics of syntax and semantics; that is, they have learned how sentences are structured and how words are used to communicate meanings. However, they are still confused by the meanings and usages of some words. Metacognitive thinking allows them to think about language; in other words, children can be described as having metalinguistic awareness. This allows them to enjoy jokes and riddles and the ambiguous use of words (e.g., using words that sound similarly or sentences that can be understood in different ways) (Schickedanz et al., 1993).

Oral language development can be occurring in more than one language. Continuing immigration to this country and concomitant diversity of cultures result in many children entering school whose primary language is not English. Schools serving these children must provide services so that they can acquire English. Because the predominant theory of second-language acquisition is that the young child learns English in the same way that he learned the first language, opportunities to hear and use English are important. The child needs to hear English modeled by other children and adults so that he can gradually use the vocabulary and sentence structure of English as well as the first language (Abramson, Seda, & Johnson, 1990; Quintero & Huerta-Macias, 1990).

Written language development in the primary grades becomes as important as oral language development. The whole-language approach to reading and writing, beginning in kindergarten, has become a sound and increasingly popular way for children to acquire literacy. Whole-language instruction proposes that elements of the language arts should not be separated but taught as a whole. This approach suggests that children need an extensive oral vocabulary prior to beginning to read. Children are encouraged to "write" stories using scribbling and invented spelling as steps to writing accurately. Written language follows the same hypothesis testing and trial and error as does oral language (Fields & Spangler, 2000; Morrow, 1997).

In the whole-language approach, reading follows a similar pattern in that children gradually obtain meaning and recognition of words from books that have become familiar through repeated readings before moving into books that have unfamiliar words. The traditional-skills approach to reading, to the contrary, includes early introduction of phonics and other beginning reading skills as part of the introduction into reading. Alphabet knowledge, letter sounds, sight-word strategies, and other decoding skills are thought to be essential to break the reading code (Freeman & Hatch, 1989).

There is adequate research into how literacy develops in young children to support the whole-language approach. Sulzby (1985), Teale (1986b), and Goodman (1986) reported on how children learn about literacy through interaction with literacy in their world and that they develop an awareness of the functions of written language. Further, new theory and research reveal that the components of literacy (reading and writing) develop simultaneously and should not be taught in isolation.

Many schools are not taking an either–or approach to reading and writing; rather, they perceive literacy as being facilitated by both approaches. The child uses natural strategies, such as the whole-language method, in reconstructing his own understanding of reading and writing. Information taught about beginning reading and writing skills facilitates an efficient acquisition of literacy (Krogh, 1990).

Social-Emotional Development

The transition into school and the new roles to be encountered are of considerable importance in the years from 5 to 8. Despite the rising numbers of children in caregiving or preschool settings outside the home during the preschool years, entry into the primary grades is an important transition socially and emotionally.

Children within this age range are entering the stage that Erikson called *industry versus inferiority.* Achievement and social acceptance become important parts of the child's life. If the child feels successful and achievement is a rewarding effort, then he develops a sense of industry. To the contrary, if the child feels unsuccessful, unpopu-

lar, and that he cannot succeed in achieving, then a sense of inferiority develops.

Children's social development is affected by their emerging social role-taking abilities. They are aware of other people's thoughts, feelings, and attitudes; in addition, they are becoming more aware and concerned about what others think about them. Children's positive or negative self-images are affected by whether they are successful in social interactions (Hartup, 1983).

Perception of social acceptance also affects self-image. Children who have established friendships have been able to develop positive social strategies that are less accessible for children who are disliked. The latter have lower self-esteem, achieve less in school, and are more likely to become antisocial, disruptive, and destructive in later elementary years unless intervention is effective in changing their behaviors and outlook (Asher & Williams, 1987).

Children's early school experiences in successful learning are particularly critical for the development of positive self-esteem and a sense of industry. Success in first grade is significant because this is the first level at which children become aware of whether they perceive themselves as competent and successful learners. It is in first grade that children receive feedback on achievement that makes a major impact on whether they believe themselves to be capable of succeeding in school.

The kind of school setting the child encounters can be an important factor in whether the child will develop a positive or negative picture of his ability (Bredekamp, 1987; Bredekamp & Copple, 1997). A school that recognizes the normal variation in children's development in this transitional period, as well as normal differences in language, motor, and social development, will organize kindergarten and primary grades to maximize the child's developmental strengths to ensure success and a positive self-image. Schools where grade-level curriculum is fixed and achievement on standardized tests controls curriculum and instruction in the primary grades are more likely to have many young students who receive negative feedback and subsequently develop a negative self-image and feelings of inferiority (Santrock, 1997).

Characteristics and Competencies in Children Ages 5 to 8 Years: Implications for Learning and Instruction

Children develop more slowly between the ages of 5 and 8 than they did previously, and characteristics of development emerge gradually over a period of years. Developmental characteristics are acquired within the remaining years of early childhood and beyond into the middle childhood years. Developmental checklists are no longer useful for charting development, because milestones are achieved gradually and continuously. Characteristics and competencies acquired between the ages of 5 and 8 are best described as evolving within the later ages of early childhood.

Because children between the ages of 5 and 8 are entering the first grades of formal schooling, it is helpful to now include a discussion of how schooling should complement developmental characteristics. Thus, this section focuses on how parents and educators should respond to rather than overlook development. Characteristics, competencies, and implications for learning and curriculum and instruction are again discussed by category of development.

Cognitive Development

Despite the gradual shift from preoperational to concrete operational thinking during this period, children are still not ready to learn in the abstract. They still need real things to focus their thinking or serve as reference points when using symbols such as words and numbers. Although they can use thinking skills to mentally manipulate concepts and ideas,

there is a continuation of the need for concrete materials and experiences in the learning process.

During these years, learning is a continuation of the reconstruction of knowledge. Experience is the method used to facilitate the construction of knowledge. Children need many opportunities to interact with concepts and use their developing thinking skills to identify and solve problems related to new information.

Emerging social and communication skills allow the child to understand and appreciate the thoughts and views of others. Consequently, these children are able to learn in small groups. Through group activities and discussions about group efforts, children can utilize the thoughts and perspectives of their peers to expand their own understanding. At the same time, they are also developing their language and social skills through group involvement in learning experiences.

Physical Development

Children between the ages of 5 and 8 are gaining better control of gross and fine motor skills. They develop longer attention spans and can maintain interest in learning activities. However, these new physical capabilities do not imply that children should be expected to sit for long periods of time engaged in passive, fine motor activities.

Physical activity is essential for children during these years. Their developing gross motor skills require generous time periods for outdoor play, both structured and unstructured. Physical action indoors and outdoors is needed to practice and enjoy new physical competencies. Because children in the primary grades become fatigued from sitting for long periods, they need to be active in the classroom. In addition, their cognitive style as active learners dictates that they interact with concrete examples for meaningful learning to occur. Therefore, physical activity is also needed for cognitive learning. Physical interactions through hands-on, center-based activities should be part of the ongoing experiences with new and familiar concepts. Children need to be actively engaged in self-initiated projects and lessons using manipulative materials as part of the learning process.

Social-Emotional Development

Social competence is a major achievement in the years between 5 and 8. Children who fail to develop social competence during these years are more likely to develop serious social and emotional problems in later years. The development of competence in achievement is also a major factor in the development of a positive self-image.

Because adults and the school environment are major factors in developing social and learning competence, teachers have an important responsibility in guiding positive acquisition of feelings of success and competence. Teachers can use direct and indirect strategies with young children to assist in the struggle for social acceptance and positive social interaction.

Teachers also can be sensitive to structuring classroom experiences to facilitate a sense of industry rather than inferiority. School-age children are able to evaluate their own efforts in learning. If they are allowed to succeed in achieving during the primary grades, then they will become self-directed and will develop a sense of industry. If they encounter frequent failure in their efforts to learn, then their self-esteem will suffer and they will develop the perception that they are failures. As a result of understanding the implications of development for learning during these years, teachers must organize learning experiences that are not beyond the child's ability to learn successfully. Activities should be carefully designed to facilitate positive motivation to learn and foster the child's belief in his or her ability to succeed.

Children are also developing a conscience and an understanding of moral rules of behavior. They are in the process of learning self-discipline and self-control. Teachers who use positive guidance techniques and model appropriate behaviors are more successful in helping children internalize rules of behavior than if they criticize and punish.

Organization of programs and classrooms for children from ages 5 to 8 will be described in Chapter 10. Planning for curriculum and instruction for children of these ages will be discussed in Chapters 11 and 12.

Summary

The years from birth to age 8 are described as the early childhood years. This period of life is most significant in terms of development. Development is more rapid during this period than during any other period in the life span. Understanding how infants and young children develop physically, cognitively, and socially and how they acquire language and literacy is necessary for adults who are rearing, providing care for, and planning learning experiences for children during this period. An understanding of how the theories of learning and development enable adults to guide the child in the early childhood years also helps adults to plan appropriate kinds of learning experiences.

The younger the child, the more rapid his growth and development. Consequently, development of infants and toddlers during the first 2 years is charted in 6 month intervals. Cognitively, babies under the age of 2 are in what Piaget termed the *sensorimotor period*. Physically, they develop from neonates to toddlers who have acquired basic locomotor skills. Socially and emotionally, they are developing an awareness of self and important others in their lives.

Older toddlers and preschool children from ages 2 to 5 are still in active periods of growth. Because these young children are in what Piaget called the *preoperational stage,* we can describe their development in three levels, rather than by age. Children in the preoperational period are rapidly developing language and concepts as they discover and explore everything they come in contact with at home, outdoors, and at locations away from home. Socially, they are developing abilities to interact and play with other children and develop a positive self-concept as they acquire social and self-help skills. They work toward independence.

Preoperational children are very active physically. They practice and enjoy both gross and fine motor movement. Two- and 3-year-olds seem to be in perpetual motion. Throughout these years, much of the children's day is spent in physical activity as they challenge themselves to achieve new physical capabilities.

At this point, children are acquiring the foundations of their language, and by age 4 or 5, they have mastered the basic language components. Their language structure has evolved from prelinguistic utterances to a language structure that is similar to that of adults. They have developed an awareness of the nature of written language and reading and may be well on their way to developing literacy.

Children from ages of 5 to 8 are in the latter stages of early childhood. They are also moving from preoperations into concrete operations. We describe these children as being in a transitional period because they are changing developmentally; moreover, they are making a transition from one level of schooling to another.

The cognitive transition to concrete operations signals new levels of thinking. The child is no longer perception bound but is now able to think using mental strategies and can think about the thought processes being used. Physical development is slower. Over a period of time, the child extends physical capabilities as body length and muscle development predominate. Regular physical activity is important for optimal continued physical development.

Sophistication in language continues. Oral language becomes more complex as the child extends vocabulary and receptive language, as well as more mature expressive language. The move toward literacy, including reading and writing, is an exciting development during the primary grades. Children master the basics of reading and can enjoy written expression and literature.

Social and emotional development are significant during this period because children have a need to become competent in social and learning interactions. It is during this period that they determine if they are popular with their peers and successful as learners.

Development during each period has its own competencies. Learning experiences provided by adults for each period need to complement the individual characteristics of each child. Developmentally appropriate curriculum and instruction are important for preschool children as well as children making the transition from preschool into primary grades. The transitional years are particularly critical for successful learning. Understanding how to match development with learning experiences is the key to successful schooling in kindergarten and primary grades if students are to develop a positive self-image, believe themselves to be competent, and become success-oriented.

Study Questions

1. How can knowledge of theories of development help to explain levels of development in children from birth to age 8?
2. How does knowledge of development inform planning for curriculum and instruction for young children?
3. How soon does language development occur in children under the age of 2? Trace language development from birth to age 2 years.
4. What is the nature of cognitive development in infants and toddlers? How can we describe "thought" in children at these ages?
5. Why would we describe the pace of physical development as significant in infants and toddlers?
6. At what stage of development do children begin to become social? How does this process emerge?
7. Why can we say that children enter school with command of their home language?

What have they mastered in language development by the age of 5?

8. Describe significant mileposts in gross and fine motor development between the ages of 3 and 6. What implications does this developmental domain have for activities planned for children at these ages?

9. How do changes in cognitive development at about ages 6 and 7 signal the end of the early childhood years? Describe this developmental process.

10. Do teachers have a responsibility to promote social and emotional development in preschool and primary children? How and why should the socioemotional domain of development be addressed?

11. How does language development affect success in literacy? What do teachers need to know about a child's language development when initiating activities for emergent literacy?

CHAPTER FIVE

Organizing Infant–Toddler Programs

CHAPTER OBJECTIVES

As a result of reading this chapter, you will be able to:

1. Describe the historical bases of infant–toddler programs.
2. Discuss how today's infant–toddler programs reflect the diversity of children's and families' needs.
3. Explain how theories of development influence models for infant–toddler programs.
4. Describe the characteristics of components of quality infant–toddler programs.
5. Discuss how experiences are designed for developmental domains of infants and toddlers.
6. Explain how thematic curriculum has a role in infant–toddler programs.
7. Discuss the role of assessment in infant–toddler programs.
8. Explain how assessment is conducted in infant–toddler programs.

Changes in societal values and practices regarding families during the past 20 years have resulted in an increasing consensus that meeting care and education goals for infants and toddlers is a societal as well as a family responsibility. Increased knowledge about early brain development and the importance of the early years for cognitive and social-emotional growth have also changed the thinking of early childhood professionals. There is now consensus that both planned and spontaneous educational experiences begin at the earliest of ages. Because such experiences require adult decision-making about their content, it is necessary to revise the traditional definition of curriculum to include both education and care perspectives.*

The idea that very young infants are alert learners is still new to many adults, even some of those who care for children. We have learned that infants are sponges for learning about the people and things in their environment. Moreover, we also know that they in turn affect those who care for them. We have come a long way from the days when babies were considered passive and helpless. The vast amount of information we have learned about early development in this century has been vital in understanding how we can develop programs for the very young. The growing need for infant and toddler care and programs has stimulated the development of models for quality programs for infants and toddlers. This chapter traces the roots of these programs and the contexts that have supported advances in infant–toddler care and learning.

The Evolution of Infant–Toddler Programs

The evolution of infant–toddler nurture and care parallels that of early childhood education; however, until recent years, the strongest trend for infants and toddlers has been custodial care. From the beginning, early childhood education for the preschool child from 3 to 5 years of age included an educational program. This was true for kindergartens, nursery schools, and private preschools. Conversely, infant and toddler care has been part of the evolution of the child-care movement; therefore, until the 1970s, care was the most significant service provided to infants and toddlers. The transition from an emphasis on care to care plus attention to developmental experiences has become more important since the 1970s. In the discussion that follows, knowledge about the development of infants and toddlers will be applied to the programs developed for their care and learning.

Infants and Toddlers Prior to the Twentieth Century

Prior to the first decades of the twentieth century, infant mortality was the most significant concern regarding infants and toddlers. In the eighteenth century, infants and young children of families emigrating to the United States rarely survived the voyage from their homeland. Physicians knew little about hygiene and how to avoid the spread of disease that contributed to the high mortality rate among infants and children under the age of 7. Parents were ignorant about child-rearing practices and proper nutrition. Midwives who delivered the infants of the poor commonly dressed the umbilical cord with snuff. They fed infants a mixture of molasses and the child's urine as a medication (Public Health Service, 1976).

In the early years of the republic, children were considered either chattel or the property of their parents. Furthermore, nineteenth-century philosophers and evangelical Christians perceived children as innately bad. Evangelical parents saw it as their responsibility to impose their will and enforce the child's unquestioning obedience, beginning in the child's first year. Greven (1977) explained further:

> From the earliest months of life through the subsequent years of childhood, evangelical parents

*From Bergen, D., Reid, R., & Torelli, L. (2001). Introduction (p. xii). In D. Bergen, R. Reid, & L. Torelli, *Educating and Caring for Very Young Children.* New York: Teachers College Press.

acted upon the assumption that parental authority was unlimited and unquestionable. Parents systematically imposed their own wills upon their infants and small children without interference from servants or grandparents. Total power of parents, total dependency and obedience of children—this was the persistent polarity. (p. 34)

In 1874, a 9-year-old child who had been whipped daily, stabbed with scissors, and tied to a bed was rescued from the brutal treatment of her guardians. Because there were no laws protecting children, the Society for the Prevention of Cruelty to Animals (SPCA) finally intervened to remove the child from the home where she was an indentured servant. In the following year, the New York Society for the Prevention of Cruelty to Children was established to protect children from inhumane treatment (Maxim, 1997).

At the turn of the century, conditions for infants and young children were still discouraging. Health experts were concerned about the ignorance concerning the health and safety of infants and toddlers. The high infant mortality rate was attributed partially to the distribution of contaminated milk from dirty supply sources. Another source of infant and toddler deaths was the ignorance of mothers. A 1904 edition of the *Ladies' Home Journal* described the practice of many mothers who gave their babies patent medicine that contained 44 percent alcohol, opium, or cocaine. Fortunately, regulated milk stations were set up to ensure the distribution of safe milk, and the Children's Bureau battled parental ignorance through the publication of pamphlets designed to inform parents about the care of their infants. The first edition of *Infant Care* was published in 1914; subsequent editions have been published continuously since then (Public Health Service, 1976). Some maltreatment of infants and young children declined during the second half of the nineteenth century. Jean-Jacques Rousseau's view of childhood was one influence that changed parenting and education in Europe and the United States. Rousseau felt that children were innately good. He proposed that babies were born with only good-

ness in their hearts, and if they were reared in an environment of regulated liberty, they would flower, or unfold. Parents and educators responded to Rousseau's influence by replacing repressive parenting and teaching with loving and nurturing environments for infants (Maxim, 1997).

Further concerns for the health, safety, and nurturance of infants and young children emerged at the end of the nineteenth century. While Rousseau's perceptions of the needs of young children were changing attitudes about the rearing of infants and toddlers, waves of immigrants were entering the United States and settling in urban areas. Widows and abandoned mothers and some wives with large families found it necessary to go to work if they and their families were to survive. With no one to care for their children, some women sent them to orphanages or foster homes or were forced to leave them unattended when they were at work. Wealthy philanthropists responded to the dilemma by opening day nurseries for unattended infants and young children. The first day-care programs provided custodial care: a safe place, nutritious meals, and places for the children to rest for 12 hours per day while their mothers were at work (Maxim, 1997).

At the beginning of the twentieth century, conditions were still very poor for infants and toddlers; in the first decade, one-fifth of the deaths in New York City were babies less than 1 year old (Public Health Service, 1976). However, further changes were occurring. Improvements in health services and medical services, the establishment of the child-study movement with its new knowledge about child development, and growing interest in programs for the very young led to improvements in conditions for infants and toddlers in the decades that followed.

Infants and Toddlers in the Twentieth Century

The work of researchers in the child-study movement begun at the turn of the century had implications for the perception and understanding of the importance of the first 2 years of a child's development. Early studies of infants and toddlers were used to describe how development progresses during the first 2 years. Arnold Gesell established developmental norms that were the first to sequence biological development in children. His developmental schedules (Gesell, 1925) were subsequently used to construct scales to measure development and developmental delay in infants and toddlers; these were, specifically, the Bayley Test of Infant Development, the Cattell Test, and the Denver Developmental Test (Weiser, 1991). During the same period, H. M. Skeels was studying the development of institutionalized infants compared with babies placed with older girls in a home for retarded children. The significant developmental difference in the babies showered with attention by the retarded girls projected the idea that environment and attention in the first 3 years affect the course of development (Skeels, 1966). Sigmund Freud's work describing the effects of the early years on the development of personality made people aware of the nature of emotional development and the importance of positive child-adult relationships in the early years (Hall & Lindzey, 1970).

The interest in a program that provided more than custodial care for very young children emerged in the first decades of the century following Margaret McMillan's work in England. McMillan had observed that although most of the babies were born healthy in England, only 20 percent entered school in good health. To counter neglect during the preschool years, she opened nursery schools for children younger than school age that provided for emotional, social, and educational growth. Beyond being given physical care and nutrition, the children were taught self-care and hygiene skills. The program included outdoor play, sensory experiences, and creative self-expression activities. Abigail Eliot transported McMillan's ideas to the United States and transformed the Ruggles Street Day Nursery in Boston into a nursery school in 1922 (Eliot, 1972). The Ruggles Street Nursery School, the first to establish

a learning program besides providing care, was soon followed by similar schools. Also, in the 1920s, other professional educators were addressing programs for infants and toddlers. Harriet Johnson wrote *Children in "the Nursery School"* (1928) and later *School Begins at Two* (1936), both of which describe programs for children under the age of 3.

During the Great Depression, nursery schools expanded through the Works Progress Administration (WPA) project that funded nursery schools to create jobs for unemployed teachers and to provide care so that mothers could contribute to family incomes. These nursery schools tended to be custodial in nature; however, training for nursery school teachers was becoming available in university home economics departments, the first having been established in 1924 at Iowa State University (Maxim, 1997).

As the WPA nursery schools were phased out at the end of the 1930s, the start of World War II initiated a new need for child care. Women went to work in large numbers in factories that produced equipment and materials for the war effort 24 hours per day, and the federal government recognized that child care was thus needed. Child-care facilities were established through passage of the Lanham Act, which provided children with food, rest, shelter, and caregivers. Infants and toddlers were served with predominantly custodial care. Exceptions were the Kaiser Child Service Centers, established at the Kaiser shipyards, which contained special innovative features that included constructive play, trained teachers, and an educational program (Braun & Edwards, 1972). Also, under the leadership of James Hymes, two outstanding centers were established that provided 24-hour-per-day care for 1000 children ages 18 months to 6 years (Dickerson, 1992). Hymes later attributed the excellent program to trained staff and adequate funding (Hymes & Stolz, 1978).

After the end of World War II, programs for infants and toddlers were affected by growth in the child-care industry as higher percentages of mothers with children under the age of 6 entered the workforce in each decade between 1950 and

1990. For infants and toddlers, custodial child care was still more common than educational programs. Studies and theories that emerged in the 1950s and 1960s led to experimental programs for minority and poverty-level infants and toddlers. The innovative programs that developed during those years changed the perception of the developmental potential of the very young child and gave new emphasis to developmental and educational components in settings that served infants and toddlers. A major concern in the 1950s and 1960s was whether preschool children, particularly infants and toddlers, should be placed in caregiving settings while their mothers worked. Finding good care for babies during the day was a major problem for working mothers.

The focus on the effects of poverty on preschool children had implications for infants and toddlers. The importance of the early years for development and learning was researched by Hunt (1961), who reported that experiences in the first years of life affect the child's intelligence. Benjamin Bloom also reported similar information that reinforced the idea that the early years are significant for the development of intelligence (Bloom, 1964). The relationship between socioeconomic status and intelligence before 3 years of age was reported by Kagan (1971) and White and Watts (1973). These and other studies reinforced the proposition that deprivation during the first 3 years has measurable effects. When federal intervention efforts for children from low-income homes were funded in the 1960s, the issues of the effects of care on infants and toddlers and the efficacy of early intervention programs for children under the age of 3 could both be addressed. The advances accomplished through the various types of infant intervention projects in the 1960s and 1970s laid the groundwork for the infant–toddler programs that served very young children in the 1990s.

The first infant intervention programs focused on the child. The model for infant–toddler care and education initiated by Bettye Caldwell and Julius Richmond in the Children's Center at Syracuse University in 1968 established a positive approach to center-based care as opposed to home care. Two additional infant–toddler programs were established by Keister at the University of North Carolina at Greensboro (Keister, 1970) and by Willis and Ricciuti (1975) at Cornell University.

Later model programs focused on parents and children. These programs emphasized the importance of the mother in the child's growth and development and addressed different approaches to working with parents and babies to enhance the child's development. Some of these parent–infant–toddler projects included the Gordon Parent Education Program in Florida, the Karnes Home Intervention Program, the Family Development Research Program developed by Lally and Honig, Levenstein's Mother-Child Program, and Schaefer's Infant Education Research Project (Cataldo, 1983; Day & Parker, 1977; Lally, 2001). These programs reinforced the understanding that parent involvement with infant care and learning is essential for the child's development. Intervention with infants alone is not effective; moreover, intervention with low-income parents is the key to permanent enhancement of the child's environment in the years before age 3.

In the 1970s and 1980s, significantly larger numbers of infants and toddlers were in need of care during the day. Working mothers, single parents, teenage mothers, and women in other low socioeconomic categories needed care for their very young children. The rapid expansion of the child-care industry led to national concerns about the quality of child care and the need for establishing standards for caregiving programs. The National Association for the Education of Young Children (NAEYC) took a leadership role in establishing a national accreditation system for preschool and child-care settings. The NAEYC National Academy of Early Childhood Programs was established in 1987 to accredit quality programs. Standards for accreditation included characteristics of quality infant and toddler programs (Recken, 1989).

Similar efforts were made to provide quality training for teachers and caregivers in early childhood programs that were not a part of the public schools which required certified teachers. A consortium of organizations that included the American Association of Elementary/Kindergarten/Nursery Educators, the Association for Childhood Education International, and the NAEYC began work on a credentialing system in 1972 named the Child Development Associate Program. This program involved training in the care of infants and toddlers. In 1975, the first credential was awarded, and by 1990 more than 30,000 teachers and caregivers had been credentialed (Phillips, 1990).

By 1990, new programs were available for intervention with high-risk infants and toddlers. One priority was for early intervention for very young children with disabilities; such a program was initiated with the passage of PL 99-457 in 1986 that included services for infants and toddlers. The intention of this federal legislation was to include provision of services to infants and toddlers with a developmental delay or a condition that is likely to result in a developmental delay (Silverstein, 1989). The federal government proposed that the funding would encourage states to develop comprehensive plans for intervention programs for infants and toddlers with disabilities and their families (Weiser, 1991).

Those who were involved with Project Head Start were focusing on intervention with infants and toddlers considered at risk because of low socioeconomic status. Head Start, originally established to serve children from ages 3 to 5, took on a new role in 1990 when the Human Services Reauthorization Act of 1990 made it possible to double the number of Head Start parent-child centers. In addition, consideration was given to extending Head Start programs to serve infants and toddlers and their families. Goals for the infant–toddler programs included parent education and training (Pizzo, 1990).

As the decade of the 1990s opened, the idea that infants and toddlers need both education and care was well-established. *Educare* had been proposed as the appropriate term for programs that included child care for infants, toddlers, and preschoolers (Caldwell, 1986, 1989; Gerber, 1981; Weiser, 1991). Models for nurturing development and learning were available; moreover, standards for developmentally appropriate care for infants and toddlers had been established by the NAEYC (Bredekamp, 1987). Programs with different goals and purposes had become available for infants and toddlers from all types of families.

Infants and toddlers in caregiving programs in the 1990s represented the diversity of families in the total population. The babies were of all ethnic and racial groups. They came from families with a variety of cultural traditions and languages. They could be from a family of the unemployed poor, or they could be the children of professional parents. Some of these infants and toddlers had disabilities or developmental delays. Others were exceptional in that they had high intellectual abilities.

Some babies lived in families that were new to this country. Not only were the infants adjusting to a new community, a new language, and new customs, but they could be frightened at the prospect of leaving the security of familiar family members to enter a caregiving situation with strangers who could not communicate with them in their home language (Packer, Milner, & Hong, 1992).

Adults in caregiving settings are challenged to understand the multiple factors that affect the infants and toddlers in their care and also to guide them in understanding each other. Because very young children begin to understand sex, race, and physical characteristics by the age of 2, their experiences in caregiving programs are important for the attitudes they are developing about themselves and others (Honig, 1983; Katz, 1982). Toddlers are capable of developing stereotypes and prejudices at a very young age; therefore, care-givers and parents have an important role in guiding their acceptance and empathy for all the children in their world. To accomplish this goal, adults also must work to accept diversity among the babies in their care. They will need to overcome their own prejudices and biases that limit their abilities to nurture each of the children they care for. They must also work at relating and responding to the uniqueness that each infant and toddler and their families bring to the program (Szanton, 2001).

Infant–Toddler Programs Today

The two major categories of settings serving infants and toddlers today are child-care and intervention programs. Parenting programs are also part of infant intervention projects, serving populations of parents and children from all socioeconomic categories. Some infant–toddler programs focus only on babies from more affluent families. The purpose of all these programs is to accelerate or facilitate development and learning or to provide enrichment for infants and toddlers. Yet the individual goals of these programs can be very diverse; they might have contrasting views of the developmental needs of infants and toddlers and the kinds of educational approaches that are most appropriate.

Infant–Toddler Child Care

In the twenty-first century there are still concerns about infants being placed in group child care before their first birthday. The basic issue has been whether out-of-home care during the first year negatively affects young infants' intellectual or emotional development. There are sometimes conflicting reasons for this reluctance to place infants in care. One belief is that the child is best cared for in the home and the early development of the infant should remain within the immediate family (Lally, 2001). From earlier concerns that infants placed in nonmaternal care before their first birthday are at risk for developmental delays (Belsky & Steinberg, 1978) to beliefs that parents are likely to perceive group care as better than in-home or family day home care (Bernstein, 1982), there are mixed feelings about the advisability of using infant and toddler care settings.

A major issue is the quality of infant care. At the end of the 1990s it was reported that only about 10 percent of infant and toddler care was of high quality; conversely, almost 40 percent of such care was considered to be harmful (Galinsky, Howes, Kontos, & Shinn, 1994; Lally, 2001). Poor-quality care can be linked to negative outcomes for children (Belsky, 1989). However, a review of the research during the same years indicated that child care causes no ill effects in infants (Clarke-Stewart, Alhusen, & Clements, 1995).

Fortunately, efforts are being made to improve care for infants and toddlers. Both the federal government and states such as California, Florida, Kansas, Nebraska, North Carolina, and Vermont are establishing comprehensive strategies for improving infant and toddler care (Fenichel, Lurie-Hurvitz, & Griffin, 1999). Improved Head Start Performance Standards were published in 1996 that cover the provision of services for pregnant women and children from birth to age 5. These standards also guide new programs for very young children called Early Head Start (Early Head Start, 2000; Lally, 2001).

Although there are still no definitive answers to these questions about out-of-home care, in the meantime, large numbers of infants are in some type of caregiving setting: in their own homes, family child-care homes, child-care centers, infant-care centers, public school centers, and child development centers.

In-Home Care. The largest percentage of infants in child care receive in-home care (48 percent in 1985) (Kelley & Surbeck, 1990). Such care is provided by a relative, a paid baby-sitter or housekeeper, a live-in nanny, or another individual who provides care in the baby's home.

Family Child Care. Family child care is the main source of out-of-home care for infants and toddlers (Eheart & Leavitt, 1989). In this arrangement, child care is provided in the home of the caregiver, who serves a small number of children in her home. The number of children served varies with licensing laws in different states; however, not all family child-care homes are licensed (Kelley & Surbeck, 1990). If the home is licensed, it must maintain health and safety standards set by the state licensing agency (Maxim, 1997).

Child-Care Centers. The number of infants and toddlers attending child-care centers is growing. Center care is expensive because of the high teacher-to-child ratio and because infants require more time and attention from caregivers (Bernstein, 1982). The adult-to-child ratio varies from state to state, ranging as high as one to eight. In addition, some centers group caregivers and infants in a single large room, a practice that Kelley and Surbeck (1990) suggest depersonalizes the care and increases the risk for illnesses, injuries, and poor caregiving practices. Some centers, however, serve only infants and seek to provide quality care by adhering to small adult-to-child ratios of one adult to three infants. The building, equipment, and materials are focused on infant and toddler care (Maxim, 1997).

Public School Centers. Public school child-care centers are being established more frequently in high schools, partly in an effort to provide high school students enrolled in vocational homemaking programs with experience in a child-care program. More significant is that such programs are set up to help teenaged mothers continue their education and provide young parents with parenting training.

One such program to provide services for teenaged mothers was established in Honolulu, Hawaii. Because of concerns that pregnant teens were dropping out of high school, the program addressed needs for prenatal, birthing, and postnatal family planning. The school established a child-care center on the high school campus staffed by early childhood educators and high

school students who had taken child development classes. At the end of the first year of operation, 14 students who otherwise would have dropped out remained in school (Thomas & Caulfield, 1998).

School-based child care is also located in elementary schools to meet community needs. Following the example of the Kramer Project in Little Rock, Arkansas, where child care and education were provided for babies as young as 6 months of age (Elardo & Caldwell, 1974), child-care facilities located at an elementary school can be convenient for parents who have older children at the school and for teachers, who can bring their infants and toddlers to school with them.

Intervention Programs for Infants and Toddlers

As more has become known about the benefits of early intervention for children at risk for development and learning problems, programs for intervention with infants and toddlers have been added to existing intervention programs for school children. As was reported earlier, both Head Start and PL 94-142 funding sevice children with disabilities as young as age 3; PL 99-457 amended PL 94-142 to include infants and toddlers. Part H of PL 99-457, passed in 1986, gave states 5 years to develop and carry out statewide plans to provide multidiscliplinary, multiagency intervention services for infants and toddlers with disabilities and their families. The programs for at-risk infants and toddlers should be provided in the type of settings where infants and toddlers without disabilities are also served. In other words, the intent is that infants and toddlers with disabilities will be served in integrated child-care, nursery school, and family child-care home environments along with children without disabilities and their families (Sexton, 1990). Existing infant–toddler programs are to be adapted to serve babies with disabilities and their families.

The disabilities to be served are the conditions of the following groups: children with a known disabling condition, such as Down syndrome, children who exhibit delay in one or more developmental areas, and infants at risk for developing a disability because of biological factors. Although most states plan to serve children with established disabilities, fewer will serve at-risk infants. If at-risk infants are to be served, then prevention of disabling conditions will be addressed in addition to intervention with existing disabilities (Graham & Scott, 1988). However, attempts to serve the large numbers of infants who could be identified with criteria for environmental and biological disabilities are cost prohibitive (Sexton, 1990).

An important component of intervention programs for infants and toddlers is the inclusive role of the family. PL 99-457 requires an Individualized Family Service Plan (IFSP), which identifies infant needs within the context of the family. The IFSP offers a family-centered approach in the services provided by the program. Intervention programs for economically deprived children, such as Head Start, also include family training and services. Indeed, many of the earlier models for infant and toddler programs were designed to counteract familial problems and to include goals for both child and parent.

Head Start was identified as a program to provide intervention for at-risk preschool children and children with disabilities. Early Head Start now extends these services to pregnant women and infants and toddlers from low-income fami-

lies. A primary purpose of Early Head Start is to promote healthy prenatal outcomes for pregnant women and to enhance the development of infants and toddlers (Early Head Start, 2000).

The Carolina Abecedarian Project (Frank Porter Graham Child Development Center, 2000) has a long history of intervention with young children, beginning in the early 1970s, to break the poverty cycle. Children from birth to age 5 were served through this program. Children received nutritional supplements in addition to a daily, year-round program that emphasized cognitive, language, and adaptive behavior skills. Although program developers found that early intervention could not replace family influence on a child's success, longitudinal follow-ups at ages 12 and 15 showed that children in the program scored significantly higher on reading tests and mathematics from primary grades through middle adolescence than peers in a control group. As adults, those who participated were more likely to still be in school and graduate from a 4-year college (Frank Porter Graham Child Development Center, 1999).

Infant–Toddler Enrichment Programs

Not all infant–toddler programs are for babies needing intervention. Many parents are interested in learning more about how their child is developing and how they can provide learning experiences. At the same time, they may need help with parenting skills. Programs designed for meeting these parental needs are available. Some have been described as enrichment programs (Cataldo, 1983); others are considered formal education (Maxim, 1997).

Enrichment programs assume that the family and infant are functioning in a normal manner. The program can enhance the child's development through enrichment experiences. Program developers have used varied approaches to informing parents how to interact with their children. Two early programs were the Nova University Play and Learn Program and the Toy Lending Library. The Nova University program offered parent manuals with suggestions for activities (Segal & Adcock, 1979), and the Toy Lending Library offered a collection of infant and preschool materials and toys that parents could use for their children's learning and development (Nimnicht, Arango, & Adcock, 1977).

A current approach to an enrichment program is used by the Crème de la Crème chain of child-care centers that serve both working parents and stay-at-home mothers. The centers include interactive television studios, computers, a water play park, and a theater for children's performances. In addition, there are rooms for more traditional curriculum such as cognitive and motor development. A controversial element of the program is a schedule that requires children to move from activity to activity every 30 minutes. Children and adults wear Crème de la Crème uniforms. The annual tuition per child is a little less than the average yearly cost of a private, 4-year college.

Crème de la Crème attracts affluent parents who are aware of brain research and the importance of early stimulating experiences for very young children. However, critics of the program question whether some elements are necessary or needed for optimum development in very young children (Galley, 1999).

Considerations for Developing Models for Infant–Toddler Programs

In Chapters 2 and 3 we considered the theories of development and learning that inform curriculum and instruction that are used with young children. We also learned about some models of early childhood programs that help us to approach alternative possibilities for developing quality programs. Now we consider the same types of information in terms of very young children, infants, and toddlers. In the next section, we will consider how classical and contemporary theories guide programs for the very youngest children.

Theoretical Bases for Infant–Toddler Programs

Arnold Gesell's (1925) maturational theory has implications for infant–toddler programs in terms of his age norms for development. The concept that certain behaviors and abilities tend to emerge sequentially and within a time range helps parents and caregivers have realistic expectations about the child's development. However, normal variations in development, particularly during the first 2 years, mean that programs for these youngest children should respond to individual development, rather than be based on group expectations.

Erikson (1963) described affective development in terms of stages. Very young children from birth to age 2 work through the first of Erikson's stages (*trust versus mistrust*) and proceed into the second stage (*autonomy versus doubt and shame*). Erikson's stages are important in terms of development of a sense of identity. The infant gradually understands that she has an identity that is separate from others. The infant's attachment to another moves from a relationship based on need to one based on love. If infants develop a secure attachment to caregivers, then they will achieve a positive adjustment in an infant program. Further, if caregivers can interact well with the infants and toddlers in their care, then the babies can also develop positive multiple attachments to them.

Behaviorist theory, particularly Bandura's social learning theory (Bandura & Walters, 1963) has a role to play in program planning for infants and toddlers. Bandura proposes that much behavior is learned through observation. Babies observe how new behaviors are performed and make adjustments following their own attempts at the modeled behavior. Children engage in self-regulation, rather than just responding to a stimulus or a reward. Parents and teachers find the behavioral approach combined with social learning helpful in management of behavior. Adults and older children have a major role in providing modeling behaviors for infants and toddlers. Babies can observe others playing with toys and putting on and removing clothing, as well as many other aspects of daily routines and play that they will learn through experience.

Skinner's (1953) behaviorist theory, on the other hand, which proposes that learning occurs as a result of reinforcement and reward systems, is seen as incompatible with the constructivist position that learning is intrinsic and can be initiated by the child. Nevertheless, programs developed for infants and toddlers using task analysis and modeling follow behaviorist and social learning theories. In task analysis, the component skills of a task are determined. Children learn one step of a skill at a time and are reinforced for successful mastery of the skills and the ultimate behavior. Modeling is used to demonstrate the desired behaviors so that the child can imitate them (Morrison, 1988). This specific skills approach is very useful for children with disabling conditions. Children with a disability may need a carefully prescribed set of activities to respond to their disability. Particular skills must be developed. Teachers and caregivers use reinforcement strategies to promote development or provide intervention in tasks designed to overcome delays in children.

Constructivists such as Piaget and Vygotsky believed in children as active learners or initiators of learning. Piaget's position on the child's reconstruction of knowledge suggests that caregivers and parents of infants and toddlers can promote development and learning through a variety of methods and materials that will build on the child's previous experiences (Kamii & DeVries, 1993). Piaget believed that developmental progress depends on both maturation and the individual's active experiences, and he thus proposed that the child's utilization of feedback from active experiences combines with maturation to further intellectual, physical, and social development.

During the first 2 years, the infant and toddler are in what Piaget termed the *sensorimotor stage of development*. The child's thinking depends on her senses and physical actions. Babies use their senses and emerging motor abilities to discover and explore within their immediate environment to learn and understand. As they become mobile, their world for learning expands, depending on how much encouragement, materials, and experiences are available to them. Teachers, parents, and caregivers who understand the cognitive-developmental process can interact with the babies and provide the kinds of opportunities that are optimal in encouraging development.

Vygotsky, like Bandura, believed that the social environment affects the child's development. The child learns from others in the environment. Parents, siblings, and caregivers provide guidance and development for infants and toddlers.

Urie Bronfenbrenner's ecological theory also supports the approach that the child's family and immediate and larger community socialize the child. The neighborhood play area, church, and child-care center are a part of the child's culture. Both Vygotsky's and Bronfenbrenner's beliefs in the importance of the child's culture have implications for the programs developed for infants and toddlers.

Programs that follow a constructivist model utilizing intrinsic learning can be described as following a discovery, or interpersonal-environmental approach. In these types of programs, the adult-child interactions and environment are significant. Developmental experiences, teacher and caregiver activities, and the environment are organized to support children's experiences that will broaden their active exploration. A prepared environment and opportunities to play are essential elements of the approach. Discovery-learning opportunities are provided in all areas of development—physical, social-emotional, and cognitive and language. Caregivers interact with the babies by asking questions, modeling, and making suggestions or comments that provide ongoing feedback. Direct instruction is used when specific behaviors or skills need to be learned; nevertheless, responsive strategies predominate as caregivers and teachers interact with individual schedules, interests, and progress of infants and toddlers.

Characteristics of a Quality Infant– Toddler Model

A quality program for infants and toddlers attends to the physical, social-emotional, and cognitive needs of very young children. To provide for these developmental needs, program must include quality caregivers, a responsive environment, developmentally appropriate program, and active parental involvement. The program includes individualized experiences and opportunities for exploration and play. Each characteristic must be present if infants and toddlers are to be nurtured appropriately, whether they receive in-home or out-of-home care. Research provides us with indicators of practices that indicate high-quality care for infants and toddlers (McMullen, 1999, p. 73):

- Use of developmentally appropriate practice as a philosophy in setting up the environment and developing the curriculum;
- Low adult-to-child ratios and group sizes that are strictly maintained;
- Health and safety recommendations and guidelines that are rigorously followed;
- Staff knowledgeable in child development and learning that is specific to the infant and toddler developmental period and who know how to use this knowledge appropriately;
- Administrative policies and workplace conditions that discourage staff turnover and thus encourage consistency of caregiving for babies;
- Staff who demonstrate that strong interpersonal skills and positive communication exist and are facilitated

among caregivers, colleagues, parents, and babies; and
- Sensitively responsive caregivers who know each baby so well that they can anticipate the babies' needs, read their verbal and nonverbal cues, and consistently respond quickly in a loving and affectionate manner to meet those needs.

The Role of Quality Caregivers

It is impossible to overstress the importance of the adults who provide care to infants and toddlers. Caregivers are the most important element of a quality program for babies. In keeping with this important responsibility, infant–toddler programs now use a system of primary caregivers. That means that the very young child is assigned to a single person as the primary caregiver. The child will also interact with other caregivers, but the primary caregiver will have the principal responsibility (Bernhardt, 2000). The infant–toddler caregiver is able to provide intensive personal interactions with each baby in her care. In the high-quality infant and toddler setting, secure attachment between the caregiver and child provides a positive basis for the caregiving experience (Raikes, 1996). The caregiver also understands that very young children have individual temperaments and schedules and the adult has the primary responsibility to initiate interactions with each infant and toddler. Some of the behaviors the quality caregiver exhibits include cuddling and carrying the baby and using loving looks and positive voice tones (Weiser, 1991).

The Role of the Environment

The physical environment in infant–toddler programs should be arranged for the unique developmental needs of very young children. Although

Quality Models in Infant–Toddler Care: Italian Centers

Like the Reggio Emilia preschool programs in Italy, infant–toddler care in that country has a long history of evolvement and improvement. Not only are these municipal programs available to parents of all backgrounds in Italian communities, but services vary according to the needs of the community and the parents and family. In addition to all-day care programs similar to Reggio Emilia that assign a single caregiver to the very young child, various other services are provided at individual centers. Some of these services are as follows (Mantovani, 2001, pp. 35–36):

- Mother-child groups (each facilitated by a professional caregiver and located near a full-day center), serving children and parents together.
- Part-time programs, offering children special activities in a setting with parental involvement.
- Parks for infants, toddlers, and preschool children, where caregivers provide socializing experiences for children and parents.
- Socializing and counseling centers for parents to meet, become oriented toward other services, and find culturally sensitive mediation services for minority groups.
- Toy libraries and children's book libraries, intended as resource centers and meeting places for children and families.
- Prenatal and postnatal parent support groups, often with activities such as infant massage, fathering groups, and other special initiatives.
- Special times and places for socialization serving immigrant mothers, often in conjunction with other services for new families.
- Training for baby-sitters and at-home caregivers.

many infant–toddler programs have environments that are more suited for older children (Lowman & Ruhmann, 1998), toddlers need environments that permit them to explore materials and move about freely. The environment should also provide a feeling of security and afford choices of materials and equipment. Some questions might be asked about the physical environment. Is there enough physical space for large-motor activities? Is there private space where children can be alone away from the group? Are an adequate number of developmentally appropriate materials available, as well as a variety of materials? Is there provision in the environment for dramatic play and discovery? (Zeavin, 1997).

Basic components of an infant–toddler indoor environment include areas for diapering, feeding, sleeping, and playing. Carpeting for the floor is essential, as well as open areas where a variety of play activities can take place. The indoor environment may be divided into separate areas using low shelving or partitions. The caregiver should be able to see every child at all times (Weiser, 1991).

Developmentally appropriate environments for both infants and toddlers are described in *Developmentally Appropriate Practice in Early Childhood Programs* (Bredekamp & Copple, 1997). See Figures 5.1 and 5.2 for examples of quality infant and toddler environments.

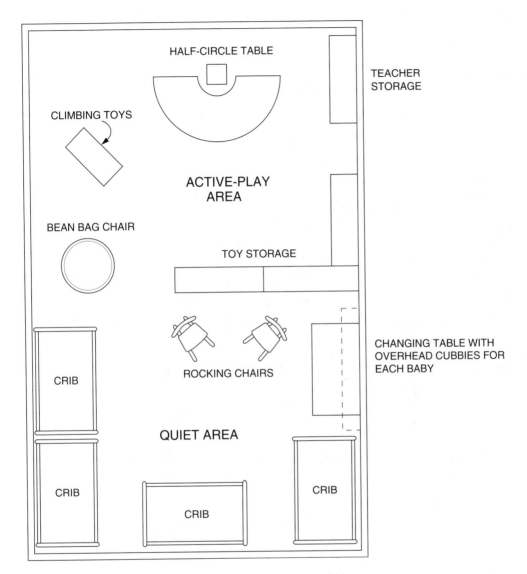

FIGURE 5.1   Indoor infant environment—6 to 12 months.

The Role of Play

Infants and toddlers spend their waking hours in some form of play. They play in interaction with adults, by themselves, near other babies, or along-side each other in first attempts to be involved with other children. The play that infants and toddlers engage in parallels their development; therefore, it is useful to discuss the role of play in terms of physical development, cognitive development, and social development. Because infants are in what Piaget called the *sensorimotor stage of de-velopment* and toddlers are progressing from the

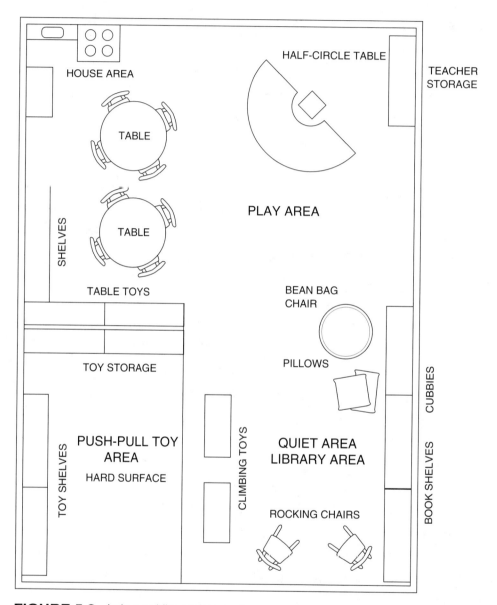

FIGURE 5.2 Indoor toddler environment.

sensorimotor to the *preoperational stage of development,* play reflects their developmental progress.

Physical Play

Physical play begins at birth, when newborns use their limited resources. They use mouth play such as bubbling saliva or mouthing a nipple (Muenchow & Seitz, 1980). As they develop more physical control over their bodies, they extend physical play to their hands, feet, and other body parts. Adults extend physical play experiences as they rock and use other movements to jiggle or swing the baby about. When the infant can grasp a toy, play is extended to objects in the environment.

Physical or motor play expands widely when the child achieves mobility and becomes a toddler. Now the child is able to extend physical play to explore the environment. The baby learns to walk and run and begins to develop better eye-hand coordination. Continual practice in physical play enables gross and fine motor skills to develop. With the decreased use of playpens in the United States, the onset of walking occurs at an earlier age than previously occurred (Garner, 1998).

Cognitive Play

Cognitive development enables the infant to combine emerging physical abilities with cognitive competencies to learn about the world. Play with objects and exploration of the environment facilitate infant cognitive development. The infant between 6 and 12 months explores the properties of toys. The child has to use sensory and motor skills to play with toys (McCune, 1986). Typically, infants mouth and visually explore toys. They may turn a toy over to examine all sides. They bang objects and focus on specific characteristics to better understand the toy. Later, infants are able to use the objects in play because they have mastered an understanding of what the toys can do.

As the older infant achieves object permanence and develops the ability to evoke images and use imitative activities, symbolic, or pretend, play emerges. The toddler can pretend one object is symbolized by another and uses this ability in make-believe play (Johnson et al., 1999). The infant can now pretend to be drinking from a cup. When the older toddler can pretend that a doll is drinking from a cup, genuine symbolic play is part of the cognitive repertoire. Pretend play activities become more complex and sophisticated as the child is provided opportunities for play with objects and materials.

Social Play

Play has an important role in social development. The infant's and toddler's individual social world has a strong influence on how they can engage in social play. The infant's first social play involves interactions with adult caregivers. The accommodating play partner engages the infant in social activities such as peekaboo or tummy tickling. The infant learns social taking of turns in interactions and communicating; through attending to and responding to social games, the infant waits for a turn and reciprocates in the give and take of the experience. Infants use these same social skills to initiate others in socialization. Smiling and vocalizations are used to attract another to interact with them (Hagens, 1997).

Toddlers can use objects to engage in social play with adults and peers. Johnson and colleagues (1999) propose that toys serve as "social butter" for mediating play between toddlers. The emergence of symbolic play enables toddlers to use pretend play with other babies.

Erikson (1963) characterized the stages of social play as *autocosmic, microspheric,* and *macrospheric*. Infant play is autocosmic because the infant's attention is focused on his or her own body. The microspheric stage evolves when the child can extend play to include toys and objects; a few significant others in the infant's environment can be included in the infant's play. Social play improves in the macrospheric stage, when the child can engage in the play of others; play structures that facilitate shared play, such as wide slides, rocking boats, and large sand boxes, encourage social interactions among toddlers.

The Outdoor Play Environment

In addition to initiating and encouraging social interactions with infants and toddlers, adults also have the responsibility of organizing the environment to facilitate physical, social, and cognitive development through play. Earlier in the chapter, the characteristics of a quality environment were explored. Examples of indoor environments for both infants and toddlers were described to include materials and toys that are developmentally appropriate for the two age groups. The equipment and toys recommended for infants and toddlers are related to the developmental progress from one age to the other that is reflected in play experiences and materials that are beneficial and enjoyable (Wortham, 2001a).

The outdoor play environment similarly provides play experiences that enhance infant and toddler development and play. Like the indoor environment, the outdoor playscape should be designed with the unique developmental needs of infants and toddlers in mind. For infants, a secure, enclosed area outdoors can provide them with opportunities to experience climate changes, landscape elements, and sensory experiences involving sun, shadows, wind, textures, and wildlife (Greenman, 1985; Miller, 1989). Infants need areas for crawling and provisions for practicing standing, cruising, and walking. Wind chimes and colored banners, hanging plants, and other natural environment features provide sensory experiences. The environment should also include toys for object play and swing sets where adults and infants can engage in social interactions during outdoor play (Wortham, 2001a).

Provisions for toddler outdoor play expand the possibilities for social, physical, and cognitive play compatible with the toddler's emerging skills and development. Pathways with different surfaces and textures; simple climbing structures that provide a slide board, steps, and a crawl-through experience; and elements that can be acted upon, such as bells, steering wheels, and chutes—all challenge toddlers' physical and cognitive growth. Greenman (1985) suggests that toddlers need outdoor spaces for developing motor skills for swinging, sliding, rolling, climbing, jumping, running, kicking, traveling, riding, and transporting. A ve-

hicle trail provides opportunities for playing with push and pull toys and wheeled vehicles.

Both small and large toys facilitate social and cognitive development. Objects that facilitate exploratory, symbolic, social, and cognitive play should be included. Toddlers are ready for materials that enhance pretend play, such as toy lawnmowers, trucks, cardboard boxes, and playhouse structures and equipment. Creative play is enhanced with facilities for sand and water play and outdoor art experiences. Figure 5.3 shows an example of the components of an outdoor infant and toddler play environment.

The Role of Routines

Adults are the primary source of care and learning for infants and toddlers. Routines are the elements of the very young child's day, whether care is provided in or out of the home. The experiences that babies have when being diapered, bathed, dressed, and fed are the opportunities for adult–child interactions that form the infant–toddler curriculum. The affectionate care and responsiveness to each individual child during the day's routines are the sources of the baby's learning.

During the first year, the adult caregiver individualizes interactive opportunities for socializing, feeding, and playing in order to be in tune with the infant's individual schedule, which Honig (1989) describes as the child's tempo. During the second year, toddlers in group care can follow scheduled times for playing, eating, and performing other brief activities with flexibility for individual needs for attention and rest. Some routines, such as diapering, are still done on an individual schedule; however, caregivers can plan for group activity and play periods and can establish times for feeding and napping for the group as a whole.

The routines followed when babies arrive and leave are also important parts of the day. The smooth transition from home to the care facility at the beginning of the day and then the change

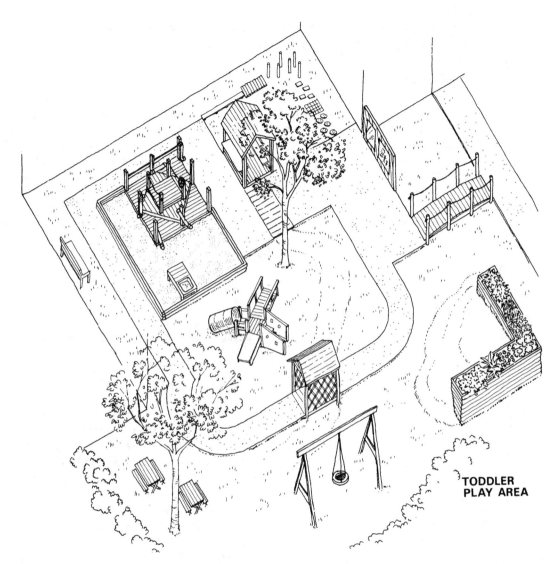

FIGURE 5.3 Infant and toddler outdoor play environment.

at the end of the day promote security and calm for babies and their families. Other transitions in routines for toddlers—for example, changing from one activity to another or washing hands before a meal—provide predictability and consistency for the daily schedule. Caregivers help toddlers anticipate changes in the routine by giving signals that help toddlers move from one activity to another. Conversations, stories, and fingerplays are also used to engage toddlers in transitions from one activity or routine to another (Morrison, 1988).

Quality Models in Infant–Toddler Care: Head Start Parent–Child Center

The Edward C. Mazique Parent-Child Center in Washington, DC, serves as a Head Start model for children under age 3. The center serves more than 500 African American and Hispanic families on a regular basis. It provides services through a home-based program, quality child care, an adolescent parents program, and early intervention for children with special needs.

The home-based program provides information and referrals for prenatal care. Information includes nutrition, parenting styles, and child development. Parents are supported until their child enters kindergarten.

High-quality center-based care is provided for infants beginning at 6 weeks of age. After the second birthday, the child can remain at the setting or enter a preschool child care program. The child can then enter a Head Start program at age 3.

The program for adolescent parents provides quality child care for children from ages 6 weeks to 3 years. At the same time, parents are given support and encouragement to continue their own education and career.

Early intervention services are provided by the center for children 6 weeks to 5 years of age who have moderate to severe developmental delays or disabilities. Services include assessment, therapy, and transportation (Carnegie Corporation of New York, 1994).

The Role of Parents

Quality infant–toddler programs support the family. Because parents are the prime adults in the child's life, close communication between caregivers and parents is particularly important. The relationship between the parents and caregivers should be a partnership; consistency between routines and child-rearing practices at home and at the caregiving setting is critical for the baby's security and development. Parents and caregivers are sharing in the child's life, and thus it is important that they discuss their roles and expectations (Bredekamp & Copple, 1997; Powell, 1989).

Parents have different needs in their relationships with staff members and caregivers in infant–toddler programs. Working parents may feel guilty and anxious about leaving their child in out-of-home care. They need reassurance about the child's daily routines and experiences, which help parents keep in touch with the child's progress and how the day went for the child and the caregiver.

Parents of infants and toddlers with disabling conditions who are in early intervention programs need ongoing progress reports and instruction on how they can contribute to the efforts being made in the child's individual program. Many parents—particularly single, teenage mothers—need supportive guidance in parenting skills.

If caregivers and other staff members in caregiving settings for infants and toddlers are responsive to cultural and language differences among the children and their families, they can learn to respond to the individual needs of parents, as well as to support the diversity of the children. Non–English-speaking parents need support and encouragement as much as their children need understanding and security (Miller, 1992; Gonzales-Mena & Bhavnagri, 2000). These parents may be unable to communicate their desires for their child's care or hesitant about using their limited English. Sensitive caregivers make efforts to help parents explain their caregiving practices. Simi-

larly, staff members seek to learn about the child's family and background.

Parents of biracial children may have concerns about their children's acceptance and identity. Single parents and teenage mothers may have questions about parenting skills. Parents of children with disabilities may have information about their children's care that needs to be shared. Others, such as parents of children with fetal alcohol syndrome, may have feelings of guilt about their involvement in their children's impediment. These parents, too, need to be accepted and involved in the program (Gargiulo & Graves, 1991).

When serving children from diverse families representing many cultures, caregivers will want to be perceptive about differences in caregiving, feeding, and other practices used in the care of babies. Parents can be asked about how they dress the baby, what sleeping patterns they expect, and what kinds of foods they prefer for their child. There are both subtle and obvious variations in caregiving among different cultures. The parents as

well as the caregivers will feel comfortable about the child who receives care outside the home if these practices are understood and followed (Gonzalez-Mena & Bhavnagri, 2000).

The caregiver in the infant–toddler program can provide ongoing support and information that can facilitate the parents' role as primary caregivers and teachers of their child. A daily report to all parents of infants and toddlers about how the child ate, slept, and played is important. This can provide consistency in the child's routines and planning between home and the program. The Integrated Components of Appropriate and Inappropriate Practice for Infants and the Integrated Components of Appropriate Practice for Toddlers (Bredekamp, 1987, p. 38) include the following characteristics of appropriate practices in staff-parent interactions:

- Parents are viewed as the child's primary source of affection and care. Staff support parents and work with them to help them feel confident as parents.

- Parents and staff talk daily to share pertinent information about the child.
- Staff help parents anticipate the child's next areas of development and prepare them to support the child.

Planning and Managing Infant-Toddler Developmental Experiences

Every day, it seems, we learn more about the capacities of newborns, the differences among very young children, the influence of family and community culture on early development, and the ability of infants and toddlers to cope with developmental challenges. We are also learning that group care of infants and toddlers presents special challenges and opportunities for promoting healthy development and supporting families . . .

Infants and toddlers thrive when they encounter challenges they can meet. Infants flourish when they are free to explore and take pleasure in their emerging interests and skills. Children's sense of belonging and ability to understand their world grow when there is continuity between the home and child care setting (Lally, et al., 1997).

Programs for very young children continue to evolve as we learn more about their capabilities and backgrounds. An infant–toddler model for care adheres to an interpersonal-environmental approach. The environment prepared for discovery and exploration through play provides experiences and adult-child interactions through daily routines. The routines and activities initiated by the adult, whether parent or caregiver, follow the needs of each child. The curriculum is developmental: adult-child interactions and experiences promote physical, social-emotional, and cognitive development matched to the child's current level of development. Therefore, planning and managing developmental experiences in group settings centers on the behaviors of the caregivers and opportunities they provide for the babies. In the following sections, suggestions are provided for

child-caregiver interactions in the domains of development. The role of the caregiver is central; nevertheless, a goal is for the child to be able to become autonomous and self-initiating. Experiences and opportunities provided should reflect a balance between adult-initiated interactions and child-initiated play activities.

Interactions and Experiences for Physical Development

During the first 3 years, children learn the skills of movement. The movement education curriculum provides guidance on interactions and experiences promoting development of gross and fine motor skills. The caregiver plans and initiates activities designed to encourage practice of physical skills. (In all descriptions of interactions, you should be aware of how caregivers include experiences as part of daily routines as well as provide planned activities.) Caregivers who perform behaviors promoting physical mastery and manipulation listed by Cataldo* (1983, pp. 81–82) do the following:

- Attempt to get young infants to look at, reach for, and kick at objects.
- Encourage young infants to hold, mouth, bang together, and examine rattles and other safe objects.
- Try to arrange toys for infants to see and to manipulate with fingers, hands, or feet when they are in a quiet state.
- Use a variety of objects and toys as playthings for exploration and manipulation; check to be certain that objects are "childproof."
- Encourage rolling over, sitting, and creeping, providing both a safe, nonrestrictive area for practice and physical support and verbal encouragement.

*From *Infant and Toddler Programs: A Guide to Very Early Childhood Education* (pp. 81–82, 84) by C. Z. Cataldo, 1983, Reading, MA: Addison-Wesley. Copyright 1983 by Addison-Wesley. Reprinted with permission.

- Arrange soft, sturdy objects so that older babies can practice standing and pulling to stand; encourage the children.
- Provide tiny, soft food objects to facilitate use of fingers and promote self-feeding by older babies.
- Use chairs, hassocks, or pushcarts, as well as abundant praise and encouragement, with toddlers who are learning to walk independently.
- Demonstrate to toddlers and assist them in gaining independent dressing and undressing skills.

Interactions and Experiences for Social and Emotional Development

Infants and toddlers have a basic need to develop social competency and a positive concept of self. The very young child has the dual task of understanding herself as an individual, unique person separate from others and becoming a social being in the company of others. The adult caregiver nutures social and emotional development through interactions that will support the development of a positive sense of self and guidance in the development of appropriate social behaviors. The adult approach to establishing an environment that provides emotional security includes the understanding that infants and toddlers must be able to develop a sense of trust. Adult-child interactions also reflect an understanding of different temperaments in infants and toddlers, which require alternative responses from adults.

There are some strategies that adults can use to promote positive social interaction between very young children (Hagens, 1997, pp. 147–148):

- Help children become more familiar with their surroundings and one another
- Maintain social groups and friendships
- Vary the number and types of toys available during any one period of time
- Control the number of children in a particular space

- Model and recognize positive social behaviors

In spite of strategies to encourage positive social interactions, this is not always the case. Frequent conflicts occur between toddlers throughout the day. There may be an environment to promote positive social interactions; however, toddlers are just beginning to learn social skills and hitting, biting, and snatching toys away from another child are common behaviors. Caregivers must find appropriate ways to intervene so that children can learn to resolve their own problems. There is concern that caregivers intervene too quickly and too frequently, thus preventing children from learning how to interact. It is proposed instead that caregivers learn to observe conflict and allow natural consequences to occur whenever it is appropriate. The caregiver must also be attentive to conflict situations and intervene to prevent injury when a child is in danger. Adults can also help children learn to resolve conflicts by modeling gentleness, staying close to a conflict, comforting each child after a conflict, and providing help so that children can solve their own problems (Da Ros & Kovach, 1998).

Interactions and Experiences for Cognitive and Language Development

The experiences provided for cognitive and language development build on what we understand about the child's role in initiating language and the internal mechanisms the child has for constructing language in increasingly complex form and content that come from continued practice with communication. The adult models new language forms and expands and extends the child's efforts at communication, thus providing vocabulary that the child can incorporate into future verbalizations. Verbal interactions initiated by the caregiver respond to the baby's interests in exploring the environment and engaging in communication episodes with the caregiver. The caregiver initiates conversations with infants and toddlers that may seem one-sided in the early months. During caregiving routines and play activities, the caregiver describes, explains, and encourages responses from the infant, even though the baby is still unable to respond using words. Later, the caregiver responds to the toddler's attempts to combine words to form communication with the adult and initiates communication experiences that will encourage the toddler to use more language.

In cognitive interactions, the adult also uses language to point out concepts and features of toys and the environment. Physical demonstration is used to show how objects and toys work. Ongoing verbalizations provide the infant and toddler with contextual explanations of activities and experiences throughout the day's routines and times for play. Examples of appropriate interactions as described by Cataldo (1983, p. 84) include the following:

- Recognizing the need to talk and sing to young infants regardless of their minimal ability to respond.
- Encouraging vocalizing, smiling, and exaggerated imitative mouth movement responses in young infants.
- Planning for crib or changing table "talk time" so that babies can listen to themselves, try out sounds, and repeat expressions before going on to other routines.
- Speaking several simple words to babies before and during routines, and repeating these frequently so that they will recognize them.
- Praising all sounds that stand for certain objects, and realizing that these are forms of early words.
- Teaching the words for body parts, foods, and diapering materials.
- Using picture books and repeating the words for objects that toddlers point to; naming details.
- Occasionally withholding objects desired by toddlers, and coaxing them to attempt to use

the words or sounds that seem appropriate for them.
- Using language to animate puppets or little toy people for toddlers, pretending and describing where they are going and what they will do.
- Using phrases and simple commands for toddlers to respond to, such as "get the ball," "pat the doggy," or "put the spoon in the cup."
- Repeating and expanding the utterances of toddlers.

The Role of Thematic Curriculum for Infants and Toddlers

Is it appropriate to design developmental learning experiences for infants and toddlers that are based on themes? If done carefully, an organized, thematic approach can be useful in helping caregivers focus on interesting experiences to share with very young children. For example, a unit on spring could easily be designed to include excursions outside to view signs of flowers and budding plants and trees during the early weeks of spring. Laminated pictures showing spring scenes could be mounted at infant-toddler eye level. Appropriate picture books could be shared with the children. Flowering, nontoxic plants could be displayed in the room and made available for careful touching and smelling.

Teachers and caregivers contemplating thematic experiences for very young toddlers should be cautious that the activities are child-centered and appropriate. The activities selected should be responsive to individual development and schedules. Art products and other activities that are beyond the child's capabilities should not be included. The guidelines for quality caregiver and child interactions should be followed; nevertheless, a thematic approach can provide an opportunity to design interesting experiences and new materials that caregivers and babies can enjoy together. (In Chapter 6, the infant-toddler curriculum will be described more specifically in terms of how caregivers and parents can design experiences to use with babies. Following an interpersonal-environmental approach, the experiences will be discussed in developmental categories that support the progress of the child's growth and learning.)

The Role of Assessment in Infant–Toddler Programs

A quality program for infants and toddlers includes provisions for assessment. Evaluation facilitates assessment and improvement. It allows program planners and staff to look at what has been accomplished and what components need to be strengthened or perhaps removed from the program. In this section, two types of assessment will be discussed. First, the child's developmental progress will be described. Evaluation of the program itself will be discussed to include the environment, experiences and activities provided for infants and toddlers, and the actions of caregivers. In addition, attention will be given to assessment of parental involvement in the program and considerations that have to be made when evaluating infants and toddlers with special needs who are served in programs for early intervention.

Assessment of Infant–Toddler Development and Competencies

Observation of infants and toddlers takes place daily as caregivers note them eating, sleeping, and eliminating during the course of the day. In high-quality programs, assessment of the infant's and toddler's progress during the day is reported to parents each afternoon when they arrive to take the child home. Assessment in this context is made to monitor the child's well-being and health each day. The caregiver can also comment on the day's activities and the child's participation.

A less frequent but equally important assessment used with infants and toddlers is that of developmental progress. Because growth and development are so rapid during the first 2 years, caregivers and parents are especially aware of the baby's developmental achievements. If infants

and toddlers are in out-of-home care during the day, parents look to caregivers to provide indicators of developmental progress in their absence.

Developmental charts or checklists similar to the ones provided in Chapter 4 are frequently used by parents and caregivers to track individual development. The infant or toddler is observed weekly or biweekly using the checklist. When a new behavior or skill is observed during the scheduled period or incidentally during the day, the achievement and the date are noted on the child's individual checklist record. Frequent reports are shared with parents; parents in turn share similar information with caregivers. Sources of developmental indicators are easily located: In addition to the Wortham Developmental Checklist for Infants and Toddlers found in Chapter 4, *Developmentally Appropriate Practice in Early Childhood Programs* (Bredekamp & Copple 1997, pp. 70–71) contains a list titled Developmental Milestones of Children from Birth to Age 3 (Lally et al., 1997). Weiser (1991) also includes the same Developmental Milestones of Children from Birth to Age 3 in Appendix B of *Infant/Toddler Care and Education.*

Portfolio assessment can be used with infants and toddlers in group care. The portfolio can be used both for assessment and program planning. An example of portfolio assessment for infant–toddler care exists at the San Antonio College (SAC) Child Development Center. SAC staff members designed a portfolio assessment system based on the center's program philosophy and program goals. After program goals were translated into program objectives, checklists were designed for developmental domains. A major decision was to determine when and how data would be collected and how checklists, anecdotal records, and other types of evaluation materials would be included in the portfolio. Parents were encouraged to contribute photos, medical forms, and other information to add to the portfolio.

A major purpose of the portfolio process was to use assessment data to plan for the child. Teachers and parents planned together for the child using an Individual Planning Profile for Infants and

Toddlers. A developmental web was used to chart the child's progress and activities to encourage further development. Figure 5.4 shows the individual planning profile for Victoria, age 10 months (Apple, Enders, & Wortham, 1998).

Assessment of Program Components

All aspects of the infant-toddler program benefit from assessment procedures. Among the components that are assessed are the environment, the experiences of and activities performed with the children, and the behavior of the adult caregiver.

Assessment of the Environment. As was described earlier, the environment planned for the infant–toddler program is organized for the specific needs of infants and toddlers. The equipment, toys, materials, and arrangement are focused on unique developmental characteristics of children younger than 3 years of age. The resulting environment is evaluated to determine whether the developmental characteristics of infants and toddlers are addressed in the room established for their care. For example, the furnishings in an infant room should include tables, infant seats, shelving, and toys that are suited to infants (Harms & Clifford, 1990). Staff members can use the indicators of an appropriate environment for infants and toddlers that are part of the Integrated Components of Developmentally Appropriate Practice for Infants and Toddlers (Lally, et al., 1997) reproduced in Figure 5.5. A rating scale with a range of indicators for the quality infant and toddler environment is available in the Infant/Toddler Environment Rating Scale (Harms, Cryer, & Clifford, 1990).

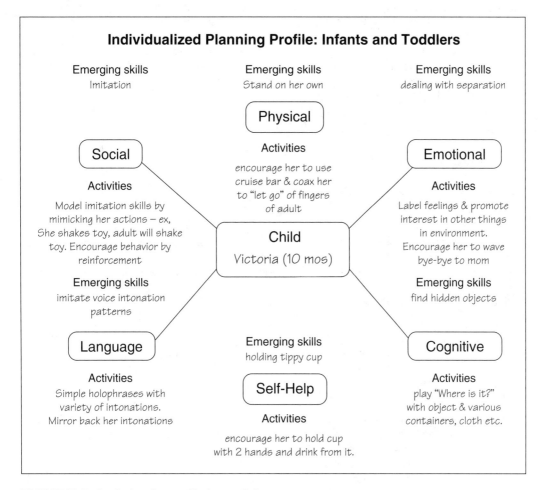

FIGURE 5.4 A planning profile for portfolio assessment.
Source: From P. Apple, S. Enders, & S. Wortham, Portfolio Assessment for Infants, Toddlers, and Preschoolers: Bridging the Gap Between Data Collection and Individualized Planning. In *Portfolio Assessment: A Handbook for Preschool and Elementary Teachers*, S. Wortham, A. Barbour, and B. Desjean-Perrotta, 1998, Olney, MD: Association for Childhood Education International. Copyright 1998 by Association for Childhood Education International. Reprinted with permission.

Assessment of Infant–Toddler Experiences and Activities. The types of activities and experiences planned and set up for infants and toddlers are also assessed. The criteria for developmentally appropriate experiences have been discussed previously. These same criteria are used to evaluate the effectiveness of the activities, which should be evaluated immediately after use to determine if they have met the child's needs and interests. Similarly, activities should be assessed to determine if they have met the purpose for which they were intended. Should an activity be used again? Does the experience need to be modified to make it more interesting or useful? Because many experiences involve adult interaction with the child, evaluation must include assessment of the adult's behaviors as well.

Appropriate Practices	Inappropriate Practices
• The play areas are comfortable; they have pillows, foam-rubber mats, and soft carpeting where babies can lie on their stomach or back and be held and read to. A hammock, rocking chair (preferably a glider for safety), overstuffed chair, and big cushions are available for caregivers or parents and infants to relax in together.	• The play areas are sterile, designed for easy cleaning, but without the different textures, levels, colors that infants need to stimulate their senses. There is not an area where an adult can sit comfortably with an infant in her arms and read or talk to the baby.
• Space is arranged so children can enjoy moments of quiet play by themselves, have ample space to roll over and move freely, and can crawl toward interesting objects. Areas for younger infants are separated from those of crawlers to promote the safe interactions of infants in similar stages of development.	• Space is cramped and unsafe for children who are learning how to move their bodies.
• Visual displays, such as mobiles, are oriented toward the infant's line of sight and designed so that the interesting sights and effects are clearly visible when the baby is lying on her back. Mobiles are removed when children can grasp them.	• Visual displays are not in an infant's line of sight. They are often used as a substitute for appropriate social interaction of infants with adults.
• Sturdy cardboard books are placed in book pockets or a sturdy book stand. Books that the adults read to the babies are on a shelf out of reach. Books show children and families of different racial and cultural backgrounds, and people of various ages and abilities.	• Books are not available or are made of paper that tears easily. Books do not contain objects familiar or interesting to children.
• Toys provided are responsive to the child's actions: a variety of grasping toys that require different types of manipulation; a varied selection of skill-development materials, including nesting and stacking materials, activity boxes, and containers to be filled and emptied; a variety of balls, bells, and rattles.	• Toys are battery powered or windup, so the baby just watches. Toys lack a variety of texture, size, and shape.
• A variety of safe household items that infants can use as play materials are available, including measuring cups, wooden spoon, nonbreakable bowls, and cardboard boxes.	• Household items that help make the infant room more homelike are not available.
• Toys are scaled to a size that enables infants to grasp, chew, and manipulate them (clutch balls, rattles, teethers, and soft washable dolls and other play animals.)	• Toys are too large to handle or so small that infants could choke on or swallow them.

FIGURE 5.5 Characteristics of an infant environment.

Source: From *Developmentally Appropriate Practice in Early Childhood Programs* (p. 75), by S. Bredekamp and C. Copple, 1997, Washington, DC: NAEYC. Copyright 1997 by NAEYC. Reprinted with Permission from the National Association for the Education of Young Children.

Assessment of the Behavior of Adult Caregivers. Two categories of adult interactions can be evaluated. The first relates to the interactions and experiences the adult initiates with the child that promote development and learning. The second category concerns the personal care routines the adult engages in with each child that concern the health, safety, and nutrition of infants and toddlers.

The Integrated Components of Developmentally Appropriate Practice for Infants and Toddlers (Lally et al., 1997) contains the contrasting indicators between appropriate and inappropriate practices used by infant-toddler caregivers in interactions and routines with babies. The caregiver's behaviors can be evaluated using the indicators related to these characteristics. The caregiver can also use the same indicators for self-evaluation and to study the characteristics of appropriate routines used with infants and toddlers. This will ensure that personal care routines and health, safety, and nutrition practices are being properly observed or carried out on a daily basis. Personal care routines and appropriate interactions and experiences can also be evaluated through use of the scales on the Infant/Toddler Environment Rating Scale (Harms et al., 1990). Interactions and activities that include language, physical skills, creative activities, social play, and cognitive skills can be evaluated using this scale.

Personal care routines used with infants and toddlers are especially important to prevent or reduce illness in very young children in out-of-home care. Staff members in locations that provide infant and toddler care will want to be very familiar with appropriate health and safety practices that are also part of personal care routines. Caregivers will want to review their practices and compare them with standards or recommended practices frequently to be sure that they are protecting the children from unsafe and unhealthy experiences. Personal care routines, especially, need ongoing attention to prevent disease and danger. Evaluators can review the indicators of appropriate practice for infants and toddlers found in the infant and toddler section (Lally et al., 1997) of *Develop-*

mentally Appropriate Practice in Early Childhood Programs (Revised) (Bredekamp & Copple, 1997) or use the appropriate rating scales in the Infant/Toddler Environment Rating Scale (Harms et al., 1990).

Assessment of Infants and Toddlers with Special Needs

According to PL 99-457, Education of the Handicapped Act Amendments of 1986, Part H, infants and toddlers (from birth to age 2) with disabilities will be served with an Individualized Family Service Plan (IFSP) that includes the specific early intervention services that are necessary to meet the individual needs of the child and the family. The plan involves the infant's or toddler's present levels of physical, cognitive, language, and psychosocial development, self-help skills, and major outcomes that are expected to be achieved for the infant and family. Included with the outcomes or objectives for the child's progress as a result of intervention are the objective criteria that will be used to measure the child's progress. Periodically, within the course of intervention services, the child's progress is assessed and decisions are made whether to continue the original plan as designed or to make needed modifications to better serve the child's intervention needs.

Assessment of Parental Involvement in Infant–Toddler Programs

If an infant–toddler program is serving children with special needs with individualized early intervention plans, the plan includes the family as well as the affected child. When the intervention program is evaluated, the parental aspect of the plan is also evaluated. A similar process should occur with programs for normal infants and toddlers who are in out-of-home care. When parental components are included in the infant–toddler program, provisions should also be made to assess and improve the parent and center relationships. If parents are involved in volunteer work at the center or in an evening parenting program, they should be given an opportunity to provide feedback on their experiences and to suggest changes they believe would be beneficial to the program. Staff members should engage in a similar process to determine the effectiveness of interactions with parents and how well they are meeting parental needs. Are the content and approach of parenting sessions meeting the parents' interests and needs? Do parents find the newsletter helpful? These and many other questions should be reviewed to assess the overall effectiveness of parental relationships and to plan future changes and additions.

Summary

Programs designed for infants and toddlers are associated with the advent of child care in this country. Although newer than preschool programs, infant–toddler programs have increased in number and have become of higher quality with the rapid growth in out-of-home care for very young children in recent years. Specialized infant–toddler programs have also emerged in the form of intervention programs for children from low-income families and infants and toddlers born with a disabling condition or who are at risk for developing a disabling condition.

Like programs for older children, infant and toddler programs are developed from theoretical bases. Theories of learning and development, particularly recent ones that emphasize the importance of the first 3 years for optimal development, form the foundations on which infant and toddler programs are organized. The purposes for the program evolve from the needs of the parents as well as the children. Some programs are used primarily for care, although experiences for development and learning are increasingly becoming a part of care. Intervention programs may serve babies of unmarried teenage mothers, low-income children who need basic experiences for language and cognitive development, and very young children who have special needs.

Regardless of the type of program established for infants and toddlers, the child's developmental characteristics usually form the background for the choices of curriculum, activities, and experiences provided. Because physical, social-emotional, and cognitive development are so important in the early years, programs for infants and toddlers focus on experiences and activities that promote development in these areas.

Adult caregivers have a key role in infant–toddler programs. Adult-child interactions are the forum for the activities conducted with the child. The interactions may occur naturally during caregiving routines and play episodes throughout the day. Because of the central nature of the adult's behavior with the child, much of the quality of the program and success of interactions and experiences depend on the qualities of the caregiver. The caregiver must be cognizant of the desired caregiving characteristics and behaviors that affect the child's experiences during the day. The caregiver needs to understand the match between experiences and interactions and the infant's or toddler's current stage of development and personality. The congruence between the child's current abilities and interests and the caregiver's choices of behaviors and activities to be used with the child form the curricular part of the infant–toddler program.

Although there is a place in infant–toddler programs for learning through imitation that follows the behaviorist and social learning models of learning, the Piagetian description of cognitive development is most closely related to the model used in this chapter. The model, described as an interpersonal-environmental approach to infant–toddler programs, is based on the Piagetian belief that learning is intrinsic. The very young child learns through discovery and interaction with the environment. For infants and toddlers, exploration of the environment and interactions with adults with appropriate materials and activities on an individual basis form the framework for their program. Although caregivers plan and initiate many of the experiences that occur with infants and toddlers each day, they also respond to the child's interest in activities with language, modeling, and encouragement. These responsive strategies reflect the caregiver's careful observations of the child and keen awareness of the kinds of interactions and experiences that will facilitate the child's development at the current stage.

The environment also is organized to promote the child's exploration and play. Equipment, furnishings, and toys are selected to fit the very young child's ability to explore and play. Room arrangement encourages emerging physical and cognitive abilities at the same time that it nurtures security and confidence. The caregiver makes appropriate experiences available and removes, adds, or rearranges toys and materials in a flexible manner to suit the changing needs of the rapidly growing child.

Parents are another key element in infant–toddler programs. Intervention programs seek to serve parental as well as child needs. The aim of child-care programs is to build a close partnership between parents and caregiver as they all share the infant's and toddler's daily life. Programs of all types may include opportunities for parents to develop parenting skills. In addition, parental involvement with the program strengthens the relationship between caregivers and parents and the overall quality of the program.

Assessment is important to the continued growth of both children and programs. Assessment of the child's developmental progress keeps parents and caregivers aware of the child's changing developmental characteristics. Awareness of developmental progress provides information that affects the nature of the program during the year as the caregiver and parents seek to respond to the child's changing developmental needs. For children with developmental delays or special needs, the intervention program based on the child's current developmental status is also evaluated based on the child's progress on the same criteria.

Other aspects of the program that benefit from assessment are the caregiver's qualities and behaviors, the quality of the parental involvement program, and the quality of the environment. With periodic assessments of all components of the programs, ongoing improvement continues the trend toward the development of a quality program for infants and toddlers.

Study Questions

1. Why has custodial care always been a factor in many programs for infants and toddlers, even at the end of the nineteenth century?
2. Why did infant mortality remain high into the first decades of the twentieth century?
3. What were some of the factors that led to the improvement of infant life and welfare after the turn of the century?
4. How did Jean-Jacques Rousseau's view of childhood differ from that of the philosophers who preceded him?
5. What specific findings in the child-study movement have affected our perception of infants and toddlers?
6. Why did the first major developments in infant–toddler programming take place after World War II?
7. A major issue since the 1950s has been whether infants should be in out-of-home care. Why is this issue still a concern today?
8. What were the contributions of the infant–toddler programs funded in the 1960s? Why were these contributions important?
9. Why are standards for infant–toddler programs and standards for the preparation of teachers and caregivers for these programs critical at this time?
10. What is the appeal of infant–toddler programs focused on enrichment or accelerated development? What are some possible problems with these programs?
11. Is there a best type of care setting for infants and toddlers? Why or why not?
12. What is the rationale for the implementation of intervention programs for infants with disabilities and their families?
13. What is meant by the interpersonal-environmental infant–toddler model? What is implied by the name of the model?

14. How and why do the caregiver's abilities control the quality of the infant–toddler program?
15. How and why is the environment of an infant–toddler program important to how the program is conducted during the whole day?
16. Why do parents need to be considered as partners in the infant–toddler program?
17. How can the infant–toddler program be affected by the quality of communication between the home and the program?
18. Why do parents of infants and toddlers in out-of-home care need a daily report on the child's progress?
19. How can caregivers assess and evaluate their behaviors to improve the infant–toddler program?
20. Why do infant–toddler intervention programs need to consider the needs of the family?

CHAPTER SIX

Infant–Toddler Curriculum: Birth to Age 2

CHAPTER OBJECTIVE

As a result of reading this chapter, you will be able to:

1. Describe examples of experiences in each developmental domain for each age group of infants and toddlers.

In Chapter 5, the evolution of educational programs for infants and toddlers was discussed. Infant–toddler child care of the past was described as having been expanded and developed into today's programs, which serve all types of very young children through educational care, intervention, and enrichment. The important role played by caregivers and the environment in providing developmental experiences for infants and toddlers was also described; play and adult–child interactions are very significant in infant–toddler programs. The curriculum for infants and toddlers was explained in terms of physical, social-emotional, and cognitive development. A developmental curriculum was described based on themes for toddlers, and the concept of an integrated curriculum was introduced that will be further developed for preschool and primary-age children in early childhood programs discussed throughout this text.

This chapter focuses on the activities and experiences that can be planned for the developmental curriculum for infants and toddlers. The curriculum for physical development, cognitive development, language development, social development, and the expressive arts will be discussed in terms of how infants and toddlers acquire each category of development. Examples of activities that are appropriate for infants and toddlers are provided. The activities described within the developmental curriculum will be matched to the developmental characteristics listed in Chapter 4 in the Wortham Developmental Checklist for Infants and Toddlers for babies from birth to 24 months.

Curriculum for Physical Development

Nurturing Physical Development in Infants and Toddlers

During the first 18 months, the infant and toddler are in what Piaget termed the *sensorimotor stage*

of development. The individual learns about the environment through his senses and by performing physical activities. As motor skills develop, so do the possibilities for experiencing the environment. The physical abilities of newborn infants are very limited. Initially, infants use reflexive movements such as blinking, swallowing, and alternately kicking the legs. These reflexes either are precursors of later skills or are protective. At about 8 months, movements become more voluntary; they are no longer automatic. Voluntary physical movements are categorized as gross motor, involving the large muscles, and fine motor, involving the small muscles (Gonzalez-Mena & Eyer, 1980).

Motor skill development occurs through movement. Much of the development in gross and fine motor skills occurs naturally as the infant and toddler use emerging physical skills to extend their possibilities to experience their surroundings. Physical action is the first medium that infants and toddlers have for communication and expression. They use movement to express their state of being and their feelings, to communicate their needs in concert with vocalization, such as cooing or crying (Weiser, 1991).

Motor skill development also occurs through the acquisition of body management skills, or body control. Body control begins with the head and neck and progresses downward along the spine in the cephalocaudal process. Body management skills are acquired from the center of the body out to the limbs in a proximodistal process. The infant is able to control the center of the body first and the hands and fingers last. In this sequence, gross motor skills precede fine motor skills (Caulfield, 1996; Gober & Franks, 1988).

Motor skills are acquired very rapidly. Much of the energy expended by infants during their waking hours involves physical activity. In the following section, experiences for infants and toddlers that will promote physical development are described. The activities are coded to the Wortham developmental checklists in Chapter 4 (Figures 4.1 to 4.4).

Experiences for Physical Development in Infants

Practicing Eye Movement

Age: Birth to 6 Months

Checklist Skill 3: Follows a Moving Person or Object with Eyes

Hold the baby in your arms or in your lap. Introduce a new toy by holding it in front of the baby's eyes. Slowly move the toy back and forth, and allow the baby to follow the movement. When the baby tires, stop the activity. If the activity is resumed, introduce a new toy or object.

Materials Needed: Infant toys

Patterns and Faces

Age: Birth to 6 Months

Checklist Skill 4: Looks at Suspended Object

Very young infants prefer looking at patterns or faces to bright colors. Patterns can be placed on the side of the crib or held for the infant to look at while he is lying in a care-taker's lap. Checkerboard and bull's-eye designs, simple geometric shapes, and large, simple faces attract the baby's visual attention.

Materials Needed: Checkerboard and bull's-eye designs; geometric shapes; drawings of simple faces

Suspended Crib Toy

Age: Birth to 6 Months

Checklist Skill 6: Moves Arms and Legs Actively

Hang a toy on the crib that will move when the baby moves his arms or legs. The more the baby moves, the more he will be rewarded by the movement of the toy. Babies also enjoy being able to activate a toy by hitting at it or kicking it.

Materials Needed: Crib toy that moves easily; brightly colored pictures suspended across the crib

Rolling Over

Age: Birth to 6 Months

Checklist Skill 9: Learns to Roll Over

As the baby begins to gain control of his arms and legs, he will begin trying to roll over. Daily opportunities to play on a pad or blanket on the floor will encourage learning to roll over. Alternately place baby on tummy and then on back. To encourage rolling from back to tummy, introduce a toy so that the baby must reach for it. Gradually move the toy farther away until the baby must roll to grasp it. Praise all efforts.

Materials Needed: Small toys to grasp

Grab It

Age: Birth to 6 Months

Checklist Skill 11: Uses Eye–Hand Coordination in Reaching

As you observe the baby during the first few months, you will notice that he is trying to reach for a toy. To accomplish this skill, eyes and hands have to be coordinated. To encourage reaching skills, hold or suspend a toy or object over the baby lying in a prone position. At first, the toy should be placed very close to the baby. As reaching skills improve, move the toy farther away.

Materials Needed: Small toy, yarn

Another Toy

Age: 6 to 12 Months

Checklist Skill 2: Transfers Object from One Hand to Another

Babies will naturally learn to transfer an object from one hand to another. Offer the baby a toy. Then offer a second toy. At first, the first toy will be dropped. Show the baby how to transfer the toy. Repeat.

Materials Needed: Small toys

Cereal Snack

Age: 6 to 12 Months

Checklist Skill 4: Picks up Small Things with Thumb and Forefinger

Place a few pieces of cereal, such as Cheerios, on the high-chair tray. Show the baby how to pick up one. When all have been grasped and eaten, place a few more on the tray.

Materials Needed: Cereal pieces

Getting Around

Age: 6 to 12 Months

Checklist Skill 9: Creeps or Gets from One Place to Another

To encourage creeping and crawling, provide the baby with opportunities to play on the floor or outside on a pad or quilt. Place a favorite toy just out of reach, and encourage baby to try to reach for the toy. Reward all attempts with smiles and approving language.

Materials Needed: Blanket, toys

Hit It

Age: 6 to 12 Months

Checklist Skill 11: Stands Holding On

Once the baby has learned to pull up to a standing position, he enjoys the opportunity to practice the new skill. To make standing fun, place two chairs facing each other. Suspend a rope between the chairs, and hang toys or household items from the rope. Encourage the baby to stand holding on to the chair and hit at the objects.

Materials Needed: Two sturdy chairs, rope, small toys or household items, yarn to attach objects to the rope

Walk the Maze

Age: 6 to 12 Months

Checklist Skill 12: Walks Holding On

Set up chairs, soft forms, or other infant furniture into a maze so that the baby can walk continuously holding on in a complete pattern. On other occasions, make different arrangements so that there will be a variety of "mazes" to experience.

Materials Needed: Sturdy furniture or plastic-covered foam shapes that can be arranged into an enclosure

Drop It

Age: 6 to 12 Months

Checklist Skill 13: Drops or Places Objects into a Container

When the baby is able to grasp and hold objects, he soon learns to drop them with some control. The adult can encourage hand control by playing a dropping game with the baby. Using small objects such as cubes and a container, the adult picks up an object and drops it in the container. The baby is then given an object and encouraged to drop it in the container. The baby should be praised for all efforts.

Materials Needed: Container such as a basket, pan, or bowl; small blocks, cubes, or toys to drop into the container

Surprise Box

Age: 6 to 12 Months

Checklist Skill 13: Drops or Places Objects into a Container

Use a shoe box or other container with a lid. Place small toys in the box. Show the baby how to remove the lid and "find" the objects. Show how to put the objects back into the container and replace the lid. Repeat with different toys.

Materials Needed: Box or large can with lid, small toys

Experiences for Physical Development in Toddlers

Throw It!

Age: 12 to 18 Months

Checklist Skill 1: Throws Ball

Toddlers love to throw, and balls are a favorite toy. Provide the toddler with a soft sponge or rubber ball that can easily be held in one hand. Take turns throwing the ball back and forth for a short distance. As the toddler gains competence, lengthen the distance. Use a larger ball requiring the toddler to use both hands for a different throwing experience.

Materials Needed: Sponge or rubber ball

I Can Build

Age: 12 to 18 Months

Checklist Skill 2: Builds Two-Block Tower

Use a set of traditional wooden blocks or plastic blocks that are about 2 inches square. Demonstrate how to line them up in a row and how to stack them. Larger, lightweight cardboard blocks can also be used to build a tower.

Materials Needed: Small wooden or plastic blocks or large cardboard blocks

What Can You Make?

Age: 12 to 18 Months

Checklist Skill 2: Builds Two-Block Tower

Gather a collection of small, sturdy cardboard boxes and other stackable containers. Cover them with Con-Tac paper. Help the toddler stack the containers. Encourage the toddler to try his own system of arranging and stacking. Round containers such as coffee cans and oatmeal boxes can also be covered and used for stacking.

Materials Needed: Empty containers covered with Con-Tac paper

Walking Here, Walking There

Age: 12 to 18 Months

Checklist Skill 3: Walks Well

Take the toddler outdoors for a walk. Find different types of walking surfaces to experience. Practice walking on sidewalks and uneven ground. Find different kinds of paved surfaces and walk up gradually sloping grassy surfaces and natural paths.

Materials Needed: None

Big Steps, Little Steps

Age: 12 to 18 Months

Checklist Skill 3: Walks Well

Walk with the toddler in an open area. Show the child how to take big steps and little steps. Practice running on tiptoe and taking running steps. Make taking the different kinds of steps into a game. Talk about the kinds of steps you are taking.

Materials Needed: None

A Little Dance

Age: 12 to 18 Months

Checklist Skill 4: Walks Backward

Put on a record or tape of slow music and try a simple dance. First take forward steps with the toddler. Occasionally take a backward step. Alert the toddler some time before a backward step is taken.

Materials Needed: Music

Learning about Spoons

Age: 12 to 18 Months

Checklist Skill 8: Uses Spoon with Little Help

Put dried beans such as pinto or large navy beans into a shallow dish. Show the toddler how to use a spoon to transfer the beans to a second dish. Start with a few beans at first and increase as dexterity is acquired.

Materials Needed: Spoon, beans, shallow dishes

Scribbling

Age: 12 to 18 Months

Checklist Skill 11: Scribbles

Give the toddler large pieces of paper and a large crayon. Show the child how to make marks on the paper. Offer a different color. Name the colors as they are used. Praise all efforts. Put the completed "pictures" where they can be admired.

Materials Needed: Large paper, large crayons

Kick It Back!

Age: 18 to 24 Months

Checklist Skill 3: Kicks Ball Forward

Engage the toddler in a game of kicking a ball back and forth. Start with a short distance and gradually move farther away. Encourage the toddler to use both feet, rather than kicking with one foot every time.

Materials Needed: Large rubber ball

Balls and Balls

Age: 18 to 24 Months

Checklist Skill 4: Throws Ball Overhand

Gather several different balls that can easily be held in one hand. Demonstrate how to throw the ball using an overhand motion. Enjoy taking turns throwing the different balls with the toddler.

Materials Needed: An assortment of small balls

Follow Me

Age: 18 to 24 Months

Checklist Skill 5: Walks Up Steps

Cut footprints the size of the toddler's feet in various bright colors. Attach them to the floor and up a three-stair climber. Have the child step on the patterns as he or she climbs up and down the stairs using alternating feet. Don't push if the toddler is not ready.

Materials Needed: Cut-outs of foot shapes on colored paper; tape; low set of stairs

Run! Run! Run!

Age: 18 to 24 Months

Checklist Skill 6: Runs

Mark three large circles with rope in an open area. With a toddler or group of toddlers, start in a circle and run to another circle. Pause, and then run to the third circle. Later, widen the distance between the circles. If a wooded area is available, toddlers can run to marked trees. On a playground, they can run from one piece of equipment to another.

Materials Needed: Lengths of rope or other materials to mark goals

Running Like the Wind

Age: 18 to 24 Months

Checklist Skill 6: Runs

Give each toddler a paper streamer or a scarf. Show them how to run holding the streamer. Use an open, grassy area for running and observing the streamer as it flutters behind.

Materials Needed: Paper streamers or scarves

Pouring Rice

Age: 18 to 24 Months

Checklist Skill 10: Drinks from Cup or Glass

To improve motor skills used to drink from a cup or glass, let the toddler pour from various types of cups and glasses. Fill a plastic dishtub half full of rice. Show the toddler how to pour the rice from one container to another. For a group of toddlers, spread an old bed sheet on the floor and provide each toddler with a plastic tub, rice, and plastic cups and glasses.

Materials Needed: Plastic dishtubs, rice, plastic cups and glasses of various sizes

Curriculum for Cognitive Development

Nurturing Cognitive Development in Infants and Toddlers

The section on physical development described infant development as involving the senses and physical actions to learn about the world. Physical movement and development of body control facilitate learning; likewise, the senses are used to take information that leads to cognitive development. Because infants use their senses and physical actions simultaneously, the two cannot be separated (Caulfield, 1996).

Cognitive development is the means for learning. Through the acquisition of cognition, infants and toddlers learn and become intelligent beings. Learning leads to understanding. Weiser (1991) proposes that understanding involves three steps: infants (1) take in information with their senses, (2) process it, and (3) use it to understand.

Caregivers and parents have a significant role in nurturing cognitive development because there are affective dimensions to learning. Infants and toddlers not only need to have the capacity to learn, they also need to be motivated to want to find out about the world. They need to have the disposition to acquire knowledge (Katz, 1988). The goal for parents and caregivers is not only to help infants and toddlers be exposed to experiences that will develop cognition but also to guide them to perceiving that learning is an enjoyable process.

In the following pages, activities that will provide cognitive experiences are explained. The activities are matched to checklist characteristics described in the Wortham developmental checklists in Chapter 4 (Figures 4.1 to 4.4).

Experiences for Cognitive Development in Infants

Propping up Baby

Age: Birth to 6 Months

Checklist Skill 3: Follows a Moving Person or Object with Eyes

Checklist Skill 10: Looks at Objects and Realistic Pictures

Just as babies need to be held in different positions, they also need to be placed in different positions so that they can observe their surroundings from different perspectives. Babies can be seated in an infant seat or on a beanbag chair or propped up in a seated position with pillows. They can observe the movement and activities of others, view pictures, and observe natural features of the outdoor environment.

Materials Needed: Beanbag chair, pillows, or infant seat

Looking and Finding

Age: Birth to 6 Months

Checklist Skill 3: Follows a Moving Person or Object With Eyes

Babies love to watch the movements of their caretaker. As they gain experience, they are able to locate adults by the location of their voice. Play a game by calling to the baby from different locations. When the baby turns his or her head to locate your voice, reward the baby with hugs and praise. The baby should be placed in different positions—on the back and tummy and in seated positions—to stimulate different kinds of movement to locate the adult playing the game.

Materials Needed: None

Crib Mobiles

Age: Birth to 6 Months

Checklist Skill 4: Looks at Suspended Object

At a very young age, babies are able to focus visually on items hanging from the crib. Interesting household items can be suspended over the baby's crib. It is important that objects are beyond the infant's ability to grasp if they can possibly be harmful. Because infants need moderate variety to maintain interest, new materials can be introduced when the baby appears to be bored with the existing objects.

Materials Needed: Strap to attach across the crib, yarn, rubber kitchen tools or toys to suspend

Looking, Looking

Age: Birth to 6 Months

Checklist Skill 10: Looks at Objects and Realistic Pictures

Babies are interested in looking at objects and pictures in their environment. When they are sitting in the caregiver's lap, they can be introduced to pictures in a magazine or picture book. They also enjoy being carried about and shown plants, grass, flowers, pets, and interesting objects. Looking activities should be accompanied by conversation about the things observed.

Materials Needed: Objects, animals, plants, and so on from the indoor and outdoor environment; pictures; picture books

What Do You Hear?

Age: Birth to 6 Months

Checklist Skill 12: Turns Head to Sound of Bell or Rattle

Infants are attentive to new sounds. To give the baby practice in hearing and listening, use a rattle or bell in a listening game. Seat the baby in the parent's or caregiver's lap. Come from behind the baby and ring the bell. The baby will soon turn toward the new sound. Reward the baby by offering the toy to be held and explored.

Materials Needed: Bell, rattle, or other toy that makes noise

Find It

Age: 6 to 12 Months

Checklist Skill 5: Uncovers Hidden Toy

Between 6 and 12 months, most babies learn object permanence. To nurture this developmental milestone, tie brightly colored ribbons to small toys. Hide the toys with the ribbon showing. Show the baby how to pull the ribbon to find the toy. Praise all efforts.

Materials Needed: Ribbons of several colors, small toys

Texture Fun

Age: 6 to 12 Months

Checklist Skill 14: Manipulates Objects

Babies love to experiment with materials that have different surfaces, textures, and sounds. Give babies wax paper, cellophane wrap, newspaper, a soft towel, or gift-wrapping paper. Supervise carefully because the materials may end up in their mouth.

Materials Needed: Cellophane wrap, paper of various colors and textures, and so on

Nesting Cups

Age: 6 to 12 Months

Checklist Skill 14: Manipulates Objects

Give the baby a set of measuring cups or toy nesting cups to explore. Show the child how to place a smaller cup into a larger one. Praise all efforts. Measuring spoons will add to the interest in the activity.

Materials Needed: Nested measuring cups or toys, measuring spoons

Simon Says

Age: 6 to 12 Months

Checklist Skill 16: Imitates Actions

In this simplified version of "Simon Says," the adult initiates activities such as clapping hands for the baby to imitate. "Patty-cake" is also an example of an imitating game. The adult first models the actions and encourages the baby to do it also. Touching and naming nose, knees, and so on can be imitated. Traditional imitating activities taught to babies include giving a kiss, throwing a kiss, and waving bye-bye.

Materials Needed: None

Experiences for Cognitive Development in Toddlers

Egg Hunt

Age: 12 to 18 Months

Checklist Skill 1: Pursues and Retrieves a Toy That Is Out of Sight

Hide plastic Easter eggs so that only part of each one is hidden. Show the toddlers how to find the eggs. At first, make the eggs fairly obvious. After more experience, leave less and less of the egg in sight.

Materials Needed: Large plastic Easter eggs or egg-shaped hosiery containers

Mailman

Age: 12 to 18 Months

Checklist Skill 1: Pursues and Retrieves a Toy That Is Out of Sight

Put toys or other interesting objects in letter envelopes or manila mailing envelopes. Put the "mail" in a large box. Invite the toddler to pick out an envelope and find what is inside. After the game has been repeated several times, change the items in the envelopes.

Materials Needed: Small and large envelopes, toys and other items to be put into the envelopes

Clothespins in the Can

Age: 12 to 18 Months

Checklist Skill 2: Puts Objects In and Out of Container

Cover a coffee can with Con-Tac paper. Cut a round hole larger than a clothespin in the plastic lid. Show the toddler how to put clothespins (try to use round clothespins) through the hole. Count the clothespins as they are placed through the hole. When all the clothespins are in the can, show the toddler how to take off the lid and dump them out. Repeat.

Materials Needed: Coffee can or other container with a plastic lid, clothespins

Ring, Ring

Age: 12 to 18 Months

Checklist Skill 3: Role Plays with Familiar Objects

Provide toddlers with old telephones or play telephones. Show them how to dial the number and "talk" on the telephone. Encourage them to call someone in their family. Become involved in the role play by pretending you are talking to someone on the telephone.

Materials Needed: Toy telephones or discarded telephones

Going Shopping

Age: 12 to 18 Months

Checklist Skill 3: Role Plays with Familiar Objects

Collect empty food containers. Put the containers on a low table or shelf. Show the toddler how to go shopping using a large basket, bag, or play grocery cart. Talk about what the toddler is going to buy. After items have been selected, name each one and encourage the toddler to take out the named item. Change items to provide variety and new vocabulary opportunities.

Materials Needed: Empty food containers; bag, basket, or cart for shopping

Hat Game

Age: 12 to 18 Months

Checklist Skill 4: Recognizes and Responds to Self in Mirror

Make a collection of old hats, the more outrageous the better. Show the toddler how to try on the hats and look in the mirror. Enjoy taking turns and recognizing each other in the funny hats. Be sure to have hats for both boys and girls, and encourage the toddler to try on all types of hats.

Materials Needed: A collection of hats

Puzzle Play

Age: 12 to 18 Months

Checklist Skill 5: Solves Simple Puzzles or Constructions

Purchase simple puzzles with two or three parts or make puzzles by mounting a picture on cardboard and cutting it into two or three pieces. Wooden puzzles should have knobs for picking up the pieces. Show toddlers how to assemble the puzzle. Praise all efforts. When the puzzles become too easy, increase the number of pieces. An endless supply of puzzles may be made from empty food boxes.

Materials Needed: Puzzles with two or three pieces, either purchased or hand constructed

Mechanical Toys

Age: 18 to 24 Months

Checklist Skill 1: Demonstrates Perception of Correct Function of Toy

Many toys require the toddler to push buttons, pull levers, or perform some other physical action to activate the toy. Introduce the toddler to such a toy and demonstrate its function. When interest lags, put the toy away for awhile and substitute another toy.

Materials Needed: Toys with mechanical function

Outside Toys

Age: 18 to 24 Months

Checklist Skill 1: Demonstrates Perception of Correct Function of Toy

Make available a variety of outdoor push and pull toys. Show the child how to "cut the grass" with a toy lawnmower, or to push a doll in a doll carriage. When the toddler is playing with a toy, talk to him about the activity and the use of the toy.

Materials Needed: Push and pull toys

More Shapes

Age: 18 to 24 Months

Checklist Skill 3: Places Correct Shape in Shape Box

Make or acquire a "shape box" with five different shapes. Invite the toddler to experiment with putting shapes into the correct holes. If the toddler finds the task too difficult, show how the shaped pieces fit.

Materials Needed: Shape toy with five or more pieces

Soap Bubbles

Age: 18 to 24 Months

Checklist Skill 4: Uses Housekeeping Toys

Fill a plastic dishpan about half full of water. Add liquid detergent. Show the toddler how to use a whisk or eggbeater to make soap bubbles. Toddlers may be more interested in playing in the soapsuds with their hands. A large piece of plastic may be needed to protect surfaces. A child's apron will protect the toddler's clothing. A water play table may be used for a group of toddlers.

Materials Needed: Dishpan, detergent, eggbeater or whisk, plastic sheeting, aprons

Playhouse

Age: 18 to 24 Months

Checklist Skill 4: Uses Housekeeping Toys

Make a playhouse by putting an old sheet over a table. Cut an opening for a door. Put play dishes, child's sleeping bag, or other dramatic play toys in the playhouse. Invite the toddler to enjoy pretending in the house.

Materials Needed: Table, old sheet, playhouse toys

Here I Am

Age: 18 to 24 Months

Checklist Skill 5: Recognizes Self in Photograph

Make a book of individual and group photographs that include pictures of the toddlers. As you look through the book together, ask toddlers to find themselves or identify another person in the pictures.

Materials Needed: A collection of photographs or photograph book

Find Another One

Age: 18 to 24 Months

Checklist Skill 6: Matches Familiar Objects by Color

Select six wooden cubes or other objects: two red, two yellow, and two blue. Put one of each color in front of the toddler. Select one of the other three cubes and show the toddler how to match it with the same color. Repeat with each of the cubes. Reward all efforts. Discuss the colors of the objects as they are matched.

Materials Needed: Two cubes or other objects of each color: red, yellow, blue

One More

Age: 18 to 24 Months

Checklist Skill 8: Understands "One More"

Engage in a game counting objects with the toddler. Stop after counting to three or four. Add one more to the group of objects and say, "One more." After repeating the activity several times, ask the toddler to give you "one more."

Materials Needed: Toys or objects to count

Put It Away

Age: 18 to 24 Months

Checklist Skill 9: Returns Toy to Correct Place

Divide a toy shelf into three or four spaces with colored tape. Choose four toys to arrange in the spaces. Find a picture of the toy in a catalog. If no picture is available, draw a simple picture to represent the toy. Play a game of putting toys on the shelf to match the picture. At the end of play times, help toddlers replace toys in the correct spot. When one shelf has been mastered, add another shelf of toys.

Materials Needed: Storage shelf, toys, pictures or drawings of toys

Feeling

Age: 18 to 24 Months

Checklist Skill (Social-Emotional Development) 5: Shows Interest in Exploring New Places

Take toddlers on a feeling expedition outdoors. Show them different elements in the playscape such as grass, sand, and tree bark. Help them to touch and experience the texture and verbally describe it for them.

Materials Needed: None

Bug Hunt

Age: 18 to 24 Months

Checklist Skill (Social-Emotional Development) 5: Shows Interest in Exploring New Places

Help toddlers be on the alert for insects in the outdoor environment. Show them how to look for bugs on the ground, on trees and flowers, or on fences. If possible, collect the bugs for them, and put them in a jar for them to observe with adult supervision.

Materials Needed: Bug nets and cages or glass jar with lid and air holes

Curriculum for Language Development

Nurturing Language Development in Infants and Toddlers

Although true vocalizations and communication using language generally do not occur before the end of the first year, the process of acquiring language begins at birth, or even before birth. The tremendous task of learning to use language to communicate with others begins with the infant's using the sense of hearing to understand the basic building blocks of sounds and language in his environment (Caulfield, 1996). Infants and toddlers must learn the sounds, or phonology, of the lan-

guage; the semantics, or meaning, of the language; the formation of words, or the syntax and grammar, in the language; and the actual logistics of communication, or pragmatics, of the language (Weiser, 1991). The process of learning all of these language components begins in the early months of the first year and continues throughout life, although the basic systems of the language are mastered by the time the young child enters school.

Theorists have different perspectives about how language is acquired. Skinner (1957) proposed that adults provide the language model that children acquire through imitation. Language and thought are initiated through interactions between adult and child. Innatists (Chomsky, 1965; Lennenberg, 1967; McNeil, 1970) believe children have an internal ability to learn language; as the child matures, language expands. Piaget (Piaget & Inhelder, 1969) proposed that language results from children's experiences with language in their world; early language reflects the child's sensory experiences. Vygotsky (1978) believed that social relationships affect the child's speech in that adult language and encouragement of the child's language match the child's need for help with language. More experienced adults provide social structure to guide children's participation in language (van Kleeck, Alexander, Vigil, & Templeton, 1996).

Infants and toddlers are encouraged to speak when they are reinforced by adults for their efforts. Likewise, they use language, once they are able to verbally communicate, to describe their actions and cognitive progress. They learn vocabulary by imitating the words they hear, although they impose their own level of syntax on the words they use. In effect, the complex nature of language acquisition is explained in part by each of the theories, although none provides a complete understanding of the process.

The role of adults is significant in the development of language in infants and toddlers. The verbal environment provided by adults and supporting interactions that include verbal communication are necessary if the child is to hear and attempt to use language. Literacy is also part of language development. The use of books and stories with infants and toddlers is part of the continuum in becoming able to read and write, in addition to being able to listen and speak (Morrow, 1997).

Very young children who come from homes where a language other than English is spoken have special needs in language development. These infants and toddlers are encountering a different language in the caregiving setting than in the home. They are being exposed to and learning two languages. Miller (1992) suggests that adults in the caregiving setting can help their non–

English-speaking children to adjust to the new language and learn to use it by following the following guidelines:

1. Build trust by helping the child feel safe and secure. To make the child feel comfortable, hold and otherwise touch the child, use eye contact, and smile at the child.
2. Use key words in the child's language. Find out from the parents how the child communicates his needs.
3. Be a good model by speaking slowly and clearly. Model the use of complete sentences and extend the child's single-word utterances.
4. Build receptive language through talking about what is happening. Talk to the child about what he is doing and the sequence of routines and events in the classroom.
5. Encourage productive language by encouraging the child to use key social words such as "thank you," "yes," "no," and "okay."
6. Try to understand nonverbal communication by observing the child's efforts to communicate through gestures and sounds and using verbalizations to interpret for the child.
7. Encourage the child to interact with other children in the classroom. Social interactions will help in socialization and provide experiences with language.

The following section presents activities that caregivers can use to implement a curriculum for language development. The activities are related to the Wortham developmental checklists in Chapter 4 (Figures 4.1 to 4.4). For infants under 6 months, the checklist items are found in the "Social-Emotional Development" section; for children 6 to 12 months, they are part of the "Physical-Cognitive Development" section; for those older than 12 months, checklist items are in the "Language Development" section.

Experiences for Language Development in Infants

Little Talks

Age: Birth to 6 Months

Checklist Skill 3: Responds to Talking, Smiling, or Touching

Checklist Skill 6: Vocalizes in Association with Pleasure, Displeasure, Eagerness, and Satisfaction

Provide frequent opportunities when the baby is rested and fed to hold and talk to him. The baby should be held close enough to view your face as you talk and smile. If the baby vocalizes, smile and reflect the vocalization. Both the infant and adult reinforce their loving attachment from positive "conversations" with each other.

Materials Needed: None

Body Parts

Age: Birth to 6 Months

Checklist Skill 3: Responds to Talking, Smiling, or Touching

Place the baby in your lap or on the floor on a blanket. Touch and pat the baby on different parts of the body as you name them. All vocal conversation should be accompanied by smiles. If the baby also vocalizes, these should be rewarded with more smiling and talk.

Materials Needed: None

Communicating Feelings

Age: Birth to 6 Months

Checklist Skill 6: Vocalizes in Association with Pleasure, Displeasure, Eagerness, and Satisfaction

During the first 6 months, the infant begins to communicate different kinds of feelings through vocalizations. On some occasions babies will coo when interacting with an adult. When babies are tired, hungry, or frustrated, they will make fretting vocalizations or cry. Respond to different kinds of communication with understanding. Talk to the baby concerning your understanding about how he feels.

Materials Needed: None

Laugh with Me

Age: Birth to 6 Months

Checklist Skill 9: Chuckles and Laughs

Babies love to "talk" with familiar people. As they gain experience with communicating, they first coo and soon chuckle or laugh. Lay baby in your lap facing you when he seems to be in a mood to "chat." Talk to baby, smiling and laughing. The infant will let you know if he wants to escalate the fun. You will soon know which kinds of conversation or physical movement on your part will bring forth chuckles and laughs. When baby tires of the activity, change to something quieter.

Materials Needed: None

Talking with Baby

Age: 6 to 12 Months

Checklist Skill 8: Imitates Speech Sounds

Although infants cannot vocalize true words at this age, they are able to vocalize and imitate sounds. You can initiate a "conversation" or respond to the infant's efforts to use sound to communicate. Hold the baby in your lap facing you, and acknowledge a sound made by the baby and imitate it. You can then initiate a sound such as "ba-ba-ba" and encourage the baby to make the same sound. All efforts should be rewarded.

Materials Needed: None

Learning New Words

Age: 6 to 12 Months

Checklist Skill 8: Imitates Speech Sounds

The infant can begin to learn names of things in the environment, although the names cannot be verbalized. While the baby is playing, introduce or name things in nearby areas. If the baby responds or tries to imitate your speech, praise and reinforce the efforts and repeat the names of the objects. Repeat the activity with the same and different items.

Materials Needed: Toys and other items in the environment

Hi and Bye-Bye

Age: 6 to 12 Months

Checklist Skill 15: Says Single Words Such as "Mama" and "Dada"

One of baby's first ways to communicate is to say "hi" and "bye-bye." Wave to the baby, saying these words, and encourage baby to imitate you. Use other familiar words, such as names of pets and siblings. Praise all efforts.

Materials Needed: None

Encouraging Language for Communication

Age: 6 to 12 Months

Checklist Skill (Social-Emotional Development) 8: Uses Motions or Gestures to Communicate (Holds out Arms to Be Picked Up)

Before infants are able to talk, they use gestures to let the caretaker know what they want. Babies will gesture or point, or perhaps whine. To encourage positive communication, ask the baby what he wants. "Do you want a banana?" "Can you say, 'banana'?" Praise efforts to verbalize. "Good. You said 'banana.' Here is the banana." Repeat for different gestures, each time modeling for the baby how to use words or positive verbalization rather than gestures or whining.

Materials Needed: None

Experiences for Language Development in Toddlers

Talk to Me

Age: 12 to 18 Months

Checklist Skill 1: Says Single Words (May Add Two and Three Words)

Before the baby can say words, he babbles, using vocalizations that sound like words. Because the baby's first words stand for a complete thought, the adult tries to determine what the baby is expressing and reflect the communication. For example, if the baby says, "light," the adult may say, "Yes, that is a light." Praise all the efforts to communicate by responding to the baby's utterances.

Materials Needed: None

Where Are Your Eyes?

Age: 12 to 18 Months

Checklist Skill 2: Points to a Body Part on Request

Before the toddler can name things, he can point to them. Toddlers are interested in their body and respond to learning the names of body parts. Adults can help toddlers learn the names by pointing to each body part and naming it. Later they can play a question game such as "Where are your eyes?" or "Show me your mouth." When the toddler has mastered pointing to major body parts, add others. When the names of the body parts can be verbalized, ask the toddler to name them as you point to them.

Materials Needed: None

Body Puzzle

Age: 12 to 18 Months

Checklist Skill 2: Points to a Body Part on Request

Make a puzzle by gluing a simple doll picture on cardboard and cutting out the body parts or gluing the picture on flannel and using it on a flannel board. Show the toddler how to assemble the puzzle. Ask the toddler to put on the arms, legs, and so on. Name the body parts, and have the toddler point to each one.

Materials Needed: Body puzzle made from a picture of a doll or human figure glued to cardboard or flannel and cut out by body parts

Names in Books

Age: 12 to 18 Months

Checklist Skill 3: Imitates Words

Select beginner books that feature objects, toys, or animals that are familiar to the baby. As you and the toddler look at the book, name each picture. Encourage the baby to say the name of the picture after you. Repeat many times with many books.

Materials Needed: Simple picture books

Where, Oh Where?

Age: 12 to 18 Months

Checklist Skill 4: Responds to a Single Request

Sing the song, "Where, oh where is dear Little _____ ?" The toddler points to himself when requested. The toddler points to the things named in the tune. In a group setting, the toddlers can point to the person named in the tune. This activity teaches vocabulary as well as how to follow a request.

Materials Needed: None

Old MacDonald

Age: 12 to 18 Months

Checklist Skill 5: Says the Names of at Least Five Things

Make a book of pictures of animals, or select an animal picture book. Adapt the song "Old MacDonald" to fit the pictures in the book. As you look at the book with the toddler, sing the song, leaving out the name of the animal in the pictures. Encourage the toddler to supply the missing name. Provide help when needed.

Materials Needed: Picture book of farm animals

Outside Talk

Age: 12 to 18 Months

Checklist Skill 5: Says the Names of at Least Five Things

When outdoors with toddlers, be alert for things in the environment they can observe. Point to a bird flying overhead and name it for the toddlers. Repeat with other elements in the environment. After many experiences, ask the toddlers to name the things that are seen.

Materials Needed: None

What Am I Doing?

Age: 18 to 24 Months

Checklist Skill 1: Combines Two to Three Different Words

Pantomime familiar activities. Ask the child to tell you what you are doing. For example, do the motions for washing your face, putting on clothing, or drinking from a glass. Show the toddler how to pantomime an action. Tell what he is doing. Repeat using other activities.

Materials Needed: None

Tell Me About Food

Age: 18 to 24 Months

Checklist Skill 1: Combines Two to Three Different Words

During mealtime or snack time, talk to the toddler about the food being eaten. Talk about the name of the foods, their color, and how they taste. Ask the toddler about the foods. Praise all responses and voluntary statements. (This process for eliciting language can be used in many everyday activities.)

Materials Needed: Mealtime foods or snacks

Here's a Ball

Age: 18 to 24 Months

Checklist Skill 1: Combines Two to Three Different Words

Learning simple fingerplays helps children to develop language. An example of a simple fingerplay is "Here's a Ball." The adult says the fingerplay and models the actions. Encourage the toddler to imitate the actions and say the words to you.

> *Here's a Ball*
>
> Here's a ball [make circle with thumb and forefinger],
> And here's a ball [make circle with both hands],
> And a great big ball I see [make circle with both arms],
> Can you count them? Are you ready?
> One [make circle with thumb and forefinger],
> Two [make circle with both hands],
> Three [make circle with both arms]!

Repeat fingerplays frequently. As toddlers become familiar with them, they enjoy being able to participate in the activity.

Materials Needed: None

Play Talk

Age: 18 to 24 Months

Checklist Skill 1: Combines Two to Three Different Words

When outdoors, talk to the toddlers about different play activities. Encourage them to talk to you about what they are doing. For example, if toddlers are digging in the sand with shovels and pails, make comments about the activity, and ask the children to tell you about it. Encourage attempts to share information about the activity.

Materials Needed: None

Names, Names

Age: 18 to 24 Months

Checklist Skill 3: Names Pictures

Construct or collect sets of pictures of categories of things such as animals, foods, furniture, and toys. Using one category of pictures, name each picture for the toddler. Ask the toddler to name them. When possible, relate the picture to the actual item. After many naming activities, go through a set of pictures and see how many the toddler can name without prompting. Praise all efforts.

Materials Needed: Sets of pictures of familiar categories of things

Stories

Age: 18 to 24 Months

Checklist Skill 3: Names Pictures

Read simple storybooks frequently. When the toddler is familiar with the story, look at the pictures and encourage the child to name things in the pictures. Ask the toddler to tell you what is happening in the picture.

Materials Needed: Storybooks

Puppets

Age: 28 to 24 Months

Checklist Skill 4: Imitates Adult Speech Without Prompting

Engage in puppet play with toddlers. Have the puppet "talk" to the child. After the toddler is familiar with the puppet, invite the toddler to make the puppet "talk" to you. Don't push if the toddler is apprehensive.

Materials Needed: Familiar puppets

Curriculum for Social Development

Nurturing Social Development in Infants and Toddlers

Social development begins as soon as the neonate engages in the first interactions with the people in his environment. Immediately after birth, the infant may be placed on the mother's abdomen and held by the father. These early interactions begin the process of bonding between the parents and the infant. Social interactions that occur in the neonate's times of wakefulness and alertness continue the process of social and emotional development.

During the first 18 months, infants are in what Erikson (1963) said was the first stage of psychosocial development: *trust versus mistrust*. The dependability and consistency of adult attention to the infant's needs form the basis of positive social and emotional development. The toddler then enters the stage of *autonomy versus shame and doubt,* when the need to develop a sense of self as an individual emerges. Adult support for exploration and independence facilitates the now mobile individual's quest for affirmation of autonomy. Many of the activities that are a part of daily routines nurture social and emotional development in infants and toddlers; however, adult caregivers may not be aware of the importance of social interactions that occur as a part of the activities. In a previous section, it was stressed that caregiver verbalizations and communications with infants and toddlers encourage language development. Social interactions likewise nurture social and emotional development. In the activities described next, attention is given to how adult interactions with infants and toddlers can support social development.

Experiences for Social Development in Infants

Ride a Cock-Horse

Age: Birth to 6 Months

Checklist Skill 1: Looks Attentively at an Adult

All babies love this game. It gives them an opportunity to gaze directly at the adult's face and interact through vocalizing as the game progresses. Place the baby in your lap facing you, and bounce the baby gently as you repeat the poem. The baby is bounced higher on the final word, "goes." Both adult and baby will enjoy the anticipation of the end of the rhyme.

> *Ride a Cock-Horse*
>
> Ride a cock-horse to Banbury Cross
> To see a fine lady upon a white horse;
> Rings on her fingers, and bells on her toes,
> She shall make music wherever she goes.

Materials Needed: None

Holding Baby

Age: Birth to 6 Months

Checklist Skill 2: Adjusts Body to the Way the Adult Holds Him or Her

Hold the baby in various positions such as on your shoulder and cradling in your arms. Place pictures, patterns, and so on within the baby's line of vision. Vary where you stand or sit so that the baby will have a variety of things to see. The baby learns trust and love by being held and cuddled. Talking to the baby reinforces the communication felt through bodily contact.

Materials Needed: Colorful patterns, pictures, or objects for the infant to see

Up and Down

Age: Birth to 6 Months

Checklist Skill 3: Responds to Talking, Smiling, Touching

The baby enjoys the play of being lifted up and down gently as the adult smiles and talks. Trust in the adult develops as the enjoyment of physical action reinforces the bond of attachment between the baby and adult. The adult should maintain eye contact with the baby as the baby is lifted gently or raised up over the adult's head in a playful gesture. The baby will respond to the adult's pleasure in the activity.

Materials Needed: None

Hold Me

Age: Birth to 6 Months

Checklist Skill 4: Quiets When Picked Up

When an infant is upset, he wants to be held. Very young babies are still adjusting to a new environment, and knowing that he will be held builds a feeling of security and trust. When the baby is upset, hold the baby close as you talk in a soothing voice. Touching, patting, and stroking also help to reassure a fretful baby. The baby is also reassured by the tactile feeling of being enclosed securely in a warm blanket.

Materials Needed: None

Baby Wants Attention

Age: Birth to 6 Months

Checklist Skill 5: Stops Crying When Someone Plays with Him

It used to be thought that picking up a young infant when he was crying would spoil the baby. Research now shows that when a baby's need for security and holding are met in the early months, the baby will demand less attention later.

When the infant cries for attention, instead of always picking the baby up, stop to play. Talk, touch, or offer a toy, letting the baby know you are there, if needed.

Materials Needed: Toy

Where Am I?

Age: Birth to 6 Months

Checklist Skill 8: Knows Familiar People or Things by Sight or Voice

Soon after birth, infants learn to discriminate between their mother or primary caregiver and less familiar adults. Play a recognition game by calling to the infant when out of sight. When the infant begins to look for you, reward the baby by appearing and engaging in talking, holding, or playing.

Materials Needed: None

Mirror Fun

Age: 6 to 12 Months

Checklist Skill 2: Plays with Image in Mirror

Place a mirror in front of the infant while he is being held in an adult's lap. Allow the baby to view his image in the mirror. Encourage the baby to interact with the image in the mirror. As an alternative, place the baby on his tummy on the floor in front of a free-standing mirror.

Materials Needed: Hand mirror or large mirror at floor level

The Hat Game

Age: 6 to 12 Months

Checklist Skill 2: Plays with Image in Mirror

Babies love to put on hats. Seat baby in front of a mirror beside you. Show the baby how to put on the hat and admire him in the mirror. Take turns putting on hats and enjoying and admiring each other.

Materials Needed: An assortment of interesting hats

A New Friend

Age: 6 to 12 Months

Checklist Skill 4: Responds to Presence of a New Person

When infants are in a period of "stranger anxiety," caution is needed when introducing a new person. Allow the baby to become familiar with the person from a secure position such as the lap of a family member or caregiver. Only when the infant indicates an interest in approaching the "new friend" should social interactions be initiated. When the baby feels comfortable with the new person, he will indicate readiness for including that person in interactions.

Materials Needed: None

Experiences for Social Development in Toddlers

See My Toy?

Age: 12 to 18 Months

Checklist Skill 2: Offers Object to Another Person

One of the first ways a toddler shows an awareness of social interactions is by approaching someone with a toy or object. The baby may want to show the toy or offer it to be held. The adult responding to the action should accept the toy and thank the baby. The gesture is usually temporary, and the baby soon expects the toy to be handed back. Often one toy after another is offered as the baby makes a game of the activity.

Materials Needed: Toys or other objects

By Myself

Age: 12 to 18 Months

Checklist Skill 3: Plays Independently or in Parallel Play

Toddlers who receive adequate attention do not always have to have an adult to engage in play with them. When the adult notices that the baby is happy playing by himself, the adult can refrain from interrupting and keep an eye on the baby from a distance. The adult can encourage or check on the activity after a short period of time.

Materials Needed: None

Setting the Table

Age: 12 to 18 Months

Checklist Skill 4: Helps with Simple Tasks

The toddler is aware of tasks that are performed in the home or in a center setting. One of the tasks that the toddler can help with is setting the table. An adult can show the toddler how to put a napkin out at each place setting. The toddler may be able to put a cup beside each napkin with adult guidance. Show appreciation for the help, even if it is time-consuming!

Materials Needed: Napkins, cups

Love the Baby

Age: 12 to 18 Months

Checklist Skill 7: Carries, Hugs Toys

Toddlers who receive plenty of affection soon learn how to express love. Parents and

caregivers can model loving behavior with a toy and show approval when the baby demonstrates affection. The adult may suggest, "Pat the baby," or, "Love the monkey."

Materials Needed: Toy doll or animal

How Are You Feeling?

Age: 18 to 24 Months

Checklist Skill 1: Uses Words to Make Wants Known or Express Feelings

Toddlers can learn to identify and express their feelings. Adults can facilitate the expression of feelings. When the child is happy, angry, or afraid, the adult can reflect the feeling in conversation by saying, for instance, "_____ is very happy." Or a question can be asked, "Are you feeling mad? Sometimes Mommy feels mad, too." If the toddler's feelings are discussed frequently, the toddler will come to understand that he or she has different feelings and that they are a normal part of living.

Materials Needed: None

Let's Put Toys Away

Age: 18 to 24 Months

Checklist Skill 2: Puts Toys Away on Request

Older toddlers are pleased to be able to respond to requests. A task in which they can easily cooperate is in putting toys away. The toys should have specific locations where they are stored. Adults can talk about where the toys belong and model how to put them away. Although the toddler is not likely to complete the task alone, he will enjoy participating in the task. Help and continued praise are essential elements of the activity.

Materials Needed: Toys

Loving You

Age: 18 to 24 Months

Checklist Skill 3: Engages in Affectionate Interchanges with Adults and Children

The toddler is developing social skills as a part of a group. Adults can encourage affection in the toddler by being loving and affectionate themselves. Toddlers need opportunities to participate in group activities. Adults can encourage affectionate interchanges among toddlers. When adults observe a child being loving toward another, they can praise the child and reward him with an affectionate gesture.

Materials Needed: None

Outings

Age: 18 to 24 Months

Checklist Skill 5: Shows Interest in Exploring New Places

As toddlers overcome their hesitation in the presence of strangers or new places, they enjoy a variety of experiences. They are avid learners and show a continued awareness of new people and places. Take toddlers to parks, puppet shows, informal musical events, and other locations where they can observe and experience. Talk about where you are and what is happening.

Materials Needed: None

Curriculum for the Expressive Arts

Nurturing Expressive Arts in Infants and Toddlers

Is it possible for infants and toddlers to develop an appreciation for the expressive arts? Can infants and toddlers participate in expressive activities? Although their limitations are obvious, these very young children can use the competencies they do possess to develop an awareness of the aesthetic quality of the natural world and man-made expressions of the expressive arts.

Infants and toddlers use their senses and physical actions to experience and understand their world. Adults can foster their awareness of sensory characteristics of their environment by providing activities that introduce them to music, beautiful elements of the natural environment, sculpture that can be touched and felt, pictures that are representative of the work of great artists, and other activities that allow them to interact with quality aesthetic examples of the fine arts.

Infants and toddlers are introduced to music and songs through nursery rhymes and other singing activities that are made a part of their daily activities. They can also be exposed to fine music when riding in the car, playing with toys, and other quiet times of the day. Parents and caregivers can rock or move about with babies in their arms to classical music pieces that are examples of different tempos and moods. Outdoor concerts can be enjoyed with the family when there are also other play opportunities available to provide diversions for short attention spans.

The value of books and story experiences can be extended to aesthetic appreciation. Adults can be selective in the kinds of books to share with infants and toddlers. In addition to concern for durability, as the toddler gains experience in caring for books, adults can look for books with quality illustrations. Picture books that contain reproductions of well-known art can be introduced with an eye to using pictures that will appeal to the very young viewer.

Nursery rhymes and finger plays introduce the very young child to poetry. Singing and telling nursery rhymes and singing songs with the babies permit them to both experience and participate in examples of interesting, melodic language. Repeated experiences with action rhymes such as "Ride a Cock-Horse" and "This Little Piggy Went to Market" allow the child to hear the rhythm and melody of language and the anticipation of physical actions that accompany the rhymes.

Aesthetic appreciation is fostered particularly through the presence of examples of beautiful living things from the natural environment. Fish in an aquarium, flowers, colorful plants, and interesting animals and birds provide infants and toddlers the opportunity to experience beautiful colors and striking combinations of color and shape. The infinite variety in flowers and plants can be viewed and often touched and smelled. Babies' sensory capabilities are stimulated and extended through many experiences with elements of nature.

Although no developmental characteristics on the checklists are specifically related to appreciation for the expressive arts, activities can be planned with attention to the inclusion of aesthetic experiences. The activities that follow can be selected for a development objective; however, they can also be planned with the intention of fostering aesthetic appreciation or expression.

Experiences for Aesthetic Appreciation and Expression in Infants and Toddlers

Looking and Listening

Age: Birth to 6 Months

Checklist Skill (Physical-Cognitive Development) 4: Looks at Suspended Object

Babies enjoy viewing and experiencing suspended objects that move and possibly make sounds. Wind chimes, colorful banners, flags, wind socks, and trees moving in a breeze are possibilities for young infants to experience the movement of suspended objects and living things.

Materials Needed: Natural elements or suspended objects that move

Looking and Listening II

Age: Birth to 6 Months

Checklist Skill (Physical-Cognitive Development) 10: Looks at Objects and Realistic Pictures

In this activity, the baby is active, and objects or natural elements are acted on. The baby is taken to or shown flowers, pets, interesting objects, and other elements in the surrounding environment. Interesting pictures on the walls or in books are viewed and discussed by the adult caregiver.

Materials Needed: Objects, pictures, and animals in the child's environment

Looking at Beautiful Books

Age: 6 to 12 Months

Checklist Skill (Physical-Cognitive Development) 6: Looks at Picture Book

Select books with quality illustrations. When viewing the pages and naming items, attention is given to aesthetic qualities in the pictures.

Materials Needed: Picture books selected for the quality of the illustrations

Moving to Music

Age: 6 to 12 Months

Checklist Skill (Physical-Cognitive Development) 16: Imitates Actions

Play a piece of music that has a distinctive tempo, such as a march. Carry the infant as you move to the tempo. Clap to the tempo, encouraging the baby to clap. Engage babies in this activity frequently, using different types of quality music with various tempos and moods.

Materials Needed: Music

Patty-Cake

Age: 6 to 12 Months

Checklist Skill (Social-Emotional Development) 7: Enjoys and Plays Games with Others

Babies enjoy playing games, particularly games that include rhyming and physical actions. Patty-cake is a favorite that has been handed down for many generations.

> *Patty-cake*
>
> Patty-cake, patty-cake, baker's man [clap baby's hands together].
> Bake me a cake as fast as you can [make whirring motion with baby's hands].
> Roll it out, cut it, and mark it with a "B" [make rolling, cutting motions].
> And put it in the oven for Baby and me [Push baby's hands gently in his or her tummy]!

Materials Needed: None

Watch Me Color!

Age: Twelve to Eighteen Months

Checklist Skill (Physical-Cognitive Development) 11: Scribbles

Felt-tipped markers make exciting strokes in bright colors. Offer the toddler a marker and a piece of paper. Let the toddler experiment with one marker at a time. Or, alternatively, put a newspaper page on the wall, and encourage the toddler to color on it. Supervision is very important. Toddlers may enjoy working in a group situation with a large piece of butcher's paper. The resulting "mural" can be mounted on the wall to be enjoyed by all.

Materials Needed: Paper, newsprint, butcher's paper, nontoxic, washable marking pens

Finger Play Fun

Age: 12 to 18 Months

Checklist Skill (Physical-Cognitive Development) 11: Scribbles

Place a small amount of pudding on a formica-topped table in front of the toddler.

Show the toddler how to experiment with scribbling with the pudding. Tasting is allowed. With older toddlers, use aerosol shaving cream and combine touching and smelling it.

Materials Needed: Pudding, shaving cream, aprons to protect clothing

Roll It Out

Age: 18 to 24 Months

Checklist Skill (Physical-Cognitive Development) 7: Pounds and Rolls Clay

Older toddlers enjoy experimenting with various forms of clay or dough. Introduce them to soft, homemade dough, which is easier to use at first than commercial dough. Let the toddler first experiment with the dough to learn how it feels and is manipulated. Later, introduce a small rolling pin or cylindrical block to roll the dough. Simple cookie cutters are fun, as well as shells, stones, toys, and objects with interesting shapes and surfaces to make prints in the dough.

Materials Needed: Dough, wet clay, cylinders or small rolling pins, cookie cutters, toys, and objects for printing

Nursery Rhymes

Age: 18 to 24 Months

**Checklist Skill (Language Development) 4:
Imitates Adult Speech Without Prompting**

Look at a nursery rhyme book with the toddler. Say the nursery rhymes until they are familiar. After the toddler knows a rhyme, say it, leaving off the last word of each line. Help the toddler supply the missing word. Encourage the toddler to say more of the rhyme with you.

Materials Needed: Nursery rhymes and rhyming storybooks

Sing Along with Me

Age: 18 to 24 Months

**Checklist Skill (Social-Emotional Development) 4:
Sings with Adults or Other Children**

Introduce toddlers to simple songs such as "Row, Row, Row Your Boat," "Mary Had a Little Lamb," and "Jack and Jill." Encourage toddlers to sing along, clap, and dance to the songs. Praise all efforts to participate.

Play simple recorded songs. Sing along with the records and praise the toddler for any attempts to sing along.

Materials Needed: Recorded songs

Rhythm Band

Age: 18 to 24 Months

Checklist Skill: None

Provide toddlers with simple rhythm band instruments such as drums, bells, or sticks. Kitchen utensils such as metal pans and wooden spoons can be substituted. Play recorded music that has a definite beat. Encourage the toddlers to match the beat of the music. Alternate with music with a different type of beat.

Materials Needed: Rhythm band instruments, pots, wooden spoons, recorded music

Summary: A Word of Caution

Infants and toddlers are active learners. They use their physical and sensory capacity to explore and understand their environment. Parents and other adults encourage the learning and development process by responding to the child's emerging abilities expressed in interesting and appropriate activities. An understanding of the developmental characteristics of infants and toddlers provides adults with clues to the types of activities that the child will enjoy and that are beneficial. This chapter has described the types of experiences that can be enjoyed by adults and infants and toddlers together. Suggested activities have been included for each age from the neonate to 2 years of age.

The nature of the very young child's approach to exploring also makes it necessary to be very alert to possible dangers in materials and places used for infant and toddler activities. Because babies rely on their senses and physical abilities to explore the toys and locations in their environment, adults need to use caution and careful planning for experiences and activities. Children under the age of 2, and often older preschool children, put everything in their mouths. This includes bugs, pebbles, paper clips, and anything else that comes their way. They require constant supervision as soon as they develop the ability to grasp. When they are mobile, new dangers are possible. They can pull things off of tables and beds, climb up the

most unlikely places, and get themselves stuck in very small spaces.

Teachers, caregivers, and parents must plan all activities and experiences with these cautions in mind. The infant who enjoys a crib toy dangling overhead becomes the infant who can reach the same toy and choke on it 2 months later. Toddlers are capable of climbing a play structure meant for preschool children and being injured in a fall, or entrapping their head between railings that are too far apart to prevent such a disaster. When planning all activities and selecting materials, adults must consider possible dangers from the materials themselves and from improper use of the materi-als. Materials with toxic paint or other possibly poisonous elements should not be used. No objects that have parts which can be dislodged and swallowed should be placed within the reach of small children. Infants and toddlers use their sensory abilities to explore, but these same capacities, combined with extreme limitations in their understanding of danger, make it necessary for adults to plan experiences and activities with the safety and health of children in mind.

CHAPTER SEVEN

A Developmental Model for Preschool Programs

CHAPTER OBJECTIVES

As a result of reading this chapter, you will be able to:

1. Discuss how goals for quality early childhood education apply to preschool programs.
2. Describe the characteristics of a quality developmental preschool model.
3. Discuss what is meant by a developmental-thematic curriculum.
4. Discuss three roles of developmental-thematic curriculum in the preschool classroom.
5. Design a developmental-thematic unit following the steps described.
6. Explain the role of assessment in preschool programs.

Introduction

This chapter, as well as Chapters 8 and 9, will discuss how to develop curriculum and instruction in preschool classrooms. Chapter 5 and 6 discussed quality programs for infants and toddlers and looked as some examples of programs that have demonstrated quality. Now we are concerned with 3- to 5-year-olds and how we can implement quality programs for preschool children.

In Chapters 2 and 3 we learned about the history of early childhood education and how classical and contemporary theorists have informed early childhood programs. We also discussed quality programs for the twenty-first century and models that are available to guide us in developing our own programs. Reggio Emilia, the Project Approach, High/Scope, and Developmentally Appropriate Practices (DAP) are all examples of excellent programs that can show us how theory has been put into practice. As we proceed into this chapter we will discuss how characteristics of quality programs, theories, and models of programs can give us ideas for developing curriculum for preschool children. We will discuss components of a quality preschool model and then study an example of how to implement curriculum and instruction for preschool children. First, we must distinguish between theories and ideals and the reality of teaching in different preschool settings with "real world" expectations.

The Differences Between Theory and Practice

In discussing the differences between theory and practice in early childhood education, one can describe the main points of major theorists and the implications for how their ideas should influence practice in the classroom. It is also plausible to cogently describe past educational movements and the ways in which schools and early childhood programs set up the curriculum suggested by certain theories and movements.

However, one is much more tentative when discussing what actually happens in the classroom. Individual understanding, acceptance, and use of theories, educational movements, and innovative approaches to instruction are difficult to see in practice in many settings. Teachers are not only bombarded with current trends and fads in education, they also have been influenced by their own experiences and thus function according to how they perceive appropriate education should progress. It is said that we often "parent as we were parented"; we also often "teach the way we were taught," not the way we were taught to teach. The individual teacher's idea of what constitutes a quality early childhood program is strongly affected by her own beliefs and experiences. Although education movements reflect in general the major influences of a period, instructional practice has ranged from one extreme to another—from quite innovative to very traditional. Despite the theories or innovations available to them, teachers throughout the history of schooling in the United States have varied in their conscious and unconscious decisions about how they would teach young children. There continues to be a significant discrepancy between the current theories and models and the way in which those ideas are transformed into practice.

During the progressive period, many primary-grade teachers continued the practice of rote learning and rigid drills. Some kindergarten teachers used Froebelian methods in spite of new progressive ideas about classroom democracy and learning centers. In the decade of the 1970s when elementary classroom teachers were trying open concept methods and team teaching, others continued round robin reading and spelling drills (Weber, 1969).

Thus, it is therefore not surprising that there are wide variations in how early childhood programs are designed and implemented today. Many theories and practices affect current thinking. Teachers, administrators, and other early childhood advocates vary widely in their understanding, acceptance, and willingness to carry out programs that are of the best quality.

We have discussed how teachers reflect their background, training, and biases in their teaching. How teachers teach young children is also influenced by the differences in administrators. Ideally, school principals should be trained to be instructional leaders. More specifically, they should have training in the education of young children in the early childhood years. Unfortunately, more administrators are trained in management of schools rather than in instructional leadership. Even fewer have been trained in the unique characteristics of early childhood education and the kinds of experiences that young children need for their stages of development and styles of learning.

The model proposed in this text reflects the current thinking that curriculum and instruction must be compatible with the developmental abilities of young children. Moreover, the cognitive-developmental theories of Jean Piaget and Lev Vygotsky, which perceive the child as an active learner with intrinsic potential to engage in learning, are the major theoretical influences for the model to be described. However, pure models following one theory rarely exist; thus, an eclectic approach building on various effective innovations and possibilities will be incorporated. Finally, although the possibilities for a quality model can be advocated in a textbook, the practices followed in individual classrooms by future teachers will also differ and will evolve continually, depending on the experiences, influences, and individual efforts of teachers to continue to sort out, interpret, and incorporate past experiences into future innovations and possibilities. Adults and teachers, like children, continue to develop; moreover, the progress of their growth as teachers will depend on their motivation to continue to search for the best ways to expedite preschool children's learning.

Considerations for Developing a Model for Preschool Education

Chapter 3 discussed goals for quality programs in the twenty-first century. Those goals included five indicators that should be considered in preschool program development: (1) principles of child development; (2) balanced curriculum; (3) parent, teacher, and child relationships; (4) assessment and accountability; and (5) diversity in children and families. How do these indicators bridge theory and practice for preschool curriculum?

Principles of Child Development

This chapter is titled "A Developmental Model for Preschool Programs," which indicates that children's development is a foundation for preschool programs. All domains of development—physical, cognitive, and socioemotional—are considered. Arnold Gesell (1925) provided the first norms of development. His studies described typical development by chronological age, which was used as a first guide for what children can do at different ages.

Cognitive Development

Through Piaget, the child's cognitive development was revisited. Piaget believed that cognitive development is influenced by both maturation and the nature of experiences encountered by the preschool child; through these encounters the child reconstructs knowledge. The child absorbs information because of interactions with the world and tries to make sense of the new information using what is known from previous experiences. The child is continually engaged in constructing knowledge by fitting new input into existing information. Each child brings different past experiences to the newly acquired knowledge and will construct further knowledge within an individual perspective.

The preschool child is in Piaget's preoperational stage of development. The preoperational child begins to use mental reasoning and forms concepts about the world. The child is egocentric, but is able to engage in symbolic thought. Children in this stage believe that inanimate objects have lifelike qualities known as *animism*.

Piaget's description of the learning process leads to a better understanding of the child as an active learner. The term *child-centered* instruction used by the models discussed in Chapter 3 has a richer meaning if we incorporate the child as actively reconstructing knowledge with how the teacher prepares the environment and plans experiences to facilitate the learning process. The teacher in a quality developmental preschool builds on a belief in child-centered, active learning and reconstruction of knowledge when organizing the curriculum (Bredekamp & Copple, 1997; Hohmann & Weikart, 1995; Malaguzzi, 1996; Staley, 1998).

Lev Vygotsky added an additional dimension to how the child acquires knowledge. For Vygotsky, cognition is a shared process. Mental processes occur in exchanges between children and between children and adults (Bodrova & Leong, 1996). The mental processes are first acquired in shared experiences and then move to individual internalization. Albert Bandura (Bandura & Walters, 1963) also viewed learning as having a social dimension. He suggested that children learn by observing others.

Active learning within the social context implies that the child learns by active involvement with information and other children or adults. New (1992) proposes that such learning is also contextualized; it has meaning and purpose. Purposeful learning has also been described as authentic learning (Newmann & Associates, 1996). Real-life problem-solving provides the context that is meaningful. For Piaget, the child experiences disequilibrium and uses assimilation and accommodation to construct new concepts. Vygotsky described cognitive conflict within the process of the zone of proximal development. Children first solve the problem with the assistance of others and eventually can resolve acquisition of new knowledge individually.

Social-Emotional Development

Erik Erikson's psychosocial theory of development provides the guide for developmental preschool classrooms. Children between the ages of 3 to 5 are in Erikson's stage of *initiative versus guilt*. Children will develop initiative if they are encouraged to engage in social play and explore. A major task for preschool children is to develop prosocial skills and be able to work and play within a social group. Quality programs are attentive to children's social development and provide guidance that will facilitate success in emotional development and social interactions.

Balanced Curriculum

A balanced curriculum for preschool children means that all domains of development are addressed as well as experiences in the expressive arts. Balance also reflects constructivism in that the child has opportunities to construct and apply knowledge in a meaningful context.

Balance is also achieved through acquisition of necessary skills. Skinner (1953), Bandura (Bandura & Walters, 1963), and Vygotsky (1978) advocated a role for teachers to use direct instruction with children to teach them specific knowledge and skills as part of a curriculum that addresses the whole child. In addition, metacognitive skills permit children to learn more deliberately through reflecting, questioning, and hypothesizing.

Parent, Teacher, and Child Relationships

Quality preschool programs engage teachers and parents as partners in the child's learning. The child is also an active participant in planning, implementing, and reflecting on the learning process. All of the models for early childhood programs discussed earlier view parents as integral participants in the preschool program through parent involvement, participation in planning and evaluation, and possibly in training provided for parents. Reggio Emilia provides an excellent model for these relationships in that parents are engaged in the administration of the schools in addition to participating in program activities (Malaguzzi, 1996). Early Head Start and Head Start Programs also include many roles and services for parents within their programs.

Assessment and Accountability

Quality preschools have a system for assessment that evaluates all facets of the program to include child progress, teaching effectiveness, and program quality. The High/Scope model has a well-established assessment system called the Child Observation Record (COR) (High/Scope Educational Foundation, 1992) that is used to document developmental progress. The DAP guidelines (Bredekamp & Copple, 1997) propose a variety of strategies to document child and program progress. Reggio Emilia and the Project Approach use displays of children's work to document child accomplishments. Later in this chapter we will learn about preschool assesment in more depth.

Diversity in Children and Families

The fifth goal for quality addresses the variety of ethnic, language, cultural, and ability differences in children who attend preschools. Quality programs provide opportunities for children and families to share their own background and learn about other cultures and practices. The curriculum reflects cultural differences as well as the individual learning needs of children with atypical abilities or disabilities. High/Scope and DAP provide guidance for addressing diversity in preschool children.

Characteristics of a Quality Developmental Model

We have just looked at goals for quality early childhood programs for the twenty-first century as they apply to preschool children. Now, we can incorporate these indicators of quality into a model that will be developed in further sections of this chapter. First we will summarize what is meant by a quality preschool program based on what we

have learned from the goals and other models that have been presented.

The general definition of a quality preschool program is that it provides the kinds of experiences that promote learning for children in the preoperational period. Further, the types of activities selected or constructed are compatible with the developmental levels of the students. Because there is an acceptance of a normal variability in development among same-age children, the activities must accommodate successful learning within those variations. Increasing diversity in the needs of children in early childhood programs makes it necessary for teachers to broaden the variety of opportunities available to young children. Including children with disabilities requires that teachers extend the range of development to include the extremes in development that might be present in a classroom. Children who are currently entering preschool classrooms are increasingly culturally diverse. Quality programs must incorporate wider differences in development and accomodate family cultures to meet the needs of current and future populations of young children. In the following sections we will look at quality characteristics of a quality preschool program that are consistent with the goals for quality in the twenty-first century and with the early childhood models we have studied.

A Quality Preschool Model: The Garden Project

The University of Michigan-Dearborn Child Care Center is an example of how a program can draw from theories and model programs to develop their own model of quality. The educators at the center that services children ages 1 through 5 have been influenced by Piaget, Vygotsky, and the Reggio Emilia approach to preschool education.

Children are given many opportrnities to encounter new knowledge through project curriculum. The environment is organized so that children

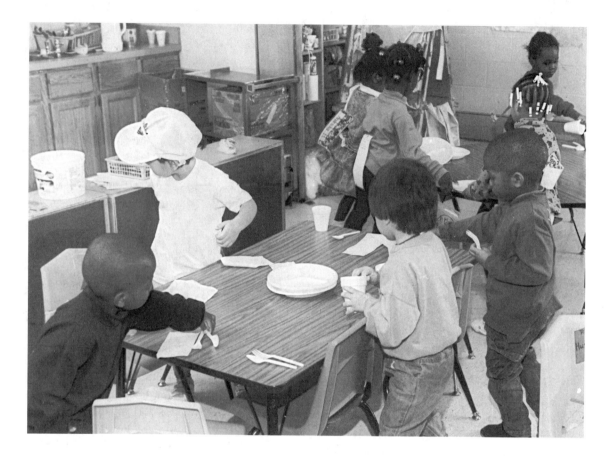

can represent their ideas and understandings in many forms. Classroom areas make it possible for children to use representation in dramatic play, constructions, drawings and other art forms, and through oral and written language.

Long-term projects are based on children's interests. Teachers document children's thinking during projects and use written language transcriptions, audiotapes, videotapes and prints, photographs, overhead transparencies, and children's productions.

The garden project was implemented with children from 4½ to 6 years of age. The project lasted from April to June and was based on children's interest in the spring season and things that were beginning to grow. In addition to class discussions and questions asked by the children, the teacher looked to website information as the process began. The children initiated many of their own investigations and used opportunities for self-initiated activities to gather information and represent what they were learning.

The interest in growing things evolved into an interest in gardens, which led to a trip to a greenhouse. Next, the children studied gardens and then planned and planted their garden using a map of the layout generated on a computer.

Throughout the work on the garden project, children's ideas and discussions drove the direction of activities. As children learned new information, project plans were revised and extended to incorporate new questions and information that emerged (Trepanier-Street, 2000). ✦

Developmentally Appropriate Practices (DAP): Using Principles of Development

The National Association for the Education of Young Children (NAEYC) describes quality preschool programs that provide curriculum that matches young children's development as developmentally appropriate practice (DAP). In the publication *Developmentally Appropriate Practice in Early Childhood Programs* (Revised) (Bredekamp & Copple, 1997), the NAEYC not only defines what is meant by *developmental appropriateness* but provides guidelines for DAP. Professionals working in high-quality programs for young children make decisions that affect the well-being and education of young children based on three kinds of knowledge: (1) what is known about child development and learning; (2) what is known about the strengths, interests, and needs of each individual child in the group; and (3) knowledge of the social and cultural contexts in which children live (Bredekamp & Copple, 1997, p. 9).

The new information on quality programs for young children in *Developmentally Appropriate Practice in Early Childhood Programs* describes current trends in early childhood education that now serve children from diverse cultural and language backgrounds and children who vary in the abilities they bring to the program. To address some criticisms of the 1987 position statement on DAP, the current position statement includes principles that embrace individual diversity in children and practices that are compatible with the complex needs of children. The following statements are given as examples of how this complexity is addressed:

- Children construct their own understanding of concepts, and they benefit from instruction by more competent peers and adults.
- Children benefit from opportunities to see connections across disciplines through integration of curriculum and from opportunities to engage in in-depth study within a content area.
- Children benefit from predictable structure and orderly routine in the learning environment and from the teacher's flexibility and spontaneity in responding to their emerging ideas, needs, and interests.
- Children benefit from opportunities to make meaningful choices about what they will do and learn and from having a clear understanding of the boundaries within which choices are permissible.
- Children benefit from situations that challenge them to work at the edge of their developing capacities and from ample opportunities to practice newly acquired skills and to acquire the disposition to persist.
- Children benefit from opportunities to collaborate with their peers and acquire a sense of being part of a community and from being treated as individuals with their own strengths, interests, and needs.
- Children need to develop a positive sense of their own self-identity and respect for other people whose perspectives and experiences may be different from their own.
- Children have an enormous capacity to learn and an almost boundless curiosity about the world, and they have recognized, age-related limits on their cognitive and linguistic capacities.
- Children benefit from engaging in self-initiated, spontaneous play and from teacher-planned and teacher-structured activities, projects, and experiences. (Bredekamp & Copple*, 1997, p. 23)

---

*From *Developmentally Appropriate Practice in Early Childhood Programs (Revised)* (p. 23), edited by S. Bredekamp and C. Copple, 1997, Washington, DC: National Association for the Education of Young Children. Copyright 1997 by the National Association for the Education of Young Children. Reprinted with permission.

The curriculum should include learning for physical, social, emotional, and cognitive development. Further, learning is described as integrated so that children can make connections between content areas in the curriculum. In other words, the child's learning takes place in a meaningful, purposeful context rather than through isolated skills acquisition. Physical development occurs through unstructured play, whereas aesthetic development results from daily opportunities for creative expression through art and music.

The Inclusive Classroom

The quality developmental model of early childhood education embraces differences in abilities in young children. Public Law 94-142, passed in 1975, mandated that children with disabilities be mainstreamed into the regular classroom as much as possible. More recently, inclusion has begun to replace "mainstreaming." Inclusion is the process of fully integrating the child into the regular classroom. Support services needed for inclusion are provided by the special education teacher, teaching assistants, and supervisors. Sometimes, the children from the regular classroom also work in the special education classroom. Quality programs for young children plan for inclusion and modify curriculum and instruction and the classroom environment to complement the needs and abilities of young children with disabilities. In addition, the teaching and management strategies used match the social and emotional objectives required by individual children. Management strategies used by the teacher are individualized to accommodate the child's needs for appropriate classroom adjustment and behaviors. Not all children will need the same level of teacher management. A child-centered instructional model is desired, with children as active learners; nevertheless,

teacher support and direction will vary for individual children.

The Culturally Responsive Classroom

A quality program for young children is sensitive to the individual culture of the home and the group culture represented by the child's family. Teachers working in a model that is culturally responsive plan curriculum and instruction that reflect the cultures present in the classroom and in the community at large. If children are predominantly from a single culture, then other cultures are included in instructional planning. The interests of the children in the classroom are a focus of the curriculum, and parents are used as resources and support for the instructional program. Parents are active partners in the educational process.

The Integrated Classroom

A quality model of early childhood education results in meaningful learning by interrelating the developmental domains or content areas in curriculum and instruction. An integrated curriculum has historical roots in early childhood education. John Dewey argued that learning could be more meaningful if content areas were blended for curriculum and instruction. Theme studies with real-life activities could lead to more relevant academic study (Dewey, 1938; New, 1992). British Infant Schools in the 1960s and 1970s were based on a child-centered, integrated curriculum that promoted projects developed and done by young children. The work of Piaget featuring child-initiated learning encourages the use of integrated curriculum based on children's ideas. Vygotsky's emphasis on the social nature of learning also supports peer interaction and meaningful activities to support learning.

Today, integrated learning is seen as the vehicle that permits teachers to design curriculum that meets the diversity in children's development and abilities and be responsive to cultural differences. Integrated curriculum makes it possible for curriculum to be child-centered and to accommodate individual interests and for children to learn from each other and the teacher.

The Teacher's Role

The teacher's role is to use the environment and teaching activities to facilitate learning. The teacher has a major role in planning and implementing instruction; however, rather than instruction being primarily teacher-directed, the focus is on possibilities for the child to take the initiative, make selections, and assume active responsibility for learning.

The teacher and children are curriculum designers. Instead of total dependence on commercial, preplanned curriculum kits and teacher guides, such manuals are used as resources, when needed, as the teacher organizes learning activities for the children. Using an integrated approach to curriculum development that evolves from a topic or theme, the teacher and children design activities that will comprise both teacher-guided lessons and child-centered and child-selected activities.

Following Vygotsky's understanding of the teacher's role in the learning process, the teacher includes a variety of teaching strategies. She recognizes that the teacher learns from the child and vice versa. Opportunities for interactions with children working on curriculum projects and activities lead to dynamic expansion of information for both child and teacher (Berk & Winsler, 1995; Bodrova & Leong, 1996). The teacher is an observer of children and uses the zone of proximal development to help children progress in their learning. The teacher motivates children to work on tasks just beyond their independent capabilities through support of the teacher and peers.

Using Piaget's idea of the preoperational child's learning process, the teacher makes a variety of activities available to help the child learn new concepts. If the child is to assimilate and accommodate new knowledge into a schema, then there must be opportunities to actively explore the information; the child must have concrete experiences with the information. The High/Scope Model (Hohmann, Banet, and Weikart, 1979) uses progressions that explain active reconstruction of knowledge. Three of these progressions include concrete to abstract, simple to complex, and experiencing to representing. More recently, the model (Hohmann and Weikart, 1995, p. 38) included ingredients of active learning that summarize the process as follows:

- *Materials.* There are abundant, age-appropriate materials that the child can use in a variety of ways. Learning grows out of the child's direct actions on the materials.
- *Manipulation.* The child has opportunities to explore, manipulate, combine, and transform the materials chosen.
- *Choice.* The child chooses what to do. Since learning results from the child's attempts to pursue personal interests and goals, the opportunity to choose activities and materials is essential.
- *Language from the child.* The child describes what he is doing. Through language, the child reflects on his actions, integrates new experiences into an existing knowledge base, and seeks the cooperation of others in his activities.
- *Adult support.* Adults recognize and encourage the child's reasoning, problem-solving, and creativity. These ingredients are used as a guide to observe children, for planning experiences, and for interacting with children. The concept of active learning is used to describe how adults initiate and use a child-centered program that is group and individually appropriate.

The Role of the Environment

The preschool classroom is arranged into learning or activity centers or areas. Learning areas should allow the children to be able to make choices and carry them out. Materials in each area are or-

ganized to support the curriculum; therefore, the child-initiated activities that are possible in each learning center facilitate self-directed learning and independence. There are many ways to arrange the classroom into centers or areas. The model described here uses the dramatic play center, language center, science and mathematics center, art center, and music and movement center.

The dramatic play center includes housekeeping equipment, an area with blocks and trucks, and provisions for puppetry and dramatic productions. The center's purpose is to provide combinations of opportunities for sociodramatic play. Prop boxes for changing themes and other rotating materials should be available, along with toys and blocks that are permanently located in the center.

The language center is the location for language and literacy development. It includes the library, listening center, materials for writing, and possibly a computer or typewriter. Language experience charts, individual slates, and various sizes of paper are just some items to be found in the center.

The science and mathematics center can incorporate equipment for sand and water play, animals and plants, materials for counting and working with other mathematical concepts, and materials for temporary projects related to topics of study. It can also house a manipulative area for materials such as puzzles and fine motor construction materials.

The art center includes easels and a variety of materials for art activities. Painting supplies, crayons, marking pens, and ample paper supplies are always available, whereas specific activities requiring particular supplies and materials are placed in the center when needed for a few days.

The music and movement center can share an area with a classroom space used for large-group activities. Record, cassette, or disc players, musical instruments, and other props for activities are located adjacent to a large rug area with ample space for physical activities.

Room arrangement is fluid and modifiable. As activities warrant, some areas may be expanded and others reduced or eliminated for a time. Teacher observation of center activities may discern a need for more extensive rearrangement because children are using space differently than anticipated. The main point is that the environment should support the children's choices and activities, not dictate them. Because the purpose of the room environment is to facilitate active learning with materials available to encourage the child's participation in self-initiated learning, the work or learning center areas are not to be used as a reward. The environment is a key to active learning; the teacher, as facilitator and resource person, uses the learning areas to encourage the progressions in the child's reconstruction of knowledge.

The teacher understands that peer collaboration and interaction support the acquisition of new knowledge. The child learns in a social environment; therefore, the teacher organizes the environment to promote peer group problem solving to include peer tutoring, cooperative learning activities, and group play (Vygotsky, 1978).

The Role of Play

The role of play is a most difficult aspect of young children's development and learning for many educators and parents to understand. Play is sometimes perceived as idleness or useless activity when contrasted with learning. For many parents and teachers, learning is associated with sitting quietly and listening to the teacher or working preschool workbook pages. To the contrary, play provides opportunities for active exploration of information, social interactions, and physical activity essential to learning and development. Furthermore, a growing body of research supports the role of play in various types of development. A few examples of activities that demonstrate the relationships between play and learning are described next.

In cognitive development, sociodramatic play and construction play may have positive relationships to IQ scores (Johnson, Ershler, & Lawton,

1982). It is also proposed that the problem-solving behaviors used in play influence general problem-solving abilities (Bruner, 1972; Simon & Smith, 1983). Vygotsky researchers determined that children's mental skills are at a higher level of the zone of proximal development during play (Berk, 1994; Elkonin, 1978). Smilansky and Shefatya (1990) correlated growth in dramatic play with gains in cognitive and social development and school-related skills. There is also a relationship between creativity and play. Lieberman (1965) conducted research that showed a possible link between play, creativity, and intelligence. Lieberman (1977) further linked creativity with early playfulness. Divergent thinking has also been linked with imaginary play (Hutt & Bhavnani, 1976; Lieberman, 1965).

Play has an important role in the development of language. As the child engages in object play, language is attached to meanings and relationships (Frost, 1992). Language is used during play to imitate adult speech, for sociodramatic play, and to organize and manage play (Smilansky, 1968; Wortham, 2001b). Young children also play with the language itself (Garvey, 1977). For example, babies sometimes sing themselves to sleep with rhyming utterances; preschoolers make up words and names and try to outdo each other with outrageous verbalizations.

Play facilitates social development. Group dramatic play requires that children plan and interact if they are to engage successfully in pretend or make-believe play episodes. As a result, sociodramatic play helps children to practice and perfect their social skills (Johnson et al., 1999). Social interaction in turn supports learning. New developmental and learning accomplishments emerge in group play followed by individual internalization by individual children (Berk, 1994; Bodrova & Leong, 1996).

More obviously, play facilitates physical development. The basic locomotor skills refined during the preschool years are acquired through daily activities involved in indoor and outdoor play. Larger and fine motor skills are also practiced

through play activities (Jambor, 1990; Mullen, 1984; Wortham, 2001b).

Play provides the experiences that enable the child to integrate and make sense of the vast amounts of information to which he is exposed each day. Because the child is in charge of play events, he can use sociodramatic, physical, and aesthetic play activities to process and understand new knowledge. The child can also practice physical, social, and language skills. The teacher will want to use indoor and outdoor play periods to support development and learning. Centers in the classroom are organized for sociodramatic play, construction play, fine motor play, and aesthetic play. Outdoor play environments can offer more than physical and social play opportunities by including sociodramatic play props and aesthetic and creative activities. Cognitive development can be encouraged through gardening, pet observation and care, and provisions for group dramatic and

literacy activities. Science experiments and natural science activities can be easily engaged in outdoors. If young children are to understand their world, the teacher needs to use the natural environment that is accessible nearby.

The Role of the Daily Schedule

Children should work individually or in small groups most of the time. Nevertheless, there will be times during the day when teachers will find that whole-group activities are useful and appropriate. The daily schedule will provide opportunities for children to plan and carry out projects and other learning and play activities. The teacher can conduct small-group and whole-group activities, and children enjoy both indoor and outdoor activities. When planning the daily schedule, the teacher will want to achieve a balance between teacher-directed and child-initiated activities. Various combinations of schedule components can be used. In this model, I will describe schedule components as large-group time, center time, small-group time, and outdoor time.

Large-group time provides opportunities for activities in which the whole group of children can participate. It may occur several times during the day, especially early in the day and after the completion of center and lesson activities. Large-group time can be used for sharing experiences, discussing plans for the day, reviewing concepts learned earlier in the year, performing music and movement activities, telling stories, reviewing what has been accomplished, and transition time between activities.

Center time occurs so that children may work in learning centers. This time is preceded by a planning period, when individuals or small groups of children describe what they will accomplish in the center. The teacher may prepare the children for center time by introducing the available activities and their purposes. The teacher may also want to give instructions on the proper use of a new toy, for example, or on material placed in the center for the first time. Some center activities may be expected to be used by all children; others can be the child's choice. The teacher also uses preparation for center time to guide children who have difficulty in making choices. During the center time, the teacher interacts with the children and assists them in making the best use of their activities. The teacher may work in a center with a small group if assistance is warranted. After center time, there is a period for cleaning up and restoring center materials to their proper location. A large-group activity can follow center time to review what the children did and how they carried out their plans.

Small-group time offers an opportunity for the teacher to guide a learning activity or engage in direct instruction. Working with a group of four or five children at a time, the teacher engages in work with concepts, discusses theme topics, conducts hands-on activities such as cooking or special art projects, and teaches lessons. Small-group times can be scheduled during center times, with the teacher alternating between facilitating center activities and conducting small-group activities. Outdoor time provides an opportunity to play or work outdoors. If the outdoor environment is perceived as a classroom, some outdoor periods may be used for large-group and small-group instruction and others for free play. Physical activities, both structured and unstructured, are planned for outdoor periods, as are field trips, neighborhood walks, and other curriculum-related activities.

Planning and Managing Instruction

In this section, planning and carrying out developmental instruction are discussed. The approach that children learn best when learning is purposeful and meaningful is used to describe planning thematic or integrated curriculum that will maximize the possibilities for children to make connections between new information and knowledge that they already understand. Using the daily schedule to set up integrated learning is also discussed.

How does the teacher plan and implement a quality instructional program that complements the developmental levels of the children? I have described the characteristics of a program designed for early childhood. Now I will explore how the classroom teacher designs and implements a quality program for preschool students. Teachers not only must consider the general developmental characteristics of their students as a group, but they must also consider the unique qualities of each individual student. Teachers analyze the diversity among their students in terms of cultural and economic backgrounds and in terms of individual differences in interests and abilities. If children with special needs are assigned to the classroom, then their individual limitations and potential are also considered in planning appropriate activities.

Many resources are available for determining goals and objectives for curriculum in early childhood classrooms. Sources for curriculum development can include developmental checklists, state-mandated curriculum objectives, commercial curriculum objectives related to adopted basal materials, and locally determined curriculum goals. All these resources help the teacher understand which curriculum goals are appropriate or expected in the educational setting where he or she teaches (Seefeldt, 1997).

The way in which one plans and manages the curriculum to achieve the desired goal can take various forms. If the program is to be developmentally appropriate, however, the curriculum design must facilitate successful learning that accommodates developmental differences within a child-centered or child-initiated approach. If learning is to be integrated and purposeful for the child, the approach for curriculum design must incorporate those characteristics. In this text, *developmental-thematic* is the term used to describe a curriculum that meets these characteristics.

Understanding Developmental-Thematic Curriculum

Teachers have been designing curricula based on themes for a long time. Every college student can remember studying Indians, community helpers, or another topic during his or her elementary school years. John Dewey introduced thematic curriculum with his project approach during the Progressive era. He felt that the classroom should be a miniature democracy and children should be engaged in projects that would help them understand their role in their community (Cremin, 1961). Themes were used for the meaningful projects that Dewey believed would engage children in learning for a purpose. Projects were activities planned by the students with a practical purpose, and problem-solving was the process used to conduct projects. For example, in making plans for a garden, students were required to make their own decisions regarding how to design the layout and plant the seeds (Parker & Temple, 1925). Later, Dewey lamented that his project approach had been reduced to a collection of activities, rather than useful experiences that would have a real purpose for the child's understanding. He described the contrast between aimless utilization of activities collected by teachers and, on the other hand, working with problems that emerged from the children's experience and were within their capacity to understand the relation of means and ends (Dewey, 1938).

Recently, Dewey's ideas have resurfaced with the new understanding of the child's role in the learning process that we have gained from Piaget. It has been called the *project approach* (Katz & Chard, 2000), *integrated learning* (New, 1992), and the concept of *thematic curriculum* (Seefeldt, 1997), among various other names. The new advocates of this type of curriculum such as Reggio Emilia, stress not only the interrelated nature of learning but also the importance of child involvement in planning and implementing the projects (Edwards, Gandini, & Forman, 1996). Moreover, the format for theme planning facilitates an understanding by both teacher and students of how different content areas are related to each other. The format demonstrates how individual activities can support learning in several areas of development and content areas.

What then is thematic curriculum? Essentially, it is a curriculum planned around a theme that students have identified as a learning topic or that the teacher has selected based on children's interests or from the curriculum. The learning activities and projects selected for the theme reflect how the students want to explore the topic or the kinds of activities they have identified that will help them acquire the knowledge or skills related to the theme. As an alternative, the teacher might do some initial brainstorming about unit activities, and the students would either select which activities are most desirable or expand on the teacher's ideas. As planning proceeds, the teacher and students use a process called *webbing*, which involves brainstorming about the possible activities and analyzing the ways in which content areas of the curriculum are being utilized or incorporated into the theme or unit plans.

The curriculum has also been identified as developmental in the early childhood years. By now, the implications of the developmental nature of thematic curriculum should be obvious. The curriculum not only will provide for integrated, purposeful learning but also will provide for the development of the students (Bredekamp, 1987; Bredekamp & Copple, 1997). In choosing the kinds of activities to design for the project or theme, the teacher will consider how learning is furthered in content areas of the curriculum; more important, however, is that the focus should be on how physical, social, and cognitive development are involved in the activities. In addition, the activities selected and developed will be planned to accommodate a range of developmental levels, so that all students will have successful experiences because of being actively involved in the theme projects (Katz & Chard, 2000). Consideration of development is an integral part of the planning and implementation process.

Roles of Developmental-Thematic Curriculum

How does developmental-thematic curriculum fit into school routines? Ideally, it could be the organizational pattern for the entire school program. It is easy to conceptualize how such a curriculum could be used in a developmentally appropriate setting for the total program; in effect, it could be used to determine the environmental arrangement, daily schedule or routines, and learning activities that will be provided in a series of units or themes throughout the year.

Many early childhood teachers, particularly those in public school settings, lack the flexibility to fully determine their schedules. For them, incorporation of the thematic-developmental curriculum into their program might take different forms. To explore several possibilities, I will discuss the developmental-thematic curriculum in terms of a primary framework for curriculum, as one of several instructional methods, and as an occasional resource for exploring special topics.

Developmental-Thematic Curriculum as the Basic Framework

When themes can be used to design the total curriculum for a preschool program, they become the framework, or scaffold, for the program. The teacher studies the educational goals or objectives for the program and correlates them with the units or themes developed during the year. Planning is carried out with the students providing their ideas and input; however, the teacher also studies the total plan and incorporates or modifies activities to ensure that desired goals are accomplished. The daily schedule for a block of days and, more probably, weeks is devoted to implementation of theme projects and activities. The time allotted in the yearly calendar is flexible and can be modified according to student interest and possible additional projects or activities that might arise during the theme. While one theme is ending, the planning process can begin for the next theme. Teachers and children can be gathering resources in anticipation of the initiation of the new theme as the planning stage comes closer to the implementation stage. In this approach, cycles of planning, implementation, and evaluation of completed themes and projects are ongoing throughout the year.

Developmental-Thematic Curriculum as One of Several Approaches

Some teachers may find themselves in a situation where a schedule for preschool already exists and must be followed. The teacher does not have the opportunity to totally determine the instructional methods that can be used. Predetermined curriculum materials might be required to provide consistency within a school or school district. Perhaps the teacher may plan and modify the schedule and curriculum within limits but may not abandon district expectations entirely.

In this type of program, the teacher tries to fit themes or projects within existing instructional practices. Project or theme curriculum is planned and organized to integrate the curriculum; however, some elements alternate with other required work. Similarly, activities or projects might have to be accomplished during scheduled times devoted to particular content areas. The teacher and students work on projects and theme activities in a consistent manner, but theme units complement rather than replace existing instructional practices in the school. Given time constraints in many schools, scheduling must be carefully planned to accomplish both theme and separate learning objectives. This approach of including themes into the curriculum might be more difficult than the first total approach; nevertheless, teachers have found that with some initial effort, they can comfortably include thematic instruction and increase its use as they become more perceptive about implementing it in a variety of combinations within the daily schedule.

Developmental-Thematic Curriculum as an Occasional Resource

Some teachers, particularly beginning teachers, may find it easier to plan only occasional units until they become more secure in managing children and the curriculum. In this context, the teacher follows the routines and curriculum in the school setting and plans a thematic unit for a special occasion or topic. A holiday or social studies topic is used as the theme. An integrated, developmental curriculum is planned around the theme, but projects and activities occur together with a subject area each day until the unit is completed. Once a unit has been completed, there may be a period before another unit is planned and set up. This approach might be considered similar to existing models of unit planning; to the contrary, it differs in the conscious inclusion of interrelated learning activities and accommodation for variations in development among the students. Another difference is the emphasis on child-planned and

child-initiated projects and opportunities for purposeful problem solving.

Each of these approaches has merit. Regardless of which approach a teacher decides to use, the principles of developmentally appropriate learning can be maintained. However, carrying out developmental-thematic curriculum as one of several approaches or as an occasional resource rather than as the basic framework provides fewer opportunities for the children to see relationships or connections in learning. The teacher will want to begin using developmental-thematic curriculum at a level that is comfortable; then, as experience makes it possible to see new avenues for integrated instruction, the teacher can increase the number of times themes are used and improve the way in which themes are planned and used in the classroom.

Designing Developmental-Thematic Curriculum Units

How, then, do the teacher and students go about planning a developmental-thematic curriculum that meets all the goals of an integrated approach to learning? Designing such a unit of work can be accomplished by following a sequence of activities from planning to implementation. The sequence begins with selection of the topic. It goes on through brainstorming, organizing ideas into a web, selecting objectives or outcomes and activities for a balanced curriculum, describing the interrelatedness of the developmental activities in the curriculum, and, finally, planning and scheduling for curriculum activities.

Selecting a Theme Topic

There are many ways to select a theme for study. In past decades, it was common for the social studies curriculum in elementary schools to be organized into themes or units. In some school systems, teachers designed the thematic curriculum to be used at each grade level.

In this context, theme topic selection is intended to be more about the teacher's and students' interests and needs within the individual classroom. If the teacher selects the topic, she may determine it from some aspect of the curriculum that needs to be covered. Ideally, the children initiate the topic, and the teacher helps them plan and carry out what is to be learned. The topic is planned to include and interrelate developmental areas in the projects and activities that are to take place. The teacher might also initiate a topic because of some event that has occurred that has meaning for the students. For example, a student in a classroom for 4-year-olds brought a pet gerbil to school. Noting the children's interest in the gerbil, the teacher and students planned the unit based on learning about gerbils and their care. In Reggio Emilia schools, thematic curriculum is described as "projects." The teacher and children work as partners to uncover the desired information. Children work together in small groups to accomplish the project work. In this context, project-based curriculum has the following characteristics (Abramson, Robinson, & Ankenman, 1994–1995, p. 198):

- The teacher role of both facilitator and partner in learning
- Topic selection based on student interests and experiences
- Collaboration among students, teachers, and parents
- Project content emerging from students' evolving understanding and not from a set of prepackaged activities.
- Multiple experiences with media to represent understandings
- Repetition of activities for different purposes
- Extended period of time devoted to a project
- Small-group rather than whole-class projects

Topics should have relevance for the population of students in an individual classroom and the area in which they live. Children living in southern regions of the United States or in Hawaii would have a different understanding of winter than would children living in northern continental states or Alaska. The cultural diversity of children in a classroom would affect the study of many topics; in addition, family differences would affect the planning of units that involve family traditions.

As much as possible, children should be the source of the topic. Students might share a bit of news that is of interest to the entire class. For example, Kevin, a student in a kindergarten classroom, brought a brightly painted clay piggy bank to school to share with the class. A general discussion about banks that other children had at home led to a unit on saving money in small and large banks.

Brainstorming a Topic

Once the topic has been selected, the teacher and students are ready to explore the information and activities that can expand their knowledge. In the case of preschool children, such a discussion might be very general, with the teacher culling suggestions from comments made by the children about the topic or guiding the discussion with ideas of her own. After gaining input from the children, the teacher can continue the brainstorming process herself.

The focus of the brainstorming should be on creating ideas for working with the topic and developing or identifying resources that will support the theme. Both teacher and students will discuss what the children want to learn about the topic; also, the teacher will try to expand the brainstorming session to include information that might be acquired as part of unit activities. The teacher will list all of the possible activities that relate to the topic. Katz and Chard (2000) suggest writing each of the possibilities on slips of paper. Whatever the method used, once the possible activities have been identified, it is time to develop a web.

A thematic unit on the topic of leaves can be used as an example. The unit was developed by Lisa, a student teacher, in response to students' curiosity about fall leaves that they were collecting on the playground. Lisa and her students live in New England, where the fall season is highly characterized by leaves turning colors and falling from the trees. (If the children lived in Hawaii or

Arizona, a different element of nature might have been chosen for the unit topic.) In designing her unit, Lisa was required to follow a unit plan format that included the following components:

Unit topic:

Overview or rationale for the unit:

Developmental stage:

Brainstorming web:

List of activities (categorized as teacher-directed, teacher-child initiated, or child-initiated):

Concepts, skills, and processes:

Unit objectives:

Summary of integrated activities:

Lisa first listed some ideas that she and the students generated about things they could do to learn about leaves. In her initial discussion with the children, they were able to make a list of the following activities:

Take a nature walk to find leaves.

Visit a botanical garden.

Draw leaves.

Rake leaves.

Make pictures with leaves.

Compare leaves.

"Write" stories about leaves.

Lisa studied the original ideas and continued the brainstorming process to expand the thematic unit possibilities. She further organized activity ideas into activities using leaves and activities about leaves. Her expanded list of possible activities included the following:

Take a nature walk.

Visit botanical garden.

Activities Using Leaves

Create leaf rubbings.

Describe characteristics of leaves.

Count sets of leaves.

Make leaf collages.

Measure leaves.

Group leaves by common characteristics.

Activities About Leaves

Dictate stories about leaves.

Dictate stories about nature walk and visit to botanical garden.

Make sponge-print pictures of trees.

Discuss leaves that are food sources.

Sing songs about leaves.

Listen to stories about leaves.

Participate in music/movement activity (e.g., pretending to be fall leaves).

Developing a Brainstorming Web

Lisa was now ready to make a brainstorming web (see Figure 7.1). She focused on developmental areas of the curriculum and placed all of the ideas in the appropriate categories of the web. Most of the activities fit into two or more categories because developmental areas were integrated in the activity. Lisa had not yet determined which of the activities would be developed for the unit. She was looking for a balance in developmental areas and was considering which activities had the most merit and the highest potential for providing meaningful, purposeful experiences that were developmentally appropriate for her students. She again worked with the children to select the activities that would be included.

Selecting Unit Activities

The next step in planning the thematic curriculum is to select the activities that will be used for the unit. The ideas and activities that were developed during the brainstorming activity and located on the brainstorming web are considered for inclusion in the final unit design. In addition, possible combinations of activities or expansion of original activity ideas are contemplated as the teacher and

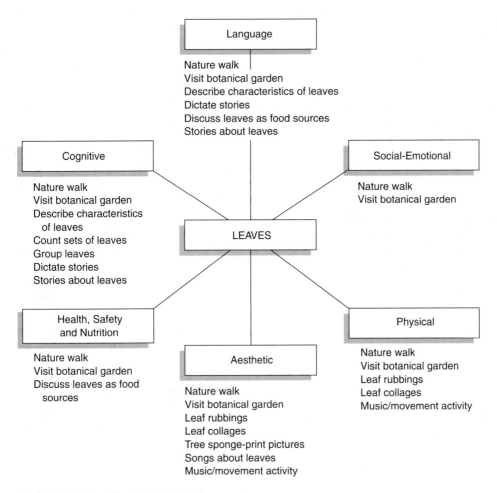

FIGURE 7.1 Brainstorming web

children begin to consider how the activities will be scheduled and set up.

Lisa decided that the leaves unit would be appropriate for a week of study. She decided that taking a field trip to the botanical garden was beyond the scope of her possibilities for activities, but taking a nature walk to find and gather leaves on the school grounds and nearby park would be a suitable way to initiate unit activities and projects. She and the children also decided to focus unit activities around the fall leaves themselves rather than to broaden the unit to include more about leaves.

The number of activities was narrowed to 12, and a final activity list was made. In the process of planning at this stage, she and the children decided that making a book of unit activities would be a good project. The tree sponge-print pictures could be used for the cover of individual books. Lisa then determined whether the activities were teacher-directed, child-initiated, or a combination of teacher- and child-initiated. She wanted to ensure that there was a balance between teacher- and child-directed activities. Lisa's final list was as follows:

1. Take a nature walk, then dictate stories about the walk (teacher-child-initiated).
2. Discuss the characteristics of leaves (teacher-directed).
3. Count, measure, and group leaves by common characteristics (teacher-child-initiated).
4. "Write" stories about leaves (child-initiated with teacher assistance).
5. Participate in movement to music (teacher-directed).
6. Sing songs about leaves (teacher-directed).
7. Rake leaves (teacher-child-initiated).
8. Draw pictures of leaves (child-initiated).
9. Create leaf rubbings (child-initiated).
10. Make leaf collages (child-initiated).
11. Make sponge-print pictures of trees (teacher-child-initiated).
12. Make individual unit booklets (teacher-directed).

Determining Concepts, Skills, and Processes

Lisa wanted to be clear about the concepts and skills that children would learn from the unit on leaves. She also wanted to review learning processes that would engage the children in interacting with information about fall leaves. She made a list that could include the following:

1. Some leaves change colors in the fall before they fall from the trees.
2. Leaves grow in different sizes, shapes, and textures.
3. Leaves can be used for counting.
4. Leaves can be sorted by common characteristics.
5. As a result of sorting leaves, we can describe their characteristics.
6. There are many ways that we can express our understanding and appreciation of fall leaves. We can make leaf rubbings, draw pictures of leaves, make leaf collages, sing songs about leaves, and move to music like leaves.
7. We can write about our experiences with leaves.

Describing Developmental-Thematic Unit Objectives

Once the teacher has determined which activities and projects will be incorporated into the unit to accomplish what both students and teachers want to learn about a topic, the teacher studies the activities to identify more specifically what will be learned. The teacher has a major decision to make: What type of objective should be used to describe the purpose for the desired learning? Traditionally, preservice students have been taught to use performance objectives (Mager, 1975). The performance objective has three elements: the behavior that the learner will exhibit, the conditions under which the behavior will occur, and the standard of performance that is minimally acceptable. For example, one of Lisa's activities for the unit on leaves was to count groups of leaves. Lisa could write an objective for the activity as follows: "As a result of a lesson using leaves for counting, the student will be able to count sets up to 5 with 100 percent accuracy." In this example, the behavior is the student's ability to count, the condition is the use of leaves in a counting activity, and the level of desired performance is 100 percent accuracy.

There is disagreement in the field of education, particularly in early childhood education, as to whether performance objectives are always appropriate for describing learning objectives for young children. Critics of performance objectives propose that they are too specific and result in breaking curriculum into fragmented elements that can be meaningless. Furthermore, an integrated curriculum that emphasizes the child's opportunity to initiate and conduct learning activities does not lend itself to description by performance objectives (Seefeldt, 1993). Proponents of the use of performance objectives point out that many schools are predominantly teacher-directed; furthermore, school districts and state education agencies might require the use of performance objectives. Schools that adopt Madeline Hunter's Instructional Theory Into Practice (ITIP) (Hunter,

1979) model are examples of settings where performance objectives are required. Individualized Education Programs (IEPs) that are used to plan curriculum objectives for children with special needs also require the use of performance objectives (Orlich, Harder, Callahan, Kauchak, Pendergrass, & Keogh, 1990).

In this text, I propose a compromise between the two positions in writing learning objectives. The standard of performance will be omitted because learning processes are more important than achieving a specific level of performance; however, the condition and desired behavior will be retained. The circumstances under which the learning occurs can be derived from the planned activities. The behaviors will be those that the child can exhibit as a result of engaging in the planned activities.

Lisa determined that as a result of engaging in unit activities in the leaves unit, her students would acquire specific concepts and abilities. The items in the behavior component of her objectives were categorized as what the students could understand and what they would be able to do. She listed them as follows:

1. As a result of taking a nature walk to find leaves, students will understand that leaves change color and fall from trees in the fall.
2. As a result of taking a nature walk to find leaves, students will understand that there are many kinds of trees and leaves.
3. Following an activity to examine and discuss the characteristics of leaves, students will understand that leaves are different colors, shapes, and sizes.
4. As a result of participating in an activity to examine and discuss the characteristics of leaves and opportunities to group leaves by a student-identified characteristic, students will understand that leaves can be organized by common characteristics.
5. As a result of participating in an activity to examine and discuss the characteristics of leaves, students will be able to describe comparative characteristics of leaves.
6. As a result of participating in group activities with fall leaves, students will be able to "write" (emergent writing) stories about leaves.

7. As a result of participating in teacher-directed and center activities with fall leaves, students will be able to count, measure, and group leaves using their own criteria.

8. As a result of working with leaves, paper, and paste in the art center, students will be able to create leaf collages.

9. As a result of working with leaves, paper, and crayons in the art center, students will be able to create leaf rubbings.

10. As a result of working with sponges cut into the shape of leaves, tempera paint, and paper, students will be able to create sponge-print pictures.

11. As a result of completing art activities, students will be able to make a book of unit activities about fall leaves.

12. Students will be able to work cooperatively in groups to rake leaves on the playground.

13. Students will be able to use appropriate behaviors during the nature walk.

Describing Integrated Unit Activities

The final step in formulating a unit plan is to write a summary of the activities that will be included in unit experiences. There are two purposes for briefly explaining the activity: to preview what will happen during the activity, and to understand how the activity provides for integration of learning.

Lisa wrote such an explanation for her unit activities. Two of those activities were described as follows:

Nature Walk

The students will be given large grocery bags and will take a walk on the playground and in the park next to the school. We will observe the different types of trees we see, the variety of leaves on the ground, and other natural characteristics that might be seen. Students will collect leaves in their bags to be used in later activities. They will also be encouraged to collect seeds and other items they might find. The teacher will have hand magnifiers available to examine interesting aspects of the environment. The activity involves cognitive development, using concepts in science. It integrates language development in the discussions that take place during the activity and social development in the use of appropriate behavior on the walking tour and social interactions used during the experience. Large and fine motor skills are used in the process of taking the walk and collecting leaves and other objects. Safety must be observed. Aesthetic development is integrated within the discussion during the walk.

Leaf Collages

Leaves and other natural items collected on the nature walk will be located in the art center. Students will be instructed on how they can create their own collage using glue to paste items on a piece of paper. The activity provides for aesthetic development as the children construct their creation. Fine motor skills are integrated when the children manipulate the materials and use the glue.

After Lisa had completed the steps in her unit design, she was ready to write her final unit plan using the format mentioned earlier. She described her rationale for developing the unit and the general development level (preoperational) of the students.

Planning Lesson Activities

Once the final unit design is completed, the teacher needs to plan the activities in detail. The unit objectives addressed by the activity, a description of the procedures for the activity, the materials needed to conduct the activity, and plans for evaluation are all considered. Students who are preparing to be teachers might be required to develop activities into lesson plans.

Lisa was required to use lesson plans for her unit on leaves. She followed a lesson plan format that included the following:

Title of plan:

Concepts, skills, processes:

Objectives addressed:

Concepts, skills, and processes used:

Activity procedures:
    Large-Group Activity
    Small-Group Activity
      Center Activities
      Cooperative Learning Activity

Materials/resources needed:

Assessment:
    Teacher Assessment:
    Activity Assessment:
    Student Assessment:

When planning a lesson, the teacher first identifies the activity by giving it a title. If more than one activity is incorporated into a plan, then the title is broader to reflect activities and objectives addressed. After determining the title, the teacher describes the concepts, skills, and processes being addressed in the lesson. The category of concepts, skills, and processes includes those described in the unit plan that are applicable to the lesson.

Under the category of objectives addressed, the teacher takes the unit objectives that relate to each individual lesson and cites them in this context.

The activity procedures describe in detail the activities to be undertaken. The teacher first de-termines which types of activities the lesson will include. Large-group activities are used with the whole class. This type of activity can be used for field trips, class discussions, and other experiences that benefit all children. Small-group activities are selected when lesson activities warrant including about five children at a time so that all can be equally involved and given individual attention. Center activities are chosen when opportunities for child-selected experiences are indicated. Most center activities should be possible for the child to engage in individually or with other children with some prior direction from the teacher. At times, the teacher or another adult is present to guide activities in a center. Some activities will involve cooperative activities that are directed by the children with the guidance of the teacher.

Whichever type of activity is chosen, the procedures are planned and described in three parts: (1) introduction, or planning; (2) development of lesson or activity; and (3) summary, or review. The introduction, or planning, procedure is the beginning of the activity. If the activity is teacher-directed, the teacher plans how the lesson will be introduced. If it is the first step for an activity that includes child planning, plans are made to solicit input from individual children or the group. If the activity is a center activity, the teacher uses this opportunity to give instructions for use of centers, and children are enabled to make their plans for selection and use of centers.

The development of the lesson or activity follows the beginning step of the learning experience. In this part of the lesson plan, the teacher describes plans for the main content of the lesson. The sequence of the lesson is explained, including questions and procedures. If a center activity is set up, the teacher serves as a facilitator as children engage in their selected activities.

The last step of the learning experience, the summary, or review, is used to conclude the activity or reach closure. If the teacher is conducting an activity, the last step is a process for summarizing the lesson. More important, it is an opportunity for the children to review and provide feedback on their understanding and reaction to the lesson. If center experiences are the type of activity used, this is the time when students conclude their activity and put materials away. Then they meet with the teacher and discuss how they carried out their plans for the centers and review the experience. If cooperative activities are included, groups report their work to the rest of the class.

In addition to planning for the body of the lesson, the teacher needs to anticipate what will be needed for successful implementation of the selected activities. In the materials/resources section of the plan, the teacher identifies what will be needed in the way of human, technological, and other materials for the lesson. Books, art materials, adult assistants, cassette tapes, videotapes, and food items are just a few of the items that would be listed as materials or resources. Needed equipment such as cooking utensils, projectors, and computers are listed.

Adapting Lesson Plans for Diversity

An important step in planning is to determine how modifications might be made in the projects, lessons, and independent activities for children in the classroom who represent various types of diversity. Are there children with language differences in the classroom who need help with vocabulary related to the unit? Do some of the activities need to be conducted in the child's home language? Better yet, is the thematic unit meaningful to children with language diversities? Does it have a multicultural dimension that is a motivating context for language use (Abramson Robinson, & Ankenman, 1994–1995)? Or, are there children in the classroom with physical limitations that might preclude their participation in an activity? How can the activity be modified for these children? It might be necessary to have an adult or other children assist those children with physical limitations in some activities or projects. Can a child with disabilities be paired with another child who can collaborate to engage in some activities? The teacher will need to think through unit

experiences that require assistance or modification for children with diverse abilities.

The last component of the lesson plan is assessment. The teacher plans how the lesson is to be appraised. Within the plan for assessment, a description is given of how the teacher's role, the activity itself, and the children's learning will be evaluated. More information on the role of assessment and how it can be conducted follows.

Planning for Assessment

This section will address how curriculum and instruction are assessed as they relate to individual lesson plans. In keeping with the assessment purposes of the lesson plan just discussed, I will describe the process of assessment of the teacher's effectiveness, the activity itself, and the children's learning.

Assessment of the Teacher. Teachers will want to conduct ongoing assessment of their effectiveness in working with the children and facilitating the desired learning. Reflection following small-group and large-group instruction can be conducted to determine success in group management, student interest in the activity, effectiveness of the materials used, and appropriate timing of the length of the activity. The teacher can note positive and negative aspects of teaching activities to constantly improve teaching and management behaviors.

Regarding Lisa's lessons, she determined how she would assess her effectiveness by asking herself specific questions. Did she adequately prepare the children to engage in the activity to make leaf collages? In talking about the leaves, did the manner in which she guided the discussion enable the children to understand how to use descriptive words to discuss the leaves?

Assessment of the Activity. Activity and curriculum assessment in preschool programs should be ongoing, whether the learning experiences are part of a thematic unit or included as a separate component of instruction. The teacher should reflect on the appropriateness of her curriculum choices before using them in the preschool classroom. Following the use of commercially designed material or participation in a teacher-designed activity, the teacher should reflect on the effectiveness of the material and activity in accomplishing objectives. Also to be considered is student interest in the activity. Decisions to use the material or activity in the future should be based on an assessment after the activity has been completed. In Lisa's sample lessons, she wanted to know if the children enjoyed making leaf collages. She also wanted to know if the activity was appropriate for her preschool children. In the lesson on describing leaves, she wanted to evaluate whether her plan for conducting the lesson was effective with her students. She also wanted to find out if the leaves she used were good samples for the children to describe, as well as whether her questions to guide the children resulted in productive descriptions in their responses. Figures 7.2 and 7.3 represent two of Lisa's lesson plans.

Assessment of Student Learning. The teacher will also want to determine if students successfully mastered the learning objectives of the unit or other developmentally based curriculum. After working on activities with the new concepts or skills, the teacher will want to conduct an assessment of individual understanding; the teacher will thus observe independent activities or tasks during a small-group time after having provided the children with sufficient opportunities with the materials.

The teacher will need to determine if student learning is expected to reach some level of mastery or if the focus is on assessing the learning process. If specific information is desired, the teacher will design a task or lesson activity that will give that kind of information about the child's achievement. For example, if the teacher wants to know that the child understands number concepts up to five, then a task would be used with the child that would allow the child to demonstrate that understanding. A certain level of performance is required of the child under those circumstances.

Similarly, some type of record keeping would be needed to maintain information on student progress.

Hopefully, the teacher and students use portfolio assessment to demonstrate the child's performance. If so, samples of the child's work will be selected to demonstrate the student's progress or mastery of skills within the unit. For Lisa's unit, samples of artwork would be an important example of the student's participation in the unit. Dictated stories would provide documentation of the child's understanding of unit concepts.

In the preschool curriculum described in this chapter, level of performance has not been required; moreover, the teacher is more interested in the child's ability to problem solve or use divergent thinking to engage in integrated activities. The teacher is using assessment to understand the child's developmental growth instead of mastery of skills as such. In Lisa's sample lesson plans, she was assessing the process of learning. There was no student assessment component of the aesthetic activity in making leaf collages. In the lesson on the description of leaves, she was interested in ascertaining how the children approached the process of describing characteristics of leaves, not in determining some level of skill development in being able to characterize similarities and differences in the leaves.

Scheduling Unit Activities

The final step in thematic unit planning is to determine how the activities will be scheduled. This step will involve making decisions about what components of the daily schedule are best suited for the activity. The teacher will need to consider whether the activity requires teacher facilitation and assistance or whether the students can conduct the activities independently with some prior preparation and planning. In addition, if the activity needs teacher instruction or direction, the teacher must decide whether it is best suited to whole-group participation or if alternating small groups would be more appropriate for all students

TITLE OF PLAN: Leaf Collages

OBJECTIVES ADDRESSED:

As a result of working with leaves, paper, and glue in the art center, students will be able to create leaf collages.

ACTIVITY PROCEDURES: Small-Group Lesson

Introduction

The activity will be explained during large-group time. The teacher will describe how leaves and other objects collected on the nature walk can be used to create a picture. Instructions for using glue and putting away materials will be reviewed.

Development of Lesson or Activity

Students will construct their collages during center time. A volunteer parent will be present to provide assistance and display the finished pictures.

Summary or Review

At large-group time following center time, the teacher and children will discuss the pictures. Children will be encouraged to explain or describe their selections and the process they used to create their picture.

MATERIALS/RESOURCES NEEDED:

Volunteer parent

Large construction paper of assorted colors

Paste or glue

Collection of leaves and other found objects

ASSESSMENT:

Teacher Assessment:

Did the children understand the activity from the explanation given?

Were materials appropriate and adequate?

Activity Assessment:

Did the children enjoy the activity?

Were the children able to carry out the activity with little assistance?

Student Assessment:

Did all students participate?

Was descriptive language used to discuss the completed pictures?

FIGURE 7.2   Example of a child-initiated lesson plan

to get the most from the experience. Once these decisions are made, the teacher can complete a schedule for the period of time that the unit will be in progress.

Lisa was student teaching in a classroom that incorporated the developmental-thematic approach to curriculum development and implementation. In charting her unit for a period of a week, she in-corporated schedule components of the approach as well as other elements of the preschool model. Figure 7.4 represents how Lisa's unit was carried out in a preschool classroom in a 5-day period. Some of her activities were scheduled for large-group time so that the whole class could partici-pate in planning, reviewing, and learning infor-mation. Some activities were set up in small-group

TITLE OF PLAN: Describing Leaves

OBJECTIVES ADDRESSED:

As a result of participating in an activity to examine and discuss the characteristics of leaves, students will be able to describe comparative characteristics of leaves.

ACTIVITY PROCEDURES: Small-Group Lesson

Introduction

After getting the students settled around the table in the science–math center, the teacher will hold up two leaves from the collection and describe them for the children. Likenesses and differences will be discussed in terms of colors, shapes, and unique characteristics.

Development of Lesson or Activity

The students will be invited to find two leaves in the collection that are interesting to them. Each is given a turn to describe their leaves and guided to look at color and shape, as well as other unique qualities. Other students will be invited to add comments after individual children have completed their descriptions.

Summary or Review

Students will be guided in summarizing what descriptive words they used to tell about their leaves. A list of words can be made on the chalkboard or a language experience chart. When the list is completed, the teacher and children will read the words together. The chart can be retained for follow-up activities.

MATERIALS/RESOURCES NEEDED:

Collection of leaves
Experience chart
Marking pen

ASSESSMENT:

Teacher Assessment:

Did the lesson proceed smoothly?
Did the lesson take an appropriate amount of time?
Were the teacher's questions effective?
Did the students understand the purpose of the activity?

Activity Assessment:

Was the activity appropriate for the students?
Did the students participate in the lesson?
Were the leaves appropriate for the discussions?

Student Assessment:

Were the students able to understand how to describe the leaves?
Were the students able to use descriptive words to describe the leaves?
Were new descriptive words used?

FIGURE 7.3 Example of a teacher-directed and child-initiated lesson plan

Schedule Component	Day 1	Day 2	Day 3	Day 4	Day 5
Large-Group Time	Plan nature walk	Plan for center time	Plan for center time	Plan for center time Songs about leaves	Plan for center time Songs about leaves
Small-Group Time		Discuss characteristics of leaves	Count, measure, classify leaves	Pressed-leaf arrangements	Make unit booklets
Center Time	*Library* Books about fall	*Art* Collages *Library* Books about fall Write leaf stories	*Art* Leaf rubbings *Library* Books about fall	*Art* Sponge rubbings *Science–Math* Count, measure, classify leaves	*Science–Math* Count, measure, classify leaves *Library* Books about fall
Large-Group Time	Songs about leaves	Reread dictated stories	Movement to music using leaves	Read book about leaves Plan for raking leaves	Movement to music
Summary and Review	Review nature walk Dictate story	Review center time activities Discuss leaves in individual collages	Review center time activities		
Outside Time	Nature walk			Rake leaves	Review unit booklets Discuss individual pictures and stories
Individual		Review individual stories about leaves		Dictate leaf stories	

FIGURE 7.4 Unit on leaves: Schedule for one week

time, giving the teacher an opportunity to facilitate an activity or engage in some direct instruction. Centers were used extensively for creative and exploratory activities. Visits to the language center were included daily to encourage the children to browse through the books related to fall leaves.

Implementing Developmental-Thematic Curriculum

Before a teacher is ready to begin a new unit, some final preparations are in order. Resources must be gathered, the environment must be arranged to accommodate the activities unique to the unit, and further planning takes place with the children to involve them in preparations to begin the new topic for learning.

Gathering Resources

If the teacher has planned carefully, needed materials and resources were listed as the thematic unit was being designed. Now it is time to study the list and determine which materials are already on hand and which need to be acquired. The art materials must be organized in preparation for the center and small-group activities that will occur during the week of the unit. A trip to the school library and other facilities is in order to find books that relate to the fall season and changes in leaves. Books that have illustrations of fall leaves can also be included in the classroom library. The teacher will want to determine which books to share with the children and which to place in the library area for browsing.

Students may be able to bring some unit materials from home. If materials for some of the activities represent items from home that can be recycled, the teacher can discuss the needs with the children and send a note home requesting that parents send the needed items. In some schools where parents have an active volunteer program, the parents will take the responsibility to help find needed resources without having to resort to purchasing materials. When purchase of some items is unavoidable, parents sometimes are

enthusiastic errand runners and offer to conserve the teacher's time. Acquired resources can be organized so that they are readily available for unit activities before the unit is initiated.

The parents themselves may be needed resources during the course of the thematic unit. If the teacher needs assistance with activities during small-group time or center time, the presence of a parent volunteer can ensure that activities go smoothly. If the preschool teacher is fortunate enough to have a teaching assistant for the classroom, parental help may not be as essential; nevertheless, with young children, an additional adult supporter is always welcome when many active projects are underway.

Planning with the Children

As was mentioned earlier, additional planning with children is important before initiation of a new unit. In addition to being involved in locating relevant resources, they will be enthusiastic supporters of activities to prepare the classroom. Children can organize the library center or other classroom areas that will be rearranged or organized for unit activities. They can also be involved in last-minute discussions about the activities that are being planned for the new theme.

Arranging the Environment

Although learning centers or areas in the preschool classroom are rearranged frequently to provide variety and maintain interest, the beginning of a new thematic unit is also a time when room arrangement is reevaluated. The teacher consults the plan to determine which center will be affected and need reorganization. Existing materials might be replaced with items required for the new unit. Art materials, prop boxes, artifacts, and other relevant resources are located in the appropriate centers or learning areas. Sometimes centers may be relocated in the classroom to better facilitate unit activities.

In the case of Lisa's unit, the theme of leaves led her to enhance a science-mathematics area in the classroom. A large table was introduced where children could measure, count, and group leaves. Small-group time to introduce the activity would be conducted at the table. Later during the week, the children could continue the activity independently during center time.

Lisa also rearranged the art area to facilitate the various creative activities using leaves. Art materials unrelated to the thematic unit remained in the area to provide choices; nevertheless, an additional space was reserved for unit-specific activities.

The Role of Assessment in Preschool Programs

In the descriptions of the process of developing unit and lesson plans presented earlier in the chapter, there were provisions for assessment. In the lesson plan description, possibilities for assessing teacher effectiveness, lesson activities, and student learning were discussed. In this section, I will discuss the broader purpose of assessment in preschool programs, the measurement of child development and learning, and the assessment of program components of preschool programs.

Assessment of Child Development and Learning

Purposes for Assessment

In Chapter 5, information was shared on how adults can monitor the development of infants and toddlers. During those years of rapid growth and development, frequent assessment of development permits monitoring of developmental progress in very young children. During the preschool years, development is slower, but awareness of developmental progress is still important. The preschool years are a significant period of development of potential for learning, as well as of physical, intellectual, and social development; therefore, information about the individual child's development is important for assessing developmental competencies, screening for delayed development, and determining possible placement in intervention programs.

Assessment of developmental competencies in the preschool years is done by parents, medical personnel, and personnel in school and child-care settings. Using developmental checklists and other instruments, the child's developmental characteristics are measured against the norms for that age. Competencies in language, motor skills, and social and cognitive development are assessed using indicators of the normal range of development. Pediatricians frequently use an instrument such as the Denver Developmental Test for a quick developmental evaluation. School and child-care center personnel might use a checklist similar to the Frost-Wortham developmental checklists found in Chapter 4. Other sources include developmental indicators used by child development centers and public schools that are locally devised or obtained from books or other texts (Beaty, 1998; Wortham, 2001d).

An important purpose for developmental assessment in the preschool years is to identify developmental delays. Children with difficulties in hearing, vision, motor, language, or cognitive development or other types of developmental delays benefit from early identification and intervention. Screening for developmental problems can be conducted with a variety of standardized instruments, such as the Early Screening Inventory (Meisels & Wiske, 1983) and the Developmental Indicators for the Assessment of Learning (3rd ed.) (DIAL-R) (Mardell-Czudnowski & Goldenberg, 1998). If indicators of delayed development are identified through use of a screening instrument, more intensive testing can be conducted by medical or psychological professionals to diagnose the delay more specifically and refer the child to the appropriate program for intervention services.

Standardized tests are frequently used with preschool children in the early childhood years for various purposes. Developmental screening tests, readiness tests, IQ tests, and other standardized instruments are used to determine if young children should be withheld from preschool programs or retained at the preschool level instead of promoted to first grade. Because of the inaccuracy of standardized test results in the preschool years and the national concern about using this kind of testing for tracking or school placement, many testing specialists, early childhood specialists, and organizations serve as advocates opposed to inappropriate testing of children in the early childhood years, particularly children in preschool programs. The NAEYC and the National Association of Early Childhood Specialists in State Departments of Education published its "Guidelines for Appropriate Curriculum Content and Assessment in Programs Serving Children Ages 3 through 8" (1991), and the Association for Childhood Education International published a position paper, "On Standardized Testing" (Perrone, 1991). Additional efforts have been made to provide information on alternatives to standardized testing for assessment and evaluation purposes (Fair Test, 1990; National Education Goals Panel, 1998; Wortham, 2001d).

Assessment of Children in Preschool Programs

Several strategies are recommended for adults who are assessing development and learning in the preschool years. Teacher observation, hands-on tasks and activities, work samples, and portfolios are informal assessment tools that can be used to determine the child's progress in development and learning.

Preschool children demonstrate growth and learning through activity. Because they learn through active work and play, observation is a primary method for understanding the child's progress and the way in which the child thinks or behaves. Teachers can schedule systematic observations of individual children at regular intervals to update information on language development or fine and gross motor skills or to conduct observations for a specific purpose, such as identify-

ing causes of inappropriate behavior. Checklists can be used for assessing developmental characteristics. Different types of observation tools, such as anecdotal records or time sampling, can be employed to obtain the desired information (Beaty, 1998; Boehm & Weinberg, 1997; Wortham, 2001d).

A more structured process for measuring learning can be accomplished through teacher-designed tasks or other hands-on tasks and activities for the children to complete. Within the context of a teacher-conducted small-group or individual lesson or activity, the teacher can ask the child to do a task and then observe the child's verbal and physical responses to determine the desired information. In a similar manner, the teacher can use discussions with children to determine ability to use language to demonstrate understanding of concepts. The teacher can also observe the child using materials in center activities for evaluation purposes (Wortham, 2001d).

Teachers are making increasing use of portfolios to collect materials to use for assessment purposes. Some type of container is designated for each child in the classroom. A list of possibilities for housing portfolios includes pizza boxes, expandable folders, paper briefcases, office supply boxes, and plastic crates (Barbour & Desjean-Perrotta, 1998). The portfolio can contain samples of artwork, emergent writing, checklists, observations, and any other relevant materials that can document the child's progress over a period of time and be shared with parents (Jervis, 1996; Wortham, 1998, 2001d).

Portfolios can also be used as part of an assessment system. In this context, there is a plan for using the portfolio to report the child's progress. In addition to including a variety of examples of the child's work that serve as documentation of progress, results of teacher assessment strategies are organized to further document what the child has accomplished. The portfolio contents become a system when a narrative report synthesizes and summarizes the child's development and learning two or three times per year (Wortham, 2001d).

Teachers serving children with special needs have specific requirements for design of intervention activities and evaluation of progress. Diagnostic assessment of the child before he enters a program identifies the characteristics and needs for intervention that are specified and addressed through an IEP. The plan identifies the strategies that will be used for intervention. Ongoing assessment is conducted to determine the effectiveness of the intervention activities and the child's developmental progress. Although there are concerns about the effectiveness of available standardized measures for diagnosis and ongoing assessment of children with disabling conditions (Fewell, 1983), Gautt (1996) recommends the Carolina Record of Individual Behavior (Simeonsson, Huntington, Short, & Ware, 1982) as an effective observational instrument to be used with young children.

Assessment of Program Components

Program assessment is an important part of the total assessment picture in preschool classrooms. The program is assessed by paying attention to the indoor and outdoor environments, the curriculum, and the teacher.

The learning environment is essential to the development and learning of preschool children. Because learning is active and physical activities are part of the child's overall development, the environment is designed and arranged to facilitate learning through play and child-centered activities. Both the indoor and outdoor environments are planned to promote physical, social-emotional, language, and cognitive development. When assessing the quality of the environment, the observer looks for characteristics of the environment that promote all categories of development. Some of the specific characteristics that are essential include plans for a variety of activities, accommodations for large- and small-group activities, and age-appropriate and developmentally appropriate materials and equipment as described in the *Guide to Accreditation* provided by the National Academy of Early Childhood Programs (1991).

The outdoor environment should also meet these criteria. In addition, criteria for safety should be met. Information for evaluation of a quality outdoor environment is also described in the *Guide to Accreditation* (National Academy of Early Childhood Programs, 1991). More comprehensive information about quality outdoor playgrounds and the way in which to evaluate a quality, safe play environment for preschool children is available in *Play and Child Development* (Frost, Wortham, & Reifel, 2001).

The effectiveness of the curriculum is also assessed as part of the assessment of overall program quality. Teachers will want to have feedback on how well the curriculum fits the learning needs of children in preschool classrooms. The *Guide to Accreditation* suggests that materials, activities, and the daily schedule are among the factors that indicate an appropriate curriculum. The daily schedule ensures a balance between active and quiet activities, as well as periods for outdoor play. There is also a balance between small-group and large-group experiences. Materials that are used have multiracial and nonsexist elements; developmentally appropriate materials include manipulatives, blocks, art materials, dramatic play materials, and sand and water toys.

Finally, assessment of the teacher and the teaching role are part of the assessment of program quality. The quality of adult interactions with children is a key to teaching effectiveness. The manner in which teachers and caregivers manage learning experiences, arrange the environment, and engage in working with the children forms the types of interactions that can be assessed. The opportunities they provide for children and the manner in which they guide language, social behaviors, routines, and work and play experiences are important indicators of the quality of the teaching role. The qualifications the teacher brings to the teaching role are equally important for evaluating the teacher (NAEYC, & National Association of Early Childhood Specialists in State Departments of Education, 1991). The appropriate training in early childhood education that was obtained as a prerequisite for employment should be nurtured with opportunities for further ongoing training throughout each school year.

Summary

Preschool early childhood programs have both a historical and a theoretical heritage. The various types of preschool settings that are currently in operation reflect a combination of many influences that affect the type of instructional program used. In addition, individual teachers also reflect the various influences and experiences that have shaped their perception of how to organize an early childhood classroom.

When designing a model for a preschool program of the highest quality, developers also consider the historical heritage and current knowledge based on research in development and learning. The best of the influences are retained and incorporated into the new model that is conceptualized and used with today's young children.

No model can be transferred intact into all preschool settings. In addition, teachers are likely to incorporate other influences into their teaching practices. To enable teachers to plan and manage instructions in a variety of settings, suggestions were made as to how to plan and manage instruction using added developmental-thematic curriculum, as well as how to adapt the process in a variety of types of preschool settings.

There are logical steps in planning thematic or integrated curriculum. Moreover, there are different ways that the curriculum can be incorporated into a daily schedule. Preschool teachers must carefully plan what activities will best meet their objectives for the unit, as well as what resources they will need to carry out the learning activities. Planning with children for unit activities is essential, as is rearrangement of the classroom environment to accommodate materials, activities, and long-term projects that will be accomplished over a period of days or weeks.

Specialists in early childhood education in the preschool years believe that young children learn best when they can see the purpose and connections in learning. The learning experiences provided for them in preschool classrooms should provide opportunities for the cognitive connections to be made through active interaction with new concepts. Developmental-thematic learning facilitates reconstruction of knowledge by young children in various types of learning settings that are developmentally appropriate. Ongoing evaluation of the curriculum, of student learning, and of teaching strategies helps the teacher to further improve and refine instructional activities for future students.

Assessment is further conducted for the preschool program as a whole. Strategies for assessment of overall development and learning of children throughout the year help guide program planning and communication with parents. Assessment of the environment provides feedback on how well the environment, both indoors and outdoors, supports the child's development and learning. The teacher and teaching role are also part of program assessment. The teacher's ability to provide developmentally appropriate equipment, materials, and activities is an indicator of teaching effectiveness. The curriculum used in the classroom should reflect effective use of developmentally appropriate activities and materials with students. The teacher's training in preparation to teach young children should also reflect a solid foundation in child development and the components of a quality educational program for preschool children.

Study Questions

1. How do contemporary models affect the nature of today's early childhood programs?
2. Which two theorists do you believe have the most influence on the development of programs for preschool classrooms? Explain your choices.

3. Why is it difficult to determine the sources of influences in many early childhood preschool classrooms?

4. Why do individual teachers vary in their perception of what constitutes a good early childhood program?

5. Why does it take many years for an innovation to be implemented in some early childhood programs?

6. How has the back-to-basics approach to instruction resulted in a conflict between theories of learning and development?

7. Why do classroom teachers find it difficult to carry out new approaches to instruction in their own teaching?

8. How does Piaget's theory of cognitive development influence current programs that are developmentally appropriate?

9. Why does the Piagetian construct of the learning process in young children support integrated curriculum development?

10. How does a preschool developmental curriculum model exemplify child-centered instruction?

11. What is meant by meaningful or purposeful learning?

12. What is the process used to design and set up a cognitive-developmental curriculum?

13. Regarding the concept of active reconstruction of knowledge, what are the ingredients of active learning?

14. Why does the learning environment in the preschool classroom need to be flexible in arrangement?

15. How does the daily schedule support child-centered learning?

16. How does a cycle of plan, do, and review facilitate the child's reconstruction of knowledge?

17. What is the origin of thematic curriculum?

18. How does the developmental-thematic curriculum incorporate an integrated approach?

19. How can a developmental-thematic curriculum be used in different types of early childhood programs?

20. Why is it helpful to use a webbing process that includes both developmental and content area categories of integrated curriculum?

21. How is student input included in the planning process of a developmental-thematic curriculum?

22. How can a brainstorming web be a vehicle for organizing early childhood curriculum?

23. Why is it important to carefully plan activities and room arrangement before beginning a thematic unit?

24. What is the role of assessment in a thematic curriculum?

CHAPTER EIGHT

Preschool Curriculum:
Ages 3 to 5

Language and Cognitive Development

CHAPTER OBJECTIVES

As a result of reading this chapter, you will be able to:

1. Explain how young children develop language.
2. Explain how young children can have language differences.
3. Describe how teachers plan for language development using listening, speaking, writing, and reading.
4. Describe how teachers plan curriculum for expressive and receptive language.
5. Define emergent literacy as contrasted with reading readiness.
6. Discuss how the environment supports language and literacy.
7. Describe examples of activities that promote reading and writing.
8. Explain how young children develop concepts.
9. Discuss how the teacher plans for concept development.
10. Explain the roles of the teacher, environment, and play for cognitive development.
11. Describe learning experiences for mathematics and science.

12. Discuss how integrated curriculum can be designed for language.
13. Discuss how cognitive curriculum is designed for children with disabilities.

Introduction

Chapter 4 introduced the nature of language development—how theorists and researchers who study the way in which humans acquire language have described the process babies and young children go through in learning to talk. It also discussed how infants and toddlers accomplish the first steps in learning to talk and what parents and other caregivers do to encourage the use of language. This chapter again emphasizes why it is important to understand how language develops, not only for designing a program for language development but also for extending or expanding the process to include literacy.

There was a period in early childhood education, from the 1930s to the 1970s, when educators believed that the process of learning to read began in the first grade. Using Gesell's maturational theory (Gesell, 1925) as a guide, it was believed that children were ready to learn to read when they were 6 years old. Preschool and kindergarten teachers were advised not to introduce formal reading instruction before the students were mature or "ready."

Newer theories of child development and learning results of studies conducted in the 1950s and 1960s began to cast doubt on the maturational approach to the process of beginning reading. Studies demonstrated that children play an active role in oral language acquisition. Language development is similar to cognitive development as proposed by Piaget (1955). The child constructs language just as the child constructs knowledge (Bloom, 1972; Brown, 1973; Cazden, 1972; Chomsky, 1965). Further research extended this theory to involve acquisition of reading. As researchers studied acquisition of literacy, they determined that young children also learn written language through constructing their own rules and

relationships. Understanding how young children learn to talk helps us to also understand how they learn to write and read (Dyson, 1985; Goodman, 1986; Snow & Tabors, 1993; Sulzby, Barnhart, & Hieshima, 1989).

In this chapter, we will be studying how young children's cognitive development helps them to acquire language and literacy and mathematics and science concepts in the preschool years. Curriculum for cognitive development will include experiences in mathematics and science in addition to language and literacy.

Curriculum for Language Development

How Young Children Develop Language

As was discussed in Chapter 4, there are various theories of how children acquire language. The behaviorist position is that language is learned through reinforcement (Skinner, 1957). Adults selectively reinforce the child's utterances; moreover, behaviorists propose that the child learns language through imitation. Speech is learned first, followed by grammar.

Researchers such as Slobin (1966), McNeil (1966), and Chomsky (1968) support a different theory, which proposes that humans are biologically equipped for language acquisition; we have an innate capacity to learn language. Proponents of this view believe that children do not imitate or reproduce what they hear. Instead, children learn a set of rules that they use to create their own utterances. They continue to try out their language and use this process to refine and elaborate their language. The rules for the language are finite, but children can generate an infinite number of sentences using the rules (Jewell & Zintz, 1986; Spodek, 1985).

The interactionist, or constructivist, approach to language is based on both maturation and interaction with language. Proponents of this theory believe children develop the ability to speak as they mature and respond to the language in their environment. Interaction with language enables them to hypothesize and try rules for communicating. Piaget (1955) believed language development paralleled the child's ability to use thought. As children progress through the sensorimotor, preoperational, concrete operational, and formal operational stages, they use their own style of thinking and language interactions to learn language.

Vygotsky also agreed that language and thought are related in the child's acquisition of language; however, he proposed that language precedes thought (Vygotsky, 1962). Children first become conscious that they can communicate through speech. According to Vygotsky, human consciousness is developed through words. He stressed the importance of the adult's role in determining the directions for the child's concept and language acquisition. Through interactions with adults, children develop their understanding of the rules and functions of language. Verbal discourse with adults supplies the context for concepts.

Although various theorists have contributed to how we understand language acquisition, there is another important element to be considered: *communicative competence*. Not only does the young child need to learn language, but she also must learn to use language appropriately. Communicative competence includes the ability to speak appropriately in different social situations and to use knowledge of linguistic rules to communicate (Genishi & Fassler, 1999). In the next section, we will look at types of linguistic rules and how the child learns to use them.

Forms of Language

Although much about the nature of language acquisition remains a mystery, we know that there are certain elements of language that all children acquire: phonology, syntax, semantics, and pragmatics. The *phonology* of the language is the sound system. The individual sound units are phonemes that are combined into meaningful utterances. The *syntax* of the language is the grammar. The child must learn the rules for how morphemes (the smallest units of meaning) can be combined in a sentence. The *semantics* of the language transmit the meaning of the communication. The child learns the cues in language that bring meaning to its spoken and written form. Every child lives in a unique community where language is used as a tool for communicating. Regardless of the variations in children's language communities, whether they are slight differences in a local English dialect or more significant, non–English-language differences, the order in which children learn the forms of language remains the same.

Pragmatics is another form of language that refers to what the speaker intends to communicate. The same utterance can convey different meanings, depending on differences in inflection, body gestures, and facial expressions. For example, a person eating a very spicy food might say, "I wish this food had more seasoning." Accompanied by an exaggerated rolling of the eyes, the speaker really intends to communicate that the food is excessively spicy.

Pragmatics is also related to effective communication. The preschool child learns how to communicate through being polite and using courteous language. When a child is told to "Say 'thank you,'" for a gift or the teacher suggests, "Ask Larry if you can play with that truck," these are examples of how the child learns to use correct types of conversation in social contexts (Snow & Tabors, 1993).

Children must understand pragmatics if they are to become competent language users. Pragmatics also includes how to take turns in a conversation, how to enter a conversation, and how to change the topic of a conversation (Christie, Enz, & Vukelich, 1997).

Language Differences in the Preschool Years

By 4 or 5 years of age, young children have acquired a basic mastery of the language spoken in their home. Although complete mastery is still to be developed, these children are well on their way to using fully grammatical sentences and pronouncing words correctly. Genishi and Fassler (1999, pp. 65–66) summarize the process:

1. Language is an enormously complex system through which people construct and convey meaning. Its main components are *semantics* (the system of meanings), *phonology* (the sound system), *syntax* (the rules for combining morphemes in sentences), and *pragmatics* (the rules underlying conversations).
2. Imitation is not the key to acquiring language. The active, thinking, meaning-seeking, and meaning-constructing child, in interaction with people and things, gradually figures out for herself the intricacies of language and communication.
3. All normal children develop communicative competence within their own communities. Different communities' ways of talking and communicating may vary widely, and re-

searchers are just beginning to study these ways in communities that are not middle-class. Thus, we cannot make judgements about what social contexts are "better" than others or what specific features in the contexts are essential for children's communicative development to occur.

It is important to note that although many children come from diverse cultures and cultural communities have their own beliefs about how their children learn to talk, children from all backgrounds and cultures learn the social and linguistic rules used therein.

Some children live in homes where a dialect different from standard English, the language used at school, is spoken. Children may thus come to school speaking a different dialect, such as Black English, which has a different structure than standard English. Once thought to be an inferior form of standard English, Black English has been found to have a sophisticated grammatical structure (Labov, 1970). Speakers of Black English use verbal games of wit that are not part of standard English (Hendrick, 1998). Speakers of Black English need to acquire standard English as a second language, as do other children who may speak a regional or subculture dialect of English. These children can maintain their home dialect and learn to determine when it is appropriate to switch to standard English.

Helping Young Children Bridge Black English and Standard English

Ms. Raney helps young African American children who speak Black English to differentiate between their dialect and standard English. Further, she provides opportunities for young students to use and understand the two types of language.

One strategy Ms. Raney uses is to videotape children in different speaking situations. Subsequently the children can hear themselves using less or more formal dialects in their classroom activities.

Dramatic play is also used to highlight the differences between dialect and standard English. Children are asked to intentionally use standard English when they are dramatizing plays. They can then compare how they use language in less formal situations when Black English is the norm.

Ms. Raney's goal is not only to have children practice using standard English, but to help children think about when more formal standard English is appropriate and when Black English is appropriate (Genishi & Dyson, 1984, p. 201, as cited in Genishi & Fassler, 1999).

Children who come from a home where a language other than English is spoken will also need to learn standard English. The most common non-English language spoken in the United States is Spanish. Other languages are spoken as well. It is not uncommon for elementary schools in urban and rural areas to have students who speak five or more different languages; moreover, they may speak different dialects of the

languages. Within the past few decades, demographic shifts have resulted in language-minority students being the majority in many major cities in the United States. In spite of recent efforts at school reform, language minority children continue to be at risk for success in school (Gutierrez, 1993).

Many young children who speak a language other than English are currently served in bilingual programs that currently focus on a transition into English, although there are also programs where the child's first language is used with the addition of English into the instruction. Other children are served in classrooms where English as a second language (ESL) is taught. The success of bilingual programs is controversial and has been eliminated in a few states, primarily California. Parents also have differing views of bilingual education for their children. Although some parents find the use of both languages in bilingual programs to be desired, other parents are more concerned that their children learn English. They reject having their children in bilingual programs (Wong-Fillmore, 1991). Regardless of the type of program serving language-minority children, there are differences in the rate at which they learn English and their willingness to learn English (Hudleson & Serna, 1997).

A more complex challenge for the teacher is the child who is limited in verbal skills and is not fluent in any language. Such a child may come from a home where adult-child interactions are very restricted. Bilingual children may be limited in their home language, as well as in English. Children who are lacking in speaking skills need special consideration, first to determine the cause of their limited language, and then to provide special activities to help them develop language. The lack of language also may be traced to social immaturity, difficulty in feeling secure and comfortable in school, a hearing impairment, or a developmental delay. Whatever the source of the problem, an appropriate preschool program is begun as early as possible to provide intervention and remediation.

Some children experience fluency disorders. They have difficulty speaking rapidly and may speak either too fast or too slow. Stuttering is one manifestation of a disfluency. Other children have articulation disorders; they have problems with pronunciation. One cause of articulation problems is loss of hearing or a brain trauma (Christie, Enz, & Vukelich, 1997). The program for language development in the preschool years facilitates language abilities in children with various types of language differences and refines the same skills in children who have already developed a rich language before entering school.

What is the best type of program to develop language in all preschool children in order to include those with cultural and language differences? If a program is to meet the needs of every child, it will have to be balanced and provide many types of experiences. Although a constructivist approach is appropriate, in itself, it is not considered to be adequate by some. The balance needs to include direct teaching of skills along with holistic and discovery language activities. The next section will discuss preschool program elements that can facilitate language development and describe curriculum experiences that can be planned for young children.

Planning for Language Development

The curriculum for language development has as its first purpose to extend the child's acquisition of oral language. The most active period of development of the ability to communicate through speech occurs from the ages of 3 through 5. During this period, the child is also continuing through the first steps of acquisition of written language. In planning for language development, the teacher conceptualizes a program that encompasses both oral and written literacy. In the following sections, we will explore the role of play and the teacher's role in language devel-

opment. Then we will learn how the environment facilitates language and literacy in preschool classrooms.

The Role of Play in Language Development

We understand that play is the vehicle for the young child's development and learning. This is particularly true for the development of language. Children use oral language in all facets of play as they communicate with each other and with adults and they use language to express themselves in play. Younger children may verbalize their activities to themselves in solitary play. While engaged in social play, they may use metacommunication, or talk about a play event interpersonally with others to negotiate or revise a play theme (Rogers & Sawyers, 1988; Wortham, 2001b). In her research of sociodramatic play, Smilansky (1968) found that children from higher income homes played a richer form of dramatic play that resulted in more successful learning later in school. She also found that adult involvement in play could extend and expand the fantasy play of children from low-income families (Johnson, Christie, & Yawkey, 1999).

Language has an important role in play, but play has an equally important role in the development of language. Language is used for make-believe, as an imitation of adult speech, and for management of play activities. Frost (1992, p. 40) cited Levy's research (1984) on the role of play in language and cognitive development as follows:

1. Play stimulates innovation in language (Bruner, 1983; Garvey, 1977).
2. Play introduces and clarifies new words and concepts (Chukovsky, 1971; Smilansky, 1968).
3. Play motivates language use and practice (Bruner, 1983; Garvey, 1977; Garvey & Hogan, 1973; Smilansky, 1968; Vygotsky, 1962).

4. Play develops metalinguistic awareness (Cazden, 1976).
5. Play encourages verbal thinking (Vygotsky, 1962).

Berk (1994) further explained how Vygotsky believed play facilitates language development. First, Vygotsky proposed that social experience influences how the child thinks. Further, language is the primary channel for communication between children. Play, particularly representational play, provides the milieu of make-believe that encourages social experience and language. According to Berk, research on sociodramatic play suggests that preschoolers who spend more time at sociodramatic play are more socially competent and are advanced in intellectual development.

The Role of the Teacher in Language Development and Literacy

The teacher acts as facilitator, instructor, and model for language development. The teacher facilitates language development through setting up the indoor and outdoor environments to support children's play. Opportunities to develop oral and written literacy are encouraged through the availability of materials for creative expression, construction play, motor play, and dramatic play. The teacher serves as an instructor through teacher-directed activities and structured experiences that incorporate concept and vocabulary development and provide opportunities for written language. The teacher is a model for language development through all verbal interactions with children. Opportunities to extend play and language are afforded through observation of children's language during play. The teacher suggests ways to extend dramatic play themes, and models how to increase language and written literacy experiences into play episodes (Johnson, Christie, & Yawkey, 1999; Morrow & Rand, 1991; Wortham, 2001b). The teacher plays alongside children in play episodes and models written language through

reading, writing, and taking dictation from children within the play experience (Fields & Hillstead, 1990). The teacher provides a variety of meaningful activities that will promote both oral and written literacy (Fields and Spangler, 2000).

The Role of Parents in Language Development

Parents play a major role in their child's development of language. Many families have an abundance of books in their home for themselves and their children, provide writing materials, talk extensively to their children, and read storybooks to them on a daily basis.

There are many things that teachers can do to motivate all parents to establish a literacy-rich home environment. Written communications and parents' workshops and classroom meetings can be used to help parents become familiar with how they can help their child learn language by reading and telling stories and engaging in conversations with their children. Teachers can also establish classroom libraries with books that can be shared with parents. Audiotapes for read-along activities can be sent home so that the parents and children can listen and follow along in the book as the audiotape is read.

Snow (1983) has reported research on the relationship between storybook reading and oral language development. Parents can learn specific strategies, including storybook reading that can facilitate language development. Tracey (2000, pp. 50–51, suggests 10 ideas that parents can use with their children:

1. *Get your children to talk!* Children learn by talking and asking questions . . .
2. *Help your children understand the story.* Sometimes children don't understand what is happening in a book. Check regularly to see whether your children understand the story . . .
3. *Praise your children.* Children love to be told nice things by their parents. Let your

children know that you are proud of them when they ask a good question, say something interesting about a book, or read well.

4. *Relate the book to your life.* Use the book as a jumping-off point to tell your children about something interesting in your life . . .
5. *Ask your children good questions during storybook reading.* Questions that will help your children the most are those that require them to talk a lot to answer . . .
6. *Wait for answers.* After you ask a question, give your children time to answer . . .
7. *With younger children, point to words when you read.* Pointing to words when you read to young children will help them learn what the words are, that we read from left to right, and that we turn pages only after we have finished reading all the words on a page . . .
8. *With older children, take turns reading.*
9. *Choose books carefully.* Many books are enjoyable, but to help your children the most it is important to choose books that are not too easy and not too difficult . . .
10. *Have fun!* Above all, try to keep the booksharing experience enjoyable!

The Role of the Environment in Language and Literacy

The preschool classroom has been described as an inviting environment for young children. It is arranged into learning or activity areas that provide for creative, constructive, dramatic, and manipulative play. The centers are arranged with materials that permit children to work on projects, express themselves through art and writing materials, and engage in pretend or role play as well as in dramatic play, including puppetry and story reenactment. Some of the activities that can be experienced in learning centers are selected by children in their own planning for work and play. Other activities are planned by the teacher and may involve the teacher's direction or indirect facilitation.

The classroom has both social and physical aspects. The physical component of the environment includes the arrangement of space and materials. The social component of the environment includes the teacher, who serves as a mediator, and the verbal and nonverbal interactions between the children. Ostrosky and Kaiser (1991, p. 124) describe four steps in providing an environmental arrangement that will prompt language as follows:

1. Focus on making language a part of children's routines.
2. Provide access to interesting materials and activities.
3. Provide adult and peer models who will encourage children to use language and respond to their attempts to do so.
4. Establish a contingent relationship between access to materials or assistance and use of language.

When considering use of the environment for language development, steps are taken to make the total area "print rich." According to Freeman and Hatch (1989), the term *print-rich environment* implies that print should be everywhere in the form of labels, lists, signs, charts, and posters. Print materials are available in play centers to support literacy in children's play. The dramatic play center includes literacy materials consistent with changing play themes. When the play or study theme involves a grocery store, for example, the center includes empty food containers with familiar labels and paper and pencils for making grocery lists and pricing items (Fields & Hillstead, 1990). A social studies theme on the post office includes mailboxes for the children, envelopes, stamps, and greeting cards (Hatch & Freeman, 1988). The art center has writing materials for writing or dictating stories about pictures and other artwork.

The library or language center is obviously the major area to support literacy development. It contains materials for all components of the language curriculum, including listening, speaking, writing, and reading. The writing area of the center has a variety of writing materials, including paper, pencils, markers, crayons, and pens. The reading area has shelves to house a large supply of picture concept books, picture storybooks, realistic literature or real-life storybooks, easy-to-read books, informational books, books with fables and folktales, wordless books, and books of poetry. Some of the shelving can be used to store a large number of books, and other shelves are open-faced, allowing children to be attracted by the covers of the books (Morrow, 1997). At least one shelf is reserved for books specific to the theme of study. Big books previously read by the teacher are also available for rereading by the children.

A listening center with cassette tapes of recorded books and a copy of the book for each headset provides opportunities for children to listen to stories throughout center activity periods. The center might also house a rocking chair and include soft seating areas with cushions, carpeting, beanbag chairs, and other arrangements that invite individuals and groups of children to browse and read.

The language center is enhanced by language experience charts, typewriters, a computer, and materials for making books. An alphabet chart is useful for children who are beginning to recognize and use letters, and a message board hung at the children's eye level can have examples of functional messages related to the school.

The teacher's role in the environment is to read to the children, engage in conversations about topics being studied, involve children in dictating contributions for language experience charts, discuss and share books and stories, and use poetry and fingerplays with the children. The child's role in the environment is to write on a daily basis, explore new books, review familiar books, listen to stories, engage in pretend and dramatic play, dictate stories, and discuss work and play activities (Freeman & Hatch, 1989; Gothard & Russell, 1990; Teale, 1987; Burns, Griffin, & Snow, 1999). More about these activities and the language development curriculum is described in the following sections on language and literacy.

Designing Curriculum for Language Development

Although the teacher is interested primarily in oral language development when planning curriculum for language development, he is also keenly aware of activities that will facilitate the transition into written language. The curriculum for oral language development can be organized into activities that will promote the child's expressive and receptive language. Expressive language is a combination of the phonetic, syntactic, and semantic and pragmatic elements that the child is able to use when speaking. Receptive language includes elements that the child has heard and understood but cannot yet use in her expressive language.

Literacy is developed when the child is able to use written language that includes writing and reading. In the preschool years, the language development program provides activities that will form the foundations for literacy. The teacher selects activities that encourage children to be actively involved in reconstructing their understanding of literacy. Children progress in becoming readers and writers through child-initiated and teacher-directed activities that lead to their making sense of how spoken language can be written and read.

Experiences That Promote Expressive Language

Expressive language development is promoted through activities that motivate the child to use oral language. When the child is engaged in play and work activities that necessitate using descriptive language and communicating with adults and other children, expressive language is being expanded and extended. Morrow (1997, p. 101) has developed objectives for the development of expressive language as follows:

1. Give children opportunities to use their own language freely at any stage of development. This could be a different dialect or mixtures

of English and Spanish. Their desire to communicate will be encouraged, accepted, and respected.

2. Encourage children to pronounce words correctly.
3. Help children to increase their speaking vocabularies.
4. Encourage children to speak in complete sentences at appropriate stages in their development.
5. Give children opportunities to expand their use of various syntactic structures, such as adjectives, adverbs, prepositional phrases, dependent clauses, plurals, past tense, and possessives.
6. Encourage children to communicate with others so that they can be understood.
7. Give children the opportunity to use language socially and psychologically by interpreting feelings, points of view, and motivation and by solving problems through generating hypotheses, summarizing events, and predicting outcomes.
8. Give children opportunities to develop language that involve mathematical and logical relations, such as describing size and amount, making comparisons, defining sets and classes, and reasoning deductively.
9. Give children the opportunity to talk in many different settings.

Arranging the classroom environment into centers for learning and play and providing generous blocks of time to engage in center activities are fundamental tasks for teachers involved in oral language development. Children use expressive language to discuss activities with their peers and the teacher and to plan and engage in play themes in the housekeeping or block center. Experiences in the art center, such as painting or working with clay, lead to expressive language, as children share their ideas or reflect on the process they are using to create a piece of art. Expressive communication occurs when children interact in the manipulative or science–math centers, asking for directions,

giving suggestions, and describing activities. The teacher is a major player in center activities as he asks questions, engages in dialogues with children who are working and playing in various centers, and offers suggestions about extending activities and thematic play.

Playing "Doctor"
"Let's play house."
"Naw, I wanna play doctor."
"OK, this is where the doctor lives."
"Yeah, and the hospital's over here."
"You be the mother."
"I don't wanna be the mother. I'm the doctor."
"Let's both be doctors!"
"Yeah!" (Ishee & Goldhaber, 1990, pp. 70–71)

Dramatic play within the housekeeping center or elsewhere offers possibly the most important opportunity for child-initiated expressive language. As children design and carry out play themes, language is used as the primary communication tool to facilitate the enactment of the fantasy or pretend play (Spodek, 1985). It should be remembered that outdoor play is essential as well. Although girls tend to engage in play focused on family themes indoors and outdoors, boys use pretend play more in outdoor than indoor environments as they engage in their preferred play themes, which include superheroes (Johnson, Christie, & Yawkey, 1999).

Teacher-directed or teacher-facilitated activities also stimulate expressive language. Class discussions during sharing times and conversations about planned or completed activities require expressive language. Teachers can encourage children to retell stories or tell about important events that have occurred. Reenactment of stories involves expressive language in dramatic play (Ishee & Goldhaber, 1990). Teacher-led discussions using wordless books likewise encourage children to use their own language to construct and describe stories to go with the pictures in the books (Raines & Isbell, 1988). Puppetry also provides a medium by which the teacher can encourage expressive oral language.

Experiences That Promote Receptive Language

Opportunities to hear language modeled are also important if the child is to extend and expand language to more closely approximate adult language. The child's receptive language will reflect the nature of the adult language that is heard. Parents and teachers who pronounce words carefully and spend time in dialogue and explanation will provide the child with models of language that can extend the child's current ability to express herself verbally. Morrow (1997, p. 101) provided objectives for the development of receptive language as follows:

1. Provide children with an atmosphere in which they will hear language frequently.
2. Children should be able to associate the language that they hear with pleasure and enjoyment.
3. Children are given the opportunity to discriminate and classify sounds they hear.
4. Children should hear a rich source of new words on a regular basis.
5. Give children the opportunity to listen to others and demonstrate that they understand what is said.
6. Provide children with opportunities for following directions.

When children enter a school setting, they spend more time listening than they do in less structured environments. It is through listening that they will acquire additions to their receptive language that will also become part of their expressive language. Teachers and parents can use many types of activities to add to the child's language.

Telling and reading stories are major activities used with young children to help them develop listening skills and receptive vocabulary. Not only are the children being exposed to new words, they are also acquiring new information (Genishi & Fassler, 1999). Opportunities to hear and "experience" stories can be enhanced through the use of cassette tapes and listening centers and video-tapes of stories. Reading poetry exposes children to a rhythmic flow of words, and fingerplays add physical actions to poetry.

Teachers use conversation throughout the school day to inform, instruct, and share information with children. Language used as part of classroom routines adds to the opportunities to model language for children. Instructional activities led by the teacher add to oral language possibilities, as do dramatic play activities that involve the teacher as a player and director and informal interactions with children in indoor and outdoor play. Taking field trips to places that are informative and interesting to young children and listening to classroom guests who relate their experiences provide additional opportunities for children to hear language modeled by adults.

Developing Foundations for Literacy

What is literacy? When does it develop? Literacy is a continuous process that begins at birth and develops as children strive to understand and use oral and written language. Having an interest in books and stories and in using conversations to communicate is part of the process. Adults serve as facilitators for oral and written literacy when they talk to children, read to them, tell them stories, model the process of writing, point out environmental print, and encourage children's interests and efforts (International Reading Association and National Association for the Education of Young Children, 1999; Teale & Yokota, 2000).

The first part of this chapter stressed the importance of language in acquiring literacy. Language is one important component of the child's development and contributes to success in becoming literate. In this section, we will look at other equally important factors that contribute to current practices used with preschool children to promote literacy. First, however, we must understand a continuing controversy over how and when children should be guided and taught in the beginning stages of reading and writing.

Resolving the Issues in Beginning Literacy Instruction

At the beginning of the chapter, I described the instructional practices that were prevalent from the 1930s through the 1970s when a child's maturation or readiness was considered to be important before beginning formal reading instruction. I also discussed how newer research into language and literacy acquisition reflected a constructivist approach to beginning reading and writing. This approach reflected the view that readiness for reading was a product of experience and that the child has a major role in acquiring literacy.

By the late 1980s, the reading readiness view was challenged by the concept of emergent literacy. This approach rejected the position that children must proceed through a reading readiness program before receiving formal reading instruction. Advocates of emergent literacy proposed that children begin the process of becoming literate very early in life; moreover, the process is a combination of reading and writing that develop in a complementary, interrelated fashion. Further, emergent literacy results from the child's active engagement with the world and through meaningful or purposeful activities involving oral and written communications (Teale & Yokota, 2000).

Whole language was another movement in the 1980s that emerged to replace traditional basal reading materials that were based on phonics and other reading skills taught in isolation. The view of the whole language approach was that reading and writing are learned best by engaging in purposeful activities, rather than in exercises. Phonics and other skills were to be taught when the need became apparent for specific children, rather than systematic instruction for the whole class. By the mid-1980s, new basal series that were literature-based became available to schools.

A reaction against the whole language approach began early in the 1990s. The concern was that while experienced teachers were able to develop strong programs, many other teachers misinterpreted the approach or lacked direction in using whole language methods in their classrooms. In addition, a series of research studies conducted by the National Institute of Child Health and Human Development (Lyon, 1998) stressed that there was a need for instruction in phonological awareness and phonics in reading. This position was reinforced by the publication *Beginning to Read: Thinking and Learning About Print* (Adams, 1990) that proposed that systematic instruction in phonics awareness and decoding should be taught in beginning reading.

Opposing views of the best way to teach beginning reading is not new. How best to teach beginning reading instruction was a matter of debate throughout the twentieth century (Chall, 1967; 1996). Unfortunately, many states currently see the issue of phonics versus whole language as similar to the controversies about reading approaches in earlier decades (Teale & Yokota, 2000). Others believe that a balanced curriculum which incorporates systematic instruction within a constructivist approach forms the basis for a quality program in beginning reading (Burns, Griffin, & Snow, 1999; Snow, Burns, & Griffin, 1998).

The approach that has been taken throughout this text and within some of the models presented in Chapter 3 supports an emergent literacy and whole language approach to beginning reading and writing. Nevertheless, the role of the teacher to guide, scaffold, and instruct remains significant, as does the role of the child to encounter, experience, and use many types of representation to reflect what is learned. The next section discusses what research tells us a child needs to know to successful in acquiring literacy.

What Does the Young Child Need to Know to Develop Literacy?

In the previous discussion of the controversies that prevail about beginning reading instruction, phonemic awareness and phonics instruction were the components at issue. Research conducted during the past few decades reinforces the complexity of the literacy process (Gambrell & Mazzoni, 1999). There are various literacy elements the young child must know to become a successful reader and writer, including vocabulary, alphabetic knowledge, phonological awareness, phonics, concept of words, and reading for meaning.

Vocabulary

The size of a child's vocabulary has been linked to reading comprehension. The larger the oral vocabulary, the easier it is to learn to read. Reading results in learning more vocabulary. The child engaged in developing literacy must be able to make the connection between the oral word and the written word. Young children can learn many words incidentally, without instruction, but some need to have intentional exposure to new words many times before those words become part of their vocabulary (Snow & Tabors, 1993). This is particularly true of children who come to preschool classrooms with a small vocabulary. Experiences for language acquisition discussed in the first part of the chapter address this important component for literacy acquisition.

Alphabetic Knowledge

A child needs to know that letters represent sounds and that words are combinations of letters and sounds. To be able to read, a child needs to be able to recognize letters and their sounds fluently (Adams, 1990; Bond & Dykstra, 1967). However, some children enter kindergarten knowing very few letters of the alphabet (Ehri, 1989). An important goal in kindergarten is for children to be able to recognize and discriminate between letter shapes with increasing fluency (Snow, Burns, & Griffin, 1998). Adams (1990) recommends that teachers start with upper-case letters that are more easily visualized followed by lower-case letters. Letters should be introduced a few at a time.

Phonological Awareness

Recognizing letters of the alphabet cannot be separated from the sounds the letters represent. The two types of letter knowledge should be taught concurrently. It is of little use to be able to recite or name the letters of the alphabet unless the child can use knowledge of letter sounds in reading contexts.

Thus, phonological awareness is the ability to hear the constituent sounds of words to include phonemes, syllables, and words (Adams, 1990; Gambrell & Mazzoni, 1999). Phonological awareness is related to reading ability. Tasks that promote phonological awareness and have been shown to predict reading performance can include phonemic segmentation, adding or deleting phonemes to create new words, blending, comparing and contrasting rhyming words, and splitting syllables in a word (Adams, 1990).

Phonics

Phonics instruction helps children to use letter knowledge and phonological awareness to read and spell words. Children's use of invented spelling are attempts to match letters with the sounds they hear in words. Although children are able to learn letter-sound correspondence in emergent literacy activities spontaneously, there is evidence that the letter-sound training facilitates reading and spelling development (Adams, 1990; Gambrell & Mazzoni, 1999; Mann, 1993).

Concept of Word

Young emergent writers and readers develop the concept of a word as a unit as well as the letters and sounds that make up a word. Children become aware of words as they are encountered in written contexts. Repeated readings of big books where teachers help children visually follow the text helps to build both vocabulary and concept of word. Teacher recording of children's dictated stories are invaluable in helping children develop word awareness, the conventions of written language, and how letter-sound relationships are used to spell words (IRA & NAEYC, 1999).

Reading as Meaning

Reading comprehension is also a basic component of literacy. Although knowledge of letters and words is essential for success in reading, the ultimate goal is for the child to gain meaning from what is read. As children engage in interpreting what is read, they are using prior knowledge and experience. In addition, the interpretation is reevaluated as the child gains new information from the reading process. The child's natural development of meaning through being read to and engaging in first attempts at reading can be enhanced through instruction in reading comprehension strategies (Gambrell & Mazzoni, 1999).

Young children can develop foundations for literacy through the inclusion of the components of literacy just discussed. Some of the knowledge they will need to become successful readers can be acquired through emergent literacy experiences. Teachers will also need to scaffold children's progress and development with meaningful, contextual instruction.

Goals for Literacy

From what we know about what children need to know to be able to acquire literacy, what should be included in a quality early literacy program? Teale and Yokota (2000, p. 7) propose the following seven points:

1. An emergent literacy approach provides the foundation.
2. Comprehension instruction is a core feature.
3. A multifaceted word study program is essential.
4. Writing—integrated and separated— is central.
5. Reading fluency must be developed.
6. Children need to practice by reading connected text.
7. The early literacy program is conceptualized as developmental.

In the sections that follow, the goals for literacy are put into action. Although literacy is described in terms of emergent writing and emergent reading, an integrated process predominates. The essential components needed for a foundation for successful reading are threaded through the examples provided. Activities for writing can include reading and vice versa. There are activities where the teacher infuses direct instruction and activities where children use writing and other expressive forms to represent what they are learning and to communicate ideas.

Emergent Writing

We know that developing literacy is an ongoing process that begins at birth and continues throughout the early childhood years. Morrow (1997) explains that the developmental process begins with learning to communicate first nonverbally and then verbally. Symbolic play follows, and then drawing emerges.

The process of using written language begins by playing with it before it is used to communicate. First attempts at writing consist of making marks on paper without understanding that the alphabet is used to symbolize speech. Later, children understand that letters are used to encode speech and that writing represents language (Ferreiro & Teberosky, 1982).

Research is being conducted to establish how children move through stages of understanding and use writing to communicate. Two groups of researchers (Sulzby, Barnhart, & Hieshima, 1989; Fields & Spangler, 2000) have characterized these stages in different ways; both characterizations of the development of written literacy are helpful in understanding how a child learns to write.

Sulzby and colleagues (1989) have established six categories of writing, rather than a developmental sequence, that demonstrate ways that children attempt to write:

1. Drawing
2. Scribbling
3. Making letterlike forms
4. Reproducing well-learned units (i.e., letter sequences that are familiar, such as those that spell the child's name)
5. Invented spelling
6. Conventional spelling

Dyson (1993) takes the position that there is no linear progression in writing development. She posits that emergent writing is part of a larger process where the children explore how to orga-nize their world within a total symbolic reper-toire. This repertoire includes opportunities to use the arts including drawing, playing, dancing, and singing. Dyson believes children and their curios-ity about the world should be the center of the curriculum, not literacy.

Although the sequences are not considered stages, the categories reveal the evolution of understanding written language and the way in which children use writing experiences to express themselves.

Fields and Spangler (2000) describe the pro-gression of written literacy in terms of written forms. Figure 8.1 is a list of these forms with ex-planations of their characteristics.

Form	Characteristics and Hypotheses
Scribbles	Random marks with no differentiation between drawing and writing
Drawing	Illustration tells a story
Linear-repetitive	Marks in a line, fairly uniform in size and shape (repetitive); looks like longhand
Copying standard writing	May or may not be linear but contains elements of actual words
Memorized forms	Frequently used and important words: love, Mom, Dad, own name, etc.
Letterlike forms	Contains elements of actual letters, looks like letters; no more than two similar forms next to one another
Quantitative principles	The number of letters is significant Reflects hypotheses about number of letters necessary for a word Big things have big names Progresses to reflect number of oral language syllables

Qualitative principles
  Beginning invented spelling
    Letter names as sounds
	Which letters are used is significant
	
	Reflects hypothesis that letters make the sound of their names

Simplified phonics	One letter per word or per syllable; only major sounds, few vowels
Advanced invented spelling	Attempts to regularize sound–symbol relationship; uses vowels; becomes readable
Standard spelling	Self-correction to match standard spelling models

FIGURE 8.1 Emergent writing forms
Source: From *Let's Begin Reading Right*, (p. 26, 4th ed.), by M. V. Fields and K. L. Spangler, © 2000. Reprinted by permission of Pearson Education, Inc. Upper Saddle River, NJ 07458.

Taking a Child's Dictation

When it comes to making sense out of print, what could be more helpful to children than seeing their own thoughts written down? That's why dictation—writing children's words exactly as they say them—is so important. It allows children to see the relationship between the words they say and the words that appear on paper. They begin to understand that print is "talk written down."

Dictation makes writing and reading meaningful and compelling to children. By working one on one to record preschoolers' words and stories, you let them know their ideas have value. Plus, because print is permanent, children see that it can be used to help them remember thoughts, feelings, and experiences. They can also see that dictation gives them a way to communicate with people who aren't near enough to hear what they say. By dictating their words, children find they can send messages to people in other rooms, at home, or even to faraway friends and relatives.

Finally, dictation gives you concrete examples to use as you observe children and talk with families about their children's development. Family members also treasure dictation because it offers them a peek into their children's thoughts and feelings while they're in your care.

Dictation Tips

Here are points to keep in mind when doing dictation:

- Use open-ended questions to invite children's dictation, such as "Tell me about that," or "What should I write?"
- Record children's words exactly as they say them.
- Match your writing speed to children's speaking as much as possible. If you can't keep up, ask children to wait a moment so you can write all their words.
- Be patient. Give children plenty of time to compose their ideas and change their minds.

When to Take Dictation

The best way to show children that print is useful is to incorporate it into their everyday activities. When it's used this way, dictation is a meaningful—not isolated—experience.

Help children solve problems. Ask children how they made a collage, designed a block structure, or figured out how to work a new puzzle. Then record their explorations and invite them to illustrate their words. Over time, show children how they can use their dictations to remind them of past ideas and situations that can be helpful in new situations.

Encourage young authors. Listen to the stories children invent during free play, at snacks and meals, and on the playground. Wait for a time when you won't be interrupting and offer to record their stories. You might write them on chart paper, put them on a few sheets in book form, or even type them. However you do it, you'll help validate children's imaginations. Invite your authors to illustrate their stories and share them with the group.

Expand communication. Talk with children about their paintings and drawings to help them further express thoughts and feelings. Maximize children's control over the experience by letting them decide where—and if—you'll write words on their artwork.

Record observations. Science activities provide natural opportunities for dictation. Write children's words on experience-chart paper as they make observations, predictions, and discoveries. Hang the charts in your science area and refer to them as you continue your investigations.

Remember fun experiences. Keep special feelings alive by writing down memories of a shared group experience such as a field trip or celebration. Invite four or five children at a time to dictate their favorite things about the event. Then gather together and read the dictation back to the whole group. (Doing group dictation with a few children at a time ensures that no one has to wait too long for his or her turn.)

Get organized. To plan an event such as a trip to the grocery store or an indoor picnic, gather in a group and make shopping and "things-to-do" lists. Then use your lists to help you get ready and carry out your plans.

FIGURE 8.2 Tips on taking a child's dictation
Source: From *SCHOLASTIC PRE-K TODAY,* January 1993. Copyright © 1993 by Scholastic Inc. Reprinted by permission of Scholastic Inc.

Activities for Promoting Emergent Writing

Children between the ages of 3 and 5 are at different levels in their progress toward written literacy. Some will be engaged in scribbling, whereas others will be interested in copying words and using invented spelling. The teacher makes available activities that encompass levels of ability within the group, as well as materials that will appeal to individual interests. In addition to providing writing opportunities and materials in the environment, planning is conducted for teacher-directed and child-centered activities. The teacher can use specific strategies to demonstrate how to write and use writing to communicate. The teacher will model writing by using it in a meaningful context the children can observe several times each day on the chalkboard or an experience chart.

Dictation is taken from the children daily, both individually and as a part of group activities. Some dictation can be in the form of writing down experience chart stories, whereby children in a small group take turns contributing items for the chart following an interesting classroom discussion. The teacher can write notes to individual children and make the children aware when notes are being written to parents or school staff (Hayes, 1990; Morrow, 1997). Sulzby (1993) provides some tips for taking children's dictation, as demonstrated in Figure 8.2

In addition to ensuring that written language is being modeled in various contexts throughout the day, the teacher can conduct other activities with the children. Suggestions for some activities are included in the following sections.

My Very Own Word

Each day, the child is invited to determine the important word of that day (Morrow, 1989). The teacher writes the important word at the top of a large piece of manila paper. The child draws a picture about the word. The child then returns to the teacher and dictates a story about the picture. The important word is also written on a file card to be put in the child's favorite-word box or bank. When 10 to 15 word pictures are completed, they are stapled into a book. Word cards are used for reviewing favorite words, copying, or recoding on a word list on the computer. The child can reread the dictated stories.

Today's Plans

Each morning during planning time, the teacher writes the day's plans on an experience chart as the day's activities are discussed. The teacher and the children read and reread the plans. Later, the experience chart is placed in a convenient place for easy access by the children who might wish to use it for their own writing and reading. They might choose to copy words or rewrite the sentences on their own sheet of paper.

Journals

This process is normally used with older students but is adaptable for younger children. Each child is given a booklet of blank pages of paper that form a journal. Every day, children and teacher write in their journals. Over a period of time, teachers and children review their entries in their journals. Young children may start with drawings and gradually develop writing skills and the use of letter forms and invented spelling.

Group Dictation

Children dictate ideas for an experience chart following a learning activity, a story, a field trip, an art experience, or an unexpected event. The dictated contributions are recorded on an experience chart using the following guidelines:

1. Each statement is recorded exactly as dictated by the child, without correction of errors.
2. Each new contribution is started on a new line.
3. Punctuation marks can be highlighted using a red marking pen.
4. For preschool children, the dictated story should be limited to five statements.
5. The teacher rereads the statement as it is being written to draw the students' attention to the relationship between the spoken and written word. When completed, the entire statement is reread with the teacher using a hand to guide the child's eye along the words from left to right.
6. When the story is completed, the entire text is reread, again with the teacher guiding the flow from left to right below the written words.

Class Books

Class books are a collection of writing and drawing efforts that are created as a result of a thematic study or special class event or project. The illustrated writing effort of each child is collected into a book and put into the library for all to enjoy. A title for the book is selected by the class to go on the book cover.

Thematic Prop Boxes

Collections of materials and objects for thematic play are organized into prop boxes. The boxes contain writing and reading materials needed for the particular dramatic play theme. Morrow and Rand (1991) suggest a newspaper office setting, with writing paper, newspaper, telephones, telephone directories, maps, typewriters, and pens and pencils to stimulate writing efforts in the dramatic play center.

Sentence Strips

Sentences from group and individual stories are written on a tagboard sentence strip. The strip is then cut apart. Children can reassemble the sentence and copy it. They can also write more sentences using the first sentence as a model.

Both teacher-planned and informal opportunities that occur during play are used for written language. Birthday cards and stories are used as part of the celebration of a birthday. Children can write or dictate thank-you notes after a special class event such as an outing or a party. Constructions or projects can be labeled, as can record keeping of work as part of integrated learning activities

(Hayes,1990). The teacher and children are constantly alert to the possibilities for using writing during classroom routines and learning experiences.

Emergent Reading

How do 3-, 4-, and 5-year-olds engage in the lifelong process of learning to read? From the time that an infant is propped up on her mother's lap to share a picture book, the reading process has begun. The young child engages in the problemsolving process of understanding the relationship between speaking and the symbols that appear on a page each time a book is read. Teale (1982) proposed that the child's involvement in reading activities in a social context with a significant person is a key to acquiring literacy. He also concluded that reading and writing are learned in real-life settings when the child participates in activities where reading and writing are used in a meaningful context (Teale, 1986a). In the preschool years, the child observes parents reading, is read to daily, sees adults writing and reading notes and letters, and begins to understand the purpose for written language.

There is evidence that understanding the purpose for written symbols comes at an early age. Toddlers become fascinated with environmental symbols; they are able to identify the golden arches of McDonald's restaurants and the graphics on the package of their favorite cereal. Understanding of environmental print and symbols expands rapidly as children are bombarded with visual symbols both inside and outside the home. Investigators have determined that children as young as age 3 are able to read common words in the environment (Hiebert, 1986; Mason, 1980).

Children who are read to frequently between the ages of 3 and 5 make significant progress in learning to read. In addition to understanding how print is organized and used, they learn about books and how they are used. Wiseman and Robeck (1983) described book knowledge that

young children acquired from reading experiences as knowing the difference between the beginning and the end of the book, where to begin reading, how to turn pages, and the difference between pictures and print, in addition to having an awareness that print moves from left to right.

What do parents and teachers do that nurtures the acquisition of reading? Jewell and Zintz (1986) described factors that occur in the home and are associated with developing the ability to read. First, not only were the children read to but the mothers also engaged in incidental reading and pointing out environmental print throughout the day; they drew the children's attention to food labels and to familiar products advertised on television. Second, there were reading materials for both parents and children in the home; books of all types—from storybooks to nursery rhymes and fairy tales—were read and reread to the children many times. Third, the parents served as reading models; parents read frequently, allowing children to observe that reading was an important, positive activity for them. Fourth, writing materials were readily available to the children; they learned to move between reading and writing as they progressed in their knowledge of letter forms and the use of letters to communicate ideas. Fifth, persons in the environment responded to and encouraged the child's attempts at reading and writing; parental help was provided not as a formal, systematic process but rather in response to incidental questions and requests for help.

The same types of experiences found in the home that nurture the acquisition of literacy are used with preschool children in group settings. The foundations for the acquisition of reading are developed through interactions with many types of books and stories and extensive experiences with environmental print.

Once the child has acquired basic knowledge about books and the ways in which they are used, how does the process evolve into recognition of words and meanings from printed materials?

Three kinds of reading behavior develop concurrently (Goodman, 1984; Mason, 1984; Morrow, 1997):

1. The child learns to understand the functions of print (such as environmental print) and family and teacher use of print (as discussed earlier).
2. The child learns about the forms of print and acquires information about names, sounds, and shapes of letters.
3. The child learns how to use the conventions of print, such as the organization of letters into words, left-to-right progression, punctuation, and use of upper- and lowercase letters.

The development of word identification is acquired in three ways (McCormick & Mason, 1981):

1. Words are identified in context.
2. Words are identified using letter-sound cues.
3. Words are sounded out.

In spite of the descriptions characterizing the process of becoming a reader, all children progress by using their own sequence and system of interpretation of reading and by using their own reading experiences as a guide. Learning to read is a complex process that cannot be easily described in stages and categories. The kinds of classroom experiences planned for children from ages 3 to 5 are based on knowledge about reading acquisition, and they accommodate individual differences in progress and interest.

Activities for Promoting Emergent Reading

Books and book reading form a central element of the journey into reading. Daily experiences with new and familiar books are the nucleus of the transition into literacy, with each child benefitting from the experiences according to her own current understanding of the reading process. Beyond the obvious need for sharing books with children, there are activities that will facilitate understanding and use of written language, which will develop into reading. The activities can be understood by recalling the categories of reading behavior introduced previously.

Activities for Understanding the Functions of Print

From their experiences with storybooks and other types of books, children learn that print is used to tell a story. They also learn that written language is used for other kinds of communication. When they engage in writing letters and notes, writing stories for their "very own words," and dictating individual or group stories, they are developing an understanding of how print is used to communicate ideas or feelings. When environmental print in the form of posters, empty product containers, and labels and other printed information is used in the classroom to give instructions and information, children become aware of how people use print to convey information. When reading and writing are used in thematic unit activities, the usefulness of print is conveyed.

Activities for Learning to Use the Forms of Print

Visual experiences with print facilitate the development of understanding of the forms and sounds of letters. Individual writing experiences, dictated stories, big-book experiences (where children can follow the print as a story is read), and follow-up experiences (where children work with individual letter sounds and symbols with a written communication) allow the child to understand and identify letters. This process can evolve from experiences with environmental print, book narratives, individual writing efforts, and other activities providing opportunities to develop an awareness of letter forms and to learn the associated sounds and names.

Activities for Learning to Use the Conventions of Print

Again, the activities used to acquire the other reading behaviors also apply to the ability to use the conventions of print. Through activities in which these conventions are used, the child learns that reading progresses from left to right, that letters are combined into words, that written statements are punctuated, and that both upper-case and lower-case letters are used in print. Dictating stories, reading big books, writing individually, and other written communication activities can be used to develop an awareness of the functions of the conventions of print. The sentence strip activities described previously in the section on written literacy can be used for understanding words, punctuation, and the use of upper-case and lower-case letters.

In addition to the strategies just described, there are activities that serve multiple purposes in facilitating the development of literacy. Four of these—story reenactments, dictated stories, big-book activities, and predictable stories—are discussed next.

Designing Language Curriculum for Children with Disabilities and Language Differences

Emergent literacy is a process of literacy acquisition that is flexible and adaptable to various levels

Story Reenactments

Story reenactment is a form of retelling a story. Story dramatization encourages oral communication as children discuss the plot, the sequence of events, and the characters' roles. Listening skills are enhanced because the children must pay careful attention to the content of the story before planning the reenactment (Han, 1991). By acting out a story, children strengthen their comprehension and memory of the story. Reenactment is a form of sociodramatic play that includes guidance and direction from the teacher. The teacher thus should help the players use fantasy play in their reenactment of the story (Ishee & Goldhaber, 1990).

A familiar story is used with this form of thematic-fantasy play. "The Three Bears" and "The Three Little Pigs" are two familiar stories commonly suggested for reenactment. The teacher has an important role in making sure that the story has been shared frequently and is well understood by the children. Props and costumes are important. The teacher determines which props are important to the story narrative. The teacher and players review the sequence of the story. During the fantasy play experience, the teacher prompts and cues as the children are guided through the sequence of the story (Johnson, Christie, & Yawkey, 1998). Because children develop their reenactment skills through practice, the reenactment is repeated several times. The teacher continues in the role of director, narrator, and actor but modifies each role as the children become more accomplished in the process (Ishee & Goldhaber, 1990).

Story reenactment helps foster social skills because children must plan and act together. They have to take turns and negotiate their parts just as they do in self-initiated fantasy play. They learn how to cooperate and participate in a group effort (Han, 1991).

Big-Book Activities

Big books are enlarged versions of books that are appropriate for young children. They serve the same purposes as any storybook; however, because of their size, they are especially suited to group activities because all children can see the pictures and print. After the text is read, the books can be used for follow-up activities similar to those applicable to dictated group stories. When the book is read and reread, the teacher follows the text with a hand, allowing the children to make the relationships between the story and the written words. As the story is reread frequently, the teacher can highlight different print conventions (such as punctuation), point out letter-sound relationships, refer to spoken and written word relationships, and test comprehension skills, such as the ability to predict what will happen next in the story. For example, when rereading a big-book story, the teacher might do one or more of the following:

1. *Call attention to punctuation marks.* Teacher and children can compare the use of periods, question marks, and exclamation points.
2. *Identify letters and words.* Given a file card with a letter or word written on it, the child can match it with the same letter or word on a page in the story.
3. *Identify letter sounds in the story.* The teacher can point out an important word

on a page and help the children identify the beginning and ending sound of the word and the letters that make the sounds.

4. *Develop book knowledge.* Children can identify such things as where reading begins on a page, when to turn a page, and where the front and back of the book are (Cassady, 1988).

5. *Identify upper-case and lower-case letters.* Given a card with both upper-case and lower-case forms of a letter, the child can find each form on a page of the big book. Discussion of the uses of upper-case and lower-case letters can be a part of the activity.

Dictated Stories

The same strategies that are used with big books can also be used with group-dictated stories. Following rereadings of the dictated story, the teacher can select the print knowledge characteristics that are addressed in the story and conduct activities that will develop the child's awareness and understanding. Any activities that can be used with big books can also be used with dictated stories. Because both use a large-size format, they are useful for group activities.

Predictable Books

Predictable books and stories have a pattern that can be chanted by the children as the teacher reads the story. The predictable pattern can also be used by the children in their own story writing. Two examples of books with predictable patterns are *The Three Billy Goats Gruff* and *Chicken Soup with Rice* (Sendak, 1962). In the poem "Over in the Meadow" (Keats, 1971), the repetitive pattern includes the sequence of numbers from 1 to 10. Through repeated readings of such poems and stories, children learn the rhythm of the poem or sentence patterns and enjoy participating in the reading. When using a repetitive pattern for their own writing, they can exercise their creativity and vocabulary in making their own repetitive statements.

of development. Its flexible nature is applicable to children who have special needs for learning in the preschool years. Little modification is needed in many classroom experiences, because no set level of participation is required. For example, Mills and Clyde (1991) describe a child with mental retardation in a preschool classroom who used paper and pencil in the housekeeping center to engage in pretend play about renting a house. He used his own level of writing skills to make an inventory of the contents of the house.

Adapting the curriculum for children who are hearing impaired or deaf requires more planning and thought because sign language differs from oral language. The musical features of rhymes are lost when translated into sign language. Dowd (1991) recommends the substitution of physical actions and visual picture clues to help children with hearing impairments make sense of Mother Goose rhymes.

Children whose first language is not English and who are limited in their ability to speak English are in the process of learning English as a second language. Because research literature supports the theory that children use the same process to learn a second language as they do to learn the first, the same emergent process to achieve literacy can be used with them (Abramson, Seda, & Johnson, 1990; Hudleson & Serna, 1997). Activities that integrate reading, writing, and language development will help these children acquire language and literacy in a meaningful context. Dictated stories, journal writing, and the use of books and stories are equally important. The teacher needs to be sensitive to limitations in language among these children and to accept the more limited vocabulary and syntax in their early efforts. Time is needed in oral conversations for these children to consider how to respond in the new language.

Children with language differences are not always provided with literacy strategies found in classrooms where children speak standard English. Misperceptions held by teachers can cause this practice. One belief is that children with language differences need remediation through structured language or skills instruction. Another perception is that these children are unready or unable to engage in emergent literacy activities because of their language limitations. There may also be the perception that there are few literacy experiences in the child's home environment that will help promote literacy activities at school (Gutierrez, 1993).

Children from diverse backgrounds benefit from the same literacy experiences as other children; however, teachers need to be knowledgeable about the child's language strengths and what kinds of literacy activities are familiar. Grocery lists, notes to friends and family, and functional reading activities might be used in the home. In addition to the regular literacy activities discussed in this chapter, teachers can focus on lessons on the functions of literacy that might be familiar from the home environment. Working with food labels and environmental print are examples of how functional literacy opportunities can be included in the curriculum (Au, 2000).

In a bilingual program in southern Texas, a family literacy project involving young children utilized a whole-language approach to achieving literacy in English. Parents who were Spanish speakers were engaged in an effort to achieve English and literacy simultaneously. The designers of the project used the same strategies that have been described in this chapter and included integrated themes in the learning process. Parents and children worked together in their writing of stories. The authors stressed the need for the acceptance of code switching (i.e., the use of both Spanish and English in language efforts) as this population of learners grew in their ability to write, speak, and read English. Code switching is a natural part of the process of mastering and using the English language (Quintero & Huerta-Macias, 1990).

The thematic curriculum used in the project follows a sequence. The theme study begins with a discussion of the topic. As part of the discussion, parents are given information on how to have meaningful conversations with the children and expand their use of the language. A learning activity following the discussion permits the parents and children to work together in a hands-on activity. Next, a language experience activity engages parent and child in writing projects. The child may dictate a story or write a message. The parent's own level of literacy will dictate how much support will be needed from the teacher. Story reading is a fourth activity, and an activity for parent and child to take and do at home ends the activities for the session. Because these activities are suitable for children who have limited use of English, they can also be used in preschool classrooms with special attention to adapting teacher language and expectations to the child's language ability. Abramson, Seda, & Johnson, (1990) propose that the teacher must use caretaker speech similar to the simplified speech used with infants and toddlers to assist the developing speaker through labeling, clarifying, and extending efforts to speak.

With careful planning, teachers can use the language curriculum with all children. The child's

level of participation will vary or may have to be modified for a specific language difference, but the process and philosophy remain the same. The teacher tunes in to the individual child's stage of learning and individual combinations of abilities and limitations and finds the activities that the child can take part in to achieve literacy.

Curriculum for Cognitive Development

In the preschool years, young children are expanding their knowledge about the world. They construct their understanding through encounters with the world. Between the ages of 3 and 5, the child's thinking process changes as the sensorimotor period proposed by Piaget is left behind and preoperational thought is used to understand experiences the child has in the world. Young children are developing their cognitive capacities in

problem-solving, reasoning, and abstract concept formation during the years from age 3 to 5 (Bredekamp & Copple, 1997). In this section, I will explore the nature of cognition between ages 3 and 5 and the way in which educators structure the environment, activities, and behaviors to foster cognitive development. I will discuss cognitive development as it applies to science and mathematics. (Social development, or cognitive development, as it is reflected in the content area of social studies, will be discussed in Chapter 9.) I will also consider an example of integrated, thematic curriculum that features language and cognitive development.

It is urgent that a quality cognitive curriculum is introduced to young children in the preschool years. Because students in the United States compare unfavorably in mathematics and science with students from other industrialized countries, there is a national effort to improve the curriculum in these areas. Moreover, the gap in learning appears as early as kindergarten and first grade (Price, 1989; Stevenson, Lee, & Stigler, 1986). The implication for educators of children in early childhood programs is that cognitive development, particularly the study of concepts in mathematics and science, should be a strong component of the preschool curriculum.

How Young Children Develop Concepts

Chapter 4 describes developmental progress in cognition in the early childhood years. The preoperational child has entered a period that includes symbolic thought; the child is able to mentally represent objects and events. Children are controlled by what they see or perceive. Because they focus on one characteristic or attribute of an object at a time (i.e., centration), they are unable to organize objects using true classification. For example, if a child is asked to study two sets of objects to determine if they are equivalent, the physical size or arrangement of the objects, rather than just the number of objects in the two sets, will affect the child's response (Dutton & Dutton, 1991). The child lacks the ability to process multiple comparisons and to conserve.

The process used by the child to construct understanding of concepts involves hands-on interactions with concrete materials. Between the ages of 3 and 5, children develop their schema about concepts through repeated experiences with a variety of materials to explore the possibilities those materials present. An explanation of concept development that reflects Piaget's theory is that when the child encounters new information, the disequilibrium or cognitive conflict that occurs will challenge the child's current understanding. However, cognitive limitations in preoperational children might prevent the child from resolving or clearly understanding new aspects of the concept. The child's innate capacities are not enough to resolve contradictions between what is known and the new information. Preschool children need scaffolding and other adult guidance, plus interactions with other children, to organize a

coherent system of understanding (Landry & Forman, 1999). To engage in this process, children need adequate time to explore, investigate, and reflect as is demonstrated in the Learning Cycle in Figure 3.3 (p. 64). The child needs skillful intervention by the teacher who uses the range of strategies described in the Teaching Continuum in Figure 3.4 (p. 65). Children also need to work in a social context where children and teachers learn as partners as exemplified by the Project Approach and the Reggio Emilia schools (Landry & Forman, 1999). Finally, children need to be introduced to and have experiences with relevant language and symbols that are part of the study of science and mathematics.

Planning for Cognitive Development

> To teach 3-year-olds, 7-year-olds, or any other age group, educators must understand how children have acquired the knowledge they already have, and how this knowledge is related to that of adolescents and adults. The only theory in existence that shows this development from birth to adolescence is Piaget's. (Kamii & Ewing, 1996, p. 261)

Extensive research has been conducted on how children acquire concepts in the preoperational period. In addition, information is available about the sequence of concept development in mathematics and science. In setting curriculum goals for cognitive development, educators must become familiar with the nature of progress in cognitive development, the way in which this understanding helps us organize instruction for cognitive curriculum, and the goals and objectives for preschool children.

Children acquire concepts through manipulation, observation, and discovery. According to Piaget, an understanding of concepts is acquired through physical knowledge—the child's physical interaction with information (Kamii & DeVries, 1993; Piaget & Inhelder, 1969).

Vygotsky believed that social transmission affected both the content of knowledge and the child's thinking process (Bodrova & Leong, 1996). Both Piaget and Vygotsky believed that children construct their own understanding from their own manipulations and discoveries. The individual child's schema of concepts varies in content and rate, depending on frequency and context of experience. The child's ability to understand concepts related to mathematics and science in the preoperational period is developed through discrimination, classification and one-to-one correspondence. Although the child lacks the ability to conserve or process multiple comparisons, she can focus on attributes and make global comparisons. The child can use discrimination to compare shapes, sizes, and colors. Discrimination of characteristics can be used to group objects and to determine what belongs or does not belong to a group.

One-to-one correspondence is a prerequisite to being able to count, add, and subtract. Matching sets of objects precedes the understanding of numbers, whereas seriation leads to the ability to order by size, texture, quantity, and other attributes. Although the child is functioning at a perceptual level, skills are being developed for higher-order cognitive development in science and mathematics.

For preoperational children, learning how to count is a major step in understanding numbers. The child moves through a succession of steps or observes principles in learning to count. First, the child learns that she needs to use the same number of counting words, or tags, as there are objects, even if the counting word order is unconventional. Next, the child understands that the sequence of counting words always follows the same order. The child can then make the connection between numbers and the process of counting (Copley, 2000; Gelman & Gallistel, 1978).

Mathematics experiences prepared for preschool children should take into account the child's cognitive limitations and present a minimum of perceptual difficulties. Dutton and Dutton (1991) advise that concrete materials must be made available to manipulate, act on, arrange,

and classify. They propose that the available objects should be familiar from the child's daily life. Buttons, keys, bottle caps, marbles, and rocks, are examples of objects from the child's environment that provide meaningful mathematical experiences. Children need to use manipulative materials in a variety of ways. Time should be allowed for children to experiment and use trial-and-error approaches. Likewise, the teacher should encourage children to find different uses for the materials and make suggestions, but should resist giving them answers to problems (Blake, Hurley, & Arenz, 1995; Copley, 2000).

Learning in science results from a store of concepts that can be used when thinking about or understanding relationships between objects, events, or situations. Through observing and discriminating, children begin to categorize their experiences. First, broad categories are developed, followed by subcategories. Thus, all four-legged animals may be identified as dogs before the child understands the category of animal and subcategories of dogs, cats, cows, horses, and so on. Through discrimination of similarities and differences, the child determines what does or does not belong in a category.

Once the child has a broad base of concepts and can see relationships among concepts, generalizations can be made. The three processes of forming concepts—differentiating, grouping, and labeling—enable children to make sense of the hands-on encounters with the environment. Daily encounters with the environment and concept-building experiences with the teacher and peers are the foundation for acquiring concepts in science (Seefeldt & Barbour, 1998).

Likewise, science concepts are learned through discovery and exploration and with experiences that are scaffolded by the teacher. Preoperational children develop a familiarity with the phenomenal world that builds a foundation for later scientific learning. As children explore and experiment with their environment, they acquire the processes of scientific thinking—forming concepts and problem-solving—at the same time that they acquire knowledge about the products of science (biological and physical sciences) (Kamii & DeVries, 1993; Landry & Forman, 1999).

Goals for Cognitive Development: Mathematics and Science

Mathematics is a science of numbers and their operations. For preoperational children, working with math is a process of constructing knowledge about mathematical concepts and engaging in problem solving. Through exploring, grouping and sorting objects, and making comparisons, young children develop understanding of numbering and its relationship to measuring quantity. The primary goal is for children to acquire understandings that evolve from established standards for mathematics (Campbell, 1999). The National Council of Teachers of Mathematics (2000) has developed standards for mathematics for prekindergarten through second grade. The categories included in the standards are: (1) numbers and operations; (2) patterns, functions, and algebra; (3) geometry and spatial sense; (4) measurement; and (5) data analysis and probability.

Another approach to organization might include a more constructivist approach such as the following:

Number
One-to-one correspondence
Counting
Numeration
Number operations

Measurement
Length
Width
Distance
Time
Money

Geometry
Shapes
Patterns

Mathematical Reasoning
Seriating
Classifying and comparing
Estimating
Problem solving

Cognitive development in science follows a slightly different process. Children construct a framework of understanding that is based on observing, thinking, and reflecting on experiences they have engaged in with phenomena in the environment. In the scientific process, children use their experiences to form hypotheses, collect data, make decisions about the hypotheses, and make generalizations about their information. The scientific process includes the following (Brewer, 1994; Seefeldt & Barbour, 1998):

- Observing: Children look for actions or information.
- Classifying and comparing: Children compare and contrast information and group or classify.
- Measuring: Data are collected through some type of measurement.
- Communicating: Children share their observations and data collections.
- Experimenting: Children manipulate conditions (e.g., trying a new way to ride a tricycle or experimenting with ways to construct bristle blocks).
- Relating, inferring, and applying: Children draw relationships or determine cause and effect.

Designing programs in science to use the scientific process with preschool children can include topics such as the following: animals, plants, space, water, air, and light. Science curricula can also be organized by categories of science: biological, physical, and earth science. Whatever scheme is used to plan the curriculum, it is organized in a meaningful, child-centered context that encourages young children to discover, explore, reflect on their experiences, and represent their understanding of what they are learning.

In summary, cognitive development does not occur in isolation. Just as mathematics and science cannot be separated, cognitive development cannot be separated from physical, social, and language development. Developmental learning is integrated; furthermore, cognitive development as reflected in science and mathematics is best learned within real-life experiences that also promote other skills and opportunities to represent and express relationships and learning.

The Role of the Teacher in Cognitive Development

The adult's role in facilitating cognitive development includes making plans for including both teacher-directed and child-directed activities and experiences. Using center time, small-group and large-group time, and other scheduled components of the day, opportunities are planned for children to engage in activities that will help them to develop and expand concepts. Keeping in mind the processes that young children use to learn, the teacher will consider how to include experiences that will permit observing, manipulating, hypotheses testing, inferring, and other procedures that will promote scientific thinking and exploration with mathematical concepts.

The teacher has a role in supporting or scaffolding the child's learning using the zone of proximal development (ZPD). The ZPD has been described as the difference between what the child can do independently and what the child can do with assistance. The teacher uses various strategies to give the child the needed assistance.

Assisted performance can come from an adult or a peer. It can result from an interaction when another person provides clues, asks questions, or demonstrates for a child. Support can come through setting up the environment with activities that will assist the child. The teacher can physically model a desired skill for a child or provide practice opportunities.

Children have individual needs for assistance using the ZPD. Some children may move ahead rapidly with minimal support, while others may need extensive support to make small gains. The teacher will use different types of structure or assistance depending on the child's strengths and interests.

The ZPD is dynamic. As the child progresses from assisted performance to independent performance, the level of the ZPD is raised. The child is now assisted at a higher level. According to Bodrova and Leong (1996), "What the child did only with assistance yesterday becomes the level of independent performance today. Then, as the child tackles more difficult tasks, a new level of assisted performance emerges" (p. 37).

The teacher will also want to keep in mind the sequences of learning that are developmentally appropriate for children in the preschool years and are logical for curriculum planning. The sequence of concrete to abstract ensures that the child will begin exploring a concept using manipulative materials or real phenomena such as plants, animals, and food items. The sequence of simple to complex will be maintained so that learning experiences follow a logical hierarchy that will guide the child's understanding of new information. For example, in working with mathematical concepts, the teacher will first include many experiences with number before adding numeral names. Likewise, the children will need to have confidence in both number and numeral names before counting and combining sets of objects and using the correct numerals with the sets.

The teacher will want to include many opportunities for children to use the sequence of experiencing and representing, particularly in working with concepts in science. Experiencing is part of the scientific process of observing, manipulating, ordering, and classifying. The child first needs to directly experience the concept. Representing is the child's opportunity to reflect on what is being understood. In science terms, inferring from data or making a decision about a hypothesis are methods of using representation to reflect knowledge being acquired. The child can use representation in math activities to practice or apply what is being learned.

The teacher will also consider how best to organize learning experiences. When is it best to plan teacher-directed activities for exploration, and when can children freely explore on their own? How much teacher guidance is needed for children to experiment with a concept? For example, if children are learning about plants, how much adult guidance is needed in planting seeds and monitoring the watering cycle? Which teacher-directed learning activities are best for small groups, and when are large-group times more effective? The processes for child-centered learning that are developmentally appropriate are combined with the unique characteristics of concept development in science and mathematics to plan meaningful, interesting activities for the children.

The Role of the Environment and Play in Cognitive Development

If children are to actively explore concepts in science and mathematics, then the environment is an essential element. The classroom needs to have a center for exploration of mathematical and scientific materials. The center needs to have a multitude of common objects for working with numbers. Collections of many different objects from the community can be used for work in mathematics. Buttons, bottle caps, dried beans, nuts, shells, and other natural objects can be used as resources for the math center.

The science center can include insect cages, small animal cages, magnifiers, a terrarium, microscopes, aquaria, rock and mineral collections, plants, and many other resources (Barufaldi, Ladd, & Moses, 1984). A changing array of additional items can be introduced as part of thematic units throughout the year. Physical science activities should be a part of the environment. Children need opportunities to explore physical properties of objects through explorations of water, sand, things that roll, and blocks (Sprung, 1996).

Patton and Kokoski (1996, p. 39) suggest that quality early childhood environments should include evidence of science, mathematics, and technology. They list the following essentials:

- A science–mathematics center
- A clearly defined library/resource center rich with science, mathematics, and technology information and literature
- Live plants and animals
- Construction materials and supplies accessible to your children and in sufficient quantities (i.e., wood chips, fabric scraps, boxes, paint, glue)
- Computers, calculators, microscopes, hand lenses, and multimedia available and in use throughout the day
- Student projects, inventions, and constructions displayed
- Running water, sinks, and sufficient electrical outlets
- A productive hum and children planning, negotiating, and moving about the room in purposeful engagement

Copley (2000) recommends that the following be part of the environment and mathematics materials in the preschool classroom:

> The physical environment, including the math materials available to children, is basic to the mathematics curriculum. Math materials include concrete manipulatives (e.g., blocks, counters, base-10 blocks, pattern blocks, attribute blocks, two-color counters, plastic people, a variety of containers, measuring materials, tangrams), symbolic materials (dice, dominoes, number lines, graphs, specific computer programs, and other visual models), and more abstract representations (plastic numerals, 100 chart, price tags from store items, grocery store lists, building plans, calculators, computers, and telephone books) (p.15).

Absent from this list are natural and found materials described earlier. A materials-rich environment would include natural items of all types that can be counted, measured, weighed, and organized using classification schemes.

Not to be forgotten is the significance of the outdoor environment. If science and mathematics are to be understood as part of the child's world, the outdoor environment should be an extended classroom where much of the work can take place.

A study of the weather would incorporate many outdoor activities. Children could explore weather phenomena such as wind, rain, sun, clouds, and weather changes (Huffman, 1996). The nearby community can also be explored for materials that expand the child's encounters with concepts.

If children are to learn through free exploration, then play is an essential ingredient in cognitive development. Much of what is learned is not the result of planned experiences but of incidental circumstances that occur during play. Children learn about weather when they observe leaves blowing in the wind or when a rain shower moves to the playground. Children playing at a water table indoors learn about the qualities of water and what objects will sink and float in water through experimentation during a play experience.

Guided discovery of concepts can also achieve a similar result. The teacher can guide water table play and discuss the concepts of floating and sinking as items with which to experiment are introduced and observed. Guided observation of wind movement can be accomplished with a group activity using paper streamers on a windy day. The point is that not all concept development occurs as a result of teacher planning. Concepts are being learned through play in all indoor learning centers and outdoors during unstructured play. The teacher can use serendipitous play opportunities to guide awareness and understanding of nature and other components of science. More significant is that the outdoor environment should be perceived as the most important location for scientific knowledge to develop.

Designing Curriculum for Cognitive Development

Cognitive development has been described here within the content areas of mathematics and science. It was pointed out that these content areas overlap, particularly in the preschool years when cognitive experiences involve the same processes. In curriculum designed for preschool children, the interrelationships in cognitive experiences reflect the nature of the preoperational child's thinking.

The activities described next are representative of the possibilities for activities that promote active involvement and child initiation. They are categorized by level and category using the Frost-Wortham developmental checklists in Chapter 4. Activities are designated as appropriate for Level III, IV, or V and related to quantitative and problem-solving, or concept, development (identification, discrimination, and classification skills). Activities are organized under mathematics and science but might be located in both categories.

Mathematics Experiences That Promote Cognitive Development: Measurement

Pretty Ribbons

Checklist Skill: Level III, Identification, Discrimination, and Classification Skills

Objective 7: Discriminates differences in the size of object (big/little, long/short)

Description of Activity: Cut six to eight different ribbons into two lengths, one obviously shorter than the other. Introduce the activity to the child by identifying one ribbon as being long and the other as short. Ask the child to find another short or long ribbon. After experiences with finding short and long ribbons, ask the child to put all the long ribbons together and all the short ribbons together.

Materials Needed: Six or eight ribbons cut to two lengths

Lady Dolls

Checklist Skill: Level IV, Quantitative and Problem Solving

Objective 6: Compares differences in dimension (taller/shorter, longer/shorter, thinner/wider).

Description of Activity: Place five nesting dolls in random order in front of the child. Demonstrate how to order the dolls from tall to short. Help the child locate the tallest doll and shortest doll. Ask the child to find a doll taller than the shortest doll and a doll shorter than the tallest doll. Put the dolls in random order. Select a doll, and ask the child to find a larger doll or shorter doll. Repeat with different dolls. Ask the child to order the dolls from tall to short or short to tall.

Materials Needed: A set of nesting dolls

Measuring Hands

Checklist Skill: Level IV, Quantitative and Problem-Solving

Objective 6: Compares differences in dimension (taller/shorter, longer/shorter, thinner/wider)

Description of Activity: Make handprints of children using tempera paint, or have the children trace an outline of their hand using crayons. Identify the handprints, and have the children cut them out. Use the prints to compare widths of hand spans. Children can compare two or more handprints to determine which is the widest and narrowest. A group of handprints can be ordered from narrow to wide. Handprints can be used to measure books or other classroom items.

Materials Needed: Paper, tempera paint or crayons, scissors

Ruler Activity

Checklist Skill: Level V, Quantitative and Problem-Solving

Objective 11: Compares distance (height, width, length) to an independent object

Description of Activity: This activity is designed to acquaint children with measurement using a ruler. The ruler is introduced to the children, and markings for measurement are discussed. A collection of items are compared with the ruler. The children must determine if each item is longer or shorter than the ruler.

Materials Needed: 12-inch ruler, 5 to 10 items that are longer or shorter than 1 foot (Tinkertoy sticks, pencils, lengths of string, paper strips, etc.)

Walking and Measuring

Checklist Skill: Level V, Quantitative and Problem-Solving

Objective 11: Compares distance (height, width, length) to an independent object

Description of Activity: Show the children how to make large measurements using walking strides. On the playground, have the children practice measuring distances between two objects such as two jump ropes or stones that have been placed several yards apart. Once the children are familiar with counting strides between two objects, have them compare distances. They can compare distances between trees, playground equipment, or other objects that have been placed different distances apart.

Materials Needed: Items that can be measured using walking strides

Mathematics Experiences That Promote Cognitive Development: Number

Egg Counting

Checklist Skill: Level III, Quantitative and Problem-Solving

Objective 2: Counts by rote from 1 to 5

Description of Activity: Using plastic Easter eggs, place one to five small items in each egg. Have children take turns opening an egg and counting the number of items. As an alternative, give children a set of eggs up to five and have them count their eggs.

Materials Needed: Plastic eggs, small items such as beans or dried corn to put inside the eggs

Matching Sets of Dishes

Checklist Skill: Level IV, Quantitative and Problem-Solving

Objective 7: Demonstrates one-to-one correspondence

Description of Activity: Using a collection of toy dishes, make sets of cups and saucers or knives, forks, and spoons. Show the child how to make sure there is a cup for each saucer. Next, vary the sets so that there are more cups or more saucers. Let the child determine which has more by putting the cups on the saucers. Repeat the activity using knives, forks, and spoons. Show the child how to use one-to-one correspondence to determine that there are the same numbers of each eating utensil. Next, vary the sets so that the children can use one-to-one correspondence to determine if there are more spoons, knives, forks, etc.

Materials Needed: Play dishes to include cups and saucers, knives, forks, and spoons.

Concentration

Checklist Skill: Level IV, Quantitative and Problem Solving

Objective 7: Demonstrates one-to-one correspondence

Description of Activity: Use a set of cards that have pairs of pictures. Place them face down and let the children take turns trying to turn two cards over to match a pair.

Materials Needed: Set of 10 to 20 cards with pairs of identical pictures

Counting Steps

Checklist Skill: Level IV, Quantitative and Problem Solving

Objective 1: Counts by rote from 1 to 10.

Description of Activity: As you climb a set of stairs, count each step with the children. Vary how many steps you climb or descend. Once the children are familiar with the process, place an item on one of the stairs, and let the children take turns counting the number of steps to the item. Let the children take turns placing the item on a step for another child.

Materials Needed: Stairs, large item such as a unit block to serve as a marker

Counting Outside

Checklist Skill: Level V, Quantitative and Problem-Solving

Objective 1: Counts to 50.

Description of Activity: Take the children outside. As a group, count objects in the environment such as swings, pieces of playground equipment, trees, windows, and so on. Let individual children choose what they want to count.

Materials Needed: None

Comparing Clothes

Checklist Skill: Level V, Quantitative and Problem-Solving

Objective 7: Compares elements of unequal sets (more than/fewer than)

Description of Activity: This activity combines one-to-one correspondence, counting, and graphing. Select items of clothing to compare. Have all the children wearing blue pants stand. Using beads and shoelaces, have a child string a bead for each blue pair of pants. Count the number of beads on the string. Repeat with other colors of pants, shirts, styles of shoes, and so on. Use a different color bead for each string. When each string is completed, hang them on a coat hanger or rod. Label each string. Let the children compare which string has the most, least, and so on. The strings can be ordered to make a graph demonstrating the comparisons in number. A similar activity could be conducted using stacks of one-inch blocks of different colors.

Materials Needed: Beads, strings, paper labels, marking pen, coat hanger or wooden rod

Egg Shake

Checklist Skill: Level IV, Quantitative and Problem-Solving

Objective 3: Orders the numerals 1 to 5

Description of Activity: Place numeral cards up to five in a plastic hosiery egg. Let children take turns shaking the egg, taking out the numerals, and ordering them.

Materials Needed: Plastic hosiery egg, numeral cards up to 5

Egg Carton Numbers

Checklist Skill: Level V, Quantitative and Problem Solving

Objective 2: Demonstrates the concept of numbers through 10

Description of Activity: Place numerals in random order in the bottom of an egg carton. Give the children beans, dried corn, or other small objects to count out for each number.

Materials Needed: Egg carton with numerals to 10 in random order; beans or other small counters

Two, Four, Six, Eight

Checklist Skill: Level V, Quantitative and Problem-Solving

Objective 6: Groups objects into sets of equal number

Description of Activity: Organize objects into sets of equal number up to 10. Give the child one of the sets, and ask the child to make two sets with the same number. Ask the child to count each set to make sure they both are the same. Repeat with other even-numbered sets.

Materials Needed: 10 objects

Mathematics Experiences That Promote Cognitive Development: Geometry

Sorting Shapes

Checklist Skill: Level III, Concept Development

Objective 6: Discriminates differences in the shape of objects (round, square, triangular)

Description of Activity: Make a collection of classroom toys, blocks, and the like that are round, square, and triangular. On pieces of construction paper, make a large drawing of each shape. Encourage the children to examine the objects and place them on the appropriate shape picture.

Materials Needed: Classroom objects that are round, square, and triangular

My Shape Book

Checklist Skill: Level IV, Concept Development

Objective 1: Points to basic shapes (circle, square, rectangle, triangle) on request.

Description of Activity: Make each child a booklet in the shape of one of the shapes to be learned. Supply the children with magazine pictures that have the desired shape. Have the children cut out the shape pictures and put them in the appropriate book. As an alternative, let the children draw pictures that include the shape.

Materials Needed: Shape books, scissors, paste, crayons

Bead Patterns

Checklist Skill: Level IV, Concept Development

Objective 5: Identifies likenesses and differences in two or more objects (shape, size, color)

Description of Activity: Have a string and collection of beads for each child. Demonstrate how to make a pattern of beads. Ask the children to duplicate your pattern. When the children are familiar with the process, let them take turns making the pattern to be copied.

Materials Needed: Strings and large assortment of wooden beads of different shapes and colors

Experiences That Promote Cognitive Development: Mathematical Reasoning

Making Stairs

Checklist Skill: Level V, Concept Development

Objective 12: Seriates (arranges) objects by size

Description of Activity: Give each child a handful of pieces of paper one inch square. Show them how to make a stair by making a series of lines of squares, each one longer than the one before. The same activity can be conducted using wooden cubes.

Materials Needed: Pieces of paper cut into inch squares; wooden inch cubes

How Tall Are You?

Checklist Skill: Level V, Concept Development

Objective 12: Seriates (arranges) objects by size

Description of Activity: Use a roll of adding machine paper to measure children. Have them lie on the floor or stand next to a wall to measure their height on the paper. Put the child's name on their strip. Tape the strips to the wall using masking tape with all strips even at the bottom. Determine who is tallest and shortest. Have the children rearrange the strips in order from tallest to shortest.

Materials Needed: Adding machine paper, marking pens, scissors, masking tape

Sorting Nuts

Checklist Skill: Level V, Concept Development

Objective 8: Classifies foods (fruits, vegetables, meats)

Description of Activity: Make a collection of different types of nuts (walnuts, peanuts, pecans, etc.). Ask the child to sort the nuts by type (all the pecans, peanuts, etc.). Then ask the child to determine a criterion for sorting (size, texture, etc.) A similar classification activity can be conducted with a collection of shells with more complex possibilities for classification.

Materials Needed: An assortment of nuts in their original shells

The Button Game

Checklist Skill: Level V, Concept Development

Objective 11: Identifies and classifies common objects by shape (circle, rectangle, triangle, oval, square)

Description of Activity: Make a large collection of buttons. Begin the game by making a set of buttons based on shape, size, or color. Ask the children to guess the common characteristic of the set. Make another set using another criterion such as number of holes or texture of the buttons. Encourage the children to take turns making sets using different characteristics of the buttons.

Materials Needed: Large collection of buttons

Science Experiences That Promote Cognitive Development: Observing

The activities that follow are described using the categories of science processes described earlier (Seefeldt & Barbour, 1998) and are not coordinated with a checklist skill. In addition, they are suitable for preschool children ages 3 to 5 with some adaptation.

Observing Fish

Description of Activity: Young children can observe many things about fish in a classroom aquarium. They can observe the likenesses and differences in different types of fish in the container. Other characteristics they might be guided to notice are the processes the fish use to breathe, the parts of the body such as fins and gills, and the way in which the body parts function. The children might observe different swimming patterns and the spots where individual fish prefer to spend their most time. They can also learn the names of the different varieties of fish and describe unique characteristics of each type.

Materials Needed: Classroom aquarium with a variety of fish

Mud Puddles

Description of Activity: On a rainy day, take the children where they can observe puddles forming in the soil. Discuss why puddles form in some locations and not in others. If the rain continues for some time, the size of the puddles can be measured and compared. After the rain is over, the puddles can continue to be observed and measured as the water evaporates. The children can also be guided to observe the drying process of the ground, trees, etc.

Materials Needed: Yardstick to measure length and width of puddles

Watching the Clouds Go By

Description of Activity: Take the children outdoors to a location where they can lie down and watch the clouds go by. Let them observe the cloud movement on a fairly

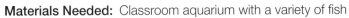

windy day so that they can see the clouds changing. They can repeat the observation several times and note differences in types of clouds, numbers of clouds, and the way clouds look when it rains. Names of types of clouds can be discussed with older children. If clouds are observed daily, a calendar might be used to record the type of clouds observed over a period of about 2 weeks.

Materials needed: None

Outdoor Sounds

Description of Activity: Take the children for a walk outdoors. Draw their attention to the sounds that they can hear. Discuss the difference between types of sounds such as bird or natural sounds versus manmade sounds from vehicles, machinery, and so on. After the walk, let the children contribute to a group-dictated story, or let each child draw a picture of something observed during the walk that made a sound and dictate a story about the picture.

Materials Needed: Paper for dictated stories, marking pen, crayons

Science Experiences That Promote Cognitive Development: Classifying and Comparing

Comparing Leaves

Description of Activity: If there are varieties of trees near the school, take children for a walk to gather as many different types of leaves as possible. Otherwise, take a collection of leaves for the children to use. Let each child select two leaves that are different and describe how they are alike and how they are different. They can then compare leaves by size, shape, texture, and so on. Older children can sort leaves into two groups using their own characteristics for classification.

Materials Needed: Large collection of leaves of many sizes and types

Sorting Types of Animals

Description of Activity: Use a collection of pictures of different types of animals such as zoo animals, farm animals, and animals that are pets. For 3-year-olds, discuss one type of animal. After discussing each animal in a group such as farm animals, mix a few farm animal pictures with zoo animal pictures. Encourage the children to decide which are farm animals and which are not farm animals. Repeat with more pictures.

For older children, three sets of animals may be compared. After discussing each set of animals separately, combine all of the pictures, and ask the children to sort them into their appropriate group. Give them a picture clue of each type of animal to guide the classification.

Materials Needed: Sets of animal pictures for zoo animals, farm animals, and pet animals

Science Experiences That Promote Cognitive Development: Measuring

Measuring Plants

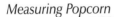

Description of Activity: Plant rapidly growing plants such as beans. Cut different colored strips of cardboard to measure 3 inches, 6 inches, 9 inches, and 12 inches. After the plants have sprouted, measure the plants once a week. Chart the growth of the plants until they have grown to 12 inches. Individual plants can be compared as to rate of growth. Children can try the different size measures to determine which is the closest to the plant's height on the day it is measured.

Materials Needed: Bean plants; measures for 3, 6, 9, and 12 inches

Measuring Popcorn

Description of Activity: The children will compare the volume of popcorn before and after it is popped. Before popping the corn, discuss what happens when corn is popped. Encourage the children to describe what happens to the corn kernels and what causes them to expand. Place the unpopped kernels in a clear container such as a large glass or clear plastic jar or pitcher. Use a marking pen to measure how high the kernels reach in the container. After popping the corn, put it back in the container and measure the volume again. Encourage the children to describe why there is now more corn in the container.

Materials Needed: Large, tall container, popcorn, popcorn popper, marking pen

Science Experiences That Promote Cognitive Development: Experimenting

Making New Colors

Description of Activity: Place shallow containers of tempera paint of the three primary colors where the children can reach them. Give each child small clear plastic cups and a spoon. Show the children how two primary colors can be mixed to make a new color. Show them how to make different combinations in their cups. Encourage them to observe and compare their color mixtures with the mixtures made by other children. Guide them to discuss why their colors are not the same. Follow up the activity with opportunities for the children to easel paint using the primary colors for further experimentation.

Materials Needed: Three containers of paint in primary colors, small plastic cups, spoons.

Experimenting with Ramps

Description of Activity: Help the children build ramps of different heights. Let them decide what types of objects to use to experiment with how fast and how far they can roll down the different ramps. Children can predict how far their object will go and then measure and record the actual distance (Sprung, 1996).

Materials Needed: Block sets and boards

Tools and Gadgets

Description of Activity: Collect discarded appliances, old clocks, discarded telephones, and so on. Give the children some pliers and screwdrivers and let them explore taking the items apart. Let them make an imaginary machine or invention with the loose parts. Discuss their observations and hypotheses about the purposes for the parts in the machinery of the objects they explore.

Materials Needed: Old clocks, appliances, telephones, etc.; pliers; screwdrivers

Cooking Tools and Machines

Description of Activity: Collect a hand electric mixer, blender, manual egg beater, and a potato masher. Explore what the children know about the use of these kitchen appliances and tools. Plan to make some scrambled eggs or mashed potatoes. Prepare some eggs in the blender or electric mixer and the manual egg beater. Discuss how each mixes the eggs and how the electric machines are the same as and different from the manual egg beater. A similar discussion can be conducted comparing the electric mixer, blender, and manual potato masher. If both foods are cooked, the children can observe and discuss why eggs are mixed or whipped before cooking and potatoes are mixed or whipped after cooking.

Materials Needed: Hand electric mixer, blender, manual egg beater, potato masher, eggs, potatoes, facilities for cooking eggs or potatoes

The Food Grinder

Description of Activity: Have available a piece of beef and ground beef. Discuss the texture of the two meats and discuss how ground beef is prepared before hamburgers are made. Help the children hypothesize how meat and other foods are ground as part of the process of preparing food. Show the children a manual food grinder that has not been assembled. Help the children assemble the grinder and predict the purpose of the different parts of the grinder. After the grinder has been assembled and attached to a surface, grind some cooked chicken or cheese to make sandwiches. Grind pickles or other ingredients as part of the grinding process. Let the children grind and mix the ground food with mayonnaise to make a sandwich spread.

Materials Needed: Hand food grinder, cooked chicken or cheese to grind, mayonnaise, mixing bowl and spoon, crackers or bread slices to make small sandwiches for sampling

The Integrated Curriculum for Language and Cognitive Development

The activities that have been described thus far for language and cognitive development in mathematics and science are examples of developmentally appropriate activities for 3-, 4-, and 5-year-old preschool children. They have also been offered to exemplify the content of language and cognitive development curriculum that forms the preschool program for preoperational children. These activities demonstrate the nature of experiences that young children can engage in to acquire new concepts. The activities require active interaction on the part of the child; moreover, they involve hands-on manipulative materials or experiences with realia or artifacts. Nevertheless, the activities as described are isolated or independent, with no necessary relationship to other components of the curriculum.

A more productive approach to developing curriculum is to place experiences into meaningful contexts. Opportunities to move from simple to complex, concrete to abstract, and experiencing to representing what has been learned result from a series of connected activities that permit the child to explore and reflect on information through a variety of encounters. In this section, I will examine how interrelated experiences that focus on language and cognitive development can encourage children to explore and understand the connectedness in learning. Integration through children's literature and through a thematic unit are two processes for developing experiences in language and cognitive development connected with activities that promote all areas of development and expression.

Using Children's Literature as a Focus for Integrated Curriculum

Children's literature provides an abundant resource for curriculum that can be based on language development in partnership with cognitive development. Although a book for children automatically serves as a resource for language development and emergent literacy, it can also be the source from which cognitive curriculum can be developed.

Children's literature can lead to knowledge about science, mathematics, or other content areas. Thematic curriculum that includes activities in small and large groups and in interest centers can begin with a book or a story. Figure 8.3 provides an example of this process. The book *Air Is All Around You,* by Franklyn M. Branley (1986), describes the properties of air and gives information about experiments that can be conducted to understand air. The authors of *Story Stretchers* (Raines & Canady, 1989), the source of this integrated curriculum, have used Branley's book and developed activities for the art and science center, as well as group activities such as a food-time or circle-time experience. Note that the activity of observing fish described earlier as an individual activity is offered as a similar experience here in the context of learning about air.

Using Thematic Units as a Focus for Integrated Curriculum

Thematic units offer more comprehensive planning for integrated curriculum that includes language and cognitive development. In a unit entitled "Seeds," a science topic, 19 activities were developed to provide a variety of experiences for children ages 3 to 5. Younger children will not be able to be successful in some of the activities; nevertheless, more advanced experiences are provided to challenge more advanced students. Ten of these activities are described next. Study of the activities discloses that a wide range of experiences has been planned to include all areas of development. In addition, the teachers who planned the unit, Michelle and Cindy, have developed activities that provide a balance between those that are directed by the teacher and those that encourage children to take responsibility for directing their own plans. The complete unit, which includes unit and lesson plans, may be found in Appendix A.

Activities for a Unit on Seeds

1. The teacher begins each lesson with a series of books that introduce the topic of the lesson, which involves seeds. Through these readings and the discussions following them, language arts are integrated into every lesson in the unit.

2. The students will take an excursion around the school grounds and collect as many different kinds of seeds as they can find. The activity involves cognitive development using concepts in science. It also integrates language, aesthetic, and social development through discussions throughout the walk. Physical development, which includes fine and gross motor skills, is addressed through the process of walking and collecting leaves.

3. The teacher and students will discuss the characteristics of a variety of seeds. They will explore size, shape, color, and texture of the seeds. They will then dissect several seeds, taking note of the differences among them. This activity involves oral language, social skills through cooperative learning, and the use of fine motor skills for dissecting.

4. Students will be guided to use a variety of seeds to construct a seed collage using glue and construction paper. The activity provides for aesthetic development as the children construct their own collage. Fine

Circle Time Presentation

Talk with the children about how they know where air is. They will mention the wind blowing and some may mention blowing out air on a cold morning and seeing a little cloud. Read *Air Is All Around You*. Then discuss again how they know air is all around them after having heard the book. Assure the children that they will have a chance to do the science experiments. Tell the children you will place the book in the science center and during free play you will be there to help anyone who wants to do the experiments.

Story Stretcher

For Art: Fish Pictures

What the children will learn—
To recognize where the fish's gills are and to incorporate this into their picture

Materials you will need—
Brightly colored construction paper, scissors, easel, fluorescent tempera paints, variety of sizes of brushes

What to do—
1. Cut the construction paper into giant fish shapes.
2. Cut a half-circle flap where the fish's gills should be.
3. Encourage the children to use many different colors to paint their fish like the ones in the class aquarium.

Something to think about—
Children respond to new information and will incorporate their new learnings into their art work. If possible, display many pictures of fish near the art area and you will see more variety in the paintings.

Story Stretcher

For Cooking and Snack Time: Orange Air

What the children will learn—
To recall the analogy of how the peel of the orange is like the air around the earth

Materials you will need—
Whole oranges

What to do—
1. Read the analogy from the book: "Air is all around you, and it is all around the earth. Air covers the earth like peel covers an orange."
2. Cut thin stripes down the orange peel from top to bottom without cutting through to the inside of the orange. Cut stripes all around the orange so the children can peel their oranges more easily.
3. Let the children peel their own oranges.

Something to think about—
It is difficult to know when to provide assistance to children. Often volunteers in the classroom will quickly take over for the child and peel the orange. However, encourage them to wait and only provide assistance after the child is having a great deal of difficulty. Then, do not peel the entire orange, but get some of the sections started. Many children will persist and need more time to finish their snacks. Do not hurry them—let them enjoy peeling the orange and savor eating it.

FIGURE 8.3   Integrated curriculum (pp. 259–261)
Source: From *Story S-t-r-e-t-c-h-e-r-s* (pp. 104–105), by Shirley C. Raines and Robert J. Canady, 1989, Mt. Rainier, MD: Gryphon House. Copyright 1989 by Gryphon House. Reprinted with permission.

For Housekeeping and Dress-up Corner: Astronauts

What the children will learn—
To pretend to be astronauts

Materials you will need—
Football helmets or bike riding helmets, large expandable hoses from a dryer connection, earphones from the listening station, down-filled jackets

What to do—
1. Show the picture of the astronaut in *Air Is All Around You.*
2. Ask the children how they might use the dress-up materials you have collected to dress up like astronauts. If possible, have several of each. If this is impossible, explain that there is only one astronaut outside the spaceship at a time and the others have their air supply inside the spaceship.

Something to think about—
Every time I see children playing astronauts, I am amazed at their inventiveness. The puffy down-filled coats reminded me of the air in the space suits; however, the idea of using the dryer air hose connection came from a child, as well as using the earphones for communication. Do not be concerned if you only have a few of the supplies, your astronauts will find what they need.

(Adapted from classroom at George Mason University's Project for the Study of Young Children.)

For Science and Nature Center: Inverted Glass Experiment

What the children will learn—
To follow directions of the experiment and observe what happens

Materials you will need—
Large clear mixing bowl, food coloring, paper napkins, glass

What to do—
1. Follow the directions in the book, which are:
   a. put water in a big bowl;
   b. color the water with a little bit of food coloring;
   c. stuff a paper napkin into the bottom of a glass;
   d. turn the glass upside down;
   e. keep the glass upside down, make sure it is straight up and down, do not tip it;
   f. push it all the way under the water;
   g. lift the glass out of the water; and
   h. turn it right side up and take out the napkin.
2. Have the children observe that the napkin is dry.
3. Let all the children who want to do the experiment have a turn.

Something to think about—
Remember that young children are hands-on learners. They will learn more if they do the experiment themselves. Many of the children will not understand what the experiment demonstrates, but they will enjoy following the directions and getting the same results as the teacher. Also, avoid referring to this experiment as magic or as a trick. While it may seem phenomenal, it is natural.

FIGURE 8.3 *(continued)*

Another Story Stretcher

For Science and Nature Center: Fishy Water

What the children will learn—
To observe the air bubbling in an aquarium and the air bubbling in water

Materials you will need—
An aquarium, two glasses filled with water, magnifying glasses

What to do—
1. For the children who are interested, reread the section of the book about the air dissolved in the water for fish. Show the pictures of the fish and point out the fish's gills.
2. Have the children look at the fish in the aquarium with their magnifying glasses and see if they can see the fishes' gills moving as the water passes through them.

3. Do the science experiment where you will fill a glass with water, wait an hour and then look with the magnifying glasses for tiny bubbles of air.
4. After an hour, fill another glass with water, and have the children search for any air bubbles in this glass.

Something to think about—
While an aquarium requires a great deal of attention, it is worth it to have living things in the classroom. Before spending school supply money on an aquarium, check with parents; often there is one in storage or one in operation that a family will donate complete with fish. Get specific instructions about its operation from the owners.

FIGURE 8.3   *(continued)*

motor skills are used in that the children must be able to manipulate materials to complete the collage.

5. The students are given a muffin tin labeled with numerals 1 through 5 or 1 through 10, depending on their development in counting. They are then instructed to place the correct number of seeds in the appropriate tin cup. If children do not yet recognize numerals, the teacher will verbally ask them to count numbers of seeds. The children will use cognitive skills for counting and fine motor skills for placing seeds in the correct spaces.

6. The students will dictate a group story on the topic of seeds to the teacher, who will in turn write the contributions as a language experience story. Expressive language and emergent reading skills will be integrated through dictation and repeated readings of the story.

7. When provided with a series of pictures showing the growth of a plant at various stages, beginning with a seed, the students will place the pictures in appropriate order. Children will be using cognitive skills, as well as language and social skills in order to discuss the task and reach consensus in their cooperative learning groups.

8. The children will be asked to pretend to be a sprouting seed; background music should be played. The children will be using physical skills, pretending, and developing appreciation for music and its different tempos.

9. Children will be given an array of seeds to compare and contrast. They will be asked to describe likenesses and differences in the seeds. The activity requires students to use oral language and cognitive skills.

10. Seeds collected from the nature walk will be used to make rhythm instruments. Students will be given a selection of containers from which to choose. The completed instruments will be used in a musical activity. Students will be developing an appreciation for tempo and music and creative and motor skills in constructing and using the instruments.

Designing Cognitive Curriculum for Children with Disabilities

The nature of cognitive activities that are planned for preschool children makes them readily adaptable to a range of development levels. Because the activities are predominantly concrete experiences, children who are developmentally delayed can also benefit from interactions that permit them opportunities to use their senses and cognitive abilities to learn. The teacher must be sensitive, however, to adaptations that might be necessary for children who have special needs.

Children who have visual limitations must substitute touch for sight. When studying a concept such as shape, they need many opportunities to trace or use tactile skills to experience the physical configuration of different shapes. Developmentally delayed children will need to spend more time engaging in experiences focused on a single shape, whereas other children, particularly 4- and 5-year-olds, may be able to work with more than one shape and discriminate between them.

Children with language differences will need opportunities to build vocabulary that accompanies new concepts. Children whose first language is not English may need to use their home language vocabulary at first and add English when they demonstrate competence with the new knowledge. All children will need many opportunities to discuss information related to cognitive learning, but children with language differences benefit

from the teacher's awareness of progress they are making in acquiring targeted vocabulary. Whatever special needs the individual child may have, the teacher can be alert to adaptations that will make an experience more accessible. Through an understanding of each child's strengths and learning style, the cognitive curriculum can be organized to be meaningful to all preschool children.

Two teachers in Indiana collaborated to develop thematic curriculum that would enhance language development for young learners who are at risk. One teacher, a language development teacher, worked with a kindergarten classroom teacher. The purpose of the combined curriculum is to provide support language and literacy growth for at-risk learners within the regular classroom environment.

An example of their thematic curriculum was a unit based on *There's a Nightmare in My Closet*, by M. Mayer (1968). One activity that was intended to assist children with limited language was to reread the story every day during the week with the result that children were verbally anticipating sentence endings. Some children were able to choral read the story from memory after a few readings. Another activity was for children to act out concepts in the book. The teachers developed prop boxes for dramatic play that reinforced concepts and events in the book. The teachers found that their own professional growth was advanced through their combined planning in an inclusive setting. They felt that their thematic curriculum approach was an effective avenue to meet needs of all children in the classroom while providing important experiences for children with language needs (Bergeron, Wermuth, Rhodes, & Rudenga, 1996).

Summary

The curriculum for language and cognitive development in the preschool years is based on our understanding of how young children acquire concepts and language. Although educators used to believe that acquisition of literacy was based on the ability to master a sequence of readiness skills leading to beginning reading, the current understanding is that it is based on a cognitive developmental process within each child. The internal cognitive mechanism that facilitates acquisition of language and other forms of cognition also explains how the child achieves literacy.

There are contrasting theories of language acquisition. It is known that children develop the ability to use language by maturing and by receiving opportunities to hear and use language. They learn a set of rules that they use to create their own utterances. Within the first 5 years, they master the forms of language that are used in their language community.

The acquisition of literacy follows a similar pattern. Literacy begins in infancy when the child is exposed to stories, books, and examples of written language. The child's progress into literacy is based on the language and literacy experiences that are available in the home environment.

By the time children enter preschool programs, they have acquired some level of language and literacy; however, they will differ because of the variations in circumstances in their home environment. The role of the teacher is to establish the school environment and curriculum to encourage further development. The teacher develops ongoing possibilities for children to use oral language and literature experiences. In addition, opportunities are provided and physical arrangements are made to encourage dramatic play, writing, art, and emergent reading activities.

The teacher uses similar planning processes to promote the child's cognitive development in science and mathematics. Piaget's cognitive development theory as it relates to the preoperational child is reflected in the categories of cognitive topics that are proposed for preschool children in mathematics and science.

The environment has an important role in the child's opportunities to learn about mathematics and science. Learning centers that offer a changing array of natural and man-made resources promote opportunities to explore, experiment, hypothesize, and reflect on phenomena and concepts in these two subjects. The outdoor area provides a natural learning center for planned and natural experiences. Weather, the path of the sun, and other elements of nature can be experienced on a regular basis.

The teacher organizes curriculum that includes a balance between child-planned and teacher-guided activities. Mathematics and science are explored within a milieu that includes a rich assortment of materials that incorporate all aspects of the curriculum.

Although individual activities that are developmentally appropriate are beneficial for learning, language and concept development experienced within an integrated approach is more meaningful. One approach to integrating curriculum involves using children's literature; another uses thematic topics as sources for curriculum development. If a book for young children serves as the stimulus for curriculum design, learning center activities and small-group and large-group activities are planned as extensions or expansions of the content of the book. A thematic unit, on the other hand, originates with a topic to be explored. The activities selected for the topic not only center on the knowledge related to the topic but also incorporate meaningful activities in all areas of development that permit application of concepts and skills. Cognitive development in language, literacy, mathematics, and science is part of this comprehensive approach to learning, which can be accomplished through adhering to integrated thematic units.

Study Questions

1. How do children acquire language? Explain the process of emergent literacy.
2. How is acquisition of literacy related to the acquisition of language?
3. Why are there differences in children's abilities to speak in the preschool years?
4. What implications do these language differences have for the language curriculum in preschool programs?
5. What forms of emergent writing do preschool children use?
6. How is play an essential part of learning to speak? Describe the role of play in language development.
7. What kinds of roles can the teacher play in encouraging the use of expressive language? How does the teacher extend receptive language?
8. What kinds of language experiences lead to literacy in reading and writing?
9. What is the difference in philosophy between reading readiness and emergent literacy? What does each approach imply for the curriculum?
10. What is the difference between emergent writing activities in preschool classrooms and formal writing lessons?
11. How do preschool children acquire their understanding of written language? What is environmental print?
12. What are the most significant activities in the home that promote literacy in the years between age 3 and age 5?
13. What do children learn about print as part of the process of acquiring literacy?
14. What is the nature of literacy development in bilingual children? Why do they have unique language and literacy needs?
15. What sequential process is involved in learning to count?
16. Why are physical experiences with manipulative materials important in the cognitive curriculum designed for preoperational children?
17. Why are goals for mathematics similar to those for science in the preschool curriculum?
18. Why are both teacher-guided and child-planned activities important in the curriculum for cognitive development?
19. What materials can be placed in learning centers for cognitive development in science and mathematics? What activities can take place in learning centers for cognitive development in these subjects?

CHAPTER NINE

Preschool Curriculum: Ages 3 to 5

Social and Physical Development

CHAPTER OBJECTIVES

As a result of reading this chapter, you will be able to:

1. Understand social development and life changes affecting social development.
2. Describe goals for social development in the preschool years.
3. List the components of social science.
4. Explain the role of the teacher, environment, and play for social development.
5. Describe curriculum designed for social development and social science.
6. Explain how integrated curriculum is designed for social science.
7. Understand physical development in the preschool years.
8. Understand the role of play, the environment, and the teacher in physical development.
9. Describe how to design curriculum for physical development.
10. Explain how physical development activities are designed for children with disabilities.

Curriculum for Social Development

Understanding Social Development

The preschool years are very important ones for social development. During this period, young children make the transition to becoming social beings. As infants and toddlers, they focused on themselves and viewed the world from that perspective. In the preschool years, young children enter the world of social interactions and learn to make a place for themselves in the social world. The first tentative steps that the toddler took toward interacting with others now evolve further. The child develops an interest in being with other children and being accepted into social groups.

During the preschool years, children are experiencing the stages that Erikson (1963) termed *autonomy versus doubt* and *initiative versus guilt*. As the child seeks autonomy, he learns self-control and self-assertion. At age 4 or 5, the child becomes more interested in reaching out to the world. The child wants to use initiative to formulate ideas for dramatic play and wants to be a part of a group in play activities. Four- and 5-year-olds are developing leadership skills. They like to participate in making plans and decisions within a group; however, they are more likely to use their enthusiasm to initiate a project than to seek satisfaction from its completion (Hendrick, 1998).

Because these children are in the preoperational period, their social development is related to their progress in cognitive development. The egocentric nature of their thinking affects their social interactions. They may be unaware of the effects their actions have on others; they are easily confused by misleading cues. For example, a young child may have difficulty in initiating a play activity with another child because he uses inappropriate behavior to get the other child's attention. The 3-year-old child may be surprised to find out that interfering with another child's efforts to mold damp sand is not appreciated. As the child becomes less egocentric during the ages of

4 and 5, he becomes more sensitive to the thoughts and feelings of others. This awareness can be transferred into social successes (Schickedanz et al., 1990).

Older preschoolers are challenged to learn how to make and keep friends. Learning how to interact with others and to adjust their actions to fit individual expectations are major tasks in establishing friendships. Moreover, children have to learn that social interactions with adults are different from those with their peers. Peer relationships are reciprocal and dynamic. Friends must negotiate the relationship and cooperate in working out boundaries. When boundaries are crossed, the individuals must make accommodations if the friendship is to continue (Burk, 1996).

The child's self-concept is an important component of social development in the preschool years. As they become less egocentric, young children develop a perception of themselves that is more stable. They have feelings about themselves and make self-evaluations about themselves that can be positive or negative. The goal is for the children to develop self-confidence and positive self-esteem. Social interactions and friendships affect the child's perception of himself as competent and successful (Bredekamp & Copple, 1997).

Social development is centered on the child's growing ability to become a part of group interactions; therefore, the use of the term *curriculum* for social development can seem awkward. Indeed, Hendrick (1998) reminds us that social development is not taught through artificially contrived group activities but emerges from the child's daily experiences with peers and adults. Development in social skills is the major goal for children between the ages of 3 and 5; at this time they are also becoming able to understand the larger world in which they live. Curriculum for preschoolers can address both types of social development.

Life Changes That Affect Social Development

In Chapter 1, the idea of diversity in children was discussed. Different types of diversity were mentioned including differences in families and changes in families that affect children. These life changes can affect the child's social development. Devall and Cahill (1995) categorized life changes into three categories: developmental change, critical change, and catastrophic change. Developmental change is normal and experienced by every child. Most children can cope with changes that occur because of development, such as entering school for the first time. Critical changes are those that cause a major adjustment in the child's life. Moving to a new home or community or experiencing the arrival of a new baby is a critical change in a child's life. Catastrophic change is a severe, unexpected event that seriously affects the child and family. Accidents, death of a family member, and experiencing violence are examples of events that result in catastrophic change.

Critical and catastrophic life changes do not affect all children, but many have become common in American culture. Among the serious events that can be categorized as critical or catastrophic are child abuse, violence, and serious illness or death in the family.

Child Abuse

Child abuse occurs in many forms that can have different effects on children's behavior. A child can be physically or sexually abused. Physical neglect and emotional maltreatment are also forms of abuse. Children who have been abused are frequently withdrawn and depressed. Physically abused children may be uncomfortable with physical contact and wear inappropriate clothing to cover their body. Sexually abused children may have poor self-esteem and be unable to interact with their peers. They may use inappropriate sex play and express seduction in their play.

Physically neglected children are frequently absent or tardy and regularly are listless or fatigued when they are at school. They might steal food when they are hungry or ask classmates for food. Emotionally maltreated children exhibit behavior extremes from passive to aggressive. They might

have habit disorders such as sucking and rocking or might be inhibited in play activities. It is difficult to detect long-term effects of abuse and neglect. Although some causes and effects have been documented, such outcomes are complex and inconclusive (Starr, 1990) Nevertheless, teachers need to be alert to social difficulties and symptoms exhibited by young children. They can provide a safe school environment and can work to ease positive social development in young abused children.

Violence

Community violence has doubled since the 1950s. Young children in many innercity neighborhoods are exposed to high rates of violence so that children's social and emotional adjustment in the classroom is affected. The presence of social support in the child's life is a positive factor in the child's adjustment. Children who have social support are less affected than children who do not have social support.

Children may also witness or be victims of domestic violence. How much children witness this violence is unknown, but children in a home where the mother is battered are more likely to be physically abused as well. Young children are vulnerable to domestic violence because they witness assaults between parents. Children who experience violence are likely to exhibit distress, immature behavior, and regressions in development (Osofsky, 1995).

Young children who repeatedly experience volent situations may begin to show signs of post-traumatic stress disorder (PTSD). Children with PTSD experience recurrent flashbacks in which the threatening event is relived and the child becomes extremely withdrawn or exhibits acting out behaviors. Children may blame themselves for the traumatic events and try to avoid triggering further events. Children suffering from PTSD also may suffer from sleep deprivation as a result of night terrors, hypervigilance, and frequent startle responses. Teachers working with traumatized children need to provide stability and predictability.

These children need healing relationships that provide security and consistency (La Cerva, 1999).

Serious Illness and Death

Many young children experience a serious illness and must be hospitalized. Some young children also experience a serious illness by a family member or friend of the family. Serious illnesses are difficult to understand. Being in the hospital or visiting someone in the hospital might be frightening for the young child. Young children need to be informed and prepared about the nature and work of hospitals. This is true whether they will be hospitalized or will visit someone who is very ill in the hospital.

Experiencing the death of a friend or loved one is even more difficult for young children. Preschool children ages 3 to 5 may not understand time and permanence and thus see death as temporary. Death may be linked with sleep. Children who have experienced death of a loved one may become anxious about separating from their parents, may be afraid to fall asleep, and may seek attention. They may want to stay home from school. If one parent has died, they might be afraid that the other parent will also die, and they do not want to be away from home (Westmoreland, 1996).

When a child dies, classmates and peer friends are affected. Many schools provide counseling and intervention for students who have experienced shock and grief because of the event. Goldman (1996) suggests that children and parents need to be informed about the facts about the child's death. They might benefit from the opportunity to participate in memorializing the child who has died.

Life changes may not be only negative. There are positive life changes that can also affect the child's social development. The reality of working mothers has forced adjustments on children, but many fathers are now taking a more active role in the home and with their children. Husbands in dual-worker families are taking on more of the child-rearing responsibilities. Fathers who want to spend more time with their children and have a

closer relationship are on the rise (Holcomb, 1994).

Not all children experience difficulties in social development because of life changes. There are major differences in how children react to significant changes in their lives. Many children are resilient; that is, they are not negatively affected by stresses caused by change. Personality characteristics affect resilience, as do the number of change factors the child experiences. The more risk factors, the more likely that a child's development will suffer. The presence of a caring adult in an on during relationship helps protect a child from the negative consequences of change (Gelman, 1991).

Rapid social changes in our society have resulted in catastrophic life changes for children; however, Elkind (1992) believes that we are moving toward a more stable society exemplified by the "vital family." The vital family is more concerned about social and parental responsibility, especially for the young and less fortunate. Parents in the vital family still are concerned with career and their need to succeed; nevertheless, they are also concerned about the need for a healthy family and each member's need to love and belong.

In this chapter, I will address the means for fostering social development and the curriculum for social science. In the section that follows, these two aspects of the social science program will be described. Goals for planning for social development and for planning the social science curriculum will be discussed as separate parts of the program for social development.

Planning for Social Development

Social science is the study of people; through the study of the social sciences, children learn about other people (Jarolimek, 1986). However, before young children can understand and appreciate other people, they must understand themselves. Thus, social development is a prerequisite for appreciating social science.

> Unless children develop positive views of self, they are not likely to develop positive views of

others; unless children appreciate their culture they are not likely to appreciate another's culture; unless children have self-respect, they are not likely to have respect for others; unless children experience success and self-worth, they are not likely to perceive others as worthy. As children look into the psychological looking glass, whatever they see in themselves, they tend to view a similar reflection of others. These mirroring effects emerge as children interact in the social world. (Schickedanz et al., 1990, pp. 282–283)

Success in social development is critical in the preschool years; consequently, the plans made for social development in the program for 3- to 5-year-olds can have a significant role. They can affect the child's growth toward the development of autonomy and industry. The foundations established through experiences in social development in turn will make it possible for the developing child to appreciate other people in his expanding understanding of the world.

Goals for Social Development

Preschool children are in the process of learning ways to live in harmony with others, both adults and other children. Social learning, then, is related to understanding how to get along with others. In planning for social development, the teacher has to keep in mind the relationship between development and learning. The goals for social development are based on children's developing social needs and might include self-concept, gender identity, socialization, and multicultural understandings and sensitivities.

Self-Concept.   Young children need to develop a good self-image. If parents and teachers can nurture this characteristic in young children, many other kinds of development are enhanced. The child's positive concept of himself results from successful encounters with the environment. The child who experiences success with people and events in life comes to value himself as an important person. Supportive adults in a supportive

environment are the ingredients needed for the establishment of self-concept.

Gender Identity.   Between the ages of 3 and 5, young children become very aware of their gender. Five-year-olds frequently discuss what boys or girls are "supposed to do." The process begins with parental behaviors that identify with the gender of the infant. During the preschool years, children develop an awareness of the appropriate behaviors expected of males and females. Much effort has been expended in recent years to encourage nonsexist relationships between parents and their young children; nevertheless, the way that parents and other adults relate to the gender of their children affects personality and self-concept. The differentiated relationship that parents and teachers have with boys and girls results in different expectations and interactions.

Awareness of ethnic identity parallels knowledge of gender identity. As children realize they are boys or girls, they begin to recognize the behaviors and expectations that are held for them. Preschool children also become aware of their ethnic identity and what gender roles their individual family and culture expect of them.

In a multicultural world, gender identity is more complex. Gender expectations vary by ethnic and cultural groups. How preschoolers perceive their gender is affected by family, peers, and their social environment. Moreover, social changes are impacting all ethnic and cultural groups. Understanding gender and ethnic identity is a complex task for preschool children. This understanding is facilitated when gender roles are not rigidly and stereotypically defined in their environment (Berk, 1996; Trawick-Smith, 1997).

Socialization.   Socialization, or the ability to get along with other people, begins very early in life. As children learn cooperating, sharing, and helping skills, they make progress in socialization. The child finds the adjustment to school or an early childhood center to be easily achieved when his socialization is compatible with the expectations of the school. If the child's socialization does not conform to the group setting or school environment, he finds the expectations and adjustments very difficult. Successful socialization development in turn depends on other developmental skills: controlling and expressing feelings appropriately, developing empathy, and developing prosocial skills.

Very young children must learn to control and express their feelings in an appropriate manner. Infants and toddlers begin this process and refine it in the preschool years. The child from age 3 to 5 has the difficult task of learning how to express anger in an appropriate manner and how to verbalize frustrating feelings to adults. In addition, the child must learn how to deal with another child's anger and frustration. Young children learn that they have many kinds of feelings: fear, happiness, anger, surprise, contentment. Being able to identify their feelings and act on them appropriately is part of the process of socialization.

As children become less egocentric and more sensitive to others, they become aware that other children may be feeling and experiencing differently than they are. Awareness and sensitivity lead to empathy. Very young children begin to develop a positive regard for others. In the preschool years, empathy can lead to generosity, compassion, and concern. Children who develop empathy are able to react appropriately to another person's feelings or circumstances. Thus, the preschooler can comfort a crying child or help a frustrated child complete a difficult puzzle. The child who can express and act on empathy is developing socialization skills.

Socialization requires additional abilities, frequently described as prosocial skills. Prosocial skills are strategies that enable the young child to enter and successfully interact with a social group. The child must learn how to ask for a toy, engage in successful sharing, gain acceptance in a group play situation, and deal with inappropriate behavior on the part of other children. The process that begins with toddlers continues into the elementary school years; nevertheless, it is during the preschool years that the pattern of success or failure in prosocial skills becomes important (Hendrick, 1998; Maxim, 1997).

Multicultural Understandings and Sensitivities. Racial bias and misunderstanding can begin at a very early age; conversely, understanding and acceptance of ethnic and cultural differences can also begin very early. Preschool children can become accustomed to differences in skin color, ethnicity, and language. They can be nurtured to accept these differences as normal and equally valued by the teacher, other children, and society at large. The preschool setting should offer dolls, books, and other materials and activities that reflect diversity in a positive manner. Children can become sensitive to and appreciative of similarities and differences in children and their families (Ramsey, 1987).

Research regarding acceptance of children of different ethnic groups is encouraging. Some studies report that peer acceptance is usually not related to ethnicity (Howes & Wu, 1990). It is thought that schools might be playing a positive role in this respect when they help children to understand each other and facilitate cross-cultural peer relationships (Trawick-Smith, 1997).

Goals for Social Science

Earlier, I mentioned that the goal for social development is for young children to develop the capability to understand and value themselves and get along with others. Social development is part of the foundation of understanding the social sciences. The major goal for social science in turn is to develop people who have self-respect and self-worth and who can become productive contributors to society. Achieving this broad goal is a life-long process that begins with the socialization of the very young child.

In the primary grades, social science is understood within a content field that includes psychology, history, geography, economics, sociology, and anthropology. These areas of study continue

throughout the years of formal schooling. Although preschool children cannot comprehend the specialized fields that are grouped within social studies, they can develop the foundations for understanding them.

Psychology.   Psychology involves the understanding of human behavior. For the young child, understanding relates to self-concept. Children can understand themselves as unique individuals who are competent. They can also come to understand that there are individual and group similarities and differences in homes, families, and individuals.

History.   History is the study of the events of the past and the forces and changes that caused the events. Young children are not able to comprehend the passage of time, but they can understand their own history and past. They can learn about themselves and changes they have gone through in their development, as well as interesting events in their family history. They are interested in hearing stories about the past and exploring artifacts from earlier times.

Geography.   Geography relates to characteristics of the earth's environment and the relationship between different environments and peoples. Young children cannot understand distant characteristics of geography, but they can relate to the more familiar and local characteristics. They can visit nearby environments and understand what is meant by geographic differences and what it means to travel from one location to another. They can become familiar with physical features and geographic differences in their community.

Economics.   Young children cannot understand the comprehensive nature of a nation's economy and the role of goods, services, and the monetary system as a vehicle of exchange; however, they can address economic concepts that affect their own lives. Young children can begin to develop an awareness of the purposes of commercials on television and other advertising media. They can come to understand the differences between acquiring things that are needed and those that are wanted. They can learn the way in which choices must be made, depending on how much money one has. They can also understand how people buy services and goods and how people depend on each other to acquire money for their needs.

Sociology. Sociology is the study of how people live in groups and communities. Young children cannot comprehend how people organize themselves into groups, communities, and nations and develop social classes and institutions. They can understand the social groups that are closest to their own experiences. They can understand the family as a social unit and extend the concept to relate to the school and immediate community near their home.

Anthropology. Anthropology is the study of cultures and diverse lifestyles; it is the study of the art, music, institutions, beliefs, dress, food, religion, and celebrations of different cultures. Although preschool children cannot address the cultural differences of unfamiliar cultures, they can relate to cultural diversities within their own community. They can learn about cultural variety by experiencing many ongoing activities. In addition, they can engage in an appreciation of cultural and social differences and the contributions of different cultural groups in their community. Teachers can promote multicultural understanding to address and prevent prejudices, discrimination, and stereotypes that are prevalent in our larger society today (Schickedanz et al., 1990; Seefeldt, 1997).

Ultimately, the goals for social development and social science are very similar. The first focuses on the child and his social world; the second focuses on social groups and how the world of social groups function. Because the young child first relates to his immediate world and social group, social development and the study of social sciences emerge from that environment and world. In the sections that follow, I will discuss the role of the teacher and the environment in promoting social development. The importance of play as a socialization tool in the child's environment will be described, especially those facets of play (such as dramatic play) that are vehicles for the child's social development.

The Role of Play in Social Development

Although infants and toddlers are more likely to play by themselves or engage in parallel play alongside another child, children between the ages of 3 and 5 enter the world of true social play. They try out social interactions in all types of play—for example, when involved in physical play on complex climbing structures, playing with wheel toys, or exploring sand and water. The richest opportunities for learning social skills, however, develop through dramatic play.

When very young children develop the ability to use pretense in their play, they can engage in dramatic play. As they move away from egocentricity and cooperate with others in pretend play, they can interact with other children in sociodramatic play. Studies of the benefits of sociodramatic play have revealed a correlation between sociodramatic play and social and cognitive competence (Garvey, 1977; Smilansky, 1968). Through fantasy play with peers, children learn social skills moreover, the amount and frequency of fantasy play predict social skills, popularity, and positive social activity (Connolly & Doyle, 1984; Johnson et al., 1999 Wortham, 2001b).

Beaty (1992) described some specific benefits of sociodramatic play. When children are involved in dramatic play roles, they are learning socialization skills. Fantasy play episodes involve peer pressure for appropriate social behaviors, as well as an understanding of the negative social effects of aggression. Children learn how to resolve interpersonal conflicts when observing other children using successful strategies. Role playing allows children to try on different roles, such as that of mother, father, sibling, or friend. As a result of engaging in planning and implementation of fantasy play themes, children learn both leader and follower roles. As they use their imagination and creativity to develop themes and roles for sociodramatic play, and they learn the difference between fantasy and reality.

Sociodramatic play permits children to express how they feel. Preschool children are unable to verbalize their feelings. Through play they can express positive feelings such as joy and contentment as well as aggressive feelings.

Play can be cathartic. Children use play to understand traumatic experiences by recreating the event over and over until their intensity of feelings has been diminished. Likewise, children can express negative feelings of aggression through play and move beyond them when they have been resolved (Landreth & Hohmeyer, 1998; Wortham, 2001b).

There are individual differences in social competence and play in preschool children. Children who are less competent in peer interactions tend to have differences in sociability in elementary school. Variations in social competence have been traced to genetic differences, parenting style and effectiveness in child rearing, and effective peer relations (Rubin & Coplan, 1998).

If teachers are to provide opportunities for sociodramatic play for preschool children, they will have to set up the environment to facilitate fantasy play themes and encourage appropriate social behaviors. In addition, they must become sensitive to their role in enabling children to develop social skills.

The Role of the Environment in Social Development

Because play is an important component for social development, the preschool classroom environment also has an important role in social development and the social science curriculum. Before children engage in sociodramatic play, space and materials must be available both indoors and outdoors. The homemaking or dramatic play center is the area most commonly thought of as the location for fantasy play themes; however, in reality, children engage in sociodramatic play in the block and truck center, art center, and other classroom areas. Outdoors, play themes can originate on the complex climbing structure or in a playhouse setting and then move to the playground as children act out the fantasy situation.

The arrangement of the environment can affect the development and use of social skills. If the classroom is organized so that children have access to play materials, then positive social behaviors are more likely to be used. Children need time and space to be able to interact appropriately; in addition, play opportunities and materials must continually challenge and interest them. Beaty (1992, p. 206) suggests that the following factors in the learning environment can cause inappropriate social behaviors:

1. Too few activities and materials
2. Activities and materials not appropriate for developmental levels of children
3. Too much room to run around
4. Activity areas not clearly defined
5. Classroom geared for total group activities rather than individual and small-group activities
6. No duplicates of favorite toys or materials
7. No change in old materials, books, toys

The daily routine or schedule can also encourage the use of social skills. Young children need the security of predictability in the routines from day to day. They are comfortable when they know what will be happening during the day. When normal routines are changed for field trips, holiday celebrations, and other special occasions, children are likely to react with excitement and difficulty in following normal expectations for behavior. When changes are unavoidable, children will respond more positively if they are prepared for schedule differences beforehand.

The need for predictability extends to classroom rules and expectations for appropriate behavior. When children know the kinds of behaviors that are acceptable for different classroom and outdoor activities, they are better prepared to demonstrate their cooperation with appropriate social skills. They need to have a voice in establishing classroom rules and frequent response to whether the rules are being followed successfully. Children between the ages of 3 and 5 need many opportunities to learn classroom procedures and benefit from reminders before their behavior gets out of control and firm measures must be taken to restore order. Young children want to use appropriate behavior. When the classroom is arranged to maximize active involvement in challenging activities, and expectations for appropriate social behaviors are clearly understood, preschool children are more likely to respond positively with their developing social skills.

The Role of the Teacher in Social Development

The teacher has a direct role in helping children acquire social skills and make progress in social development. The teacher must prepare the environment for sociodramatic play and appropriate social behaviors, but young children also need help in controlling their behavior. The teacher will need to develop strategies for helping children manage their behavior, develop activities for fostering and improving sociodramatic play, and plan the social science curriculum.

In spite of the teacher's best efforts to set the tone of the classroom to encourage prosocial skills, young children have difficulty in maintaining appropriate behaviors. As a result, the teacher is forced to intervene when unsocial impulses cause a child to misbehave. When children break rules for appropriate behavior, the teacher must take steps to correct the situation. If a child attempts to use physical aggression to hurt another child, immediate steps must be taken to prohibit the child from making further attempts to use the behavior. To help the child acquire more long-term controls, the teacher can initiate steps that will lead toward the goal. The child can be reminded of the rule and the consequences for breaking it; redirected to a more appropriate activity; isolated and given the opportunity to discuss feelings; asked to indicate when he feels able to return to an activity and use appropriate behavior; or help to choose another activity (Hendrick, 1998). Children need to know what to expect when they lose control and feel assured that the teacher will take steps to help them stay within the limits for appropriate social behaviors.

Sometimes children use inappropriate behaviors because they do not know how to use prosocial skills. They do not know how to use positive alternatives to interact with other children. These children need direct suggestions for using successful behaviors. Children can be shown how to offer to contribute to a play group or play alongside a play activity until accepted into a group. They can be taught how to ask for a turn with a toy and to apologize when they are responsible for accidentally (or deliberately) hurting another child. The teacher shows approval and gives positive response when positive behaviors are used.

The preschool teacher's goal is to help students become socially competent. There are many strategies teachers can use to accomplish this goal to include making children aware of others' feelings and helping children enter ongoing discussions in an appropriate manner. Teachers can increase social competence by guiding children in improving their interactive skills in order to develop positive relationships. Children can also be taught to take turns, to negotiate with others, and to use positive language when rejecting a request by another child to play or engage in an activity together. Most important, teachers can work to minimize inappropriate forms of teasing and bullying (Katz & McClellan, 1997).

Similar direct and indirect teacher behaviors can be used to nurture and extend children's sociodramatic play. Although teachers should avoid excessive intervention in children's play, observation can indicate when children would benefit from adult involvement to extend and further develop their play. The teacher can join a play episode as a co-player but can leave the children in charge of the play theme. Suggestions can be made about materials or equipment that could extend the play. The adult can model new approaches for dramatic play or tutor the children by demonstrating possibilities through questions or responding to children's actions and verbalizations. Most important, the teacher can encourage further sociodramatic play by showing approval of the play activity and demonstrating appreciation for the children's development of fantasy play themes (Johnson, Christie & Yawkey, 1999).

The teacher's role in developing the social science curriculum is also significant. Many teachers believe that preschool children are too young to learn about social studies because they lack the experience and cognitive abilities to relate to the components of the curriculum. Teachers of young children can involve them in social science at their own level, which will not only further their development as members of their immediate social group but also add to their experiences in the social world in which they and their family live.

Designing Curriculum for Social Development

Fostering Social Development

I have discussed the meaning of social development in the preschool years and the goals for social development in preschool children. I have also explained that the curriculum for social development is the social learning that young children acquire from daily experiences in their environment. There is no written curriculum or curriculum topic that teachers organize into group activities so that children can learn how to get along with others. There are, however, categories of social development skills that teachers and children can address in the preschool classroom. Two major social accomplishments that young children must master in their social world are self-management skills and social participation skills. To this end, there are strategies teachers can use to develop these competencies in young children within group discussions and play experiences. Following are some activities teachers can use to foster social development in preschool children; these activities are based on research of preschool children's peer acceptance and social interaction (Kemple, 1991).

Activities for Fostering Social Interactions

Fostering Social Skills

Children who are lacking social skills can learn them from children who are socially competent. The teacher can organize special play sessions where less effective children are paired with children who have acquired effective social skills. Through play experiences, the less skilled child can learn to play more effectively.

Overcoming Social Isolation

Some children may understand social skills but are unable to use them. Sometimes pairing these children with a younger child will give them the confidence they need. When socially isolated children are exposed to play sessions with younger children, they may become more socially involved because they feel comfortable with younger children.

Learning Social Alternatives

Many children use aggression because they do not understand alternative strategies to resolve conflicts. Planned activities can be used to teach children alternative strategies that are more successful than aggression. The teacher can initiate

skits, puppet activities, and group discussions involving hypothetical situations. Children can become involved in the problem and in determining alternative solutions. Children are encouraged to increase the number of appropriate strategies they might try.

Learning Prosocial and Empathic Behavior

Children who are popular are helpful and cooperative. Many children are not helpful because they do not recognize situations in which they can be of assistance. Through observation, teachers can determine whether students are empathic and how they can be helped to cooperate and offer assistance. The teacher can create opportunities for a child to demonstrate helpfulness or point out situations when the child can be helpful to another child who is in need or in distress.

Can I Play?

Many young children have difficulty entering a play group. One solution may be for the teacher to guide the isolated child to a smaller play group or a more cooperative group. The teacher can tutor the child to identify the play theme and think of a role that can be played that would contribute to the group's play.

Improving Social Communication Skills

Children who have difficulty maintaining a play episode are unable to communicate effectively with playmates. Teachers can provide guidance on how to clarify communication within the play episode. The teacher can instruct a child to be more specific in an explanation. An unpopular child can be guided to be sensitive to the negative emotional cues that indicate that another child does not like the unpopular child's behavior or actions.

Helping Children Who Have No Friends

Peers should not be forced to play with a child; however, there are ways that teachers can facilitate that child's acceptance into the peer group. The teacher can interpret the child's positive intentions to the other children and guide them toward helping the child successfully play with them. Teacher strategies can facilitate peer understanding and empathy for the child who has difficulty in making friends. The peer group can then help the child become more successful in play interactions.

Designing Curriculum for Social Science

In a previous section, I discussed the components of the social science curriculum and the way in which it applies to young children of ages 3 to 5. In this section, I will describe how those components are carried out into learning experiences that are developmentally appropriate. Because children have their own limitations in cognition and experience, there are certain criteria for curriculum design: (1) the curriculum should emphasize direct activities, such as taking field trips, utilizing resource persons, and examining real things; and (2) the curriculum should focus on the children.

Young children learn best about the social world in meaningful contexts; therefore, integrated curriculum is the best framework to use for planning. The teacher should plan units based on social science themes that permit young children to use their senses and receptive and expressive language to reflect on the information they are encountering. If the curriculum is to be based on the children themselves, the units of study should center on their life histories, families, homes, and feelings. They can also extend their social world to include their peers, the school, and the society of the community. Schickedanz, York, Stewart, and White (1990) suggest that the social science curriculum be organized around two major categories: (1) understanding self and family and (2) understanding people and society. These two categories are further divided into major theme possibilities as follows:

Understanding Se.lf and Family
Understanding Self
Each Individual Has Worth and Dignity
Personal History
Feelings Can Be Expressed in Acceptable Ways
Death as a Part of Life
Divorce and the Young Child
Coping with Crisis Situations

Understanding People and Society
The Family Unit Is Basic in a Society
People Have Rights
People Have Responsibilities
People Have Needs and Desires
Rules Are Necessary When People Live in Groups
People Live in Communities
People Produce and Consume Goods and Services
People Do Different Types of Work

People Travel in Various Ways and Send Messages
People Represent Many Cultures
Important People of the Past and Present
Understanding Cultural Diversity
Values, Customs, and Traditions

These topics would have to be further simplified to make them applicable for preschool children age 5 and younger; nevertheless, they represent many of the significant topics in the social science curriculum that have been discussed earlier. When planning a unit, the teacher will plan unit activities with the children so that all may express their interest in the unit and the kinds of information they would like to find out from working on unit experiences and activities. In the activities described next, examples are given of some of the topics related to the social world of children that will extend their understanding of social science concepts. Then, an example of an integrated thematic topic will be described to demonstrate how social science activities can be enriched by being integrated with other areas of development using direct experiences.

Designing Integrated Curriculum in Social Science

Social science concepts are learned best in a meaningful context. Preschoolers need to be involved in real experiences if they are to understand concepts about their social world. It is recommended that social science activities for preschool children be closely related to their personal lives. One topic that is pertinent to young children is that of their own family. In the integrated social science curriculum described next, the unit on families can be related to the social science topic entitled "The Family Unit Is Basic in Society." The activities related to families center on the book *Daddy Makes the Best Spaghetti,* by Anna Grossnickle Hines (1986). The book should be particularly appealing because Daddy does the cooking and shares in caring for his chil

Activities for Social Science

Understanding Historical Time

Preschoolers have a very limited understanding of past and future time. Because of their preoperational mode of thinking, they can understand past and future events only when they are described in relation to the present day. They can understand the passage of time based on the events of each day. Activities that include discussions of what happened earlier in the day and will happen later in the day help them to attend to the nature of passing time.

Celebrating birthdays and marking a monthly calendar can help older children build an awareness of the passage of days. Children can develop a foundation for historical perspective by taking part in activities that include the ages of different members of the family and their ranks based on time that has passed (Vukelich & Thornton, 1990).

Grandparents and Oral History

Children are interested in things that have happened to their family a long time ago. Children are fascinated by stories told of real-life experiences related to family history; resource people who can tell such stories are integral to this activity. If grandparents or surrogate grandparents can bring artifacts that represent their earlier life and share them with young children, the children gain a meaningful awareness of their social heritage. For example, a grandmother in Iowa brought a butter churn to the classroom. She demonstrated with the children how it was used to make butter. She showed a picture of the house she lived in when she was a little girl. The children were able to discuss how homes today compare with their grandmother's house; they could also compare the way we get butter today at a store with the way the grandmother had to churn her own butter when she was a child.

Death and the Life Cycle

Even young children need to understand that there is a cycle in life that ends in death. Many young children have experienced the death of a pet or seen a dead insect or plant. An experience with growing plants can help them to understand the life cycle. Teachers and children can plant seeds, nurture the growing plants, and enjoy the flowers that bloom when the plants are mature. Furman (1990) suggests that children need to experience the rest of the cycle, when the plant dies and decays. They can discuss what has happened to the plant and how seeds can be harvested from the flowers to make future plants. They can have a similar experience with a gourd or melon vine or a potato plant.

Understanding Transportation

All children notice different types of vehicles that pass their school, child-care center, or own home. They can learn the transportation purposes that different kinds of vehicles serve. Children can discuss the different types of vehicles that pass a corner for

a given period of time. The teacher can record the names of the vehicles or photograph them. The children can then study the photos and determine what was transported in the vehicle. They can decide whether the vehicle's purpose is to transport people or some type of goods or is used to perform a service.

Neighborhood Structures

A similar activity can be conducted with buildings in the neighborhood. Children can note the types of buildings they see on a brief walk and decide whether they are homes or stores or serve another purpose. They can discuss the many kinds of buildings in a community. As a follow-up activity, they might construct their own community structures with blocks or make models out of cardboard boxes.

Understand Change

One way to teach children what happens with the passage of time and how people live together in a community is to provide them with activities that show how things change. Children might take a walk near the school or center and note locations that are in the process of being built or changed. Next, they might search for places that indicate wear and aging, such as cracks or potholes in the street or paint that is peeling from a building. Areas being remodeled or renewed can be identified. The purpose is for the child to understand that change is a part of life.

Want and Need

Children need to differentiate between things that they want and things that they need. After a discussion of the difference, children might look through magazines for pictures and make a collage of things they would like to have on one side and things they need on the other side. As an alternative activity, a group mural could be constructed.

School Workers

Children can become aware of the different people who provide a service for them at their school or center. The teacher can take them to visit workers and observe what they do. The worker can then visit the classroom and discuss how the children are served through their efforts. The children can dictate stories about each worker and illustrate the story. A class book can be made of the stories.

dren. Because spaghetti is a favorite with young children, cooking and eating spaghetti will be an exciting event.

The family-life theme activities engaged in can center on such ideas as the way in which families eat together and the different types of family groups. The family-oriented activities that include favorite bedtime storybooks and pots, pans, and cooking spoons for a kitchen band experience are taken from *More Story Stretchers* (Raines & Canady, 1991). Figure 9.1 describes the activities and interest centers that can be incorporated into a thematic unit.

Circle Time Presentation

Show the children the cover of Corey and Dad marching and making music with pots and pans. Ask the children to predict what they think the story is about. After reading the title, *Daddy Makes the Best Spaghetti,* ask if anyone wants to change their minds about what will happen in the story. Read *Daddy Makes the Best Spaghetti* and pause for the children to giggle at Dad's impersonations of "Bathman" and the delightful suspense as Corey tries to find Dad while almost losing his bath towel. At the end of the reading, several children probably will volunteer some descriptions of funny games their parents play. Encourage them to also talk about cooking with their dads.

Story Stretcher

For Cooking and Snack Time: Making the Best Spaghetti

What the children will learn—
To assist in making spaghetti

Materials you will need—
Prepared sauce or ingredients for your own sauce, range or hot plate, spaghetti, water, salt, butter, one large saucepan and one large pot, wooden spoons, colander, plates, silverware, brightly colored napkins and tablecloths

What to do—
1. Divide the children into four groups of chef's assistants. Discuss with each group what their task will include.
2. Make a rebus chart, a combination of words and symbols, for each group's instructions and the spaghetti recipe. Post the chart and refer to it throughout the cooking experience.
3. If possible, have a parent come to the classroom and prepare his or her favorite spaghetti sauce with the help of a small group of children acting as chef's assistants. If this is not possible, let this group help warm up the sauce in a large saucepan or place it in a microwave to heat.
4. Let another small group of children cook the spaghetti by boiling water, adding salt and butter, cooking the noodles, and, finally, draining them in a colander.
5. Have the third group of children set the table with brightly colored napkins and tablecloth.
6. Ask the fourth group of chef's assistants to serve the spaghetti to the rest of the class and parents.

Something to think about—
While cooking hot foods with young children takes extra preparation and caution, the pride of accomplishment the children feel and the valuable learning experiences are worth the extra efforts.

Another Story Stretcher

For Cooking and Snack Time: Families Setting the Table and Eating Together

What the children will learn—
To pretend to be families during snack time and how to set the table

Materials you will need—
If possible, real silverware, dishes, glassware, napkins and placemats or tablecloths

What to do—
1. Look again at the illustration of the family eating together in the book.
2. Ask the children to sit at the snack table; then at random ask children to pretend to be the father, mother, grandfather, grandmother, and children. At some tables there might not be a mother and at others there might not be a father. Discuss that we are still families even if one of our parents is not present.

FIGURE 9.1   Integrated social studies curriculum (pp. 280–282)
Source: From *More Story S-t-r-e-t-c-h-e-r-s* (pp. 40–41), by S. Raines and R. Canady, 1989, Mt. Rainer, MD: Gryphon House. Copyright 1991 by Gryphon House. Reprinted with permission of the publisher.

3. Have these children sit together as families throughout the week during snack time.
4. Let different members of the family take turns setting the table.

Something to think about—
With older children, encourage table conversations with each person maintaining their role. With younger children, since snack time is not usually a pretending time, a teacher, aide, or volunteer may need to sit at the table to encourage conversation.

Story Stretcher

For Housekeeping and Dress-up Corner: Grocery Store

What the children will learn—
To set up the area, improvise props, play the roles involved

Materials you will need—
Canned and boxed foods, grocery bags, aprons, cash register, cents-off coupons, newspaper ads, scratch pads, pencils, posterboard, markers (optional—grocery carts)

What to do—
1. In the parent newsletter, announce the grocery store center and ask for empty cans and boxes.
2. After the cans and boxes have arrived, collect cents-off coupons and newspaper ads that correspond to the containers.
3. Give the players in the area the coupons, ads, scratch pads, pencils, posterboard, and markers. Ask them what they can do with these materials to make the area look like a real grocery store. Expect to see them make posters guiding the shoppers to the food displays and matching the cents-off coupons to the food. Eventually, as they shop, expect them to use the scratch pads to write checks for their groceries.

4. After the grocery store is set up, let the arrangers become the first customers, cashiers, produce managers, and baggers.

Something to think about—
A grocery store is a wonderfully rich center for learning about community helpers, emergent literacy, nutrition, mathematics, and social studies as the children play the roles.

Story Stretcher

For Library Corner: Our Favorite Bedtime Books

What the children will learn—
To select a favorite bedtime book

Materials you will need—
Collection of books about bedtime, naptime, nighttime, or family experiences

What to do—
1. Show the illustration from *Daddy Makes the Best Spaghetti* where the little boy and his father are listening to his mother read a bedtime story.
2. Read one of your favorite bedtime or naptime books in a lowered, calm voice.
   Talk with the children about how it makes you relax when you read the book.
3. Ask the children to bring a copy of a book from home, one of their favorite books that helps them relax and go to sleep.
4. During the week, select bedtime books to read aloud in the library corner and at times during the day when a relaxing mood is needed.

Something to think about—
If some of your children have few books at home, let these children go with you to the school or city library and check out books for the rest of the class.

Story Stretcher

For Music and Movement: Pots and Pans for Our Kitchen Band

What the children will learn—
To march and keep the beat on their kitchen utensils and pots and pans

Materials you will need—
Large cardboard box, pots and pans, lids, coffee cans, large metal and wooden serving spoons, tablespoons, cassette recording of march music, tape player

What to do—
1. Collect all the instruments, pots and pans, and utensils for the kitchen band and place them in a large cardboard box.
2. During a second circle time of the day, play some march music and let the children parade around the edge of the circle time rug, marching and clapping their hands.
3. Have the children sit on the circle time rug again and at random, call out the names of the children to come up and select an instrument for the kitchen band.
4. March around the room, leading the kitchen band as they keep time with the march music.

Something to think about—
Banging around on pots and pans and coffee cans certainly is not real music; however, the improvised pretend band can enjoy the movement of the activity.

FIGURE 9.1   *(continued)*

Designing Integrated Curriculum for Children's Life Changes

The integrated curriculum described here includes the concept of multiple types of family groups. It is sensitive to the reality that many children do not live in the traditional family unit composed of father, mother, and children. Other variations in children's lives must also be accommodated into integrated curriculum. Such a unit for social science is described by Wellhousen (1996). A study of homes is an appropriate topic for young children; nevertheless, children live in many types of homes. Some children are homeless and live in a shelter. A web used to demonstrate how children from diverse home settings can understand the concept of home includes types of homes and who lives in homes. In Figure 9.2 types of homes include shelters, mobile homes, and condominiums. This is one example of a curriculum topic that incorporates life changes that children experience.

I have also discussed in previous chapters that integrated curriculum units should originate with children's interests and needs. Curriculum should be centered in children's planning rather than always being planned by the teacher. Unit topics can focus on life changes that children in the classroom are encountering. Themes of study can emerge from critical events in the students' lives. Devall and Cahill (1995) have developed thematic projects that can use play as a focus for experiences. In Figure 9.3, different life changes are listed in the first column. Suggestions for child-centered activities for each project or topic are listed in four columns.

Integrated units in the preschool years can have their origin in any category of development; however, as has been pointed out several times, other types of development are also interfaced with integrated curriculum. This is especially true of physical development. Preschool children are physically involved when they are learning and playing. Nonetheless, the preschool program should include curriculum for physical development that extends beyond self-initiated or informal play activities to include activities that involve gross and fine motor skills. The next section discusses the

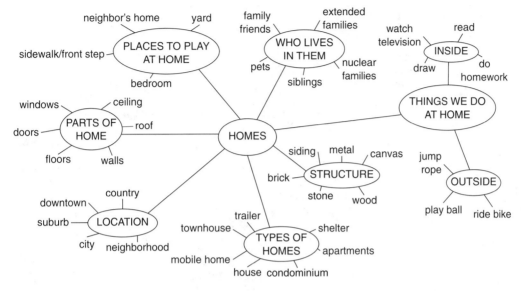

FIGURE 9.2   A sample web on homes
Source: From "Be It Ever So Humble: Developing A Study of Homes for Today's Diverse
Society," by K. Wellhousen, *Young Children,* 52, (November), p. 74. Copyright 1996 by
Young Children. Reprinted with permission from the National Association for the Education
of Young Children.

nature of physical development in the preschool
years and appropriate curriculum to encourage
physical activities.

Curriculum for Physical Development

 Peter Paul and Amos

*Peter Paul and Amos are sitting under a tree en-
joying a glass of lemonade. They have been playing chase around the trees in the backyard of Peter
Paul's house and are thirsty. They are munching on
peanut butter cookies that Peter Paul's mother
brought them for a snack. When Amos is finished,
he pulls himself onto a low limb and looks for
more limbs he can use to climb. "I can climb very*

*high," he announces to Peter Paul. Not to be out-
done, Peter Paul abandons his lemonade and runs
to another nearby tree.*

"I can, too," he calls to Amos.

"Not as high as I can," challenges Amos.

*There is silence for a few minutes as each boy
slowly makes his way up a few feet more.
"I am as high as a jet," Amos calls to Peter Paul.*

*"I am as high as the sky," Peter Paul re-
sponds.* ✦

The preschool years are significant for physical development. The emerging locomotor skills
practiced by infants and toddlers are improved
and refined during the preschool years. Preschoolers spend many hours in active play that
exercises gross and fine motor skills. They need
abundant time for play, both indoors and outdoors. In this part of the chapter, I will discuss

Project topics[a]	Dramatic play props	Literacy props	Display ideas	Field trips and visitors	Comments
The children themselves Babies—the birth of a sibling	Cribs, dolls, changing table, diapers, clothes, bottles, baby food, bathtub, washcloths and towel	"Parenting" books with photos, baby announcement cards	Baby photos of children and teachers	Invite parents with infants to share care routines; visit nursery at local hospital	
The children themselves Families— marriage, remarriage, and adoption	Items from a variety of tradi- tions: candles, bouquets, "fancy" clothing, music, foods	Paper for writing invitations and thank-you cards	Photos of family adoption ceremonies; wedding and anniversary celebrations		As with all dramatic play, allow children to choose own roles
Local community Hospital—going to the hospital	Stethoscope, bandages, gowns, surgical outfits, dolls, food, trays, bed, flowers, "X-ray machines"	Get-well cards, prescription pads, "med- icine" bottles with written di- rections, recep- tionist materials	Photographs of children's doctors, nurses and dentists and of interior and exterior of local hospital	Field trip to hospital; tour facility; ride gurney, wheelchair, meet the staff	
Local community Elementary school— transition to a new school	Construct a school bus from large boxes and chairs; bus driver outfit; backpacks, lunch boxes	Class roster for taking attendance, map of local school route, "school" props	Photographs of local elementary school, various kindergarten classrooms, kindergarten teachers	Visit kinder- garten classes at local schools; ride school bus; invite last year's class to talk about kindergarten	
Local community The vet's office—death of a pet	Stuffed animals, leashes, blan- kets, bandages, stethoscope, strip thermom- eter, "X-ray machines"	Prescription pad, telephone, phone books, message pads, calendar, ap- pointment book	Photographs of family pets, favorite animals	Visit a local vet office or animal hospital	Reenactment of pet funeral, *only* if idea emerges from children
Place Neighborhood— moving to a new home	Suitcases, cardboard boxes, tape, paper for wrapping items	Markers, labels for identifying boxes, change- of-address cards	Photographs of homes of children and teachers; pictures of all types of homes	Invite local moving com- pany to bring moving van, dolly, etc.; sim- ulate a garage sale; construct a moving van	

[a] Adapted from project topics suggested by Katz and Chard (1990).

FIGURE 9.3   Projects and activities on life changes
Source: From "Addressing Children's Life Changes in the Early Childhood Curriculum" by E. L. Devall and B. J. Cahill, 1995, *Early Childhood Education Journal, 23,* p. 59. Copyright 1995 by Plenum. Reprinted with permission.

how physical development is part of the curriculum for three- to five-year-olds and how the teacher can prepare the environment and plan opportunities for children to exercise their bodies to develop physical abilities.

Understanding Physical Development

Physical development is referred to as motor development because the young child is using fine and gross motor movement in physical activities. It is also described as perceptual-motor development because there is interdependency between perception and motor skills. Motor be- havior and changes in motor abilities follow perceptual actions (Williams, 1983).

In Chapter 4, I described the characteristics of physical development in three- to five-year-olds. The Frost-Wortham developmental checklists describe major milestones in fine and gross motor skills at each developmental level. In this chapter, I will address physical development as it involves perceptual-motor development. As the child develops the capacity to manage more complex sensory input, more skillful motor behavior follows (Jambor, 1990). The components of these interactive elements of sensory and physical actions constitute perceptual-motor development.

Components of Perceptual-Motor Development

Fundamental movement skills are developed during the preschool years. Frost (1992, p. 46) describes these movement skills as follows:

Gross motor activities: Throwing, catching, kicking, jumping, swinging

Fine motor activities: Cutting lace, hammering, buttoning, pouring

Body awareness activities: Naming, pointing, identifying, moving, and performing tasks using body parts

Spatial awareness activities: Moving, exploring, locating, comparing, and identifying using walking, running, catching, rolling, and going through tunnels and mazes

Directional awareness activities: Moving, stationing, pointing, identifying, and imitating using body objects and apparatuses

Balance activities: Walking, bounding, and clapping using balance beams and boards, trampoline, and spring boards

Integration activities: Hitting moving ball, tracking moving objects, matching visual and motor responses, responding to auditory signals

Expressive activities: Working with art, music, dance, and dramatic play

These categories of skills can be further explained as follows (Gallahue, 1993):

Gross motor skills: Locomotor skills; movements using large motor abilities

Fine motor skills: Skills using fingers and hands that promote development of strength and flexibility in the fingers

Body awareness: The capacity to discriminate among the parts of the body and to understand how the body works—what parts of the body can do

Spatial awareness: Perceptual-motor development that permits children to orient themselves in space; includes understanding how much space their body occupies and how to locate themselves and objects in space

Directional awareness: Refers to directionality and laterality; the child is able to understand location and direction as it relates to the position of his or her body (left and right, up and down, front and back); also refers to the ability to see or understand direction in space; children must be able to perceive directionality of print on the page in the English language to be able to read

Temporal awareness: Refers to the relatedness between the body and time; related to physical coordination; rhythm, synchrony, and sequencing necessary for coordinated physical performance

Children's ability to control their bodies affects all other areas of development. The ability to use fine and gross motor skills affects the child's feeling of competence and is carried over to other areas of development. Self-image is related to mastery of physical skills. Children who perceive themselves as having good physical abilities can use their success for gaining confidence in addressing social and cognitive activities.

Gallahue (1993) proposes that young children follow a developmental progression in the acquisition of their motor skills. Failure to properly develop these skills in the early childhood years can lead to later failure in games and sports. He believes that the motor and perceptual development cannot be left to chance. Fundamental movement skills are basic to the motor development and movement education program for young children. Developmental sequences for these fundamental movement skills form the framework for the program in physical development. Young children vary in the acquisition of fundamental movements depending on the kinds of physical experiences they have had as well as hereditary factors. Therefore, the developmental movement programs should emphasize sequential movement skill acquisition and increased physical competence that is individualized to the individual developmental level of each child.

Planning for Physical Development

Children vary in their rate of physical development, just as they do in language, cognitive, and social development. Teachers need to be aware of these differences when planning environment arrangements and experiences for physical development. A range of experiences should be planned for perceptual-motor and movement activities that will promote physical development in young children.

Although children acquire many motor skills through normal working and playing activities in the indoor and outdoor environment, the teacher also plans for comprehensive physical development. The teacher identifies current levels of physical abilities in individual students and selects specific fine and gross motor skills that can be addressed in planned daily activities. Thus, the teacher might decide to put out boards, blocks, or a walking beam to help children develop balancing skills; or the teacher might plan a cutting activity to practice using scissors. Attention is given to both fine and gross motor skills that are developmentally appropriate for preschoolers.

When planning activities that provide for gross and fine motor skills, the teacher might make a choice from a list of activities such as the following (Beaty, 2000):

Large Motor Activities
Walking
Throwing, catching
Balancing
Hopping, jumping, leaping
Running, galloping, skipping
Climbing
Crawling, creeping, scooting
Using wheeled vehicles

Fine Motor Activities
Zipping, buttoning, tying
Twisting, turning
Pouring
Cutting
Holding and printing, tracing, painting
Inserting

Large motor skills activities for preschool children should be provided indoors as well as outdoors. Obstacle courses, indoor climbing equipment, and flexible motor skills apparatuses can be arranged for use in the activities to be included in the daily schedule. Other center activities, teacher-directed lessons, and small-group activities planned for the day or week can be analyzed for the type of fine and gross motor skills that will be used. Through a combination of planned activities and natural play opportunities during the day, children can have a balance of perceptual-motor experiences that permit them to refine and extend physical development (Hendrick, 1998).

The Role of Play in Physical Development

Play has an important role in all categories of development; however, its benefits for physical development may be more obvious for most teachers and parents. Physical exercise is associated with outdoor play, and traditional playground equipment used throughout most of the twentieth century has been designed to exercise motor skills.

For our concerns, the role of play for preschool children is more than that for providing gross motor exercise. Fine motor skills are considered as well within the understanding the importance of play. Three- to 5-year-olds spend much of their day in play. If they are in a caregiving or preschool setting, indoor and outdoor play periods should be alternated with more structured activities. During play opportunities, children combine language practice, socialization, and cognitive exploration with fine and gross motor activities. The child selects the play activities; thus, play events are self-directed or group directed. Some children take leadership roles in play, and the physical activities engaged in are supportive to the child's purpose for the play activity.

The Role of the Environment in Physical Development

The quality of the play environment affects the benefits of physical play. A primary concern is that the playscape is safe (Frost, 2001). Beyond consideration for safety of design and construction of equipment for physical play, the child's play activities are related to the type of space where the play takes place, the materials that are available for the play, and the way in which the play space is arranged (Johnson, Christie, & Yawkey, 1999).

Children play differently indoors than outdoors. Large motor play is more likely to occur outdoors, where there is more space and where play equipment encourages gross motor activity. Construction play is more frequent indoors, where there is an abundance of blocks, manipulative materials, and art and writing activities (Henniger, 1985). Boys and girls play differently indoors and outdoors. Preschool boys prefer playing outdoors more than do girls; moreover, they engage in more make-believe play outdoors. Girls, on the other hand, prefer to play indoors. They engage in more dramatic play indoors and are more likely to engage in fine motor activities than are boys (Johnson, Christie, & Yawkey, 1999).

The Indoor Environment

A well-planned indoor environment is well-stocked and arranged for both gross and fine motor activities. Materials and ideas for fine motor activities are always available in the art center, language center, and manipulative center.

In the art center, all activities will nurture fine motor skills. Painting, cutting, and pasting; mold-

ing play dough; constructing collages; and working with chalk and crayons are examples of expressive activities that nurture many fine motor movements. Hands and fingers are exercised and used differently for each of these activities.

The manipulative center also can facilitate varied fine motor actions. Puzzles, bristle blocks, Legos, and other such construction materials help develop fine motor coordination as children explore possibilities for working with the materials. The sensory nature of Montessori materials makes them particularly useful for fine motor experiences. Lacing, zipping, buttoning, and using snaps can be practiced in activities that teach dressing skills. The manipulative nature of Montessori materials for cognitive activities also incorporates physical manipulation of curriculum experiences.

The language center in a preschool classroom provides opportunities to use fine motor skills. Writing activities require fine motor exercise, as do emergent literacy games.

Gross motor skills should also be nurtured indoors. In addition to the portable climbing equipment and temporary obstacle courses mentioned earlier, gross motor activities can be engaged in through playing with sand and water and with different sizes of blocks and vehicles in the block center. Workbench activities also attract both girls and boys to opportunities for sawing, hammering, and drilling, using both gross and fine muscle skills.

Beaty (1992) recommends that the indoor classroom have a large motor center where activities can be planned for gross motor skills. She suggests that changing equipment arrangements be placed in the center to encourage specific gross motor exercise. Teacher-directed activities to promote large motor skills can supplement the options for child-initiated gross motor play.

The Outdoor Environment

Many gross motor activities can be planned and encouraged indoors; nevertheless, the outdoor environment is where all gross motor actions can take place naturally. Outdoors, preschool children

can run, jump, gallop, and so on most freely. The freedom of a large space permits many gross motor activities. In addition, equipment and design features provide more variety in physical activity opportunities.

A complex climbing structure, or superstructure, is a central feature of the playscape for physical exercise. The structure contains decks and attached apparatus that provide for a range of gross motor actions; such apparatus can include slides, fireman's poles, steps, clatter bridges, trapeze bar, and ramps. The opportunities offered by complex climbing structures include options for both upper torso and lower torso exercise. Swingsets are another standard piece of equipment that provides enjoyable gross motor activity. A path where vehicles can be ridden or pushed and pulled is also important on preschool playgrounds.

Natural features can also provide possibilities for climbing, running, sliding, balancing, and rolling. The site can be planned to include mounds, small hills, tree stumps, and large dead trees; other natural features arranged in a large open area

also encourage vigorous movement in play (Frost, 2001).

Preschool playscapes should also include opportunities for fine motor activities. Many art and craft activities are enjoyed in the outdoor environment. Outdoor sand and water activities promote both fine and gross motor movement, as do gardening and some dramatic play activities.

Both the indoor and outdoor environments for preschool children should include provisions for perceptual–motor development. Some activities will occur naturally as a result of having the facilities and materials available in the planned environment. Other experiences will require conscious planning on the teacher's part.

The Role of the Teacher in Physical Development

Perhaps the most important responsibility the teacher assumes when considering how to plan for physical development is for carefully planning how the learning environment and outdoor play area will nurture gross and fine motor skills. As described earlier, the teacher's understanding of the role of play in physical development and the effect of the environment on exercising emerging physical abilities must be translated into physical arrangements indoors and outdoors that will encourage the range of physical movement in preschool children.

The second important responsibility of the teacher is to be informed of the physical development needs of individual children. Through daily observation when children are at play, the teacher is alert to the physical skills the children are mastering. For example, the teacher may note that a child is having difficulty with play equipment or a locomotor skill; demonstration, modeling, and guided instruction can enable a child to try the fireman's pole or climb a ladder to the complex climbing structure. Similarly, the teacher can show a child how to hold a plastic bat to hit a sponge ball off a tee and can monitor the child's efforts to hit the ball successfully. The teacher needs to be actively involved in large and small motor activities to provide guidance and encouragement when needed.

The teacher's third responsibility is to plan curriculum activities. Some will be planned to be carried out indoors, whereas others will take place outdoors. Some activities will be planned for a motor activity period, and others will be integrated with activities in other developmental areas. The significant factor is that the teacher is sensitive to the importance of motor development and does not relegate outdoor free play periods as the only options for physical exercise. The preschool teacher who is enthusiastic about incorporating language, social, and cognitive experiences in integrated, thematic curriculum can be equally competent and interested in incorporating physical development into planned units. The section that follows discusses how the teacher can set up perceptual-motor experiences for preschool children.

Despite the important role that teachers play in promoting physical development, it is important to remember that preschool children need abundant amounts of time for free play, particularly outdoor play. Children need time and space for spontaneous, natural play that will permit them to engage in play activities alone or with their friends. In addition, they need to engage in social, socio-dramatic, and cognitive elements in play that are possible within physical play. Because many

---

Walking
Follow the leader
Walk like an animal
Rocking boat
Walking trail

Balancing
Follow the leader
Hollow blocks
Be an animal
Balance beam
Block beam
Con-Tac paper footprints
Balance board

Hopping, Jumping, Leaping
Footprint trail
Hopscotch
Jump over the river
Jumping jack period

Running, Galloping, Skipping
Follow the leader
Relay race
Action chants

Climbing
Jungle gym
Rung ladder
Nesting climber
Dome climber
Tires
Swiss cheese board
Rowboat
Tree stumps
Cable spools

Crawling, Creeping, Scooting
Spooky music
Tambourine
Tunnels of cardboard
Barrels
Styrofoam tunnel
Masking tape obstacle course
Scooter
Wooden vehicles

Picking Up/Carrying
Large hollow blocks
Boxes
Furniture
Large toys

FIGURE 9.4 Equipment and activities for motor development
Source: From *Skills for Preschool Teachers* (4th ed., pp. 90–91) by J. J. Beaty, copyright © 1996. Reprinted by permission of Pearson Education, Inc. Upper Saddle River, NJ 07458.

preschool children are in structured after-school settings while their parents work, or cannot play outdoors because the outdoor environment is dangerous, it is particularly important that preschool settings provide for free play time as part of their overall physical development program (Wortham, 2001b).

Designing Curriculum for Physical Development

Teachers may be very familiar with the materials and equipment they need for cognitive and language development in the classroom. They may also be secure in their understanding of how the block and manipulative centers promote gross and fine motor skills. However, they may be less knowledgeable about how they can ensure that they have acquired the materials and equipment needed to carry out a comprehensive program for physical development. Beaty (1992) suggests materials and activities that address the basic gross and fine motor skills that are part of the preschool physical curriculum, Figure 9.4 lists these suggestions. Although the majority of the activities described are more likely to be used indoors, many suggestions are also part of outdoor playground activities.

Jambor (1990) describes perceptual-motor activities for young children that are intended to promote kinesthetic and sensory development in outdoor experiences (Figure 9.5). He describes activities and equipment needed for locomotion, balance, body and space perception, rhythm and temporal awareness, rebound and airborne movement, and projections and reception movement. Although most of these suggestions for physical development are best conducted outdoors, many are also suitable for indoors.

Throwing/Catching
Beanbags
Ring toss
Sponge balls
Yarn balls
Beach balls
Rubber balls

Twisting/Turning
Eggbeaters
Food mills
Can openers
Bottle and screw tops
Bolt boards
Orange squeezer

Pouring
Small pitchers
Rice, salt, sand

Cutting
Table knife and cooked vegetables
Paring knife and raw vegetables
Shredder
Grater
Melon baller

Holding and Printing/Tracing/Painting
Pencil, crayon
Felt-tip pen **Wheeled**
Equipment
Tricycle
Big Wheel
Large wooden vehicles
Scooter
Conveyer belt trike path

Inserting
Shoe box collections
Egg carton
Wooden-knob puzzles
Legos
Pegboards
Golf tees
Geoboard
Frame puzzles
Photo puzzles

Zipping
Clothing with zippers
Zipper board

Locomotion
- Rolling in various directions on flat and sloped grassy areas with arms in different positions
- Creeping, crawling, and walking on or across textured surfaces (to increase sensory input)
- Crawling through "space-holes": barrels, open-ended boxes, single mounted tires, tire tunnels, low playhouse windows
- Crawling across a wide plank
- Climbing on hills, ramps, stairs, platform levels, connected tire formations, rope nets, ladders, multipurpose structures, low limb tree branches, overhead and multidirectional ropes
- Stepping up on graduated levels: platforms, logs, tires, stumps, large wide blocks
- Jumping/bouncing on flat springboards, large flexible horizontal tires, inner tubes, mattresses (trampolines are considered dangerous and not recommended)
- Jumping from varying heights: tires, wooden platforms, stone/earth ledges, stumps, spring boards
- Hurdling over "natural" objects, objects prepared by adults (e.g., a horizontal bamboo pole between two adjustable vertical support points)
- Hopping in place with both feet, then with one foot at a time; hopping, back and forth over lines, between rungs of a wooden ladder on the ground
- Running and walking across bridges, up and down natural slopes and man-made ramps, in open grassy areas
- Chasing and "tag" games that utilize most play apparatus and available space
- Crossing "hand-over-hand" on overhead ladder
- Pumping a swing
- Pulling or pushing a wagon
- Wheel toys that coordinate alternate pumping and steering with feet and hands; obstacle course routes that challenge the coordination of perceptual and motor skills

Many of these actions and activities, as well as those that follow, can be controlled and enhanced by listening for music cues for stopping, starting, and intensity of action.

Balance
- Standing and balancing (both feet, then only one) on walking beam, vertical in-ground tire, moving bridge, suspended horizontal rope with overhead hand support; close eyes for added sensation
- Walking various heights, widths, and spans of wooden beams, vertical in-ground tires, large diameter rope and fire hose (with overhead supports to keep upright)
- Walking on wide beams with arms extended holding a weighted object in one hand or both

FIGURE 9.5 Outdoor activities for perceptual–motor development
Source: From Promoting perceptual–motor development in young children's play (pp. 159–162), by T. Jambor, 1990. In *Playgrounds for Young Children,* S. C. Wortham & J. L. Frost (Eds.), Reston, VA: American Alliance for Health, Physical Education, Recreation and Dance. Reprinted with permission of the publisher.

- Walking on a line or thin diameter rope configuration on ground
- Walking with one foot on and one off a ground-level beam, on a curb edge, on an edge of a ladder lying on ground, around the edge of a large-diameter horizontal tire
- Following the leader on a spontaneous or preplanned obstacle course throughout playground

Body and Space Perception
- Large mirror area for viewing self and specific body parts and experimenting with ways these parts can function
- Identifying body parts and relating them to a function of movement activity
- Responding to requests to use a body part(s) on climbing or balancing apparatus
- Coordinating body parts to perform physical feats of strength and agility in play spaces and on equipment
- Using arm and leg movements to create "snow/sand angels"
- Pushing someone on a swing
- Fitting into spaces; boxes, large tire opening, wagon, playhouse, play boat or car, across a bridge span, on a swivel tire, at top of a slide (number and size relationship concept)
- Coordinating running and movement activities within a limited space
- Climbing on, under, around, through, etc.; going to the left or to the right (body-objects relationships and directionality)
- Any activity requiring movement in space!

Rhythm and Temporal Awareness
- Recurring rhythm: swing (standard infant and strap seats, suspended tire or rope, swivel tire, vestibular platform, porch style); rocking boats, etc.; wheel toys
- Methodic, rhythmic bouncing on large tires, inner tubes, springboards
- Jumping over stationary rope or one swung in a quarter arc to a rhythmic beat
- Galloping, marching through playground to music, with rhythm instruments or hand claps
- Accelerating and decelerating physical movement to given tempo
- Running up or down diagonal ramps and hills
- Tossing, catching, kicking, dodging objects (e.g., various size balls, beanbags, balloons)

Rebound and Airborne Movement
- Bouncing on springboards, mattresses, large flexible tires, inner tubes (music varies the variety and tempo of action)
- Jumping onto a mattress or into sand, pea gravel, or other resilient ground base from varying heights
- Hanging by hands or legs from climbers, chinning bars, low tree branches, etc.
- Swinging on vertical rope; pushing off of objects to continue or vary movement

The Integrated Curriculum for Physical Development

Preschool teachers can use Beaty's (2000) and Jambor's (1990) guides to develop a quality physical development program for preschool children; in addition, attention can be given to incorporating activities for physical development into the total curriculum. Many skills will be encouraged through ongoing center and teacher-directed activities in art, language, and mathematics and science. They naturally occur as part of the overall preschool curriculum. Other opportunities result from conscious attempts to correlate learning across developmental areas. The teacher deliberately uses physical activity options to help children integrate cognitive concepts; for example, perhaps an art activity is combined with emergent writing to address fine motor skills.

Trostle and Yawkey (1990) developed a handbook of integrated learning activities for young children. They classified integrated experiences into chapters and broad unit categories. One chapter, on transportation, provides particularly helpful advice for interrelating physical development with other curriculum components. Two integrated experiences in the chapter on transportation exemplify how physical development can be integrated with other areas of the curriculum. The activity titled "Wiggling Feet" (Figure 9.6) describes how naming and moving body parts is part of language arts. Moving their bodies to songs and then having discussions help children understand names of body parts, relationships between parts of the body, and the way in which the body moves.

The second activity, "Shape Jumping" (Figure 9.7) combines playing with shapes with jumping activities. To engage in a hopscotch shape activity, children must also use skills in patterning and sequence. Children use fine motor skills to make the shapes used in the activities. In addition, the children must use listening skills to follow directions and use divergent thinking skills to develop a transportation story.

Motor skills activities can be planned for thematic units. Herr and Libby (1990) developed a handbook of thematic units for preschool classrooms. Some of the units provide for specific body movement activities. A unit titled "Music" focuses on musical instruments. Activities are suggested for various areas of the curriculum such as using water in crystal glasses to make music and constructing instruments out of various materials. For large muscle activities, the authors suggest the following (Herr & Libby, 1990, p. 357):

The thematic units developed for preschool classrooms in this text that include kindergarten also incorporate physical activity experiences. In the unit described in Chapter 8 titled "Seeds," students make and use musical instruments using seeds they have collected in rhythm band activities (see Appendix A). In addition to fine motor activities related to art activities, the students also engage in a music and movement activity. Another preschool unit, "Farm Animals" (Appendix B), correlates

WIGGLING FEET (Language Arts)

Overview: Children use body movements and practice movement as direction. In Target, they move parts of their bodies to soft and mood music. In Moving Ahead, they move their bodies to the rhythm of common, familiar songs.

Objective: Naming and moving parts of the body

Supplies: Audio recording of soft or mood music; audio recorder

Words You'll Like: movement, body, body parts, direction, music, soft, practice, connect, opposite

Getting Started

The children talk about and name their body parts, such as arms, toes, fingers, and so forth. After the discussion, the youngsters name several body parts of their choice and show how each part moves. The children invent and show new movements for each body part. For example, they shake their heads back and forth and swing their legs at the knees.

Target

The children lie on their backs on the floor and place their hands over their heads. The youngsters identify the body part opposite their heads. They wiggle their toes to show this point. The children think about the body part connected to their arms; then they move their shoulders. Repeat the questioning using different body parts as the youngsters demonstrate the appropriate movements. Try this activity while playing music. Introduce "Heads, Shoulders, Knees, and Toes," a favorite movement song among children everywhere.

Moving Ahead

The children sing and practice familiar songs involving movement, such as the "Hokey Pokey" or "The Farmer in the Dell." The children sing the song using the familiar body movements. Next, the children identify and practice several original movements to these songs using different body parts. Finally, the youngsters identify the new body parts they used in the movement songs. For example, using "Hokey Pokey" the youngsters might substitute thumbs, wrists, ankles, knees, calves, and necks for the traditional body parts.

Let's Talk

1. After the youngsters listen to and move their bodies to music or song, they describe their feelings as they performed these activities. Have them close their eyes as they perform. Compare differences in how they feel when their eyes are opened and closed.
2. Talk about fish and streams using nautical terms. If available, use a rocking boat (or use a rocking chair) for a fishing expedition. Provide poles and magnetic paper fish. As a variation, draw a body part on each fish. As children "catch" the fish, they name the body part drawn on it and move that body part. Others join in and "follow the leader" by also moving that body part.

FIGURE 9.6   Integrated curriculum for physical development
Source: From *Integrated Learning Activities for Young Children* (p. 258), by S. L. Trostle and T. D. Yawkey, 1990, Boston: Allyn & Bacon. Copyright 1990 by Allyn & Bacon. Reprinted with permission.

SHAPE JUMPING (Physical Education)

Overview: Children draw shapes and use them in hopping exercises to develop muscles, movements, and coordinations. First, the youngsters draw and color shapes and then use them in a hopping activity. Then they hop to shapes in circular and other arrangements. They discuss transportation as it relates to these activities.

Objective: Jumping to shapes in various arrangements.

Supplies: Poster board, oak tag, or other durable material; ruler; crayons; tape

Words You'll Like: drawing, hopping, order, rectangle, circle, square, rhombus, ellipse, triangle, pretend

Getting Started

The children draw shapes, such as circles, triangles, squares, ellipses, and rectangles on pieces of poster board, oak tag, or other durable paper. After coloring the shapes, the children place the shapes on the floor to make a straight path about one inch apart. They help tape down the shapes to secure them while the youngsters are hopping. Have the children hop forward and back on the shapes, stating the shapes' names as the children go.

Target

Using more durable paper, the children draw two of each of the following: triangle, circle, square, rhombus, and ellipse. After outlining and coloring these shapes, they tape the shapes on the floor making a straight path about eight inches apart in the following order: triangle, circle, square, ellipse, rhombus, triangle, circle, square, ellipse, rhombus. The children stand at one end of the path on the triangle. Call out a series of shapes indicating to the children where they jump next. For example, call "circle, ellipse, rhombus."

Continue by changing the patterns where the children are jumping. The children can also identify jumping patterns. As the youngsters become more skillful, add rectangles and increase the space between the shapes. Finally, the youngsters jump from shape to shape and, as they land, add a new line to a pretend story about traveling. As they tell their stories, they give characteristics of their transportation vehicles and destinations.

Moving Ahead

The children arrange and secure all their shapes in one large circle in a specified order. For example, the children arrange and jump from circle, to square, to rectangle, to ellipse, to circle, to square, to rectangle, to ellipse. Repeat each pattern several times. The children anticipate what shape comes next and identify jumping patterns. After they hop around a circle, try forming other shapes such as a large square or rectangle.

Let's Talk

1. The youngsters decide if they would like to always hop, jump, or fly rather than walk from one place to another. They talk about hopping, jumping, and flying forms of transportation. The children explain why they would or would not like to use these modes of transportation.
2. The children name several animals that primarily use hopping for transportation, such as the rabbit, frog, toad, grasshopper, and kangaroo. After naming the different animals, the children imitate the animals' movements. Try other types of animal movements and exercise, such as crawling, and follow the same steps.

FIGURE 9.7   Integrated curriculum for physical development
Source: From *Integrated Learning Activities for Young Children* (pp. 268–269), by S. L. Trostle and T. D. Yawkey, 1990, Boston: Allyn & Bacon. Copyright 1990 by Allyn & Bacon. Reprinted with permission.

mathematics and body movement in a duck walk game. Children are also taught a simple square dance that integrates music and movement. In addition, the students must coordinate different steps in the dance, follow directions, and move in time with the rest of the group.

Designing Physical Development Activities for Children with Disabilities

Children with disabilities experience difficulty in engaging in motor activities, especially physical play. Children with physical disabilities have restricted abilities to participate in motor activities; consideration must be made to accommodate activities to match the physical characteristics of individual preschool children. The play environment also must be adapted to individual disabili-

ties. The adult may need to prepare the child for physical activities.

Children with visual disabilities can be helped to orient themselves to space and time and participate in motor activities, with attention being paid to their visual impairment. The following are suggestions for planning activities for children with disabilities (Wortham, 2001e):

- Adults can assist by planning a play activity with the child in terms of what is available: play materials, other children, special equipment.
- The playground should offer sensory clues such as different textures on walking surfaces that will guide the child to play opportunities. The teacher can help the child orient himself toward the equipment or materials the child wishes to use.
- Before play, the adult can help the child practice with materials or equipment that will be used.
- The adult supports and encourages the child during play activities.

Children with motor disabilities have difficulty participating in physical activities and using environments that have not been adapted for such limitations. In spite of restrictions in movement, these children are able to participate in some activities. The play environment should be modified to allow the child access to play experiences, to allow the teacher to physically locate the immobile child in a play experience, and to allow the teacher to develop broadened opportunities for the physically limited child's physical development. The goal is to develop alternative ways for children with physical disabilities to participate in activities that require mobility. The play environment should be studied for accessibility. Accessibility considerations are different for children who use a wheelchair for mobility and those who are able to use a walker. Accessibility to play equipment and activities is adapted differently depending on the child's physical limitations.

Body Movement Rhythms

Introduce a simple body movement. Then have the children repeat it until they develop a rhythm. Examples include the following:

> stamp foot, clap hands, stamp foot, clap hands
> clap, clap, stamp, stamp
> clap, stamp, clap, stamp
> clap, clap, snap fingers
> clap, clap, stamp, clap, clap, stamp

Body Percussion

Instruct the children to stand in a circle. Repeat the following rhythmic speech:

> We walk and we walk and we stop [rest].
> We walk and we walk and we stop [rest].
> We walk and we walk and we walk and we walk,
> We walk and we walk and we stop [stop].

March

Play different rhythm beats on a piano or another instrument. Examples include beats that provoke hopping, skipping, gliding, walking, running, tiptoeing, and galloping. The children can move to the rhythm.

Summary

Preschool children are busy becoming social beings. They are learning how to live in a world of many people who have their own feelings and ideas. Young children are learning that some of the ways they use to interact with others are more successful than others. They want to be accepted into group play and are feeling their way in developing successful skills to get along with their peers and in behaving appropriately to meet adult expectations.

One goal for the preschool curriculum for social development is to help children become comfortable with themselves and others. The social development curriculum is based on an environmental setting and activities that assist children in living and playing in harmony.

The child's socialization involves the ability to control and express feelings appropriately, develop empathy, and use prosocial skills. Children must learn how to understand their own feelings and how to act on those feelings in an acceptable manner. They learn to recognize similar feelings in other children and how to respond to those emotions. When they can respond to another child in a sympathetic way, they have begun to experience empathy.

The teacher has an important role in helping children develop social skills. There are certain strategies the teacher can use to make socialization easier. The classroom, routines, and daily activities can be organized to facilitate harmony and minimize conflicts among children. However, because young children are just learning successful behaviors, the teacher has to take an active role in guiding them. Children who are angry, aggressive, or otherwise behave inappropriately need adult intervention and redirection to learn the correct behaviors.

The teacher also has a role in guiding children to understand and accept multicultural differences. Because racial bias begins early in life, the teacher nurtures a sense of value toward different cultures. The preschool setting and social development curriculum reflect multicultural diversity in a positive manner.

Social development also encompasses the social sciences. Learning to get along with others is part of a larger goal of understanding and participating in the larger society. Foundations for later study of history, geography, economics, sociology, and anthropology are established through the social science curriculum in the preschool program. The social science curriculum is best learned in an integrated, meaningful context; therefore, experiences that are planned help extend the child's understanding of him- or herself and others and relate to the child's life and experiences. Learning about social science topics within thematic units enables children to understand their membership in society in more depth and breadth.

Great strides are made in physical development in the preschool years. Children between the ages of 3 and 5 are extremely active and energetic in exercising their bodies through play. Perceptual-motor development, which depends on the interaction of sensory and physical advances, results in more complex sensory input accompanied by more skillful motor behaviors.

The child's physical development involves gross and fine motor skills, body awareness, locomotor skills, and body, spatial, temporal, and directional awareness. Both the indoor and outdoor environments should be planned and equipped for these kinds of perceptual-motor development to be encouraged. Also, the teacher plans activities to promote development, particularly in gross and fine motor activities. In addition to ensuring that children have substantial time for indoor and outdoor play, the teacher plans a balance of gross and fine motor activities as part of the physical development curriculum.

The teacher must be aware of the individual needs of children for physical activities. Because children vary in level of physical development and opportunities for physical activities outside the group setting, the teacher provides opportunities for physical exercise and practice that meet individual differences. Opportunities for fine and gross motor activities occur naturally during the day through participation in ongoing preschool activities. Motor skills are developed through center activities, play periods, and teacher-planned activities. Activities can also be planned within thematic units.

Special consideration needs to be given to children who have physical limitations. Outdoor play equipment needs to be accessible to children who have no mobility or must use a walker or wheelchair. Curriculum activities that require physical movement may need to be modified or adapted for children with physical disabilities. The teacher's goal should be to make it possible for the child with special needs to participate as much as possible in some capacity.

Study Questions

1. Why do preschool children need play experiences each day to help them develop social skills?
2. How do preschool children develop successful behaviors in interacting with others?
3. How does cognitive development help the child acquire empathy?
4. What is the nature of a "curriculum" for social development in the preschool program?
5. How does a good self-image affect development of socialization skills?
6. What kinds of behaviors does a child have to use for successful socialization?
7. What kinds of behaviors do children use when they have developed empathy?
8. How does the teacher nurture multicultural sensitivity in preschool children?
9. What are the goals for a social science curriculum in preschool classrooms?
10. Why is sociodramatic play important for both socialization and the social science curriculum?

11. How does inappropriate organization of the classroom environment result in inappropriate behaviors in young children?

12. What kinds of strategies can the teacher use to minimize or eliminate inappropriate behaviors?

13. What kinds of activities best help children understand social science concepts?

14. Why do social science experiences need to relate to the child's life experiences?

15. What is perceptual-motor development?

16. What kinds of activities promote perceptual-motor development?

17. Should the teacher consider daily outdoor play adequate for meeting physical development needs?

18. How can the indoor environment be arranged to foster gross motor skills?

19. What are some strategies that the teacher uses to develop a comprehensive perceptual-motor development program that achieves a balance between gross and fine motor skills?

20. What features need to be included in the outdoor environment to nurture both fine and gross motor development?

21. Why is teacher observation of children's play important when planning physical development experiences?

22. Can physical development activities be part of the integrated curriculum? Explain.

23. How should preschool teachers consider including children with physical disabilities in physical activities?

24. How should the outdoor playground be modified for children with physical disabilities?

25. Why do children's individual disabilities make a difference when the teacher is planning how to modify a playground for children with physical limitations?

26. How should preschool teachers consider including children with physical disabilities in physical activities?

CHAPTER TEN

A Model for Programs for Children Ages 5 to 8

CHAPTER OBJECTIVES

As a result of reading this chapter, you will be able to:

1. Understand how developmental changes in the primary grades influence learning.
2. Understand the role of play in the primary grades.
3. Describe appropriate curriculum for developmental needs in the primary grades.
4. Describe components of models for children ages 5 to 8.
5. Explain the components of an ungraded primary model.
6. Explain the steps in designing thematic curriculum in the primary grades.
7. Explain how systematic instruction is a part of thematic instruction.
8. Describe the role of assessment in kindergarten and primary grades.
9. Explain the purposes of assessment in kindergarten and primary grades.
10. Describe types of assessments that can be used in kindergarten and primary grades.

In this chapter, the design and implementation of curriculum for students in the primary grades are considered. I have stressed throughout the book that development and learning are continuous, especially as children move from preschool into the primary grades. I have also described how an understanding of the course of development in children is particularly important as teachers plan curriculum that is developmentally suitable for students in the latter years of early childhood. In Chapter 4, I describe these years as transitional because children are making important changes in areas of development, as well as making the transition to a different level of schooling.

One might question why the age of 5 is included in both preschool and primary grade curriculum. There is a need to establish bridges across the preschool and primary years and to emphasize the continuity through the years of early childhood. In addition, different early childhood settings use one organization or the other; that is, either they have programs for 3-, 4-, and 5-year olds or the 5-year-olds are in kindergarten before they enter first grade. Private and church-related settings frequently do not go beyond preschool. It is logical to place 4- and 5-year-old children together for those settings. Public schools, on the other hand, may have a variety of possibilities for organizing early childhood programs. For schools that do not have prekindergarten, kindergarten may be the level of entry into the school system. In this chapter, designing curriculum for the primary grades is considered as a continuum that begins in kindergarten. Although it is important to understand how developmental changes allow children to use more sophisticated and complex thinking, keep in mind that they are making a transition along a continuum in their development. Therefore, it is also important for teachers to deepen their understanding of how developmental advances help the use of broader possibilities for instructional strategies. Teachers want to be able to design curriculum that will be adaptable for individual differences in development to ensure success for all students. This chapter will explore how to provide a balance between systematic instruction and integrated, or thematic, curriculum. A model for a quality program in the primary grades, known as the ungraded primary, will be described; designing and implementing curriculum within the model are also described.

The Significance of Developmental Changes in the Primary Grades

Overall growth and development occur more slowly between the ages of 5 and 8 than during earlier years; however, significant developmental changes occur that permit acquisition of reading and writing skills during the primary grades. Because of the normal variations in development, children's individual timetables have implications for how teachers build in flexibility for curriculum and instruction.

Physical Development

Children entering the primary grades continue the process of developing control over their bodies. They are able to sit and work at tasks for longer periods of time. They become skilled in many physical games requiring gross motor skills, such as Frisbee, baseball, and soccer. Fine motor skills are developed through working with crafts, building models, and playing a musical instrument (Schickedanz et al., 1993; Santrock, 1997).

Because primary-age children are in the process of continuing their development of motor skills, they need to be physically active during the school day. They need frequent opportunities for physical activities if their gross motor skills are to be refined (Bredekamp, 1987; Bredekamp & Copple, 1997). Daily participation in physical activities is essential for the development of motor coordination and body strength. In addition, physical activity helps in a general feeling of well-being. Current emphasis on academic skills has resulted in diminished attention to physical development. Schools in many parts of the country are restricting both physical education periods and unstructured free play or recess periods in favor of spending more time teaching reading and other categories of academic instruction (Manning, 1998).

At issue is whether school-aged children need time for recess and unstructured play. Proponents of recess express concern that many children do not have opportunities for free play outside of school hours. They also believe there are social as well as physical benefits. Opponents of recess and free play describe concerns about aggression, bullying, and time away from academic curriculum (Smith, 1998; Wortham, 2001c).

Involvement in organized sports should be approached with caution during kindergarten and primary school years. Although children become interested and adept at physical games, their bones and muscles are immature. Extensive stress can cause strain and injury to developing bones and muscles. Prolonged use of one area of the body can lead to injuries such as sprains and stress fractures or result in accelerated bone growth (Harvey, 1982; Stoner, 1978). Participation in games and sports by all children is important; nevertheless, overemphasis on competition in organized sports with extended practice periods can be damaging to gross motor development.

Cognitive Development

I have previously discussed how children gradually shift from preoperational to concrete operational thinking between the ages of 5 and 7. A major cognitive achievement in young children entering the concrete operational stage is the acquisition of the mental ability to think about and solve problems. As this mental ability, or metacognition, develops, children become able to develop systems to organize and remember information. When children are able to use metacognition, they can plan strategies for games, understand riddles, and address how others think and feel. An appropriate primary-grade curriculum is designed with the understanding that cognitive change is gradual and subject to individual variations. These young students still need to actively reconstruct knowledge. The opportunity to use hands-on, manipulative materials allows them to have concrete reference points in their encounters with new information (Katz & Chard, 2000). Written assignments to supplement concrete materials should be designed for emerging writers in various stages.

The first years of school between kindergarten and third grade are also significant in the development of motivation to learn. Emerging cognitive abilities allow young children to assess and reflect on whether they are successful or experiencing failure in school. Children become quite aware of whether they are proficient students and whether they are able to control their success (Rotter, 1954). Children vary in how they perceive their competence and are also affected both positively and negatively by parental and teacher feedback in response to their learning efforts.

Inappropriate curriculum materials and teaching strategies that assume all children in first grade have achieved concrete operations put many students at risk for failure and inability to perceive themselves as being in control of their learning. The curriculum in kindergarten and first, second, and third grades should help the shift from preoperational thinking; at the same time, opportunities to use manipulative materials should always be included as part of instruction to ensure that possibilities for successful learning are maximized for children who are making the transition in cognitive development at different rates (Berk, 1996; Schickedanz et al., 1993).

Social and Emotional Development

A major task for children in the primary grades is to be able to work and interact effectively with their peers. Children who are unsuccessful in establishing positive peer relationships tend to have low self-esteem and achieve less in school, and they may have more problems later in life. Teachers and parents play a significant role in the child's development of self-control and social skills between the ages of 5 and 8. Research has shown that adult intervention can be effective in helping children develop successful social relationships with their peers. Teachers who use positive guidance techniques can help children develop social competence. By modeling appropriate behaviors, involving children in developing classroom rules, and engaging students in cooperative group learning activities, teachers can have an active influence on student acceptance of self-control and responsibility (Katz & McClellan, 1997).

Failure to develop a sense of competence because of inappropriate teaching practices can also affect social and emotional development. When children are expected to learn skills beyond their ability, they experience failure because they have not mastered a skill as quickly as have other students. Moreover, they may develop low self-esteem because they perceive themselves as unsuccessful learners (Elkind, 1987). According to Erikson's (1963) stages of psychosocial development described in Chapter 2, the child will either develop a sense of industry or a sense of inferiority during these years. Just as teachers need to incorporate flexibility in the learning program to adjust for variations in cognitive and motor development, they also need to respond to individual differences in social and moral development. Sensitivity to differences in social and emotional development in the primary grades can result in teaching and management practices that will support social competence in young students.

The Role of Play in the Primary Grades

As children progress through kindergarten and the primary grades, their cognitive, social, and physical development results in a shift in their approach to play. In the preschool years, socio-dramatic play and preoperational thinking predominated. As children develop toward and into concrete operational thinking, their play interests gradually change. In earlier years, play on various structures

supported physical activities and play themes. Mastery of physical skills was accomplished through play. As children move into the primary grades, games with rules and organized sports become more important.

There is a tendency in some elementary schools for teachers to perceive outdoor periods as a part of the daily curriculum. Structured physical education periods directed by an adult are considered enough for the child's physical development. However, teachers who share this perception ignore the purposes of play in a period of continuing development that goes beyond physical skills. Children's social and cognitive development during these years is also facilitated through play. Moreover, this is a period when peer relationships become increasingly important. Peer social groups develop and change as children participate in undirected play; in addition, such groups are the major socializing agent for children in the elementary grades (Hartup, 1983; Coplan & Rubin, 1998).

The peer culture is transmitted through play. Children learn from other children. Physical and social skills that are necessary for group acceptance are learned through play (Bodrova & Leong, 1996). The more experienced children in a peer group teach slang expressions, jokes, stories, riddles, and group games to newer members of the group. Hughes (1991) reminds us that parents may teach their children how to ride a bicycle, but it is members of the peer group who teach them how to do "wheelies" or jump across a ditch.

Play can be a source of either positive or negative self-concept during these years. Children who do not excel in academic areas might be skilled in physical activities. Their emerging need for competence and acceptance might be fulfilled through outdoor play activities, where their proficiency can be acknowledged by peers. The sense of competence gained from proficiency in physical activities can carry over to mastery of more difficult academic skills in the classroom. On the other hand, social acceptance or rejection in outdoor play can be based on physical ability. In a study of second-grade children, Barbour (1993) found that those with poor physical skills were not selected for teams in games organized by children. The importance of contribution to a group effort through physical skills needed for a sport or game had replaced acceptance based on social skills in the preschool years.

Adults working with children in the primary grades can take advantage of the emerging ability of children to teach each other through play, both indoors, and outdoors. Opportunity to take leadership roles and work through cooperative planning can be nurtured through structured and unstructured play periods during the school day. Similarly, parents and teachers can be cognizant of the child's success or difficulty in play situations and facilitate improvement in peer acceptance. It should not be assumed that free play periods are no longer needed for the child's development. Physical, social, and cognitive development changes in nature during the later early childhood years, but each type is equally important. Play that results from peer groups and is not directed by adults during these years continues to be significant and important (Wortham, 2001C).

Describing Appropriate Curriculum for Children Ages 5 to 8

If we accept that variations in development in the period between 5 and 8 years of age are normal, then schooling for children between kindergarten and third grade should reflect their developmental needs at those ages. More specifically, curriculum in first-, second-, and third-grade classrooms should accommodate developmental differences rather than describe achievement expectations within a narrow framework of required skills. We also need to be able to extend our understanding of variations in development to include children who have more extreme characteristics from the norms. Gifted children are at one extreme, while children with mental retardation are at the other

extreme. Children with physical disabilities also are beyond the range of normal variations.

Teaching practices with children from ages 5 to 8 allow for the unique background and level of development that each child brings to the classroom. Bredekamp and Copple (1997) describe the sources for the complex decisions that teachers must make when addressing complexity in development and culture presented by their students. They base appropriate practices on the following:

>   1. What is known about child development and learning—knowledge of age-related human characteristics that permits general predictions within an age range about what activities, materials, interactions, or experiences will be safe, healthy, interesting, achievable, and also challenging to children
>   2. What is known about the strengths, interests, and needs of each individual child in the group to be able to adapt for and be responsive to inevitable individual variation
>   3. Knowledge of the social and cultural contexts in which children live to ensure that learning experiences are meaningful, relevant, and respectful for the participating children and their families. (p. 36)

Describing a Curriculum for Continuing Developmental Needs

When describing developmental learning needs of the young child in the primary grades, one can point out many similarities among them. These students are active learners who reconstruct knowledge through individual involvement with information. They come to school from various backgrounds and previous experiences. They vary in physical, social-emotional, and cognitive development. They have different learning and socialization styles. They may also have different cultural backgrounds and family experiences that affect their approach to schooling.

Most important, these children are moving through the last years of early childhood. They are in the latter stages of preoperational thinking and moving into concrete operational thinking. Although they are developing skills in reading and writing, their individual progress in the transition to literacy necessitates curriculum that ensures success for all. Children at this stage of development are eager to succeed in school and are becoming aware of limits in abilities. Their comparison of themselves with other children can be either favorable or unfavorable and in turn affects their motivation to learn (Hills, 1986). They are acquiring dispositions about learning such as the desire to read or motivation to use mathematics skills that they have learned (Bredekamp & Copple, 1997).

Curriculum to meet continuing developmental needs in the primary grades accounts for a range in individual development. In addition, it facilitates child-initiated experiences to provide for reconstruction of knowledge. As emphasized in the discussion about preschool children, connections and relationships in learning are stressed through meaningful and purposeful activities. The relationships in knowledge are developed through an integrated curriculum that provides a meaningful context for learning. At the same time, the integrated curriculum allows children to select activities that permit them to work cooperatively and independently so that their developmental differences are complementary rather than competitive.

Integrated curriculum can provide a supportive environment for students who are at risk. The classroom that includes integrated curriculum provides opportunities for developing a sense of community in children that can help children who are at risk for success in school. When students are engaged in cooperative learning through thematic projects, they are continually interacting and collaborating within small groups in a learning community (Wolk, 1994). The classroom can reduce the impact of life changes on children by providing necessary components that might be missing in the child's home life (Charbonneau & Reider, 1995).

Systematic instruction is also needed in the primary grades as a balance is achieved between child-initiated and teacher-directed instruction. Increasingly in the primary grades, it is necessary for children to acquire specific skills and knowledge (Seefeldt, 1999). Systematic instruction is composed of lessons planned by the teacher to introduce and practice specific skills and concepts. In some contexts, the skills and concepts are sequential or hierarchical; that is, there is an order in which they are learned. For example, children must have number and numeral concepts before they can address learning how to add. In other instances, the teacher is aware that children will need to understand a concept or skill as a tool to other learning. For example, in a third-grade social studies unit, students needed to be able to look up addresses in a phone book. The teacher conducted a series of lessons on alphabetical order using the telephone directory before implementation of the activity in the unit.

The teacher introduces systematic instruction to ensure that children are mastering skills that will enable them to progress. Through systematic teaching activities, the teacher maintains meaningful instruction and teaches related skills when they are relevant to achieving proficiency (Helm & Katz, 2001; Katz & Chard, 2000). The primary-grade curriculum achieves a balance between informal child-initiated instruction and systematic teacher-designed instruction within a meaningful context.

There are concerns, and rightfully so, that skills development might be neglected in constructivist classrooms. Advocates of whole language and integrated curriculum might feel that students will learn needed skills in context within meaningful curriculum. Although this might be true for some students, others require more extensive, structured instruction if needed skills are to be mastered. This does not imply that integrated curriculum should be abandoned in favor of teaching skills, but it does mean that both explicit instruction and integrated learning are appropriate (Harris & Graham, 1996).

Primary-grade teachers cannot assume that students can acquire all skills presented within thematic curriculum. The increasingly complex skills associated with reading and mathematics require specific planning and instruction on the part of the teacher. The teacher also continuously assesses student learning needs and teaches complex academic skills through teacher-selected tasks and instruction (Katz & Chard, 2000). Bredekamp and Copple (1997), in *Developmentally Appropriate Practice in Early Childhood Programs* (Revised), describe how teachers use a variety of strategies to ensure that all children in the classroom learn appropriately. Figure 10.1 shows appropriate strategies that can be used by teachers.

The Ungraded Primary: A Model for Children Ages 5 to 8

Educators across the United States have been searching in recent years for alternatives to the present structure of three primary grades in the elementary school. The search for an alternative structure has resulted from the problems encountered by children within the school reform movement whereby schools have accelerated expectations for achievement in the primary

grades. As higher percentages of children have been identified as being at risk for failing in the primary grades, particularly in first grade, efforts to better meet the needs of students have been launched.

A common practice that became popular in the mid-1980s was the prefirst-grade, or transitional, classroom, which provided an additional grade between kindergarten and first grade for children who were felt to be at risk, or not ready for first-grade curriculum. Children were evaluated during the kindergarten year using various types of standardized tests or more informal measures to determine whether they were developmentally ready to successfully complete first grade. This practice was implemented to a lesser extent with younger and older children in prekindergarten and presecond-grade classrooms in some school districts.

The problems associated with these transitional programs soon became apparent. The tests used to identify "immature" students were questionable in terms of reliability and validity (Shepard & Smith, 1986). Accountability for accuracy in identification was lacking (Bredekamp & Shepard, 1989; Meisels, 1989). The focus on the child as being unready rather than on the curriculum as being inappropriate at these grade levels was also questioned. Instead of the curriculum being

- Teachers use a variety of strategies for ensuring each child's progress in accomplishing the expected, age-appropriate learning objectives. Teachers are aware of the continuum of learning in each curriculum area (such as literacy, mathematics, science, and social studies) and adapt instruction for individual children who are having difficulty as well as for those who are capable of more advanced levels of competence.
- To help children learn and develop, teachers use a variety of active, intellectually engaging strategies, including posing problems or discrepancies, asking thought-provoking questions, adding complexity to tasks, and engaging in reciprocal discussion in which they take children's ideas seriously. Teachers also use modeling, demonstrating, and explaining, and provide the information, coaching, direct instruction, and other assistance that a child needs to progress.

FIGURE 10.1 Teaching strategies for children ages 5 to 8
Source: From *Developmentally Appropriate Practice in Early Childhood Programs* (rev. ed.) (p. 65), by S. Bredekamp and C. Copple (Eds.), 1997, Washington, DC: NAEYC. Copyright 1997 by NAEYC. Reprinted with permission from the National Association for the Education of Young Children.

designed to fit the varied developmental levels of the students, children were expected to fit the curriculum (Day, 1988). Finally, the extra-year programs were a form of retention in themselves (Smith & Shepard, 1987). Although the transitional programs were designed to prevent failure, they added an extra year to the elementary school grades; in effect, many young students perceived that they were failures (National Association of Early Childhood Specialists in State Departments of Education, 1987).

The search for a better solution to the issue of preventing children from being at risk in the primary grades now focuses on effective ways to design curriculum and instruction between the ages of 5 and 8 (ASCD Early Childhood Education Policy Panel, 1988). The early childhood unit that groups preschool and primary classrooms as separate wings in a building or separate schools in a district is one alternative that is being advocated. Such organizational patterns can group children together in the early childhood years. Teachers and

administrators in these units can restructure curriculum to focus on the developmental nature of children in early childhood education and use developmentally appropriate curriculum materials (NAEYC & National Association of Early Childhood Specialists in State Departments of Education, 1991; National Association of Elementary School Principals, 1990).

Another alternative is the ungraded primary, in which the age-related grade levels are removed and the school is restructured to provide developmentally appropriate curriculum and instruction (Day, 1988). It is this type of alternative structure that is used to develop the model for primary-grade children in this chapter. There is more than one possibility for restructuring the primary grades. Potential arrangements include a 3-year experience with a single teacher or a team of teachers and some form of multiage grouping in an ungraded setting. None of these possibilities is new. All of the examples I will describe have been in use with elementary-age children in the United States as well as in other countries. They are being reconsidered again as alternatives to the graded, academic approach that predominates in U.S. schools at the present time.

The British Infant School Model

British infant schools have had an ungraded structure for many years. Children enter school when they turn 5 and stay with the same teacher until age 7. A teacher has students ranging across the three age levels, loses some older students each year, and gains others when they have their fifth birthday. The teacher plans the curriculum for the needs of individual students by responding to their individual interests, development, and level of achievement. Small-group and large-group instruction and activities are conducted, but children are also able to engage in individual projects for portions of the school day. Using a concept called the *integrated day,* teachers relate the subjects by integrating content areas through topics of study. Large blocks of the day are devoted to the integrated curriculum (Rothenberg, 1989).

For the purposes of this chapter, an adaptation of this structure for an ungraded model in the primary grades has students enter a classroom and stay with a teacher or a team of teachers for 3 years. The age range is from 5 to 7 or 6 to 8. Children engage in thematic study for much of the curriculum, with activities designed for a range of development and achievement levels. Students work on projects and theme activities individually and in groups as interests and the characteristics of theme experiences permit. At the end of the 3 years, students are evaluated for their achievement relative to typical expectations for students completing third-grade curriculum. If a school follows a practice of continuous progress or outcome-based education, all children move to intermediate grades, with instruction adapted to their current level of achievement. Retention would be a reality in schools where a minimum level of achievement must be attained for promotion.

Systematic instruction, both group and individual, is conducted to support the child's progress through required objectives of the curriculum. Additional planning requirements for teachers are offset by possibilities for peer teaching by students and small cooperative learning groups of students with mixed achievement and abilities. Peer teaching involves pairs of students discussing information and providing feedback about information being learned. Also, a student who is more advanced than other students could conduct study sessions to practice skills. Cooperative learning groups are particularly useful in problem-solving activities, especially for thematic experiences. Mixed groups of students could work together to find and report on information about a topic. Groups plan and set up a unit project, with differentiated responsibilities determined under teacher guidance and supervision. There is a strong emphasis on student-initiated experiences and student responsibility in attending to learning activities and managing the environment.

Team Teaching

Teams of teachers focusing on an ungraded primary class could organize a modification of the 3-year experience. The same students remain with each other for the span of 3 years; however, a multiple-class organization prevails. Two or three classes are grouped together according to the team organization desired. Teachers share classroom environments and planning and teaching responsibilities for thematic and systematic instruction. Individual teachers focus on specific content areas for systematic instruction.

Much of the curriculum is designed through thematic units that incorporate topics suitable for three grade levels. Topics selected and skills taught over the 3-year period incorporate overlapping objectives for the three grade levels that might be repeated in a traditional, separated primary-grade organization. In the ungraded primary, similar learning objectives in some content areas are introduced to all of the students regardless of grade level. Objectives are covered several times during the 3-year span using different approaches. Application of the skills or concepts for different grade levels is incorporated into thematic experiences, supplemented with systematic instruction when needed.

Team teaching, using integrated themes, and implementing systematic instruction that accommodates for different achievement and ability levels is more time efficient than planning for separate grade levels. Teachers can plan for continuity of learning experiences rather than conceptualize instruction for a span of a single year. For example, in typical curriculum planning, instruction is planned for a single grade level. A theme in social studies might be designated for a particular grade level and taught only at that level. (In some school districts, topics for themes are designated for particular grade levels.) In an ungraded situation, a team of teachers can plan curriculum for a broad range of student abilities. Because the same children are in the class for more than 1 year, a topic can be expanded and explored in more depth, building on experiences from the previous year.

Multiage Grouping

Multiage grouping in the ungraded primary groups children of more than one chronological age together for a single year (Nachbar, 1989). In this pattern of organization, students are placed by developmental similarities, rather than by chronological age. Curriculum is flexibly designed to facilitate achievement in learning on a continuum for a three-grade range, rather than for a single grade level. This is especially important for children from diverse backgrounds. Opportunities are provided for children to learn at their personal rate, rather than according to a set curriculum (Lolli, 1992). Students are regrouped for each of the three years. The goal is to move the children through the curriculum objectives taught through systematic instruction complemented by ongoing thematic instruction. Students complete third-grade curriculum by the end of the third year; however, the emphasis is on matching the type of learning ex-

periences selected with the shared developmental characteristics of the students. In any of the ungraded structures discussed, the issue of retention is not totally solved. Although development is more stable and evened out by third grade, there would still be some students who would not complete the third-grade curriculum with their peers. The school system would need to determine what would be done with students who need additional remediation or retention before moving into the intermediate elementary grades.

Team teaching could also be used for multiage grouping. Multiple classes are combined or teachers conduct cooperative teaching with separate classes. There are combined thematic activities and exchanges of students for systematic instruction to match individual learning needs. Groups are flexible, and frequent regrouping ensures that student progress is encouraged.

There is a precedent in United States education for both multiage classrooms and team teaching, in addition to multiage groupings found in British infant schools. One-room rural schools at the turn of the century had multiple ages learning together. In the 1970s, multiage grouping and team teaching were used in open classrooms and conventional school facilities. Some schools retained these practices into the 1990s.

Some recent studies show that multiage grouping can have positive outcomes in student achievement, particularly when team teaching, cooperative groups, integrated curriculum, and developmentally appropriate strategies are used (Kinsey, 2001; Johnson & Johnson, 1994). Interaction among classmates can provide a support system for improved learning; however, the classroom teacher's intentional facilitation of cross-age learning activities is a key to successful multiage classrooms.

Cooperative learning groups and peer teaching could be incorporated into multiage grouping: Class groups are not organized by grade levels. The multiage groups engage in a continuous curriculum that cuts across grade levels. Thematic curriculum is the source of cohesion of instruction during the school year.

Characteristics of the Ungraded Primary Model

Regardless of the organizational pattern found in the ungraded primary model, such a restructuring of the primary grades has common characteristics. One primary purpose of all styles of ungraded organizations is to provide developmentally appropriate curriculum to adjust for the normal variations found in primary-age children moving from the preoperational stage in cognitive development to the concrete operational stage. All such models adopt some form of continuity in curriculum that eliminate traditional grade levels. These common characteristics are described more specifically in the next section.

Ungraded Classrooms

The ungraded primary model is characterized by the elimination of the traditional grade levels organized by chronological age. This type of restructuring of the primary grades is no more radical than the change from ungraded one-room rural schools to urban graded schools at the beginning of the twentieth century. Children are grouped to permit flexibility in instruction to accommodate for variation in development between the ages of 5 and 8. Placement of 5-year-olds in the nongraded organization could vary. Whatever the organizational plan, the student moves through the 3-year span without being assessed for promotion or failure from one level to another. Instead, curriculum and instruction support individual achievement and development and are designed to provide experiences that allow for spurts and lags in developmental growth (Shanker, 1993).

Developmental Curriculum

The ungraded primary model is characterized by a developmental curriculum, which takes into account the abilities of students between the ages of 5 to 8. Learning experiences include manipulatives, problem-solving, creative activities, and other hands-on activities to facilitate the child's role as an active learner. At the same time, these active experiences promote child-initiated learning and ensure success for children who vary in cognitive, motor, and social development. The learning experiences are open-ended and flexible enough that children at various stages in the acquisition of reading and writing can work together successfully.

Integrated Curriculum

The ungraded primary model curriculum is integrated. Thematic units that include all content areas of the curriculum—reading, mathematics, science, social studies, health and safety, fine arts, and physical education—in meaningful context form a large part of the overall curriculum. Because this type of curriculum involves planning on the part of the students, experiences and activities incorporate student interests and competencies. Children gain an understanding of the connections between content areas, rather than assuming they are separate, unrelated categories. In addition, the whole-language approach to the language arts enables students to use their own interests and ideas in reading and writing to develop their competencies in these areas. Activities completed within integrated curriculum minimize developmental differences between students and ensure successful involvement by all.

One route to success is through the use of unit projects. Students select the projects that they will complete. All students experience success because projects enable students of different abilities and interests to work in a complementary fashion. Because students have a choice in what they will explore, they are intrinsically motivated to engage in their projects (Wolk, 1994).

Systematic Instruction

The curriculum also includes instruction in the content areas taught separately from thematic units. Although there are opportunities in thematic curriculum to gain information and learn skills related to the topic being studied, comprehensive instruction may also be indicated in content areas that require planning for instruction of skills in a sequential manner, such as mathematics and, in some instances, reading. For example, in mathematics there is a sequential or hierarchical pattern to how concepts are acquired. The student must master the concepts and skills related to addition before multiplication is introduced. The teacher uses systematic instruction to ensure that each concept is understood and practice provided for mastery. The ungraded primary model includes scheduling for systematic instruction; the teacher plans activities to introduce and work with identified concepts and skills in teacher-directed lessons and then provides opportunities for students to practice and achieve competence. Skills instruction will be incorporated into integrated thematic curriculum as much as possible; nevertheless, because of the increasing quantity of specific concepts and skills that are part of curriculum objectives in the primary school, systematic instruction is included to ensure steady progress. Organized instruction is matched to individual needs and progress. Skills instruction in mathematics and reading combines planned instruction in skills and concepts that is compatible with contextual instruction within thematic learning. Whole-group systematic instruction is infrequent. Small-group and one-to-one instruction are more relevant for individual learning needs.

Cooperative Learning Groups

Cooperative learning is a practice whereby small groups or committees of students engage in accomplishing learning activities. Students with a range of achievement, learning styles, and abilities work together in a cooperative effort to solve and report on a learning objective. The group engages in brainstorming and problem solving before reaching consensus on the solution. For example, in the first grade, cooperative learning groups could brainstorm to come up with as many words as possible beginning with a consonant during a limited time period; in the third grade, groups could collaborate on finding locations on a map.

Students in the ungraded primary unit are capable of working together in learning activities. Because of the transitions occurring in their cognitive and social development, they are able to benefit from group interaction to enhance their own learning and to be of assistance to others. Differences in ability to read and write can be used in a cooperative, rather than a competitive manner as students use their emerging abilities for different tasks within group activities. Students who are more advanced in reading and writing skills can take a leadership role in reading and recording information. Students who are moving more slowly in acquiring literacy skills might take a leadership role in art projects or activities requiring organization of materials. Students will facilitate the learning of others as they work together in solving problems and completing projects and assignments. The teacher guides planning and implementation of activities so that all students have leadership roles and achieve success in cooperative activities.

Peer Teaching

Students in the ungraded primary unit can develop leadership roles by engaging in teaching responsibilities. Because students of different ages and developmental stages will be grouped together, they can use their competencies to serve as peer teachers. All students can take leadership roles according to their individual strengths; nevertheless, older students or students with more advanced skills in reading, writing, and mathematics can serve as tutors or guides for younger or less advanced students. Age differences are minimized as all students are encouraged to take responsibility for activities and tasks within their ability to perform.

Planning and Managing Instruction

Earlier in the chapter, I discussed the need for both thematic and systematic instruction in the primary grades. In this section, I will discuss how to plan and carry out each type of instruction within an ungraded school structure. The roles of the teacher and students will be explained, as well as how both thematic and systematic instruction still maintain the approach that learning must involve the student as an active learner who needs opportunities for self-directed or child-initiated choices. I will also describe the organization of the classroom environment for developmentally appropriate instruction.

The Role of the Environment

The classrooms that serve children ages 5 to 8 or some combination of these age ranges must have materials and resources that facilitate learning at several developmental and academic levels. Because the environment will be used for both systematic learning and thematic curriculum, organization of space must include provisions for all types of activities—group projects, individual work, small-group instruction, and large-group experiences. Flexibility in arrangement will accommodate changing needs as thematic units are designed and carried out.

Room Arrangement

There are various ways to describe the classroom environment. All of the descriptions have characteristics in common that help the teacher understand the possibilities for arrangement to provide for activities that reflect student interests. Just as in the preschool classroom, the primary classroom uses spaces for students to work, play, and engage in teacher-directed lessons. The classroom can be arranged to take into account certain areas of interest, or learning centers can be set up, so that various types of activities can occur simultaneously.

The importance of using learning areas or centers in the primary grades should be stressed at this point. Although centers have a long history in preschool classrooms, primary grade teachers have not always felt that they are appropriate in the

elementary school. Project work and thematic curriculum require many spaces for accessing materials and engaging in individual and group activities. With more emphasis on exploration of concepts and ideas, working spaces become necessary. Some different conceptualizations of room arrangements are described in the following paragraphs.

Seefeldt (1999) characterized the classroom as a small community or workshop. Although she perceived the classroom as an artificial environment, compared with the natural outdoor environment, she proposed that the room be arranged into clearly defined areas that would allow children to engage in meaningful learning in groups or individually. She also suggested that both preschool and primary classrooms should include areas that offer materials for sociodramatic play, mathematics, art, reading, manipulative play, sand and water play, woodworking, music, and writing.

We can describe learning activities in terms of individual and group projects. The room can be arranged to accommodate large projects conducted to accomplish three types of activities: construction activities, investigation activities, and dramatic play. They also support activities being engaged in by individual students, thus necessitating spaces in which one person could work at a time (Helm & Katz, 2001; Katz & Chard, 2000).

The concept of open and closed spaces was proposed by Day (1983). He believed that a balance between open space (which gives children freedom to move) and closed space (which provides security and privacy) should be met when arranging the classroom. Among the criteria Day proposed for evaluating the room environment with open and closed spaces were whether the learning areas supported the goals of the program; whether the arrangement provided for large-group, small-group, and individual activities; and whether the children used the areas as they were intended to be used.

One way to organize primary-grade interest areas is to arrange a few centers to encompass a wide spectrum of activities. Thus, one large area accommodates the language arts center. Within that interest area is space for writing activities, a library, listening center equipment and resources, and other reading instruction materials. A similar center houses science, math, and manipulatives. Space for both group investigations and individual work is included in that learning center.

Art and creative dramatics occupy yet another center. Changing role-play materials, puppets, and other materials for dramatic play share space with art materials and working surfaces for group and individual creative activities. Provisions for sand and water and blocks extend creative and construction play (Seefeldt, 1999).

Ideally, tables of various sizes replace the individual desks frequently found in primary classrooms. Students work at various tables during the day and store their books and materials in individual cubbies. If desks must remain, they are clustered in groups of four to six to provide for group efforts and larger working surfaces.

If the large combined center concept is used, three center areas are located in each of three corners of the room. The center of the room is used for large-group activities and larger project work. The fourth corner houses the teacher's desk and teaching materials and includes arrangements for small-group and individual work and instruction. Student cubbies are located adjacent to this area so that students have access to their learning materials when needed.

Primary grade teachers who have never used centers might benefit from the following tips:

1. Organize and implement one center at a time. Make sure one center is operating smoothly before setting up another center.
2. Develop procedures or rules for each center. Make sure children understand how to work in that area and how many children the area will accommodate.
3. Centers can be organized in small spaces. A teacher's desk, closet, or cluster of student desks or tables can become a center. Display

areas can be designed using a fabric wall hanging, or a large appliance box. Teachers are creative in using found and inexpensive materials to make working areas attractive and functional.

Whatever arrangement is chosen, two additional factors need to be considered when organizing the environment. One is the inclusion of the students in planning for and setting up arrangement of the classroom environment. This is also important when the room is reorganized for each thematic unit. In addition, the use of the outdoor environment is an important factor. Because the indoor environment is artificial, students should engage in activities outdoors whenever it is relevant to do so. Noisy projects, science and art activities, creative dramatics, and many language arts activities can be done outdoors.

Designing Thematic Curriculum

Thematic curriculum is particularly appropriate for instruction in ungraded and multiage classes in primary grades. Because a variety of projects and activities is included for a unit, certain activities are appropriate for students who vary widely in their developmental and academic progress. Students of different ages and abilities can work together on projects, with younger students learning from older classmates. Younger students and students working at less advanced academic levels will find activities that are motivating and can be accomplished successfully. Older and more advanced students will find challenging activities and will be able to plan experiences and projects that are of interest to them. The curriculum is planned by the teacher and students; consequently, consideration can be made for cultural diversity within the classroom, or diversity can be included because the theme lends itself to cultural differences and contributions.

Chase (1995) described a unit on pumpkin growing in Maine that continues throughout the school year. The teachers can have a long-term project because their students stay with them for 3 years. The project begins with planting the pumpkins in the spring in late May. During the summer, the plants are thinned and weeded but are mostly on their own. In the fall, they are harvested and sold to students at the school. Because this project is repeated each year, students can compare harvests of different years, plan how to spend the money earned for classroom needs, and plan for improvements with the next crop.

Because thematic curriculum is completed over a period of time, there is opportunity for exploration, investigation, and representation of learning in an unhurried environment. The unhurried nature of the units makes it possible to include experiences for children with special needs. If children with disabilities are mainstreamed or included in the class, the teacher can plan to adapt activities to address their special needs. This is done whether they have physical disabilities or are emotionally disturbed or gifted. The unit plans are analyzed to determine how each student can play a special role in the learning activities designed for the unit curriculum.

There are obvious similarities between preschool and primary thematic curriculum. Webbing is used to design the topic and its activities. Children are involved in planning, and the curriculum is integrated. Nevertheless, because of the advancing capabilities of the children, their active participation in the process is increased. Also, more complex concepts can be addressed, the unit can extend for a longer period of time, and more activities can be incorporated to match individual interests. Opportunities for children to work together can be ongoing, with children of varying abilities supporting and helping each other in project activities. The teacher has a major role in conceptualizing, planning, and managing unit work, but student contribution and initiative are more extensive, at both the planning stage and the implementation stage.

Selecting a Theme Topic

As is true with preschool thematic units, different approaches can be used to identify a theme topic.

Teachers can also use a content area approach. The focus of the unit is on a content area of the curriculum such as science, mathematics, social studies, or language arts. The chosen topic has as its major focus that area of the curriculum, although all other content areas are integrated into the unit.

Another approach is to begin with an important event or celebration. The annual celebration of Valentine's Day could lead to a study of Valentine's Day cards or the origin of Valentine's Day. Also, many communities and states have annual celebrations that reflect their history and community characteristics. Some aspect of the celebration can be studied to help students understand and broaden their concepts about their local history and culture.

Incidental sources of interest can lead to a learning project. A child's unique experience or discovery of a natural phenomenon can lead to a project of interest to the whole class. Similarly, an interesting topic can occur to the teacher through professional reading, watching an interesting program on television, or another unexpected source. Katz and Chard (2000) suggest that criteria for selecting a topic should include whether the topic is relevant to the children's lives, whether the needed materials and equipment are available, and whether there is access to needed resources in the school and community. Dearden's (1983) criteria for topic selection include opportunities for children to make sense of their experiences, particularly in their own community; topics that give students opportunities to extend their knowledge and skills; and topics that are helpful in preparing them for later life. A common characteristic of all of the approaches to topic selection is that they provide the students with opportunities for meaningful and purposeful learning experiences in acquiring and extending knowledge and skills.

Brainstorming a Topic and Developing a Brainstorming Web

Once the topic has been selected, the teacher is ready to begin the brainstorming stage for ideas for the unit. As with the preschool unit, the teacher uses his or her own brainstorming and incorporates the children's contributions as well. With primary-grade children, however, the teacher can engage them in the webbing process. The first brainstorming web will be an outgrowth of the brainstorming activity. The teacher might begin the initial generation of ideas herself and include the children when ready to explore their ideas, which will include possibilities for projects. The teacher also considers topics that are relevant to the local community, preferably near the school.

An example of thematic curriculum developed for kindergarten through third grade is a unit developed by Mary Ann Roser, a teacher in an ungraded primary classroom. Her classroom is self-contained and arranged into flexible learning centers that are changed to reflect the unit being studied. She uses thematic curriculum throughout the year, but also incorporates systematic instruction into the daily schedule. Mary Ann's unit plan format includes the following:

Unit topic:

Overview or rationale for the unit:

Developmental stage:

Brainstorming webs:

List of activities and projects (categorized as teacher-directed, teacher–child-initiated, or child-initiated):

Unit objectives:

Concepts, skills, and processes

Curriculum web:

Summary of integrated activities and projects:

Mary Ann selected the topic of bakeries for a thematic unit focused on social studies. She considered the wide varieties in the types of bakeries the children might study. Because she taught in a large, urban community, she considered the types of baked goods that were available in local bakeries, which ranged from common sliced breads and rolls produced by commercial bakeries to ethnic foods such as pita bread, Italian bread sticks, bagels, and tortillas. A bakery, Trevino's, was located near the school; therefore, Mary Ann focused on the types of baked goods available in that bakery. Trevino's was located in a culturally diverse neighborhood with a strong Hispanic influence. In addition to typical American breads and pastries, items reflecting Hispanic traditions were sold. Mary Ann did some initial brainstorming and determined four subcat-

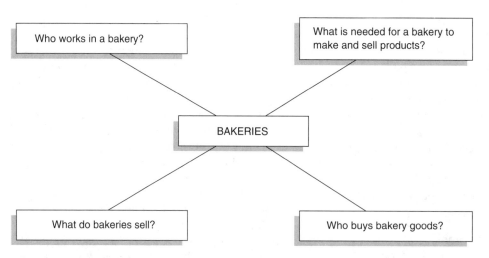

FIGURE 10.2 Initial brainstorming web

egories that she would like her students to learn about bakeries. In her initial brainstorming web she organized the four subtopics as follows: people who work in bakeries; products sold in bakeries; items that bakeries need to make and sell products, and people who buy bakery goods. Mary Ann's initial brainstorming web is pictured in Figure 10.2.

Next, Mary Ann was ready to extend the brainstorming process with the students. She conducted a discussion of the cookies that had been served for lunch the previous day and explored the topic with the children. Once bakeries had been identified as a source for cookies and other baked products, the class was ready to work on the web. Included in the discussion was talk of baked goods from different cultures and bakeries that specialized in breads and goods from different cultures. Each subtopic was discussed separately, with extension and expansion of the web as the conversation continued. Mary Ann wrote the children's contributions on a chalkboard so that the students could follow the progress of the web. When the web was completed, the students were ready to move to a discussion of the activities and projects they would like to pursue to learn more about bakeries. Figure 10.3 shows Mary Ann's final brainstorming web.

Planning with Students and Selecting Unit Activities

As Mary Ann and the students talked about what they wanted to learn, they listed ways to find out more about bakeries and bakery products. As students suggested things they might like to pursue, Mary Ann made a list of activities and projects. The first list included the following:

Visit bakery.

Find recipes for bakery products.

Make bread, cookies, cupcakes, and pies.

Find out about bakery jobs.

Make a classroom bakery.

Write stories about the visit to the bakery.

Read books about bakeries and bakery products.

Learn how different products are made.

Make recipe books.

Mary Ann later studied the list and refined and further organized it. She arranged the unit into projects and individual activities that did not fit into a project. She further categorized each item on the list to indicate whether it was teacher-directed, teacher–child-initiated, or child-initiated. Her revised list was organized as follows:

Activities

Visit bakery (teacher–child-initiated).

Write stories about the bakery visit (child-initiated).

Make a book of recipes (teacher–child-initiated).

Make a mural about bakery jobs (teacher–child-initiated).

Projects

Construct a classroom bakery (teacher–child-initiated).

Conduct a bakery day to sell products (teacher–child-initiated).

Bake cupcakes, cookies, and tortillas (teacher–child-initiated).

> *Collect recipes.*
> *Collect equipment needed for baking.*
> *Make list of ingredients needed for baking each type of product.*
> *Shop for baking ingredients.*
> *Bake and package products.*
> *Sell products to school students on bakery day.*

In making her final list, Mary Ann determined which activities could accommodate her students' abilities; she included all of them in different parts of the curriculum. She also determined what was manageable for the students to bake. She selected cupcakes, cookies, and tortillas because they were

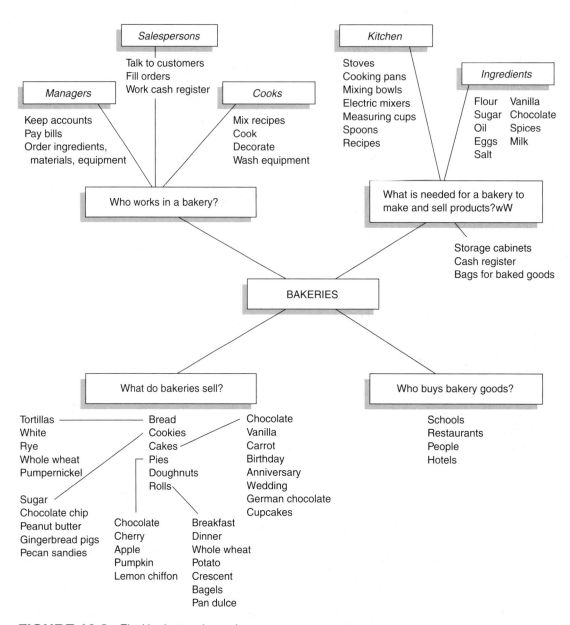

FIGURE 10.3 Final brainstorming web

easy to make and represented different types of ingredients and products. She included cookies that were traditional in certain cultures: Mexican gingerbread pigs, Chinese almond cookies, and Scotch shortbread recipes were solicited from par-

ents. The cookies each had different textures and were mixed and prepared for baking differently.

Mary Ann added the activity that involved representing jobs in a bakery because she wanted to offer a creative way for all the students to

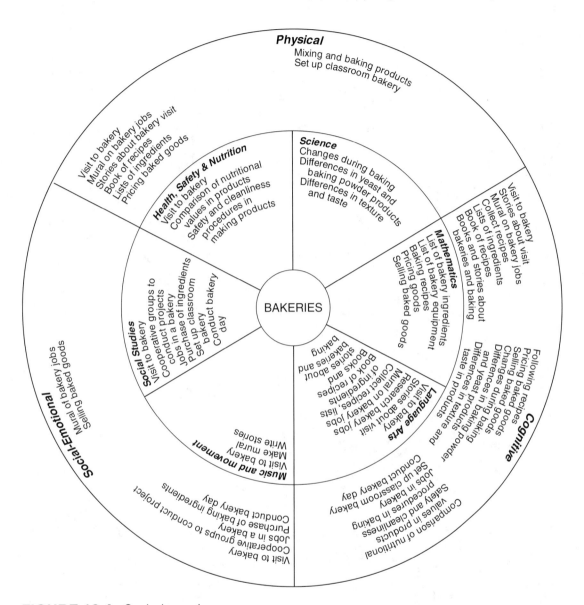

FIGURE 10.4 Curriculum web

participate in some capacity. To determine how the unit experiences would include a balanced, integrated curriculum, Mary Ann developed a curriculum web; it allowed her to organize the unit experiences into content and developmental categories. Figure 10.4 shows Mary Ann's curriculum web. She was pleased with the distribution of activities and felt that coverage of content areas and connections between the content and developmental areas were well defined. Mary Ann could also have used a grid to chart and compare activities. Figure 10.5 shows a grid arrangement. With decisions made about what the students would learn about bakeries, Mary Ann and the

Unit Activities Grid

	Language Arts	Math	Science	Social Studies	Expressive Arts	Health/Safety
Cognitive	Visit to bakery Stories about visit Research bakery jobs Mural on bakery jobs Collect recipes, lists of ingredients Book of recipes Books and stories about bakeries and baking	List of bakery ingredients List of bakery equipment Baking recipes Pricing goods Selling baked goods	Changes during baking Differences in yeast and baking powder products Differences in texture and taste	Visit to bakery Cooperative groups to conduct projects Jobs in a bakery Purchase of ingredients Set up classroom bakery Conduct bakery day	Visit to bakery Make mural Write story	Visit to bakery Comparison of nutritional values in products Safety and cleanliness procedures in making products
Social/Emotional	Visit to bakery			Cooperative groups to conduct project Jobs in a bakery Conduct bakery day		
Physical	Visit to bakery Stories about bakery visit Book of recipes Lists of ingredients Pricing baked goods Mixing and baking products	Lists of ingredients Lists of baking equipment			Mural on bakery jobs	

FIGURE 10.5 Curriculum grid

students were first able to transform the learning ideas into concepts, skills, and processes. Mary Ann was then ready to develop unit objectives.

Determining Concepts, Skills, and Processes

Because of the comprehensive nature of the unit, there were many concepts, skills, and processes that the children could learn. Mary Ann and the students decided on the following:

1. There are many different roles in a bakery.
2. Bakeries sell a variety of baked products.
3. Special equipment is needed to prepare large quantities of baked goods.
4. Each type of baked goods has its own recipe.
5. Bakery cooks must follow recipes carefully if baked goods are to be of a consistent quality.
6. The amount of baked goods to be produced must be planned carefully if there is to be enough but not too much each day.
7. Baked goods to be prepared will vary depending on the time of the year and before holidays.

Developing Unit Objectives

Because the thematic unit objectives were designed for students of varied ages and abilities, Mary Ann described them in general terms. She categorized the objectives according to what students would understand and what they would be able to do. The same process of describing the condition and the behavior as was used in Chapter 7 was followed. Mary Ann's unit objectives were as follows:

1. As a result of visiting a bakery and observing bakery products, students will understand that a variety of baked goods are sold in a bakery.
2. As a result of visiting a bakery and observing bakery employees, students will understand that workers in a bakery have different responsibilities.
3. As a result of visiting a bakery and observing bakery operations, students will understand

what equipment and materials are needed to run a bakery.

4. Following a visit to a bakery and discussions with bakery employees, students will be able to describe responsibilities of bakery workers.
5. As a result of visiting a bakery and studying recipes, students will be able to determine what ingredients and cooking equipment are needed to bake cookies and cupcakes.
6. Following a planning session with the teacher, students will be able to construct a classroom bakery and conduct bakery sales.
7. As a result of studying recipes and discussing how to interpret recipe terminology, students will be able to follow a recipe to make bakery products.
8. As a result of cooperatively planning unit projects, students will be able to work in groups to complete the planned projects.
9. As a result of practicing how to price baked products and make change, students will be able to conduct simple money transactions to sell bakery products.
10. After visiting a bakery, participating in discussions about bakeries, and reading stories about bakeries, students will be able to write stories about bakeries.
11. As a result of studying cookbooks and recipes donated by parents, students will be able to select recipes for cookies, cupcakes, and tortillas.
12. Following the baking of cookies, cupcakes, and tortillas and discussions about how much to charge for baked products, students will be able to package and price bakery products.
13. As a result of selecting and using recipes for cookies and cupcakes, students will be able to make a book of recipes.
14. After discussing bakery jobs and planning how to represent them, students will be able to make a mural describing the responsibilities of bakery workers.

15. After completing cooperative group projects to make a mural, construct a classroom bakery, and bake cookies, cupcakes, and tortillas, students will be able to participate in bakery day to sell baked products to students from other classrooms.

Planning Lesson Activities and Projects

The planning process is not complete until the projects and activities are explored in more detail. The teacher will consider all of the procedures and materials needed for each activity and project. She will also determine when and how the activity will fit into the schedule. In the case of unit projects, the teacher will need to consider how much time should be set aside for the project and how the students can choose to be involved in planning and doing the project. Activities will be described so that the teacher and students will understand specifically what will occur.

Mary Ann studied her unit activities and wrote a description of each one. Each activity was described and discussed in terms of how it incorporated different content areas of the curriculum. She described the visit to the bakery as follows:

Visit to Trevino's Bakery.
After planning what to look for at the bakery, students, teacher, and volunteer parents will walk two blocks to the bakery. The manager will meet the group, and explain how bakery goods are made in the kitchen and sold in the sales area. Students will be prepared to observe different equipment in the kitchen and the varied bakery products in the sales shelves. Groups of students will have assignments to learn the different kinds of breads, cookies, cakes, and pies sold at the bakery. Some groups will be prepared to find out how different products are mixed, baked, and frosted or decorated by the cooks. The activity focuses on social studies; there will be discussion about the different roles people have in contributing to the needs of the community. Specifically, the contributions of the bakery to the local community are discussed. In addition, the activity includes language arts;

oral discussions are conducted, and students will record the types of products that are sold at this particular bakery.

Each of the activities was summarized in a similar fashion; projects, however, required more extensive planning. Mary Ann worked with the students in discussing each project and what would be necessary to complete each one. Students discussed their interests in being a part of certain projects. They were encouraged to select a project with which they would like to work. Because all of the students wanted to take part in cooking, the class was divided into groups to cook either cupcakes, tortillas, or cookies. Other responsibilities for collecting recipes, mixing and baking equipment, and ingredients for baking were also divided among the groups. Students were given responsibilities according to their ability and interest. Students of different levels of achievement were grouped together, with group leaders selected to be responsible for helping to identify responsibilities for each of the group members.

When plans were completed for unit activities and projects, Mary Ann was able to complete the unit plan. The format used was the same general format used in the preschool unit plan. However, Mary Ann had the additional curriculum web to assist her in interpreting how she was relating and integrating experiences across the curriculum.

Mary Ann could also describe the final unit plans in terms of individual lessons. She included the lesson or project activities, a description of the procedures for the lesson, the materials needed to conduct the activity or project, and plans for assessment. Mary Ann used the following format:

Title of plan:

Objectives addressed:

Concepts, processes, skills to be developed:

Activity procedures:

> *Large-Group Activity (teacher-directed):*
> *Small-Group Activity (teacher–child-initiated):*
> *Center Activities (child-initiated):*

Materials/resources needed:

Assessment:

   Teacher Assessment:
   Activity Assessment:
   Student Assessment:

There were some differences between Mary Ann's plans for the primary grades and Lisa's plans for preschool children (refer to Chapter 7 for a discussion of Lisa's plans). Mary Ann included systematic instruction lessons under small-group activities. Projects and cooperative group activities could also be organized under the small-group category. Children could be more involved in evaluation procedures; students would be able to evaluate their own learning and assess the success of group projects with the group and the teacher.

Mary Ann's plans had many similarities to preschool plans. Within the activity category, three-part procedures can again be used to describe the sections of the lesson: (1) introduction, or planning; (2) development of lesson or activity; and (3) summary, or review.

There are many ways that a plan can be described. If a teacher-directed lesson is to be used rather than a teacher–child-initiated activity, then lesson procedures might be more detailed than activity procedures. An example follows:

Lesson Procedures:

Introduction of the lesson

  a. *Focusing Activity:* What will be done to get students' attention.
  b. *Objective:* Discuss with the students what they will know or be able to do at the end of the lesson.
  c. *Tie in prior learning:* How the lesson will be related to a previous lesson or other unit activities

Development of the lesson

  a. *Explanation:* (models or modeling, definitions, examples, process steps, etc.)
  b. *Guided practice:* (manipulative or hands-on activities, written practice, etc.)
  c. *Challenge activity:* An activity that permits students to apply the information or skill they are learning. Can be done alone, in pairs, or in groups.
  d. *Adaptations:* Modifications that can be made in the lesson to enhance the learning of children with diverse needs or abilities or developmental levels in the classroom.
  e. *Reteaching activity:* (if needed)

TITLE OF PLAN: Understanding Recipes

OBJECTIVES ADDRESSED:

As a result of studying recipes and discussing how to interpret recipe terminology, students will be able to follow a recipe to make bakery products.

CONCEPTS, SKILLS, AND PROCESSES USED:

Each type of baked goods has its own recipe.

Bakery cooks must follow recipes carefully if baked goods are to be of a consistent quality.

ACTIVITY PROCEDURES:

Large-group activity (teacher-initiated, small cooperative groups) The lesson will be conducted with the class divided into cooperative groups to learn how to understand and follow a recipe.

Introduction

The teacher will write the recipe on a large chart tablet or overhead transparency. Rebus pictures will be used in addition to written measurements for young and less advanced readers.

Development of Lesson or Activity

Step 1

The teacher and students will read the recipe together

Peanut Butter Cookies

1 cup shortening

1 cup granulated sugar

1 cup brown sugar

2 eggs

1 teaspoon vanilla

1 cup peanut butter

3 cups enriched flour

2 teaspoons soda

½ teaspoon salt

Thoroughly cream together 1 cup shortening, 1 cup granulated sugar, 1 cup brown sugar, 2 eggs, and 1 teaspoon vanilla. Stir in 1 cup peanut butter.

Sift together 3 cups sifted enriched flour, 2 teaspoons soda, and ½ teaspoon salt. Stir into creamed mixture.

FIGURE 10.6   Example plan for a cooperative group lesson

f. *Closure:* How the lesson will be concluded so that it makes sense to the students. This activity might take the form of a review discussion with the students, a written chart where the children will dictate what was learned in the lesson, etc.

Following this description of how the lesson will be conducted, the format can then be resumed to include the materials and resources needed and procedures for assessment.

As was true in preschool lessons, each category can be adapted to fit the type of activity and the size of the group involved, as well as the flexible

Drop by rounded teaspoons on ungreased cookie sheet. Press with back of floured fork to make crisscross. Bake at 350° about 10 minutes or until light brown. Makes about 5 dozen cookies.

Step 2

Teachers and students will discuss the ingredients that they will need to make the cookies. Each cooperative group will make a list of ingredients that will be needed by studying the recipe. Their lists will be compared with the teacher's list.

Step 3

The recipe will be read again. Teacher and students will focus on what will need to be measured, sifted, etc. The cooperative groups will list the measuring, mixing, and baking utensils that will be needed.

Step 4

The recipe will now be studied for the processes that will be needed to make the cookie dough and bake the cookies. The teacher will underline the steps and processes to be followed. Cooperative groups then will list the processes and describe what each means. Individual lists will be compared with the teacher's list.

Summary or Review

The recipe will be read one final time. The teacher will guide the groups to identify kitchen items not specified in the recipe that will be needed to prepare the cookies (e.g., potholders, storage container, etc.).

MATERIALS/RESOURCES NEEDED:

Recipe

Chart tablet or overhead transparencies and projector

Pencils and paper for student responses

ASSESSMENT:

Teacher Assessment:

Could the students understand the recipe and procedures? Were they able to complete the group assignments with a minimum of teacher assistance? Could all students participate regardless of learning differences?

Student Assessment:

Did all students contribute to group activities? Were they interested in helping their group complete the assignments in an effective manner?

Activity Assessment:

Could the students understand the recipe and procedures? Were they able to complete the group assignments with a minimum of teacher assistance? Could all students participate, regardless of learning differences?

role of the teacher. A teacher-directed lesson begins with a strategy to introduce the purpose for the lesson, continues with the procedures used to help children learn the lesson, and ends with a summary of the main points of the lesson. A group project begins with the teacher and the group planning the activity, followed by actual work on the project. At the end of the work period, the work area is restored and materials are put away; this is followed by an opportunity to review and evaluate progress and make adjustments if needed. Figure 10.6 provides an example of Mary Ann's plan for a cooperative group lesson.

Planning for Assessment

As can be seen in Mary Ann's sample lesson, she conducted three types of evaluation to assess the effectiveness of curriculum and instruction in her classroom. She considered assessment of the teaching role, assessment of student learning, and assessment of the quality of the activities used for the lesson.

Assessment of the Teacher. Mary Ann had a plan to assess her effectiveness in the teaching role as a part of every group activity or lesson. When conducting thematic experiences, she used the role of facilitator more frequently than she engaged in teacher-directed responsibilities. As facilitator and guide, she wanted to reflect on how well she enabled the students to accomplish the objectives of the activity. She assessed how well she was able to serve as a resource for ideas and processes to accomplish child-planned activities.

When she had a more directive role in systematic instruction, she evaluated herself in terms of student success in learning. She was sometimes interested in student mastery of specific skills. Teachers who are required to give grades would have to be very specific about how well students performed in acquiring information and skills. Assessment of teaching effectiveness following systematic instruction relates to how effective instructional experiences were in helping students achieve success in learning. In the example of Mary Ann's teaching described earlier, she used assessment to determine her success in helping students acquire the skills needed to engage in a unit cooking activity and at the same time assessed the children's growth in working in groups to accomplish learning objectives.

Assessment of Student Learning. Mary Ann also wanted to determine how well students were learning. Again, her objectives for assessment varied depending on the nature of the learning objective. In this lesson, she wanted to assess how successful the students were in leadership, problem solving, and other processes involved in cooperative assignments requiring student collaboration.

Mary Ann was also evaluating students' acquisition of specific knowledge and skills. She wanted to determine whether the students had adequately learned the information and skills presented. She wanted to assess how well the students learned the objective of the lesson.

Assessment of the Curriculum. Mary Ann had more than one type of curriculum to evaluate in her classroom. When she assessed thematic curriculum, she considered the effectiveness of the activities, materials, and equipment used for experiences and projects. She looked at the length of time needed for thematic activities and evaluated whether time and value of the activity were compatible.

When Mary Ann was engaged in systematic instruction, she assessed whether her teacher-designed or commercial materials were appropriate and whether she accomplished the objectives she had set for learning. Mary Ann wanted to know whether she had made good choices regarding the activities she used for children in their attempts to acquire specific knowledge or skills. She also wanted to know whether adequate time and activities had been planned for student learning.

Figure 10.6 describes Mary Ann's plans for assessing her lesson. The strategies she used were representative of some of the purposes and processes for evaluation with primary-age students. More about assessment in primary grades will be discussed at the end of the chapter.

Implementing Thematic Curriculum

Planning with Students and Parents

Mary Ann extended planning with the students as she prepared to set up the unit on bakeries. At this point, she contacted parent volunteers to help her in the final stages of decision making. Parents helped to identify where to acquire the resources needed to carry out the unit activities and projects. Individual parents accepted responsibilities for project activities or agreed to work in centers with

Schedule	Monday	Tuesday	Wednesday	Thursday	Friday	Learning Center Arts
8:00–8:15 Large group planning	Plan trip to bakery	Plans to begin group projects	Plans for the day	Plans for the day	Plans for the day	*Language Arts* Tuesday – Individual stories about trip to bakery / Recipe Group Tuesday – Wednesday / Research cookbooks / Select and copy recipes on experience charts / Mural Group / Research bakery worker responsibilities
8:15–8:30 Group plans	Group plans for bakery information	1) Bakery construction group 2) Recipes group 3) Mural group	Problem solving for group projects	Meetings with project groups 4) Cooking committee	Cooking committees	Library books / Books and stories about bakeries and bakery products
8:30–9:30 Small group instruction	Visit to bakery →	Mathematics / Systematic Instruction	Mathematics / Systematic Instruction	Reading / Systematic Instruction	Reading / Systematic Instruction	*Art /Creative Dramatics* Classroom Bakery Group / Plan and construct bakery / Mural Group / Design mural panel for each bakery job / List responsibilities in each panel / Coordinate decoration of panels
9:30–10:00 Individual Help		Systematic Instruction	Systematic Instruction	Systematic Instruction	Systematic Instruction	
10:00–10:45 Project work	Write bakery stories	Monitor cooperative group activities			Group reports on projects / Review bakery stories	*Math/Science/Manipulatives* Recipe Group / Select recipes / Copy recipes / Determine ingredients needed
10:45–11:15 Large group Review morning activities Plan for following day	Review trip Discuss plans for Tuesday	Review group projects	Review morning activities	Review morning activities	Plan for new and continued activities for following week	*Cooking Groups* Study recipe charts / Determine cooking equipment needed

FIGURE 10.7 Weekly schedule

children for art and language arts activities. Students were allowed to volunteer for leadership roles in projects, with parents acting as resources and supporters for facilitating successful completion of activities needing adult guidance.

Adults and children planned together how to get the room ready for the new unit. Mary Ann and the parents guided the children in discussing how to construct a bakery and the steps involved in setting up the bakery area. The students also discussed how to research recipes and make recipe books. Plans were made as to when and how needed resources for all of the projects and activities would be acquired. Arrangements were made to borrow the school's cooking cart and use the ovens in the school kitchen to bake in the afternoons when school cooks were finished for the day.

Scheduling

Planning and carrying out the weekly and daily schedule required periodic times for planning and review. Mary Ann made a weekly plan that reflected her activities, including group projects, small-group instruction, and individual interaction and working with project groups. As was true in the preschool model, the sequence of planning activities and reviewing after activities were completed was incorporated into the schedule each day. Figure 10.7 shows Mary Ann's schedule for the first week of implementation of the unit on bakeries.

Mary Ann scheduled the entire morning for unit work and instruction combined. Afternoons were reserved for instruction that could not fit into thematic work times and needed to continue in content areas. She started each morning with 15 minutes for planning with the entire group. The next 15 minutes was used for planning with the project groups. Each day for an hour, she worked with small groups in systematic instruction, followed by an hour of interaction with individuals. She might spend the time conducting assessments, working on skills that were causing difficulties for individual students, or helping students complete work or try new methods to attack a problem.

According to this week's schedule, she worked for 2 days in mathematics and then switched to reading for the following 2 days.

After the periods of systematic instruction, she spent 45 minutes facilitating and working as a resource for the project groups. Students alternated among center activities, projects, and systematic instruction and related assignments during the morning. The children might work from contracts or follow group schedules put on the board during planning time. The project groups functioned as cooperative groups. Small-group instruction could be conducted with cooperative groups working at different levels in the curriculum according to ability and achievement. These flexible groups could be reorganized when needed to meet individual needs or to allow children to progress at a different rate.

The section of the schedule devoted to learning center areas listed the activities that might take place on a daily or weekly basis. Some activities were for individual children to complete, whereas others were conducted by project groups. In the case of the recipe group, project research began in the library center and then moved to the mathematics-science-manipulatives area when it came time to use the recipes to get ready for cooking projects the following week.

The first day of the unit was used to plan and take the trip to the bakery. Students were prepared for the information they needed to find while touring the bakery. Upon returning from the bakery, they were given time to begin their stories about the experience, which could be continued the following day in the language arts area.

At the end of the morning, the class completed a review session during large-group time to discuss the day's progress and make preliminary plans for the following day. At the end of Friday morning, the whole class reviewed the week's activities and discussed project progress with the respective committees. Before the review period ended on Friday, Mary Ann and the class made plans for the second week of the project, which would include baking cookies, cupcakes, and tortillas and selling the products in the classroom bakery the following Friday.

This particular unit was planned for 2 weeks. Another thematic curriculum could be longer or shorter, depending on the topic. It is obvious that this unit, although very interesting, would require a great deal of preparation on the part of the teacher, volunteer parents, and students. If the teacher wished to have ongoing units, she might want to plan less extensive units after the more demanding ones. This type of unit also might be planned infrequently, and then time could be provided for smaller projects until the teacher would be able to begin the planning process for the next theme. A team of teachers working together could alternate, taking the major responsibility for planning a unit, with the other teachers acting as resource people. With this plan, it is possible to have a more continuous flow from one thematic unit to another, perhaps alternating among the content areas of the curriculum as the major focus.

Incorporating Systematic Instruction

When commercial producers began publishing curriculum materials around the turn of the century, they made it possible for state boards of education to set the curriculum for school districts across the state. Before that, individual school districts and local boards of education had determined the curriculum for their children. With urbanization, consolidation, and construction of large school buildings with many classrooms, the purchase of curriculum materials that had been developed by specialists was a form of insurance for a centralized standard of instruction (Cremin, 1988).

Since the advent of commercial curriculum materials, the industry has grown; many large corporations now produce teaching resources for all grade levels, including preschool classrooms. Over the years, teachers have become very comfortable following the sequence of the curriculum as organized in the basal reader program, language arts text, mathematics series, and other

content area resources. Unfortunately, the various texts and kits for each grade level were developed independently of each other and may have little in common in terms of content or approach to teaching.

Curriculum and instruction practices in early childhood classrooms were criticized earlier in this text because of accelerated content in the early grades that requires young children to perform in a manner that is not developmentally appropriate. If one studies the commercial resources available in a particular school for the primary grades, it becomes readily apparent that at least some of the materials teach concepts and skills without any obvious connection to how the skills are applied for a purpose. Using thematic curriculum fills this gap by making connections between skills and how they are applied. It also demonstrates the relationships between content and developmental areas. The problem is in how to incorporate basal texts for systematic instruction. The task can be difficult because the teacher may need to use the adopted textbooks for this type of instruction. Nevertheless, the same principles according to which young children learn must be applied to systematic instruction, and the teacher must be able to adapt existing resources so that students can reconstruct knowledge and have ample opportunities to work through acquisition of concepts with hand-on activities.

Managing Systematic Instruction

When a teacher chooses to use systematic instruction, she knows there are some concepts or skills that need to be taught that have not or will not be covered in thematic curriculum. Perhaps the child has been having difficulty in decoding words or is not attending to endings on words. Some activities with the skills would strengthen the child's understanding and application of the needed skills. In mathematics, the teacher may be following a sequence of skills and through informal assessment has determined which students in the class need instruction on certain skills; the teacher organizes small groups that she has identified and plans a series of lessons to help these students acquire the math objective. Still another source of identification for systematic instruction is thematic curriculum. In the course of carrying out unit activities, the teacher identifies a student who is having difficulty in accomplishing a unit project that requires a skill. The teacher provides systematic instruction to facilitate the child's ability in the needed skill. In Mary Ann's unit, she might notice children were unable to understand the measurements in a recipe. She could plan lessons and let the children practice using measuring cups and spoons to help them acquire confidence in completing the correct measurements.

Regardless of the source of the need for systematic instruction, the teacher plans lessons to match the need for active learning and reconstruction of knowledge. This process is further explained in "Guidelines for Appropriate Curriculum Content and Assessment in Programs Serving Children Ages 3 through 8" (NAEYC & National Association of Early Childhood Specialists in State Departments of Education, 1991, p. 25) as follows:

> Children need to form their own hypotheses and keep trying them out through mental actions and physical manipulations—observing what happens, comparing their findings, asking questions, and discovering answers. When objects and events resist the working model that the child has mentally constructed, the child is forced to adjust the model or alter the mental structures to account for the new information.

The guidelines further describe the learning process as a cycle that includes awareness generated from experience, exploration of what is being learned, and utilization, whereby children are able to use or apply what they have learned. The cycle demonstrates how children use child-initiated learning to acquire new knowledge. The point is that systematic instruction does not imply that the teacher is disseminating information for the child to absorb and master. There is a definite difference between systematic instruction and teacher-directed instruction. In teacher-directed instruction, the teacher directs and controls the process; in systematic instruction, the teacher plans the activities with a definite learning objective in mind, although the activities encourage the children to acquire the information using their own capacities for learning.

Thus, the teacher's responsibility is to introduce the child to the concept or skill to be learned—to develop the child's awareness. Exploration with the skill or concept is promoted through hands-on and other sensory experiences so that it becomes personally meaningful. True understanding comes when the child is able to use the new concept or skill in various applications; the child is able to apply the learning to new situations (NAEYC & National Association of Early Childhood Specialists in State Departments of Education, 1991).

Whether the teacher is developing her own teaching strategies or using commercial materials for systematic instruction, she will want to provide experiences that meet the characteristics explained earlier. In both cases, the teacher will evaluate the activities being planned to determine how purposeful they are for the child. If the commercial resources do not provide a variety of hands-on exploratory activities to pursue the concept, the teacher must modify the lessons to include them. Similarly, if the learning activities include pencil-and-paper drill exercises but no meaningful application, opportunities for working with the skill or concept in a purposeful context should be provided.

Balancing Thematic and Systematic Instruction

No matter how the teacher decides to employ thematic curriculum and systematic instruction in her classroom, a balance needs to be established between the two approaches. If thematic curriculum is used as an ongoing part of the program, many of the skills in a state-mandated set of curriculum objectives will be covered through theme units. Systematic instruction will supplement thematic activities. The less often thematic curriculum is used, the more often systematic in-

struction will be incorporated into the program. If theme units are used only occasionally, systematic instruction will become the major source for instruction, whereas thematic curriculum will serve as the source for supplementary activities. Whichever combination is used, the teacher needs to keep firmly in mind the process by which young children learn, which is fostered through developmentally appropriate instruction that is child centered and meaningful.

The Role of Assessment in Kindergarten and Primary Grades

The role of assessment was discussed in Chapter 7 in the context of preschool classrooms. Evaluations of thematic units, of the teacher's effectiveness, and of student learning were included as components of evaluation of the school program. The same elements remain when assessing in the primary grades; however, evaluation of student learning becomes more significant as student achievement is measured for various purposes.

In Chapter 3, I discussed the use of standardized tests with young children and the misuse of these tests for purposes of placing children in programs, excluding them from programs, and retaining them at certain levels. Standardized tests are also used to measure student learning in the primary grades; however, group achievement tests have limitations in measuring individual student learning. Other methods of assessment are more appropriate for measuring and reporting individual student achievement. As children enter the primary grades, assessment may be used to assess and report student progress in learning, to evaluate and improve the instructional program, to identify and address learning problems, and to report to parents.

The Purposes of Assessment in Kindergarten and Primary Grades

Assessing and Reporting Progress in Learning
Parents, teachers, and other school personnel must have information about students' progress in learning in kindergarten and primary grades. The

information is needed to determine whether the individual child is progressing adequately in the instructional program, what individual and group instructional needs are, and how effectively the instructional program is serving to instruct the students. School districts commonly use standardized achievement tests to assess individual and group progress in learning; however, such tests are less effective for assessing achievement in the primary grades, especially individual achievement. They can be an indicator of the quality of the instructional program in language arts and mathematics when comparing group achievement.

Informal types of assessment are more useful than standardized tests to measure student learning. They are available when needed, can be revised by the teacher when needed, and can be a natural part of ongoing instruction. Informal assessment can stem from observation, representative work by the children, completion of tasks within small-group instruction, and other activities during the school day. The teacher tries as often as possible to conduct assessment as an ongoing process within natural classroom routines rather than taking separate periods of time to conduct testing (Wortham, 2001d).

Informal strategies for assessment can include teacher-designed assessments, commercially designed assessments, observations, interviews, directed assignments, work samples, project work, and student portfolios.

Teacher-Designed Assessments

In Chapter 6, teacher-designed concrete tasks were described as developmentally appropriate for evaluating the learning progress of preschool children. This type of assessment activity continues to be appropriate for kindergarten and primary children. The teacher uses objects or pictures for the child to manipulate or otherwise indicate a response to a learning task. As children enter the primary grades, acquisition of reading and writing skills makes it possible for students to begin to respond to learning experiences with pencil-and-paper tasks. This transition is gradual and dependent on the child's competence in working with pictured, rather than real, objects. Also, the use of printed words is gradual, with prior orientation by the teacher to the written task. Children are asked to circle, make an X by, or underline, the correct response (Wortham, 2001d). Later they can fill in a missing word and move to more extensive written responses. Through the primary grades, the use of written assessments is approached carefully; the teacher studies the design of written teacher assessments for specificity and appropriate level of written response on the part of the student.

Commercially Designed Assessments

Commercial instructional materials are frequently accompanied by written paper-and-pencil assessments to be used with the students. They may take various forms, such as end-of-unit assessments in science, assessments of mathematical skills, and tests at the end of a basal reader. Many of these assessments are well designed; nevertheless, others are neither useful nor appropriate. When deciding to administer a pencil-and-paper test to kindergarten and primary children, the teacher needs to determine whether it is the best method of assessment and whether it is appropriate for the information desired about the child's learning. A teacher-designed concrete task or written worksheet might be more specific for the objective to be assessed.

Observations

Observation is a natural strategy for teachers to use when they are conducting a lesson, working with children in centers or assigned tasks, or observing classroom routines. Observations can be planned or used because a moment for evaluation presents itself. Observations can be conducted involving individual children or a small group of children. The teacher needs some type of method to record what is being observed; this can include an anecdotal note of the event or accomplishment, a checklist or rating scale, or another type of record-keeping form. Observations can be used for all types of learning, particularly to document progress that is not being acquired through some type of written evaluation. Teachers use observation to record reading behaviors when children are reading to a small group, to document understanding of a process in mathematics when children are working on mathematics assignments, or successful efforts to work in a cooperative group (Hills, 1992; Wortham, 2001d).

Interviews

In an interview, the teacher questions a student to determine understanding and the thought processes the child is using with an activity. Instead of giving a paper-and-pencil test to measure problem solving in mathematics, the teacher talks to the child and asks how the child went about solving the problem.

Interviews may be planned or unstructured. In a planned interview, the teacher determines what questions will be asked before the child is approached. In an unplanned or unstructured interview, the teacher happens upon a significant activity and decides to talk to the children about the activity in which they are engaged (Seefeldt, 1999; Wortham, 2001d).

Directed Assignments

A directed assignment is designed for assessment purposes. The teacher instructs students to carry out a specific activity that will be used to assess progress and mastery. A directed assignment can be a work sheet or a task located in a learning center. The assignment can be the same for all students or differentiated depending on individual progress. The assignment can be written or a manipulative task.

Work Samples

Students complete assignments every day. They also engage in self-selected activities because of their own interests. Any type of work product can become a tool for assessment. Work sheets are commonly thought of as the typical work sample,

but many other forms of work can be collected. Examples of art, stories, or book reports written by the student, and results of cooperative group activities can be collected for a work sample. The sample is selected because it is a good representation of the student's progress.

Project Work

Project samples are similar to work samples; however, they are likely to represent work over a period of time. When engaging in thematic units, students often devise projects that they would like to conduct to learn unit objectives. Students might plant a garden, conduct research, and record their findings; engage in some type of extended art work to represent their learning; or construct a model. All of these projects can be used to represent progress in learning (Katz & Chard, 2000).

Portfolios

Portfolios provide an opportunity to review what a student has accomplished or learned over a period of time using a variety of materials that reflect the student's activities and work. The teacher and student begin collecting samples of the student's work early in the school year and materials are added periodically as the year progresses. Samples of writing, art, classroom assessments, and records of individual, group, and project work can be included in the portfolio. The teacher and student can review the materials periodically to assess progress and decide which samples should remain in the portfolio.

Portfolios can have different purposes. The type of entries will depend on the purpose that has been designated. A showcase portfolio is meant to highlight a student's best work. Entries are selected primarily by the student and are meant to be shared with other students, teachers and, particularly, parents. An evaluative portfolio is the purpose that is most commonly known. The evaluative portfolio has as its primary purpose to provide documentation for student assessment. Evaluative portfolio entries might be selected by the teacher, but the selection is best when the teacher and student collaborate on what entries best reflect the student's progress and accomplishments. If the portfolio will contribute to a grade on a report card, then contents will include various types of assessments and instruments such as rubrics to document level of achievement.

A portfolio can start out as a working portfolio. In this type of collection, entries are made without determining the value of the work. Later, when the portfolio is organized for assessment or to showcase the student's work, entries are reviewed and selections are made from the contents. The entries that are not to be used can be taken home (Barbour & Desjean-Perrotta, 1998).

Portfolios can be organized for a specific content area or to include all content areas. A portfolio can also be used to document project or unit work. All of the contents reflect the student's efforts and contributions toward implementation and completion of the project. Entries for project work might include photographs, audiotapes, videotapes, and other materials to show student work in progress, problem-solving, and completed projects. Written narratives might be included to explain the student's role in the project, and learning that was accomplished through project work (Helm & Katz, 2001; Wortham, 2001d).

Whenever possible, parents should be involved in portfolio assessment. Although the topic of using portfolios to report progress to parents is discussed in the next section, parents can also be involved in selecting materials and contributing their own information about the child's progress as reflected in activities that have occured at home.

Reporting Progress to Parents

Although early childhood educators tend to be against giving grades, especially before third grade, progress reports have to be made to parents and administrators. If report cards are required, teachers are accountable for conducting periodic assessment for reporting purposes. If report cards are not used, assessment of learning is still important for planning appropriate instruction for individual students and measuring successful accomplishment in completing curriculum objectives. Progress reports to parents need to be accurate, whether or not report cards are used. Assessment is closely tied to instruction, whether thematic or systematic. If done in a developmentally appropriate manner, assessment will provide essential information about the student that will help guide plans for future learning experiences.

Effective reporting of student progress can include reports from teacher observation, informal teacher-designed assessments, or results of commercial tests. Student portfolios can be shared with parents and administrators who are interested in reports on student learning. Parents not only are interested in the child's work but also appreciate information about the child's learning through thematic units. Photographs taken during unit projects and group activities help parents visualize what their child participated in and learned about during unit experiences. Classroom displays of unit projects also add to the parents' appreciation of the benefits of thematic units.

The teacher will very likely be instructing children who come from different types of family backgrounds. As a result, the style of reporting may be different, depending on the interests and needs of the parents concerned. Parents with no ability or limited ability in English may need help in understanding how the child is learning and progressing. Parents who are professionals may be more interested in results of standardized tests or the significance of integrated learning. Other parents may be most interested in the child's participation in class projects and the way in which it relates to academic progress. Many parents focus on the child's reading level and need information on the worth of other types of evaluation. The teacher will want to be prepared to respond to differences among parents in how they perceive the child's learning and achievement. All parents are interested primarily in knowing whether the child is learning successfully. The teacher has the responsibility to communicate the child's progress in a manner that is helpful to each parent.

Identifying and Addressing Learning Problems

In kindergarten and the primary grades, some students begin to encounter serious problems in learning, which will go beyond normal developmental differences during the latter early childhood years. As was mentioned earlier, attempts are made in infancy and the preschool years to identify and remediate disabilities resulting from birth defects and other disabling conditions. Children with such disabilities are identified and referred to intervention programs as early as possible to obtain services that can minimize the disabilities and improve the children's chances of overcoming the problem or finding alternative avenues for learning.

In spite of these services, there are children who enter school in kindergarten or first grade who do not initially exhibit serious learning difficulties but after a few months in school begin to exhibit symptoms of difficulty. Some children have trouble learning to read or are unable to comprehend concepts that most children are able to understand. When teachers begin to notice learning difficulties, there are steps that can be taken to assist the child. The teacher can begin by observing the child frequently to attempt to identify more specifically what difficulties the child is having and why they are present.

A next step is to have a specialist observe the child to confirm the symptoms of learning difficulties that the child is presenting. If more intensive diagnosis is indicated, the child is referred for individual testing through a series of standardized tests to identify the nature of the learning problem and the best strategies for assistance. If the child is to be served through the special education program funded under PL 94-142 explained earlier, services will be provided by both the classroom teacher and educational specialists (Meyen, 1996b).

Summary

The philosophy of teaching children from ages 5 to 8 is an extension of the philosophy regarding learning in the preschool years. Students in kindergarten through third grade are in the later early childhood years and are making the transition from the preoperational stage of thinking to the concrete operational stage. Developmental changes make it possible for them to acquire reading and writing skills at their own individual pace. Learning is centered within the child, who needs learning experiences that will extend her understanding of the world in a developmentally appropriate manner.

Because pace of development varies widely during these years from kindergarten through the primary grades, instruction must accommodate a range of abilities in students. The present structure of graded classrooms limits teachers' opportunities to be flexible in instructional planning that nurtures successful learning in students, regardless of their developmental variations. As a result, attention is given to other options for school organization for children age 5 to 8; these options include ungraded classrooms and multiage grouping.

The model chosen for this text is based on the multiage organization first developed for British infant schools. A modified approach more suitable for schools in this country groups students from kindergarten through the primary grades in multiage classrooms. A teacher or team of teachers plans and carries out instruction that includes experiences at different levels of achievement to allow students to participate in learning activities based on individual development rather than chronological age.

Although thematic curriculum is used within the model to facilitate child-initiated learning and to accommodate developmental differences, systematic instruction is also appropriate at these grade levels to ensure that students are acquiring the necessary skills for continued academic progress in individual achievement. At the same time that the teacher plans for instruction for individual needs (which requires planning and assessment of individual progress), the age range within the classroom and the levels of social development make it possible for the students themselves to take active responsibility in the teaching and learning roles. Cooperative learning groups can be organized for group accomplishment of learning tasks. The cooperative groups can be selected to include a range of student abilities. The students use their individual strengths and talents to contribute to the group effort. Peer tutoring and matching older students (as leaders) with younger ones facilitates growth in confidence in more advanced students, while the younger children benefit from more sources of attention and instruction.

When planning for instructional design and implementation, the teacher must consider how to balance teacher-directed and child-initiated instruction. At the same time, decisions must be made as to how to manage thematic curriculum with systematic instruction. Developmental advances make it possible for the students to take a more active role in the development of thematic curriculum. And, they can also assume more responsibility for gathering resources and arranging the classroom environment as the thematic topic moves from the planning stage to the implementation stage. The teacher or team of teachers must determine to what extent the two types of curriculum will be used in the classroom. School district requirements, personal teaching styles, and expectations about how instruction will be organized will affect how much teachers stress thematic curriculum or systematic instruction. Regardless of the emphasis, developmentally appropriate methods are used, which may necessitate adaptation of commercial curriculum resources for use in the program that has been designed for the various age groups represented in the classroom.

Scheduling the school day includes consideration of both types of curriculum and includes the various roles the teacher must play to manage a variety of activities interfaced with organized instruction for individuals, small groups, and the entire class. The teacher and students plan each day together to organize management of thematic curriculum and systematic instruction within the schedule. Students are able to make choices for the activities and projects in which they wish to participate. At the same time, all must plan for how they will carry out their responsibilities for their own assignments and the activities where they will work with and help other students.

Study Questions

1. Why is it possible to include kindergarten children either with 4-year-olds or with children in first, second, and third grades?
2. How can the significant developmental changes be characterized for children between the ages of 5 and 8?
3. Why is it important for teachers of children in these grades to understand that development is gradual and takes place on individual timetables?
4. What are the implications of the nature of development during these years for the design of appropriate curriculum?
5. What kinds of problems emerge when inappropriate teaching methods are used with these children?
6. How do teaching practices affect the child's motivation to learn and the child's development of a sense of competence?
7. How does the teacher consider different levels of ability, development, and learning styles when designing learning experiences for students between the ages of 5 and 8?
8. Why is it difficult to accommodate for these student differences in the typical graded classroom?
9. How are thematic curriculum and systematic instruction complementary?
10. What different approaches to planning and implementing instruction are required by

teachers who work with thematic curriculum and systematic instruction?

11. Why is an alternative organization to graded classrooms needed for children in the primary grades?

12. How would an alternative structure of organization answer the problem of using transitional classrooms before kindergarten or first grade?

13. Why do the ungraded classroom or multiage grouping provide a positive alternative to graded classrooms?

14. How does thematic curriculum help bridge developmental differences in students in multiage classrooms?

15. Does the ungraded approach help solve the issue of retention in the early grades? If so, how?

16. How do cooperative learning groups and peer teaching help the teacher to improve the use of time for instruction?

17. How is the classroom environment that uses thematic curriculum similar to the pre-school environment? How is it different?

18. What is the role of students in developing and implementing thematic curriculum?

19. How does student involvement in developing the brainstorming web facilitate their understanding of the connections between content areas in integrated curriculum?

20. How do student choices in selecting theme projects and activities enhance their social development and sense of responsibility?

21. Why does the teacher need to extensively involve students and parents in planning for implementation of unit projects?

22. What considerations must the teacher include when scheduling thematic curriculum and systematic instruction in the ungraded or multiage classroom?

23. What adaptations might the teacher consider to ensure that commercial material resources are developmentally appropriate?

24. How might commercial material resources be adapted for thematic curriculum units?

25. How can the teacher ensure that systematic instruction is included as needed, both within thematic curriculum and as a separate component of the daily schedule?

26. Why does assessment of individual progress become more important when planning and carrying out instruction for children between the ages of 5 and 8?

27. How are assessment and teaching for individual needs related?

The Transitional Curriculum: Ages 5 to 8

Language Arts, Mathematics, and Science

CHAPTER OBJECTIVES

As a result of reading this chapter, you will be able to:

1. Describe how language development evolves in children ages 5 to 8.
2. Understand the language needs of children with language differences.
3. Design curriculum for language development.
4. Understand how literacy develops in kindergarten and the primary grades.
5. Explain the role of the environment, the teacher, and technology in the language arts program.
6. Describe the stages of literacy acquisition.
7. Explain alternative approaches to organizing the language arts program.
8. Describe examples of experiences that promote reading and writing.
9. Explain how curriculum is designed to accommodate student learning differences.
10. Describe trends and issues in mathematics.

11. Describe how to plan and organize the mathematics program.
12. Describe how to plan experiences in mathematics.
13. Explain how young children learn about science.
14. Describe trends and issues in science.
15. Explain how to plan and organize the science program.
16. Describe the role of the environment and the teacher in organizing the science program.
17. Discuss how to use integrated curriculum in the language arts, mathematics, and science in kindergarten and the primary grades.

The ages between 5 and 8 are exciting ones for children in the first years of school. I have described them as transitional years because at this time children make the transition from preoperational to concrete operational thinking. Children are also making the transition toward literacy. They will become true readers and writers during these years of kindergarten and the primary grades. This chapter discusses languages arts, mathematics, and science curriculum and instruction for children who are making the transition from preschool into the primary grades. The language arts curriculum will be discussed first, followed by mathematics, and the science.

Curriculum for Language Arts

In Chapter 8, I discussed the acquisition of literacy in terms of language development. I described language skill as the ability to speak, listen, write, and read. The importance of understanding how children acquire the ability to write and read. I explained the interrelated nature of language development, and the individual nature and pace of literacy acquisition. The issue of whether language development and literacy should be taught from a skills approach or as a natural, emerging process was debated. Activities for promoting language development, including receptive and expressive oral language, writing, and reading, were suggested; in addition, integrated approaches, including that of thematic curriculum, were described.

In this chapter, I will discuss the continuation of language development and literacy in kindergarten and the primary grades and later stages of early childhood education. The span of development that occurs between the ages of five and eight, or from kindergarten through third grade, as was described in Chapter 10, is the range that will be included in this discussion. During these years, the child moves from preoperational thinking to concrete operational thinking. In language arts, the movement is from emergent literacy to independent reading and writing.

The teaching of language changes from a developmental to a content-area approach in the primary grades, beginning with kindergarten. Therefore, for preschool programs, the acquisition of oral and written literacy was discussed in terms of language development. Regarding the later ages of early childhood, it is described as the language arts.

Languages arts include listening, speaking, writing, and reading. The process of learning about these components is interrelated, just as it is in the preschool curriculum. Each component of the language arts curriculum depends on and contributes to progress and growth in the others; therefore, experiences in the language arts program are described in holistic terms, rather than as separate areas of study.

In the sections that follow, the language arts curriculum for students ages 5 to 8 is described as a transitional process. There is much similarity with the curriculum for the preschool years. The kinds of experiences that children need build on the foundations developed for 3- and 4-year-old children. Nevertheless, as students extend their abilities in literacy, competencies in reading and writing build rapidly. Certain stages in the transition toward competence and the kinds of experiences and activities that promote further progress in literacy can be described.

Oral language and concept understanding continue to develop. I will therefore discuss the importance of addressing continuing acquisition of receptive and expressive language. The issue of a skills approach as opposed to a developmental approach to reading in the preschool years continues as an issue in the primary grades; I define it as a controversy between the whole-language approach and the skills approach in reading instruction. I will discuss the role of the teacher, the environment, instructional materials, and also appropriate activities for promoting development in writing skills. Finally, I will explore integrated curriculum in the language arts based on thematic units. I will include a description of the balance between thematic and systematic instruction as it applies to the language arts.

The Continuing Process of Language Development

Although much of the child's acquisition of the language of her home and community is acquired before kindergarten and first grade, children continue to add to their language ability. Five- to 8-year-olds have developed a good control of their language. They can use language creatively and generally are able to articulate well as they verbalize their thoughts, give directions, and ask questions. During the primary grades, they will develop larger vocabularies, develop new meanings for words they already use, and use more complex language structure. As their cognitive abilities continue to expand, they will express more complex thought in their language (Seefeldt & Barbour, 1994).

Contrary to the practice in many elementary schools, the emphasis on reading instruction in the latter early childhood years does not preclude a need for further opportunities to develop oral language. No matter how well children are able to express themselves, language development should continue. Genishi and Fassler (1999, p. 75) suggest ways to nurture talk and language:

1. Talk between adults and children and between children serves a variety of purposes and functions. That is, language is used to inform, tell stories, question, pretend, have fun, discuss, plan, and so on.
2. Because talk flows when people have something to talk about or tell each other, teachers provide for and engage the children in activities and experiences that are the focus of talk.
3. Conversations are comfortable for both child and teacher. Talk is fluent because the communicators are absorbed in getting their messages across, and their conversations are meaning-oriented, not form-oriented.

Children need to engage in many activities firsthand and need opportunities to talk about their experiences in their learning activities. The rich experiences with language will lead to literacy. Children will respond to learning activities from their individual levels of development. Some will be able to express themselves in written form, whereas others will use mostly oral language at first to reflect on what they have encountered. Regardless of the child's level, the opportunities to acquire concepts and language permit the child to move into literacy individually from a language base (Graves, 1983).

Addressing the Language Needs of Diverse Speakers

Children who are speakers of non-English languages or other dialects especially need opportunities to further develop their oral language. Because these children learn language through communicating, they need daily activities that will facilitate the acquisition of language along with new information (Abramson, Robinson, & Ankenman, 1990).

The best method for assisting children who are learning a second language is a current issue. For many years, bilingual scholars proposed that children learning English needed to be taught academic subjects in their home language for several years while they are learning English. Further, they believe that a strong foundation in the first language supports the child in learning English (Cummins, 1994).

There have been serious challenges to this approach to language education. One concern has been the small amount of time spent in teaching English in bilingual programs (Tanamachi, 1998; Traub, 1999). And as was mentioned in Chapter 8, not all parents of bilingual children want their child in a bilingual program.

In 1998, then Secretary of Education Richard Riley changed the policy in bilingual education. He called for a goal of English proficiency in 3 years. California had already repealed bilingual statutes in 1987, and Texas and Illinois had revised their policies (Green, 1997).

Research to support appropriate language instruction for non–English-speaking children fails to provide direction as to the best approach. Program evaluations are politicized and flawed (Gersten, 1999). As a result, conflict and controversy prevail. Regardless of the lack of direction for the most effective bilingual education, there are suggestions that can assist teachers of young children in kindergarten and the primary grades.

Specific strategies can be used with bilingual and second-language learners. First, children should be supported in developing literacy in their native language before becoming literate in English. Their native language should be used to bridge understanding in English. Teachers should use natural, predictable texts for beginning reading instruction in both languages. Similarly, predictable books should be used for shared reading and small-group reading lessons. Children should be

given opportunities to self-select for independent reading; additionally, they should be encouraged to write in both their native language and in English (Serna & Hudelson, 1997). Oral collaboration between skilled English speakers and second-language or dialect speakers during literacy instruction helps many speakers acquire English (Enright & McCloskey, 1985). Similarly, when native speakers and bilingual students share their journals, this enhances the limited speaker's acquisition of new vocabulary and emergent writing (Urzua, 1987). Further, Hudelson (1984) found that these kinds of writing activities enabled students who were limited in English to read and write in English before expressing themselves orally. Finally, teachers should observe their second-language learners in reading and writing activities to respond to their literacy progress in both languages (Serna & Hudelson, 1997).

Developers of an English literacy project that involved parents and preprimary and primary-age children assumed that social interactions were a vehicle for oral language development and literacy for limited-English speakers and second-language speakers. The researchers proposed the following assumptions, based on their review of the literature (Quintero & Velarde, 1990, p. 11):

1. Social context is of utmost importance in the child's learning in general and in literacy development specifically.
2. Use of oral language is an integral part of the literacy development process. Oral language is also strongly affected by social context.
3. Learners enter school knowing that written language has meaning, but they cannot understand print usage when it is presented to them as isolated letters and sounds.
4. Literacy behaviors are not restricted to the use of books but rather encompass many social and linguistic activities.

Finally, teachers need to ensure that children become competent communicators in English. They need to learn "school talk" to be able to participate in the social environment of the classroom. It is the social environment that will support acquisition of competency (Genishi & Fassler, 1999; Gutierrez, 1993).

In the sections that follow, guidelines and examples are given of experiences that will promote oral language in all speakers in the later early childhood years. The oral language curriculum follows the assumptions made by Quintero and Velarde (1990) that children developing oral language skills benefit from the social context of the kindergarten and primary-grade classroom.

Designing Curriculum for Language Development

Children develop their oral language by talking to their peers and to adults. The teacher's goal in designing curriculum for oral language development is to include speaking opportunities in learning activities. Although this may seem obvious, a visit to many elementary schools might demonstrate that verbal discussions are not the norm in primary classrooms. In a school where quiet classrooms are valued, children may have little opportunity to exchange ideas and participate in discussions. Further, reading instruction periods can be dominated by individual work, with more time spent on practicing reading skills in written form than on using conversational language. Daily oral discussions of many types are required for language competency to continue to expand and improve.

Following are some of the types of classroom (and outdoor) activities that foster oral language in kindergarten and primary-grade children. The length and form of the activities vary depending on the age of the students, their prior experiences, and their confidence levels. Nevertheless, they can be used with some adaptation at all grade levels that serve children from 5 to 8 years old.

Group Discussions

There are many occasions when the entire class can engage in a group discussion. The discussion could follow a common group experience, an unusual local event that interests the children, or an opportunity to solve a problem. For example, an unexpected storm swept a local community without warning early one morning as the children were arriving at school. Soon after class began, the teacher gathered the children to discuss their experiences with the storm as they traveled to school Witnessing the unusual darkness of the sky, high winds, flooded streets, and other phenomena gave the children the opportunity to use descriptive language as the class discussed the storm and its effects on the community. In another instance, in a second-grade classroom, students had become careless with keeping the working areas organized. The teacher and students discussed the problem and decided which suggestions for improving the appearance and arrangement of classroom materials would be carried out.

Class Projects

Projects related to unit or content study activities lend themselves to oral language experiences. Groups of students engaged in the projects can be asked to discuss and report the results of their project. Students might talk about the problems they encountered and solved in completing their project, the steps required to accomplish their goal, the reasons for choosing the project, and so on. The larger group can be encouraged to ask questions, make observations about the group's work, and reflect on what was learned about the topic studied.

Dramatic Productions

Kindergarten and first-grade students enjoy acting out a familiar fairy tale or popular children's story. Older students in the second and third grades enjoy writing a play and presenting it to the rest of the class. Whichever form of production is used, students can plan the production, improvise costumes, practice parts, and otherwise engage in extensive language to prepare the dramatic production. The teacher may be needed to guide the process with younger children but may serve only as a resource person for older students who have experience in initiating and carrying out activities in a small group. The dramatic activity requires extensive use of oral language as children develop dialogue and roles for the type of dramatic event they will present.

Field Trips

Every field trip that focuses on a new experience—whether a walk outside the school or a trip with a distance of many miles—is an opportunity to develop new vocabulary. Before the trip, the teacher can set the stage for important new words that children will encounter. The children can be alerted to notice new information and words before the field trip begins. For example, a kindergarten class was studying trees. As part of the study of how trees are used, the children visited a lumberyard to see how lumber products are used in construction. The teacher asked the children to notice the products that are made of wood and to remember new words. After they returned from the lumberyard, children were asked to recall what they saw. They made a list of products made of wood, and then they told language experience stories. The teacher prompted the children to remember many new words, such as *lumber,* names of tools used to work with wood construction, and other words related to a lumberyard.

Children's Literature

Children's books offer endless opportunities to develop and use oral language. One major goal for language development through children's literature is to appreciate the creative and aesthetic use of language in books. Neuman & Bredekamp, (2000) describe the opportunities books offer for language development, including exposing children to mature language, listening to varied syntax, enjoying figurative language, hearing different dialects, introducing new vocabulary in context, presenting new words, sharing books that em-

phasize word meanings, and playing with language. Glazer (1986) used the stories *The Little Engine that Could* and *Millions of Cats* as examples of classic children's books that involve play with patterns of language.

Cooperative Learning Groups

Cooperative learning group activities provide natural opportunities to use conversation and discussion. Because the students must interact to complete the activity, members of the group will be engaged in individual ideas as the problem or exercise is resolved. Mixing students who have varied language abilities will enhance the exchange of vocabulary and syntax during frequent verbal exchanges.

Curriculum for language development is not organized as a separate component of the language arts curriculum. Nor is it separate from activities in other content areas. In the suggestions

Activities That Promote Language Development

Memory Game

This memory game is frequently found in Montessori classrooms. The teacher assembles a number of objects or pictures related to a new concept. The objects are placed on a tray, and the child is asked to study them. The objects are then covered, and the child is asked to name them. More objects or pictures are added, a few at a time, and the exercise is repeated. Examples of objects that can be used include vegetables, articles of clothing, solid shapes, and pictures of furniture items.

Imaginary Creatures

Students are asked to make an imaginary creature using play dough, crayons and paper, or scraps of recycled materials. They are asked to describe to the rest of the group such things as what the creature looks like and where it lives.

What Is It?

This activity promotes divergent thinking and expressive language. The teacher finds objects that are interesting and unfamiliar to the children. Old household utensils such as coffee grinders or a rug beater are examples of objects that can be described. The children are asked to examine the object and describe its characteristics such as how it is made, what materials it is made of, and what its qualities are. After the children have exhausted descriptive characteristics, they are asked to decide how the object could be used. They are not asked to identify the purpose of the object but rather to invent a use for it. At the end of the experience, the teacher can tell the children the actual purpose and function of the object.

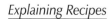

Explaining Recipes

Simple recipes offer rich opportunities for expressive language. After children engage in a cooking project, they can orally describe the cooking process and the changes in the foods that were prepared. Good examples of such activities include making butter, peanut butter, and popcorn. The children not only can explain what happens when popcorn pops or peanuts are put in the blender or food processor, they can also describe the steps involved in the process of preparation and the necessary equipment and ingredients needed.

Sequencing Stories

Oral comprehension and expression language are used when retelling or sequencing a story. Kindergarten children enjoy retelling or sequencing by using flannel board pictures of a well-known story such as *The Three Little Pigs* or a nursery rhyme. The flannel pictures provide props for retelling the story. Older children can make up their own story or retell a story they have read. They enjoy making cartoon pictures of the story, perhaps including the dialogue, and sharing it with the other students.

put forth earlier, oral language activities are interwoven into ongoing classroom methods and strategies related to the total curriculum; the specific activities suggested serve this purpose. They involve concept development, art, problem-solving, science, and language arts. They are more likely to involve an individual student or a small group, rather than large-group efforts.

The Continuing Process of Literacy Development

The Nature of Literacy Acquisition in Kindergarten and the Primary Grades

What are the differences between the kinds of experiences that promote literacy in preschool and kindergarten and those that promote literacy in the primary grades? In some schools, a developmental approach to literacy is advocated for preschool classrooms for 4-year-olds but is abandoned in kindergarten, when "serious learning" must begin. Language experience stories and big-book activities give way to basal reader lessons reinforced with workbooks and dittoed skills sheets.

The years between kindergarten and third grade are the most critical in determining whether the child will become a successful reader, will enjoy reading, and will be able to use the acquired reading and writing skills to become a competent and effective learner. The child crosses the bridge into literacy and continues to refine competence as a reader and writer. How successfully the child acquires literacy depends on the kinds of experiences that are provided and whether the child perceives him- or herself as a competent student. If a developmental philosophy prevails, the teacher will continue to provide literacy activities that facilitate the child's progress within an individual timeline. If a skills approach is advocated, much time may be spent in teacher-directed lessons using formal instruction in reading and writing. A problem that teachers in these grade levels must address is how to determine the best practices for their students. How can the teacher structure the curriculum to best ensure that kindergarten and primary-grade students will make a positive transition into literacy? In Chapter 8 the history of the controversy between whole language and phonics was discussed. The debate centered on a reading program that either used whole language strategies or featured phonics as the core of beginning reading instruction. In reality, quality reading programs are based on a balanced approach to reading instruction, rather than using one or the other. Increasingly, teachers are learning how to incorporate the best of both sides of the controversy. In achieving a balanced language arts program for their classroom from kindergarten to third grade, they have developed an understanding of the philosophy and practices of the whole language approach and how to balance their instruction between skills instruction and child-initiated literacy efforts.

The development of literacy in kindergarten through third grade is also a continuation of the process that began when children were infants and toddlers. The process of emerging literacy continues as the child acquires the ability to read and write. In the next section, we will look at the language arts program for children ages 5 to 8. We will first understand the elements of a quality language arts program for children who are developing literacy and then discuss the roles that contribute to a successful program.

The Language Arts Program for Children Ages 5 to 8

In Chapter 8, I described the preschool curriculum for language development. I emphasized the importance of oral language development for literacy in the arrangement of the environment, the role of play, the role of the teacher, and the experiences that could be provided to facilitate language and literacy. I also discussed how meaningful experiences in book reading and storytelling, participating in integrated thematic units, and other daily experiences can promote the child's emerging literacy.

Earlier in this chapter, I stressed the continuing importance of oral language and vocabulary as a

foundation for competent readers and writers in the beginning elementary grades. In this section, I will discuss the language arts program as it relates to reading and writing. The goal is to develop a balanced program that combines child-initiated and teacher-directed activities that will incorporate all of the experiences that are needed for a quality language arts curriculum. The balanced program also includes informal, contextual experiences, as well as regularly scheduled systematic instruction for students who need assistance in acquiring literacy skills. Within this curriculum framework, the teacher will provide formal and informal activities that will permit children to make progress toward literacy through both individual and group activities.

What do effective teachers do to develop a quality language arts program for young children? A study of kindergarten, first-grade, and second-grade teachers determined that there are eight practices used by these outstanding teachers (Pressley, Rankin, & Yokoi, 1996). Their literacy in-

struction included the following characteristics (Gambrell & Mazzoni, 1999, pp. 96–97):

1. There is a literate environment.
2. Outstanding children's literature is read.
3. Students read aloud to others.
4. Students read along with the teacher.
5. Students engage in writing.
6. Literacy instruction is integrated across the curriculum.
7. Many skills are taught.
8. There is a home-school connection.

In the next part of the chapter, we will look at how the language arts program can address these characteristics.

The Role of the Environment

In Chapter 8, I described the preschool classroom environment for emergent literacy, including center arrangements that foster listening, speaking, writing, and reading skills. In kindergarten and primary grades, a similar arrangement is appropriate. A large language arts center with collections of books of all types, including books written by the children, can be organized and displayed for easy perusal. Areas for listening to taped books, areas that are comfortable for reading, and quiet spaces for reading and thinking provide a relaxed ambience. An area for writing and illustrating written work contains writing materials; marking pens; crayons; a variety of art media such as chalk, watercolors, and tempera paints; and a selection of writing paper. Typewriters, computers, and book-making materials broaden opportunities for composing and reading.

The room might also accommodate a project, study, and planning and instruction center. The project center can contain materials for changing projects related to thematic work. Book-making materials might also be located here, rather than in the library center. The study center is a quiet area where students can conduct individual work. A study table could seat several students who need to complete assignments or read. Individual desks can be transformed into carrels using cardboard dividers. The planning and instruction center is a larger area where the whole class can gather for planning and feedback sessions. Small-group instruction can also be conducted in this area.

The Role of the Teacher

The teacher in kindergarten and primary grades still serves as guide and facilitator of learning. In addition, the role of assessor and evaluator of the child's learning is expanded as the need to track the child's strengths and to instruct or guide the child in language arts skills becomes more evident.

The role of the teacher is to provide assistance. In keeping with Vygotsky's views of assisted performance versus independent performance, the teacher determines the child's zone of proximal development (ZPD) and offers assistance to the child so that progress is maximized. Children's interests and progress into literacy are closely observed, and the teacher provides steps in reading and writing just beyond the child's ability by modeling for the child or guiding the child's own work (Tharp & Gallimore, 1988). For example, the child is using invented spelling in writing stories. The teacher might select some of the child's words that are close to the correct spelling and provide the child with the correct models. Similarly, if a child is consistently selecting books that are now too easy, the teacher might suggest a slightly more difficult book and read it to the child, and then with the child.

Much of the work is informal and incidental when the child asks for assistance or the teacher observes the child's progress during small-group instruction. At other times, the teacher will need to introduce a skill to some or all of the class or model forms in composition that the children are ready to use but that they have not developed through their individual reading and writing efforts.

The teacher conducts much instruction informally within whole-language and integrated thematic activities. Periodic or regular systematic instruction focuses on specific objectives or skills. Jewell and Zintz (1986) offered some guidelines to the teacher's role as children move into literacy in a meaningful, enjoyable manner. The teacher's role includes the following, adapted from their list (Jewell & Zintz, 1986, pp. 94–95):

1. Read materials to children that they cannot read for themselves.
2. Read from a variety of materials with a high interest level.
3. Provide a reading environment by having an abundance of reading materials readily available in the classroom.
4. Have older, proficient readers tape stories and store the cassettes for children to use in the listening center.
5. Provide flannel boards with appropriate cutouts for children to use to tell stories to themselves or to others.
6. Have writing materials readily available: pencils, crayons, and paper.

7. Have a scrap or "attic" box filled with a collection of odds and ends for children to sort through, touch, and talk about in whatever way they choose.
8. Provide time to engage in all of the above activities.
9. Provide a multitude of hands-on activities for children to participate in and talk about.
10. With the emergence of reading behaviors, provide information and help as children request them.
11. Begin to prepare language experience stories by recording the children talking about an experience in the classroom.
12. As children develop additional competencies and interests in reading, provide more time in frequently spaced periods for them to read.
13. Continue to share books with the whole group by reading daily.

The Role of Technology

As more schools acquire computers for the classroom, educators have become interested in how computer technology can be useful in the language arts program. Much of the original software developed for kindergarten and primary-grade classrooms was meant for work with reading readiness and reading skills. Drill activities that replicated the same kinds of skill reinforcement found in reading workbooks prevailed.

The computer can be a useful tool for beginning literacy. Simple word processing programs are available that can be used by younger children who are able to use the keyboard to write. As they become more proficient in the process of composing their writing, they can use editing features such as spell checking. An advantage of the computer for beginning writers is that correcting mistakes or making changes is much easier, thus minimizing frustrations.

Current uses of the computer include new ways to approach literacy or "electronic" literacy (Labbo, Reinking, & McKenna, 1999). Teachers and their students can use multimedia composing, and sociodramatic play enhanced by the computer. The main caution for teachers is to avoid getting caught up in the attractiveness of software; they should instead make purchases and decisions based on the usefulness of the program for students in their classroom. Moreover, computer technology cannot replace a good quality literacy program in the classroom (Teale & Yokota, 2000).

Stages of Literacy Acquisition

The transition into literacy in the later early childhood years is gradual and individual. If the teacher understands the nature of this accomplishment, developmentally appropriate materials and experiences can be planned to facilitate progress for each child. In the sections that follow, I will discuss literacy acquisition within three stages. Each stage has implications for the kinds of instruction and skills development that can complement natural experiences that nurture literacy.

The ages from 5 to 8 are the years when most young children achieve literacy in reading and writing. Mastery of their home language is basically acquired by age 5; likewise, the major steps into literacy are mastered between age 5 and 8. Literacy can be described as occurring in three overlapping stages: setting foundations for literacy, learning about print and understanding printed language, and becoming independent readers.

Stage One: Setting Foundations for Literacy. The first stage, setting foundations for literacy, begins when the child is an infant and proceeds throughout the preschool years. Children acquire information about the processes of speaking, writing, and reading through activities in which they can experiment and express themselves in preliteracy steps of writing and reading. Through use of oral language and opportunities for emergent writing and reading, each child acquires many of the characteristics of literacy at an individual rate. By age 5, as they enter kindergarten, children have progressed into literacy at their own individual rate. The first stage gradually becomes the second stage, learning about print and understanding printed language.

Stage Two: Learning About Print and Understanding Printed Language. In stage two, the child masters the components of written language and becomes a reader and writer of English. Although the process of true mastery of reading and writing is a life-long task, understanding and using printed language is the major accomplishment in this stage.

To master literacy, the child must attend to features of printed language that include phonic elements, grammar, and punctuation. Major steps toward this goal were already made in the foundations stage, when the child developed an awareness of how letters are formed and put together into words to express thoughts. There is likewise an awareness of how punctuation is used to enable others to understand what one has expressed in written language. In this second stage, the child continues to learn about print and how it is used. Language experience stories used in stage one to develop awareness of printed language are continued in stage two to practice the elements of printed language. The skills used in relating to printed language that can be learned through language experience stories in stage two include the following:

1. Match letters, upper case and lower case.
2. Match words.
3. Match sentences.
4. Practice word recognition when the teacher frames individual words.
5. Practice phonic, structural, and context clues to locate letters and words and identify them.
6. Identify different types of punctuation.
7. Reread stories and share reading with a buddy.
8. Make similar sentences using the syntax model in a sentence.

Chapman (1996) identified other classroom literacy experiences that promote stage two of literacy to include the following:

News time when children write news collaboratively

Shared reading experiences using enlarged texts or charts

Reading and writing time when children choose independent activities that involve reading and writing

Author's circle when individual children share their own writing (p. 33)

The specific reading skills that young children acquire in the primary grades can be categorized as recognizing sight words and understanding phonics, word analysis, context clues, and the mechanics of reading and writing (Fields & Spangler, 2000). Although language experience stories are one vehicle for facilitating practice with the skills, the child's own reading and writing processes will incorporate others. The teacher can supple-

---

Sight Words—instantly recognizable words

Phonics—learning about letters and the sounds they represent

Word Analysis—learning parts of words
    compound words (bedroom)
    inflections–possessives (*'s*), plurals, endings (*ed, s, ing*)
    roots, prefixes (*un*), suffixes (*ful, less, ly*)

Context Clues—learning words from their location in a sentence

FIGURE 11.1 Beginning reading skills

ment these natural experiences for acquiring competence with the printed language with systematic instruction. Figure 11.1 lists the basic beginning reading skills.

Although the child engages in activities that provide practice in the elements of printed language that will facilitate the ability to read, the transition into reading requires many experiences in reading. In the foundations stage, the children engaged in big-book and other read-along activities that led them to begin to put the pieces of the reading process into place. They learned that in English, print moves from left to right, and they became able to follow along and turn the pages when favorite stories were read. They contributed to group-dictated stories in addition to engaging in individual "reading" efforts with familiar books (Neuman & Bredekamp, 2000).

In stage two, children continue to advance in their ability to understand how to read print until they are able to read on their own. The transition into reading begins in stage one, with repeated readings of big books or shared books (Neuman & Bredekamp, 2000). The process continues with assisted reading. Hoskisson (1975) described three stages of assisted reading: (1) the child is asked to repeat a phrase or sentence after it has been read; (2) the child is asked to fill in a word that occurs repeatedly in a story; and (3) the child takes over more of the reading process and the adult prompts the words the child has trouble recognizing. In each step, the child takes over more of the reading process until the teacher assists only as needed.

After some proficiency has been achieved in reading, more formal activities can be used that target or reinforce specific elements or skills. Workbooks and computer drill programs are used sparingly for practice to supplement the use of the skill in the child's own reading and writing efforts. In a similar manner, teacher-directed instruction is selected based on learners' needs, rather than as routine lessons that are scheduled whether or not they are needed (Fields & Spangler, 2000).

Morrow (2000) describes a language arts block that uses independent center activities to accomplish some of the components of a quality literacy classroom. For example, children might engage in partner reading, a writing activity, a working with words activity, or listening center activity in one segment of the language arts block. In another part of the language arts time period, the teacher engages in small-group instruction when children are taught based on the skills instruction that they need.

✦ Using Writing to Communicate About Mathematics

A first-grade teacher used journal writing with her first-grade students to help them become aware of how mathematics had relevance in their lives. The teacher first brainstormed with the children about how they could use mathematics in situations outside school. The children were asked to be aware of ways that they used mathematics over a period of days outside of school. On a Monday morning, the children spent time writing about their uses of mathematics in their individual journals. After their entries had been made, each child shared one journal entry with the class. Class members were encouraged to comment or ask questions. The teacher then modeled how a journal entry could be transformed into a mathematics word problem. The class solved the problem and then used an example in their own journal or one shared in class to write their own word problem. Children worked in pairs to read and edit the word problems to determine if they made sense and were worded correctly. Finally the word problems were rewritten from the editing process and recorded on file cards. The cards were then used by the class to solve all of the word problems. (Brown, 1997) ✦

Stage Three: Becoming Independent Readers. Children need extensive reading experiences to master the reading and writing process. When they have developed competence in the beginning stages of literacy, they make the transition to independence in reading and writing. As they continue to use the features of written language, their competence and confidence also increase. Instruction in reading continues but is now based on individual needs. Whole-group instruction decreases, and small-group and individual instruction increases.

The teacher's role increasingly becomes that of facilitator, and the teacher is less focused on basic instruction. Books and reading materials are made available for all types of reading. Children need a balance between narrative and expository reading. The classroom library should include easy nonfiction, with books about animals, places to visit, famous people, and nature (Sanacore, 1991; Morrow, 2000). Books from trips to the school library and public library are supplemented with books from home. The teacher continues to read to the children but moves to longer books that are read in chapters. Reading in the content areas is used extensively as children study thematic units and seek out resources for developing class projects, assignments, and reports. Reading for problem-solving is engaged in frequently, and skills for beginning research are developed as students search for information related to unit activities.

Organizing the Language Arts Program

How, then, do teachers determine how to organize the classroom for instruction as children move through the stages of literacy in the later years of early childhood? In the pages that follow, examples are given of how some teachers decided to design their language arts program. In each of the examples, the teachers studied and analyzed what processes they believed would best provide their students with a language arts program that has a balance between whole-language, basal, and phonics instruction. The examples come from a first-grade classroom that was not grouped, a literature-based model, content-area grouping, and a reading workshop.

A Non–Ability-Grouped, Multilevel, First-Grade Classroom

Three teachers established a model for a first-grade classroom (Cunningham, Hall, & DeFee, 1991). The children are grouped in three classrooms, with similar ranges of ability in each room. The teachers decided to include the four major approaches to reading: the basal approach, the phonics approach, implementing real books, and writing. They studied these approaches, determined that some children respond best to one particular approach, and built their program around four components, or blocks, based on the benefits of the four approaches. Children were told of the activities and were provided instruction in each of the four blocks.

In the basal block, children were given daily guided instruction in a basal reading series. The instruction included workbook activities, partner reading, whole-group instruction, and feedback activities at the end of the block.

A working-with-words block involved a "Word Wall" and "Making Words" activity. Each day, five words from the basal reading lessons were added to the Word Wall on a bulletin board. The children learned to read, spell, and alphabetize the words. A variety of group activities were conducted with the words each day. The Making Words activity involved making words from letters. The children were given a limited selection of letters at their desk. In some instances, the teacher called out the word to be made. In other activities, the children were told to make words out of some or all of the letters.

The writing block began with a short writing lesson modeled by the teacher. Next, the children engaged in their own individual writing activity. The teacher helped children edit and revise their work. The lesson ended with a brief period during which children could share their work with the class.

The fourth block, the real-books block, involved self-selected reading and reading aloud by the teacher. Children could select from a variety of books and could read alone or with a friend (Hall, Prevatte, & Cunningham, 1995).

The three teachers combined whole-language and basal materials and activities for their reading program. They achieved a balance between teacher-directed and child-initiated work during the language arts period. They permitted students to develop literacy at their own rate, but at the same time they felt ensured that they were working with beginning reading and writing skills in a systematic fashion (Cunningham, Hall, & DeFee, 1991).

Literature-Based Instruction

A second-grade language arts classroom described by Fields and Spangler (2000) was based on good books. The teacher conducted the program both to meet individual interests and to conduct group topics in science or social studies. He helped individual children select books that would support what they were trying to learn or do. He wanted the students to have control of their learning. His belief was that children learn and practice reading and writing through the study of content that they are interested in. He concentrated on the progress of each individual student and used responsive teaching to guide students in the development of reading and writing skills.

While reading and writing were conducted throughout the day, the teacher prepared skills instruction for small groups or individual children. He used basal materials or constructed his own activities to use with the children. Reports of student needs and progress were kept in individual folders. The folder contained daily journal and other written work, as well as projects the child had in progress or had completed. The teacher used the folders for planning with individual children and for assessing their instructional needs.

This classroom was offered reading and writing experiences through class projects and studies of topics in science and social studies. The class library became a source of reading materials as the teacher, librarian, and students found resources

that could be consulted for the topic being studied. Again, as the teacher identified reading and writing problems during topic activities, systematic instruction was planned to address needs of identified students.

Content-Area Grouping

Content-area instruction and cooperative learning groups were used in a third-grade classroom to replace ability grouping and traditional reading instruction (Pardo & Raphael, 1991). The teacher was interested in developing independent learners who could extend their strategies for reading and learning. Reading and writing activities were used to study subject matter. Students selected the topics to be studied; developed a general concept about the topic; gathered, organized, synthesized, and reported information about the topic; and used their emerging reading and writing skills to share information about the topic.

Teacher-led whole-class discussions were used to introduce learning strategies and topic concepts and to develop background knowledge before exploring a topic. The teacher also used whole-group instruction to work with difficult text and conduct enrichment activities.

Small cooperative learning group activities afforded opportunities for students to practice and use new learning strategies and to work on topic activities. The groups gathered information and wrote reports on their findings. They generated and answered questions about the topic being studied or worked on a subtopic related to the larger class topic.

Individual work was undertaken to set individual goals and purposes related to study topics and to apply and practice reading and writing strategies. Students recorded their thoughts and reflections in dialogue journals. They responded to focus questions posed by the teacher and shared individual ideas, along with participating in other individual activities.

Because the students designed the topics to be studied, the teacher in this third-grade classroom maintained a role as facilitator and guide. She helped students map or web the information they wished to acquire from content-area topics. She introduced and modeled strategies that students needed to pursue and report on information developed through large-group and cooperative-group activities. She also was able to work extensively with individual students to extend their skills as independent readers and writers.

The Reading Workshop

Teachers of the reading workshop in another third-grade classroom used a more directive approach to reading instruction (Reutzel & Cooter, 1991). They wished to achieve a balance between providing meaningful activities for the students and ensuring that instructional time was constructive and well managed. They used a 70-minute reading workshop approach to organize their classroom. Through the workshop, they established a classroom environment that integrated reading with writing, speaking, and listening. Student-selected books were the focus of workshop activities, with regular demonstrations of reading and writing strategies.

The reading workshop consisted of periods for sharing (5 to 10 minutes), a minilesson (5 to 10 minutes), state-of-the-class activities (5 minutes), and self-selected reading and responses (35 to 45 minutes). Sharing time was an introductory period used by the teacher to share new discoveries in literature. Minilessons followed sharing time and were short, teacher-designed whole-group in-structional sessions to demonstrate reading strategies. The minilessons were derived from observed student needs or learning objectives from the school district reading curriculum objectives. State-of-the-class activities were used to update the teacher on individual student progress. The teacher could assess the effectiveness of the student's work and adaptations made when needed.

The major period of the reading workshop was devoted to self-selected reading and responses. During this period, the class engaged in sustained silent reading (SSR), some groups of children met with the teacher in literature response groups, and some participated in individual reading conferences. Students engaged in individual reading and writing activities with their self-selected reading materials if and when they were not meeting with the teacher in a group activity. Many different types of projects were planned and conducted by students within their reading and writing activities that had been planned previously with the teacher. At the end of the self-selected reading and response period, the whole class met for a few minutes to share their work as a culminating activity of the reading workshop.

The models just presented represent several approaches to language arts instruction in primary-grade classrooms that serve students in stages two and three, discussed earlier. The models range from predominantly whole-language orientation to more structured combinations that incorporate both basal and whole-language strategies. In the sections that follow, I will present examples of activities suitable for beginning and independent readers. Many of the examples can be used in some or all of the models described.

Experiences That Promote Reading

Reading Buddies

Pairs composed of two students or a student and an adult are established for reading experiences. The buddies meet daily or on a regular basis to read together. They take turns reading from the same book or read from different books. Cross-age buddies can also be formed, whereby students from a higher grade have a buddy in kindergarten or the primary grades. The older buddy listens to the younger child read and reads books selected by the younger buddy. Writing activities can also be conducted. The younger child can dictate a story to the older buddy or receive help in writing a story. Same-age buddies can collaborate on a writing activity.

Read-Along Tapes

Tapes of familiar books are recorded. The child plays the tape as the book is read and reads along with the tape. The activity can be repeated many times until the student has mastered the story. Basal reader stories can be recorded. Many read-along tapes are also available from commercial resources.

Sustained Silent Reading (SSR)

A time is provided for all children to read on their own. Regardless of individual reading levels, all students participate. The book is usually self-selected, and the following guidelines are recommended (McCracken & McCracken, 1979, p. 35):

1. Begin with the whole class.
2. Each child selects one book.
3. Each child must read silently.
4. The teacher reads silently.
5. A timer is used.
6. There are absolutely no reports or records of any kind.

Poem Picture Books

Poem picture books can be used in a manner similar to picture storybooks in the classroom. After they have been introduced and repeated with the children several times, poem picture books can, for example, be used as a read-along source; the poems can be chanted, accompanied by rhythm sticks or drums; or they can be illustrated. Children can make up similar poetry following the pattern of a poem and write their own poems (Glazer & Lamme, 1990).

Creating Nonsense Words

Provide the child with a selection of vowels and consonants. Ask the child to create nonsense words. Have the child "create" an animal or object to match the nonsense word.

Substitute Words

Select a word that is familiar to the children, such as *walk.* Ask the children to generate substitute words for the key word. Examples include *run, jump, tiptoe,* and *creep.* Use *walk* in a sentence. Substitute the word list in the sentence, and have children read the sentence.

Word Games

Use a secret code by substituting numerals for letters in a message. Give the children the numeral code and have them "decode" the message. Another game uses palindromes, or words that are spelled the same frontward and backward (e.g., *wow.*) See how many palindromes students can think of (Danielson, 1990).

Oral Reading to Share Information

Children can read together to share information. The following activities are suggested (Fields & Spangler, 2000, p. 256):

1. Children can read the lunch menu, daily bulletin, and newspaper items.
2. Children can confirm an answer by reading it from a book.
3. One child (a good reader) can read out loud while others listen with their textbooks closed.
4. Children can read passages from reference books or trade books.

Experiences That Promote Writing

Journal Writing

Students write daily in a journal. The journal can be a part of the language arts program or used more broadly for the whole school day. The child records ideas, feelings, reactions to activities, and so on. The teacher reads the journal and responds to the child. Mechanics of writing are not corrected. The teacher is interested in the child's expression of thoughts.

Story Starters

Children are given many opportunities to write their own stories and illustrate them. When they are stumped for ideas, story starters can be used. One form of a starter is a sentence that can be used as the first one in a story, for example, "The noise came closer and closer." Another way to spark a story is to have a collection of pictures, and ask the child to select a picture and write a story about it.

Messages

Responding to messages can trigger interesting writing efforts. The teacher can give each child a mysterious message and ask the child to respond. Another type of mes-

sage is curriculum related. The teacher can leave a message for the child to respond to a question that has been posed. For example, a small container of beans is placed in the mathematics center. The students are left a message to estimate the number of beans and record their name and estimate below the message. The next day, the students can respond to a message asking them to count the number of beans and again record their name and the number they counted.

Lists

All kinds of lists can be generated. For example, students can be asked to write a list of foods they like the least or the best; or they can be asked to keep a list of the books they have read or the names of as many people in their family as they can remember.

Writing Workshop

Children in the primary grades who have become independent writers can use the processes of the writing workshop to improve their writing efforts. The student engages in a series of steps to initiate, improve, and evaluate the writing effort. The process is used each time students are asked to write a composition that will be edited and improved until the teacher and child are satisfied with the quality. Figure 11.2 lists the steps in the writing process (Fields & Spangler, 2000, p. 213).

Prewrite	Participate in an experience Talk about the experience Brainstorm Think about audience, form, and purpose Webbing	
Fastwrite	Put notes and ideas on paper Prepare "sloppy copy," or first draft	
Share, Respond, and Revise	Read and share first draft with others Receive feedback Change and rewrite draft using feedback	This stage may be repeated more than once
Copyread	Proofread and correct details of final draft	
Publish	Prepare final copy Share with others	
Evaluate	Assess effectiveness of process and product	

FIGURE 11.2 Steps in the writing process
Source: From *Let's Begin Reading Right* (4th ed.), (p. 213), by M. V. Fields and K. L. Spangler, © 2000. Reprinted by permission of Pearson Education, Inc. Upper Saddle River, NJ 07458.

Accommodating the Learning Differences of Students with Special Needs

In spite of efforts to provide children in kindergarten and the primary grades with a quality language arts program, some children encounter difficulties in learning to read. It is important that these children be identified as soon as possible and efforts made to correct the problem.

Reading achievement in the first 3 years of school is critical for later achievement. If low-achieving students can be identified and brought up to grade level in the primary grades, they are more likely to remain at grade level than if remediation comes in later grades (Adams, 1990; Carter, 1984; Clay, 1979). The importance of the early years for later learning was also advocated in *Becoming a Nation of Readers* (Commission on Reading, National Academy of Education, 1985) and *Preventing Reading Difficulties in Young Children* (Snow, Burns, & Griffin, 1998); ability to read determines the level of achievement in secondary education.

Prevention of reading difficulties through early intervention is a key to successfully assisting young students who are encountering problems in beginning to read. The students who are unable to progress in literacy are experiencing frustrations in processing print. They are unable to recognize words quickly and effortlessly and thus fall behind in reading comprehension (Adams, 1990; Gaskins, Gaskins, & Gaskins, 1991; Hill & Hale, 1991; Snow, Burns, Griffin, 1998). Programs for early intervention focus on intensive instruction to help the student become successful as soon as possible.

Reading Recovery is an early intervention program designed for 6-year-olds who are low achievers. The children receive intensive one-on-one instruction 30 minutes per day for 12 to 20 weeks. The purpose of the program is to help the child acquire the strategies used by good readers. Instruction includes reading activities using natural language and predictable texts. Writing activities are based on the child's experience or presented as an extension of text readings (Hill & Hale, 1991). The lowest-performing students are selected for the program; they are replaced with other students at the completion of the program, after they have begun performing comfortably with average children in the classroom. Reading Recovery does not replace regular classroom instruction in reading but rather complements the child's other language arts activities.

Marie Clay, the designer of Reading Recovery, describes the program as a second chance to learn. She attributes the success of the program to three elements: individual instruction, daily, intensive instruction, and acceleration of progress. Individual instruction allows the teacher to plan for the child's individual strengths and weaknesses with specific activities to correct problems. Acceleration is accomplished as the child develops skills and reading abilities at a more rapid pace than is possible with group instruction in the regular classroom. Daily, intensive instruction permits the teacher to closely monitor the child's responses and prompt the child accordingly (Clay, 1993).

The Benchmark Word Identification Program is another method designed to identify students who have difficulty in processing print (Gaskins, Gaskins, & Gaskins, 1991). Originally designed at Benchmark, a school for poor readers, the program focuses on helping poor students with poor reading skills develop word identification skills. One strategy used with beginning readers is to immerse them in a rich language environment compatible with whole-language strategies. In addition, students are instructed in methods that will lead to effective decoding of words using sight vocabulary, phonological awareness, and word analysis. In the beginning program for nonreaders who are up to the second-grade level, word identification activities previously described for the nonability-grouped, multilevel first-grade model (Cunningham, Hall, & DeFee, 1991) are used.

The programs just described are only two intervention programs that have been developed to correct early reading problems. Both incorpo-

rate whole-language strategies that are child centered along with intensive work in specific reading skills that will assist the child in being able to process written language. Both are designed to achieve quick results before the child has experienced extensive failure; both methods have been successful in enabling students to reverse their low achievement in beginning reading.

Success For All is a prevention program designed at the Johns Hopkins University's Center for Research on the Education of Students Placed at Risk (CRESPAR) (Slavin, 1996). Like the Reading Recovery program, it uses one-to-one tutoring. However, it is different in that it begins with children at age 5 and focuses on perceptual skills in addition to reading. The purpose of the program is to prevent students from getting behind by attending to intensive intervention before first grade. The program uses cooperative learning, a balanced reading program, and a strong parent involvement program. Success For All is funded by Chapter I funds and sometimes is supplemented with special education funds. The intention is to prevent children with potential disabilities from becoming candidates for special education programs in the primary grades.

Curriculum for Mathematics

When cognitive development in the preschool years was discussed in Chapter 8, concepts in mathematics and science were explained from a developmental perspective in terms of how the preoperational child learns. In this chapter, I will discuss mathematics and science as content areas approached with the child's development in mind.

Between the ages of 5 and 8, the child moves from the preoperational stage to the concrete operational stage of thinking. The child moves from thinking that is dominated by perceptual content to thinking that is logical, which allows them to use mental schema to make an operation that previously required concrete objects. Although the child needs concrete materials to understand new concepts, she no longer has to rely only on manipulating the objects; mental schema can also be used to classify, seriate, count, and perform other functions. In mathematics, this mental ability in the concrete operational stage is represented in conservation and reversibility. The ability to conserve and reverse operations allows the child to do mathematical problems using mental schema (Copley, 2000).

Curriculum in mathematics for children from age 5 to 8 reflects this progression from preoperational to concrete operational thinking. Curriculum for 5-year-olds is a continuation of the preschool curriculum. It is a continuum that becomes more complex as the child accumulates experience. The same categories are still used to organize the curriculum. Moreover, repeated experiences with concepts previously introduced are required for the child to be able to internalize and apply mathematical principles. If one looks at mathematical curriculum from a grade-level point of view, mathematical concepts are reviewed and practiced at each level before moving to more complex applications. Mathematics is a continuum, but it is also hierarchical and sequential: Complex concepts build on a foundation of prior concepts and skills. Thus, simple addition follows understanding of number, and more complex addition of several digits follows simple addition (National Council of Teachers of Mathematics [NCTM], 2000).

Trends and Issues in Mathematics

In recent decades the concern of mathematics specialists was that mathematics curriculum focused on basic skills that did not prepare students who would live and work in the twenty-first century. More specifically, they took the position that much of the emphasis on drill had become obsolete with the advent of calculators and computers. Their position was that workers of the future would need to be able to solve unconventional problems (Steen, 1990).

In 1989 the National Council of Teachers of Mathematics (NCTM) issued *Curriculum and Evaluation Standards for School Mathematics* which proposed dramatic changes in mathematics curriculum and instruction. The standards specify that mathematics instruction should involve hands-on experiences, calculators and computers, manipulatives, and cooperative learning groups. The curriculum should emphasize making connections between math topics, problem-solving, and communicating about mathematics (Willis, 1992). In 2000, NCTM issued *Principles and Standards for School Mathematics* (NCTM, 2000) to further improve curriculum and instruction in mathematics in the twenty-first century. The principles and standards reflected the new emphasis on diversity in learners, the growing importance of technology, and the continuing need to be able to use mathematics in everyday life and in the workplace. NCTM expressed the future needs for mathematics in a changing world to include the following (NCTM, 2000, p. 3):

- *Mathematics for life.* Knowing mathematics can be personally satisfying and empowering. The underpinnings of everyday life are increasingly mathematical and technological. For instance, making purchasing decisions, choosing insurance or a health plan, and voting knowledgeably all call for quantitative sophistication.
- *Mathematics as a part of cultural heritage.* Mathematics is one of the greatest cultural and intellectual achievements of humankind, and citizens should develop an appreciation and understanding of that achievement, including its aesthetic and even recreational aspects.
- *Mathematics for the workplace.* Just as the level of mathematics needed for intelligent citizenship has increased dramatically, so too has the level of mathematical thinking and problem solving needed in the workplace, in professional areas ranging from health care to graphic design.
- *Mathematics for the scientific and technical community.* Although all careers require a foundation of mathematical knowledge, some are mathematics intensive. More students must pursue an educational path that will prepare them for lifelong work as mathematicians, statisticians, engineers, and scientists.

Work of members of the mathematics education community reflects four themes related to mathematics and mathematical knowledge (Campbell, 1999, p. 107):

1. Mathematics is a growing, dynamic discipline.
2. Students actively construct mathematical knowledge.
3. Understanding in mathematics comes from perceiving relationships either between or within mathematical ideas.
4. Knowledge may be fostered through social interaction.

Like language development, acquisition of mathematical knowledge begins early in life and continues throughout preschool years and elementary, secondary, and higher education. Children learn mathematics in the preschool years through exploring their environment and through everyday experiences when they encounter mathematical concepts in daily life. Children enter kindergarten and the primary grades with different levels of mathematics understanding. Teachers need to acknowledge these differences in young children and plan experiences that will extend their individual foundations for further acquisition of mathematical concepts. These concepts will be developed at different times and different rates. To be successful, young students must have adequate time and opportunity to construct, test, and reflect on their growing understanding of mathematics (NCTM, 2000).

What, then, should children in kindergarten and the primary grades be taught in a balanced mathematics curriculum? The curriculum should include such topics as number sense, constructs of quantity to include counting and number operations, geometry, measurement, and data analysis or statistics, and abilities in problem-solving. They should be able to apply mathematical concepts and skills in finding solutions to real problems and situations (Campbell, 1999; NCTM, 2000).

In the next section, I present a mathematics program for children from age 5 to 8 which incorpo-

rates the principles and standards advocated by the NCTM. I will discuss a mathematics program that is appropriate for children in the primary grades and describe how the environment and teacher support curriculum and instruction. Next, I describe the organization of the mathematics program following NCTM Principles and Standards, including components of the curriculum. Finally, I present examples of activities that represent the new directions suggested in the NCTM Principles and Standards (NCTM, 2000).

Planning the Mathematics Program

Goals for the Mathematics Program.

> The mathematics program is designed to help children acquire and apply understanding of mathematics concepts and skills. Teachers plan for children to learn mathematical concepts through solving meaningful problems. Math skills and problem-solving are the focus of instruction and are also fostered through spontaneous play, projects, and situations of daily living. A variety of math manipulatives and games is provided and used to aid concept development and application of mathematics. Noncompetitive, oral "math-stumper" and number games are played for the practice. Math activities are integrated with other relevant projects, such as those in science and social studies. (Bredekamp & Copple, 1997, p. 173).

The developmentally appropriate mathematics curriculum for ages 5 to 8 just cited is from *Developmentally Appropriate Practice in Early Childhood Programs*. It describes a program that is child-centered and connected to real, problem-solving activities. Children are active participants in constructing math schema based on experiences that incorporate concrete to abstract thinking. Mathematical knowledge is reconstructed by experiencing and acting on objects in the environment and the process of reflection and, later, logical thinking (Kamii, 1982, 2000).

The key to a quality program in mathematics is to design experiences that bridge preoperational into concrete operational thinking. A present danger in kindergarten and the primary grades is that children are pushed into abstract functioning before they have the cognitive capacity. They are asked to use mental schema for operations in mathematics before they are able to do so. It is common to see children in primary classrooms counting on their fingers as they solve written addition problems. These students still require concrete referents for solving addition problems because they have not internalized the concepts of addition as a mental process. Children should be allowed to move at their own pace with concrete materials, followed by paper-and-pencil practice when they are ready (Charlesworth & Lind, 1990).

The goals for the mathematics program are based on both the child's cognitive development and the elements of mathematics that are part of the overall components recommended by the NCTM (2000). The goals of the mathematics program in kindergarten and the primary grades lead to competence in the larger goals of society and adult living in the next century.

The 10 standards are in the following categories:

1. Number and operations
2. Algebra
3. Geometry
4. Measurement
5. Data analysis and probability
6. Problem solving
7. Reasoning and proof
8. Communications
9. Connections
10. Representation

However, the standards for prekindergarten through second grade include the first five standards. More information on the standards and expectations for prekindergarten through second grade will be described later in the chapter.

The Role of the Environment and the Teacher

The classroom environment is organized so that children can investigate mathematics through many types of hands-on experiences. The arrangement must be conducive to individual, small-group, and whole-group activities. The areas designed for these types of activities in the language arts program are also suitable for the mathematics program. An important requirement is a work and play area for mathematics activities and materials. The mathematics area, sometimes combined with the science area, contains the many materials needed for investigation and practice of mathematical concepts.

The math center should be organized so that children can participate in different types of activities. Items such as objects for counting, construction materials, unifix cubes, and other multipurpose materials are accessible for ongoing use. Other materials are placed in the center for a particular unit of study or for thematic projects. For example, balance scales and objects to weigh and compare could be placed in a learning station during the study of measurement of weight. Books related to time and different types of clocks (wind-up clocks, digital clocks, sand timer, stove timer, etc.) could be organized in an area with specific problems suggested for investigation during a unit on measuring time.

Whereas kindergarten teachers may find the use of a mathematics center easy to coordinate with mathematics curriculum, primary teachers unfamiliar with using centers may have to systematically plan how to include concrete, real-life activities to work with concepts if the adopted basal program focuses on whole-group instruction and workbook practice. Hands-on activities using materials in the mathematics center should be developed to ensure experiences that will facilitate the child's construction of new concepts.

The teacher has a key role in developing the kind of mathematical experiences that will fulfill the goals of a quality mathematics program. Two basic considerations guide the learning experiences: the developmental characteristics of the students and inclusion of the new standards set forth by the NCTM (2000).

An understanding of the progressions of concrete to abstract, simple to complex, and experiencing to representing introduced in Chapter 6 is particularly useful when applied to mathematics instruction with students who are moving from preoperational to concrete operational thinking. Teachers will want to design activities that facilitate these progressions to accommodate the nature of the child's cognitive processes.

The teacher also has a responsibility to make decisions as to when to use systematic instruction and when informal, integrated, or real-life, meaningful activities are the most appropriate. Some of the curriculum and instruction that is planned will attend to the scope and sequence of instruction. The teacher will plan to introduce concepts that will build on concepts already acquired or lay the foundation for future units of work. Systematic, teacher-directed instruction to provide students with hands-on experiences with concepts will follow a sequential plan to make mathematical knowledge meaningful and logical.

In the primary grades, the teacher would consider how to include concrete activities before abstract practice within systematic instruction. For example, when learning place value, students can work with wooden cubes of different colors to represent tens and ones before moving to a flip book with pictured representations of place value and a pencil-and-paper exercise on place value.

Informal, practical experiences encourage the child to apply mathematical concepts when working with realistic problems. For example, children in a first-grade classroom using an adding machine or a calculator to add up purchases in a grocery store set up in the mathematics area would be learning real-life purposes for math. At the same time, they would be using technology used for mathematical problem-solving in today's world.

Integrated, thematic units would also provide opportunities for applying mathematical concepts for useful purposes. Kindergarten children could use measurement when following a simple recipe in a unit on cooking. In a unit on field games,

second-grade students could use a stop watch to measure the time individual students required to run a measured distance; then they could graph the time recorded.

In the next section, I will describe the components of mathematics for kindergarten and the primary grades; then I will present suggestions for activities that promote the development of mathematical concepts. The teacher can include these components when organizing systematic and informal instruction with students in a nongraded primary school or in a self-contained classroom serving students of a single grade or age.

The Role of Technology in the Mathematics Program

Calculators and computers are part of the young child's world. They are now a given resource in learning mathematics. Children should be introduced to these technological resources in the preschool years, and this equipment should be integrated into the mathematics curriculum for children from ages 5 to 8.

At age 5, children should learn the importance of calculators through free play and exploration. Dutton and Dutton (1991, p. 91) propose that 5-year-olds can also engage in the following:

1. Learn to display numbers 1 through 9 and clear the display after each entry.
2. Increase numbers such as 5 or 6 by adding 1 to each number.
3. Subtract by taking away one number from a previous number.
4. Begin to enter two-digit numbers—first 10, and then 10 and one more.

Thereafter, children should be able to extend their use of the calculator with whatever skills and concepts they have learned. Once children have learned how to use an operation, they can use the calculator to increase their speed and accuracy. Educators must also learn to use the calculator appropriately with children. It is a tool that can enhance mathematical abilities; however, it is not meant to replace the child's understanding of mathematical processes and how to apply them.

Computers also have an important role in the mathematics curriculum because every young child needs to become computer literate beginning at age 3 or 4. Computer software for teaching mathematics is being developed at a rapid rate. In addition to the materials being developed by commercial companies, the U.S. Department of Education helps schools learn about innovative programs through the National Diffusion Network (NDN) (Dutton & Dutton, 1991).

Seymour Papert has pioneered the use of computers in mathematical and language literacy with young children. Papert (1980) believes that children can become programmers and learn to communicate through computers. Using his background study at Piaget's Center for Genetic Epistemology in Geneva, Switzerland, Papert developed the LOGO computer language to enable children to communicate with computers. The use of the "Turtle" with LOGO enables children to use manipulation to give commands to the computer.

The National Science Foundation (NSF) advocated the use of computers in *Educating America for the 21st Century* (NSF, 1983). The NSF stated that children should learn through computers, learn with computers, and use computers to learn about computers. One of the themes of the NCTM Principles and Standards is technology. The NCTM (2000, p. 4) proposed: "Technology is essential in teaching and learning mathematics; it influences the mathematics that is taught and enhances students' learning.

Clements (1987) reviewed the efficacy of using computers with young children. Among his findings were that although computers can enhance learning, they are not a panacea; they have the same benefit as other valuable learning strategies and materials. Clements made two critical points about children using computers for mathematics and problem solving. He proposed that (1) children should understand concepts before they use computers for practice and (2) the teacher must

play an active role in mediating the child's interaction with the computer.

Another caution regards the selection of developmentally appropriate software for young children. Haugland and Shade (1988) found that much of the available software does not reflect a developmental approach to teaching and learning. Teachers should review and evaluate software carefully before using it with young children.

Calculators and computers are part of the future in mathematics instruction. Teachers of young children need to become competent in the use of these resources. In addition, they need training in how to incorporate these tools effectively in the mathematics program designed for young children.

Organizing the Mathematics Program

The mathematics program for kindergarten and the primary grades includes 5 of the 10 standards established by the NCTM introduced earlier. The standards are described using goals and expectations for grades pre-kindergarten through second grade. Figure 11.3 shows the standards and expectations.

It should be noted that expectations are described in a hierarchy of simple to more complex rather than divided by grade level. In some categories the expectations are sequential; that is, the first expectation must be understood or mastered before working on the next expectation. In other categories, the expectations can be engaged in simultaneously.

The mathematics program as described in Figure 11.3 is more of a guide to the hierarchical nature of mathematics than a prescriptive sequence that dictates what should be taught at an age or grade level. Teachers and children will progress through the curriculum based on the abilities and interests of the class. Moreover, in an ungraded or multilevel school organization pattern, children can work on the same objective at different age and ability levels through cooperative learning groups or paired student interactions. The teacher

Number and operations standard

Instructional programs from prekindergarten through grade 12 should enable all students to—	Expectations for grade pre-K–2 *In prekindergarten through grade 2 all students should—*
Understand numbers, ways of representing numbers, relationships among numbers, and number systems	• count with understanding and recognize "how many" in sets of objects • use multiple models to develop initial understandings of place value and the base-ten number system • develop understanding of the relative position and magnitude of whole numbers and of ordinal and cardinal numbers and their connections • develop a sense of whole numbers and represent and use them in flexible ways, including relating, composing, and decomposing numbers • connect number words and numerals to the quantities they represent, using various physical models and representations • understand and represent commonly used fractions, such as $\frac{1}{4}, \frac{1}{3},$ and $\frac{1}{2}$
Understand meanings of operations and how they relate to one another	• understand various meanings of addition and subtraction of whole numbers and the relationship between the two operations • understand the effects of adding and subtracting whole numbers • understand situations that entail multiplication and division, such as equal groupings of objects and sharing equally.
Compute fluently and make reasonable estimates	• develop and use strategies for whole-number computations, with a focus on addition and subtraction • develop fluency with basic number combinations for addition and subtraction • use a variety of methods and tools to compute, including objects, mental computation, estimation, paper and pencil, and calculators.

FIGURE 11.3 NCTM principles and standards prekindergarten through second grade
Source: From *Principles and Standards of School Mathematics,* (pp. 78, 90, 96, 102), National Council of Teachers of Mathematics, 2000, Reston, VA: NCTM. Copyright 2000 by NCTM. Used with permission.

Algebra standard

Instructional programs from prekindergarten through grade 12 should enable all students to—	Expectations for grades pre-K–2 *In prekindergarten through grade 2 all students should—*
Understand patterns, relations, and functions	• sort, classify, and order objects by size, number, and other properties • recognize, describe, and extend patterns such as sequences of sounds and shapes or simple numeric patterns and translate from one representation to another • analyze how both repeating and growing patterns are generated
Represent and analyze mathematical situations and structures using algebraic symbols	• illustrate general principles and properties of operations, such as commutativity, using specific numbers • use concrete, pictorial, and verbal representations to develop an understanding of invented and conventional symbolic notations
Use mathematical models to represent and understand quantitative relationships	• model situations that involve the addition and subtraction of whole numbers, using objects, pictures, and symbols
Analyze change in various contexts	• describe qualitative change, such as a student's growing taller; describe quantitative change, such as a student's growing two inches in one year

Geometry standard

Instructional programs from prekindergarten through grade 12 should enable all students to—	Expectations for grades pre-K–2 *In prekindergarten through grade 2 all students should—*
Analyze characteristics and properties of two- and three-dimensional geometric shapes and develop mathematical arguments about geometric relationships	• recognize, name, build, draw, compare, and sort two- and three-dimensional shapes • describe attributes and parts of two- and three-dimensional shapes • investigate and predict the results of putting together and taking apart two- and three-dimensional shapes
Specify locations and describe spatial relationships using coordinate geometry and other representational systems	• describe, name, and interpret relative positions in space and apply ideas about relative position • describe, name, and interpret direction and distance in navigating space and apply ideas about direction and distance • find and name locations with simple relationships such as "near to" and in coordinate systems such as maps
Apply transformations and use symmetry to analyze mathematical situations	• recognize and apply slides, flips, and turns • recognize and create shapes that have symmetry

FIGURE 11.3 *(continued)*

Geometry standard *(continued)*

Use visualization, spatial reasoning, and geometric modeling to solve problems	• create mental images of geometric shapes using spatial memory and spatial visualization • recognize and represent shapes from different perspectives • relate ideas in geometry to ideas in number and measurement • recognize geometric shapes and structures in the environment and specify their location

Measurement standard

Instructional programs from prekindergarten through grade 12 should enable all students to—	**Expectations for grades pre-K–2** *In prekindergarten through grade 2 all students should—*
Understand measurable attributes of objects and the units, systems, and processes of measurement	• recognize the attributes of length, volume, weight, area, and time • compare and order objects according to these attributes • understand how to measure using nonstandard and standard units • select an appropriate unit and tool for the attribute being measured
Apply appropriate techniques, tools, and formulas to determine measurements	• measure with multiple copies of units of the same size, such as paper clips laid end to end • use repetition of a single unit to measure something larger than the unit, for instance, measuring the length of a room with a single meterstick • use tools to measure • develop common referents for measures to make comparisons and estimates

Data analysis and probability standard

Instructional programs from prekindergarten through grade 12 should enable all students to—	**Expectations for grades pre-K–2** *In prekindergarten through grade 2 all students should—*
Formulate questions that can be addressed with data and collect, organize, and display relevant data to answer them	• pose questions and gather data about themselves and their surroundings • sort and classify objects according to their attributes and organize data about the objects • represent data using concrete objects, pictures, and graphs
Select and use appropriate statistical methods to analyze data	• describe parts of the data and the set of data as a whole to determine what the data show
Develop and evaluate inferences and predictions that are based on data	• discuss events related to students' experiences as likely or unlikely
Understand and apply basic concepts of probability	

needs to understand the nature of the scope and sequence of the curriculum, however, so that planning for systematic and informal, integrated curriculum will include the content and types of experiences students will need to meet the NCTM standards.

 ## A Project to Collect and Represent Mathematical Data

Two university professors and a third grade teacher engaged in a project with third grade students to help them learn how to ask mathematical questions, collect data, and then represent their findings. The students had to learn how to ask appropriate questions, how to collect data, and how to chart their findings. After learning that teacher-designed questions were uninteresting to the students, the teachers brainstormed with the children on things they wondered about at school or in the surrounding community. After many discussions, and listing of question ideas, the class pursued the question: "How many kids choose 2%, chocolate, whole, or skim milk for lunch?" The class divided itself into groups and pursued different ways to collect the data. One group counted each type milk as children moved through the lunch line while another group went to each classroom and had children raise their hands as to their choice of type of milk.

A major challenge was analyzing and reporting data. The students were working with very large numbers and had to learn how to use 10s and 20s to graph their findings. Some students used calculators to finalize and graph their numbers. The teachers learned that their students were capable of initiating and conducting their investigations with assistance, rather than direction from the teachers. (Hutchison, Ellsworth, & Yovich, 2000) ✦

Designing Curriculum for the Mathematics Program

When designing curriculum for kindergarten and primary classrooms, the teacher considers whether the activity will be a part of a teacher-directed lesson, a center opportunity, an assignment for a cooperative learning group, a whole-class investigation, or a game to be selected by a pair or small group of learners. The activities that follow are only a small representative example of some of the activities a teacher can design for young students. The activities are drawn from different components of the curriculum for different levels of complexity. Because some of the activities can be adapted for either more complexity or more simplicity, they are not identified by age or grade level.

Experiences That Promote Mathematics

Counting Games

Math Component: Number and Numeration

Description: Children can make games for game boards. Introduce children to a game that involves a spinner and numbered cards in a deck. Discuss how counting is used to play the game and determine the winner. Solicit suggestions for different themes that could be used for a counting game, as well as what will be needed for the game. Have pairs of students or cooperative groups come up with a game idea, make the game, and play it several times. Laminate the games to be put into the mathematics center.

Materials Needed: Large sheets of paper or tagboard, marking pens, spinners or cards, game pieces

Domino Doubles Addition

Math Component: Operations of Whole Numbers

Description: Teach the children how to play a simple version of dominoes, where they draw the dominoes and take turns attempting to make matches of number patterns. When they are able to make a match, have them make a larger set using the combined numbers with counting objects.

Materials Needed: Dominoes, objects for making sets

Numeral Treasure Hunt

Math Component: Number and Numeration

Description: Divide the class into cooperative groups. Discuss how they can search for examples of numerals around the school and outdoors. Have each group tour the school environment and record as many examples of numerals as they can during a 15-minute period. When the activity has been completed, have each group report the numerals they found. The group with the most examples is the winner of the activity. Discuss why the numerals were needed in each example.

Materials Needed: Pencils and notepads to record data

Number Bingo

Math Component: Number and Numeration

Description: Make assorted bingo cards with sixteen numerals ranging from 1 to 20 or higher. Use a set of cards with dots corresponding to all of the possible numerals on the cards. The game is played by having the students in a small group take turns drawing a card. They must determine which numeral matches their card and whether they have that numeral on their bingo card. The first player to make a horizontal or vertical line is the winner.

Materials Needed: Numbered Bingo cards

Odd and Even

Math Component: Rational Numbers

Description: Give pairs of students a small handful of counters, such as beans or poker chips. The goal of the activity is for the students to decide whether they have an odd or even number of objects. Ask the students to divide the objects between them. Then ask them to report whether they have an odd number or even number of items and justify why they came to the answer. They should be able to respond based on whether they have the same or different numbers of items.

Materials Needed: Counting objects

Container Multiplication

Math Component: Operations of Whole Numbers

Description: Collect a group of containers such as berry baskets or juice cans and counting objects such as sticks, crayons, cubes, or other objects. Select up to five cans. Ask a child to put the same number of items in each can, either two or three items. Demonstrate how the child can add the number of items in each can to get a total or multiply them to get the same total. For example, if four containers are used and three counters are put in the can, the child can add 3 plus 3 plus 3 plus 3 equals 12 or can multiply 4 times 3 equals 12. Repeat the activity several times using different combinations. Let the children make the addition and multiplication sentence for each combination. The activity can be made either simple or complex, depending on the abilities and experiences of the students.

Materials Needed: Containers such as berry baskets or juice cans, counting objects

Egg Carton Division

Math Component: Operations of Whole Numbers

Description: Use egg cartons with a dozen plastic eggs. The students will divide the eggs into equivalent groups and determine the appropriate division sentence. For example, the students might be asked to make the eggs into groups of three, four, or six. Ask them to determine how many groups of each total twelve. Demonstrate how a division expression can be written to describe the number of smaller sets in twelve. For example, 12 divided by 3 equals 4 and so on.

Materials Needed: Egg cartons; plastic eggs for each carton

Sand Buckets

Math Component: Measuring

Description: Have students put varying amounts of sand in sand pails or other containers. Use measuring cups to measure how many cups of sand are in each container. Have the children measure fractions of a cup to the nearest half cup. As a follow-up, have the students graph the measured amounts.

Materials Needed: Sand buckets or other containers, measuring cups, pencils, paper, sand

Sorting Solid Shapes

Math Components: Geometry, Problem-Solving

Description: Give students an array of solid shapes. Ask them to sort the shapes by some attribute. Have the students compare individual sorting criteria. Ask them to identify how the solid shapes are used for practical purposes in the environment.

Materials Needed: Enough solid shapes for several children to have at least five

Shape Symmetry

Math Components: Shapes, Symmetry

Description: Give the students an array of two-dimensional shapes cut from paper, or have them trace a variety of common shapes, triangles, squares, circles rectangles, ovals, and so on. Ask the students to fold the shapes in half so that each shape has two equal sides. Define the term *symmetrical,* and ask the students to explain how their shapes are symmetrical. As a follow-up activity, ask the students to think of things in the environment that are symmetrical (e.g., butterflies, the human body, books).

Materials Needed: Paper shapes, scissors

Shape Fractions

Math Components: Shapes, Rational Numbers

Description: Use the same shapes as for the previous activity. Have the students determine how the shape has been divided into two equal parts, or into halves. Introduce the fraction one-half. Have the students divide the shapes once again so that there are four parts. Discuss the fraction one-quarter. Ask the students to show you one-half of the shape and one-quarter of the shape.

Materials Needed: Paper shapes, scissors

Accommodating Learning Differences Among Students

Special attention has been given to the need for curriculum and instruction that is appropriate in mathematics, especially in ensuring that learning experiences include the progression from concrete to abstract. This is especially relevant when working with children who are developmentally delayed or have cognitive-ability disabilities. Children who are delayed will not have made the transition from preoperational into concrete operational thinking. As a result, the teacher will need to assess the child's developmental status and design curriculum experiences based on development rather than on chronological grade or age.

Another difficulty children encounter occurs when asked to apply a concept without first having developed the necessary understanding of the concept. This can happen whether or not students have a learning disability. Students may be taught how to execute a mathematical operation without acquiring the underlying concept. The result is that when the child needs to use the concept in a real-life situation, problem-solving strategies cannot be applied to the concept. For example, a student may have learned the mechanics of simple division and completed many practice exercises. However, when asked how many loaves of bread can be purchased for $3.00, the child does not understand how division can be used to find the answer.

Children with learning differences may have difficulties in processing or expressing information about mathematics. Young children may have difficulty in expressing their mathematical understanding verbally because they lack the expressive vocabulary to describe the mathematical knowledge. Children whose first language is not English or who are otherwise limited in the ability to speak English may experience frustration when asked to use verbal responses. They need to have nonverbal opportunities to point to or manipulate objects to express their ability to use a concept.

A child may lack the motor skills to perform paper-and-pencil tasks to express mathematical knowledge or skills. The child may be delayed in fine motor skills or have difficulty with reversals. Instead of concluding that the child is unable to understand the mathematical process being studied, the teacher needs to determine whether the written expression required is causing the child's difficulty in responding appropriately.

Some young children experience receptive problems; that is, they cannot understand oral discussions of a concept or have difficulty in attending to printed information. Children may have difficulty discriminating between figure and ground on the printed page, which results in difficulty attending to and interpreting visual information.

Many children who experience receptive and expressive difficulties in mathematics will overcome the problem over time. They have a temporary delay that normal development will eliminate. For other young children, the difficulty is more permanent. The teacher will need to be alert to the child's learning differences and find alternative avenues to facilitate the child's ability to acquire mathematical concepts and express understanding.

Curriculum for Science

The science curriculum for children ages 5 to 8 continues to build on the experiences children had in the preschool years. Unlike mathematics, which has sequential characteristics, science is holistic in nature. Children are continually encountering information about the work and adding to their schema, or store of knowledge. Children's natural interest and curiosity make them avid explorers of scientific phenomena during these years.

How Young Children Learn About Science

The science curriculum can be predominantly child-centered and child-initiated because knowledge is acquired best through firsthand investigation and experimentation. A requirement for preoperational and concrete operational thinking, an understanding of science should be approached from hands-on study at all ages. The nature of the child's thinking in each of these stages has implications for how the science program is planned.

Preoperational children of ages 5 and 6 learn about science within their cognitive limitations. Because they cannot mentally reason about concepts, they must carry out actions to understand their importance. But even with concrete actions, their perceptions limit their understanding. For example, even though a preoperational child can pour a container of liquid into vessels of two different shapes, she is influenced by the appearance of a change in quantity and does not understand that the quantity remains the same. Children at this stage are also affected by their level of egocentricity. They focus on their own view of events and can address only one aspect of a situation at a time.

Five- and 6-year-olds cannot anticipate results or consequences of future actions. This limits their ability to predict what they have not yet experienced. The question, "What do you think might happen if . . . ?" is very difficult for them to grasp. Likewise, this limitation makes if difficult for children to link cause and effect or see a pattern in a series of events. The science curriculum for preoperational children should be composed of firsthand experience and exploration of objects.

As children make the transition from preoperational to concrete operational thinking, they can use thought instead of, or in addition to, action to approach their understanding of science. They can grasp the entirety of a process, as well as the individual parts or steps. They are able to understand how more than one variable or characteristic of a phenomenon can affect an outcome. They begin to understand another person's viewpoint or physical perspective of an event or object. Because the transition to concrete operational thinking is gradual, the ability to use rational thinking is first possible with familiar concepts and information. The more complex a problem or situation, the less likely it is that the child will be able to use rational thinking to reach a solution. Physical manipulation of the information will be needed.

Children in the primary grades also bring developing literacy and social skills to the science curriculum. They can use numbers and written words to express their reflections on science investigations. They can extend their period of work and collaborate with their peers in taking turns, making predictions, and discussing their findings.

In Chapter 8, I discussed the cognitive limitations in preschool children that might prevent

them from fully exploring and investigating science concepts. They would not be able to act on cognitive conflict without the teacher to facilitate or scaffold their thinking.

Primary-grade children are emerging from these cognitive limitations, but still need guidance and support when learning science concepts. The science program should include components of quality early childhood programs discussed in earlier chapters to include:

1. Children learn science concepts through active involvement with science phenomena that include exploration, investigation, reflection, and representation.
2. Children learn science concepts in a social milieu. While observing and working with other children in learning centers, cooperative groups, and paired activities, children exchange ideas, engage in science projects, and discuss their findings.
3. Children learn concepts with the teacher as a partner. The teacher scaffolds and facilitates the direction of science experiences and guides children in reaching higher levels of understanding and problem solving.

Trends and Issues in Science

Concern about the low quality of science curriculum in American schools has been expressed for many years. The criticism about poor science instruction includes comments about elementary school science programs. Numerous reports on science education described the curriculum used in the 1980s to be obsolete. Allan Bromley, science adviser to President George Bush declared, "In a great many cases, precollege education in the past decade has been literally perpetuating a fraud on the younger generation" (Bromley, 1989, p. 203).

Bromley's observation was supported by the 1986 study of school science conducted by the NAEP (Mullis & Jenkins, 1988). Not only did American students perform more poorly than students from other countries, but girls lagged behind boys, and African American and Hispanic students' performance was lower than that of their white peers.

The poor quality of science instruction at the elementary level had been reported earlier. Dueschl (1983) reported that science instruction at the elementary level was infrequent and ineffective. Causes of poor science instruction had been attributed by elementary teachers to inadequate background in science, inadequate time and space, and inadequate science equipment (Hove, 1970); researchers in the late 1980s felt little had changed since these conditions were reported (Tilgner, 1990).

In 1987, the National Science Teachers Association (NSTA) developed criteria for excellence that addressed the requirements for a quality science program for students, curriculum, instruction, and teachers in kindergarten through third grade.

In 1995 the association published new standards, *National Science Education Standards* (NSTA, 1995) with the goal of improving science education for all students. The content standards included the following categories:

Content as Inquiry

Physical Science

Life Science

Earth and Space Science

Science and Technology

Science in Personal and Social Perspectives

History of Science

Unifying Concepts and Processes

The National Science Foundation (NSF) funded an effort to reform science education in U.S. elementary and secondary schools. Project 2061 suggests doing four common themes—materials, energy, information, and systems—that are introduced in kindergarten and studied throughout the school years (Tilgner, 1990). This project and other efforts to improve science curriculum seek to meet the criteria of an exemplary science program proposed by the NSTA. In 2001, Project 2061 and NSTA published an update to Project 2061, *Atlas of Science Literacy* (Project 2061 & NSTA, 2001). The atlas describes connections among the learning goals for Project 2061.

A given in science education reform is the use of hands-on activities. Inquiry-based, hands-on instruction is considered to be an effective way for young students to learn (Sivertsen, 1993). However, educators have different rationales and interpretations of hands-on activities. A project for science educators to investigate how reform is translated into practice defines science teaching as hands-on instruction. Nine science educators in the project defined a hands-on, inquiry-based curriculum as follows:

- The curriculum focuses on student understanding of science concepts and processes, rather than memorization of facts.
- Students learn to "do" science using science process skills.
- Instruction is experience-based; students are regularly engaged in hands-on activities and exploration (Penta, Mitchell, & Franklin, 1993, cited by Vesilind & Jones, 1996, p. 378).

Planning the Science Program

Goals for the Science Program

The main goal for the science program for children ages 5 to 8 is to help children understand the world around them. To accomplish this major goal, three subgoals should be met: children should understand the ideas or concepts of science; they should acquire science process skills; and they should establish certain attitudes about science. Some of the experiences that nurture acquisition of science concepts include the following (Rakow & Bell, 1998, pp. 165–166):

1. Children are encouraged to work together to identify and solve relevant problems, rather than passively and individually acquiring arbitrary information.

2. Children have ready access to a wide variety of equipment and materials that allow them to interact with the natural world of their backyards, neighborhoods and communities.
3. An inquiry approach to science teaching places investigations at the center of the science program. Students learn through their own investigations about the natural world.

The way in which children learn about their world involves the use of the science process, including observing, classifying and comparing, measuring, communicating, experimenting, and relating, inferring, or applying. In Chapter 8, I described the science process in terms of preschool experiences. In this chapter, I will discuss the process in terms of curriculum for 5- to 8-year-old children.

Incorporating the Science Process

The science program for young children is designed around the science process. Whether students are engaging in a single experience or conducting a series of experiences for a broader topic, some or all of the process skills may be applied. Figure 11.4 explains the process skills as they apply to kindergarten and primary-grade children.

One example of a science activity is a nature walk to observe plants. Two science processes that children will use are observing and communicating. On the walk, the students will use observation skills to explore the variety of plants in the immediate environment. On returning to the classroom, they can communicate their thoughts on their observations by discussing, drawing pictures, or writing about their findings.

A longer project to study seeds can incorporate more process skills. Students can classify types of seeds and plants and observe progress of growth. They can predict which seeds will have the largest plants, measure plant growth and control variables by varying the amount of moisture and light that plants will receive, and observe the effect on the plants. Teacher and students should consciously plan to use science process skills and actively think about the components of the process as they are incorporated into science curriculum experiences.

The Role of the Environment

A quality science program requires a large amount of storage space. The classroom science center will need to have adequate space for small groups and individuals to be able to conduct investigations and other science activities. The center will need to have a number of locations where materials can be stored. Table-tops, bulletin boards, and storage cabinet surfaces will be needed for exhibits, projects that are in progress, and permanent components of the science program, such as pets, terraria, aquaria, and insect cages. Not to be forgotten are the essential elements needed for science activities: natural light, a source of water, electricity, and reference materials.

Rotating science materials will be a frequent task for the teacher and students. As materials are brought to the classroom, they are made available for examination and exploration. When work is completed for a thematic unit, materials and equipment that are no longer needed are returned to storage to be replaced by items needed for new topics of study.

With the various types of activities that may be occurring at the same time, careful planning is necessary for traffic flow and management of different types of activities. Display areas should be separated from working areas. Storage facilities should be located in an area that is accessible for the appropriate activities.

The science center requires a management plan. Hands-on activities will require that students know how to use science equipment and materials safely. Procedures for conducting investigations and appropriate behaviors to use when working in the center should be clearly understood

Scientific Processes for Young Children	
Observing:	Using the senses (seeing, hearing, touching, tasting, smelling) to learn about the characteristics of the environment
Comparing:	Measuring, counting, quantifying, and / or examining objects and events in terms of similarities and differences
Classifying:	Grouping and sorting according to properties, such as size, shape, color, and use
Measuring:	Quantitative descriptions made either directly, through observation, or indirectly, with a unit of measure
Communicating:	Naming, recording, and sharing observations and findings, orally or in written form (e.g., pictures, maps, graphs or journals), so others can understand what was learned.

FIGURE 11.4 Scientific processes for young children
Source: From "Making the Connections: Science and Literacy," By K. Barclay, C. Benelli, and S. Schoon, 1999, *Childhood Education,* 75, p.147. Copyright 1999 by *Childhood Education.* Reprinted with permission.

and observed by the students. Planned activities should be reviewed to determine whether they can be conducted independently or whether adult guidance or supervision is required.

The teacher will need additional storage beyond what is available in the center. If the teacher is fortunate enough to have a storage closet, materials and equipment should be organized and stored in clearly labeled containers inside. A school resource area may be available at many sites, but teachers frequently find themselves transporting needed items back and forth from home when space for storage is not available at school.

Teachers will also need to plan to acquire materials needed for classroom science activities. Much of the permanent equipment will be supplied by the school as part of classroom resources. Materials can also be salvaged from home and recycled for the classroom. Parents frequently are helpful in locating free and low-cost materials. If newsletters are sent home well ahead of implementation of science activities, parents can save and send items needed by the teacher.

Not to be overlooked is the outdoor environment as a natural resource for science experiences. Many investigations can easily be transported outdoors, where there is room to move about. Of course, some activities should be conducted outdoors only. Many times, commercial resources present science activities in an artificial format; such activities could be better learned by going outside and experiencing things firsthand. For example, a lesson on different types of clouds accompanied by pictures is a poor substitute for observing clouds over a period of days or weeks until all types of clouds have been observed.

The Role of the Teacher

The teacher is actively involved as a guide, respondent, and facilitator in carrying out the science curriculum. When children are engaged in observation, investigation, and experimentation, the teacher observes and questions as the children conduct the activity. As observer, the teacher determines when children need additional resources or would benefit from responding to careful questioning. A primary responsibility for the teacher is to observe and record the evolution of student thinking. Teachers can organize science instruction using a "play-debrief-replay." strategy to fulfill the teaching role (Wassermann, 2000).

In the first part of the strategy—play—the teacher designs an experiences whereby students study a concept in a cooperative learning group. The group members are "players" in the active, investigative work. The teacher's role is to observe, rather than participate or direct.

During the second part of the strategy, debriefing, the teacher helps the children reflect on their investigation activities and better understand the ideas they were exploring. The debrief period is an opportunity for the teacher to provide scaffolding information to help children make sense of their activities and findings. The teacher can use questioning strategies to help students address discrepancies in their thinking and move toward new insights and understandings. The teacher might ask (Wassermann, 2000, p. 30):

What observations did you make?

How did you know that?

How did you figure that out?

How did you get that to work?

The last phase of the play-debrief-replay strategy is replay. Over the next few days children can engage in repetition of the investigation. New materials might be used. Replay provides practice with the concept where findings can be replicated or the investigation can move into a new direction.

The teacher also needs to anticipate the kind of time and grouping that is required for science activities. At times, children should pursue their own interests individually; at other times, a cooperative group effort will enhance learning opportunities. Before whole-class or teacher-directed activities, the teacher will want to plan demonstrations or otherwise prepare students for a science activity. The teacher needs to be aware of which process skills will facilitate students in acquiring knowledge from activities and must guide them accordingly on how to use the skills in the procedures they will follow. If rules or policies need to be established, the teacher needs to make sure that the children understand how to proceed before the activity begins.

Organizing the Science Program

Components of the Science Program

The world of science offers unlimited possibilities for organizing the science program. In the large field of biological and physical sciences, the teacher and students have many interesting topics from which to select. Science topics should be selected from the ideas in which students are most interested. There needs to be a balance between biological and physical sciences, because children tend to be more interested in biological topics (Seefeldt & Barbour, 1994).

The content standards of the *National Science Education Standards* (1995) provide a framework for components of a science program that is appropriate for kindergarten and primary grade children (Rakow & Bell, 1998, pp. 166–167):

Physical Science
  Properties of objects and materials
  Position and motion of objects
  Light, heat, electricity and magnetism
Life Science
  The characteristics of organisms
  Life cycles of organisms
  Organisms and environments
Science and Technology

It should be obvious that the possibilities for selecting topics and organizing the science program are open-ended. The important consideration is that the science program be structured in such a way that the children are empowered through hands-on child-directed experiences to be active learners along with the teacher. Equally important is the nature of local or regional science opportunities that occur as a result of climate and geography. Children will be more interested in science experiences that directly relate to where they live. Lindberg summarized the ultimate goal as "students experiencing the process of science while they sought to answer questions *they* wanted to know the answers to, discovering in the process that science was something you do" (Lindberg, 1990, p. 80).

Designing Curriculum for the Science Program

The science curriculum just described is organized as a content area; that is, the activities are focused on the teaching of science concepts. Various types of activities from other content areas may be included in the range of experiences, but the predominant focus is on learning science.

A significant alternative method is to design the curriculum within thematic topics, where all content areas are equally important to the exploration, and knowledge is derived from the thematic experiences. Science concepts are learned within the larger context of the unit theme. Growth in all content areas through integrated, thematic experiences is the major goal of the curriculum. Through this process, the child comes to understand the connections in learning and the holistic nature of learning about the world.

The curriculum activities presented next reflect these two approaches. The first section includes individual activities that can be used with any age group from 5 to 8. We will explain a variety of interesting activities from science topics. The second section of science curriculum will be representative of science integrated with other content areas. We will describe examples of science units that are based on a theme or special topic in science.

Experiences That Promote Science

Dried Apples

Science Topic: Plants

Science Processes Used: Observation, predicting, communicating, and inferring

Description: Have students peel apples with a potato peeler, remove the core, and slice the apples. String the slices in bright sunlight and observe them over a period of time as they dry. When the children sample dry apple slices, have them slice a fresh apple and compare them for color, texture, and taste.

Materials Needed: Apples, potato peelers, knives, string (Barufaldi, Ladd, & Moses, 1984)

Comparing Seeds

Science Topic: Plants

Science Processes Used: Predicting, classifying, and inferring

Description: Collect a variety of fruits, such as apples, pears, peaches, cherries, melons, and strawberries. Cut open the fruit, and have the children locate and describe the seeds. Have them compare the number and type of seeds and where they are located on or in the fruit.

Materials Needed: Fruits of several types, knives, paper plates or paper towels

Seed Collections

Science Topic: Plants

Science Processes Used: Collecting data, classifying, and communicating

Description: Take a nature walk in the fall to collect seeds. Give each child a shopping bag, and have the children collect as many different seeds as they can find. Have the children work in small groups to compare the types of seeds they found for similarities and differences. Combine all of the seeds in each group, and ask the children to group the seeds from each type of plant together. Let each pick a seed to describe. As an extension of the activity, children could count and graph the number of seeds they found for six or seven types of seeds.

Materials Needed: Shopping bags, large paper, marking pens for graphing

Bug Models

Science Topic: Animals (insects)

Science Processes Used: Observing, identifying, and communicating

Description: Use collected insects to encourage children to make model representations. Let the children examine the insects in an insect cage or small jar. Provide magnifying glasses for examination of the insect's body parts. Encourage the children to make a model of the insect using play dough and scrap materials. Upon completion, the children can explain their model or write about the insect and their model.

Materials Needed: Play dough, scrap materials, insects, paper, and pencils (Westley, 1988)

Bark Rubbings

Science Topic: Plants

Science Processes Used: Observing and communicating

Description: Following a discussion about trees, tree parts, and the characteristics of bark, take children out to observe the bark of different trees. Give each child a large piece of paper and a large beginner's crayon. Have the child choose the tree for a rubbing. Attach the paper to the tree and show the child how to use the side of the crayon to make the rubbing. Children can compare the completed drawings and discuss the comparisons of the trees.

Materials Needed: Large sheets of paper, wax crayons (Richards, 1989)

Watching Shadows

Science Topic: Light and Shadows

Science Processes Used: Observing, experimenting, and inferring

Description: Children are interested in shadows. They can trace the movement of the

sun and earth and describe the way shadows are affected. Take them out several times during a sunny day, and let them compare the size and directions of the shadows. Let them experiment with different objects and the shadows they can make.

Materials Needed: None

Making Shadows

Science Topic: Light and Shadows

Science Processes Used: Observing, experimenting, and inferring

Description: Children can experiment with shadows indoors. Project a strong light on a white wall or newsprint. Encourage the children to experiment with the shadows they can make with their bodies. Encourage them to make puppets out of paper taped to a Popsicle stick or attached to their fingers. Show the children how to vary the types of shadows they can make by varying the distance between the light and the wall.

Materials Needed: Light, white surface on a wall, paper, scissors, tape, Popsicle sticks

Introduction to Magnets

Science Topic: Magnets

Science Processes Used: Observing, experimenting, and inferring

Description: Give each child a magnet. Place a collection of small objects, both metal and nonmetal, on the table. Let the children experiment with the objects that are attracted to the magnet. Have the children sort the objects into two piles: those that are attracted by the magnet and those that are not attracted by the magnet. Encourage the children to hypothesize why objects are attracted to a magnet.

Materials needed: Magnets, small classroom objects

Integrated Experiences That Promote Science

The science activities described in the previous section can be meaningful in themselves or used as part of a series of activities to explore a broader concept. Science is meaningful in a more comprehensive manner when experiences are correlated with other content areas. Moreover, science can be a starting point for cross-disciplinary curriculum. Science is excellent as the core of integrated curriculum because children love science as a content area, it lends itself to involvement and hands-on activities, and all subject areas are enhanced by the thinking skills used with the science processes. Figure 11.5 illustrates how Mechling and Kepler (1991) charted science process skills used across the curriculum.

A unit of studying the September harvest moon demonstrates how a science topic can be the focus of a unit that integrates science across the curriculum. Students observe the cycle of one new moon to another during the period of one month. They observe and sketch the moon each night to record its phases. In a second activity, the students compare the sizes of the rising full moon with its appearance higher in the sky by tracing the moon on a paper held up to a window.

PROCESS SKILLS ACROSS THE CURRICULUM
Read left to right and see how process skills are used across the curriculum.

Science	Reading	Math	Social Science
Classifying	Comparing and contrasting characteristics	Sorting, sequencing	Comparing ideas
Collecting data	Taking notes	Collecting data	Collecting data
Interpreting data	Organizing facts, recognizing cause and effect	Analyzing	Interpreting data
Communicating results	Logically arranging information	Graphing, constructing tables	Making maps
Predicting	Predicting	Predicting	Predicting

FIGURE 11.5 Integrating science process skills
Source: From *Instructor*, March 1991 issue. Copyright © 1991 by Scholastic Inc. Reprinted by permission of Scholastic, Inc.

To extend the understanding of the significance of the moon, for social studies, students can study historical lore connecting the phases of the moon to weather changes; for art they can conduct a nighttime art project by the light of the moon; and for math they can compare how the moon's different gravitational force would affect the weight of objects. These are only some of the many activities that can be designed to make a study of the moon more interesting and informative (Kepler, 1991).

Integrating Curriculum in Language Arts, Mathematics, and Science

There are many ways to integrate learning across the curriculum. The most frequently discussed model in this text is the integrated, thematic unit.

It is also possible to integrate curriculum outside of developing a theme of study.

A motivating way to encourage emerging writers is to integrate art and literacy. Olshansky (1995) described an art project used with first-grade children. The project, Image-Making Within the Writing Process, combines expression through art materials with writing of imaginative stories. Children are first asked to create a personal portfolio of hand-painted, textured papers. Using a variety of art materials, the children paint, make collages, and use other strategies to create textured papers. The next step is to encourage the children to find images in the papers that can lead to an imaginative story idea. Identifying a visual image helps the children to use colorful language in their story. A study of the project found that stories written and illustrated by the young authors contained a fuller expression of ideas compared to other stories without the art component.

A natural integration process is science and mathematics. *Integrating Mathematics and Science for Kindergarten and Primary Children* (Kellough, 1996) provides a wealth of information on how integration can be achieved. An example of such integration is a series of three activities on water evaporation. The three activities, Why Does Water Appear to Disappear?, Measuring Needless Waste of Water, and Make Your Own Water Cycle, engage children in the scientific process in completing the activities to answer their questions or hypotheses. Figure 11.6 shows the three integrated activities in their entirety.

An integrated unit designed for first grade originated with children's literature. *If You Give a Mouse a Cookie*, by Laura Joffe Numeroff, was used as the focus for a unit on mice. As part of the science content, students observed and measured a mouse. They wrote their own mouse stories for a book in language arts and discussed the kinds of food that mice like to eat. Many of the activities designed for the unit integrated several areas of the

curriculum. The Summary of Activities section of their unit, presented next, gives a description of the Activities. (See Appendix C for the complete unit and lesson plans.) An added section of each lesson plan is labeled Adaptations. Under this section, the planner determined what adaptations would be needed for children who were diverse in development or ability.

Summary of Activities

1. *Mouse observation.* Both language arts and science are integrated in this activity of observing a real mouse. Children will use the language arts skills of listening and answering questions, along with following directions. Science will be experienced through observing the different characteristics of the mouse and classifying differences and similarities between a real mouse and a fictional one.

2. *Mice puppets.* Integration of language arts, social studies, and art can be experienced through this activity of creating mice puppets. The chil-

dren will use their language arts skills of listening and following directions. Social studies will be represented through cooperation and sharing by the children. The art activity will include drawing and coloring the mice and gluing them to paper bags. Theater arts can be incorporated through play acting *If You Give a Mouse a Cookie*.

3. *Mouse shapes and sizes.* This activity integrates art, math, science, and language arts. The art activity involves drawing different sizes and shapes of mice. Students use math when they measure the different mice and compare them with real mice. Science is incorporated through measuring and predicting.

4. *Mouse story.* This activity involves dictating a mouse story to the teacher and drawing pictures to illustrate the story. It integrates language arts and fine arts

5. *Mouse party.* This activity integrates health and physical education, social studies, music, and mathematics. Nutrition is studied through the different foods brought to the mouse party. Movement and music are experienced as children sign and dance to mouse songs. Art is involved in making the costumes and decorations for the party. Social studies is incorporated through a discussion of proper party manners, and math is integrated when measuring different ingredients for the mouse food.

Summary

This chapter described the curriculum in language arts, mathematics, and science suitable for children ages 5 to 8. At these ages, children are in a transitional period; the curriculum also undergoes a transition. Children are making the transition from the preoperational period to the concrete operational period in the later early childhood years. They are also making a transition from preschool into elementary school. The curriculum is transitional in language arts, as literacy becomes well established in most children by the time they are 8 years old and in the third grade. Mathematics and science curricula also are designed to complement the emerging literacy and cognitive abilities of the children.

Although acquisition of literacy is a major accomplishment during this period, children also continue to add to and refine their ability to speak. Oral language development is important in continuing the language foundation needed to acquire and use concepts and apply them to written language. Therefore, the curriculum in kindergarten and primary grades includes emphasis on oral language development.

Children who have special language needs particularly need attention to language development. Whether they are speakers of a dialect or speakers of another language, they need abundant opportunities to add Standard English to their speaking vocabulary. These children need to interact with peers who are skilled speakers of English. Through social and instructional contexts, they benefit from opportunities to listen and speak throughout the day. Group discussions, projects, teacher-led lessons, and working periods in learning centers all afford children from various language backgrounds opportunities to speak about things based on common interests.

The process of emerging literacy continues within each child. Some will progress more rapidly than others, depending on the type of home environment and the available preschool experiences. The emergent literacy or whole-language activities used in the preschool continue in kindergarten. As children approach the stage where the ability to interpret written language from books becomes a reality, teachers must make decisions about the role of phonics and beginning reading skills in their reading program. The philosophy of the nature of beginning reading and the conflict between skills approaches to reading versus the whole-language approach cause further conflict in many school districts.

Although there is no definitive resolution regarding the opposing philosophies, teachers need to understand the causes of the disagreement so that they can make informed decisions about how they think a quality reading program should be designed. To that end, I described several possibilities for primary-grade language arts programs, which ranged from totally whole-language instruction to a blend of whole-language and reading skills instruction.

To further assist teachers in developing an appropriate language arts program, I described stages of literacy acquisition, beginning with the foundations stage, when children experiment with emergent writing and reading and acquire many of the characteristics of literacy on an individual basis. In the second stage, they master the forms of printed language. They learn to use phonic elements, grammar, and punctuation in their writing and reading efforts. Through extensive practice in reading and writing, they are able to put together the elements of printed language until they are able to read on their own,

SET 3:
WATER

ACTIVITY 3.1	**Why Does Water Appear to Disappear?**
What Concepts Might Students Discover or Construct?	A liquid appears to disappear when it changes to an invisible gas when heated. The term to describe this process is *evaporation*.
What Will We Need?	An aquarium, paint jars, and containers of water Measuring cup Meter- or yardstick and/or a wire coat hanger Paper clips $3'' \times 3'' \times 1''$ sponge Masking tape and/or marking pens
What Will We Discuss?	*Where does the water level in the uncovered aquarium go down?* *What caused the water level to change?* *Why do wet things take longer to dry on wet days?* *How can we measure how much water a sponge holds?* *What are some ways to speed up how fast wet objects dry?*

PROCESSES

What Will Students Do?
Measuring

Observing
Measuring
Recording
Hypothesizing

PART I

1. Using masking tape or marking pens, mark the beginning water levels of some uncovered water containers, such as an aquarium, a paint jar, a water jar used for plant cuttings, etc.
2. Check the water levels each morning and, using a measuring cup, add enough water to the containers to bring the water levels back up to original water level marks you made.
3. Keep a record of how much water was added to your containers each week. *Where did the water go?*

PART II

Constructing

1. Using the meterstick or yardstick, wire coat hanger, and paper clips, build either of the balances shown.

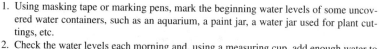

FIGURE 11.6   Integrated activities on water evaporation (pp. 386–388)
Source: From *Integrating Mathematics and Science for Kindergarten and Primary School Children*, by R. D. Kellough, Copyright © 1996. Reprinted by permission of Pearson Education, Inc. Upper Saddle River, NJ 07458.

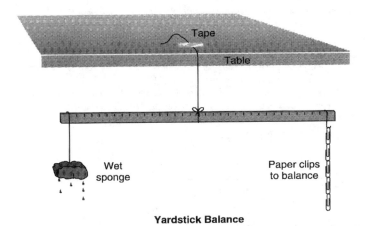

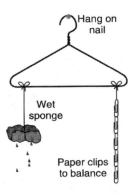

Yardstick Balance

Wire Coat Hanger Balance

2. Soak your piece of sponge until it is dripping water, then hang it with an "S"-shaped paper clip to one end of your balance. Add paper clips to the other end until the balance is level. *How many clips did it take?*   *Measuring*

3. Every 15 minutes, check to see if the balance is level.
   What do you see happening after several observations?   *Observing*
   Why do you think the paper clip end of the balance is lower?   *Hypothesizing*
   Keep a written record of what happens.

4. At each 15-minute observation, take off and record how many paper clips must be removed to keep the balance level.

5. When the sponge is dry, take your written observations and plot a line graph with the data. Set up your graph like the one shown.   *Graphing*

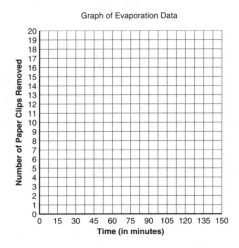

6. *What are some variables that might affect how quickly the water in the sponge evaporates?*   *Hypothesizing*
   How could you set up an experiment to test these variables?   *Designing an Investigation*

Some of the variables that affect the rate of evaporation are type of liquid, evaporation temperature of the liquid, air temperature, wind velocity, relative humidity, etc. Guide students in gathering data and in recording and graphing the results in the same way as was done in this activity.

What Must I Know?/Where Do I Find It?

385

How Will Students Use or Apply What They Discover?	*Why does water evaporate faster from your hands when you vigorously rub them together?*
	Why does your hair dry faster on a dry day than on a wet one?
	Why will a wet towel dry faster if it is spread out rather than crumpled in a ball?

ACTIVITY 3.2   **Measuring Needless Waste of Water.**

Adjust a faucet so that there is a steady drip of water. See how much water will drip into a measuring cup in 1 hour. Calculate the amount of water that would be wasted in 1 day. Multiply this by the probable number of water users in your community. List other ways in which water is wasted needlessly.

ACTIVITY 3.3   **Make Your Own Water Cycle.**

Start with: a commercial-size mayonnaise jar with a screw-on cap
small stones
sand
soil from outside or bought at a plant store
small plants such as mosses, ivy, baby ferns, or other plants found in the woods
a shell or large bottle cap
water

Step 1: Layer in the bottom of the jar:
stones—one-fourth inch deep
sand—to cover stones
soil—about four inches deep

Step 2: Create a nice arrangement for the plants and bury the roots in the soil.

Step 3: Fill the shell or cap with water to create a lake in the terrarium. Tightly screw the lid on the terrarium.

Find a shady place to keep the terrarium. You will see that the water condenses on the lid, falls back down into the soil and lake, evaporates into the air, and then starts all over again.

FIGURE 11.6   (continued)

During stage three, children become independent readers. They refine their knowledge about printed language and can use their emerging skills in more complex and lengthy reading and writing experiences. They engage in extended practice and become interested in both narrative and expository reading and writing.

The mathematics curriculum also enables students to progress to more complex levels using higher levels of cognition as concrete operational thinking is acquired. The sequence of concrete to abstract and simple to complex is particularly significant as children encounter new mathematical concepts. Because mathematics is sequential in nature, the teacher needs to understand how concepts build on previous mathematical experiences. Extensive use is made of concrete materials when learning new skills, and many opportunities are made available for children to apply their mathematical skills and problem-solving abilities in real-life applications. Like the language arts curriculum, the trend in mathematics is to its application in context and not as a set of isolated skills. In addition, the importance of immersing young children in the use of technological tools and applications is part of the curriculum from the preschool years through higher education.

Science curriculum, conversely, is more holistic. Children need ongoing encounters with the same science concepts in many contexts to fully understand the implications and applications of the science process. Whether children are in the preschool years, kindergarten, or the primary grades, they are using the science processes of observing, classifying and comparing, measuring, communicating, experimenting, and relating, inferring, or applying as part of their basis of understanding scientific phenomena.

There are extensive possibilities in physical and biological science that teachers and children can pursue. Although children tend to favor biological themes, they need a balance of both in the curriculum. Young children benefit from integrated experiences with science when all components of the curriculum can contribute to the child's understanding and use of the science process. As national efforts are made to improve the quality of the science curriculum, beginning with very young children, teachers are placing more emphasis on planning and implementing improved curriculum in their classrooms. This includes the design of units of study based on science topics that facilitate comprehensive experiences in a variety of activities over a period of time, including real experiences with living things and materials and phenomena of the surrounding world.

Study Questions

1. In what way are children age 5 to 8 considered transitional learners?
2. Why is it important to continue oral language development after students have begun the transition to literacy?
3. How do teachers attend to the needs of diverse speakers whose strongest language is not standard English?
4. How can oral language be strengthened and extended within classroom experiences and instruction?
5. Why do kindergarten and primary-grade teachers face a dilemma when organizing the language arts program?
6. What issues must these teachers resolve when deciding how to best teach children who are making the transition to literacy?
7. What are some possibilities for resolving the whole-language versus phonics debate in reading instruction?
8. How would you organize the language arts program in kindergarten and the primary grades using the models described in the chapter?
9. How does the beginning reader move through stages of reading ability between kindergarten and third grade? What implications do these stages have for instruction?
10. How does the teacher achieve a balance between systematic instruction and

child-initiated experiences in the language arts program?

11. Why is early intervention important for children who experience difficulty learning to read?

12. Why can the mathematics program be described as a continuum between preschool and primary years?

13. Why are mathematics specialists recommending a different approach to mathematics instruction for future students?

14. What kinds of changes are recommended?

15. Why does the mathematics program need to be developmentally appropriate?

16. Why are integrated or real-life experiences particularly significant in mathematics?

17. How should students learn about computer and calculator technology in mathematics activities?

18. Why should teachers be cautious about selecting and using computer software?

19. In what way is the mathematics curriculum hierarchical and sequential?

20. What difficulties do students with learning disabilities encounter when trying to understand and perform in mathematics? How can the teacher help them?

CHAPTER TWELVE

The Transitional Curriculum: Ages 5 to 8

Social Studies and Physical Education

CHAPTER OBJECTIVES

As a result of reading this chapter, you will be able to:

1. Understand the importance of social development in kindergarten and the primary grades.
2. Describe activities the teacher can use to nurture social development.
3. Describe the social studies curriculum in kindergarten and the primary grades.
4. Explain the components of the social studies curriculum.
5. Explain how to design curriculum in social studies.
6. Describe how to design integrated, thematic curriculum in social studies.
7. Explain how physical development continues in children ages 5 to 8.
8. Discuss how to plan for physical development.
9. Describe the role of the teacher and physical education teacher in designing curriculum for physical development.
10. Describe the integrated curriculum for physical development.

Curriculum for Social Studies

In the preschool years, social development is the basis for devising the social science curriculum. In the years between age 5 and age 8, the curriculum for social development or social science is commonly labeled as *social studies;* however, the major components or topics are similar to the categories used with young children. Social development is still an important consideration in the kindergarten and primary grades. In addition to expanding socialization skills, students in the later early childhood years are developing attitudes and values about themselves and other people. The curriculum for social studies includes activities for both advancing socialization skills and broadening students' understanding about the world and its people.

Social Development for Ages 5 to 8

Chapter 9 described the preschool child as gradually becoming less egocentric and developing the ability to understand that others may think and feel differently than he does. As the young child enters school, this ability continues to mature and enables the child's social cognition to include social role taking, or the ability to put oneself in another's place and anticipate what another person may feel or think. Development of social cognition allows children to better understand others and themselves, leading to interests in initiating friendships. Children also understand that people interpret situations differently, though they may not understand the source or cause of those differences (Berk, 1996; Feldman, 2000).

As young children enter school, they are moving into what Erikson called the stage of *industry versus inferiority*. Until they reach puberty, these young children will be developing a sense of adequacy as they become adept at reading, writing, and mathematics. If they are successful academi-

cally, they come to see themselves as competent learners. Likewise, if they are successful in using their social skills, they perceive themselves as liked by their peers. Children who do not overcome barriers to successful adaptation to school or fail to learn satisfactorily can develop a sense of inferiority or a lack of self-esteem.

> A child who is socially and emotionally ready for school and thus ready to learn has many, though not all, of the following characteristics: he or she is confident, friendly, has developed or will be able to develop good relationships with peers, and is able to concentrate on and persist at challenging tasks. The child must also be able to effectively communicate frustrations, anger, and joy and must be able to listen to instructions and be attentive.*

Unfortunately, not all children achieve social and academic success. Many factors can affect the child's positive socialization in the first years of school. Differences in child-rearing practices and value systems can make it difficult for some children to fit into the school structure, which traditionally has reflected a middle-class perspective. Diversity among family structures, economic conditions among families, and ethnic and cultural variations in the child's background can make it difficult for the child to feel comfortable in the school environment (Hale-Benson, 1986; Lane, 1986). Children who have been neglected and abused and children with disabilities have special challenges in their efforts to feel successful and accepted (Meddin & Rosen, 1986; White & Phair, 1986). Although these factors affect socialization in preschool years, they can be even more significant during early elementary school years. When children enter the primary grades, they are more aware of the need to conform to the social standards of their class and school and to expectations for behavior. They are also more perceptive as to whether they are accepted by their peers as part of a classroom social group.

---

*(The Child Mental Health Foundations and Agencies Network [FAN], 2000, p. vii)

Children who are not socially and emotionally competent when they enter kindergarten are frequently unsuccessful in the primary grades. They can encounter behavioral, academic, and emotional and social problems that continue throughout childhood into adulthood (FAN, 2000). Grade retention can result in behavioral problems. Children who have poor academic achievement in the early grades are also at risk for antisocial behavior (Huffman, Mehlinger, & Kerivan, 2000).

Peer rejection can have major consequences for the child in the primary grades. When considering Vygotsky's emphasis on the social components of learning, children who are rejected by their peers are at a disadvantage for learning through socialization. It also can deny them access to learning events where spontaneous groups engage in activities (Matthews, 1996).

The school is a major force for socialization, and the teacher plays an important role in guiding all children toward becoming successful members of the classroom community (FAN, 2000). There are practices the teacher can use to maximize positive socialization in students in kindergarten and primary classrooms. First, the teacher must assess friendship and sociometric patterns in the classroom (Matthews, 1996). Cooperative and sharing behaviors can be acquired through teacher modeling and guidance. The teacher can use coaching, direct teaching, and reinforcing to nurture appropriate social behaviors. Frequent group experiences, including activities among cooperative learning groups, can help children understand that they can work together and support one another (Deutsch, 1963; Kamii, 1986; Roopnarine & Honig, 1986; Veach, 1986; Manning, 1998).

The ages between 5 and 8 are also important for moral development (Kamii, 1986). Whereas children have previously made objective judgments in moral reasoning, they now become more subjective; that is, they consider the other person's intentions when making moral judgments about them. Learning to understand the intention of others is a difficult process, which continues through adulthood (Kamii, 1986; Kohlberg, 1973).

There seems to be a relationship between the development of moral reasoning and social behavior. In a study of first-grade students, those with indications of higher moral reasoning were also more successful socially (Enright & Sutterfield, 1980). Children who had good social skills were better able to judge the intentions of other children and were able to take their needs into account (Dodge, Murphy, & Buchsbaum, 1984). Children who were more advanced in moral reasoning had more successful social interactions and were sought out or approached more frequently by other children.

Paralleling moral development is the formation of attitudes and values. Values and attitudes are learned; moreover, they are acquired through the attitudes and values that are experienced by children through interactions with the people they come in contact with in their family and community (Seefeldt, 1999). The child's formation of values and attitudes begins in very early childhood years and is influenced by family, school peers, adults at the school, and other groups outside the school. Young children learn the values and habits of their family and immediate community through daily life. They likewise learn the values of the school culture through daily experiences in the school community. Therefore, it is important that parents and teachers take seriously their role in establishing values and attitudes. This is especially true in teaching the values and attitudes of living in a democratic society. In our society, we wish to promote the idea that all are equal and have equal rights to dignity and respect.

Not everyone in our society receives equal treatment, and children can become prejudiced at a very young age (Allport, 1952). Children can be influenced by stereotypes, prejudices, and discriminatory practices as early as age 2 (Derman-Sparks, 1992). Prejudice is a serious problem in this country, especially against minorities. Teachers can work toward establishing an environment that ensures equal treatment for all students. They will want to understand that diversity among children includes differences in gender, abilities, linguistic capabilities, class, and culture (Byrnes & Kiger, 1992). A first step in this process is for teachers to develop their own awareness of differences in the backgrounds of their children and how it affects them as they live and learn together. Cultural differences can include perceptions about gender roles, orderliness, noise level, and the importance of the group, rather than competition between individuals. Toward eliminating prejudice, as their understanding of differences develops, teachers can better model and teach equality and fairness toward all students and expect the same attitudes from the children (Greenberg, 1992; Seefeldt, 1999; Wells & Crain, 1984; West, 1992).

Activities for Nurturing Continued Social Development

Social development in kindergarten and primary classrooms is nurtured through the daily process of living, playing, learning, and working together. Social and moral development as well as the formation of values and attitudes occur within the environment and within practices for social living and learning that are established by the teacher. The major goals for social development are for children to extend their own socialization skills and to develop an appreciation for themselves and others through membership in their school community. The teacher helps students reach these goals through modeling appropriate attitudes and behaviors and establishing classroom practices and activities that enable students to practice social role taking and cooperation in a democratic environment.

The teacher's initial task is to establish a classroom climate that nurtures cooperation and mutual respect. A conscious effort is made to establish a noncompetitive atmosphere where all children participate in shared learning. The teacher's orientation and leadership shift the emphasis from teacher-directed instruction to mediated leadership that fosters peer interaction (Feldman, 2000).

The desired classroom climate established by the teacher promotes self-esteem and respect for self and others. Students learn how to be good citizens in the process of acquiring democratic values and behaviors. Through participating in group life, communicating with others, and solving problems cooperatively, students experience social and academic success (Holmes, 1991). A sense of belonging and self-worth develops from learning together through participatory roles facilitated by the teacher (Johnson & Johnson, 1987).

The teacher uses several strategies to actualize the noncompetitive, shared learning environment. These strategies involve discussions, cooperative learning groups, and democratic decision making.

Class Discussions

Class discussions are a vehicle whereby teachers can help students learn rights and responsibilities and develop respect for themselves and others. Through the medium of discussion, children can express their developing awareness of the many differences and similarities among people in the United States, as well as those represented by children in their classroom. They can share their family life-styles and traditions with one another and broaden their understanding and appreciation of individual and group differences.

Cooperative Learning Groups

Cooperative learning groups facilitate shared learning and group interactions. Instead of working alone, students work in small groups that are heterogeneous in development, ability, background, and gender. To function successfully in the group, students must learn and use interpersonal skills. The teacher plans activities that will build group cohesiveness and positive interactions. Through successful participation in group efforts, low-achieving students can feel they are making positive contributions to the group, while more able students can try out leadership roles (Lyman & Foyle, 1990). Students learn from each other as they observe, imitate, and discuss ideas with their peers (Atkinson & Green, 1990).

Democratic Decision-Making

Democratic values are learned through democratic decision-making in group living and learning. Throughout the school year, students and teachers work together in setting learning goals and classroom rules and solving social problems that arise in the classroom. Choices are made about what and how they will learn, particularly when planning projects or thematic units. When a unit of study is developed, the process of brainstorming together and planning and implementing activities to accomplish unit learning objectives actualize democratic practices in learning. Individual and group work that is planned includes assigning varied responsibilities, monitoring progress of unit activities, and reporting the final results (Lenhoff & Huber, 2000).

Social problem-solving can be addressed in democratic decision-making activities. The teacher can lead group discussions intended to elicit suggestions for resolving the issue at hand. Class meeting techniques can be used (Glasser, 1969) to ensure that each child has the opportunity to speak, that children are guided in seeing and understanding the view-points of others, and that a solution to the problem is reached through consideration of the consequences of making suggestions and reaching conclusions.

Citizenship learning and socialization skills are part of the total school curriculum, but they are also part of the social studies curriculum. In the next section, I will consider how to organize or structure social studies in kindergarten through third grade, as well the major role of integrated learning in the social science curriculum.

Social Studies Curriculum in Kindergarten and the Primary Grades

The preschool social science curriculum is divided into the categories of history, geography, economics, sociology, and anthropology; these subjects also form the framework for social studies in elementary and secondary school. Earlier chapters explained that studies in these areas are adapted to the experiences and abilities of children in the preoperational stage of development. In this chapter, social studies will be discussed using the same categories, but learning experiences for kindergarten and primary-grade children will reflect their growing ability to understand concepts from a broader and more complex perspective. Moreover, social studies curriculum design will be approached from an integrated organization, reflecting the most meaningful way that young children can learn about themselves and others in their world.

The social studies curriculum emerges from the children in the individual classroom. The ethnic and cultural backgrounds of the students and the makeup of their larger community and region form the foundation for the topics and content to be studied. For example, children who live in Arizona will attend classes that have a different mix of cultures than would be found in Alaska or Wisconsin. Differences within cultures and ethnic groups can also be affected by where children live. The Hispanic culture in southern Florida may be affected by influences from Cuba and South America, whereas the Hispanic culture in California and Texas may have stronger influences and traditions from Mexico. When developing goals for social studies, teachers must keep in mind that the unique characteristics of each region's student population will affect the learning experiences that will be planned.

Goals for Social Studies

In 1994 the National Council for the Social Studies (NCSS) published *Expectations of Excellence: Curriculum Standards for Social Studies* (NCSS, 1994). Although it is not the only organization setting such standards in social studies, it is the professional organization that advocates for social studies in the public schools (Jantz & Seefeldt, 1999). The NCSS Standards are concerned with developing good citizens. They also reflect constructivism and the integrated nature of learning. The introduction to the Standards explains the intent of the social studies (NCSS, 1994, pp. 1–2):

1. Social studies programs have as a major purpose the promotion of civic competence-which is the knowledge, skills, and attitudes required of students to be able to assume the office of citizen (as Thomas Jefferson called it) in our democratic republic.
2. K–12 social studies programs integrate knowledge, skills, and attitudes within and across disciplines.
3. Social students programs help students construct a knowledge base and attitudes drawn from academic disciplines as specialized ways of viewing reality.
4. Social studies programs reflect the changing nature of knowledge, fostering entirely new and highly integrated approaches of resolving issues of significance to humanity.

The NCSS further proposed that children at the primary levels should learn through highly integrated experiences across disciplines that could be constructed around themes. In the area of academic disciplines, history, geography, political science, and sociology were described as the categories of discipline-based knowledge.

The standards for social studies are organized into 10 themes:

Culture

Time, Continuity and Change

People, Places and Environments

Individual Development and Identity

Individuals, Groups, and Institutions

Power, Authority, and Governance

Production, Distribution, and Consumption

Science, Technology, and Society

Global Connections

Civic Ideals and Practices

The academic disciplines listed in the standards are appropriate for the curriculum for children in kindergarten and the primary grades. In the following sections, history, geography, economics,

sociology, and anthropology will be discussed when describing goals for social studies.

History

Children in kindergarten and the primary grades are beginning to develop concepts related to history. Two of the concepts, change and time, help children understand the notion of the past. Children first understand the passage of time through understanding the role of routines during the day. They can move from experiences measuring time to understanding that history is the study of things that happened in time that has passed. A sense of change that occurs over time also leads to an understanding of the meaning of history. Children can move from understanding changes in themselves to recognizing changes in their home and neighborhood. Through intergenerational contacts, they learn about continuity in life and that people of different ages represent the passage of time (Seefeldt, 1999). Holidays mark the passage of time during a calendar year, as well as celebrations people observe today that were also observed in the past.

Geography

Learning geography helps children understand that the earth is the home of humans. Geography helps them to be able to locate where places and things can be found on Earth. As children move toward concrete operational thinking, they begin to discriminate between living and nonliving things. They begin to understand that nonliving things cannot move themselves but can be moved by an outside force (Piaget, 1932,1965).

Some concepts that can be understood between ages 5 and 8 include the following: the land and water surfaces on Earth, Earth as a part of the solar system, the way seasonal and climatic changes occur on Earth, and spatial directions. With an understanding of location and spatial directions, children can be introduced to the use of simple maps. They can learn how to represent places and locations by using such things as blocks

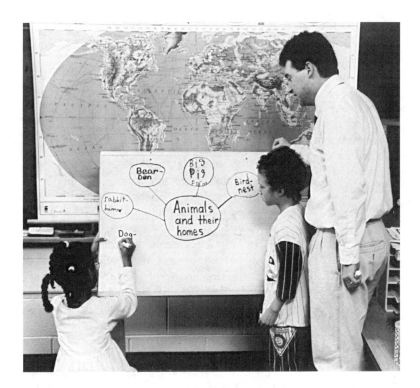

and boxes. For example, kindergartners enjoy laying out an outline of a house using unit blocks. Drawing streets for small vehicles are also possibilities for beginning mapping experiences.

Geography concepts can be applied first within the local community and then within the immediate neighborhood surrounding the school. Nearby land and water surfaces, characteristics of local climate, and mapping of community places in relationship to the location of the school can lead to mapping more varied area characteristics at farther distances from the school and community.

✦ Learning How To Make Maps

A second-grade class engaged in a project to learn about mapmaking. Three concepts in geography were developed within the mapping unit: (1) rep- *resentation and symbolization; (2) perspective; and (3) scale. All three concepts supported the purpose and use of maps. The teachers used sequences of concrete to abstract and experiencing and representing to help students understand unit concepts. The students constructed models of the classroom in small groups followed by drawn maps. The children's representations in the drawings included a combination of different perspectives. Children were then asked to draw a map of their bedroom.*

In the next phase of mapping, children developed an awareness of their community. A community map was enlarged to 3 feet by 4 feet. Children were able to place their houses on the map using milk cartons for the constructions. The children became aware of the logic of the bus routes related to location of homes and how near or far they lived to another students. Students picked another student's home and drew a map between the two homes and wrote about this discovery.

At the most abstract level, students discussed how they could map the sequence of events in their day. The class first discussed the schedule of their day in the classroom and made an experience chart to "map" the activities that occurred in the schedule. Then each student designed and drew a map of their own day.

Some children had difficulty with the concept of scale. They were not able to maintain proportion in objects they drew. The most important objects were larger than other objects in their drawings. (Lenhoff & Huber, 2000) ✦

Economics

Preschool children can understand what is involved in the buying and selling of goods and services. They have all gone shopping at some point in their lives and have experienced the exchanges of money, bank checks, and charge cards for groceries or clothes. Kindergarten and primary-grade children can understand the relationship between labor and production of goods and the economic characteristics of neighborhoods. They can understand, for example, the need to work to earn money, the concept of supply and demand, the implications of overproduction and scarcity, and the idea of savings (Seefeldt, 1999). Learning activities that will foster an understanding of these concepts include field trips to grocery stores, freight yards, banks, drug stores, construction sites, and shopping malls.

Children can explore what it means to be a consumer. They can learn how consumers become informed about goods that are available for purchase through advertising and the difference between producing goods and providing services.

Young elementary students can also learn about businesses and how they function. In 1992, Junior Achievement introduced the Elementary School Program for kindergarten through sixth grade as a pilot project. Sequentially integrated themes were used. The kindergarten theme, "Ourselves," is followed by "Our Families" in first grade and "Our Community" in second grade. A goal of the program is for students to understand economic principles and engage in problem solving (Van Scotter, Van Dusen, & Worthen, 1996).

Sociology and Anthropology

Young children need to learn about people and how they organize themselves into groups and communities. Preschool children can understand the family as the basic social unit, and primary-grade children can learn about communities beyond the local level. Children can also relate to how people live in other countries. They can become aware that we need to understand the similarities and differences in how people live in the nearby community as well as other parts of the world. Children in transition from preoperational thinking to concrete operational thinking can begin to use reasoning to understand the causes of war and the implications of racial and ethnic differences. Children need to discuss international topics so they can have a perception of people beyond U.S. stereotypes. Discussing global topics will facilitate acquisition of international concepts. These studies must begin with young children if they are to build positive attitudes toward the diversity of people in the United States and other countries and avoid prejudices that can influence their points of view (Moyer, 1970).

Current Issues

Information in social studies is constantly changing. We live in a rapidly changing world; and because of the availability of visual information about current events on television, children can develop an awareness of changing situations and conditions in countries that are nearby as well as distant. For example, primary-grade children may be made aware of information about new countries that are being carved out of the former Soviet Union or are seeking to regain the historic status they had before the world wars. Current issues, such as ecology and environmental protection, being addressed by various media resources and local community groups and organizations are also part of young children's awareness.

Primary-grade children are able to study topics about their own community that can relate to topics in other parts of the world. They can develop an awareness of why economic issues can affect how countries react to the way they use their environment. By being shown concrete examples of conflicting needs of different populations in their own community, children can be guided in beginning to understand conflicts in other nations. For example, awareness of a local controversy over the location of a garbage dump site or an issue about the amount of garbage that accumulates in the community can establish a foundation for understanding that there are various types of pollution in the world that are addressed differently in individual countries because of differing circumstances.

Young children can understand principles of patriotism. They can appreciate why flags are used as symbols for a state or country, why we recite the "Pledge of Allegiance," and why countries have a national anthem. Especially now, children can become aware that countries experience change and that change in government can result in changes in how people live and work.

Although the NCSS standards call for a curriculum that should be a basic component in public school education, the reality is that social studies is not considered to be as important as other subjects. There is also the issue of teachers' commitment to social studies. With the emphasis on basic skills and standardized testing, teachers spend a majority of their time on reading, language arts and mathematics. The fact that competing organizations are calling for different curriculum topics such as multiculturalism and gender issues results in unclear directions for teachers in social studies (Thornton, & Houser, 1997; Jarolimek, 1996; Jantz & Seefeldt, 1999).

Designing Curriculum for Social Studies

How, then, do teachers of young children from ages 5 to 8 plan and implement curriculum for social studies? To be consistent with the focus of this text, the social studies curriculum described will build on developmental continuity between the preschool and primary years. The social science topics will be developed to include topics that explore the elements of social studies discussed earlier in more depth.

The topics will be developed with the students' cognitive abilities in mind. I will consider the child's development toward using written language and making cognitive advances into concrete operational thinking, as well as the principles of learning that have been basic to all curriculum development throughout the text. Reconstruction of knowledge through active participation in hands-on learning and student involvement in planning are basic to the way the curriculum is organized. The topics discussed next focus on having global awareness, integrating social science with whole language, and celebrating holidays. Then a thematic, integrated unit designed according to the model used in Chapter 10 will be introduced to exemplify social studies as integrated curriculum.

Topics in Global Awareness

One of the goals of the social science curriculum is for young children to understand people from other cultures and countries. Three topics for global awareness are designed for different levels of development as children make the transition from preschool into the primary grades. The topics—Silkworms and the Orient, Toys, and the Global Community—involve activities that complement changing development and experiences in learning about other cultures.

Topics Integrating Whole Language and Literature

Language and literature can be the vehicles for designing social studies topics. In the four examples beginning on p. 401, principles from whole language are used to investigate topics that integrate social studies and language arts. Two of the topics could lead children to become involved in social action. Children's literature is used as a source of understanding and appreciating cultural differences.

Silkworms and the Orient

This study of silkworms integrates science and social studies and is suitable for kindergarten children (Cole, 1988). It originates with how silkworm thread was discovered in China and developed to make silk fabric. Children are introduced to the topic through a story about silkworms. The unit focuses on growing silkworms in the classroom and observing their life cycle from eggs to adult moths. The students can make some of the cocoons into silk thread and see the eggs laid by the moths after they emerge from the cocoon. Cole gives information on how to obtain silk-worm eggs and how to care for and feed the worms until they spin their cocoon. Science concepts learned from following the life cycle of the moth are important in building foundations for understanding other types of life cycles, the process of metamorphosis, and the care of silkworms at different stages of the life cycle.

Cole suggests other activities that help children develop an appreciation for people from an Oriental culture. Field trips to such places as an Oriental garden or market would familiarize children with Oriental customs and foods. Community members from the Far East can be invited to visit the classroom to share information about their native country. Children can also be invited to bring household items from their home that are from China, Japan, or other Far Eastern countries. Cooking experiences should include preparation of Oriental dishes. Books about boys and girls from Oriental cultures should be read to the class and placed in the library center.

Toys

A study of toys and play can help children understand that toys are universals that are present in all cultures around the world. Students can understand similarities and differences among people through a unit study of toys and the roles they play in children's lives (Swiniarski, 1991). A unit on toys could be organized around different types of toys. Animal toys, fashion toys, war toys, toys as national symbols, and toys as representative of folklore or fairy tales are just a few of the types of toys that can be studied.

Toys such as Babar and Pinocchio offer insights into children's literature from other countries. Toys from popular culture—such as Mickey Mouse and Barbie from the United States and Sooty from Great Britain—can be recognized by children in many countries.

Some toys are more classic and reflect the historical heritage of a country. Nested dolls from the former Soviet Union, Chinese kites, and dragon puppets are traditional toys from various parts of the world. Cultures can be compared through toys that are representative of a country's traditions or customs. Bride and groom dolls, toy vehicles, miniature dwellings, and toy environments such as farms or medieval castles can be used to compare current and historical lifestyles.

With toys of various types as the core of a unit, experiences can be developed to integrate learning across the curriculum. Children can make toys from various media, explore children's literature related to toys, and make puppets representing other cultures.

The study of toys from an international perspective can be developed into extended projects and used as sources for writing stories and reports and discussing social issues. Swiniarski (1991) reported on a first-grade project that involved making a catalog of international toys that the class had collected and an exhibit of the collected toys. The toys reflected the ethnic and racial backgrounds of the children in the class.

A Global Community Study

A unit for third-grade students (Peters, 1991) had as its purpose to introduce students to different cultures and physical environments from a global perspective. A strategy called Student Awareness of Global Environments (SAGE) was used to gather and report information about other cultures and environments. Working in small, cooperative groups, students worked to research and interpret data on culture traits such as diet, clothing, shelter, education, and family structures of different cultures. The types of physical characteristics of a country—such as vegetation, wildlife, weather, temperature, rainfall, and natural resources—were matched with the environmental characteristics of the country. Data on natural and cultural characteristics were used to understand the people who occupy the area. The effects of the country's physical characteristics on the cultural traits were explored for relationships between the two; the reverse issue could also be applied, regarding how the inhabitants of an area affect the natural environment of the country.

Biographical Studies

One way for students to learn social studies through integration with literacy is to write biographies about leaders in the social studies topic they are studying. For example, children might study explorers as a topic. They might develop biographies on Columbus, Marco Polo, or Lewis and Clark. If they were to study heroes, they might write about George Washington, Nelson Mandela, or Crazy Horse. Through writing about leaders, they would learn about history and political science while expanding and refining their reading and writing skills (Roberts, 1996).

Whole-Language Lessons for Promoting Social Action

Freeman and Freeman (1991), the authors of this curriculum topic, promoting social action, support the thesis that students should be involved in their own learning and that authentic learning materials are the best source of information for social studies curriculum. They present a model of social studies that addresses the inclusion of whole-language principles in social studies instruction.

Freeman and Freeman draw a parallel between instruction in language and instruction in social studies in the shift from education that transmits knowledge to

education as construction of knowledge. They further propose that cooperative groups investigating long-term projects place students as active players in their own learning. Moreover, they believe that students can put knowledge into action by initiating social change. Freeman and Freeman believe this approach is particularly suitable for students who have limited English proficiency and who benefit from engaging in learning that is related to their own lives. For these students, active involvement in cooperative projects creates more opportunities to develop second-language proficiency.

The model the authors propose centers on a study of the community. As they study the community, students can focus on how the environment affects community life. To better understand the characteristics of the community, students can examine and compare two communities and determine the advantages and disadvantages of living in each community. Language and vocabulary development are used in reporting the analysis. Reading can be used to further understand how various environments affect how people live.

As students conduct an in-depth study of the quality of life in their community, they can identify ways in which their community can be improved; further, they can design an action plan where they can contribute to the desired improvement.

Whole-language activities related to the topic include class discussions, group research and writing, and definitions of what students can do to improve the quality of life. Talking, reading, and writing will be used to accomplish all the goals of their investigation. The approach to learning uses the students' background knowledge and facilitates the development of proficiency in oral and written language.

Students in a large urban city in Texas studied two areas within the city to compare what was available for elementary students to do after school. The students discovered that one area they studied had many resources, whereas the other did not. The students devised a plan for after-school activities for children in the targeted area and approached two churches with their concern. One church not only became interested but coordinated efforts with the neighborhood elementary school to conduct after-school activities both at the church and at the school. The students studied their community from the perspective of the availability of the quality of life for children in different areas of the city. When they understood that there was a lack of resources for children in one of the areas, they designed a plan that engaged them in the process of social action to improve the situation.

Children's Literature and Social Studies

Children's literature can foster social science concepts, especially in developing an understanding and appreciation of multiple cultures. Barnes (1991) proposed that, in addition to understanding cultural differences, children can understand how cultures are the same—that is, the universals that all cultures share. Some of the cultural universals that can be explored include language, government, economic systems, religion, family, and education.

Barnes suggests that children's literature is more meaningful than are texts that supposedly help people learn about their own culture. Children's books can be helpful in learning about the form that cultural universals take, no matter which culture the

child is in. Barnes suggests books that will familiarize children with cultural understanding; his suggestions include topics that are related to family relationships, daily living, race, and cultural rituals such as weddings, funerals, graduations, and christenings. Each of these acculturation topics can be developed into a thematic unit using topical literature and related, integrated experiences.

Multicultural literature written for children can be used to meet the goal of helping children grow in their understanding of themselves and others (Norton, 1990). Using Native American literature as an example, Norton suggests a comprehensive sequence of study that includes traditional literature; autobiographies; biographies; historical fiction and nonfiction; and contemporary fiction, biography, and poetry, in five phases of study. The sequence is followed to study one cultural group at a time. Although the process is most appropriate for upper elementary and secondary students, second- and third-grade students could engage in the process with literature written for primary-grade children.

Holiday Celebrations

When teachers of young children consider social studies, one of the topics they usually think of is the celebration of holidays. Although there is an abundance of ideas on how to study and experience holiday celebrations, many of the existing activities have become stereotyped or sterile. Curriculum themes for holidays can be fresh and innovative if teachers and children plan thematic units based on children's interests and backgrounds.

One way to get a new perspective is to have a brainstorming session at the beginning of the year to include parents, children, and teachers. The planning group can focus on theme ideas that are appealing to them and can bring new approaches to understanding holidays (Nunnelley, 1990). The unit developed for the theme can follow the same steps as in Chapter 9, with parents taking an active part in all steps, including planning and implementation. It is recommended that each theme involve one main event, such as a field trip, party, production of a play, or celebration of a special event.

Older children can take a broader, global approach to holiday observances. For example, a group of teachers and students planned a 2-month study of holiday celebrations around the world in November and December. Between November 1 and December 31, they observed 15 celebrations from Mexico, England, the United States, Germany, Africa, Japan, Vietnam, Israel, Sweden, and Poland. The unit, called "Holiday Express," involved research, writing, learning geographic locations, and learning about cultural differences in important holidays and observances. In addition to making and posting a master plan for all the countries they would "visit," the students participated in the National Geographic Kids Network and exchanged information about traditional holiday celebrations by computer with students from other countries (Beach, Hinojosa, & Tedford, 1991).

Designing Integrated, Thematic Units in Social Studies

Earlier, I discussed how literature can serve as the source of information to learn about other cultures. In one example, in a unit planned for primary-grade children and initiated with children's literature, activities were planned that would involve learning about life on a different continent and dealing with frustration. Laurel, a second-grade teacher, designed a thematic unit that integrated social studies and language arts with her class. She used *Alexander and the Terrible, Horrible, No Good, Very Bad Day,* by Judith Viorst (1972), as the focus of her unit. (The entire unit, including the unit plan and the lesson plans, is described in Appendix D.) Students in her class were able to learn about Australia and how people speak and live differently in that country. Among the unit activities Laurel and her students planned were those that involved learning how to waltz, to sing the song "Waltzing Matilda," and to participate in singing the song and waltzing as a music activity. Students learned new vocabulary words that are unique to Australia and participated in related activities that incorporate other content areas into the unit experiences. Laurel listed the following activities for five lessons in the unit:

1. The teacher will read to the class the literature selection *Alexander and the Terrible, Horrible, No Good, Very Bad Day,* followed by a discussion of the story. The children will write and illustrate a sequel to the story, describing what might have happened the next day.

2. The class will locate the continent of Australia on a map and draw a map of the continent. This will be followed by an identification game in which children select a picture, identify it, and become familiar with the person, place, or thing that is characteristic of Australia.

3. A dentist (maybe a student's parent) will visit the class to discuss the importance of caring for one's teeth (in the story, Alexander has to go to the dentist). The class will participate by using a model of teeth and demonstrating proper dental hygiene techniques.

4. The children will construct a graph charting the least favorite vegetable of the class.

5. The children will become familiar with an Australian song through singing and dancing.

Both social development and social studies objectives were fulfilled through this unit. Children learned how to cope with feelings at the same time that they were learning about people in Australia. They learned that Australian children speak and live differently than children in the United States. At the same time, they were made aware of the similarities between children in both countries when they try to deal with difficult days in their lives.

Curriculum for Physical Education

Although much attention is paid to the need for play in the preschool years, the same cannot be said for the elementary school years; moreover, the emphasis on play periods for 5-year-olds may be very different among programs at different settings. Childcare centers and private schools are more likely to devote time for unstructured play than are public schools. Five- to 8-year-olds continue in their need for activities that promote motor development; however, schools and homes do not always provide the kinds of physical activities that are desirable.

Physical Development of Children Ages 5 to 8

I have described motor development in the preschool years more specifically as perceptual motor development, and I divided the skills into fine motor and gross motor skills. Play for preschool children was discussed in terms of physical play and its relationship to social and cognitive development. The indoor and outdoor preschool play environments provide for fine and gross motor skills in a context of play experiences that encompass sociodramatic play, cognitive play, and creative expression.

Gross motor and fine motor skills, body awareness, spatial awareness, balancing, and integrated movement as described for preschool children continue to develop in the early elementary years. The rapid rate of growth during the preschool years slows down with major development now occurring in the trunk and limbs. Childhood obesity can occur, a condition that is prevalent and increasing among children of these ages (Berk, 1996; Epstein, Wing, & Valosi, 1985; Wortham, 2001c).

Motor development during these years is a process of improving fine and gross motor skills. Children acquire improved skills rapidly and become competent at physical games. Gallahue (1993) describes motor development and movement skill acquisition in terms of stages and age periods of development. He describes children in kindergarten and the primary grades as moving from the fundamental movement phase into the specialized movement phase. They are moving from the mature stage of fundamental movement to the transition state of specialized movement.

The child in the primary grades enjoys demonstrating the skills that are being acquired. Hughes (1991) gives the example of the young boy who begged his parents for a skateboard and then derived much satisfaction from daily performances of the latest accomplishments that had been mastered. Children become interested in gymnastics, dance lessons, and organized sports. Improvement in fine motor skills makes hobbies possible, such as assembling models, sewing, making crafts, and participating in other activities that require dexterity. Many children become adept at writing and are able to use smaller writing. However, not all children develop this fine motor maturity and are penalized if school expectations for handwriting are too difficult for their level of fine motor development.

Motor development is interrelated with social and cognitive development. As children move from preoperational to concrete operational thinking, their emerging cognitive and social-emotional needs affect their play interests. In the primary grades, children become more aware of peer approval. It is very important to them to be accepted by the group. Cognitive abilities make it possible for children to engage in games with rules, increasing the opportunities to engage in group activities and enjoy organized sports, which require group efforts and competition.

Games with rules can involve gross or fine motor skills. The typical games familiar in American culture, such as baseball, soccer, hide-and-seek, and hopscotch, exercise gross motor skills. Marbles, checkers, and jacks require fine motor skills, whereas Monopoly and other board games advance intellectual skills. Children between the ages of 5 and 8 enjoy all of these opportunities for participating in physical activity and games that require physical and mental competence.

There are issues and lack of agreement concerning what kinds of physical activities should be promoted and how much importance should be given to physical development in kindergarten and primary grades. The issues that are most common relate to the following questions: What emphasis should be placed on physical education in the primary grades? Should physical education curriculum involve structured or unstructured play periods? And what is the appropriate role for organized sports in the early elementary grades?

Planning for Physical Development

The preschool teacher has the primary responsibility for all areas of the curriculum in most program settings. This organization changes radically in elementary schools as specialist teachers assume some of the instruction of young students. As early as kindergarten, children may be served by a music teacher, physical education teacher, computer center technologist, and art teacher. If the school is limited in special teachers, the physical education teacher is the specialist most likely to be hired. The common perception, then, is that physical education is a separate subject of the curriculum. The physical education teacher plans the physical education program as a structured curriculum with goals and objectives for motor development and physical fitness. The classroom teacher no longer has the responsibility for physical development beyond fine motor skills related to classroom experiences. It is possible that no one has the responsibility for the child's total physical development and for providing a balance between exercise and fitness and play opportunities that foster the interrelated benefits of social, cognitive, expressive, and physical play.

Furthermore, there is great concern that physical development is neglected in elementary schools. Concurrent with the back-to-basics movement in the latter 1980s, less time was devoted to physical education and more time was scheduled for academic instruction. There is evidence that physical fitness has declined in the last decades. Kenneth Cooper, a prominent fitness expert, reported that children in 1986 were heavier, fatter, and in poorer aerobic condition than were children in 1976 (Dart, 1990). Although some of the problem is attributed to increased television watching and poor diet, decreased emphasis in the public schools on physical education is also a major factor (Coop & Rotella, 1991).

Gallahue (1993) proposes that the motor and perceptual development of young children should not be left to chance. He suggests that children follow a progression in the development of movement skills. If children fail to develop and refine those skills, it will lead to later frustration and failure in sports and recreational activities. Bad movement habits can develop that are difficult to correct beyond the early childhood years.

The issue of participation in organized sports in early elementary years is another concern in planning for physical development in elementary schools. In past decades, unstructured play periods were part of the school day. Children had time to be outdoors and to select their own play activity. Although they were likely to organize group games during these periods, the activities were supervised by, but not directed by, adults. In schools today, most outdoor periods are limited to adult-directed physical education periods. Adults select and direct the activities, and children are required to participate. In addition, many primary-grade children participate in organized sports after school. Time for unstructured play after school and on weekends has diminished for many children. As a result, some of the advantages of unstructured, child-initiated play are lost. Games that are initiated and conducted by children promote social and psychological development in addition to physical development. Children create the games and rules and learn leadership skills, diplomacy, and compromise within the social group engaged in the games. These possibilities are lost in adult-directed sports. Not only is the child relegated to an adult-controlled world, but the spontaneous qualities of child-initiated play and games are lost to school-age children (Pellegrini & Bjorkland, 1996).

There are negative physical consequences of overemphasis on organized sports. Children who participate excessively in organized sports can experience burnout (Rotella, Hanson, & Coop, 1991). In addition, they are subject to sports injuries (Taft, 1991). Young children who participate in organized sports may experience injuries from overuse, such as tendinitis and stress fractures. Taft states that children seldom experience this kind of injury in free-play sports because children will stop playing when they are tired or feel pain. In organized sports, however, adults tend to encourage children to train, exercise, and compete at a level that is not appropriate to their level of development. Moreover, when parents encourage children to participate in more than one organized sport, the possibilities for injury or overuse of muscles and tendons may be compounded. There are, however, elements of play in sports. In addition to interest in winning the game, children also engage in playful pranks, verbal banters, and trading insults. Sports allow children to enjoy being with their friends and engaging in playful behaviors (Hilliard, 1998).

Designing Curriculum for Physical Development and Education

The Role of the Teacher

Although the classroom teacher may not have a responsibility for developing a curriculum for physical development, the teacher should be responsible for ensuring that kindergarten and primary-grade children have a balance between unstructured and structured play during the school day. If present policies preclude outdoor play periods for young kindergarten and elementary children, then the teacher should seek to inform administrators about the need for unstructured play. Developmentally, these children need the social, cognitive, and physical benefits of outdoor play on a well-designed, safe playground just as much as do younger preschool children. Although primary-grade students are interested in organized games, they still engage in sociodramatic play during these years. After they are 8 or 9 years old, this interest diminishes; nevertheless, kindergarten, first-grade, and second-grade children still benefit from sociodramatic play in overall development.

The classroom teacher can plan and develop physical activities that are suitable for children who are making the transition to the primary-grade years. With the child's advancing abilities in physical skills and changing interests in games with rules, the teacher organizes the classroom and outdoor environment to accommodate a range in children's physical and cognitive development and interests. Many of the activities used with preschool children are appropriate for 5- to 8-year-olds. As school-age children begin to need more challenges in materials and equipment, new possibilities are added to the opportunities available for play.

The emerging ability to concentrate on games with rules creates a demand for board and card games. The teacher begins with easy games with simple rules that are easily understood and followed. Carpentry tools requiring more physical coordination can be added to the simple tools made available to preschool children. Small motor abilities can be fostered through handicraft materials for leather work, embroidery, beadwork, and painting and glazing child-made clay pieces. These activities also promote creativity and pride in accomplishment. More complex manipulative materials that focus on higher cognitive skills are enjoyed, as well as more challenging art activities and drawing materials.

Large motor skills also develop through an evolving interest in games with rules. Although the children may be most interested in baseball, other games also encourage beginning group play and motor skill development. Croquet, tetherball, volleyball, and basketball are commonly available. Badminton is another possible game for beginners (Eliason & Jenkins, 1999). The classroom teacher can see that these large motor games are accessible for outdoor play periods.

The Role of the Physical Education Teacher

There are guidelines for organized curriculum for exercise and fitness for young elementary school children. Responding to information that young American children are declining in fitness, the President's Council on Physical Fitness and Sports conducted a nationwide study confirming that American youth are not in good physical condition. The report proposed that schools need to again emphasize physical education. Primary-age children need daily physical education periods that provide exercise and physical fitness. A typical physical education period includes both fitness and exercise. Figure 12.1 lists suggestions for activities presented in a typical physical education class (Greene & Adeyanju, 1991).

It is recommended that physical fitness and exercise activities used with elementary school children be those that students are most likely to continue as adults. Walking, aerobic dance, calisthenics, swimming, bicycling, and jogging are among the possibilities that children will enjoy and continue later in life.

The physical education program should also inform students about fitness and health. Children need to know why they need to engage in physical activities and exercise and how they can lead a healthy lifestyle. The lesson format in Figure 12.1 begins with an opportunity that allows the teacher to introduce and explain health and fitness concepts. The goal of promoting a healthy lifestyle should be encouraged through observance of the following guidelines (Greene & Adeyanju, 1991, p. 442):

1. Stress the importance of aerobic conditioning and total body fitness, and promote an understanding of the physiological concepts of fitness.

2. Teach children to become responsible for their own fitness. Demonstrate to them the importance of sufficient physical activity to stimulate normal growth and development.
3. Provide experiences that will enable children to understand the necessity of maintaining good health-related fitness.
4. Incorporate motivational schemes to promote positive attitudes toward physical fitness.
5. Discuss with students the immediate and long-term effects of health-related fitness.
6. Provide information on running economy and pacing oneself when exercising.
7. Allow children to test their knowledge about health-related fitness and total fitness.

Although the guidelines just mentioned were designed for physical education teachers, they can apply to classroom teachers as well. All teachers can promote healthy lifestyles and stress the need for physical fitness. Physical education and regular classroom teachers can work together in planning and providing activities for fine and gross motor skills and health and physical fitness.

The Integrated Curriculum for Physical Development

Can integrated curriculum that centers on physical development and education be designed in kindergarten and the primary grades? Many resources on curriculum design do not include motor development as one of the content areas to be addressed in curriculum development. Physical movement is sometimes identified merely as movement and grouped with music. The categorization of physical education as a component of education separate from classroom instruction also reduces the interest in using physical development and education as a focus for integrated curriculum design. There are good examples of how integrated curriculum can be designed and implemented, however. *Integrated Learning Activities for Young Children* (Trostle & Yawkey, 1990) contains many examples of activities that feature

Activity	Time (minutes)
Presentation of fitness or health concept:	
Teacher discussion and explanation	1–2
Student participation and related activity	1–2
Brief discussion	1–2
Warm-up or muscular fitness exercise	2–3
Aerobic exercise	6–10
Skill development	9–17
Cool down	2

FIGURE 12.1 Typical physical education class activities
Source: From "Exercise and Fitness Guidelines for Elementary and Middle School Children" by L. Greene and M. Adeyanju, 1991, *The Elementary School Journal, 91*, p. 441. Copyright 1991 by The University of Chicago Press. Reprinted with permission.

or incorporate physical education or movement education. Two examples from this resource are provided in Figures 12.2 and 12.3. The first, titled "Physical Education" (Figure 12.2), has children use an art activity to create movement pictures. In a writing activity, the children describe exercise routines that are compiled into a booklet. The class selects a sport and exercise routine they wish to learn. Other related activities include language experience stories and discussions about the process of learning a sport.

The second activity, "In the Air" (Figure 12.3), is related to basketball. Students engage in an activity to keep balloons in the air and pretend to be Harlem Globetrotters. Games are played that involve passing the balloon in creative ways. In addition, air-filled balloons are compared with helium-filled balloons. Written messages are put into balloons for another child in the class to read.

Many other topics come to mind that can correlate physical education with other components of the curriculum. The history of baseball can be studied to explore changes in rules, equipment, and uniforms. Students might learn about early baseball fields and how foods served at baseball games became popular. Students might visit a local school team or professional team workout to learn the role of physical fitness in preparing for participation in a sport. Books describing what has been learned can be written for the class library, and a mural depicting a baseball game might be created. Biographies can be written about sports heroes.

Another unit might be based on jump ropes and jump rope chants. Children might look to other children and older members of the community for different chants that are used for jumping rope. They could also research print resources with the librarian's assistance. Different types of jump ropes could be studied, as well as jumping with a single rope or a pair of ropes. Contests might be conducted for the highest number of completed jumps, most improved jumper, and so on. Students might write letters to another class inviting them to come and learn new chants.

Brainstorming with parents and other teachers could result in a number of interesting topics that integrate physical education with other content areas. Once an interesting topic has been planned and implemented, others will follow. The physical education teacher is a valuable resource for planning integrated units. The librarian can also be helpful in researching information and locating books on famous athletes, stories about sports that include children, and other books that relate to a physical education topic.

PHYSICAL EDUCATION (Movement Education)

Overview: The children learn how nice it is to feel good physically. They depict movement activities in a creatively pictorial way and then learn the steps involved in their favorite sport. Later, they write exercise routine booklets so all the children can play.

Objective: Expanding physical education knowledge and creativity.

Supplies: Construction paper; glue or paste; small tan or brown circles; mats; crayons or felt-tip markers

Words You'll Like: *sports, sportswear, circle, movement, physical exercise, routine, booklet, authors*

Getting Started

Distribute ten tan or brown one-inch circles to each youngster. Also provide colored construction paper, crayons, and glue. The children randomly paste the circles on the colored paper. They draw faces, hats, sportswear, and scenery around and on the circles to depict their favorite or imaginary movement or sport. Help them write titles for their movement pictures at the bottom of the page. Titles for the movement pictures from one group of creative first-graders included Playing Football, Strike One, Super Skaters, Physical Ed., Bowling Boys, and Swim and Sun.

Target

Ask the youngsters to display their pictures from *Getting Started*. They imitate the sport or movement they have drawn. Then vote on one activity that they would most like to learn. Compile with the youngsters a set of written directions for mastering the skills involved in the sport. Provide the equipment or supplies, if possible. Youngsters may wish to learn somersaulting, bowling, kite flying, bicycle riding, skipping, rope jumping, ball throwing, or basket weaving. Invite them to pretend that they are a famous person while they perform each.

Moving Ahead

The children become authors. They work in teams of three or four and compile an exercise routine booklet. In the booklet, they write the exercises they feel are most interesting for their classmates. The list might include As If exercises or skills, such as *Make believe that you are a famous gymnast:*

1. Do a forward roll.
2. Do a backward roll.
3. Hop ten times on your left foot.
4. Do a headstand.
5. Count to twenty while standing on one foot.

Let's Talk

1. Ask each child to relate an experience to his or her Getting Started picture. Write one sentence on a language experience chart for each storyteller.
2. Discuss feelings (a) when we cannot perform an exercise or sport, (b) when we are learning the sport, and (c) after we have succeeded in mastering skills.
3. Invite the youngsters to locate pictures of famous athletes. Discuss the achievements and contributions of each famous athlete.

FIGURE 12.2 Integrated curriculum for physical education
Source: From *Integrated Learning Activities for Young Children* (pp. 97–98) by S. L. Trostle and T. D. Yawkey, 1990, Boston: Allyn & Bacon. Copyright 1990 by Allyn & Bacon. Reprinted with permission.

IN THE AIR (Physical Education)

Overview: The youngsters pass air-filled balloons and basketballs as team members and team leaders. Pretending to be famous pilots and the Globetrotters enhances the activities.

Objective: Cooperating with teammates to manipulate balloons and basketballs.

Supplies: Air-filled balloons; floor mats; two basketballs

Words You'll Like: *balloon, flight, airplane, pilot, Harlem Globetrotters, airport, helium, parallel*

Getting Started

Ask the youngsters to pretend that an air-filled balloon is an airplane that contains many frightened passengers, and they are the pilots. It is up to them to keep the plane in flight at all times. The youngsters stand in a circle as they bounce and toss the balloon from one pilot to another.

Target

Divide the youngsters into two equal groups. The children pretend to be the Harlem Globetrotters. Each group chooses a leader. Place a basketball in front of the straight line of children. The leader sends one basketball down the line in three unique ways, such as bouncing twice between children, bouncing under the leg, or bouncing behind the back. Each of the three times the leader sends the ball to the others in his or her group, the ball travels a new way. The last child in line to receive the ball runs the ball to the front of the line. A new leader takes the front of the line after the previous leader has had three turns to send the ball. The other line of children passes a second ball in a similar fashion. Which team was faster?

Moving Ahead

The youngsters, divided into two teams, form two parallel lines. The first child in line, the leader, passes a balloon (an airplane) to the next child in the line in a unique way. The airplane must not touch the ground and no hands are allowed. Play the game like the *Target* ball game; now each team member serves as a leader (or pilot) once. The others pass the balloon in the same fashion as the team leader. The first team to complete passing the balloon, with every child being a leader one time, is named "Champion Pilots." Ideas for no-hands balloon passing include passing under the chin, under the arm, between the feet, from head to head, or between the knees.

Let's Talk

1. Observe and compare a helium-filled balloon with a regular, air-filled balloon. Discuss the properties of a variety of gases.
2. Obtain several helium balloons. Help the youngsters to think of messages that they would like to send to others. The messages are written on small slips of paper, along with the names of the children in the classroom. The messages are inserted into the balloons. Release the balloons into the classroom. Each child finds a new balloon and reads the message inside.

FIGURE 12.3 Integrated curriculum for physical education
Source: From *Integrated Learning Activities for Young Children* (pp. 101–102), by S. L. Trostle and T. D. Yawkey, 1990, Boston: Allyn & Bacon. Copyright 1990 by Allyn & Bacon. Reprinted with permission.

The units that appear in the appendixes all contain examples of physical development activities that support the theme of the unit. Activities that require the children to use fine or gross motor skills have been described for each unit in the curriculum web and summary of activities. In addition, attention has been given to the inclusion of activities for health, safety, and nutrition. Through incorporation of physical education in integrated curriculum, children can be reminded of the importance of physical exercise and fitness.

Summary

Children who are making the transition from preschool into kindergarten and the primary grades are in the later years of early childhood education. The curriculum that is planned for them reflects the continuing importance of development, both to ensure that experiences are developmentally appropriate and to accommodate curriculum activities to changing development.

Children ages 5 to 8 are continuing to acquire social skills. They are more aware of peer perception and acceptance. They are developing moral reasoning in the process of developing attitudes and values. In addition to acquiring their own values, they are becoming aware of the values and attitudes of others. Teachers have the responsibility to guide children in avoiding prejudice and stereotypic attitudes toward students from different ethnic and economic groups. This goal of equality and fairness for all students is nurtured through a positive classroom climate that nurtures cooperation, mutual respect, self-esteem, and good citizenship practices.

The social studies curriculum also addresses the goal of helping students to understand themselves and others. The social studies components of history, geography, economics, sociology, and anthropology are taught within an integrated organization of content. Examples of topics ranging from Oriental silkworms to untraditional ways to celebrate holidays were described as approaches to integrating the curriculum.

The curriculum for physical development and physical education changes as children move from preschool to elementary school programs. One difference is that the need for play and physical activity may not receive the priority that it should have. Another difference is that the physical education teacher usually has the responsibility for developing the curriculum for physical development.

There are issues regarding physical education and development in the primary grades. One concern is the poor fitness level of American children and the recommendation that public schools devote more time and effort to helping children develop fitness programs and healthy lifestyles. Another concern is whether physical activities should be limited to formal physical education periods.

Because children in kindergarten and the primary grades benefit from unstructured outdoor play periods, there is a need for teachers and other school personnel to advocate for young children to have the opportunity for daily outdoor play beyond formal physical education periods. Parents and teachers also need to be aware of potential problems in overstressing organized sports for primary-grade children and seek to ensure opportunities for unstructured play outside of school.

Curriculum for physical development and physical education should respond to the changing physical and cognitive abilities of the students. Opportunities for games with rules for fine motor and gross motor skills should be provided. Although much of the time devoted to providing opportunities to engage in games with rules falls within the physical education curriculum, the classroom teacher can also help ensure a balanced curriculum in physical development and make equipment and materials available for group games.

The integrated curriculum is appropriate for physical education topics. Although teachers may be less familiar with using the process with physical education, many topics can be designed into thematic units with supportive experiences drawn from other content areas.

Study Questions

1. How does the social studies curriculum for the primary grades differ from the preschool curriculum? How is it similar?
2. Why is Erikson's industry versus inferiority stage significant for young children in the primary grades?
3. How does peer approval affect social behaviors of young children entering elementary school?
4. What role should the teacher have in the young child's moral development?
5. How can an attitude of prejudice be prevented in young children?
6. Why are class discussions effective for developing democratic values and practices?
7. How does decision making facilitate understanding of the democratic process?
8. How do young children ages 5 to 8 learn about history?
9. Can primary-grade children construct maps? What kinds?
10. Why do young children need to be conscientious consumers?
11. Why do young children need to understand changes in countries at the present time?
12. What are some current social studies issues that young children could address (beyond the examples given in the text)?
13. What is meant by a literacy curriculum in social studies?
14. Why does the social studies curriculum need to include topics from a global perspective?
15. Why is children's literature especially helpful in planning integrated social studies curriculum?
16. Why do public schools devote less time for outdoor play than other school settings that serve children 5 to 8 years old?
17. What does motor development imply for curriculum development in the early elementary grades?
18. How do games with rules relate to cognitive and physical development in kindergarten and primary-grade children?
19. Why should the physical education program focus on physical fitness and exercise?
20. Why are public schools accused of neglecting physical development in elementary schools?
21. What kinds of games do young children in kindergarten and the primary grades enjoy? How should the teacher introduce games with rules?
22. Why do kindergarten and primary-grade children need free play in addition to a period for physical education?

23. How would you describe a quality program for physical fitness and exercise for children in the primary grades?
24. What is the classroom teacher's role in nurturing physical development?

25. Why should the physical education program stress long-term health and fitness?

Teaching in the Real World

In this book, I have tried to help teachers and future teachers of young children in the early childhood years become informed about quality educational programs. I have discussed some of the issues, problems, and possibilities involved with the practices used with curriculum and instruction in early childhood programs today. One purpose of this book has been to describe how teachers can develop curriculum and learning experiences that are appropriate for the young children they teach.

Undergraduate students are often confused and frustrated when they engage in field experiences because they observe situations that are not the same as described in their texts. Even though universities are increasing the types of field activities and the time that students spend in early childhood classrooms, students expect that all classrooms will reflect the "ideals" that they learned in their university-based course work.

Because there are various types of early childhood settings and because early childhood programs vary within a community, between communities, and among different areas of the nation, early childhood teachers work under diverse kinds of circumstances. How teachers in early childhood programs design and implement curriculum and instruction in their own program setting depends on their unique backgrounds and experiences and the way in which their individual teaching styles fit into the particular environment where they work with young children. The early childhood teacher seeking employment will want to be aware of the different possibilities available in the community. In addition, the teacher entering the profession will want to be aware of the philosophy and approach being used in the early childhood setting where employment is sought, to determine what type of a program is in place or being developed. Many teachers feel that they have no choice, that they must take whatever teaching opportunity is available. If this is the case, and the program is not appropriate, the teacher might work toward improving the situation or seek a better position in another setting. On the other hand, the teacher might have the opportunity to join a group of teachers who are in the process of restructuring their program and curriculum to be developmentally appropriate. Moreover, there are early childhood settings in many states that have been offering developmentally appropriate quality programs for many years. The teachers hired to join this type of setting have the advantage of being able to learn from fellow teachers.

In the following sections, 10 early childhood educators are introduced. Their stories can serve to illustrate the opportunities and realities that exist in current programs for young children. The reader is invited to evaluate the potential for developing, improving, or advocating a developmentally appropriate early childhood program in each setting.

Beth

Beth has been teaching first grade in a suburban school district for 6 years. She is working on a master's degree in early childhood education. She considers herself well-informed about issues and practices in the field. Although her school district has a reputation for being progressive and is highly respected in the immediate area, Beth is frustrated. She has a new principal who is very concerned with her own success as an administrator. The principal is worried about achievement test scores in her school and how they will reflect on her effectiveness as an administrator. She expects teachers in her school to focus on a skills approach to teaching and learning that will result in good test scores. Beth is particularly frustrated with the new principal because the school district encourages her to attend staff development sessions on whole language and strategies for implementing integrated curriculum with a child-centered approach. Beth knows that the school district supports developmentally appropriate curriculum, but it is discouraged in her particular school. She resists using precious time and energy so that she can be an assertive advocate for an appropriate program for her first-grade children.

Beth is uncertain how to proceed with curriculum planning because she is not clear about the future direction of her particular school and how much of her recent training she should try to implement with her students. The school has two vacancies for teachers in first-grade classrooms. Beth will be involved in interviewing candidates. She is uncertain about what information she should share about the school with prospective teachers during their visits.

Renee

Renee teaches kindergarten in the same school district as Beth. She originally taught in a child development laboratory school in a university in the Midwest. She has relocated to the Southwest because there are more teaching opportunities in this area, where the population is steadily increasing each year. When Renee first arrived, she was discouraged because the school where she was teaching was very academically oriented and she found the program to be rigid and demanding compared with the developmental program she taught previously. When the school district opened a new school at the beginning of the current year, Renee was chosen to be one of the kindergarten teachers. The principal had a background in early childhood education; moreover, the school had applied for and received a grant to develop innovative programs. Renee is very pleased to be able to try new approaches in her classroom. She is confident that she and her fellow teachers are creating an exciting program for young children. However, she sometimes has moments of doubt because standardized achievement tests are administered in her school. She and her colleagues are afraid that if test scores drop they will be required to return to a more academic approach. Usually, though, she enjoys the opportunity to be the kind of teacher she has envisioned being. Another kindergarten teacher will be hired for a new classroom next year. Renee hopes that the new teacher will be knowledgeable about a developmentally based program and will bring new ideas and strategies to share with her and the other early childhood teachers.

Yolanda

Yolanda has taught for 20 years, most of which she has spent working with young Hispanic children in a small rural school district. Yolanda is Hispanic herself and feels that she can help these young children in her preschool classroom for 4-year-olds. Although the school district has limited funds, and the children come from families who are poorly paid farm workers, Yolanda's school has been recognized as an exemplary school by the state. For several years the school has served as a family resource center in the community. Families are an important part of the program, and parents volunteer regularly to assist in classrooms. Yolanda and her fellow teachers design the curriculum to reflect the children's backgrounds and learning levels and the population of the community. They look to parents and community businesses to help them provide learning experiences that will broaden the world where these young children live. Walking field trips to nearby locations are a frequent activity. Yolanda uses thematic curriculum for social studies but also believes that structured teaching, using direct strategies, is important. She uses commercial curriculum materials and learning centers to extend learning experiences for her children. Yolanda hopes that new teachers hired for her school will understand the cultural backgrounds of the children in her community and be prepared to continue the type of program that nurtures this particular population of children.

Susan

Susan is a teacher in a private early childhood center that combines a preschool program with child care. The center calls itself a child enrichment center. It is located in a community of professional parents. The center is new and well-equipped. There is a beautiful playscape, and each classroom has computers and an abundance of software. Susan has a degree in music but no teaching certificate. Her training for her position has been primarily through local workshops given by a junior college. Susan is very interested in using the fine arts in her classroom. She supplements supplies that the center provides with materials that she buys herself. Susan also buys resource and idea books through catalogs at the center. She is beginning to understand a little about designing curriculum around a theme. She is currently trying out some ideas she found in one of her books. She is thinking about the possibility of contacting a nearby university to work toward becoming certified, but she likes the freedom she has to pursue her own ideas as a teacher at the center. The pay is poor compared with the salaries of public school teachers; however, Susan enjoys her small class of children, which would be much larger in a public school setting in her community. She also has an interest in opening her own center and further developing the expressive arts for young children. One frustration that Susan encounters is the frequent change in teachers at the center. The turnover is so high that teachers do not have time to adjust to the children and the program before they have moved on to find a position that offers higher pay.

Rollo and Nancy

Rollo operates his own early childhood center. He lives in a small city on the East Coast. Rollo and his wife, Nancy, have two children in elementary school. They are very interested in new trends in lifestyles and in teaching children to be socially responsible. Rollo opened the New Age School for children ages 2 to 5. He perceives his program to be suitable for parents who want a school that reflects the values of their upper-middle-class culture. Children attend the preschool program for a half-day. Child-care services are not a part of the program.

Rollo's background is in psychology, and Nancy has a master's degree in English. Both of them have taken courses in early childhood education through an extension program offered by a local college. They opened the school originally for their own children. The program features expressive experiences and trips to museums and other cultural centers, activities that Rollo and Nancy believe are missing in other preschool settings. The curriculum reflects an awareness of ecology, animal rights, natural foods, and the fine arts. They prefer to hire teachers with a liberal arts background who agree with their philosophy of education. This is possible because policies requiring teacher certification do not apply to private and parochial schools in their state. They train their staff themselves and hold several orientation sessions each year for prospective parents. The school has a waiting list; therefore, Rollo and Nancy are considering opening a second center or expanding the current program.

Gladys

Gladys is an African American teacher at a public school in Oregon that serves children from many cultural backgrounds. The school includes a program for non–English-speaking 4-year-olds, as well as kindergarten through third grade. The school is located within a housing development for low-income families. Because all types of families seek work in the area, the children represent 12 different cultural backgrounds. Language acquisition is the most important component of the curriculum. Curriculum development is usually centered on different cultures represented by the children in the school. Gladys teaches second grade. Most of her children have acquired some facility in English, but there are a few every year who are still very limited in the use of expressive English or are unfamiliar with standard English. Gladys and her fellow teachers do a great deal of team planning. They also exchange children throughout the day to better place the children in activities that are appropriate for their level of language and cognitive development. Curriculum planning is done by teams of teachers representing at least two grade levels; but, frequently, multiage grouping across three grade levels is more useful for the children. Several new teachers will be hired for the coming school year. Gladys and her colleagues hope the new teachers will quickly adjust to the style of teaching they have developed in the school. They have also heard rumors that their principal will be transferred to a larger school. They are uneasy about having a new principal next year who might not understand and support their program.

Hector

Hector retired from the military as a result of downsizing at his airforce base. He and many other exmilitary personnel received their training to become teachers in an alternative certification program that accelerates teacher preparation and requires many fewer hours of course work before beginning an internship in the schools. Hector had many questions about pursuing alternative certification. First, it was very expensive. Second, he did not receive college credit for the course work. Third, he was uncertain if he was ready when he entered the classroom after completing four courses. It was not easy to acquire the first teaching position that also served as the internship year. Hector lives in an urban area that has many school districts. Some of the districts will not consider teachers trained in the alternative certification program. Others have reputations for poor educational programs and many problems with parents and students. In addition, most districts that hire alternative certification program participants are in high-crime neighborhoods. Hector took the elementary preparation program that also included kindergarten in the certification. He was hired in a classroom for 4-year-olds in a school with a 98% poverty level. The first week of school, he lost one of his children after recess. The physical education teacher for the upper grades found the child crying after the class had left the play-

ground. During the first year, Hector learned about young children, how to manage a classroom and discipline, and finally felt he understood the curriculum. His children, who were Spanish-speaking, adored having a man teacher. Hector found he was able to nurture and enjoy very young children. At the end of the first year, Hector was approved for elementary certification. After much thought, he has decided to apply for a transfer to an intermediate grade. His fellow early childhood teachers are disappointed with his decision. They feel that they have helped in his training and were looking forward to working with him next year.

Loretta

Loretta is the principal in an innercity elementary school. Her school includes kindergarten through fifth grade. In addition, an early childhood wing for children with various disabilities has programs for 3- to 5-year-olds; these children also participate in regular classroom activities. Until recently, the school district required an academic approach to curriculum and instruction. Loretta belongs to a national early childhood organization, as does the early childhood supervisor for the district. As a result of the efforts of Loretta and the supervisor to inform district administrators about the inappropriate practices that are currently in use in early childhood classrooms, the district has decided to develop a model early childhood program in Loretta's school that will use multiage grouping to try to eliminate the high numbers of children failing the primary grades. Although all of Loretta's teachers in kindergarten through third grade have expressed an interest in the training being offered to prepare for implementing the new program, Loretta has some concerns. She believes that some of her teachers are reluctant to leave self-contained classrooms and a more traditional curriculum. She is considering suggesting that some teachers might like to transfer to another school in the district and then replacing them with either new or experienced teachers who have a more flexible approach to teaching. She is also concerned that she will not have time to participate in the training and curriculum development process. Her school experiences crises frequently, and Loretta has a Reading Recovery program starting up this semester as well. She is looking for volunteers to serve as reading tutors and makes frequent visits to local organizations that might be interested in helping. Loretta sometimes feels that she is trying to implement more than she and the teachers can manage. On the other hand, she feels she owes it to the students and parents to provide the best early childhood education possible. She and the teachers are hoping that the district will be able to provide financial support for the materials needed to implement the new model that will be developed.

Loisa

Loisa has been teaching for 5 years. She is married and has three children; two are in high school and one is in middle school. Loisa completed her training to become an elementary teacher 20 years ago but did not begin teaching until her children were well along in school. Loisa teaches first grade. The state education agency recently rewrote learning objectives for kindergarten and the primary grades that focus on development rather than skills. Loisa is uneasy about using the new objectives. She believes she is a competent teacher, a firm believer in giving children a good start in the first grade. Loisa feels very comfortable with the commercial textbooks and materials purchased by her school and uses them to make sure that her children acquire the skills they need to achieve in school. However, the school district is pushing a developmental approach using the developmental objectives that will require her to design her own curriculum. She has studied the new objectives and finds them to be very general and vague. Loisa has agreed to attend meetings where the new developmental objectives will be explained and where there will be discussions about how the objectives can be used to design curriculum experiences for children with different rates of de-

velopment. Loisa has her doubts about the changes that are being discussed and is concerned that too much work will be required to prepare for teaching. She wants to keep an open mind but is confused by the many terms—such as *alternative assessments, emergent literacy,* and *outcome-based learning*—that are being discussed by her fellow teachers. She feels that it has taken her this long to master how to teach first grade and does not want to have to start over with some new fad that probably will change yet again.

Teachers who are moving into professional teaching positions may find themselves teaching with early childhood educators similar to those described in this chapter. They may find that teaching in the real world is either very similar to or different from approaches to teaching suggested in this text. Whatever the educational environment in which teachers of young children find themselves, there will be opportunities to work toward developing a quality program in their classroom. They may find themselves in the position of becoming advocates for the type of program they believe is best for young children. As professionals in the field of early childhood education, they will want to maintain currency with new developments. To achieve this status, they will want to consider joining two organizations that address issues and disseminate information about early childhood education in the United States. Both the Association for Childhood Education International and the National Association for the Education of Young Children welcome new members and publish excellent journals and educational materials.

Today's new teachers will become tomorrow's educational leaders. There is much work to be done to improve early childhood education in this country. Early childhood educators in the twenty-first century will be continually adjusting their programs as society, children, and educational resources continue to evolve and change. The early childhood educator can make a difference in the lives and learning of very young children. The challenge is awesome, as is the opportunity.

Preschool Unit: Seeds

Unit Plan Outline

Unit Topic: Seeds

Overview or rationale for the unit.   To motivate, stimulate, and interest the children in learning about seeds. They can learn that all plants originate from a seed. They can explore different types of seeds, how they grow, and how many seeds are a source of food.

Developmental Stage.   Cognitive Development

Grade Level.   Kindergarten

Brainstorming Web.   See Figure A.1.

List of Activities to Be Used
for Five Lesson Plans

1. Stories about seeds (teacher-directed)
2. Seed walk excursion (teacher-child-initiated)
3. Examining and dissecting seeds (teacher-child-initiated)
4. Seed collage (child-initiated)
5. Counting seeds (child-initiated)
6. Dictated story (teacher-child initiated)
7. Picture-card sequence of seed growth (child-initiated)
8. Songs about seeds (teacher-child-initiated)
9. Pretending to be seeds: music/movement (teacher-child-initiated)
10. Compare and contrast different seeds (child-initiated)

11. Seed shaker instruments (child-initiated)
12. Classify different seeds (child-initiated)
13. Musical chairs activity with seed packages (teacher-child-initiated)
14. Visitor: guest gardener (teacher/guest directed)
15. Planting and growing seeds (teacher-child-initiated)
16. Pretending to be a gardener in dramatic play (child-initiated)
17. Charting the growth of seeds (teacher-directed)
18. Discuss seeds as food sources (teacher-child-initiated)
19. Cooking/eating seeds (teacher-child-initiated)

Concepts, Skills/Processes

1. Seeds come from many plants, trees, and vegetation and vary in size, color, shape, and texture.
2. Seeds can be classified by color, shape, size, and texture.
3. The growth of seeds can be observed and charted.
4. Seeds are used as a source of food.

Unit Objectives

1. As a result of reading and listening to stories about seeds and going on a seed walk, students will be able to dictate their thoughts about seeds in story form.
2. As a result of taking a nature walk to find seeds, students will understand that seeds come from many plants, trees, and other

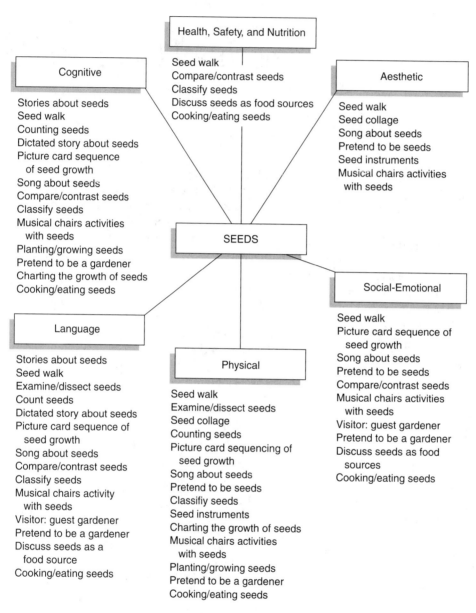

FIGURE A.1 Brainstorming web

vegetation and that they vary tremendously in size, color, shape, and texture.

3. By examining and dissecting seeds, the students will develop a general understanding of the complexity of seeds.

4. Students will be able to make unique seed collages with a variety of seeds after comparing and contrasting their different types.

5. After discussing and reading about the growth process of seeds, children will be

able to place sequence cards of seed growth in order.

6. As a result of learning a song about the growth of seeds, students will be able to pretend to be seeds; musical background will accompany.

7. Following an activity in examining and dissecting seeds, students will understand that seeds can be organized or classified according to their color, shape, size, and texture.

8. As a result of collecting seeds on the nature walk, students will be able to make rhythm instruments using a variety of seeds.

9. By classifying seeds, students will be able to participate in a musical chairs activity with seed packages.

10. As a result of visiting with a gardener, the students will be able to plant their own seeds.

11. The students will be able to chart the growth of their own seeds as a result of planting seeds.

12. By observing the actions of the guest gardener, students will be able to pretend to be a gardener in dramatic play.

13. Through listening to stories about seeds that are eaten, children will be able to participate in a discussion about seeds as a food source.

14. As a result of participating in a cooking activity with seeds, the children will learn of the nutritional value of seeds.

Assumptions About Previous Knowledge

1. Knowledge of story structure
2. Knowledge of the terms *before* and *after*

Summary of Activities

1. The teacher begins each lesson with a series of books that introduce the topic, which involves seeds in a unique way. Through these readings and the discussions that follow, language arts are integrated into every lesson in the unit.

2. The students will take an excursion around the school grounds and collect as many different kinds of seeds as they can find. The activity involves cognitive development using concepts in science. It also integrates language, aesthetic, and social development through discussions among the students. Physical skills are used in the process of walking and collecting leaves.

3. The teacher and the students will discuss the characteristics of a variety of seeds. They will look at size, shape, color, texture, and the parent plant. They will then dissect several seeds, taking note of the differences among them. This activity involves oral language, social skills through cooperative activities, and fine motor skills for dissecting the seeds.

4. Students will be encouraged to construct a seed collage using seeds, glue, and construction paper. The activity provides for aesthetic development as the children construct their unique collage. Fine motor skills are integrated in that the children must be able to manipulate the materials and use the glue.

5. The students are given a muffin tin labeled with the numbers 1 through 10. They are then instructed to place the correct amount of seeds in the appropriate cup. The children will use cognitive skills when counting and fine motor skills for handling the seeds.

6. As a class, the students will dictate a story to the teacher, who will, in turn, write the children's thoughts in story form.

7. When provided with a series of pictures showing the growth of a seed at various stages, the students will place them in appropriate order. In doing so, children will use cognitive thinking skills as well as language and social skills to reach a consensus within their cooperative learning group.

8. The teacher will introduce a song about seeds. Language skills will be integrated into this expressive arts activity.

9. The children will be asked to pretend to be a sprouting seed; background music will be provided. They will use motor skills and develop an appreciation for music and its different tempos.

10. The teacher will read to the children about the differences between seeds. The children will then be given a variety of seeds to compare and contrast in a group discussion. Speaking and cognitive skills will be used.

11. The seeds collected on the nature excursion will be used to make rhythm instruments. Children will play their instruments to pieces of recorded music. They will develop aesthetic appreciation for a variety of forms of music and using motor skills to construct and use the instruments.

12. Students will use the muffin tins and seeds that were used in a counting activity for a classification experience. They will classify seeds according to color, shape, size, and texture. Both cognitive and fine motor skills will be used.

13. Children will be given a selection of seeds to use in an adapted version of musical chairs. The teacher will stop the music at various intervals and ask those who have a seed with a specific characteristic to sit down. Students will use cognitive skills to identify their seeds. Social skills will be integrated through participation in the group activity.

14. The guest gardener will read books to the children on planting and growing seeds. The group will then discuss the process of planting seeds. Students will demonstrate listening skills, show respect for others who are speaking, and actively participate in the discussion.

15. Children will work under the direction and supervision of the teacher and guest gardener in planting their own seeds. Students will be required to listen carefully and follow directions in order to successfully complete the task. They will use fine motor skills to plant their seeds and oral language to explain the steps they took in the planting process.

16. The children will be provided with various gardening supplies for use in the dramatic play center. They will use motor skills and symbolic play to engage in sociodramatic experiences.

17. After their seeds begin to grow, students will discuss the changes and will record the growth of their seeds on a chart. Language and cognitive skills will be used in conjunction with working with peers.

18. After listening to stories about seeds that we eat, children will be allowed to share individual experiences they have had with eating various seeds. Socialization skills will be used in the group discussion.

19. During the cooking activity, the teacher will ask the children to gather the necessary ingredients for making peanut butter. They will measure and add ingredients under the teacher's direction. They will use cognitive, socialization, and physical skills.

Lesson Plan 1

Lesson Title: An Introduction to Seeds

Concepts, Skills, and Processes

1. Seeds come from many plants, trees, and vegetation and vary in size, color, shape, and texture.

Lesson Objectives

1. As a result of reading and listening to stories about seeds and going on a seed walk, students will be able to dictate their thoughts about seeds in story form.

2. As a result of taking a nature walk to find seeds, students will understand that seeds come from many plants, trees, and other vegetation and that they vary tremendously in size, color, shape, and texture.
3. By examining and dissecting seeds, the students will develop a general understanding of the complexity of seeds.
4. Students will be able to make unique seed collages with a variety of seeds.

Developmental and/or content areas that have been integrated.   Cognitive, physical, social-emotional, language, and aesthetic experiences have been integrated into the lesson.

Lesson Procedures

1. In a whole-group setting, read *Seeds and More Seeds,* by Millicent E. Selsam (1959). Discuss the book, and plan the nature excursion to be taken. Describe things the students can look for, and write them on a chart.
2. Take a nature walk around the school grounds, looking for seeds. Let the children collect into a shopping bag any seeds they find. Encourage conversation among the children.
3. In small groups, have the children talk about what they saw on the walk or collected in their bags. Then guide the children in cutting an apple and examining the seeds and the star shape made by the seeds. Show other types of seeds, and discuss edible versus inedible seeds. Guide the children in discussing differences in size, shape, and color of the seeds. Children can have their apple for a snack.
4. In the art center, provide the children with an array of seeds, and let them make their seed collage.
5. Place in the mathematics center a muffin tin that is labeled with the numbers 1 to 10.

Show the children how to place the correct number of seeds in each cup.

Materials Needed

Shopping bag

Book
    Seeds and More Seeds, by Millicent E. Selsam (1959)

Apples

Bird seed

Glue

Muffin tin (labeled 1 through 10)

Large paper

Writing utensil

Evaluation

Teacher
    Were the activities developmentally appropriate?
    Did the children acquire an understanding of seeds?

Activity
    Were the children interested?
    Did the children participate?

Students
    What comments and actions did the student use that suggest a broader understanding of the nature and function of seeds?

Lesson Plan 2

Lesson Title: Seed Growth

Concepts, Skills, and Processes

1. The growth of seeds can be observed and charted.

Lesson Objectives

1. After discussing and reading about the growth process of seeds, children will be able

to place sequence cards of seed growth in order.

2. As a result of learning a song about the growth of seeds, students will be able to pretend to be seeds.

Developmental and/or content areas that have been integrated. Cognitive, physical, aesthetic, social-emotional, and language activities have been integrated.

Lesson Procedures

1. The teacher reads from the following books:

   The Tiny Seed, by Eric Carle (1987)

   How a Seed Grows, by H. Jordan (1992)

   A discussion of seeds follows.

2. Children will work in small groups to determine the growth sequence of plants. The teacher provides a series of sequence cards showing the development of a plant from a seed. Children work cooperatively to put the cards in their correct sequence.

3. The teacher guides the students in learning "The Garden Song" to a record. The song describes the seed as a tiny, still object; then it slowly begins to grow with the help of sun and water.

4. After learning the garden song, children are asked to pretend that they are the little seed that gradually grows. As the song is played, the children assume a position as a tiny seed. As they sing along, they act out the growing process. The teacher participates with the children as they move and pantomime the actions suggested by the song.

Materials Needed

Books

   The Tiny Seed, by Eric Carle (1987)

   How a Seed Grows, by H. Jordan (1992)

Sequence cards

Record

   "The Garden Song"

Evaluation

Teacher

   Did the students understand stages of a seed's growth into a plant from the stories and discussion?

Activity

   Did the children enjoy the activities?

   Did the activity spark the children's desire to grow their own seeds?

Students

   Did the students work cooperatively in the center activity?

   Were the students interested in the activity?

Lesson Plan 3

Lesson Title: Seeds Are Different

Concepts, Skills, Processes

1. Seeds can be classified by color, shape, size, and texture.

Lesson Objectives

1. Following an activity in examining and dissecting seeds, students will understand that seeds can be organized or classified according to their color, shape, size, and texture.

2. As a result of collecting seeds on the nature walk, students will be able to make rhythm instruments using a variety of seeds.

3. By classifying seeds, the students will be able to participate in a musical chairs activity with seed packages.

Developmental and/or content areas that have been integrated. Cognitive and physical development have been integrated.

Lesson Procedures

1. In a whole-group setting, read *Bean and Plant,* by Christine Back (1986). Discuss the differences and similarities among seeds.

2. Have the children classify seeds in a muffin tin by some category, including size, shape, color, or texture.
3. Play musical chairs in a large-group activity. Place seed packages on chairs. When the music stops, the teacher will call out a characteristic of seeds to identify. If the chair has seeds with that characteristic, the child may sit down. For example, the teacher may say, "Everyone who has black seeds may sit down."
4. Place a variety of books about seeds and plants in the class library.
5. Have the children make their own rhythm instruments using seeds in the art center. Paper rolls from toilet tissue may be used to construct a seed shaker. Instruments are played to several musical pieces.

Materials Needed

Book
> *Bean and Plant,* by Christine Back
> *(1986)*

Muffin tins

Collection of seeds

Glue

Music

Evaluation

Teacher
> *Were the activities developmentally appropriate?*
> *Did the children understand that seeds can have differences and similarities?*

Activity
> *Were the children interested?*
> *Did they participate?*

Students
> *Did the children participate?*
> *Did they demonstrate an understanding of how to classify seeds?*

Lesson Plan 4

Lesson Title: Planting and Growing Seeds

Concepts, Skills, and Processes

1. The growth of seeds can be observed and charted

Lesson Objectives

1. As a result of visiting with a gardener, the students will be able to plant their own seeds.
2. The students will be able to chart the growth of their own seeds.
3. By observing the actions of the guest gardener, the students will be able to pretend to be a gardener in a dramatic play.

Developmental and/or content areas that have been integrated. Cognitive, physical, aesthetic, social-emotional, and language activities have been integrated.

Lesson Procedures

1. The teacher introduces the class visitor, a gardener in the community. The gardener first asks the children what they already know about seeds and then reads to the class from *Seeds and More Seeds,* by Millicent Selsam (1959). The guest gardener and students discuss what is involved in planting seeds. The children are asked what they believe to be the magic of seeds.
2. In small-group activities, students are asked to sort and match a mixture of seeds by color and shape. They are asked to select some seeds for planting.
3. Children are assisted in planting their seeds in small containers. Throughout the process, questioning and discussing are constant. Following the activity, students are asked to explain the process to another child.
4. The teacher introduces a chart on which students measure and record the growth of

their plant. Growth on charts of the same seed types will be compared, as well as growth on charts of different seed types.
5. Tools and equipment for gardening are placed in the dramatic play center for role-playing activities.

Materials Needed
Books
  Seeds and More Seeds by Millicent Selsam (1959)

Assortment of seeds

Soil, water, containers

Growth charts

For dramatic play:
  Gloves
  Hat or bonnet
  Small hand shovel
  Buckets
  Water sprinkler

Evaluation
Teacher
  Did the children understand the gardener's questions?
  Did they understand how to plant and care for their seeds?

Activity
  Did the children enjoy interacting with the gardener?
  Did they enjoy planting their seeds?

Students
  Could the students sort and match their seed assortment?
  Did they work cooperatively with the other students?
  Were they able to describe the planting process?

Lesson Plan 5

Lesson Title: We Eat Some Seeds

Concepts, Skills, Processes
1. Seeds are used as a source of food.

Lesson Objectives
1. Through listening to stories about seeds that are eaten, children will be able to participate in a discussion about seeds as food sources.
2. As a result of participating in a cooking activity with seeds, the children will learn of the nutritional value of seeds.

Developmental and/or content areas that have been integrated.   Cognitive, physical, social-emotional, language, and nutrition activities have been integrated.

Lesson Procedures
1. The teacher reads a section from *Science Fun with Peanuts and Popcorn* (Wyler, 1986). The teacher and the children share their experiences in eating seeds.
2. The teacher introduces the activity of making peanut butter to small groups. She asks the students to recall the ingredients that are needed. Students are then assigned to different tasks for making peanut butter. Some will shell peanuts and remove skins, others will gather the supplies needed, and so on.
3. The teacher asks the children to review the process of making peanut butter. For each cup of peanuts, students will measure one teaspoonful of vegetable oil and add it before placing the ingredients in a food processor.
4. After the peanut butter is made, students make their own sandwiches to enjoy.

Materials Needed

Books

    Science Fun with Peanuts and Popcorn, by
      Rose Wyler (1986)

Peanuts

Vegetable oil

Measuring spoons

Food processor

Butter knives

Bread

Evaluation

Teacher

    Were the children provided with plenty of
      examples of seeds that are eaten?
    Did the children have sufficient opportunity to
      participate?

Activity

    Did the children enjoy the activities?
    Were they able to follow the directions
      for making peanut butter and work
      cooperatively?

Preschool Unit: Farm Animals

Unit Plan Outline

Unit Topic: Farm Animals

Overview or Rationale for the Unit. Because children generally like animals and have an innate curiosity about them, implementing a farm animal unit is a way to channel their interest and facilitate a rich learning experience. The suggested trip to a farm will especially help to build a larger background knowledge base for future learning.

Developmental Stage. Preoperational

Grade Level. Kindergarten

Brainstorming Web. See Figure B.1.

List of Activities to Be Used
for Five Lesson Plans

1. Visit a farm.
2. Make a big book, using pictures from the field trip.
3. Observe eggs in an incubator set up in the science center.
4. Sing "Old McDonald."
5. Chart students' favorite animals from the song.
6. Work with number line made of duck feet shapes on the floor.
7. Write "I Went Walking" story.
8. Make a mural: use fingerpaint with grain, use animal sponge painting.
9. Square dance.
10. Reenact *Barn Dance!* (Martin & Archambault, 1986) in dramatic play center.
11. Match pictures to animal sounds tape.
12. Make pancakes.

Concepts, Skills, Processes

1. Chickens are developed in eggs.
2. Objects can be organized into sets from one to ten and matched to the appropriate numeral.
3. Stories can be used to make predictions.
4. We can write our own stories about animals.
5. We can learn to do a square dance.
6. Animal pictures can be matched to their sounds.
7. Measuring and mixing ingredients are necessary to make pancakes.

Unit Objectives

1. As a result of visiting a farm, children will be able to contribute something of their experience to a big book story.
2. As a result of watching eggs in an incubator, children will gain an understanding of how chicks are developed in eggs.
3. As a result of choosing their favorite animal from the song "Old McDonald," children will be able to determine the class's overall favorite.
4. As a result of working with manipulatives and a number line, children will be able to match the numeral to the set to which it corresponds for sets of objects from one to ten.

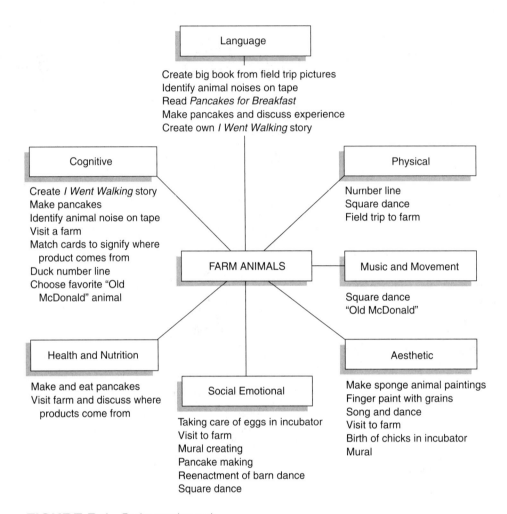

FIGURE B.1   Brainstorming web

5. As a result of listening to the story *I went Walking* (S. Williams, 1992), children will be able to make predictions and finish repetitive sentences.

6. As a result of participating in the reading of *I Went Walking* in class, children will be able to "write" (using emergent literacy) their own story about the animal that was looking at them at the farm.

7. As a result of working with paint, paper, yarn, hay, sponges, and so on, children will be able to contribute to the creation of a class mural.

8. As a result of listening to the story *Barn Dance!* (Martin & Archambault, 1986), and being given square dancing directions, children will participate in a simple dance.

9. As a result of listening to *Barn Dance!* and using associated props, children will recreate the story during center time.

10. As a result of listening to a tape of animal sounds, children will be able to identify the

animal and match the corresponding picture to the sound.

11. After hearing *Pancakes for Breakfast* (dePaola, 1978), children will be able to recall where the ingredients for pancakes come from.

12. As a result of making pancakes, children will understand how to use a measuring cup and measurement terms.

Assumptions About Previous Knowledge

We assume that the child has an adequate vocabulary and language skills to participate in the activities and that the child has had some previous experience with art activities.

Summary of Activities

1. *Visit a farm.* Students will visit a farm and be shown pigs, cows, horses, ducks, and sheep. They will pet the animals, feed the chickens, and see a cow being milked. This activity involves cognitive development as the children observe the animals. It integrates language development in the discussions that take place during the field trip, and social development is facilitated in the children's interactions. Motor skills are being used as the children walk on the farm and feed the animals.

2. *Make a big book.* During the field trip, the teacher will take pictures to be displayed in the classroom. The children will sequence the pictures according to the day's activities and then dictate a story reenacting their trip. The teacher will record their responses and give them each one page of the story to illustrate. The pages will be put together to form a class big book that will be put in the reading center. This activity uses cognitive and language skills when the children recall their farm experiences in sequence. Fine motor skills are developed as the children create their illustrations, which also promotes aesthetic development.

3. *Observe eggs in an incubator.* The teacher will set up eggs in an incubator to be kept in the science center. She will discuss the concept of "Touching only with the eyes." She will place a calendar in the center, and the children will mark off each date and count how many days the eggs had been there before they hatched. This activity encourages cognitive and language development as the children observe and discuss what is happening each day. It also facilitates social development as the children exercise control and care for the eggs. Observing new life is an aesthetic experience that can be woven into discussion. After the chicks have hatched, the teacher and children can discuss proper care of the chicks.

4. *Sing "Old McDonald," and chart the favorite animal.* The class will sing "Old McDonald" together. Then they will place their name card under their favorite animal drawn on a large chart. The class will determine which animal has the largest number of names under it and thus identify it as the favorite animal. Second and third choices will also be determined. This activity promotes language development, because the children are expressing which is their favorite animal. Cognitive skills are being used to determine the favorite animals. The music enhances aesthetic development.

5. *Duck feet number line.* A large number line will be placed on the floor with the numbers 1 to 10 written on duck feet. The child will stand on the first footprint, and the teacher will give the child a set of plastic ducks, ranging in quantity from 1 to 10. The child will be asked to waddle to the number that corresponds to the number of ducks he or she is given. This activity can also be done with two children instead of a teacher. This activity uses physical skills as the child waddles to the correct number. It uses cognitive skills as the child matches the

numeral to the corresponding set. If this activity is done with two children, they will develop socially as a result of their interactions.

6. *Write an "I Went Walking" story.* The teacher will read *I Went Walking* (S. Williams, 1992) to the class and then ask the children to choose an animal that was looking at them when they went to the farm and "write" a story about it. This activity facilitates the children's cognitive and language development when they create their own story and recall the story they heard. Sharing their stories with one another integrates their social and emotional development, while the actual creation of their story uses motor skills.

7. *Make a mural.* During large-group time, the teacher will provide a large farm scene backdrop made on butcher paper and give instructions for the children to add their favorite farm animal or the one they wrote about in the walking story. The mural will be completed in small groups with the help of a parent. This activity facilitates children's cognitive and language development when they create their own animal for the mural and when they work together cooperatively. Fine motor skills are being used, and the art activity stimulates their aesthetic development.

8. *Square Dance.* The teacher will read *Barn Dance!* by Bill Martin, Jr., and John Archambault (1986). Then the children will listen to a square dance tape and specific commands, such as the Virginia Reel, and the teacher will explain and demonstrate the caller's directions. Students will learn and participate in the square dance. Dancing facilitates the social development of the children, as well as their physical development. Aesthetic development is enhanced as children respond to music with body movement.

9. *Reenact Barn dance in the dramatic play center.* The dramatic play center should be arranged as a simulation of the barn in the book *Barn Dance!* A table with a red-and-white checkered tablecloth, a small bale of hay, and a prop box complete with cowboy boots, hats, kerchiefs, and child-sized musical instruments (such as fiddles or guitars) will encourage the children to reenact the book in their dramatic play. This activity facilitates the children's social development through play and enhances their language development as they role play.

10. *Match pictures to animal sounds.* In the listening center, children will listen to a tape of farm animal sounds and pick the corresponding animal from animal pictures. The answer will be given after each sound so that the child can self-correct his or her choice. This listening activity promotes cognitive, listening, and language development skills.

11. *Pancake party.* The teacher will read *Pancakes for Breakfast,* by Tomi dePaola (1978). After the reading, the teacher will write the correct measurements of the ingredients on a large chart. The children will divide into small groups and follow the directions on the chart with the help of volunteer fifth graders. Cognitive and language development are encouraged as children "read" the recipe chart and measure the ingredients. Vocabulary is developed as groups discuss the ingredients and cooking and measuring terms. Nutrition and health concepts are also incorporated into the activity. Social development is involved as children interact with other students.

Lesson Plan 1

Lesson Title: Field Trip to Farm

Concepts, Skills, and Processes Used

1. Chickens are developed in eggs.
2. We can write our own stories about animals.

Lesson Objectives

1. As a result of visiting a farm, children will be able to contribute something of their experience to a big book story.
2. As a result of watching eggs in an incubator, children will gain an understanding of how chicks are developed in eggs.

Developmental and/or content areas that have been integrated. This lesson involves cognitive development in observing scientific concepts. Language development is facilitated through the children's interactions. Physical skills will be used as children walk on the farm, and an appreciation for the beauty found in their environment will be facilitated through observation and conversation during the field trip.

Lesson Procedures

Introduction. Students will visit a farm, and pet and feed the animals. They will be encouraged to notice sounds and movements of the animals. The teacher will take pictures of the day's activities. When the class returns, the teacher will mount the pictures on tagboard and display them at large-group time.

Development. Students will be encouraged to describe what is happening in the photos and to arrange them in sequential order as a reenactment of the day's events. Together they will then dictate a story retelling their experience on the farm.

The teacher will give each student one page of the story and allow them to illustrate it. Then the teacher will build a big book and make it available in the reading center for the children.

The teacher will set up eggs in an incubator in the science center. The teacher will discuss with the children what the incubator is and the importance of "touching only with their eyes." The teacher will place a calendar in the center, and each day the children can mark off the date and count how many days the eggs had been there before they hatched.

Summary Review. At large-group time, children will read together the big book and further discuss their field trip. Children will be encouraged to explain their illustrations and share observations of the eggs in the incubator.

Materials Needed

Tagboard

Marking pens

Photographs

Crayons

Incubator

Viable chicken eggs

Calendar

Paper

Evaluation

Teacher

> *Did the children understand the activities from the explanations given?*
> *Were materials used appropriate and adequate?*

Activity

> *Did the children enjoy the activity?*
> *Were the children able to carry out the activity?*
> *Were the children able to carry out the activity with little assistance?*

Students

> *Did all students participate? Were the children able to use descriptive language to discuss the field trip and contribute to the big book story?*

Lesson Plan 2

Lesson Title: Graphing Children's Favorite Farm Animals

Concepts, Skills, and Processes Used

1. Objects can be organized into sets from one to ten and matched to the appropriate numeral.

Lesson Objectives

1. As a result of choosing their favorite animal from the song "Old McDonald," children will be able to determine the class's overall favorite.
2. As a result of working with manipulatives and a number line, children will be able to match the numeral to the set to which it corresponds for sets of objects from 1 to 10.

Developmental and/or content areas that have been integrated. This lesson promotes cognitive development through counting, sequencing, and corresponding number to numeral. Physical development is integrated as children waddle, imitating a duck's movement. Aesthetic appreciation is incorporated through the song.

Lesson Procedures

Introduction. Children will sing "Old McDonald" as a class. Then they will be asked which was their favorite farm animal and be instructed to place their name strip under a picture of that animal on a wall chart.

Development. The children will then count together to see which was the class favorite, the second favorite, and so on. Then they will sing the song again with the favorite animal first, the second favorite next, and so on. In the math center, a large number line will be placed on the floor with the numerals 1 to 10 written on duck prints. Working in pairs, one child will give the other child a number of ducks, and the second child will waddle to the corresponding numeral.

Materials Needed

Classroom chart of farm animals

Name strips

Plastic ducks

Duck footprints

Evaluation

Teacher
> *Did the children understand how to do the activities?*
> *Were the materials appropriate and adequate?*

Activity
> *Did the children enjoy the activities?*
> *Were the children able to carry out the activities successfully?*

Students
> *Did all the students participate? Was descriptive language used to compare choices for the animal chart?*
> *Were children able to match the set of ducks to the appropriate numeral?*

Lesson Plan 3

Lesson Title: I Went Walking

Concepts, Skills, and Processes Used

1. Stories can be used to make predictions.
2. We can write our own stories about animals.

Lesson Objectives

1. As a result of listening to the story *I Went Walking* (S. Williams, 1992), the children will be able to make predictions and finish repetitive sentences.
2. As a result of participating in the reading of *I Went Walking,* the children will be able to "write" (using emergent literacy) their own story about the animal that was looking at them at the farm.
3. As a result of working with paint, paper, yarn, dried hay, sponges, grains, colors, and so on, the children will be able to contribute to the creation of a class farm mural.

Developmental and/or content areas that have been integrated. This activity facilitates the children's cognitive and language development when they create their own story of an animal they could see looking at them. Sharing their stories with one another and working cooperatively to create a class mural develops their social skills. Fine motor skills are used in both activities, and the art activity stimulates their aesthetic development.

Lesson Procedures

Introduction. Students will listen as the teacher reads the story *I Went Walking,* by Sue Williams (1992). The teacher will encourage students to predict what will happen and will use the repetitive structure of the story to facilitate the children "reading" along.

Development

1. The book *I Went Walking* will be put in the writing center, and children will be supplied with paper, pencils, and colors to "write" their own "I Went Walking" story. The teacher can encourage the students to write about an animal they saw at the farm.
2. In large-group time, children can share their stories with one another. The teacher can ask questions that will encourage them to elaborate on their stories, thereby extending their language skills.
3. While still in large-group time, the teacher will provide a large farm scene backdrop made on butcher paper to which the children will add their favorite farm animal. The teacher will give directions for the use of animal-shaped sponges, paint, construction paper, paste, and scissors. Yarn, cotton, and straw will be provided for them to add creative details of their choosing. The teacher will point out that the green finger-paint has grains in it, representing what the animals eat. Children can use the paint to create the grass for their animal creation.
4. The children will be divided into small groups and will take turns working on the

mural. A volunteer parent will provide assistance and stimulate the children to talk about what they are doing.

Summary. During large-group time, after the mural is finished, the process of creating the mural will be discussed by the class. Then the teacher can reenact the story *I Went Walking.* The teacher can point to a particular animal on the mural and ask, "I went walking, and what did I see?" The child who created the animal the teacher is pointing to can complete the question with, "I saw a _____ looking at me."

Materials Needed

Book
   I Went Walking, by Sue Williams (1992)

Construction paper

Finger paint

Grains (oats or wheat)

Butcher paper

Yarn, straw, paste, cotton

Scissors

Animal-shaped sponges

Evaluation

Teacher
   Did the children understand how to participate in the activities?
   Were there enough materials?
   Were they appropriate?

Activity
   Did the children enjoy writing their story and making the mural?
   Could they use the materials with little difficulty?

Students
   Did all the students participate?
   Did their stories give indications of development and progress?
   Did they use expanded language in their conversations?

Lesson Plan 4

Lesson Title: Barn Dance!

Concepts, Skills, and Processes Used

1. We can learn to square dance.
2. Animal pictures can be matched to their sounds.

Lesson Objectives

1. As a result of listening to *Barn Dance!* (Martin & Archambault, 1986) and being given square dancing directions, children will participate in a simple dance.
2. As a result of listening to *Barn Dance!* and using associated props, children will recreate the story during center time.
3. As a result of listening to a tape of animals sounds, children will be able to guess the animal and match the corresponding picture to the sound.

Developmental and/or content areas that have been integrated. This lesson facilitates the social development of the children as they play act the story in their center. The dance also facilitates social development and physical development. Aesthetic development is enhanced as children respond to music with body movement. Listening to animal sounds on a tape helps the children develop listening and cognitive skills.

Lesson Procedures

Introduction. The teacher will read *Barn Dance!* by Bill Martin, Jr., and John Archambault (1986). As the story is read, the teacher will point out the rhythm and rhyme of the language in the story and the beauty of the illustrations.

Development

1. During large-group time, the children will listen to a square dance tape with simple commands, such as the Virginia Reel. The teacher will explain and demonstrate the caller's directions and help the children participate in a square dance.
2. In the listening center, children will listen to a tape of farm animal sounds and pick the corresponding animal from animal pictures. The answer will be given after each sound so that children can self-correct their answers.
3. The dramatic play/housekeeping center will be arranged as a simulation of the barn in *Barn Dance!* A table with a red-and-white checkered tablecloth, a small bale of hay, and a prop box complete with cowboy boots, hats, kerchiefs, and child-sized musical instruments (such as guitars or fiddles) will encourage the children to reenact the story in their dramatic play.

Summary. During large-group time, after the children have had a chance to work in the centers, the teacher will guide them to summarize the caller's commands from the square dance tape. A list of commands can be made on the chalkboard, and the children can come up two at a time to demonstrate each command.

Materials Needed

Book
> *Barn Dance!*, by Bill Martin, Jr., and John Archambault (1986)

Tape of animal sounds

Square dance tape

Props for housekeeping center

Evaluation

Teacher
> *Did the children understand how to do the square dance steps?*
> *Were the dance instructions simple enough and demonstrated clearly enough for the children to successfully participate in the dance activity?*

Activity

> *Did the children voluntarily participate in the barn dance dramatic play opportunity?*
> *Were the children able to follow the caller's instructions for the square dance on the tape?*

Students

> *Were all of the children able to participate in following the directions on the square dance tape?*
> *Did all of the students voluntarily participate in the dance activity?*
> *Did the students match the correct pictures to the animal sounds?*

Lesson Plan 5

Lesson Title: Pancake Party

Concepts, Skills, and Processes Used

1. Measuring and mixing ingredients are necessary to make pancakes

Lesson Objectives

1. After listening to *Pancakes for Breakfast* (dePaola, 1978) the children will be able to identify where the ingredients for pancakes come from.
2. As a result of making pancakes, the children will understand how to use a measuring cup and measurement terms.

Developmental and/or content areas that have been integrated. Cognitive and language development are encouraged as children "read" the recipe on the large chart and measure the ingredients. Vocabulary is developed as groups discuss where the ingredients came from and as they use cooking and measuring terms. Nutrition and health concepts are also discussed during this activity, as well as when the children eat their pancakes. Social development is also involved as children interact during the activity.

Lesson Procedures

Introduction. During large-group time, the teacher will read *Pancakes for Breakfast,* by Tomi dePaola (1978). After the reading, the teacher will help students recall information about the story by asking questions such as the following:

What did the lady use to make her pancakes?

Where did she get the eggs, milk, butter, and syrup?

What happened to her pancakes?

Did she still get to have pancakes for breakfast?

Development

1. While still in large-group time, the children will discuss how pancakes are made at their respective houses. The teacher will record the children's responses on a large recipe chart. The teacher will adapt their contributions to include correct measurements and ingredients for pancakes.
2. After the chart is completed, the class will divide into small groups. With the help of fifth-grade students, each group will follow the directions to mix and make pancakes. After they have finished cooking, the children will eat the pancakes.

Summary and Review. During large-group time, the teacher will encourage the students to talk about their cooking experience. The teacher will ask them to describe the sequence of the mixing and cooking and evaluate how well they did in making the pancakes.

Materials Needed

Cooking utensils

Griddles

Spoons

Bowls

Measuring cups

Ingredients for pancakes

Milk

Butter

Pancake mix

Eggs

Book

> *Pancakes for Breakfast,* by Tomi dePaola (1978)

Evaluation

Teacher

> *Were there adequate materials for the cooking activity?*
>
> *Were the questions appropriate for the study and did they encourage recall and discussion?*
>
> *Were the fifth-grade students able to lead their group?*

Activity

> *Did the children enjoy making and eating the pancakes?*

> *Were the children able to work successfully with older students?*
>
> *Were adequate measures taken for the safety of the children while they were cooking?*
>
> *Were all of the students included in the mixing and cooking?*

Students

> *Were the students able to retell the story and learn about the origin of the ingredients for pancakes?*
>
> *Did all children participate?*
>
> *Did the students measure ingredients properly?*
>
> *Did they understand measurement procedures?*

Kindergarten-Primary Unit: If You Give a Mouse a Cookie

Unit Plan Outline

Unit Topic: Mice

Overview or rationale for the unit. The unit is based on the story *If You Give a Mouse a Cookie* (Numeroff, 1985). Students will be able to learn about the differences and similarities between a real and a fictional mouse.

Developmental Stage. Preoperational and Concrete Operational

Grade Level. First Grade

Brainstorming Web. See Figure C.1

List of Activities to Be Used
for Five Lesson Plans

1. Observe real mouse.
2. Sing songs about mice.
3. Discuss different foods mice eat. Have children make and eat food.
4. Talk about manners and how we should ask for things we want.
5. Create mice puppets to be used in dramatization of the book.
6. Have children dictate stories to the teacher about mice.
7. Count how many different things the mouse asked for.
8. Move to music and role play mouse movements.
9. "Draw what you would want if you were a mouse. Explain why you would want these things."
10. Measure a real mouse.

Curriculum Web. See Figure C.2.

Concepts, Skills, and Processes

1. Mice have distinct physical characteristics.
2. Animals can be measured to determine their size.
3. We can write our own stories about what we have learned about mice.
4. We can learn what mice eat.
5. We can describe the differences between real mice and fantasy mice.

Unit Objectives

1. As a result of observing a mouse, students will understand different characteristics of mice.
2. As a result of observing a mouse and listening to the story *If You Give a Mouse a Cookie* (Numeroff, 1985), students will understand and be able to discuss the differences and similarities between a real mouse and a storybook mouse.
3. As a result of observing a mouse, listening to the story *If You Give a Mouse a Cookie,* and participating in an art activity, students will be able to create mice puppets and cut out a picture representing the thing they would desire if they were a mouse.
4. As a result of drawing and measuring mice of different sizes, students will understand how mice can be measured.
5. As a result of studying individual mice drawings, students will be able to discuss a mouse's shape.
6. As a result of measuring a real mouse, students will be able to determine the length of the mouse's tail and the size of the body.

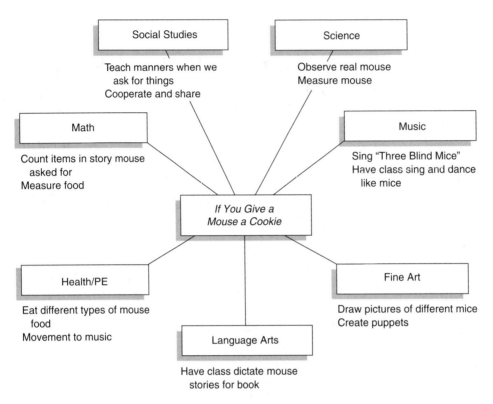

FIGURE C.1 Brainstorming web

7. As a result of their experiences with mice, students will be able to dictate or write and illustrate their own story about mice.

8. As a result of observing a mouse and listening to the story *If You Give a Mouse a Cookie,* students will be able to distinguish between what a real mouse and a storybook mouse would eat.

9. As a result of participating in a music activity with the song "Three Blind Mice," students will be able to sing and role play mouse movements to the music.

Assumptions about previous knowledge. Students will know what mice are. Students will have had previous experiences with mice or have heard stories about mice.

Summary of Activities

1. *Mouse observation.* Both language arts and science are integrated in this activity of observing a real mouse. Children will use language arts skills of listening and answering questions, along with following directions. Science can be seen through the actual manipulation of the real mouse, observance of the different characterists of the mouse, and classification of the differences and similarities between a real and fictional mouse.

2. *Mice puppets.* The integration of language arts, social studies, and art can be seen in this activity of creating mice puppets. The children will use their language art skills of listening and following directions. Social studies will be observed through cooperation and

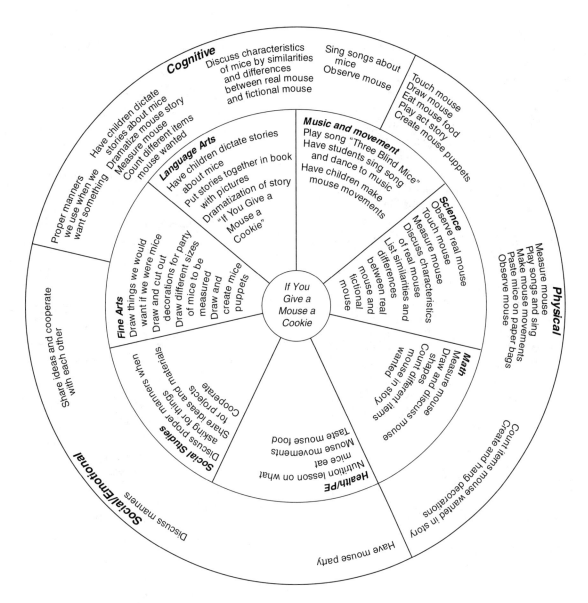

FIGURE C.2 Curriculum web

sharing skills. The art activity in this lesson will include drawing the mice, gluing them on the paper bags, and coloring the mice. The theater arts can be incorporated through role playing the story *If You Give a Mouse a Cookie*.

3. *Mouse shapes and sizes.* This activity integrates art, mathematics, science, and language arts. The art activity is the drawing of different sizes and shapes of mice. The math activity involves measuring the drawn mice and comparing the measurement with that of

a real mouse. Language arts are again experienced through listening and speaking skills. Science is incorporated through measuring and predicting.

4. *Mouse Story.* This activity of dictating or writing individual mouse stories and drawing pictures to illustrate the story integrates language arts and fine arts. Students use their creative abilities for creating and illustrating the story.

5. *Mouse Party.* The integration of health, social studies, music, fine arts, and math can be observed through this activity. The study of nutrition occurs as a result of the different foods used at the mouse party. Physical education can be seen in the movement that the children use as they dance and act like mice. Music is incorporated in the music and movement as they sing along to the song. Art is involved in the making of the decorations and costumes for the party. Social studies occurs in socialization skills during the party and the discussion of proper manners. Math is integrated through measurement of different ingredients for the mouse food.

Lesson Plan 1

Lesson Title: Mouse Observation

Concepts, Skills, and Processes Used

1. Mice have distinct physical characteristics.
2. We can describe the differences between real mice and fantasy mice.

Lesson Objectives

1. As a result of observing a mouse, students will understand different characteristics of mice.
2. As a result of observing a mouse and listening to the story *If You Give a Mouse a Cookie* (Numeroff, 1985), students will understand

and be able to discuss the differences and similarities between a real mouse and a storybook mouse.

Developmental and/or content areas that have been integrated. The content areas of science and language arts will be integrated. The activity will involve science through observation and deductions made through the observation. The activity will be physical in that children will be allowed to touch and hold the mouse. Language arts are integrated through the discussion about the similarities and differences between the real and fictional mouse.

Lesson Procedures

1. *Planning Time.* Students and teacher will discuss what they know about mice. They will then discuss observing a real mouse before it is brought to class. The teacher will discuss rules about how to handle the mouse and things to avoid when holding the mouse.
2. *Observation Time.* The teacher will bring a real mouse to class in a glass aquarium. Students will be allowed to come to the science center in groups of five. Students will be allowed to hold and pet the mouse during the observation. The teacher will point out different characteristics of the mouse and encourage the children to discuss their own observation.
3. *Recall Time.* The teacher will conduct the class in a discussion of the different characteristics of mice. The characteristics will be listed on the board. The children will be encouraged to suggest differences and similarities between the real and the fictional mouse. The differences and similarities will be listed on the board.

Materials Needed

Mouse
Mouse house (aquarium)

Book

> *If You Give a Mouse a Cookie* (Numeroff, 1985)

Evaluation

Teacher

> *Were the activities conducted in a meaningful way with the students?*
>
> *Was the teacher able to maintain the students' interest in the activities?*

Activity

> *Did the children enjoy participating in the activities?*
>
> *Were the children interested in observing and holding the mouse?*
>
> *Did the children understand how to compare the real and fictional mouse?*

Students

> *Did each student handle the mouse carefully?*
>
> *Did each student contribute to the discussions?*

Adaptations

1. *Diversity.* For children who have limited English, vocabulary words related to the storybook will be emphasized.
2. *Developmental Levels.* The planned activities are adaptable to all developmental levels since the observation is concrete and no writing is required.

Lesson Plan 2

Lesson Title: Mice Puppets

Lesson objectives. As a result of observing a mouse, listening to the story *If You Give a Mouse a Cookie,* and participating in an art activity, students will be able to create mice puppets and cut out a picture representing the thing they would desire if they were a mouse.

Developmental and/or content areas that have been integrated. This lesson integrates art with social studies and language arts. It requires that students use their creative abilities to draw and create mice puppets. It will also require the students to work together and be involved in socialization activities. Children will use language arts as they talk to each other and the teacher, and they will use listening skills to follow directions.

Lesson Procedures

1. *Planning Time.* Students will talk about the story and start to think about what they would want if they were a mouse. The teacher will give the class directions about how they will go about creating their puppets and drawing a mouse with one item they would want if they were a mouse.
2. *Activity Time.* The students will each get a brown paper bag, which they will be able to transform into mice puppets. Every student will receive drawing paper and crayons to draw their mouse and the one thing they would ask for if they were a mouse. The students then will cut out their mice and glue them on the brown paper bag. They will also cut out the item that they would ask for if they were a mouse. The class will role play the story *If You Give a Mouse a Cookie* with their puppets, but instead of saying the items the mouse in the story asked for, they will use the items that they drew in class.
3. *Discussion Time.* Students will talk about why they chose the items they selected for the activity. The teacher will ask the students to contribute responses to the other students' ideas.

Materials Needed

Brown paper bags

Scissors

Glue

Drawing paper

Crayons

Evaluation

Teacher

> *Was enough time provided for completing the puppets?*
> *Was the class managed so that all students participated in the role play?*
> *Were all students included in the discussion?*

Activity

> *Were the students able to manage the materials to construct the puppets?*
> *Did the students seem interested in the role-play activity?*

Students

> *Did all students participate in the activities?*
> *Did the students work in a cooperative manner?*

Adaptations

1. *Diversity.* Children with language differences might have more difficulty in engaging in the discussion about the story and what they would want if they were a mouse. All attempts to contribute will be accepted equally. Children with motor skill delay might need help making puppets.
2. *Developmental levels.* Children with less developed fine motor skills will need encouragement and suggestions in making their mouse puppets.

Lesson Plan 3

Lesson Title: Mouse Shapes and Sizes

Concepts, Skills, and Processes Used

1. Animals can be measured to determine their size.

Lesson Objectives

1. As a result of drawing and measuring mice of difference sizes, students will understand how mice can be measured.
2. As a result of studying individual mice drawings, students will be able to discuss a mouse's shape.
3. As a result of measuring a real mouse, students will be able to determine the length of the mouse's tail and the size of the body.

Developmental and/or content areas that have been integrated. This lesson includes the integration of art, mathematics, science, and language arts. Children use social and emotional skills in co-operating and sharing materials and information. Science and math are used in measuring different parts of the mouse's body. Art is used in drawing mice.

Lesson Procedures

1. *Planning time.* The teacher will plan the activity of measuring the mouse with the class by first talking about and predicting how big the children think mice are. The responses can be written on a large chart or chalk board. The teacher will provide appropriate instructions for drawing mice.
2. *Activity time.* Students will draw mice of different shapes and sizes. They will cut out their mice and tape them on the board. Students will use a ruler or measuring tape to measure the mice. The teacher will assist in the measuring process. The real mouse will be measured and the measurements put on the board next to the students' earlier predictions. The class will discuss the predictions compared with the measuring results.
3. *Discussion time.* The class will discuss the different measurements of their mice and compare measurements of the real mouse with drawn mice.

Materials Needed

Scissors

Drawing paper

Crayons

Measuring tape or ruler

Real mouse

Evaluation

Teacher

Did the students understand the purpose for drawing mice?

Did they understand the value in measuring the real mouse?

Was the measuring activity conducted so that all students could feel involved?

Activity

How did comparing the measurements of the drawn mice with those of the real mouse benefit the students?

Were they interested in discussing the different mice drawings?

Students

Were all students engaged in attending to the measuring activities?

Did all students exhibit an interest in using the ruler or tape measure?

Did students understand how to use a measuring tool?

Adaptations

1. *Developmental levels.* Children will be paired or grouped to measure the mouse. Some children may lack experiences in how to use a measuring tape or ruler. One partner of the pair will be able to guide the measuring activity.

Lesson Plan 4

Lesson Title: Mouse Story

Concepts, Skills, and Processes Used

1. We can write our own stories about mice.

Lesson objectives. As a result of their experiences with mice, students will be able to dictate or write and illustrate their own story about mice.

Developmental and/or content areas that have been integrated. This lesson integrates art and language arts. Fine motor skills are used for writing and illustrating the story. Art is integrated in the illustration, and language arts are involved in dictating or writing the story.

Lesson Procedures

1. *Planning time.* The teacher and students will discuss some ideas for writing or dictating a story about mice. Some of the ideas can be listed on the board. Students are encouraged to be creative in extending their own ideas for a story.
2. *Activity time.* The students individually work on writing or dictating their story. Each child then illustrates his or her story. Completed stories are bound into a class book.
3. *Discussion time.* Students can read or tell their stories and discuss their pictures. Children are encouraged to respond to other students' stories. Suggestions might be made to revise or extend stories.

Materials Needed

Drawing paper

Crayons

Notebook or materials to construct a book for the stories

Evaluation

Teacher

Was the teacher able to manage dictation from individual students?

Were students encouraged to work at their own ability level in writing or dictating their stories?

Activity

> *Did all of the students seem interested in creating a story and illustration?*
>
> *Were the students able to give supportive and constructive comments to other students' stories?*

Students

> *Did all of the students complete their story?*
> *Did each student use the time well?*

Adaptations

1. *Developmental levels.* Some children might have difficulty using ideas written on the board for writing their story. Similarly, they might have difficulty in writing their own story. Those needing help will be guided in using written ideas and will be able to dictate their story if they prefer.

Lesson Plan 5

Lesson Title: Mouse Party

Concepts, Skills, and Processes Used

1. We can learn what mice eat.

Lesson Objectives

1. As a result of observing a mouse and listening to the story *If You Give a Mouse a Cookie* (Numeroff, 1985), students will be able to distinguish between what a real mouse and a storybook mouse would eat.
2. As a result of participating in a music activity with the song "Three Blind Mice," students will be able to sing and role play mouse movements to the music.

Developmental and/or content areas that have been integrated. This lesson integrates health, social studies, mathematics, music, and movement. Social studies involve the use of proper manners at a meal. Music and movement involve the song and dance movements. Math is incorporated through measuring ingredients for food, and health involves eating different types of foods.

Lesson Procedures

1. *Planning time.* Students and teacher will discuss and plan the mouse party. The students will each participate in creating the decorations for the party, as well as their costumes. The teacher will help set the guidelines for behavior during the party.
2. *Activity time.* Students will cut out mice ears and tails, which they will wear to the party. They will create decorations for the party, which will be hung around the room. In small groups, food trays will be prepared for the party. Two trays of food will be made. One tray will have the items the mouse in *If You Give a Mouse a Cookie* wanted. The other tray will have what real mice will eat.

   Following the eating activity, the teacher will play the song "Three Blind Mice." The students will sing along and dance and role play mice movements to the music.

3. *Recall and review time.* The class will review what they have learned about what mice eat. They will compare the types of food the real mouse eats with the types of food the fictional mouse eats.

Materials Needed

Mouse

Food (cheese, grains, cookies, milk, etc.)

Record of "Three Blind Mice"

Colored paper for tails and ears

Materials for room decorations

Evaluation

Teacher

> *Were the students prepared appropriately for the activities?*
>
> *Was the teacher able to manage the activities smoothly?*

Were all students able to participate in food preparation?

Was enough time allotted for the activities related to the party?

Activity

Was there enough food for all to sample?

Did the students enjoy role playing mice?

Students

Were all students actively involved in the activities?

Did each student contribute to the review at the end of the activities?

Adaptations

1. *Developmental levels.* Some children might need assistance in the cutting activity. All should be able to assist in preparing food trays.

Primary Unit: Alexander and the Terrible, Horrible, No Good, Very Bad Day

Unit Plan Outline

Unit Topic: Alexander and the Terrible, Horrible, No Good, Very Bad Day, *by Judith Viorst (1972)*

Overview or rationale for the unit. Alexander and the Terrible, Horrible, No Good, Very Bad Day is a familiar story to most children who have experienced days when nothing seems to go quite right. Children will relate to Alexander and realize that life does, indeed, have its ups and downs but that in some situations they can control the outcome and in other situations the result is simply unavoidable—even if you live in Australia! The goals of this unit are to incorporate meaningful activities to develop the children's knowledge and skills in all of the cognitive, social-emotional, and physical development areas; to develop self-esteem, a sense of competence, and positive feelings toward learning; and to view each child at different levels of ability as well as integrate all of the content areas of language arts, social studies, science, mathematics, and fine arts that are woven throughout the story.

Developmental stage. Transitional period moving from preoperational to concrete operation (5- to 8-years-old).

Grade level. Second Grade

Brainstorming web. See Figure D.1.

List of Activities to Be Used for Five Lesson Plans

1. The teacher will read to the class the literature selection, *Alexander and the Terrible, Horrible, No Good, Very Bad Day,* (Viorst, 1972), followed by a discussion of the story. The children will write and illustrate a sequel to the story of what might have happened the next day.
2. The class will locate the continent of Australia on a map, and the children can draw a map of the continent. This will be followed by an identification game in which children select a picture, identify it, and become familiar with the person, place, or thing that is characteristic of Australia.
3. A dentist will visit the class to discuss the importance of care for the teeth. The class will participate using a model of teeth and demonstrating proper dental hygiene techniques.
4. The children will construct a graph charting the least favorite vegetable of the class.
5. The children will become familiar with an Australian song through singing and dancing.

Curriculum Web. See Figure D.2.

Concepts, Skills, and Processes

1. Everyone has bad days.
2. Good dental hygiene helps prevent cavities.
3. Australia is a country and a continent.
4. We can use bar graphs to compare amounts.
5. We can learn to waltz.

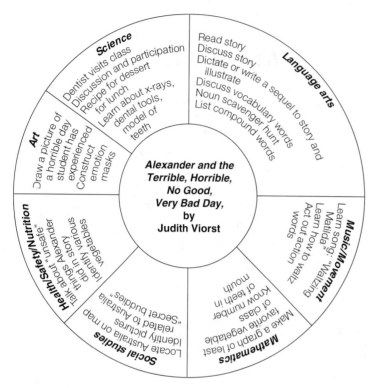

FIGURE D.1 Brainstorming web

Unit Objectives

1. Students will understand that it is not unusual to have a bad day.
2. Students will be able to distinguish between safe and unsafe practices.
3. Students will understand the importance of proper dental hygiene and the way to avoid cavities.
4. Students will be able to locate Australia on a map; will know that it is not only a separate country, but also one of the seven continents; and will be familiar with certain characteristics of the country.
5. Students will be able to construct a graph charting the least favorite vegetable of the class.
6. Students will be able to understand the process of creative thinking when writing a sequel to the story.
7. Students will be exposed to Australian idioms in the lyrics of the song "Waltzing Matilda."
8. Students will have an opportunity to dance a waltz to "Waltzing Matilda."

Assumptions About Previous Knowledge

1. Students should be familiar with daily practices that promote oral hygiene.
2. Students should have basic familiarity with safe and unsafe practices.
3. Students should be familiar with construction of graphs.
4. Students should know basic geography skills concerning direction and location.
5. Students should have a basic interest in the topic of literature selection and knowledge of listening, discussing, reading, and writing skills.

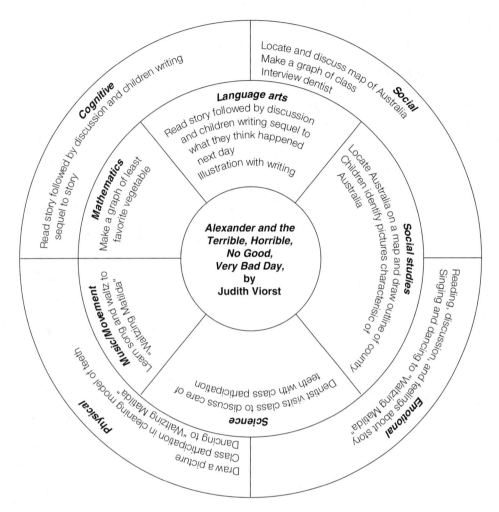

FIGURE D.2   Curriculum web

6. Students will have had some exposure to music and movement to music.

Summary of Activities

Physical Activities

1. *Music/Movement.* Students will become familiar with the Australian song "Waltzing Matilda" and will become acquainted with the steps to the waltz. This activity will initially be teacher-directed, with the words to the song being taught by the teacher or played on

a record or tape. Special terms will be defined for the student. Basic steps to the waltz will be demonstrated for the students. The students will then divide into pairs, singing and dancing to the song (teacher directed).

2. *Science.* The dentist will discuss the importance of caring for the teeth with class participation using a model of teeth and demonstrating proper dental hygiene techniques. This activity will initially be teacher directed, with discussion, but will be followed by a hands-on activity of brushing

and flossing the large model of teeth. Each child will receive his or her own personal toothbrush and floss from the dentist.

3. *Language Arts.* The students will use creative thinking abilities to write a sequel to the story of what might have happened to Alexander the next day. This activity will be an informal handwriting exercise providing flexibility in fine motor skills in a less structured environment (child initiated).

Cognitive Activities

1. *Language Arts.* The teacher will read the literature selection, followed by a class discussion of the story. The children will write a sequel to the story of what might have happened the next day and will include an illustration. This activity will be done in a reading circle with all of the children. It will begin as a teacher-directed activity with reading of the story, followed by discussion in comprehension, safety practices, vocabulary words, nouns, and compound words. As a child-initiated activity, children will use their own creative thinking abilities by writing a sequel to the story of what they think might have happened to Alexander on the next day. This exercise will accommodate children as emerging writers at various stages of development and with varying ability to actively reconstruct knowledge.

2. *Mathematics.* Students will construct a graph charting the least favorite vegetable of the class. Discussion will begin with a teacher-directed question, such as when the class remembered the vegetable that Alexander hated in the story. After students respond to the question, the discussion will lead to other vegetables that the children consider their least favorite. The students will be divided into small groups to decide what is the least favorite vegetable of the whole group. The results from the groups will be given to the teacher, who will then graph a large chart of the least favorite vegetables in the class.

Social-Emotional Activities

1. *Social studies.* Students will locate Australia on a map or globe and will draw a map of the continent. This will be followed by an identification game. A large Manila envelope containing various pictures of persons, places, and things is passed around to each child. Each child selects a picture from the envelope and identifies it, and the class then discusses its relevance to Australia.

2. *Language arts.* The class will discuss the story. This activity touches on many aspects of social studies learning by exploring Alexander's day, his experiences with friends and his teacher, his relationship with his family, and the dentist, and so on. By discussing Alexander's social experiences, the students are able to understand the importance of positive peer relationships, class rules, and self-control.

Lesson Plan 1

Lesson Title: Have You Ever Had a Bad Day?

Concepts, Skills, and Processes Used
1. Everyone has bad days.

Lesson Objectives
1. The students will understand that it is not unusual to have a bad day.
2. The students will be able to distinguish between safe and unsafe practices.
3. The students will be able to understand the process of creative thinking when writing a sequel to the story.

Developmental and/or content areas that have been integrated. Language arts, social studies, and art activities have been integrated into the lesson.

Lesson procedures. Students will be read the literature selection *Alexander's Terrible, Horrible, No Good, Very Bad Day* by Judith Viorst (1972).

This will be followed by discussion of the story with such topics as what unsafe actions Alexander performed that could have been prevented; what his relationships were with family, friends, and teachers; why his trip to the dentist's office was unpleasant, and so on. The students would then have an opportunity to write a sequel to the story and imagine what they think might have happened to Alexander the next day. The students will create an illustration to go with their sequel.

Materials Needed

Book

> *Alexander and the Terrible, Horrible, No Good, Very Bad Day,* by Judith Viorst (1972)

Chalkboard and chalk or easel with large writing tablet with marker

Paper and pencil

Evaluation

Teacher

> *Was the discussion led in such a manner that most of the students felt they were actively involved?*

Activity

> *Did the students enjoy the story?*
> *Were the children interested in writing and illustrating the sequel to the story?*

Students

> *Did each student attempt to do his or her best in writing and illustrating the sequel to the story?*
> *Did each student focus on the discussion that followed the reading of the story?*

Lesson Plan 2

Lesson Title: Where IS Australia, Anyway?

Concepts, Skills, and Processes Used

1. Australia is a country and a continent.

Lesson objectives. Students will be able to locate the country of Australia on a map; they will know that it is not only a separate country but also one of the seven continents; and they will be familiar with certain characteristics of the country.

Development and/or content areas that have been integrated. Language arts, social studies, and art activities have been integrated into the lesson.

Lesson Procedures. The lesson will begin with a discussion of Alexander's references to going to Australia whenever he is unhappy with a situation. The students will then find Australia on a map and be able to draw an outline of the country. The class will play a game in which a large Manila envelope containing various magazine pictures of persons, places, and things that are characteristic of Australia will be passed to each student. The student will identify the picture and understand its association with Australia.

Materials Needed

Large world map showing the country of Australia

Paper and crayons or markers

Large Manila envelope

Magazine pictures of persons, places, or things characteristic of Australia

Evaluation

Teacher

> *Was the discussion conducted in a relevant manner?*
> *Were the students encouraged to participate in the discussion?*

Activity

> *Were the students interested in the discussion and the game?*
> *Were the pictures used for the game relevant to Australia?*

Students

> *Was each student able to locate and draw an outline of Australia?*
> *Did each student actively participate in the game?*

Lesson Plan 3

Lesson Title: Cavities Make for a Very Bad Day!

Lesson objectives. Students will understand the importance of proper dental hygiene and the way to avoid cavities.

Developmental and/or content areas that have been integrated. Science, social studies, language arts, and mathematics activities have been integrated into the lesson.

Lesson procedures. A dentist will visit the class to discuss the importance of proper dental hygiene. The dentist will show various charts, x-rays taken of patients' teeth, and examples of tools used in the office. A hands-on model of teeth will be displayed for the children to look at and will be used by the dentist to show the proper procedure for cleaning the teeth with a toothbrush and floss. The students will learn the total number of teeth in the human mouth. The children will also be able to participate in cleaning a model of the teeth. At the close of the visit, the dentist will give each of the students his or her own toothbrush and floss to take home.

Materials Needed

Dental charts

x-rays

Dental tools

Model of teeth

Toothbrushes

Floss

Chalkboard and chalk

Evaluation

Teacher
> *Was the dentist able to communicate effectively with the students?*

Activity
> *Were all students able to participate in the lesson procedures?*

Students
> *Did the students understand the importance of regular brushing and flossing?*
> *Could the students demonstrate the proper way to brush their teeth?*

Lesson Plan 4

Lesson Title: Terrible, Horrible, No Good, Very Bad Veggies!

Concepts, Skills, and Processes Used

1. We can use graphs to compare amounts.

Lesson objectives. Students will be able to construct a graph charting the least favorite vegetable of the class.

Developmental and/or content areas that have been integrated. Mathematics, language arts, science, and social studies activities have been integrated into the lesson. Lesson Procedures. Students will be asked if they remember what vegetable (lima beans) Alexander hated in the story. The students will then be told they are going to construct a graph to show which vegetable is the least favorite of the class. Various common vegetables will be shown to the students through pictures or actual vegetables bought at the store. The students will initially be divided into small groups to decide which is their least favorite vegetable among their own group. Then the results will be given to the teacher to be graphed on a class chart to determine the least favorite vegetable of the whole class.

Materials Needed

Pictures of vegetables or actual vegetables bought at store

Mimeographed copies of graphing chart for individual students

Large graphing chart in front of room for showing totals of least favorite vegetables

Evaluation

Teacher
> *Was the teacher able to clearly explain the procedures for making the chart?*

Activity
> *Were all of the students able to participate in the graphing activity?*

Students
> *Were the students able to complete the graphing chart within their small group?*

Lesson Plan 5

Lesson Title: "Waltzing Matilda"

Concepts, Skills, and Processes Used

1. We can learn to waltz.

Lesson Objectives

1. Students will be exposed to Australian idioms in the lyrics of the song "Waltzing Matilda."
2. Students will have an opportunity to dance a waltz to "Waltzing Matilda."

Developmental and/or content areas that have been integrated. Music and movement, language arts, and social studies activities have been integrated into the lesson.

Lesson Procedures. Students will become familiar with the words and tune to the Australian song "Waltzing Matilda." There will be a discussion of unfamiliar terms such as *swagman* (hobo), *billabong* (pond), *billy* (small pot of water), *jimbucks* (sheep), and *tuckerbag* (travel sack) included in the song and an explanation of their meaning. After becoming familiar with the song, the students will be divided in pairs to learn how to do a waltz. The students will then try waltzing to the song.

Materials Needed

Words to "Waltzing Matilda"

Tape or record of "Waltzing Matilda"

Evaluation

Teacher
> *Was the teacher able to clearly explain the unfamiliar terms during the discussion?*
> *Was the teacher able to teach the students how to do a waltz?*

Activity
> *Was the waltz within the students' ability level?*

Students
> *Did each student participate in singing the song and waltzing?*

References

Abramson, S., Robinson R., & Ankenman, K. (1994–1995). Project work with diverse students: Adapting curriculum based on the Reggio Emilia approach. *Childhood Education, 71,* 197–202.

Abramson, S., Seda, I., & Johnson, C. (1990). Literacy development in a multilingual kindergarten classroom. *Childhood Education, 67,* 68–72.

Adams, M. J. (1990). *Beginning to read: Thinking and learning about print.* Cambridge, MA: MIT Press.

Adler, J. (1998, November 2). Tomorrow's child. *Newsweek,* pp. 54–57, 60–63.

Allport, G. (1952). *The nature of prejudice.* New York: Doubleday Anchor.

Anglin, J. (1973). Introduction. In J. Anglin (Ed.), *Jerome S. Bruner. Beyond the information given* (pp. xiii–xxiii). New York: W. W. Norton.

Apple, P., Enders, S., & Wortham, S. (1998). Portfolio assessment for infants, toddlers, and preschoolers: Bridging the gap between data collection and individualized planning. In S. C. Wortham, A. Barbour, & B. Desjean-Perrotta, *Portfolio assessment: A handbook for preschool and elementary educators* (pp. 31–44). Olney, MD: Association for Childhood Education International.

ASCD Early Childhood Education Policy Panel. (1988). Analysis of issues concerning public school involvement in early childhood education. In C. Warger (Ed.), *A resource guide to public school early childhood programs* (pp. 99–115). Alexandria, VA: Association for Super-vision and Curriculum Development.

Asher, S. R., & Williams, G. A. (1987). Helping children without friends in home and school contexts. In *Children's social development: Information for teachers and parents* (pp. 1–26). Urbana, IL: ERIC Clearinghouse on Elementary and Early Childhood Education.

Atkinson, A. H., & Green, V. P. (1990). Cooperative learning: The teacher's role. *Childhood Education, 66,* 280–284.

Au, K. H. (2000). Literacy instruction for young children of diverse backgrounds. In D. S. Strickland & L. M. Morrow (Eds.), *Beginning reading and writing* (pp. 35–45). New York: Teachers College Press.

Au, K. H., & Kawakami, A. J. (1991). Culture and ownership: Schooling of minority students. *Childhood Education, 67,* 280–284.

Austin, J. S. (2000). When a child discloses sexual abuse: Immediate and appropriate teacher responses. *Childhood Education, 77,* 2–5.

Back, C. (1986). *Bean and plant.* Parsippany, NJ: Silver Burdett.

Baker, P., & Raban, B. (1991). Reading before and after the early days of schooling. *Reading, 25,* 6–13.

Bandura, A., & Walters, R. (1963). *Social learning and personality development.* New York: Holt, Rinehart, & Winston.

Barbour, A. (1993). *Physical competence and peer relations: Case studies of eight second-graders.* Unpublished doctoral dissertation, University of Texas at Austin.

Barbour, A., & Desjean-Perrotta. (1998). The basics of portfolio assessment. In S. Wortham, A. Barbour, & B. Desjean-Perrotta, *Portfolio assessment. A handbook for preschool and elementary teachers* (pp. 15–27). Olney, MD: Association for Childhood Education International.

Barbour, N. H., & Seefeldt, C. (1993). *Developmental continuity across preschool and primary grades.* Wheaton, MD: Association for Childhood Education International.

Barclay, K., Benelli, C., & Schoon, S. (1999). Making the connection: Science and literacy. *Childhood Education, 75,* 147–149.

Barkeley, R. (1989). Attention deficit disorders: History, definition, diagnosis. In M. Lewis & S. Miller (Eds.), *Handbook of developmental psychopathology,* (pp. 65–76). New York: Plenum Press.

Barnes, B. R. (1991). Using children's literature in the early anthropology curriculum. *Social Education, 55,* 17–18.

Barnett, S. W., & Escobar, C. M. (1990). Economic costs and benefits of early intervention. In S. J. Meisels & J. P. Shonkoff (Eds.), *Handbook of early childhood intervention* (pp. 560–582). New York: Cambridge University Press.

Barufaldi, J. P., Ladd, K. G. T., & Moses, A. J. (1984). *Health science* [Level K]. Lexington, MA: D. C. Heath.

Baumrind, D. (1971). Current patterns of parental authority. *Developmental Psychology Monographs, 4* (1, Pt. 2).

Beach, L., Hinojosa, B. L., & Tedford, A. C. (1991, November/December). Holiday express: A cross-curricular, multicultural geography unit on holidays around the world. *Instructor,* pp. 25–29.

Beaty, J. J. (1998). *Observing development of the young child.* Upper Saddle River, NJ: Merrill/Prentice Hall.

Beaty, J. J. (1992). *Preschool appropriate practices.* Fort Worth: Harcourt Brace Jovanovich.

Beaty, J. J. (2000). *Skills for preschool teachers* (6th ed.). Upper Saddle River, NJ: Merrill/Prentice Hall.

Beilin, H. (1989). Piagetian theory. In R. Vasta (Ed.), *Annals of child development* (Vol. 6). Greenwich, CT: JAI Press.

Belsky, J. (1989). Infant-parent attachment and day care: In defense of the strange situation. In J. S. Lande, S. Scar, & N. Gunzenhauser (Eds.), *Caring for children: Challenge to America.* Hillsdale, NJ: Erlbaum.

Belsky, J., & Steinberg, L. (1978). The effects of day care: A critical review. *Child Development, 49,* 929–949.

Bergen, D., Reed, R., & Torelli, L. (200). Introduction. In D. Bergen, R. Reid, & L. Torelli, *Educating and caring for very young children. The infant/toddler curriculum.* New York: Teachers College Press.

Bergeron, B. S., Wermuth, S., Rhodes, M., & Rudenga, E. A. (1996). Language development and thematic instruction. Supporting young learners at risk. *Childhood Education, 72,* 141–145. *Handbook of developmental psychopathology.* New York: Plenum.

Berk, L. E. (1994). Vygotsky's theory: The importance of make-believe play. *Young Children, 50,* 30–38.

Berk, L. E. (1996). *Infants, children, and adolescents* (2nd ed.). Boston: Allyn & Bacon.

Berk, L. E., & Winsler, A. (1995). *Scaffolding children's learning: Vygotsky and early childhood education.* Washington, DC: National Association for the Education of Young Children.

Bernhardt, J. L. (2000). A primary caregiving system for infants and toddlers: Best for everyone involved. *Young Children, 55,* 74–80.

Bernstein, N. (1982, April 16). Infant day care: Controversial, expensive, and scarce. *Milwaukee Journal.*

Berrueta-Clement, J. R., Schweinhart, L. J., Barrett, W. S., Epstein, A. S., & Weikart, D. P. (1984). Changed lives: The effects of the Perry Preschool programs on youths through age 19. *Monographs of the High/Scope Educational Research Foundation, 8.* Ypsilanti, MI: High/Scope Press.

Better Homes Fund. (1999). *Homeless children: America's new outcasts.* Newton, MA: Author.

Blake, S., Hurley, S., & Arenz, B. (1995). Mathematical problem solving and young children. *Early Childhood Education Journal, 23,* 81–84.

Bloom, B. (1964). *Stability and change in human characteristics.* New York: John Wiley.

Bloom, B. (1972). *Language development: Form and function in emerging grammars.* Cambridge, MA: MIT Press.

Bodrova, E., & Leong, D. J. (1996). *Tools of the mind. The Vygotskian approach to early childhood education.* Upper Saddle River, NJ: Merrill/Prentice Hall.

Boehm, A. E., & Weinberg, R. A. (1997). *The classroom observer. Developing observation skills in early childhood classrooms.* New York: Teachers College Press.

Bond, G. L., & Dykstra, R. (1967). The cooperative research program in first-grade reading instruction. *Reading Research Quarterly, 2,* 5–142.

Bonn, M. (1976). An American paradox. In E. H. Grotberg (Ed.), *200 years of children* (pp. 160–169). Washington, DC: U.S. Department of Health, Education, & Welfare.

Bowman, B. T. (1992). Reaching potentials of minority children through developmentally and culturally appropriate practices. In S. Bredekamp & T. Rosegrant (Eds.), *Reaching potentials: Appropriate curriculum and assessment for young children* (pp. 128–135). Washington, DC: National Association for the Education of Young Children.

Bowman, B. T. (1999). Achieving excellence in education. *Center for Early Education at Rutgers. Conference Special Issue, 1,* 1–7.

Bowman, B. T., & Stott, F. M. (1994). Understanding development in a cultural context: The challenge for teachers. In B. L. Mallory & R. S. New (Eds.), *Diversity and developmentally appropriate practices,* (pp. 119–134). New York: Teachers College Press.

Bowman, B., Donovan, S., & Burns, M. S. (Eds.) (Committee on Early Childhood Pedagogy). (2000). *Eager to learn: Educating our preschoolers.* Washington, DC: National Academy Press.

Boyer, E. L. (1989). What teachers say about children in America. *Educational Leadership, 46,* 73–75.

Branley, F. M. (1986). *Air is all around you.* New York: Harper & Row.

Braun, S. J., & Edwards, E. P. (1972). *History and theory of early childhood education.* Belmont, CA: Wadsworth.

Brazelton, T. B. (1985, December). Do you really want a superkid? *Family Circle,* p. 75.

Brazelton, T. B. (1989, February 3). Working parents. *Newsweek,* pp. 66–70.

Bredekamp, S. (Ed.). (1987). *Developmentally appropriate practice in early childhood programs serving children from birth through age 8.* Washington, DC: National Association for the Education of Young Children.

Bredekamp, S. (1993). The relationship between early childhood education and early childhood special education: Healthy marriage or family feud? *Topics in Early Childhood Special Education, 13,* 258–273.

Bredekamp, S., & Copple, C. (Eds.). (1997). *Developmentally appropriate practice in early childhood programs* (Revised). Washington, DC: National Association for the Education of Young Children.

Bredekamp, S., & Rosegrant, T. (Eds.). (1992). *Reaching potentials: Appropriate curriculum and assessment for young children* (Vol. 1). Washington, DC: National Association for the Education of Young Children.

Bredekamp, S., & Rosegrant, T. (Eds.). (1995). *Reaching potentials: Transforming early childhood curriculum and assessment* (Vol. 2). Washington, DC: National Association for the Education of Young Children.

Bredekamp, S., & Shepard, S. (1989). How to best protect children from inappropriate school expectations, practices, and policies. *Young Children, 44,* 14–24.

Brewer, J. A. (1994). *Introduction to early childhood education.* Boston: Allyn & Bacon.

Bromley, D. A. (1989). A conversation with D. Allen Bromley by B. J. Culliton. *Science, 246,* 203.

Bronfenbrenner, U. (1979). Contexts of child rearing: Problems and prospects. *American Psychologist, 34,* 844–850.

Bronfenbrenner, U. (1986). Ecology of the family as a context for human development: Research perspectives. *Developmental Psychology, 22,* 723–742.

Brown, F., & Yoshida, R. K. (1996). Children with mental retardation. In E. L. Meyen (Ed.), *Exceptional children in today's schools* (3rd ed., pp. 433–464). Denver: Love.

Brown, R. (1973). *A first language: The early stages.* Cambridge, MA: Harvard University Press.

Brown, S. (1997). First graders write to discover mathematics relevancy. *Young Children, 52,* 51–53.

Bruer, J. T. (1999, May). In search of . . . brain-based education. *Phi Delta Kappan,* 649–657.

Bruner, J. S. (1972). The nature and uses of immaturity. *American Psychologist, 27,* 687–708.

Bruner, J. S. (1983). Play, thought, and language. *Peabody Journal of Education, 60,* 6–69.

Buchoff, R. (1990). Attention deficit disorder: Help for the classroom teacher. *Childhood Education, 67,* 86–90.

Burk, D. I. (1996). Understanding friendship and social interaction. *Childhood Education, 72,* 282–285.

Burns, M. S., Griffin, P., & Snow, C. E. (Eds.). (1999). *Starting out right: A guide to promoting children's reading success.* Washington, DC: National Academy Press. (http://bob.nap.edu/readingroom/books/sor/sor-int.htm).

Byrnes, D. A., & Kiger, G. (1992). *Common bonds: Anti-bias teaching in a diverse society.* Wheaton, MD: Association for Childhood Education International.

Cadwell, L. B. (1997). *Bringing Reggio Emilia home.* New York: Teachers College Press.

Caldwell, B. (1986). Day care and the public schools—Natural allies, natural enemies. *Educational Leadership, 44,* 34–39.

Caldwell, B. M. (1989). A comprehensive model for integrating child care and early childhood education. *Teachers College Record, 90,* 404–414.

Campbell, P. E. (1999). Fostering each child's understanding of mathematics. In C. Seefeldt (Ed.), *The early childhood curriculum. Current findings in theory and practice,* (pp. 106–132). New York: Teachers College Press.

Carle, E. *The tiny seed*. Saxonville, MA: Picture Book Studio.

Carnegie Corporation of New York (Carnegie Task Force on Meeting the Needs of Young Children). (1994). *Starting points. Meeting the needs of our youngest children*. New York: Author.

Carnegie Corporation of New York (Carnegie Task Force on learning in the Primary Grades). (1996). *Years of promise. A comprehensive learning strategy for America's children*. New York: Author.

Carta, J. J. (1995). Developmentally appropriate practices: A critical analysis as applied to young children with disabilities. *Focus on Exceptional Children, 27*, 1–14.

Carta, J. J., Atwater, J. B., Schwartz, I. S., & McConnell, S. R. (1993). A reaction to Johnson, & McChesney Johnson. *Topics in Early Childhood Special Education, 13*, 243–254.

Carter, L. G. (1984). The sustaining effects of compensatory and elementary education. *Educational Researcher*, 4–13.

Cassady, J. K. (1988). Beginning reading with big books. *Childhood Education, 65*, 18–23.

Cataldo, C. Z. (1983). *Infant and toddler programs: A guide to very early childhood education*. Reading, MA: Addison-Wesley.

Caulfield, R. (1996). Physical and cognitive development in the first two years. *Early Childhood Education Journal, 23*, 239–242.

Cazden, C. (1972). *Child language and education*. New York: Holt, Rinehart, & Winston.

Cazden, C. (1976). Play and language and metalinguistic awareness. In J. Bruner, A. Jolly, & K. Slyva (Eds.), *Play: Its development and evolution*. New York: Basic Books.

Chall, J. (1967). *Learning to read: The great debate*. New York: McGraw-Hill.

Chall, J. (1983). *Learning to read: The great debate* (Updated ed.). New York: McGraw-Hill.

Chall, J. S. (1996). *Learning to read: The great debate* (3rd ed.). Fort Worth, TX: Harcourt Brace.

Chapman, M. L. (1996). The development of phonemic awareness in young children: Some insights from a case study of a first-grade writer. *Young Children, 51*, 31–37.

Charbonneau, M. P., & Reider, B. E. (1995). *The integrated elementary classroom. A developmental model of education for the 21st century*. Boston: Allyn & Bacon.

Chard, S. C. (1992). *The Project Approach: A practical guide for teachers*. Edmonton, Alberta, Canada: University of Alberta.

Chard, S. C. (1994a). *The Project Approach: A second practical guide for teachers*. Edmonton, Alberta, Canada: University of Alberta.

Chard, S. C. (1994b). *The Project Approach: A practical course for teachers*. Edmonton, Alberta, Canada: University of Alberta.

Charlesworth, R., & Lind, K. K. (1990). *Math and science for young children*. Albany, NY: Delmar.

Chase, P. (1995). A harvest of learning for a multiage class. *Educational Leadership, 53*, 58–61.

Checkley, K. (1997). The first seven . . . And the eighth: A conversation with Howard Gardner. *Educational Leadership, 55*, 8–13.

Chess, S., & Thomas, A. (1977). Temperamental individuality from childhood to adolescence. *Journal of Child Psychiatry, 16*, 218–226.

Child Mental Health Foundations and Agencies Network (FAN). (2000). *A good beginning. Sending America's children to school with the social and emotional competencies they need*. Bethesda, MD: National Institute of Mental Health.

Children's Defense Fund. (1989). *A vision for America's future*. Washington, DC: Author.

Children's Defense Fund. (1991). *The state of America's children: 1991*. Washington, DC: Author.

Children's Defense Fund. (1994). *The state of America's children yearbook 1994*. Washington, DC: Author.

Children's Defense Fund. (2000). *The state of America's children*. Washington, DC: Author.

Chomsky, C. (1965). *Aspects of a theory of syntax*. Cambridge, MA: MIT Press.

Chomsky, C. (1972). Stages in language development and reading. *Harvard Educational Review, 42*, 1–33.

Chomsky, N. (1968). *Language and mind*. New York: Harcourt Brace Jovanovich.

Christie, J., Enz, B., & Vukelich, C. (1997). *Teaching language and literacy*. New York: Longman.

Chukovsky, K. (1971). *From two to five*. Los Angeles: University of California Press.

Clark, E. (1983). Meanings and concepts. J. H. Flavell & E. Markman (Eds.), Vol. 3. *Cognitive development*. New York: John Wiley & Sons.

Clarke-Stewart, K. A. (1989, January). Single-parent families: How bad for the children? *NEA Today*, pp. 60–64.

Clarke-Stewart, K. A., Alhusen, V. D., & Clements, D. C. (1995). Nonparental caregiving. In M. H. Bornstein (Ed.), *Handbook of parenting* (Vol. 3). Hillsdale, NJ: Erlbaum.

Clay, M. M. (1993). *Reading recovery: A guidebook for teachers in training.* Portsmouth, NH: Heinemann.

Clewett, A. S. (1988). Guidance and discipline: Teaching young children appropriate behavior. *Young Children, 43,* 26–31.

Cliatt, M. J. P., & Shaw, J. M. (1992). *Helping children explore science.* Upper Saddle River, NJ: Merrill/ Prentice Hall.

Clifford, R., Early, D., & Hills, T. (1999). Almost a million children in school before kindergarten: Who is responsible for early childhood services? *Young Children, 53,* 48–51.

Cole, E. (1988, Spring). Silkworms and the Orient. *Texas Child Care Quarterly,* pp. 28–33.

Coleman, M. (1990). Planning public preschools. *Dimensions, 19,* 7–9.

Connell, J. P., & Goldsmith, H. H. (1982). A structural modeling approach to the study of attachment and strange situation behaviors. In R. J. Emde & R. J. Harmon (Eds.), *The development of attachment and affiliative systems* (pp. 213–243). New York: Plenum.

Conolly, J. A., & Doyle, A. B. (1984). Relation of social fantasy play to social competence in preschoolers. *Developmental Psychology, 20,* 797–806.

Coop, R. H., & Rotella, R. J. (1991). Sport and physical skill development in elementary schools: An overview. *The Elementary School Journal, 91,* 409–412.

Coplan, R. J., & Rubin, K. H. (1998). Social play. In D. Fromberg & D. Bergen (Eds.), *Play from birth to twelve and beyond* (pp. 368–377). New York: Garland.

Copley, J. V. (2000). *The young child and mathematics.* Washington, DC: National Association for the Education of Young Children.

Cremin, L. A. (1961). *The transformation of the school.* New York: Alfred A. Knopf.

Cremin, L. A. (1988). *American education: The metropolitan experience 1876–1980.* New York: Harper & Row.

Croom, L. L. (1993). The relationship between the construction of multidimensional self-concept in second grade children and the level of teacher endorsement of developmentally appropriate practice. Unpublished thesis (ED 373 871).

Cummins, J. (1994). Primary language instruction and the education of language minority students. In *Schools and language minority students: A theoretical framework* (2nd ed.). California State University National Evaluation, Dissimination, and Assessment Center.

Cunningham, P. M., Hall, D. P., & DeFee, M. (1991). Non-ability grouped, multilevel instruction: A year in a first-grade classroom. *The Reading Teacher, 44,* 566–571.

Curry, N. E. (1990). Presentation to the Pennsylvania State Board of Education. *Young Children, 45,* 17–23.

Dailey, K. A. (1991). Writing in kindergarten. *Childhood Education, 67,* 170–175.

Da Ros, D. A., & Kovach, B. A. (1998). Assisting toddlers and caregivers during conflict resolutions. Interactions that promote socialization. *Childhood Education, 75,* 25–30.

Dart, B. (1990, January 19). Exercise urged for youngsters. *News and Observer,* p. 1D.

Davis, L. (1993). Developmentally appropriate practice and implications for knowledge construction. Unpublished thesis (ED 390 590).

Day, B. (1988). What's happening in early childhood programs in the United States? In C. Warger (Ed.), *A resource guide to public school early childhood programs* (pp. 3–31). Alexandria, VA: Association for Supervision and Curriculum Development.

Day, D. (1983). *Early childhood education: A human ecological approach.* Glenview, IL: Scott, Foresman.

Day, M. C., & Parker, R. K. (Eds.). (1977). *The preschool in action* (2nd ed.). Boston: Allyn & Bacon.

Dearden, R. R. (1983). *Theory and practice in education.* London: Routledge & Kegan Paul.

Deiner, P. L. (1993). *Resources for teaching children with diverse abilities.* Fort Worth: Harcourt Brace Jovanovich.

dePaola, T. (1978). *Pancakes for breakfast.* New York: Harcourt Brace Jovanovich.

Derman-Sparks, L. (1992). Reaching potentials through antibias, multicultural curriculum. In S. Bredekamp & T. Rosegrant (Eds.), *Reaching potentials: Appropriate curriculum and instruction for young children* (pp. 114–127). Washington, DC: National Association for the Education of Young Children.

Deutsch, M. (1963). Minority group and class status as related to social and personality factors in scholastic achievement. In M. Grossack (Ed.), *Mental health and segregation* (pp. 64–75). New York: Springer.

Devall, E. L., & Cahill, B. J. (1995). Addressing children's life changes in the early childhood curriculum. *Early Childhood Education Journal, 23,* 57–62.

DeVries, R., & Kohlberg, L. (1990). *Constructivist early education: Overview and comparison with other programs.* Washington, DC: National Association for the Education of Young Children.

Dewey, J. (1899). *The school and society.* Chicago: University of Chicago Press.

Dewey, J. (1938). *Experience and education.* New York: Macmillan.

Diaz-Soto, L. (1999). *The multicultural worlds of childhood in postmodern America.* In C. Seefeldt (Ed.), *The early childhood curriculum* (pp. 218–242). New York: Teachers College Press.

Dickerson, M. (1992). James L. Hymes, Jr. In Association for Childhood Education International, *Profiles in childhood education 1931–1960* (pp. 82–90). Wheaton, MD: Author.

DiMartino, E. C. (1989). Understanding children from other cultures. *Childhood Education, 66,* 30–32.

DiPietro, J. A. (1981). Rough and tumble play: A function of gender. *Developmental Psychology, 17,* 50–58.

Dodge, K., Murphy, R. R., & Buchsbaum, K. (1984). The assessment of intention-cue detection skills in children. Implications for developmental psychopathology. *Child Development, 55,* 163–173.

Doescher, S. M., & Sugawara, A. I. (1989). Encouraging prosocial behavior in young children. *Childhood Education, 65,* 213–216.

Dowd, F. S. (1991). Mother Goose goes to school. *Childhood Education, 67,* 218–222.

Dueschl, R. A. (1983). The elementary level science methods course: Breeding ground of an apprehension toward science? A case study. *Journal of Research in Science Teaching, 20,* 322–326.

Dutton, W. H., & Dutton, A. (1991). *Mathematics children use and understand.* Mountain View, CA: Mayfield.

Dweck, C. S. (1986). Motivational processes affecting learning. *American Psychologist, 41,* 1040–1048.

Dyson, A. H. (1985). Individual differences in emerging writing. In M. Farr (Ed.), *Advances in writing research* (Vol 1). *Children's early writing development* (pp. 54–126). Norwood, NJ: Ablex.

Dyson, A. H. (1993). From prop to mediator: The changing role of written language in children's symbolic repertoire. In B. Spodek & O. N. Saracho (Eds.), *Language and literacy in early childhood education,* (pp. 21–41). New York: Teachers College Press.

Early Head Start. (2000, December). What Is Early Head Start? *http://www.ehsnrc.org/ehs.htm.*

Eddowes, E. A., & Hranitz, J. R. (1989). Educating children of the homeless. *Childhood Education, 66,* 197–200.

Edelman, M. W. (1989). Economic issues related to child care and early childhood education. *Teachers College Record, 90,* 342–351.

Edwards, C., Gandini, L., & Forman, G. (1996). *The hundred languages of children: The Reggio Emilia approach to early childhood education.* Norwood, NJ: Ablex.

Edwards, L. L., & Simpson, J. D. (1996). Emotional disturbance. In E. L. Meyen (Ed.), *Exceptional children in today's schools* (2nd ed., pp. 251–280). Denver: Love.

Eheart, B. K., & Leavitt, R. L. (1989). Family day care: Discrepancies between intended and observed child care practices. *Early Childhood Research Quarterly, 4,* 145–162.

Ehri, L. C. (1989). Movement into word-reading and spelling. How spelling contributes to reading. In J. M. Mason (Ed.), *Reading and writing connections* (pp. 65–81). Boston: Allyn & Bacon.

Elardo, P., & Caldwell, B. (1974). The Kramer adventure: A school for the future? *Childhood Education, 50,* 143–152.

Eliason, C. F., & Jenkins, L. (1999). *A practical guide to early childhood curriculum* (6th ed.). Upper Saddle River, NJ: Merrill/Prentice Hall.

Eliot, A. A. (1972). Nursery schools fifty years ago. *Young Children, 27,* 210–214.

Elkind, D. (1986). Formal education and early childhood education: an essential difference. *Phi Delta Kappan, 67,* 631–636.

Elkind, D. (1987). *Miseducation: Preschoolers at risk.* New York: Alfred A. Knopf.

Elkind, D. (1989, October). Developmentally appropriate practice: Philosophical and practical implications. *Phi Delta Kappan,* 113–117.

Elkind, D. (1993a). Overwhelmed at an early age. In D. Elkind, *Images of the young child,* (pp. 77–83). Washington, DC: National Association for the Education of Young Children.

Elkind, D. (1993b). Resistance to developmentally appropriate practice: A case study of educational inertia. In D. Elkind, *Images of the young child,* (pp. 55–64). Washington, DC: National Association for the Education of Young Children.

Elkind, D. (1997, November). The death of child nature: Education in the post-modern world. *Phi Delta Kappan, 241–245.*

Elkonin, D. (1978). *The psychology of play.* Moscow: Pedagogika.

Enright, D. S., & McCloskey, M. L. (1985). Yes Talking! Organizing the classroom to promote second language acquisition. *TESOL Quarterly, 15,* 431–453.

Epstein, L. H., Wing, R. R., & Valosi, A. (1985). Childhood obesity. *Pediatric Clinics of North America, 32,* 363–379.

Erikson, E. (1963). *Childhood and society.* New York: Norton.

Fair Test. (1990). *Standardized tests and our children: A guide to testing reform.* Cambridge MA: The National Center for Fair & Open Testing.

Farmer, J. (1976). Toward equal opportunity. In E. H. Grotburg (Ed.), *2000 years of children* (pp. 189–199). Washington, DC: U. S. Government Printing Office.

Fenichel, E., Lurie-Hurvitz, E., & Griffin, A. (1999). Seizing the moment to build momentum for quality infant/toddler child care. *Zero to Three, 19,* 3–17.

Ferreiro, E. K., & Teberosky, A. (1982). *Literacy before schooling.* Exeter, NH: Heinemann.

Fewell, R. (1983). Assessing handicapped infants. In S. G. Garwood & R. R. Fewell (Eds.), *Educating handicapped infants: Issues in development and intervention,* (pp. 257–297). Rockville, MD: Aspen.

Fields, M. V., & Hillstead, D. V. (1990). Whole language in the play store. *Young Children, 67,* 73–76.

Fields, M. V., & Spangler, K. L. (2000). *Let's begin reading right: Developmentally appropriate beginning literacy* (4th ed.) Upper Saddle River, NJ: Merrill/Prentice Hall.

Feldman, R. S. (2001). *Child development.* Upper Saddle River, NJ: Merrill/Prentice Hall.

Filippini, T. (1996). The role of the *Pedagogista.* In C. Edwards, L. Gandini, & G. Forman (Eds.), *The hundred languages of children,* (pp. 113–118). Norwood, NJ: Ablex.

Forman, G., Lee, M., Wrisley, L., & Langley, J. (1996). The city in the snow: Applying the multisymbolic approach in Massachusetts. In C. Edwards, L. Gandini, & G. Forman (Eds.), *The hundred languages of children,* (pp. 233–250). Norwood, NJ: Ablex.

Frank Porter Graham Child Development Center (1999). *Early learning, later success: The Abecedarian study. Executive Summary.* Chapel Hill, NC: University of North Carolina.

Frank Porter Graham Child Development Center (2000). The Carolina Abecedarian Project. *http://fpg.unc.edu/overview/abc/abc-ov.htm.*

Freeman, E. B. (1990). Issues in kindergarten policy and practice. *Young Children, 45,* 29–34.

Freeman, E. B., & Hatch, J. A. (1989). Emergent literacy: Reconceptualizing kindergarten practice. *Childhood Education, 66,* 21–24.

Freeman, D. E., & Freeman, Y. S. (1991). Doing social studies: Whole language lessons to promote social action. *Social Education, 55,* 29–32.

Freud, S. (1925). Instincts and their "vicissitudes." In S. Freud, *Collected papers* (Vol. 4). London: Institutes for Psycho-analysis & Hogarth Press.

Frost, J. L. (1986). Children in a changing society. *Childhood Education, 62,* 242–249.

Frost, J. L. (1992). *Play and playscapes.* Albany, NY: Delmar.

Frost, J. L. (2001). *Child safety in public places.* In J. L. Frost, S. Wortham, & S. Reifel, *Play and child development,* (pp. 462–505). Upper Saddle River, NJ: Merrill/Prentice Hall.

Frost, J. L., Wortham. S., & Reifel, S. (2001). *Play and child development.* Upper Saddle River, NJ: Merrill/Prentice Hall.

Galinsky, E., Howes, C., Kantos, S., & Shinn, M. (1994). *The study of children in family child care and relative care.* New York: Families and Work Institute.

Gallahue, D. L. (1993). Motor development and movement skill acquisition in early childhood. In B. Spodek (Ed.), *Handbook of research on the education of young children* (pp. 24–41). Upper Saddle River, NJ: Merrill/Prentice Hall.

Galley, M. (1999, September, 22). The petite elite. *Education Week, 19,* 24–29.

Gambrell, L. B., & Mazzoni, S. A. (1999). Emergent literacy: What research reveals about learning to read. In C. Seefeldt (Ed.), *The early childhood curriculum. Current findings in theory and practice* (pp. 80–105). New York: Teachers College Press.

Gandini, L. (1993). Fundamentals of the Reggio approach to early childhood education. *Young Children, 49,* 4–8.

Gandini, L. (1996). Educational and caring spaces. In C. Edwards, L. Gandini, & G. Forman (Eds.), *The hundred languages of children* (pp. 135–150). Norwood, NJ: Ablex.

Garcia, E. E. (1995). The impact of linguistic and cultural diversity on America's schools. In M. C. Wang & M. C. Reynolds (Eds.), *Making a difference for students at risk.* Thousand Oaks, CA: Corwin Press.

Gardner, H. (1983). *Frames of mind.* New York: Basic Books.

Gardner, H. (1996). Forward: Complementary perspectives on Reggio Emilia. In C. Edwards, L. Gandini, & G. Forman (Eds.), *The hundred language of children* (pp. ix–xiii). Norwood, NJ: Ablex.

Gargiulo, R. M., & Graves, S. B. (1991). Parental feelings: The forgotten component when working with parents of handicapped preschool children. *Childhood Education, 67,* 176–178.

Garner, B. P. (1998). Play development from birth to age four. In D. P. Fromberg & D. Bergen (Eds.), *Play from birth to twelve and beyond* (pp. 137–145). New York: Garland.

Garvey, C. (1977). *Play.* Cambridge, MA: Harvard University Press.

Garvey, C., & Hogan, R. (1973). Social speech and social interaction: Egocentrism revisited. *Child Development, 44,* 565–568.

Gaskins, R. W., Gaskins, J. C., & Gaskins, I. W. (1991). A decoding program for poor readers—and the rest of the class, too. *Language Arts, 68,* 213–225.

Gautt, S. W. (1996). Early childhood special education. In E. L. Meyen (Ed.), *Exceptional children in today's schools* (3rd. Ed., pp. 153–194). Denver: Love.

Gelman, R., & Gallistel, C. R. (1978). *The child's understanding of number.* Cambridge, MA: Harvard University Press.

Genishi, C., & Dyson, A. H. (1984). *Language assessment in the early years.* Norwood, NJ: Ablex.

Genishi, C., & Fassler, R. (1999). Oral language in the early childhood classroom: Building on diverse foundations. In C. Seefeldt (Ed.), *The early childhood curriculum: Current findings in theory and practice* (pp. 54–79). New York: Teachers College Press.

George, C., & Main, M. (1979). Social interactions of young abused children: Approach, avoidance, aggression. *Child Development, 50,* 306–318.

Gerber, M. (1981). What is appropriate curriculum for infants and toddlers? In B. Weissbourd & J. Musick (Eds.), *Infants: Their social environments* (pp. 77–85). Washington, DC: National Association for the Education of Young Children.

Gersten, R. (1999). The changing face of bilingual education. *Educational Leadership, 56,* 41–45.

Gesell, A. (1925). *The mental growth of the preschool child.* New York: Macmillan.

Gesell, A., & Ilg, F. A. (1946). *The child from five to ten.* New York: Harper.

Gillespie, C. W. (2000). Six Head Start classrooms begin to explore the Reggio Emilia approach. *Young Children, 55,* 21–27.

Glasser, W. (1969). *Schools without failure.* New York: Harper & Row.

Glazer, J. I. (1986). *Literature for young children* (2nd. ed.). Upper Saddle River, NJ: Merrill/Prentice Hall.

Gleason, J. B. (1988). Language and socialization. In F. Kessel (Ed.), *The development of language and language researchers* (pp. 269–280). Hillsdale, NJ: Erlbaum.

Gober, B. E., & Franks, B. D. (1988, September) Physical and fitness education of young children. *Journal of Physical Education, Recreation and Dance,* pp. 57–61.

Goldman, L. E. (1996). We can help children grieve: A child-oriented model for memorializing. *Young Children, 51,* 69–73.

Gonzalez-Mena, J., & Bhavnagri, N. P. (2000). Diversity and infant/toddler caregiving. *Young Children, 55,* 31–35.

Gonzalez-Mena, J., & Eyer, D. W. (1980). *Infancy and caregiving.* Palo Alto, CA: Mayfield.

Goodman, Y. (1984). The development of initial literacy. In H. Goelman, A. Oberg, & F. Smith (Eds.), *Awakening to literacy* (pp. 102–109). Exeter, NH: Heinemann.

Goodman, Y. (1986). Children coming to know literacy. In W. H. Teale & E. Sulzby (Eds.), *Emergent literacy: reading and writing* (pp. 1–14). Norwood, NJ: Ablex.

Gothard, H. M., & Russel, S. M. (1990). A tale of two teachers (or how our children led us into whole language). *Childhood Education, 66,* 214–218.

Grace, C., & Shores, E. F. (1991). *The portfolio and its use.* Little Rock: Southern Association on Children Under Six.

Graham, M. S., & Scott, K. G. (1988). The impact of definitions of high risk on services to infants and toddlers. *Topics in Early Childhood Special Education, 8,* 23–28.

Graham, S., Harris, K. R., Reid, R., & Kandel, M. (1996). Learning disabilities. In E. L. Meyen (Ed.), *Excep-*

tional Children in today's schools (3rd ed.), (pp. 221–250). Denver: Love.

Granucci, P. L. (1990). Kindergarten teachers: Working through our identity crisis. *Young Children, 45,* 6–11.

Graves, D. H. (1983). *Writing: Teachers and children at work.* Portsmouth, NH: Heinemann.

Gredler, G. R. (1984). Transition classes: A viable alternative for the at-risk child? *Psychology in the Schools, 21,* 463–470.

Green, E. J. (1997). Guidelines for serving linguistically and culturally diverse young children. *Early Childhood Education Journal, 24,* 147–154.

Green, L, & Adeyanju, M. (1991). Exercise and fitness guidelines for elementary and middle school children. *The Elementary School Journal, 91,* 437–444.

Greenman, J. (1985, Summer). Babies get out: Outdoor settings for infant toddler play. *Beginnings,* pp. 7–10.

Greven, P. (1977). *The Protestant temperament.* New York: Alfred A. Knopf.

Gross, R., & Gross, B. (1976). Lifelong learning. In E. H. Grotberg (Ed.), *200 years of children* (pp. 178–187). Washington, DC: U. S. Government Printing Office.

Gulliford, A. (1984). *America's country schools.* Washington, DC: Preservation Press.

Gullo, F. (1990). The changing family context: Implications for the development of all-day kindergartens. *Young Children, 45,* 35–39.

Guralnick, M. J. (1989). Recent developments in early intervention efficacy research: Implications for family involvement in PL 99-457. *Topics in Early Childhood Special Education, 9,* 1–17.

Gutierrez, K. D. (1993). Biliteracy and the language minority child. In B. Spodek & O. N. Saracho (Eds.), *Language and literacy in early childhood education* (pp. 82–101). New York: Teachers College Press.

Hagens, H. E. (1997). Strategies for encouraging peer interactions in infant/toddler programs. *Early Childhood Education Journal, 25,* 147–149.

Hale-Benson, J. (1986). Research in review: Black children: Their roots, culture, and learning styles. In J. B. McCracken (Ed.), *Reducing stress in young children's lives* (pp. 122–129). Washington, DC: National Association for the Education of Young Children.

Hall, C. S., & Lindzey, G. (1970). *Theories of personality* (2nd ed.). New York: Wiley.

Hall, D. P., Prevatte, C., & Cunningham, P. M. (1995). Eliminating ability grouping and reducing failure in the primary grades. In R. L Allington & S. A. Walm-

sly, *No quick fix* (pp. 137–158). New York: Teachers College Press.

Hall, G. S. (1883, May). The contents of children's minds. *The Princeton Review, 11,* 249–253.

Han, E. P. (1991). "You be the baby bear." Story re-enactments by young children. *Dimensions, 19,* 14–21.

Hanson, M. J., & Lynch, E. W. (1989). *Early intervention: Implementing child and family services for infants and toddler who are at-risk or disabled.* Austin, TX: Pro-Ed.

Harlan, J. D., & Rivkin, M. S. (1996). *Science experiences for the early childhood years.* Upper Saddle River, NJ: Merrill/Prentice Hall.

Harms, T., & Clifford, R. (1998). *Early childhood environment rating scale (Revised edition).* New York: Teacher's College Press.

Harms, T., Cryer, D., & Clifford, R. (1990). *Infant/toddler environmental rating scale.* New York: Teacher's College Press.

Harris, K. R., & Graham, S. (1996). Memo to Constructivists: Skills count, too. *Educational Leadership, 53,* 26–29.

Hartup, W. W. (1983). Peer relations. In P. H. Mussen (Ed.), *Handbook of child psychology* (4th ed., Vol. 4). New York: Wiley.

Harvey, J. H. (1982). Overuse syndromes in young athletes. *Pediatric Clinics of North America, 29,* 1369–1381.

Hatch, J. A., & Freeman, E. B. (1988). Kindergarten philosophies and practices: Perspectives of teachers, principals, and supervisors. *Early Childhood Research Quarterly, 3,* 151–166.

Haugland, S. W., & Shade, D. D. (1988). Developmentally appropriate software for young children. *Young Children, 43,* 37–43

Haycock, K. (1991). Reaching for the year 2000. *Childhood Education, 65,* 276–279.

Hayes, L. F. (1990). From scribbling to writing: Smoothing the way. *Young Children, 45,* 62–68.

Helm, J. H., & Katz, L. (2001). *Young investigators. The Project Approach in the early years.* New York: Teachers College Press.

Hendrick, J. (1998). *Total learning* (5th ed.). Upper Saddle River, NJ: Merrill/Prentice Hall.

Herr, J., & Libby, Y. (1990). *Creative resources for the early childhood classroom.* Albany, NY: Delmar.

Hiebert, E. H. (1986). Using environmental print in beginning reading instruction. In M. R. Sampson

(Ed.), *The pursuit of literacy: Early reading and writing* (pp. 73–80). Dubuque, IA: Kendall/Hunt.

High/Scope Educational Research Foundation. (1992). *Assessment Booklet Child Observation Record (COR).* Ypsilanti: Author.

Hill, L. B., & Hale, M. G. (1991). Reading recovery: Questions classroom teachers ask. *The Reading Teacher, 44,* 480–483.

Hilliard, D. C. (1998). Sport as play (and work). In D. P. Fromberg & D. Bergen (Eds.), *Play from birth to twelve and beyond* (pp. 416–423). New York: Garland.

Hills, T. (1986). *Classroom motivation: Helping students want to learn and achieve in school.* Trenton: New Jersey Department of Education.

Hills, T. W. (1992). Reaching potentials through appropriate assessment. In S. Bredekamp & T. Rosegrant (Eds.), *Reaching potentials: Appropriate curriculum and assessment for young children* (pp. 43–61). Washington, DC: National Association for the Education of Young Children.

Hinkle, D. (2000). *School involvement in early childhood.* Washington, DC: National Institute on Early Childhood Development and Education, U.S. Department of Education.

Hohmann, M., Banet, B., & Weikart, D. (1979). *Young children in action.* Ypsilanti: High/Scope Press.

Hohmann, M., & Weikart, D. (1995). *Educating young children: Active learning activities in preschool and child care programs.* Ypsilanti: High/Scope Press.

Holcomb, B. (1994, July). How families are changing. *Working Mother,* pp. 29–36.

Holmes, E. E. (1991). Democracy in elementary school classes. *Social Education, 55,* 176–178.

Honig, A. S. (1983). Sex role socialization in early childhood. *Young Children, 38,* 57–70.

Honig, A. S. (1989). Quality infant/toddler caregiving: Are there magic recipes? *Young Children, 44,* 4–10.

Hoskisson, K. (1975). The many facets of assisted reading. *Elementary English, 52,* 312–315.

Hove, E. (1970). Science scarecrows. *School Science and Mathematics, 70,* 322–326.

Howes, C., & Wu, F. (1990). Peer interactions and friendships in an ethnically diverse school setting. *Child Development, 61,* 537–541.

Hudelson, S. (1984). Kan ret and rayt in Ingles: Children become literate in English as a second language. *TESOL Quarterly, 18,* 221–238.

Hudelson, S., & Serna, I. (1997). Young children's second language development. In J. Christie, B. Enz, & C. Vukelich, *Teaching language and literacy* (pp. 45–50). New York: Longman.

Huffman, A. B. (1996). Beyond the weather chart: Weathering new experiences. *Young Children, 51,* 34–37.

Huffman, L. C., Mehlinger, S. L., & Kerivan, A. S. (2000). Risk factors for academic and behavioral problems at the beginning of school. In *Off to a good start: Research and the risk factors for early school problems and selected federal policies affecting children's social and emotional development and their readiness for school.* Chapel Hill, NC: University of North Carolina, FPG Child Development Center.

Hughes, F. P. (1991). *Children, play, and development.* Boston: Allyn & Bacon.

Hunt, J. M. (1961). *Intelligence and experience.* New York: Ronald Press.

Hunter, M. (1979). Teaching is decision-making. *Educational Leadership, 37,* 62–64, 67.

Hutchinson, J. (1991). What crack does to babies. *American Educator, 15,* 31–32.

Hutchison, L., Ellsworth, J., & Yovich, S. (2000). Third-grade students investigate and represent data. *Early Childhood Education Journal, 27,* 213–218.

Hutt, C., & Bhavnani, R. (1976). Predictions from play. In J. S. Bruner, A. Jolly, & K. Sylva (Eds.), *Play: Its role in development and evolution* (pp. 216–221). Upper Saddle River, NJ: Merrill/Prentice Hall.

Hymes, J. L. (1990). *Early childhood education. The year in review. A look at 1989.* Washington, DC: National Association for the Education of Young Children.

Hymes J., & Stolz, L. M. (1978). The Kaiser Child Service Centers. In J. L. Hymes (Ed.), *Living history interviews. Book 2: Care of the children of working mothers* (pp. 26–56). Carmel, CA: Hacienda Press.

International Reading Association and National Association for the Education of Young Children. (1999). *Learning to read and write. Developmentally appropriate practices for young children. A joint position statement of the International Reading Association (IRA) and the National Association for the Education of Young Children (NAEYC).* In S. B. Neuman, C. Copple, & S. Bredekamp (Eds.), *Learning to read and write: Developmentally appropriate practices for young children* (pp. 3–26). Washington,

DC: National Association for the Education of Young Children.

Isaacs, S. (1966). *Intellectual growth in young children.* New York: Schocken Books.

Ishee, N., & Goldhaber, J. (1990). Story re-enactment: Let the play begin! *Young Children, 45,* 70–75.

Jacobs, F. H., & Davies, M. W. (1991, Winter). Rhetoric or reality? Child and family policy in the United States. *Social Policy Report, Society for Research in Child Development,* pp. 1–25.

Jambor, T. (1990). Promoting perceptual-motor development in young children's play. In S. C. Wortham & J. L. Frost (Eds.), *Playgrounds for young children: National survey and perspectives* (pp. 147–166). Reston, VA: American Alliance for Health, Physical Education, Recreation and Dance.

James, W. H., Smith, A. J., & Mann, R. (1991). Educating homeless children. *Childhood Education, 67,* 4–7.

Jantz, R. K., & Seefeldt, C. (1999). Early childhood social studies. In C. Seefeldt (Ed.), *The early childhood curriculum: Current findings in theory and practice* (3rd ed., pp. 159–178). New York: Teachers College Press.

Jarolimek, J. (1996). NCSS and elementary social studies. In J. Davis, (Ed.), *NCSS in retrospect* (Bulletin No. 92) (pp. 103–110). Washington, DC: National Council for the Social Studies.

Jenkins-Friedman, R., & Nielson, M. E. (1996). Gifted and talented students. In E. L. Meyen (Ed.), *Exceptional children in today's schools* (3rd ed., pp. 493–536). Denver: Love.

Jervis, K. (1996). *Eyes on the child: Three portfolio stories.* New York: Teachers College Press.

Jewell, M. G., & Zintz, M. V. (1986). *Learning to read naturally.* Dubuque, IA: Kendall/Hunt.

Johnson, H. M. (1928). *Children in "the nursery school."* New York: Agathon.

Johnson, H. M. (1936). *School begins at two.* New York: New Republic.

Johnson, J. E., Christie, J. F., & Yawkey, T. D. (1999). *Play and early childhood development.* New York: Longman.

Johnson, J. E. Ershler, J., & Lawton, J. T. (1982). Intellective correlates of preschoolers' spontaneous play. *Journal of General Psychology, 106,* 115–122.

Johnson, R. H., & Johnson, R. T. (1994). *Learning together and alone: Cooperative, competitive, and individualistic learning.* Boston: Allyn & Bacon.

Johnson, S. Q., & Johnson, R. (1987). *Learning together and alone: Cooperative, competitive, and individualistic learning* (2nd. Ed.). Upper Saddle River, NJ: Merrill/Prentice Hall.

Jordan, H. (1992). *How a seed grows.* New York: HarperCollins Children's Books.

Kagan, J. (1971). *Change and continuity in infants.* New York: Wiley & Sons.

Kagan, S. (1989, October). Early care and education: Beyond the schoolhouse doors. *Phi Delta Kappan,* 107–112.

Kagan, S. L., & Neuman, M. J. (1997). Highlights of the Quality 2000 Initiative: Not by chance. *Young Children, 52,* 54–62.

Kagan, S., & Rivers, A. M. (1991). Collaboration in early care and education: What can and should we expect? *Young Children, 47,* 51–56.

Kamii, C. (1982). *Number in the preschool and kindergarten.* Washington, DC: National Association for the Education of Young Children.

Kamii, C. (1986). Viewpoint: Obedience is not enough. In J. B. McCracken (Ed.), *Reducing stress in young children's lives* (pp. 93–95). Washington, DC: National Association for the Education of Young Children.

Kamii, C. (Ed.). (1990). *Achievement testing in the early grades.* Washington, DC: National Association for the Education of Young Children.

Kamii, C. (2000). *Young children reinvent arithmetic. Implications of Piaget's theory* (2nd ed.). New York: Teachers College Press.

Kamii, C., & DeVries, R. (1993). *Physical knowledge in preschool education: Implications of Piaget's theory.* New York: Teachers College Press.

Kamii, C., & Ewing, J. K. (1996). Basing teaching on Piaget's constructivism. *Childhood Education, 72,* 260–264.

Katz, L. G. (1988). What should young children be doing? *American Educator, 12,* 28–33, 44–45.

Katz, L. G. (1994). *The Project Approach.* Champaign, IL: ERIC Clearinghouse on Elementary and Early Childhood Education.

Katz, L. G. (1996). What can we learn from Reggio Emilia? In C. Edwards, L. Gandini, & G. Forman (Eds.), *The hundred languages of children* (pp. 19–40). Norwood, NJ: Ablex.

Katz, L. G., & Chard, S. C. (1989). *Engaging children's minds: The Project Approach.* Norwood, NJ: Ablex.

Katz, L. G., & Chard, S. C. (2000). *Engaging children's minds: The Project Approach* (2nd ed.). Stamford, CT: Ablex.

Katz, L. G., & McClellan, D. E. (1997). *Fostering children's social competence: The teacher's role.* Washington, DC: National Association for the Education of Young Children.

Katz, P. (1982). Development of children's racial awareness and intergroup attitudes. In L. Katz (Ed.), *Current topics in early childhood education* (Vol. 4, pp. 17–54). Norwood, NJ: Ablex.

Keats, E. J. (1971). *Over in the meadow.* New York: Scholastic.

Keister, M. E. (1970). *"The good life" for infants and toddlers.* Washington, DC: National Association for the Education of Young Children.

Kelley, M. F., & Surbeck, K. E. (1990). Infant day care. In E. Surbeck & M. F. Kelley, (Eds.), *Personalizing care with infants, toddlers, and families* (pp. 62–70). Wheaton, MD: Association for Childhood Education International.

Kellough, R. D. (1996). *Integrating mathematics and science for kindergarten and primary children.* Upper Saddle River, NJ: Merrill/Prentice Hall.

Kemple, K. M. (1991). Preschool children's peer acceptance and social interactions. *Young Children, 46,* 47–94.

King, E. W., Chipman, M., & Cruz-Janzen, M. (1994). *Educating young children in a diverse society.* Boston: Allyn & Bacon.

Kinsey, S. J. (2000). *The relationship between prosocial behaviors and academic achievement in the primary multiage classroom.* Unpublished doctoral dissertation, Loyola University, Chicago.

Kinsey, S. J. (2001). Multiage grouping and academic achievement in elementary school. *eric/eece Newsletter, 13,* 1–2.

Krogh, S. (1990). *The integrated early childhood curriculum.* New York: McGraw-Hill.

Labbo, L. D., Reinking, D., & McKenna, M. C. (1999). The use of technology in literacy programs. In L. Grambrell, L. M. Morrow, B. Neuman, & M. Pressley (Eds.), *Best practices in literacy instruction* (pp. 311–327). New York: Guilford Press.

Labov, W. (1970). The logic of nonstandard English. In F. Williams (Ed.), *Language and poverty* (pp. 153–189). Chicago: Markham.

La Cerva, V. (1999, November). Adverse affects of witnessing violence. *Child Care Information Exchange,* 44–47.

Lally, J. R. (2001). Infant care in the United States and how the Italian experience can help. In L. Gendini & C. P. Edwards (Eds.), *Bambini. The Italian approach to infant/toddler care.* (pp. 15–22). New York: Teachers College Press.

Lally, J. R., Griffin, A., Fenichel, E., Segal, M., Szanton, E., & Weissbourd, B. (1997). Development in the first three years of life. In S. Bredekamp & C. Copple (Eds.), *Developmentally appropriate practice in early childhood programs* (pp. 17–33). Washington, DC: National Association for the Education of Young Children.

Landreth, G., & Hohmeyer, L. (1998). Play as the language of children's feelings. In D. P. Fromberg & D. Bergen (Eds.), *Play from birth to twelve and beyond* (pp. 193–198). New York: Garland.

Landry, C. E., & Forman, G. (1999). Research on early science education. In C. Seefeldt (Ed.), *The early childhood curriculum. Current findings in theory and practice* (pp. 133–158). New York: Teachers College Press.

Lane, M. (1986). Reaffirmations: Speaking out for children. A child's right to the valuing of diversity. In J. B. McCracken (Ed.), *Reducing stress in children's lives* (p. 130). Washington, DC: National Association for the Education of Young Children.

Lanser, S., & McDonnell, L. (1991). Creating quality curriculum yet not buying out the store. *Young Children, 47,* 4–10.

Lawton, J. T. (1988). *Introduction to child care and early childhood education.* Glenview, IL: Scott, Foresman.

Lazar, I., & Darlington, R. (1982). Lasting effects of early education: A report from the Consortium for Longitudinal Studies. *Monograph of the Society for Research in Child Development, 47,* 2–3, Serial No. 195.

LeeKeenan, D., & Nimmo, J. (1996). Connections: Using the Project Approach with 2- and 3-year-olds in a university laboratory school. In C. Edwards, L. Gandini, & G. Forman (Eds.), *The hundred languages of children* (pp. 251–268). Norwood, NJ: Ablex.

Lenhoff, R., & Huber, L. (2000). Young children make maps. *Young Children, 55,* 6–12.

Lennenberg, E. (1967). *Biological foundations of language*. New York: Wiley.

Levy, A. K. (1984). The language of play: The role of play in language development. *Early Childhood Development and Care, 17*, 49–62.

Lewin, A. (1995). *The fundamentals of the Reggio approach*. Presentation to visiting delegation at the Model Learning Center, Washington, DC.

Lieberman, J. N. (1965). Playfulness and divergent thinking: An investigation of their relationship at the kindergarten level. *Journal of Genetic Psychology, 107*, 219–224.

Lieberman, J. N. (1977). *Playfulness: Its relationship to imagination and creativity*. New York: Academic Press.

Lindberg, D. L. (1990). What goes 'round comes 'round. Doing science. *Childhood Education, 67*, 79–91.

Lindfors, J. W. (1987). *Children's language and learning* (2nd ed.). Upper Saddle River, NJ: Prentice Hall.

Lowman, L., & Ruhmann, L. H. (1998). Simply sensational spaces: A multi-"s" approach to toddler environments. *Young Children, 53*, 11–17.

Lyman, L., & Foyle, H. C. (1990). *Cooperative grouping interactive learning: Students, teachers, administrators*. Washington, DC: National Education Association.

Lyon, G. R. (1998). Why reading is not a natural process. *Educational Leadership, 55*, 14–18.

Maccoby, E. E., & Martin, J. A. (1983). Socialization in the context of the family: Parent-child interactions. In P. H. Mussen (Ed.), *Handbook of child pyschology* (4th ed., Vol. 4). New York: Wiley.

Mager, R. F. (1975). *Preparing instructional objectives* (2nd ed.). Belmont, CA: Fearon.

Magid, R. Y. (1989). The consequences of employer involvement in child care. *Teachers College Record, 90*, 434–443.

Malaguzzi, L. (1996). History, ideas, and basic philosophy. In C. Edwards, L. Gandini, & G. Forman (Eds.), *The hundred languages of children* (pp. 41–90). Norwood, NJ: Ablex.

Mallory, B. L., & New, R. S. (1994). *Diversity and developmentally appropriate practices*. New York: Teachers College Press.

Manley-Casimir, M., & Wassermann, S. (1989). The teacher as decision-maker. *Childhood Education, 65*, 288–293.

Mann, V. A. (1993). Phoneme awareness and future reading ability. *Journal of Learning Disabilities, 26*, 259–269.

Manning, M. L. (1998). Play development from ages eight to twelve. In D. P. Fromberg & D. Bergen (Eds.), *Play from birth to twelve and beyond* (pp. 154–162). New York: Garland.

Manning, M., Manning, G., & Kamii, C. (1988). Early phonics instruction: Its effect on literacy development. *Young Children, 44*, 4–8.

Mantovani, S. (2001). Infant-toddler centers in Italy today: Tradition and innovation. In L. Gandini & C. P. Edwards (Eds.). *Bambini. The Italian approach to Infant/Toddler Care*. (pp. 23–37). New York: Teachers College Press.

Mardell-Czudnowski, C. D., & Goldenberg, D. S. (1998). *Developmental Indicators for the Assessment of Learning* (3rd ed.). Circle Pines MN: American Guidance Service.

Mason, J. (1980). When do children begin to read: An exploration of four year old children's letter and word reading competencies. *Reading Research Quarterly, 15*, 203–227.

Mason, J. (1984). Early reading from a development perspective. In P. D. Pearson (Ed.), *Handbook of reading research* (pp. 505–543). New York: Longmen.

Mavrogenes, N. A. (1990). Helping parents help their children become literate. *Young Children 45*, 4–9.

Maxim, G. W. (1997). *The very young* (4th ed.). Upper Saddle River, NJ: Merrill/Prentice Hall.

Mayer, M. (1968). *There's a nightmare in my closet*. New York: Dial Books for Young Readers.

Mayer, M. H. (1996). Hearing impairment. In E. L. Meyen (Ed.), *Exceptional children in today's schools* (3rd ed., pp. 315–350). Denver: Love.

McCarthy, M. A., & Houston, J. P. (1980). *Fundamentals of early childhood education*. Cambridge, MA: Winthrop.

McCormick, C., & Mason, J. (1981). What happens to kindergarten children's knowledge about reading after summer vacation? *The Reading Teacher, 35*, 164–172.

McCormick, J. (1990, Fall/Winter). Where are the parents? *Newsweek*, pp. 54–55, 58.

McCormick, L., & Holden, R. (1992). Homeless children: A special challenge. *Young Children, 47*, 61–67.

McCune, L. (1986). Symbolic development in normal and atypical infants. In G. Fein & M. Rivkin (Eds.), *The young child at play* (pp. 45–62). Washington, DC: National Association for the Education of Young Children.

McMullen, M. B. (1999). Achieving the best practices in infant and toddler care and education. *Young Children, 54,* 69–76.

McNeil, D. (1966). Developmental psycholinguistics. In F. Smith & G. A. Miller (Eds.), *The genesis of language: A psycholinguistic approach* (pp. 15–82). Cambridge, MA: MIT Press.

McNeil, D. (1970). *The acquisition of language: The study of developmental psycholinguistics.* New York: Harper & Row.

Mechling, K. R., & Kepler, L. E. (1991, March), Start with science. *Instructor,* pp. 35–37.

Meddin, B. J., & Rosen, A. L. (1986). Child abuse and neglect: Prevention and reporting. In J. B. McCracken (Ed.), *Reducing stress in young children's lives* (pp. 78–82). Washington, DC: National Association for the Education of Young Children.

Meisels, S. J. (1987). Uses and abuses of developmental screening and school readiness testing. *Young Children, 42,* 4–6, 68–73.

Meisels, S. J. (1989). *High-stakes testing in kindergarten. Educational Leadership, 46,* 16–22.

Meisels, S. J., & Wiske, M. S. (1983). *The Early Screening Inventory.* New York: Teachers College Press.

Menyuk, P. (1969). *Language and maturation.* Cambridge, MA: MIT Press.

Mercer, J. (1973). *Labeling the mentally retarded.* Berkeley, CA: University of California Press.

Meyen, E. L. (1996a). Educating exceptional children. In E. L. Meyen (Ed.), *Exceptional children in today's schools* (3rd. ed. pp. 1–46). Denver: Love.

Meyen, E. L. (Ed.). (1996b). *Exceptional children in today's schools* (3rd ed). Denver: Love.

Miller, K. (1989, Summer). Infants and toddlers outside. *Texas Child Care Quarterly,* pp. 22–29.

Miller, K. (1992). Guidelines for helping non–English-speaking children adjust and communicate. In B. Neugebauer (Ed.), *Alike and different: Exploring our humanity with young children* (pp. 50–53). Washington, DC: National Association for the Education of Young Children.

Mills, H., & Clyde, J. A. (1991). For rent: The housekeeping area. *Dimensions, 19,* 26–27.

Mitchell, A. (1989, May). Old baggage, new visions: Shaping policy for early childhood programs. *Phi Delta Kappan,* pp. 665–672.

Mitchell, A., & Modigliani, K. (1989). Young children in public schools? *Young Children, 44,* 55–61.

Montovani, S. (2001). Infant-toddler centers in Italy today: Tradition and innovation. In L. Gandini & C. P. Edwards (Eds.), *Bambini. The Italian approach to infant/toddler care* (pp. 23–37). New York: Teachers College Press.

Moran, M. R. (1996). Speech and language disorders. In E. L. Morgan, G. (1989, Winter). Stalemate or consensus? Barriers to national policy. *Theory into Practice,* pp. 41–46.

Morrison, G. S. (1988). *Education and development of infants, toddlers, and preschoolers.* Glenview, IL: Scott, Foresman.

Morrow, L. M. (1997). *Literacy development in the early years* (3rd ed.). Boston: Allyn & Bacon.

Morrow, L. M. (2000). Organizing and managing a language arts block. In D. S. Strickland & L. M. Morrow (Eds.), *Beginning reading and writing* (pp. 83–98). New York: Teachers College Press.

Morrow, L. M., & Rand, M. K. (1991). Promoting literacy during play by designing early childhood classroom environments. *The Reading Teacher, 44,* 396–401.

Moyer, J. (1970). *Bases for world understanding and cooperation.* Washington, DC: Association for Supervision and Curriculum Development.

Muenchow, S., & Seitz, V. (1980, September). How play begins. *Parents,* pp. 61–64.

Mullen, M. R. (1984). Motor development and child's play. In T. D. Yawkey & A. D. Pellegrini (Eds.), *Child's play and play therapy* (pp. 7–16). Lancaster, PA: TECHNOMIC.

Mullis, I. V. S., & Jenkins, L. B. (1988). *The science report card: Elements of risk and recovery: Trends and achievement base on the 1986 national assessment.* Princeton, NJ: Educational Testing Service.

Nason, R. B. (1991). Retaining children: Is it the right decision? *Childhood Education, 67,* 300–304.

National Academy of Early Childhood Programs. (1991). *Guide to accreditation.* Washington, DC: National Association for the Education of Young Children.

National Association for the Education of Young Children. (1996). *Guidelines for preparation of early childhood professionals.* Washington, DC: Author.

National Association for the Education of Young Children & National Association of Early Childhood Specialists in State Departments of Education. (1991). Guidelines for appropriate curriculum content and assessment in programs serving children ages 3 through 8. *Young Children 46,* 21–38.

National Association of Early Childhood Specialists in State Department of Education. (1987). *Unacceptable trends in kindergarten entry and placement: A position statement.* (ERIC Document Reproduction Service No. 297–856).

National Association of Early Childhood Specialists in State Departments of Education (2000). *Still! Unacceptable trends in kindergarten entry and placement. A position statement developed by the National Association of Early Childhood Specialists in State Departments of Education.* Washington, DC: Author.

National Center for Children in Poverty. (1990). *Five million children: A statistical profile for our poorest young citizens.* New York: Columbia University, School of Public Health.

National Council for Teachers of Mathematics. (2000). *Standards for grades pre-K–2, Principles and standards for school mathematics.* Reston, VA: Author.

National Council for the Social Studies (NCSS). (1994). *Expectations of excellence: Curriculum standards for the social studies.* Washington, DC: Author.

National Education Goals Panel. (1998). *Principles and recommendations for early childhood assessments.* Washington, DC: Author.

National Science Foundation. (1983). *Educating America for the 21st century: A report to the American people and the National Science Board.* Washington, DC: Author.

National Science Teachers Association. (2001). *Atlas of science literacy.* Arlington, VA: Author.

National Science Teacher's Association (1995). *National science education standards.* Arlington, VA: Author.

Neuman, S. B., & Bredekamp, S. (2000). Becoming a reader: A developmentally appropriate approach. In D. S. Strickland & L. M. Morrow (Eds.), *Beginning reading and writing* (pp. 22–35). New York: Teachers College Press.

New, R. (1992). The integrated early childhood curriculum: New interpretations based on research and practice. In C. Seefeldt (Ed.), *The early childhood curriculum: A review of current research* (2nd ed.), (pp. 286–325). New York: Teachers College Press.

New, R. (1993). Cultural variations on developmentally appropriate practices. In C. Edwards, L. Gandini, and G. Forman (Eds.), *The hundred languages of children: The Reggio Emilia approach to early childhood education.* Norwood, NJ: Ablex.

New, R. (1994). Culture, child development, and developmentally appropriate practices: Teachers as collaborative researchers. In B. L. Mallory & R. S. New (Eds.), *Diversity and developmentally appropriate practices* (pp. 84–106). New York: Teachers College Press.

New, R. (1996). Cultural variations on Developmentally Appropriate Practice: Challenges to theory and practice. In C. Edwards, L. Gandini, & G. Forman (Eds.), *The hundred languages of children: The Reggio Emilia approach to early childhood education* (pp. 215–232). Norwood, NJ: Ablex.

Newman, L. F., & Buka, S. L. (1991). Clipped wings. *American Educator, 15,* 27–33, 42.

Newmann, F. M., & Associates. (1996). *Authentic achievement. Restructuring schools for intellectual quality.* San Fransisco: Jossey-Bass.

Nimnicht, G., Arango, M., & Adcock, D. (1977). The parent/child toy library. In M. Day & R. Parker (Eds.), *The preschool in action* (2nd ed., pp. 129–148). Boston: Allyn & Bacon.

Norton, D. E. (1990). Teaching multicultural literature in the reading curriculum. *The Reading Teacher, 44,* 45–46.

Nuckolls, M. E. (1991). Expanding students' potential through family literacy. *Educational Leadership, 49,* 45–46.

Nunnelley, J. C. (1990). Beyond turkeys, santas, snowmen and hearts: How to plan innovative curriculum themes. *Young Children, 45,* 24–29.

O'Brien, S. (1991). How do you raise respectful children in a disrespectful world? *Childhood Education, 67,* 183–184.

Odem, S. L., & Diamond, K. E. (1998). Inclusion of young children with special needs in early childhood education: The research base. *Early Childhood Research Quarterly, 13,* 3–25.

O'Donnell, N. S. (1999, March). Using early childhood brain development research. *Child Care Information Exchange,* pp. 58–62.

Olshansky, B. (1995). Children who witness domestic violence. The invisible victims. *Social Policy Report, 9,* 1–16.

O'Neil, D., & Foster, S. (2000). On-site child care: "Home being where the job is . . ." *ACEI Focus on Infants and Toddlers, 13,* 1–2.

O'Neil, J. (1991). A generation adrift? *Educational Leadership, 49,* 4–10.

Orlich, D. C., Harder, R. J., Callahan, R. C., Kauchak, D. P., Pendergrass, R. A., & Keogh, A. J. (1990). *Teaching strategies: A guide to better instruction.* Lexington, MA: D.C. Heath.

Osofsky, J. D. (1995). Children who witness domestic violence. The invisible victims. *Social Policy Report, 9,* 1–16.

Ostrosky, M. M., & Kaiser, A. P. (1991, Summer). Preschool environments that promote communication. *Teaching Exceptional Children,* pp. 6–10.

Packer, A. B., Milner, S. C.. & Hong, M. H. (1992). Lost in a distant land: the foreign child's dilemma in child care. In B. Neugebauer (Ed.), *Alike and different: Exploring our humanity with young children* (pp. 42–49). Washington, DC: National Association for the Education of Young Children.

Pardo, L. S., & Raphael, T. E. (1991). Classroom organization for instruction in content areas. *The Reading Teacher, 44,* 556–565.

Parker, S. C., & Temple, A. (1925). *Unified kindergarten and first grade teaching.* Boston: Ginn.

Patterson, K., & Wright, A. E. (1990). The speech, language or hearing-impaired child: At-risk academically. *Childhood Education, 67,* 91–95.

Patton, M. M., & Kokoski, T. M. (1996). How good is your early childhood science, mathematics, and technology program? Strategies for extending your curriculum. *Young Children, 51,* 38–43.

Pellegrini, A. D. (1991). A critique of the concept of at risk as applied to emergent literacy. *Language Arts, 68,* 380–385.

Pellegrini, A. D., & Bjorklund, D. (1996, Fall/Winter). The place of recess in school: Issues in the role of recess in children's education and development. *Journal of Research in Childhood Education, 11,* 5–13.

Penta, M. O., Mitchell, J. W., & Franklin, M. E. (1993, January). *Reliability studies of a needs assessment instrument for elementary school mathematics and science programs in North Carolina.* Paper presented at the meeting of the North Carolina Association for Research in Education, Greensboro, NC.

Perrone, V. (1991). On standardized testing. *Childhood Education, 67,* 131–142.

Peters, R. (1991, February). Introducing students to the global community. *Teaching K–8,* pp. 61–62.

Peth-Pierce, R. (2000). A good beginning. Sending America's children to school with the social and emotional competence they need to succeed. Washington, DC: The Child Mental Health Foundations and Agency Network (FAN).

Phillips, C. B. (1990). The Child Development Associate Program: Entering a new era. *Young Children, 45,* 24–27.

Piaget, J. (1955). *The language and thought of the child.* New York: Noonday.

Piaget, J. (1963). *The origins of intelligence in children* (M. Cook, Trans.). New York: W. W. Norton.

Piaget, J. (1965). *The moral judgment of the child.* (M. Gabain, Trans.). New York: W. W. Norton.

Piaget, J., & Inhelder, B. (1969). *The psychology of the child.* New York: Basic Books.

Pizzo, P. D. (1990). Family-centered Head Start for infants and toddlers: A renewed direction for Project Head Start. *Young Children, 45,* 30–35.

Powell, D. R. (1989). *Families and early childhood programs.* Washington, DC: National Association for the Education of Young Children.

Powell, D. R. (1994). Parents, pluralism, and the NAEYC statement on developmentally appropriate practice. In B. L. Mallory & R. S. New (Eds.), *Diversity and developmentally appropriate practices* (pp. 166–182). New York: Teachers College Press.

Pressley, M. C., Rankin, J., & Yokoi, Y. (1996). A survey of instructional practices of primary teachers nominated as effective in promoting literacy. *Elementary School Journal, 96,* 363–384.

Price, G. G. (1989). Mathematics in early childhood. *Young Children, 44,* 53–58.

Public Health Service (1976). 200 years of child health in America. In E. H. Grotberg (Ed.), *200 years of children* (pp. 61–122). Washington, DC: U.S. Government Printing Office.

Quint, S. (1994). *Schooling homeless children.* New York: Teachers College Press.

Quintero, E., & Huerta-Macias, A. (1990). All in the family: Bilingualism and biliteracy. *The Reading Teacher, 44,* 304–309.

Quintero, E., & Velarde, M. C. (1990). Intergenerational literacy: A developmental, bilingual approach. *Young Children, 45,* 10–15.

Raikes, H. (1996). A secure base for babies: Applying attachment concepts to the infant care setting. *Young Children, 51,* 59–67.

Raines, S. C., & Canady, R. J. (1989). *Story stretchers.* Mt. Rainier, MD: Gryphon House.

Raines, S. C., & Canady, R. J. (1991). *More story stretchers.* Mt. Rainier, MD: Gryphon House.

Raines, S. C., & Isbell, R. (1988). Tuck talking about wordless book into your classroom *Young Children, 43,* 24–25.

Rakow, S. J., & Bell, M. J. (1998). Science and young children: The message from the National Science Education Standards. *Childhood Education, 74,* 164–167.

Ramsey, P. (1987). *Teaching and learning in a diverse world: Multicultural education for young children.* New York: Teachers College Press.

Recken, R. (1989). Accreditation update: Who gets accredited? *Young Children, 44,* 11–12.

Reed, S., & Sauter, R. C. (1990, June). Children of poverty. *Phi Delta Kappan,* K1–K12.

Reutzel, D. R., & Cooter, R. B. (1991). Organizing for effective instruction: The reading workshop. *The Reading Teacher, 44,* 548–555.

Rinaldi, C. (1996). The emergent curriculum and social constructivism. In C. Edwards, L. Gandini, & G. Forman (Eds.), *The hundred languages of children* (pp. 101–112). Norwood, NJ: Ablex.

Roberts, P. L. (1996). *Integrating language arts and social studies for kindergarten and primary grades.* Upper Saddle River, NJ: Merrill/Prentice Hall.

Rogers, C. S., & Sawyers, J. K. (1988). *Play in the lives of children.* Washington, DC: National Association for the Education of Young Children.

Rogoff, B., & Chavajay, P. (1995). What's become of research on the cultural basis of cognitive development? *American Psychologist, 50,* 859–877.

Rohner, R. P. (1998, October). Father love and child development: History and current evidence. *Psychological Science,* pp. 157–161.

Roopnarine, J. L., & Honig, A. (1986). Research in Review: The unpopular child. In J. B. McCracken (Ed.), *Reducing stress in young children's lives* (pp.

110–115). Washington, DC: National Association for the Education of Young Children.

Rotella, R. J., Hanson, T., & Coop, R. H. (1991). Burnout in youth sports. *The Elementary School Journal, 91,* 421–428.

Rothenberg, T. (1989). The open classroom reconsidered. *The Elementary School Journal, 90,* 69–86.

Rotter, J. G. (1954). *Social learning and clinical psychology.* Upper Saddle River, NJ: Merrill/Prentice Hall.

Rousseau, J. J. (1911). *Emile* (B. Foxley, Trans.). London: J. M. Dent & Sons.

Rubin, K. H., & Copland, R. (1998). Social and nonsocial play in childhood: An individual differences perspective. In O. N. N. Saracho & B. Spodek (Eds.), *Multiple perspectives on play in early childhood education* (pp. 144–170). Albany: Albany State University of New York Press.

Sanacore, J. (1991). Expository and narrative text: Balancing young children's reading experiences. *Childhood Education, 67,* 211–214.

Santrock, J. W. (1997). *Children.* Dubuque, IA: Brown & Benchmark.

Schickedanz, J. A., Schickedanz, D. I., J. A., Hansen, K., & Forsyth, P. D. (1993). *Understanding children.* Mountain View, CA: Mayfield.

Schickedanz, J. A., York, M. E., Stewart, I. S., & White, D. A. (1990). *Strategies for teaching young children.* Upper Saddle River, NJ: Merrill Prentice Hall.

Schorr, L. B. (1989). Early interventions to reduce intergenerational disadvantage: The new policy context. *Teachers College Record, 90,* 362–374.

Schulman, K., Blank, H., & Ewen, D. (1999). *Seeds of success: State prekindergarten initiatives 1998–99.* Washington, DC: Children's Defense Fund.

Schultz, K. A. (1989). Early interventions to reduce intergenerational disadvantage: The new policy context. *Teachers College Record, 90,* 362–374.

Schwartz, S. L., & Robinson, H. F. (1982). *Designing curriculum for early childhood.* Boston: Allyn & Bacon.

Schweinhart, L. J. (1989, Winter). Early childhood programs in the U.S today. *High/Scope Resource, 1,* 9–14.

Schweinhart, L. J., Barnes, H. V., & Weikart, D. P. (1993). *Significant benefits: The High/Scope Perry preschool study through age 27.* Ypsilanti: High/Scope Press.

Schweinhart, L. J., & Weikart, D. (1985, April). Evidence that good early childhood programs work. *Phi Delta Kappan,* 545–553.

Schweinhart, L. J., Weikart, D. P., & Larner, M. B. (1986). Consequences of three preschool curriculum models through age 15. *Early Childhood Research Quarterly, 1,* 15–45.

Seefeldt, C. (1997). *Social studies for the preschool-primary child* (5th ed.). Upper Saddle River, NJ: Merrill/Prentice Hall.

Seefeldt, C., & Galper, A. (1998). *Continuing issues in early childhood education* (2nd ed.). Upper Saddle River, NJ: Merrill/Prentice Hall.

Seefeldt, C., & Barbour, N. (1988). "They said I had to . . .": Working with mandates. *Young Children, 43,* 4–8.

Seefeldt, C., & Barbour, N. (1998). *Early childhood education: An introduction* (4th ed.). Upper Saddle River, NJ: Merrill/Prentice Hall.

Segal., M., & Adcock, D. (1979). *From birth to one year/From one to two years.* Rolling Hills Estates, CA: B. L. Winch and Associates.

Selsam, M. E. (1959). *Seeds and more seeds.* New York: Harper & Row.

Sendak, M. (1962). *Chicken soup with rice.* New York: Harper & Row.

Serna, I. A., & Hudelson, S. (1997). Alicia's biliteracy development in first and second grade. In J. Christie, B. Enz, & C. Vukelich, *Teaching language and literacy* (pp. 255–263). New York: Longman.

Sexton, D. (1990). Quality integrated programs for infants and toddlers with special needs. In E. Surbeck & M. F. Kelly (Eds.), *Personalizing care with infants, toddlers, and families* (pp. 41–51). Wheaton, MD: Association for Childhood Education International.

Shantz, C. U. (1975). The development of social cognition. In E. M. Hetherington (Ed.), *Reviews of child development research* (Vol. 5, pp. 257–323). Chicago: University of Chicago Press.

Shepard, L. A., & Smith, M. L. (1986). Synthesis of research on school readiness and kindergarten retention. *Educational Leadership, 48,* 78–86.

Shepard, L. A., & Smith, M. L. (1987). Effects of kindergarten retention at the end of first grade. *Psychology in the Schools, 24,* 346–357.

Shepard, L. A., & Smith, M. L. (1988). Escalating academic demand in kindergarten. Counterproductive policies. *The Elementary School Journal, 89,* 135–145.

Shepard, L. A., & Smith, M. L. (1989). *Escalating kindergarten curriculum.* Urbana, IL: ERIC Clearinghouse on Elementary and Early Childhood Education.

Shepard, L. A., & Smith, M. L. (1990). Synthesis of research on grade retention. *Educational Leadership, 52,* 84–88.

Silberman, R. K. (1996). Visual impairments. In E. L. Meyen (Ed.), *Exceptional children in today's schools* (3rd ed., pp. 351–398). Denver: Love.

Silverstein, R. (1989). *The intent and spirit of P. L. 99-457: A sourcebook.* Washington, DC: National Center for Clinical Infant Programs.

Simeonsson, R., Huntington, G., Short, R., & Ware, W. (1982). The Carolina record of individual behavior: Characteristics of handicapped infants and children. *Topics in Early Childhood Special Education, 2,* 114–136.

Simon, T., & Smith, P. K. (1983). The study of play and problemsolving in preschool children: Have experimenter effects been responsible for previous results? *British Journal of Developmental Psychology, 1,* 289–297.

Sivertsen, M. L. (1993). *State of the art: Transforming ideas for teaching and learning science.* Washington, DC: U.S. Department of Education.

Skeels, H. M. (1966). Adult status of children with contrasting early life experiences. *Monographs of the Society for Research in Child Development, 31* (Serial N. 105).

Skinner, B. F. (1953). *Science and human behavior.* New York: Macmillan.

Skinner, B. F. (1957). *Verbal behavior.* Boston: Appleton-Century-Crofts.

Slavin, R. E. (1996). Neverstreaming: Preventing learning disabilities. *Educational Leadership, 53,* 46–54.

Sleeter, C. (1986). Learning disabilities: The social construction of a special education category. *Exceptional Children, 63,* 46–54.

Slobin, D. I. (1966). Comments on developmental psycholinguistics. In F. Smith & G. A. Miller (Eds.), *The genesis of language: A psycholinguistic approach* (pp. 85–92). Cambridge, MA: MIT Press.

Smilansky, S. (1968). *The effects of sociodramatic play on disadvantaged preschool children.* New York: Wiley.

Smilansky, S., & Shefatya, L. (1990). *Facilitating play: A medium for promoting cognitive, socio-emotional, and academic development in young children.* Gaithersburg, MD: Psychosocial and Educational Publications.

Smith, M. L., & Shepard, L. A. (1987). What doesn't work. Explaining policies of retention in the early grades. *Phi Delta Kappan, 69,* 129–134.

Smith, M. M. (1989, Spring). Excellence and equity for America's children. *Tennessee's Children,* pp. 5–12.

Smith, S. T. (1998, July 26). Recess isn't what it used to be *Boston Globe,* p. F5.

Snapper, K. J. (1976). The American legacy. In E. H. Grotberg (Ed.), *200 years of children.* Washington, DC: U. S. Government Printing Office.

Snow, C. E. (1983). Literacy and language: Relationships during the preschool years. *Harvard Educational Review, 53,* 165–189.

Snow, C. E., Burns, M. S., & Griffin, P. (Eds.). (1998). *Preventing reading difficulties in young children.* Washington, DC: National Academy Press.

Snow, C. E., & Tabors, P. O. (1993). Language skills that relate to literacy development. In B. Spodek & O. N. Saracho (Eds.), *Language and literacy in early childhood education* (pp. 1–20). New York: Teachers College Press.

Snyder, A. (1972). *Dauntless women in childhood education, 1856–1931.* Washington, DC: Association for Childhood Education International.

Soderman, A. K. (1985). Dealing with difficult young children. *Young Children, 40,* 15–20.

Spaggiari, S. (1996). The community-teacher partnership in the governance of the schools. In C. Edwards, L. Gandini, & G. Forman (Eds.), *The hundred languages of children.* (pp. 91–100). Norwood, NJ: Ablex.

Spodek, B. (1985). *Teaching in the early years* (3rd ed.). Upper Saddle River, NJ: Prentice Hall.

Sprung, B. (1996). Physics is fun, physics is important, and physics belongs in the early childhood curriculum. *Young Children, 51,* 29–33.

Staley, L. (1998). Beginning to implement the Reggio philosophy. *Young Children, 53,* 20–25.

Starr, R. H. (1990, June). The lasting effects of child maltreatment. *The World and I,* 484–489.

Steen, L. A. (1990, April). Making math matter. *Instructor,* 21–23.

Stein, J. U. (1993). Critical issues: Risk management, informed consent, and participant safety. In S. J. Grosse & D. Thompson (Eds.), *Leisure opportunities for individuals with disabilities: Legal issues* (pp. 37–54). Reston, VA: American Alliance for Health, Physical Education, Recreation and Dance.

Stevenson, H. W., Lee, S. Y., & Stigler, J. W. (1986). Mathematics achievement of Chinese, Japanese, and American children. *Science, 231,* 693–699.

Stewart, J. (1986). *The making of the primary school.* Milton Keynes, England: Open University Press.

Stoner, L. J. (1978). Selecting physical activities for the young child, with an understanding of bone growth and development. *Research for Practitioners and Parents, 1,* 32–42.

Sulzby, E. (1985). Kindergartners as writers and readers. In M. Farr (Ed.), *Advances in writing research* (Vol. 1). Norwood, NJ: Ablex.

Sulzby, E. (1993, January). I can write! Encouraging emergent writers. *Scholastic Pre-K Today,* pp. 30–33.

Sulzby, E., Barnhart, J., & Hieshima, J. (1989). Forms of writing and rereading from writing: A preliminary report. In J. Mason (Ed.), *Reading and writing connections* (pp. 63–79). Boston: Allyn & Bacon.

Swiniarski, L. (1991). Toys: Universals for teaching global education. *Childhood Education, 67,* 161–163.

Szanton, E. S. (2001). For America's infants and toddlers, Are important values threatened by our zeal to "teach"? *Young Children, 56,* 15–32.

Taft, N. (1991). Sports injuries in children. *The Elementary School Journal, 91,* 429–436.

Tanamachi, C. (1998, July 18). Educators poll: Set bilingual time limit. *Austin American Statesman,* p. B1.

Taylor, R. L., Willits, P., & Lieberman, N. (1990). Identification of preschool children with mild handicaps: The importance of cooperative effort. *Childhood Education, 67,* 26–31.

Teale, W. H. (1982). Toward a theory of how children learn to read and write naturally. *Language Arts, 59,* 555–570.

Teale, W. H. (1986a). Home background and young children's literacy development. In W. H. Teale & E. Sulzby (Eds.), *Emergent literacy: Reading and writing* (pp. 173–206). Norwood, NJ: Ablex.

Teale, W. H. (1986b). The beginning of reading and writing: Written language development during the preschool and kindergarten years. In M. Sampson (Ed.), *The pursuit of literacy: Early reading and writing* (pp. 1–29). Dubuque, IA: Kendall/Hunt.

Teale, W. H. (1987). The emergent literacy classroom. *Reading Today, 7,* 14.

Teale, W. H., & Yokota, J. (2000). Beginning reading and writing: Perspectives on instruction. In D. S. Strickland & L. M. Morrow (Eds.), *Beginning reading and writing* (pp. 3–21). New York: Teachers College Press.

Tharp, R. G., & Gallimore, R. (1988). *Rousing minds to life.* Cambridge: Cambridge University Press.

Thomas, A., Chess, S., & Birch, H. (1970, August). The origin of personality. *Scientific American, 223,* 102–109.

Thomas, M., & Caulfield, R. (1998). Teen pregnancy and parenthood: Infants and toddlers who need care. *Early Childhood Education Journal, 25,* 203–206.

Thornton, S., & Hauser, N. (1997, June). The status of elementary social studies in Delaware: A view from the field. *Resources in Education, 132*–139.

Tilgner, P. J. (1990). Avoiding science in the elementary school. *Science Education, 74,* 421–431.

Tracey, D. H. (2000). Enhancing literacy growth through home-school connections. In D. S. Strickland & L. M. Morrow (Eds.), *Beginning reading and writing* (pp. 46–57). New York: Teachers College Press.

Traub, J. (1999, January 31). The bilingual barrier. *The New York Times Magazine,* pp. 32–35.

Trawick-Smith, J. (1997). *Early childhood development. A multicultural perspective.* Upper Saddle River, NJ: Merrill/Prentice Hall.

Trepanier-Street, M. (2000). Multiple forms of representation in long-term projects. The garden project. *Childhood Education, 78,* 18–25.

Trostle, S. L., & Yawkey, T. D. (1990). *Integrated learning activities for young children.* Boston: Allyn & Bacon.

Troy, M., & Sroufe, L. A. (1987). Victimization among preschoolers: Role of attachment relationship history. *Journal of the American Academy of Child and Adolescent Psychiatry, 26,* 166–172.

Udell, T., Peters, J., & Templeman, T. P. (1998, January/February). From philosophy to practice in inclusive early childhood programs. *Teaching Exceptional Children,* pp. 44–49.

U.S. Department of Education (undated). *Education for homeless children and youth program report to Congress, FY 1997.* Washington, DC: Author.

U.S. Department of Education. (2000). Double Oaks Program ensures bright beginnings. *U.S. Department of Education Community Update, 80,* 6–7.

Urzua, C. (1987). "You stopped too soon": Second language children composing and revising. *TESOL Quarterly, 21,* 279–303.

Vandell, D. L., & Corassaniti, M. A. (1988). Variations in early child care: Do they predict subsequent social, emotional, and cognitive differences? *Child Development, 48,* 176–186.

van Kleeck, A., Alexander, E. I., Vigil, A., & Templeton, K. E. (1996). Verbally modeling thinking for infants: Middle-class mothers' presentation of information structures during book sharing. *Journal of Research in Childhood Education, 10,* 101–113.

Van Scotter, R., Van Dusen, L, & Worthen, B. (1996). Starting early: Junior Achievement's elementary school program. *Educational Leadership, 53,* 33–37.

Veach, D. M. (1986). Choice with responsibility. In J. B. McCracken (Ed.), *Reducing stress in young children's lives* (pp. 96–98). Washington, DC: National Association for the Education of Young Children.

Vecchi, V. (1996). The role of the *Atelierista.* In C. Edwards, L. Gandini, & G. Forman (Eds.), *The hundred languages of children* (pp. 119–127). Norwood, NJ: Ablex.

Vesilind, E. M., & Jones, M. G. (1996). Hands-on Science education reform. *Journal of Teacher Education, 47,* 375–385.

Viorst, J. (1972). *Alexander and the terrible, horrible, no good, very bad day.* New York: Atheneum.

Vygotsky, L. (1932). *Thought and language.* Cambridge, MA: MIT Press.

Vygotsky, L. (1978). *Mind in society: The development of psychological processes.* Cambridge, MA: Harvard University Press.

Wallach, V., & Caulfield, R. (1998). Attachment and at-risk infants: Theoretical perspectives and clinical implications. *Early Childhood Education Journal, 26,* 125–129.

Wallerstein, J., Lewis, J., & Blakeslee, S. (2000). *The unexpected legacy of divorce: A 25 year landmark study.* Boston: Hyperion.

Wang, M. C., Reynolds, M. C., & Walberg, H. J. (1994–1995). Serving students at the margins. *Educational Leadership, 52,* 12–17.

Wardle, F. (1990). Endorsing children's differences: Meeting the needs of adopted minority children. *Young Children, 45,* 44–46.

Wassermann, S. (2000). *Serious players in the classroom.* New York: Teachers College Press.

Weber, E. (1969). *The kindergarten.* New York: Teachers College Press.

Weber, E. (1970). *Early childhood education: Perspectives on change.* New York: Teachers College Press.

Weber, E. (1984). *Ideas influencing early childhood education.* New York: Teachers College Press.

Weikart, D. P., Epstein, A. S., Schweinhart, L. J., & Bond, J. T. (1978). *The Ypsilanti Preschool Curriculum Demonstration Project: Preschool years and longitudinal results.* Ypsilanti: High/Scope Press.

Weikart, D. P., Rogers, L., Adcock, C., & McClelland, D. (1971). *The cognitively oriented curriculum: A framework for teachers.* Urbana, IL: ERIC-NAEYC.

Weiser, M. G. (1987). *Group care and education of infants and toddlers.* St. Louis: C. V. Mosby.

Weiser, M. G. (1991). *Infant/toddler care and education* (2nd ed.). Upper Saddle River, NJ: Merrill/Prentice Hall.

Wellhousen, K. (1996). Be it ever so humble: Developing a study of homes for today's diverse society. *Young Children, 52,* 72–74.

West, B. (1992). Children are caught—between home and school, culture and school. In B. Neugebauer, (Ed.), *Alike and different: Exploring our humanity with young children* (pp. 127–139). Washington, DC: National Association for the Education of Young Children.

Westley, J. (1988). *Insects and other crawlers.* Sunnyvale, CA: Creative Publications.

Westmoreland, P. (1996). Coping with death: Helping students grieve. *Childhood Education, 72,* 157–163.

White, B. L., & Watts, J. C. (1973). *Experience and environment: Major influences on the development of the young child* (Vol. 1). Englewood Cliffs, NJ: Prentice-Hall.

White, B. P., & Phair, M. A. (1986). "It'll be a challenge!" Managing emotional stress in teaching disabled children. In J. B. McCracken (Ed.), *Reducing stress in young children's lives* (pp. 136–140). Washington, DC: National Association for the Education of Young Children.

Williams, L. R. (1999). Determining the early childhood curriculum: The evolution of goals and strategies through consonance and controversy. In C. Seefeldt (Ed.), *The early childhood curriculum: Current findings in theory and practice* (3rd ed., pp. 1–26). New York: Teachers College Press.

Williams, S. (1992). *I went walking.* San Diego: Harcourt Brace.

Willer, B., & Bredekamp, S. (1990). Redefining readiness: An essential requisite for educational reform. *Young Children, 45,* 22–24.

Willis, A., & Ricciuti, H. (1975). *A good beginning for babies: Guidelines for group care.* Washington, DC: National Association for the Education of Young Children.

Willis, S. (1992, January). Mathematics education standards 'Revolution' takes hold. *ASCD Curriculum Update,* pp. 1–3.

Wiseman, D. E., & Robeck, C. P. (1983). The written language behavior of two socio-economic groups of preschool children. *Reading Psychology, 4,* 349–363,

Wishon, P. M., & Spangler, R. S. (1990). The education of children in Japanese-American internment camps during WWII. Focus on kindergarten. Unpublished manuscript.

Wolery, M. (1994). Implementing instruction for young children with special needs in early childhood classrooms. In M. Wolery & J. S. Wilbers (Eds.), *Including children with special needs in early childhood programs* (pp. 151–166). Washington, DC: National Association for the Education of Young Children.

Wolery, M., Strain, P. S., & Bailey, D. B. (1992). Reaching potentials of children with special needs. In S. Bredekamp & T. Rosegrant (Eds.), *Reaching potentials: Appropriate curriculum and assessment for young children* (Vol. 1, pp. 92–111). Washington, DC: National Association for the Education of Young Children.

Wolery, M., & Wilbers, J. S. (Eds.). (1994). *Including children with special needs in early childhood programs.* Washington, DC: National Association for the Education of Young Children.

Wolfe, L. (1992). Reaching potentials through bilingual education. In S. Bredekamp & T. Rosegrant (Eds.), *Reaching potentials: Appropriate curriculum and assessment for young children* (Vol. 1, pp. 139–144). Washington, DC: National Association for the Education of Young Children.

Wolk, S. (1994). Project-based learning: Pursuits with a purpose. *Educational Leadership, 52,* 42–45.

Wong-Fillmore, L. (1991). Language and cultural issues in early education. In S. L. Kagan (Ed.), *The care and education of America's young children: Obstacles and opportunities* (Part I, pp. 30–49). Chicago: National Society for the Study of Education.

Wortham, S. (1984). *Organizing instruction in early childhood.* Boston: Allyn & Bacon.

Wortham, S. C. (1990). Infant-toddler playgrounds. In S. C. Wortham & J. L. Frost (Eds.), *Playgrounds for young children: National survey and perspectives* (pp. 69–88). Reston, VA: American Alliance for Health, Physical Education, Recreation, and Dance.

Wortham, S. C. (1992). *Childhood 1892–1992.* Wheaton, MD: Association For Childhood Education International.

Wortham, S. (1998). A model of portfolio assessment in prekindergarten through primary grades. In S. Wortham, A. Barbour, & Desjean-Perrotta, B., *Portfolio assessment: A handbook for preschool and elementary teachers* (pp. 45–60).

Wortham, S. (2001a). Play. Infants and toddlers. In J. L. Frost, S. Wortham, & S. Reifel, *Play and child development* (pp. 116–159). Upper Saddle River, NJ: Merrill/Prentice Hall.

Wortham, S. (2001b). Play in the preschool years. In J. L. Frost, S. Wortham, & S. Reifel, *Play and child development* (pp. 160–213). Upper Saddle River, NJ: Merrill/Prentice Hall.

Wortham, S. (2001c). Play and the school-age child. In J. Frost, S. Wortham, & S. Reifel, *Play and child development* (pp. 214–259). Upper Saddle River, NJ: Merrill/Prentice Hall.

Wortham,. S. C. (2001d). *Assessment in early childhood education* (3rd ed.). Upper Saddle River, NJ: Merrill/Prentice Hall.

Wortham, S. C. (2001e). Play and children with disabilities. In J. L. Frost, S. Wortham, & S. Reifel, *Play and Child development* (pp. 340–385). Upper Saddle River, NJ: Merrill/Prentice Hall.

Wortham, S. C. & Frost, J. L. (Eds.). (1990). *Playgrounds for young children: National survey and perspectives.* Reston, VA: American Alliance for Health, Physical Education, Recreation, and Dance.

Wyler, R. (1986). *Science fun with peanuts and popcorn.* Parsippany, NJ: Silver Burdett Press.

Youcha, G. (1995). *Minding the children.* New York: Scribner.

Zeavin, C. (1997). Toddlers at play: Environments at work. *Young Children, 52,* 72–77.

Zero to Three & The Ounce of Prevention Fund. (2000). *Starting smart: How early experiences affect brain development.* Washington, DC: Authors.

Name Index

Abramson, S., 109, 199, 206, 240, 342
Adams, M. J., 228, 229, 358
Adcock, C., 64, 65
Adcock, D., 125
Adeyanju, M., 406, 407
Adler, J., 2
Alexander, E. I., 164
Alhusen, V. D., 122
Allport, G., 391
Anglin, J., 30
Ankenman, K., 199, 206, 342
Apple, P., 140
Arango, M., 125
Archimbault, J., 429, 430, 432, 436, 449
Arenz, B., 243
Asher, S. R., 110
Atkinson, A. H., 392
Au, K. H., 19, 240
Austin, J. S., 11

Back, C., 425
Bandura, A., 39, 125, 126, 186
Banet, B., 65, 192
Barbour, A., 60, 213, 305, 334
Barbour, N., 81, 243, 244, 253, 341, 377
Barclay, K., 376
Barnes, B. R., 400
Barnett, S. W., 35
Barnhart, J., 218, 230
Barrett, W. S., 30
Barufaldi, J. P., 246, 378
Baumrind, D., 95
Beach, L., 401
Beaty, J. J., 212, 213, 272, 273, 287, 288, 290, 291, 294
Beilin, H., 108
Bell, M. J., 374, 377
Belsky, J., 121, 122
Benelli, C., 376

Bergen, D., 116
Bergeron, B. S., 262
Berk, L. E., 42, 191, 193, 223, 269, 303, 390, 403
Bernhardt, J. L., 127
Bernstein, N., 122
Berrueta-Clement, J. R., 30
Bhavnagri, N. P., 134, 135
Bhavnani, R., 193
Birch, H., 84
Bjorkland, D., 405
Blake, S., 243
Blakeslee, S., 8
Bloom, B., 30, 119, 218
Blow, S., 27
Bodrova, E., 42, 55, 56, 61, 186, 191, 194, 243, 245, 304
Boehm, A. E., 213
Bond, G. L., 229
Bond, J., 64
Bonn, M., 25
Bowman, B., 2, 16, 17, 19
Bowman, B. T., 52, 53, 54, 62
Boyer, E. L., 10, 19
Branley, F. M., 258
Braun, S. J., 26, 27, 30, 118
Bredekamp, S., 43, 60, 61, 62, 63, 64, 65, 97, 108, 110, 121, 128, 134, 135, 139, 142, 143, 186, 187, 189, 197, 241, 266, 302, 305–307, 344, 351, 361
Brewer, J. A., 244
Bromley, D. A., 373
Bronfenbrenner, U., 56, 68, 126
Brown, F., 12
Brown, J., 93, 218
Brown, S., 351
Bruer, J. T., 103
Bruner, J., 30, 69
Bruner, J. S., 193, 222
Buchoff, R., 12
Buchsaum, K., 391

Burk, D. I., 266
Burns, M. S., 2, 16, 17, 19, 53, 54, 228, 229, 358
Byrnes, D. A., 392

Cadwell, L. B., 69, 71, 72
Cahill, B. J., 267, 282, 284
Caldwell, B., 121, 123
Callahan, R. C., 203
Campbell, P. E., 244, 361
Canady, R. J., 258, 259–261, 279, 280
Carle, E., 424
Carter, L. G., 358
Cassady, J. K., 239
Cataldo, C. Z., 120, 123, 136, 138
Caulfield, R., 81, 123, 148, 155, 163
Cazden, C., 218, 223
Chall, J. S., 228
Chapman, M. L., 350
Charbonneau, M. P., 306
Chard, S. C., 72, 73, 74, 75, 196, 197, 199, 284, 303, 306, 307, 313, 315, 333
Charlesworth, R., 362
Chase, P., 314
Chavajay, P., 40
Checkley, K., 58
Chess, S., 84
Chipman, M., 34
Chomsky, C., 163, 218
Christie, J. F., 93, 131, 219, 222, 223, 226, 238, 272, 275, 288
Chukovsky, K., 222
Ciari, B., 67
Clarke-Stewart, K. A., 8, 122
Clay, M. M., 358
Clements, D. C., 122
Clements, D. H., 364
Clewett, A. S., 95
Clifford, R., 16–17
Clifford, R. M., 140, 143

Clyde, J. A., 239
Cole, E., 398
Coleman, M., 14
Connell, J. P., 81
Connolly, J. A., 272
Coop, R. H., 404, 405
Cooter, R. B., 354
Coplan, R., 273
Coplan, R. J., 304
Copley, J. V., 243, 246, 360
Copple, C., 43, 62, 63, 108, 110, 128,
    134, 139, 142, 143, 186, 187,
    189, 197, 241, 266, 302,
    305–307, 361
Cremin, L., 196
Cremin, L. A., 29, 34, 329
Cruz-Janzen, M., 34
Cryer, D., 140, 143
Cummins, J., 342
Cunningham, P. M., 352, 353, 358

Da Ros, D. A., 137
Dailey, K. A., 94
Darlington, R., 35
Dart, B., 404
Day, B., 60, 308
Day, D., 313
Day, M. C., 120
De Vries, R., 242, 244
Dearden, R. F., 315
DeFee, M., 352, 353, 358
Deiner, P. L., 34
dePaola, T., 431, 432, 437, 440
Derman-Sparks, L., 62, 391
Desjean-Perrotta, B., 213, 334
Deutsch, M., 391
Devall, E. L., 267, 282, 284
DeVries, R., 126
Dewey, J., 28, 42, 67, 72, 191, 196
Diaz-Soto, L., 18
Dickerson, M., 118
DiMartino, E. C., 5
DiPietro, J. A., 93
Dodge, K., 391
Doescher, S. M., 95
Donovan, S., 2, 16, 17, 19, 53, 54
Dowd, F. S., 239
Doyle, A. B., 272
Dueschl, R. A., 374
Dutton, A., 242, 243, 363, 364
Dutton, W. H., 242, 243, 363,
    364
Dweck, C. S., 73
Dykstra, R., 229
Dyson, A. H., 218, 221, 231

Early, D., 16–17
Eddowes, E. A., 9, 10
Edelman, M. W., 6
Edwards, C., 67, 69, 70
Edwards, D., 196
Edwards, E. P., 26, 27, 30, 118
Edwards, L. L., 11
Eheart, B. K., 122
Ehri, L. C., 229
Elardo, P., 123
Eliason, C. F., 406, 407
Eliot, A. A., 118
Elkind, D., 3, 44, 268, 304
Elkonin, D., 193
Ellsworth, J., 368
Enders, S., 140
Enright, D. S., 342
Enright, R. D., 391
Enz, B., 219, 222
Epstein, A. S., 30, 64
Epstein, L. H., 403
Erickson, E., 68
Erikson, E., 37, 55, 61, 125, 131, 171,
    186, 266, 304
Ershler, J., 193, 194
Escobar, C. M., 35
Ewing, J. K., 242
Eyer, D. W., 148

Farmer, J., 32
Fassler, R., 219, 220, 221, 341, 343
Feldman, R. S., 390, 392
Fenichel, E., 122, 136, 139, 140,
    143
Ferreiro, E. K., 230
Fewell, R., 214
Fields, M. V., 94, 109, 223, 230, 231,
    351, 353, 356, 357
Filippini, T., 71
Fisher, J., 33
Forman, G., 67, 72, 196, 242, 244
Forsyth, P. D., 30, 37, 38, 82, 93, 108,
    109, 302, 303
Foster, S., 16
Foyle, H. C., 392
Franklin, M. E., 374
Franks, B. D., 148
Freeman, D. E., 399
Freeman, E. B., 110, 224–225
Freeman, Y. A., 399
Freinet, C., 67
Freud, S., 37, 118
Froebel, F., 26–27, 67
Frost, J. L., 93, 193, 214, 222, 286,
    288, 289, 292

Galinsky, E., 45, 122
Gallahue, D. L., 286, 403, 404
Gallaudet, T., 33
Galley, M., 125
Gallimore, R., 348
Gallistel, C. R., 243
Gambrell, L. B., 229, 230, 347
Gandini, L., 67, 69, 70, 196
Garcia, E., 4
Gardner, H., 56, 58, 67, 69
Gargiulo, R. M., 135
Garner, B. P., 131
Garvey, C., 193, 222, 272
Gaskins, I. W., 358
Gaskins, J. C., 358
Gaskins, R. W., 358
Gautt, S. W., 214
Gelman, G., 268
Gelman, R., 243
Genish, C., 341, 343
Genishi, C., 219, 220, 221
George, C., 81
Gerber, M., 121
Gersten, R., 342
Gesell, A., 28, 35, 36, 54, 55, 118,
    125, 185, 218
Gilbert, G. G., 303
Gillespie, C. W., 72
Glasser, W., 393
Glazer, J. I., 344, 355
Gleason, J. B., 94
Gober, B. E., 148
Goldenberg, D. S., 212
Goldhaber, J., 226, 238
Goldsmith, H. H., 81
Gonzalez-Mena, J., 134, 135, 148
Goodman, Y., 110, 218, 236
Gothard, H. M., 225
Graham, M. S., 124
Graham, S., 12, 306
Granucci, P. L., 30
Graves, D. H., 341
Graves, S. B., 135
Green, L., 342
Green, V. P., 392
Greenberg, P., 392
Greene, L., 406
Greenman, J., 132
Greven, P., 116
Griffin, A., 122, 136, 139, 140, 143
Griffin, P., 228, 229, 358
Gross, B., 34
Gross, R., 34
Gulliford, A., 26
Gullo, F., 44

Guralnick, M. J., 35
Gutierrez, K. D., 221, 240, 343

Hagens, H. E., 131, 137
Hale, M. G., 358
Hale-Benson, M. J., 390
Hall, C. S., 118
Hall, D. P., 352, 353, 358
Han, E. P., 238
Hansen, K., 30, 37, 38, 82, 93, 108, 109, 302, 303
Hanson, M. J., 35
Hanson, T., 405
Harder, R. J., 203
Harms, T., 140, 143
Harris, K. R., 12, 306
Harris, W. T., 27
Hartup, W. W., 110, 304
Harvey, J. G., 303
Hatch, B., 110
Hatch, J. A., 224–225
Haugland, S. W., 364
Hayes, L. F., 233, 235
Helm, J. H., 72, 73, 74, 75, 306, 313, 334
Hendrick, J., 220, 266, 270, 274, 287
Henniger, M. L., 288
Herr, J., 294
Hiebert, E. H., 235
Hieshima, J., 218, 230
Hill, L. B., 358
Hill, P. S., 28
Hilliard, D. C., 405
Hills, T., 16–17, 306
Hills, T. W., 62, 333
Hillstead, D. V., 223, 224
Hines, A. G., 277
Hinkle, D., 19
Hinojosa, B. L., 401
Hogan, R., 222
Hohmann, M., 65, 66, 68, 186, 192
Hohmeyer, L., 273
Holcomb, B., 268
Holden, R., 10
Holmes, E. E., 392
Hong, M. H., 121
Honig, A. S., 120, 121, 132, 391
Hoskisson, K., 351
Houser, N., 397
Houston, J. P., 30, 34
Hove, E., 374
Howes, C., 45, 122, 270
Hranitz, J. R., 9, 10
Huber, L., 396
Hudelson, S., 221, 240, 342

Huerta-Macias, A., 109, 240
Huffman, A. B., 247
Huffman, L. C., 391
Hughes, F. P., 304, 403
Hunt, J. M., 30, 66, 119
Hunt, M., 30
Hunter, M., 202
Huntington, G., 214
Hurley, S., 243
Hutchinson, L., 368
Hutt, C., 193
Hymes, J. L., 45, 118

Ilg, F. A., 28, 35, 54
Inhelder, B., 164, 242
Isaacs, S., 72
Isbell, R., 226
Ishee, N., 226, 238

Jambor, T., 194, 285, 291, 294
Jantz, R. K., 393, 397
Jarolimek, J., 268, 397
Jenkins, L., 373, 406
Jervis, K., 213
Jewell, M. G., 218, 235, 348
Johnson, C., 109, 240
Johnson, D. W., 392
Johnson, H., 118
Johnson, J. E., 93, 131, 193, 194, 222, 223, 226, 238, 272, 275, 288
Johnson, R., 392
Johnson, R. H., 310
Johnson, R. T., 310
Jones, M. G., 374
Jordan, H., 424

Kagan, J., 119
Kagan, S., 15, 44, 46
Kagan, S. L., 2, 20, 51, 52, 53, 54
Kaiser, A. P., 224
Kamii, C., 126, 242, 244, 361, 391
Kandel, M., 12
Katz, L. G., 71, 72, 73, 74, 75, 155, 196, 197, 199, 274, 284, 303, 304, 306, 307, 313, 315, 333, 334
Katz, P., 121
Kauchak, D. P., 203
Kawakami, A. J., 19
Keats, E. J., 239
Keister, M. E., 120
Kelley, M. F., 122
Kellough, R. D., 382, 384
Kemple, K. M., 275

Keogh, A. J., 203
Kepler, L., 380
Kerivan, A. S., 391
Kiger, G., 392
Kilpatrick, W. H., 28, 72
King, E. W., 34
Kinsey, S. J., 310
Kohlberg, L., 391
Kokoski, T. M., 246
Kontos, S., 45, 122
Kovach, B. A., 137
Krogh, S., 110

La Cerva, V., 268
Labbo, L. D., 349
Labov, W., 220
Ladd, K. G. T., 246, 378
Lally, J. R., 120, 121, 122, 136, 139, 140, 143
Lamme, L. L., 355
Landreth, G., 273
Landry, C. E., 242, 244
Lane, E. W., 390
Langley, J., 72
Lanser, S., 42
Larner, M. B., 64
Lawton, J. T., 81, 193, 194
Lazar, I., 35
Leavitt, R. L., 122
Lee, M., 72
Lee, S. Y., 242
LeeKeenan, D., 72
Lenhoff, R., 396
Lennenberg, E., 163
Leong, D. J., 42, 55, 56, 61, 186, 191, 194, 243, 245, 304
Levy, A. K., 222
Lewin, A., 69, 70
Lewis, J., 8
Libby, Y., 294
Lieberman, J. N., 193
Lieberman, N., 12
Lind, K. K., 362
Lindberg, D. L., 378
Lindfors, J. W., 94
Lindzey, G., 118
Lowman, L., 128
Lurie-Hurvitz, E., 122
Lyman, L., 392
Lynch, E. W., 35
Lyon, G. R., 228

Maccoby, E. E., 95
Mager, R. F., 202
Magid, R. Y., 16

Main, M., 81
Malaguzzi, L., 67, 68, 69, 186, 187
Mallory, B. L., 43
Mann, V. A., 229
Manning, M. L., 303, 391
Mantovani, S., 128
Mardell-Czudnowski, C. D., 212
Martin, B., Jr., 429, 430, 432, 436, 449
Martin, J. A., 95
Mason, J., 235, 236
Matthews, M. W., 391
Mavrogenes, N. A., 94
Maxim, G. W., 117, 118, 122, 123, 270
Mayer, M., 11, 262
Mazzoni, S. A., 229, 230, 347
McCarthy, M. A., 30, 34
McClellan, D. E., 274, 304
McClelland, D., 64, 65
McCloskey, M. L., 342
McCormick, C., 236
McCormick, J., 20
McCormick, L., 10
McCracken, M., 355
McCracken, R. A., 355
McCune, L., 131
McDonnell, L., 42
McKenna, M. C., 349
McMillan, M., 118
McMullen, M. B., 45, 127
McNeil, D., 164, 218
Meddin, B. J., 390
Mehlinger, S. L., 391
Meisels, S. J., 212, 307
Menyuk, P., 81
Mercer, J., 34
Meyen, E. L., 12, 335
Miller, K., 132, 134, 164
Mills, H., 239
Milner, S. C., 121
Mitchell, A., 43, 44, 45, 46
Mitchell, J. W., 374
Moran, M. R., 11
Morgan, G., 31
Morrison, G. S., 37, 38, 80, 81, 126, 133
Morrow, L. M., 94, 109, 164, 223, 225, 227, 230, 233, 234, 236, 351, 352
Moses, A. J., 246, 378
Moyer, J., 396
Muenchow, S., 131
Mullen, M., 194
Mullis, I. V. S., 373
Murphy, R. R., 391

Nachbar, R. R., 310
Nason, R. B., 60
Neuman, S. B., 344, 351
Neumann, M. J., 2, 20
New, R., 72, 196
New, R. S., 43, 55, 186
Newman, M. J., 51, 52, 53, 54
Newmann, F. M., & Associates, 186
Nimmo, J., 72
Nimnicht, G., 125
Norton, D. E., 401
Numeroff, L. J., 439–447
Nunnelley, J. C., 401

O'Brien, S., 95
O'Donnell, N. S., 103
O'Neil, D., 16
O'Neil, J., 6
Olshansky, B., 381
Orlich, D. C., 203
Osofsky, J. D., 267
Ostrosky, M. M., 224

Packer, A. B., 121
Papert, S., 364
Pardo, L. S., 353
Parker, F., 28
Parker, R. K., 120
Parker, S. C., 196
Patterson, K., 11
Patton, M. M., 246
Pellegrini, A. D., 405
Pendergrass, R. A., 203
Penta, M. O., 374
Perrone, V., 213
Pestalozzi, J., 26–27
Peters, R., 399
Peth-Pierce, R., 13
Phair, M. A., 390
Phillips, C. B., 120
Piaget, J., 27, 30, 39, 40, 61, 66, 67, 68, 69, 80, 126, 129, 164, 185–186, 218, 219, 242, 243, 394
Pizzo, P. D., 120
Powell, D. R., 134
Pressley, M. C., 347
Prevatte, C., 353
Price, G. G., 242

Quint, S., 9
Quintero, E., 109, 240, 342, 343

Raikes, H., 127
Raines, S. C., 226, 258, 259–261, 279, 280

Rakow, S. J., 374, 377
Ramsey, P., 270
Rand, M. K., 223, 234
Rankin, J., 347
Raphael, T. E., 353
Recken, R., 120
Reid, R., 12, 116
Reider, B. E., 306
Reifel, S., 214
Reinking, D., 349
Reutzel, D. R., 354
Reynolds, M. C., 4, 12
Rhodes, M., 262
Ricciuti, H., 120
Rinaldi, C., 72
Rivers, A. M., 46
Robeck, C. P., 235
Roberts, P. L., 399
Robinson, R., 199, 206, 342
Robison, H. F., 81
Rogers, C. S., 222
Rogers, L., 64, 65
Rogoff, B., 40
Rohner, R. P., 44
Roopnarine, J. L., 391
Rosegrant, T., 60, 61, 62, 63, 64, 65
Rosen, A. L., 390
Rotella, R. J., 404, 405
Rothenberg, T., 309
Rotter, J. G., 303
Rousseau, J., 26, 117
Rubin, K. H., 273, 304
Rudenga, E. A., 262
Ruhmann, L. H., 128
Russell, S. M., 225

Sanacore, J., 352
Santrock, J. W., 57, 81, 92–94, 108–109, 302
Sawyers, J. K., 222
Schickedanz, D. I., 30, 37, 38, 82, 93, 108, 109, 302, 303
Schickedanz, J. A., 30, 37, 38, 82, 93, 108, 109, 266, 269, 272, 277, 302, 303
Schoon, S., 376
Schorr, L. B., 13
Schwartz, S. L., 81
Schweinhart, L. J., 30, 35, 64
Scott, K. G., 124
Seda, I., 109, 240
Seefeldt, C., 60, 81, 196, 202, 243, 244, 253, 272, 306, 313, 314, 333, 341, 377, 391, 392, 393, 396, 397

Segal, M., 125, 136, 139, 140, 143
Seitz, V., 131
Selsam, M. E., 423, 426
Sendak, M., 239
Serna, I., 221, 240, 342
Sexton, D., 124
Shade, D. D., 364
Shanker, A., 311
Shefatya, L., 193
Shepard, L. A., 60, 307, 308
Shepard, S., 60, 307
Shinn, M., 45, 122
Short, R., 214
Silberman, R. K., 11
Silverstein, R., 120
Simeonsson, R., 214
Simon, T., 193
Simpson, J. D., 11
Sivertsen, R., 374
Skeels, H. M., 118
Skinner, B. F., 38, 126, 163, 186, 218
Slavin, R. E., 359
Sleeter, C., 34
Slobin, D. I., 218
Smilansky, S., 193, 222, 272
Smith, A. J., 9
Smith, M. L., 60, 307, 308
Smith, P. K., 193
Smith, S. T., 303
Snapper, K. J., 33
Snow, C. E., 218, 223, 228, 229, 358
Snyder, A., 25, 27, 28
Soderman, A. K., 84, 96
Spaggiari, S., 70
Spangler, K. L., 94, 109, 223, 230, 231, 351, 353, 356, 357
Spangler, R. S., 33
Spodek, B., 218, 226
Sprung, B., 246, 256
Sroufe, L. A., 82
Staley, L., 67, 69, 72, 186
Starr, R. H., 267
Steen, L. A., 360
Stein, J. U., 46
Steinberg, L., 121
Stevenson, H. W., 242
Stewart, I. S., 266, 269, 272, 277
Stewart, J., 72
Stigler, J. W., 242
Stolz, L. M., 118
Stoner, L. J., 303
Sugawara, A. K., 95
Sulzby, E., 110, 218, 230, 231, 233
Surbeck, K. E., 122
Sutterfield, S. J., 391

Swiniarski, L., 398
Szanton, E., 136, 139, 140, 143
Szanton, E. S., 121

Tabors, P. O., 218, 229
Taft, N., 405
Tanamachi, C., 342
Taylor, R. L., 12
Teale, W. H., 110, 227, 228, 230, 235, 349
Teberosky, A., 230
Tedford, A. C., 401
Temple, A., 28, 196
Templeton, K. E., 164
Tharp, R. G., 348
Thomas, A., 84
Thomas, M., 123
Thornton, S., 397
Tilgner, P. J., 374
Torelli, L., 116
Tracey, D. H., 223
Traub, J., 342
Trawick-Smith, J., 269, 270
Trepanier-Street, M., 188
Trostle, S. L., 294, 295, 296, 406, 408–409
Troy, M., 82

Urzua, C., 342

Valosi, A., 403
Van Dusen, L., 396
van Kleeck, A., 164
Van Scotter, R., 396
Veach, D. M., 391
Vecchi, V., 71
Velarde, M. C., 342, 343
Vesilind, E. M., 374
Vigil, A., 164
Viorst, J., 402, 449–455
Vukelich, C., 219, 222
Vygotsky, L. S., 27, 40, 55, 56, 61, 68, 69, 126, 164, 186, 193, 219, 222, 223, 242, 243

Walberg, H. J., 12
Wallach, V., 81
Wallerstein, J., 8
Walters, R., 39, 125, 186
Wang, M. C., 4, 12
Wardle, F., 5
Ware, W., 214
Wasserman, S., 377
Watts, J. C., 89, 119

Weber, E., 27, 29, 36, 40, 184
Weikart, D., 30, 35, 186, 192
Weikart, D. P., 64, 65, 66, 68
Weinberg, R. A., 213
Weiser, M. G., 89, 118, 120, 121, 127, 128, 139, 155, 163
Weissbourd, B., 136, 139, 140, 143
Wellhousen, K., 282, 283
Wermuth, S., 262
West, B., 392
Westley, J., 379
Westmoreland, P., 268
White, B. L., 89, 119
White, B. P., 390
White, D. A., 266, 269, 272, 277
Wilbers, J. S., 46
Williams, G. A., 110
Williams, H. G., 285
Williams, L. R., 27, 43
Williams, S., 430, 432, 434, 435
Willis, A., 120, 360
Willits, P., 12
Wing, R. R., 403
Winsler, A., 42, 191
Wiseman, D. E., 235
Wishon, P. M., 33
Wiske, M. S., 212
Wolery, M., 14, 46
Wolfe, L., 62
Wolk, S., 306, 311
Wong-Fillmore, L., 221
Wortham, S. C., 29, 32, 33, 54, 93, 132, 140, 193, 194, 212, 213, 214, 222, 223, 272, 273, 274, 291, 292, 297, 303, 305, 332, 333, 334, 403
Worthen, B., 396
Wright, A. E., 11
Wrisley, L., 72
Wu, F., 270
Wyler, R., 426, 427

Yawkey, T. D., 93, 131, 222, 223, 226, 238, 272, 275, 288, 294, 295, 296, 406, 408–409
Yokoi, Y., 347
Yokota, J., 227, 228, 230, 349
York, M. E., 266, 269, 272, 277
Yoshida, R. K., 12
Youcha, G., 29
Yovich, S., 368

Zeavin, C., 128
Zintz, M. V., 218, 235, 348

Subject Index

Abuse or neglect, child, 10–11, 267
Acceptance needs, 110, 304–305
Accuracy of tests, 56, 213
Achievement, importance in child's life, 110
Active learning, 186
   practices for preschool and childcare programs, 65
Active reconstruction of knowledge, 192
Aesthetic appreciation, fostering, 176–177
African Americans
   historical roots of early childhood education, 32
Aid to Families with Dependent Children (AFDC), 43
Air Is All Around You (Branley), 258
Alcohol abuse, 10
Alexander and the Terrible, Horrible, No Good, Very Bad Day (Viorst), 402, 449–455
Alphabetic knowledge, 229
American Association of Elementary/Kindergarten/Nursery Educators, 120
American Asylum for the Deaf, 33
Americans with Disabilities Act (ADA), 46
Animism, 186
Anthropology, 272, 396
Antisocial behavior, 391
Anxious ambivalent/avoidant children, 81
Art center, 192
Articulation disorders, 222
Assessment
   developmental-thematic curriculum, 206–207
   Head Start, 35
   infant–toddler programs, 139–144
   preschool programs, 213–214

primary-age children (5 to 8), 331–335
   program components, 214
   purposes of, 212–213
   software, computer, 364
   teachers, 206–207, 214, 326
   thematic curriculum, 326
Assisted performance, 41
Assisted reading, 351
Association for Childhood Education International (ACEI), 27, 60, 120, 213
At-risk children. *See also* Diversity of student populations
   evolution of early programs for, 31–35
   explaining term, 7–13
   Head Start, 15–16
   homelessness, 9
   infant–toddler programs, 120–121, 124
Attention deficit hyperactivity disorder (ADHD), 12, 37
Attitudes and values, formation of, 391
Authoritarian parents, 95
Autocosmic stage, 131
Autonomy *vs.* shame and doubt, 37

Babbling, 81, 84
Back-to-basics movement, 60
Balance activities, 286
Bandura, Albert, 39
Banet, Bernard, 65
Barn Dance, The (Martin & Archimbault), 429, 430, 432, 436
Bayley Test of Infant Development, 118
Bean and Plant (Back), 424, 425
Beginning to Read: Thinking and Learning About Print (Adams), 228

Behaviorist theory, 37–39, 55–56, 125, 126, 218
Bell, Alexander G., 33
Bible, the, 25
Big books, 225, 229, 238–239, 351
Bilingual programs, 13–18, 221, 342
Biographical studies, 399
Biracial children, 135
Black English, 220–221
Bladder control, 81
Bloom, Benjamin, 30, 119
Blow, Susan, 27–28
Body awareness, 286
Books, children's, 344, 353, 400–401
Bowel control, 81
Brain research
   implications of, 103
Brainstorming topics
   developmental-thematic curriculum, 198–200
   preschool unit plans, 420, 430
   primary unit plans, 440, 450
   thematic curriculum, 315–317
   transitional curriculum: ages 5 to 8 (physical education), 407
Bright Beginnings Initiative, 17
British infant schools, 191, 309
Bromley, Allan, 373
Bronfenbrenner, Urie, 68
Bruner, Jerome, 30, 69
Bullying, 274, 303

Calculators, 363
Caldwell, Bettye, 120
Caregivers and infant–toddler programs, 127, 134–136, 143–144
Carolina Abecedarian Project, 124
Carolina Record of Individual Behavior, 214
Carpentry tools, 405
Categorizing, 243

Categorizing children, biases in, 34
Center child care, 122
Center for Genetic Epistemology, 364
Center for Research on the Education
    of Students Placed at Risk
    (CRESPAR), 359
Centers. *See* Learning centers
Change as part of life, 4, 279
Checkley, K., 58
Checklists, developmental. *See also*
    Wortham Developmental
    Checklist for Infants and Toddlers
    developmental model for preschool
        programs, 212–213
    Frost-Wortham developmental
        checklists for preschool years,
        96–107, 247
    individual development, 139
Chicken Soup with Rice (Sendak), 239
Child abuse, 10–11, 267
Child-care programs
    employer-sponsored, 16
    expansion of, 44–45
    infant–toddler programs, 121–125
    mothers entering the work force,
        118
    origins, 29, 117
    World War II, 118
Child-centered approach to curriculum
    design, 18–20
Child-centered instruction, 186
Child Development Associate (CDA)
    credential, 51
Child Development Associate Program,
    120
Child labor, 31–32
Children in the Nursery School
    (Johnson), 118
Children (Santrock), 57
Children's Center at Syracuse
    University, 120
Children's Defense Fund, 45
Chronological development, 54
Ciari, Bruno, 67
Citizenship learning, 393
Civil Rights Movement, 34
Class books, 234
Class discussions, 392
Classifying and comparing, 243, 244,
    254
Class projects, 343
Clay, Marie, 358
Cognitive development, 185
    preoperational stage, 185

Cognitive-developmental theory, 30,
    39–42, 55. *See also*
    Developmental characteristics
    (birth to 8 years); Preschool
    curriculum: ages 3 to 5 (cognitive
    development)
    concrete operational period, 111
    developmental model for preschool
        programs, 185–186
    infant–toddler curriculum, 155–162
    infant–toddler programs, 123–124,
        137–138
    motor development, 402
    play, 129–132
    preoperational period, 92–93.
    primary-age children (5 to 8), 303
Cognitively Oriented Curriculum. *See*
    High/Scope model
Cold War, 30–31
Commercially designed assessments,
    332
Communication skills, 276
Community structures, 279
Community violence, 10, 267
Compensatory programs, 31, 34–35
Competence, emerging need for,
    304–305
Competency-based instruction, 31
Complexity in preschool programs,
    16–18
Computers, 363–364
Concepts
    developmental-thematic curriculum,
        202
    preschool curriculum: ages 3 to 5
        (cognitive development), 242
    preschool unit plans, 419, 429
    primary unit plans, 439, 449–450
    processes used to understand, 242
    skills/processes and, determining,
        320
    spontaneous, 61
Concepts, processes of forming, 243
    differentiating, 243
    grouping, 243
    labeling, 243
Concrete operational period, 40,
    107–111, 359–360. *See also*
    Developmental characteristics
    (birth to 8 years); Transitional
    curriculum *listings*
Conforming to social standards, 390
Conscience, developing a, 112
Construction play, 193

Constructivist approach to language
    acquisition, 219. *See also*
    Cognitive-developmental theory;
    Developmental characteristics
    (birth to 8 years)
Content-area grouping, 353–354
Contents of Children's Minds (Hall),
    35
Context cues, 350
Cooper, Kenneth, 404
Cooperative learning
    British infant schools, 309
    developmental model for preschool
        programs, 95
    Japanese preschool classrooms, 55
    multiage grouping, 310
    primary-age children (5 to 8), 312,
        323–325
    transitional curriculum: ages 5 to 8
        (language arts), 346, 353–354
    transitional curriculum: ages 5 to 8
        (social studies), 391, 392
Cornell University, 120
Corporations and child-care programs,
    16
Counting, 242, 243, 249–251, 368
Credentialing system for early
    childhood programs, 120
Crème de la Crème childcare centers,
    124
Crying, 84
Cultural differences, 3–5. *See also*
    Diversity of student populations
Cultural diversity, 54
Current issues, awareness of, 396–397
Curriculum. *See also* Developmentally
    appropriate practices (DAP);
    Infant–toddler curriculum;
    Preschool curriculum *listings*;
    Transitional curriculum *listings*
    child-centered approach to
        designing, 18
    diversity of student populations, 18
    family involvement in planning,
        19–20, 326–328
    inappropriate, 58–60
    theory and practice, conflicts
        between, 20
*Curriculum and Evaluation Standards
    for School Mathematics*, 359–360

Daddy Makes the Best Spaghetti
    (Hines), 280
Daily schedule, 194

Dame Schools, 25
DAP. *See* Developmentally appropriate practices
Death and the life cycle, 268, 278
Decision making, democratic, 393
Delays, developmental, 212
Democratic decision making, 393
Denver Developmental Test, 118, 212
Developmental characteristics (birth to 8 years)
    birth to 6 months, 83, 85
    concrete operational period, 107–111
    18 to 24 months, 87–91
    5 to 8 years, 111–112
    preoperational period, 92–96
    preschool learning, implications for, 98–107
    sensorimotor stage, 80–83
    6 to 12 months, 84, 86
    study questions, 113–114
    summary, 112–113
    12 to 18 months, 87
    2 to 5 years, 96–98
Developmental Continuity across Preschool and Primary Grades, 60
Developmental delays, 212
Developmental Indicators for the Assessment of Learning-Revised (DIAL-R), 212
Developmentally appropriate environments
    infants and toddlers, 128
Developmentally Appropriate Practice in Early Childhood Programs (Bredekamp & Copple), 62, 128, 139, 142, 143, 189, 306
Developmentally Appropriate Practice in Early Childhood Programs Serving Children from Birth through Age 8 (Bredekamp), 60
Developmentally appropriate practices (DAP), 43, 73, 187
    developmental model for preschool programs, 189–190
    inappropriate practices, issues leading to, 60
    infant–toddler programs, 136–138, 143
    primary-age children (5 to 8), 305–307
    refining, 62
    software, 364

study questions, 77
    summary, 75–76
Developmental model for preschool programs. *See also* Preschool curriculum *listings;* Developmental-thematic curriculum
    cognitive-developmental theory, 185–186
    culturally responsive classroom, 191
    daily schedule, 194
    developmentally appropriate practices, 189–190
    environment, 192–193
    evaluation, 212–215
    inclusive classroom, 190–191
    integrated classroom, 191
    play, 193–194
    study questions, 215–216
    summary, 215
    teacher's role, 191–192
    theory and practice, differences between, 184–185
Developmental progress. *See also* Cognitive-developmental theory; Physical development; Social-emotional development; Theoretical bases of development
    Gesell's views, 118
    infant–toddler programs, 139–140
Developmental-thematic curriculum
    brainstorming a topic, 198–200
    concepts/skills/processes, determining, 202
    diversity, adapting lesson plans for, 206
    evaluation, 206–207
    implementing, 211–212
    implications for, 197
    integrated approach to curriculum development, 195
    objectives, describing, 202–204
    planning lesson activities, 205–206
    roles of, 197
    scheduling unit activities, 207, 210
    selecting unit activities, 200–202
    summarizing activities to be included, 204–205
    topic selection, 197–198
Developmental theories, 54
    applying classical, 54–58
Dewey, John, 28, 42, 67, 72, 191
Dictated stories, 239
Dictation, 232–233, 234

Directed assignments, 333
Direct instruction, 126
Directional awareness, 286
Disabilities, children with. *See* Special needs, children with
Discovery, 242, 247
Discrimination, 391–392
Discussions, group/class, 343, 392
Diversity of student populations
    cultural/ethnic differences, 3–5
    developmental model for preschool programs, 191
    developmental-thematic curriculum, 206
    family environments, 5–7
    historical roots of early childhood education, 33
    infant–toddler programs, 135
    learning needs, 7
    multicultural understandings and sensitivities, 270
    school environment, adaptation to the, 390
    settings, complex nature of, 1–18
    special education programs, trapped in, 34
    standard English, 220, 221
    study questions, 21–22
    summary, 20–21
    teachers' preparation for the, 18
    transitional curriculum: ages 5 to 8 (language arts), 341–343
Division for Early Childhood of the Council for Exceptional Children (DEC/CEC), 62
Divorce, 6, 7–8
Domestic violence, 10–11, 267–268
Dramatic play/productions, 193–194, 226, 272–273, 343–344
Drug abuse, 10

Eager to Learn: Educating Our Preschoolers, 45
Early Childhood Education Journal, 284
Early childhood programs
    expanding role of, 43
Early Head Start, 122, 124
Early Screening Inventory, 212
Ecological theory, 56–57
Economics, 271, 396
Educare, 121
Educating America for the 21st Century, 364
Egocentrism, 92, 266

Elementary School Journal, The, 407

Elementary School Program, 396. *See also* Primary-age children (5 to 8); Transitional curriculum *listings*

Eliot, Abigail, 118

Emergent literacy, 227–239, 340–341. *See also* Language development; Preschool curriculum: ages 3 to 5 (cognitive development); Preschool curriculum: ages 3 to 5 (language development); Transitional curriculum: ages 5 to 8 (language arts)

Emile (Rousseau), 26

Emotionally disturbed children, 14. *See also* Social–emotional development

Empathic behavior, 276

Employment
  child-care programs, employer-sponsored, 16
  child labor, 31–32
  mothers entering the workforce, 6, 118

Engaging Children's Minds: The Project Approach, 72, 73

English as a second language (ESL), 221

Enrichment programs, infant-toddler, 124–125

Environment
  assessment, 140
  developmental model for preschool programs, 192–193
  developmental-thematic curriculum, 211–212
  infant–toddler programs, 127–128
  play, indoor/outdoor, 93, 131–132
  preschool curriculum: ages 3 to 5 (cognitive development), 246–247
  preschool curriculum: ages 3 to 5 (language development), 224–225
  preschool curriculum: ages 3 to 5 (physical development), 288–289
  preschool curriculum: ages 3 to 5 (social development), 273–274
  primary-age children (5 to 8), 313–314
  transitional curriculum: ages 5 to 8 (language arts), 347–348
  transitional curriculum: ages 5 to 8 (mathematics), 362–363

transitional curriculum: ages 5 to 8 (science), 375–376

Erikson, Erik, 37, 55, 68, 186

Ethnic differences, 3–5. *See also* Diversity of student populations

Ethnic identity, 269

Evaluation. *See* Assessment

Evangelical parents, 116

Even Start, 46

Exosystem, 56–57

Expectations of Excellence: Curriculum Standards for Social Studies, 393

Experiences during early years, role of, 30

Experimentation, 244, 255–256

Explore, opportunities to, 93, 192, 242

Expressive arts/activities, 176–180, 286

Expressive language development, 223, 225–226

Extended-care programs, 14–15

Extra-year programs, 307–308

Facial expressions, 84

Families
  curriculum development, involvement in, 19–20, 326–328
  destructive parenting practices, 116–117
  divorce, 6, 7–8
  domestic violence, 10–11, 267–268
  homelessness, 9
  infant–toddler programs, 134–136, 143–144
  intervention programs for infants/toddlers, 120–121, 123–124
  learning in the early years, interest in, 43–44
  parenting styles, 95
  preschool curriculum: ages 3 to 5 (language development), 235
  reporting progress to parents, 334
  single-parent homes, 6
  stress, members feeling, 10
  substance abuse, 10
  teenage parents, 8–9
  thematic curriculum, 326–329
  vital family, 268
  working parents, 6

Family Development Research Program, 120

Fantasy play, 272

Farm animals, preschool unit plan on, 429–438

Farrell, Elizabeth, 34

Federally funded initiatives
  historical roots of early childhood education, 42–43
  innovative period (1950s and 1960s), 30–32

Field trips, 344

Finger plays, 176

Fisher, John D., 33

Fluency disorders, 222

Follow Through program, 30

Frank Porter Graham Child Development Center, 124

Free play, 291

Freinet, Celestin, 67

Freud, Sigmund, 36–37, 118

Froebel, Friedrich, 14, 26–27

Frost-Wortham developmental checklists for preschool years, 96–107, 247

Funding sources, 50, 52

Gallaudet, Thomas, 33

Gardner, Howard, 67, 69

Gardner's theory of intelligence, 56, 58

Gender and physical development, 93

Geography, 271, 394–395

Geometry, 251–252

Gesell, Arnold, 28–29, 35–36, 54–55, 118, 185

Gifted and talented children, 14

Gifts and occupations, 26

Global awareness, 397, 401

Goals
  preschool curriculum: ages 3 to 5 (cognitive development), 244
  preschool curriculum: ages 3 to 5 (social development), 269, 270–272
  transitional curriculum: ages 5 to 8 (mathematics), 361–362
  transitional curriculum: ages 5 to 8 (science), 374
  transitional curriculum: ages 5 to 8 (social studies), 393–397

Gordon Parent Education program, 120

Grandparents and oral history, 278

Group discussions, 343

Guided discovery/observation, 247

Guidelines for Appropriate Curriculum Content and Assessment in

Programs Serving Children Ages 3 Through 8, 60, 330
Guidelines for Preparation of Early Childhood Professionals, 62
Guide to Accreditation, 214

Hall, G. Stanley, 28, 35
Harris, William T., 27
Harvard University, 24
Head Start, 50, 64, 187
  at-risk children, 15–16
  Civil Rights Movement, 34
  Early Head Start, 122, 124
  evaluation, 35
  improved performance standards, 122
  innovative period (1960s), 30
  new role, taking on a, 120
High/Scope model, 63, 64–68, 187
  criteria for, 66
  elementary school applications, 65
  elements of, 66–67
  international adaptations, 65
High/Scope Preschool Education Approach. *See* High/Scope model
Hill, Patty S., 28
Hispanic Americans. *See* Latinos
Historical roots of early childhood education
  African Americans, 32
  at-risk children, 31–35
  evolutionary steps, 26–28
  historical influence revisited, 42–46
  innovative period (1950s and 1960s), 30–32
  Latinos, 32–33
  Montessori, 30
  Native Americans, 33
  nursery school and child-care movements, 29
  Progressive Era, 28–29
  rural schools, 25–26
  study questions, 48
  summary, 46–47
  urbanization of public schools, 30
Historical time, understanding, 271, 278, 394
Hohmann, Mary, 65, 66
Holiday celebrations, 401
Holophrastic speech, 81
Homelessness, 9
Housing, low-cost, 9
How a Seed Grows (Jordan), 424

Hunt, J. McVicker, 30, 66, 119
Hymes, James, 118

Identifying/addressing learning problems, 335, 371–372
If You Give a Mouse a Cookie (Numeroff), 439–447
Illness, serious, 268
Image-Making within the Writing Process project, 381
Inappropriate practices, issues leading to, 60. *See also* Developmentally appropriate practices (DAP)
Inclusion, 12, 34–35, 190–191
Independent performance 44, 351–352
Individualized educational programs (IEPs), 14, 83, 214
Individualized family service plans (IFSPs), 124, 143
Individually guided education, 31
Individuals with Disabilities Act, 46
Indoor environments, well-planned, 288. *See also* Environment
Infant Care, 117
Infant development, 80–86, 89–91. *See also* Developmental characteristics (birth to 8 years)
Infant Education Research Project, 120
Infants and Toddlers program, 83
Infant/Toddler Care and Education, 139
Infant–toddler curriculum
  cognitive development, 155–162
  expressive arts, 176–180
  language development, 163–170
  learning, implications for, 89–92
  physical development, 148–155
  social-emotional development, 171–176
  summary, 180–181
Infant/Toddler Environment Rating Scale, 143
Infant–toddler programs
  assessment, 139–144
  caregivers, 127
  child care programs, 121–125
  curriculum, thematic, 138–139
  developing models for, 125–127
  developmentally appropriate practices, 136–138
  environment, 127–128
  evolution of, 116–125

  families, 134–136
  language development, 137–138
  physical development, 136–137
  play, 129–132
  routines, 132–133
  social-emotional development, 137
  study questions, 145–146
  summary, 144–145
  theoretical bases, 125–127
Inferring, 244
In-home child care, 122
Initiative *vs.* guilt, 37, 186
Innovative period
  (1950s and 1960s), 30–32
  (1960s and 1970s), 42
Inquiry-based curriculum, 374
Instructional Theory into Practice (ITIP), 202
Integrated Approach to Curriculum Development
  developmental model for preschool programs, 191
  developmental-thematic curriculum, 196
  development of, 73–74
  elements of, 74–75
  history of, 72–74
  preschool curriculum: ages 3 to 5 (language/cognitive development), 257–262
  preschool curriculum: ages 3 to 5 (physical development), 294–297
  preschool curriculum: ages 3 to 5 (social development), 277–283
  systematic instruction, concerns about, 306
  transitional curriculum: ages 5 to 8 (language arts/mathematics/science), 380–383
  transitional curriculum: ages 5 to 8 (physical education), 406–410
  transitional curriculum: ages 5 to 8 (social studies), 402
  ungraded primary model, 311
Integrated Components of Appropriate and Inappropriate Practice for Infants and Toddlers, 135, 143
Integrated Learning Activities for Young Children (Trostle & Yawkey), 295, 296, 406, 408–409
Integrating Mathematics and Science for Kindergarten and Primary Children (Kellough), 384

Integration activities for perceptual-motor development, 286
Integration and children with special needs, 12, 34–35, 190–191
Intelligence
    Gardner's theory of, 56, 58
    poverty influencing, 119
Intelligence and Experience, 66
Interactionist approach to language acquisition, 219
International Kindergarten Union (IKU), 27
Intervention programs, 34–35, 36–37. *See also* Federally funded initiatives; Head Start
    at-risk children, 12
    importance of, 12–13
    infant–toddler programs, 120–122
    innovative period (1960s), 31
    origins, 120
Interviews, 333
Iowa State University, 118
Isolation, overcoming social, 275
I Went Walking (Williams), 430, 432, 434, 435

Japan, cooperative preschool classrooms in, 55
Japanese Americans and historical roots of early childhood education, 33
Johns Hopkins University, 359
Journal writing, 233, 356
Junior Achievement, 396

Kaiser Child Service, 118
Karnes Home Intervention Program, 120
Kilpatrick, William H., 28
Kindergarten. *See also* Transitional curriculum *listings*
    assessment, 331–335
    Blow's views, 27–28
    extending from half-day to full-day, 42
    Froebel's views, 26–27
    Hill's views, 28
    origins of, 14
    prekindergarten programs in public schools, 14
Kramer Project, 123

Language centers, 288
Language development. *See also*

Preschool curriculum: ages 3 to 5 (language development); Transitional curriculum: ages 5 to 8 (language arts)
Alexander and the Terrible, Horrible, No Good, Very Bad Day (Viorst), 452
developmental model for preschool programs, 192
infants, 81
infant–toddler curriculum, 163–170
infant–toddler programs, 137–138
play, 193–194
preoperational period, 93
toddlers, 87–88
Language Training Curriculum (Direct Instruction Model), 64
Latinos
    historical roots of early childhood education, 32–33
Learning centers, 313
    developmental model for preschool programs, 193
    innovative period (1950s and 1960s), 31
    organizing primary-grade interest, 313–314
    preschool curriculum: ages 3 to 5 (physical development), 288
    tips for implementing, 314
Learning needs, diversity in, 7
Learning problems, identifying/addressing, 335, 371–372
Legislative acts
    Americans with Disabilities Act, 46
    Bilingual Education Act of 1974, 34
    Child Care and Development Block Grant, 45
    Education for All Handicapped Children Act, 34
    Elementary and Secondary Education Act of 1965, 34
    Elementary and Secondary School Improvement Act of 1988, 46
    Fair Labor Standards Act of 1938, 32
    Human Services Reauthorization Act of 1990, 120
    Individuals with Disabilities Act, 46
    Lanham Act, 118
    Northwest Ordinances of 1784, 25

Social Services Block Grant (Title XX), 45
Lesson procedures, 323–324
Life changes affecting social development, 266–268
Lists, 357
Literacy
    developing foundations for, 227
    goals for, 230
Literacy, emergent, 227–239, 340–341. *See also* Language development; Preschool curriculum: ages 3 to 5 (cognitive development); Preschool curriculum: ages 3 to 5 (language development); Transitional curriculum: ages 5 to 8 (language arts)
Literature-based instruction, 258, 344, 353, 400–401
Little Engine that Could, The, 344
Logical-mathematical knowledge, 61
LOGO computer language, 364

Macrospheric stage, 131
Mainstreaming, 12, 34–35, 190–191
Malaguzzi, Loris, 67, 68
Manipulation, 242, 288
Mapmaking, 395
Mathematics, 192, 242–244, 247–253, 452. *See also* Transitional curriculum: ages 5 to 8 (mathematics)
Maturational theory, 28–29, 35–36, 54–55, 125
McMillan, Margaret, 118
McMillan sisters, 29
Meaning in reading, 230
Measurement, 244, 247–248, 255
Mental retardation, 11–12
Mercer, Jane, 34
Mesosystem, 56, 57
Messages, responding to, 356–357
Metacognition, 108, 109
Mice, learning differences between real and fictional, 439–447
Microspheric stage, 131
Microsystem, 56, 57
Migrant students, 34
Millions of Cats, 344
Minority education. *See* Diversity of student populations
Modeling appropriate behaviors, 304
Montessori, Maria, 30

Moral development, 112, 391
More Story Stretchers (Raines & Canady), 280
Morphemes, 219
Mortality rates for children, 116, 117
Mother-Child program, 120
Mothers entering the workforce, 6, 118
Motor skills. *See also* Physical development
  gross/fine, 286–287, 288, 402–403, 406
  outdoor play and, 93
  perceptual-motor development, 286–287
Multiage grouping, 310
Multicultural understandings and sensitivities, 19–20, 62, 270. *See also* Diversity of student populations
Music, 176, 192

National Academy of Early Childhood Programs, 120
National Association for the Education of Young Children (NAEYC), 43, 45, 58, 60, 62, 63, 73, 120, 213
National Association of Early Childhood Specialists in State Departments of Education (NAECSSDE), 60, 213
National Association of Elementary School Principals, 60
National Association of State Boards of Education, 60
National Board for Professional Teaching Standards (NBPTS), 62
National Council for the Social Studies (NCSS), 393
National Council of Teachers of Mathematics (NCTM), 60, 244, 360, 361, 362
National Education Association, 33
National Education Goals Panel, 213
National Institute of Child Health and Human Development, 228
National Science Foundation (NSF), 364, 374
Native Americans and historical roots of early childhood education, 33
Negative reinforcement, 37–39
Neighborhood structures, 279
Neighborhood violence, 10–11, 267
New England Asylum for the Blind, 33

New York Society for the Prevention of Cruelty to Children, 117
Nonsense words, 355
Nova University Play and Learn program, 124
Numbers, 243, 244, 249–251, 369
Nursery rhymes, 176
Nursery schools, 29, 118

Objectives
  developmental-thematic curriculum, 202–204
  preschool unit plans, 419–421, 429–431
  primary unit plans, 439–440, 450
  thematic curriculum, 321, 322
Observation, 242, 253–254, 332–333
One-to-one correspondence, 243
Open and closed spaces, concept of, 313
Open classroom, 31
Oral history, 278
Oral reading to share information, 356
Outdoor play
  infant–toddler programs, 131–132
  motor skills, developing, 93
  preschool curriculum: ages 3 to 5 (physical development), 288–289
  sociodramatic play, 194
  transitional curriculum: ages 5 to 8 (physical education), 404
Over in the Meadow (Keats), 239

Pancakes for Breakfast (dePaola), 431, 432, 437
Papert, Seymour, 364
Parental styles, 95. *See also* Families
Parents
  preschool curriculum: ages 3 to 5 (language development), 223–224
Parker, Francis, 28
Patriotism, 397
Pavlov, Ivan, 37–38
Peers
  collaboration, 193
  culture transmitted through play, 304
  rejection, 391
  teaching, 312
Perceptual-motor development, 286–287. *See also* Physical development
Performance objectives, 202–203

Permissive parents, 95
Perry Preschool Project, 64, 66
Pestalozzi, Johann, 26–27, 42
Phonics, 229, 350
Phonological awareness, 229
Phonology, 219, 220
Physical development. *See also* Preschool curriculum: ages 3 to 5 (physical development); Transitional curriculum: ages 5 to 8 (physical education)
  concrete operational period, 109, 111–112
  infants, 81, 90
  infant–toddler curriculum, 148–155
  infant–toddler programs, 136–137
  play, 193
  preoperational period, 93
  primary-age children (5 to 8), 302–303
  toddlers, 90
Physical impairments, 11. *See also* Special needs, children with
Piaget, Jean, 30, 39–40, 55, 185–186, 242, 243. *See also* Cognitive–developmental theory
Plan, do, review process, 66, 67
Play
  cognitive, 131
  developmental model for preschool programs, 193–194
  environments, indoor and outdoor, 93, 131–132, 194, 288–289
  infant–toddler programs, 129–132
  physical, 130
  preschool curriculum: ages 3 to 5 (language development), 222
  preschool curriculum: ages 3 to 5 (physical development), 287
  preschool curriculum: ages 3 to 5 (social development), 272–273
  primary-age children (5 to 8), 304–305
  transitional curriculum: ages 5 to 8 (physical education), 402, 404–405
Play, unstructured, 303, 305
Play and Child Development, 214
Playgrounds for Young Children (Wortham & Frost), 292
Playpens, decreased use of, 131
Poem picture books, 355
Portfolio assessment, 139–141
Portfolios, student, 213, 333–334

Positive reinforcement, 37–39
Post-traumatic stress disorder (PTSD), 267
Poverty
  at-risk children, 9–10
  intelligence influenced by, 119
  working poor, 9
Pragmatics, 219, 220
Predictable books, 239
Prejudice, 391–392
Prekindergarten programs in public schools, 14
Preoperational period, 40, 92–96, 192, 242, 359–360. *See also* Developmental characteristics (birth to 8 years); Developmental model for preschool programs; Preschool curriculum *listings*
Preschool. *See also* Developmental characteristics (birth to 8 years); Developmental model for preschool programs
  assessment, 213–214
  Frost-Wortham developmental checklists, 96–107, 247
  physical development, 93
  primary and preschool thematic curriculum, similarities between, 315
  public schools, expansion of programs in, 45
  social-emotional development, 98, 102
Preschool curriculum: ages 3 to 5 (cognitive development)
  classifying and comparing, 254
  concepts, processes used to understand, 242
  environment, 246–247
  experimentation, 255–256
  geometry, 251–252
  goals, 244
  integrated curriculum, 257–262
  mathematical reasoning, 252–253
  measurement, 247–248, 255
  numbers, 249–251
  observation, 253–254
  special needs, children with, 262
  study questions, 264
  summary, 263
  symbolic thought, 242–243
  teacher's role, 245–246
Preschool curriculum: ages 3 to 5 (language development)
  acquisition of language, 218–219

  conflict between reading readiness and emergent literacy, 228
  designing curriculum, 225–227
  environment, 224–225
  forms of language, 219
  integrated approach to curriculum development, 257–262
  language differences, 220–222
  play, 222
  reading, emergent, 235–239
  special needs, children with, 239–241
  study questions, 264
  summary, 263
  teacher's role, 223, 225
  writing, emergent, 230–235
Preschool curriculum: ages 3 to 5 (physical development)
  designing curriculum, 291–298
  environment, 288–289
  integrated approach to curriculum development, 294–297
  perceptual-motor development, 286–287
  planning, 287
  play, 287
  special needs, children with, 297
  study questions, 299–300
  summary, 298–299
  teacher's role, 289–291
Preschool curriculum: ages 3 to 5 (social development), 268–270, planning
  designing curriculum, 275–279
  egocentrism, 266
  environment, 273–274
  goals, 269, 270–272
  integrated approach to curriculum development, 277–283
  life changes, critical, 266–268
  play, 272–273
  social interactions, activities fostering, 275–276
  study questions, 299–300
  summary, 298–299
  teacher's role, 274–275
Preschool Curriculum Demonstration Project, 64
Preschool unit plans
  farm animals, 429–438
  seeds, 419–428
President's Council on Physical Fitness and Sports, 406
Pretend play activities, 131

Previous knowledge, assumptions about, 421, 431, 440, 450–451
Primary-age children (5 to 8). *See also* Transitional curriculum *listings;* Thematic curriculum
  assessment, 331–335
  British infant schools, 309
  cognitive development, 303
  developmentally appropriate practices, 305–307
  environment, 313–314
  multiage grouping, 310
  physical development, 302–303
  play, 304–305
  preschool and primary thematic curriculum, similarities between, 315
  social-emotional development, 303–304
  study questions, 336–337
  summary, 335–336
  systematic instruction, incorporating, 329–331
  team teaching, 309, 310
  transitional programs, 307–308
  ungraded primary model, characteristics of, 311
Primary circular reactions, 80
Primary unit plans
  Alexander and the Terrible, Horrible, No Good, Very Bad Day (Viorst), 449–455
  mice, learning differences between real and fictional, 439–447
Print-rich environment, 224, 237
Private school programs, 14
Problem-solving, 243
Problem-solving activities, 88
Progressive Era, 28–29, 42, 184
Project 2061, 374
Project Approach: A Practical Course for Teachers, The, 72
Project Approach: A Practical Guide for Teachers, The, 72
Project Approach: A Second Practical Guide for Teachers, The, 72
Project Approach, The, 63, 72-75, 187. *See also* Integrated approach to curriculum development
  development of, 73–74
  elements of, 74–75
  history of, 72–74
Project work, 333
Prop boxes, thematic, 234

Prosocial behavior, 276
Psychoanalytic theory, 36–37
Psychology, 271
Psychosocial theory, 37, 55
Public school programs
    child-care centers, 122–123
    expansion of, 45
    settings for, 13–14
Punishment, 39

Quality early childhood programs. *See*
    Developmentally appropriate
    practices (DAP)
Quality in early childhood education
    programs
    accountability of, 54
    assessment of, 54
    challenges to, 50
    characteristics of, 52
    goals of, 51
Quality infant and toddler programs,
    127
    caregivers, 127
    environment, 127
    Head Start Parent-Child Center,
    134
    Italian centers, 128
Quality language arts programs,
    elements of, 347
Quality preschool programs
    assessment and accountability, 187
    cultural diversity, 187
    models of, 187
Quality 2000 Initiative, 51

Reaching Potentials: Appropriate
    Curriculum and Assessment for
    Young Children (Bredekamp &
    Rosegrant), 61, 62
Reaching Potentials: Transforming Early
    Curriculum and Assessment
    (Bredekamp & Rosegrant), 61, 62
Reading. *See also* Language
    development; Transitional
    curriculum: ages 5 to 8 (language
    arts)
    conflict between readiness and
    emergent literacy, 228
    emergent, 235–239
    Recovery program, 358
Reading programs, balanced approach
    to, 346
Receptive language, 227
Recess, 303
Reflexive actions, 80

Reggio Emilia, 63, 186, 187, 242
Reggio Emilia model, 67–72, 69–70
    development of, 69
    elements of, 70–77
    history of, 67–69
Reggio Emilia schools, 55, 199
Rehearsal of information, 108
Reinforcement, 37–39
Resources, gathering, 211
Richmond, Julius, 120
Room arrangement, 192, 313–314
Rough-and-tumble play, 93
Rousseau, Jean-Jacques, 26, 42, 117
Routines and infant–toddler programs,
    132–133
Ruggles Street Day Nursery, 118
Rural schools, 25–26

Scaffolding, 42, 242, 243
Scheduling unit activities, 207, 210,
    328–329
Schema, 40, 183–184
School-based child care, 122–123
School workers, 279
Science, 192, 242–244, 452. *See also*
    Transitional curriculum: ages 5 to
    8 (science)
Science, concepts in, 243
Science Fun with Peanuts and Popcorn
    (Wyler), 426, 427
Screening for developmental problems,
    212
Scribbling, 92, 94, 231
Secondary circular reactions, 80
Seeds, preschool unit plans on,
    419–428
Seeds and More Seeds (Selsam), 423,
    425, 426
Self-concept, 266, 269, 304
Self-esteem, 390, 392
Semantics, 219, 220
Sensorimotor stage, 40, 80–83
Sentence strips, 234
Settings for early childhood programs,
    13–18
Seventeenth century, colonial
    education in, 24–25
Sex-role identity, 269
Sharing behavior, 95
Shelters, 10
Sight words, 350
Single-parent homes, 6
Skeels, H. M., 118
Skills for Preschool Teachers (Beaty),
    290

Skinner, B. F., 38–39
Sleeter, Christine, 34
Social-conventional knowledge, 61
Social-emotional development. *See*
    also Preschool curriculum: ages 3
    to 5 (social development);
    Transitional curriculum: ages 5 to
    8 (social studies)
    Alexander and the Terrible,
    Horrible, No Good, Very Bad
    Day (Viorst), 452
    concrete operational period,
    111–112
    infants, 81–82, 84, 91
    infant–toddler curriculum, 171–
    176
    infant–toddler programs, 137
    play, 193
    preoperational period, 94–96
Social-emotional development. *See*
    also Preschool curriculum: ages 3
    to 5 (social development);
    Transitional curriculum: ages 5 to
    8 (social studies)
    preschoolers, 98, 102
    primary-age children (5 to 8),
    303–304
    toddlers, 88, 91
Socialization, 270
Social learning theory, 39
Social play, 131
Social Services Block Grant (Title XX),
    45
Society for the Prevention of Cruelty to
    Animals (SPCA), 117
Sociodramatic play, 193–194,
    272–273
Sociology, 272, 396
Software, computer, 364
Songs, 176
Spanish language, 221
Spatial awareness, 286
Special needs, children with
    assessment, 143
    categorizing children, biases in, 34
    curriculum for, 19
    emotional disturbances, 11–12
    evaluation, 214
    historical roots of early childhood
    education, 33–34
    inclusion, 12, 34–35, 190–191
    infant–toddler programs, 120–121,
    124
    learning problems,
    identifying/addressing, 335

Special needs, children with,
continued
  mental retardation, 11
  physical impairments, 11
  preschool curriculum: ages 3 to 5
    (cognitive development), 262
  preschool curriculum: ages 3 to 5
    (language development),
    239–241
  preschool curriculum: ages 3 to 5
    (physical development), 297
  programs for, 14
  transitional curriculum: ages 5 to 8
    (language arts), 358–359
  visual impairments, 11
Spelling, invented, 109
Spontaneous concepts, 61
Sports, organized, 404–405
Sputnik, launching of, 31
Standard English, 220, 221
Standardized tests, 54, 60, 212–
  213
Stimulus-response theory, 38
Story experiences, 176
Story reenactments, 238
Story starters, 356
Story Stretchers (Raines & Canady),
  258
Student involvement in planning
  curriculum/activities, 317,
  326–328
Substance abuse, 10
Substitute words, 356
Success For All program, 359
Supervision, toddler, 88
Sustained silent reading (SSR), 355
Symbolic representation, 81, 92,
  242–243
Syntax, 219, 220
Systematic instruction, 306–307, 309,
  311, 312, 329–331

Tapes, read-along, 355
Teachers
  assessment, 326
  developmental model for preschool
    programs, 191–192
  diverse populations, curriculum
    development for, 18
  evaluating, 206–207, 214
  family involvement in curriculum
    development, 19–20
  independent readers, 351–352
  licensing, 51–52
  peer teaching, 312

  preschool curriculum: ages 3 to 5
    (cognitive development),
    245–246
  preschool curriculum: ages 3 to 5
    (language development), 223,
    225
  preschool curriculum: ages 3 to 5
    (physical development), 289–291
  preschool curriculum: ages 3 to 5
    (social development), 274–275
  salaries, 50–51
  social-emotional development in
    concrete operational period, 112
  team teaching, 309, 310
  theory and practice in curriculum
    development, 20
  training and preparation, 50, 51, 52
  transitional curriculum: ages 5 to 8
    (language arts), 348–349
  transitional curriculum: ages 5 to 8
    (mathematics), 362–363
  transitional curriculum: ages 5 to 8
    (physical education), 405–406
  transitional curriculum: ages 5 to 8
    (science), 376–377, 378
  transitional curriculum: ages 5 to 8
    (social studies), 391
Teachers' individual stories
  Beth, 414–415
  Gladys, 416–417
  Hector, 417
  Loisa, 418
  Loretta, 417–418
  Renee, 415
  Rollo and Nancy, 416
  Susan, 415–416
  Yolanda, 415
Team teaching, 309, 310
Technology
  transitional curriculum: ages 5 to 8
    (language arts), 349
  transitional curriculum: ages 5 to 8
    (mathematics), 363–364
Teenage parents, 8–9
Teething, 81
Temple, Alice, 28
Temporal awareness, 286
Tertiary circular reactions, 80, 81
Testing, increase in, 58, 60
Thematic curriculum,192-194. See
  also Developmental-thematic
  curriculum, 326–328
  assessment, 326
  balancing systematic instruction
    and, 330–331

  brainstorming, 315–317
  concepts/skills/processes,
    determining, 320
  families and students, planning with,
    326–328
  objectives, developing unit, 321,
    322
  planning lesson activities and
    projects, 322–326
  preschool and primary, similarities
    between, 315
  scheduling, 328–329
  student involvement in selecting
    activities, 317, 326–328
  topic selection, 315
Theoretical bases of development. *See
  also* Cognitive-developmental
  theory; Developmentally
  appropriate practices (DAP)
  behaviorist theory, 37–39, 218
  infant–toddler programs, 125–127
  maturational theory, 28–29, 35–36
  psychoanalytic theory, 36–37
  psychosocial theory, 37
  social learning theory, 39
  study questions, 48
  summary, 46–47
Theory and practice, differences
  between, 20, 184–185
Theory of cognitive development, 69
There's a Nightmare in My Closet
  (Mayer), 262
Thought and Language (Vygotsky), 40
Three Bears, The, 238
Three Billy Goats Gruff, The (Sendak),
  239
Three Little Pigs, 238
Tiny Seed, The (Carle), 424
Toddler development, 87–92. *See also*
  Developmental characteristics
  (birth to 8 years); Infant–toddler
  listings
Topics, brainstorming/selecting,
  198–200, 315–317
Toy Lending Library, 125
Toys, 88
Transitional curriculum: ages 5 to 8
  (language arts)
  activities promoting language
    development, 345
  class projects, 343
  content-area grouping, 353–354
  cooperative learning groups,
    344–346, 353–354
  designing curriculum, 343

diversity of student populations, 341–343
dramatic productions, 343–344
emergent literacy to independent reading/writing, 340–341
environment, 347–348
field trips, 344
group discussions, 343
integrated approach to curriculum development, 381–383
literacy acquisition, nature/stages of, 346, 349–351
literature-based instruction, 344, 353
non-ability-grouped/multilevel first-grade classroom, 352–353
organizing language arts program, 352–353
reading, experiences promoting, 355–356
reading workshop, 354
special needs, children with, 358–359
study questions, 387–388
summary, 383–387
teacher's role, 348–349
technology, 349
writing, experiences promoting, 356–357
Transitional curriculum: ages 5 to 8 (mathematics)
designing curriculum, 368
environment, 362–363
experiences that promote mathematics, 368–371
goals, 361–362
integrated approach to curriculum development, 381–383
learning differences among students, 371–372
organizing the mathematics program, 364–368
preoperational to concrete operational stages, 359–360
study questions, 387–388
summary, 383–387
technology, 363–364
trends and issues in mathematics, 360
Transitional curriculum: ages 5 to 8 (physical education)
integrated approach to curriculum development, 406–410
motor skills, fine and gross, 402–403

planning, 404–405
study questions, 411–412
summary, 410–411
teacher's role, 405–406
Transitional curriculum: ages 5 to 8 (science)
building on past experiences, 372
designing curriculum, 378
environment, 375–376
experiences that promote science, 378–380
goals, 374
how young children learn science, 372–373
incorporating the science process, 375
integrated approach to curriculum development, 380–383
organizing the science program, 377–378
study questions, 387–388
summary, 383–387
teacher's role, 376–377
trends and issues in science, 373–274
Transitional curriculum: ages 5 to 8 (social studies)
activities for nurturing social development, 392–393
conforming to social standards, 390
current issues, 396–397
designing curriculum, 397–402
economics, 396
geography, 394–395
global awareness, 397–399, 401
goals, 393–397
history, 394
industry vs. inferiority, 390
integrated approach to curriculum development, 402
moral development, 391
prejudice, 391–392
study questions, 411
summary, 410
whole language and literature, 397, 399–401
Transitional programs, 307–308
Transitions and infant-toddler programs, 132–133
Transportation, understanding, 278–279
Trial-and-error, 243
Trust vs. mistrust, 37

Ungraded primary, the, 311. *See also* Primary–age children (5 to 8)
Unit-Based Curriculum (Nursery School Model), 64
Unit plans. See Preschool unit plans; Primary unit plans
University of North Carolina at Greensboro, 120
Unstructured play, 402, 404–405
Urbanization of public schools, 30

Values and attitudes, formation of, 391
Violence, domestic, 10–11, 267–268
Visual impairments, 11
Vital family, 268
Vocabulary, 229
Vygotsky, Lev, 40–42, 55, 68, 184, 185, 191, 242–243

Webbing, 74, 196, 315, 316, 441, 451
Weekly schedule, 327
Western view on cooperative play, 55
Whole language approach, 110, 397, 399–401
William and Mary, College of, 24
Word analysis, 350
Word games, 356
Words, as concept, 229
Workbench activities, 288
Working parents, 6
Work samples, 333
Works Progress Administration (WPA), 118
World War II, 118
Wortham Developmental Checklist for Infants and Toddlers
birth to 6 months, 85
18 to 24 months, 90–91
6 to 12 months, 86
12 to 18 months, 88–89
Writing. *See also* Language development; Transitional curriculum: ages 5 to 8 (language arts)
emergent, 230–235
journals, 233, 356
workshop, 357

Young Children, 60
Young Children in Action, 65
Young Investigators: The Project Approach in the Early Years, 73

Zone of proximal development (ZPD), 41, 69, 186, 245, 348